Credit Derivatives Pricing Models

Wiley Finance Series

Credit Derivatives Pricing Models

Models, Pricing and Implementation

Philipp J. Schönbucher

WILEY

Other Wiley Editorial Offices

John Wiley & Sons Inc., 111 River Street, Hoboken, NJ 07030, USA

Jossey-Bass, 989 Market Street, San Francisco, CA 94103-1741, USA

Wiley-VCH Verlag GmbH, Boschstr. 12, D-69469 Weinheim, Germany

John Wiley & Sons Australia Ltd, 33 Park Road, Milton, Queensland 4064, Australia

John Wiley & Sons (Asia) Pte Ltd, 2 Clementi Loop #02-01, Jin Xing Distripark, Singapore 129809

John Wiley & Sons Canada Ltd, 22 Worcester Road, Etobicoke, Ontario, Canada M9W 1L1

Wiley also publishes its books in a variety of electronic formats. Some content that
appears in print may not be available in electronic books.

British Library Cataloguing in Publication Data

A catalogue record for this book is available from the British Library

ISBN 10: 0-470-84291-1 (H/B)
ISBN 13: 978-0-470-84291-1 (H/B)

Typeset in 10/12 pt Times by TechBooks, New Delhi, India.
Printed and bound in Great Britain by Antony Rowe Ltd, Chippenham, Wiltshire.
This book is printed on acid-free paper responsibly manufactured from sustainable forestry
in which at least two trees are planted for each one used for paper production.

Contents

Preface

This book grew out of a series of training courses for practitioners that I taught on credit derivatives pricing, credit risk modelling and credit portfolio modelling. The aim of the book is to show how currently traded credit derivatives can be priced and risk-managed. As there is no such thing as *the* credit risk, and given the large variety of traded credit derivatives, different models will be appropriate for different tasks. I aimed to present the most important modelling approaches and to clearly point out the strengths and potential weaknesses of the different modelling approaches.

Even more than in other areas, a clear intuitive understanding of the mechanics of a pricing model is essential in credit markets. As credit markets are usually incomplete, it is dangerous to rely on a model that is not fully understood. One important function of the pricing model is to provide an aid to the intuition by reducing the problem of building an opinion on a complex quantity (like the price of a credit derivative) to the forming of an opinion on more fundamental quantities which are much better understood. Furthermore, a formal pricing model makes this process consistent so that arbitrages across the prices of different instruments are not possible. For this reason much time is spent on the explanation of the implications of different modelling assumptions and the meaning of the models' parameters.

A second function of credit derivatives pricing models is to provide a framework for the assessment of the risk involved in one particular credit derivative transaction or a whole portfolio of such instruments. Here the model's output is not just one number (the price) but rather a whole return distribution. If the model is to be used for hedging, the output is a consistent description of the price dynamics of the credit derivative and the underlying hedge instruments.

Like the market for credit derivatives, the field of credit risk modelling is expanding rapidly and still in flux. Thus, only in rare cases is it possible to give a definitive recipe for a given problem, and again an intuitive understanding of the essential features of a given modelling approach is necessary in order to assess other models that may be encountered later on.

In the past few years, credit derivatives have fundamentally transformed the way banks and other financial institutions view and manage credit risks.

The key feature of credit derivatives is that they allow the transfer of credit risks in an efficient, simple and standardised way and open up a market for these risks in which everybody can participate. Credit derivatives allow active risk transfer for credit risk managers, the management (some say arbitrage) of regulatory capital requirements for banks, new funding opportunities for banks through the securitisation of loan portfolios, portfolio optimisation for bond and loan portfolio managers, highly leveraged investment vehicles for speculators and hedge funds, and the structuring of previously unavailable risk–return profiles.

Thus it is no surprise that the market of credit derivatives has seen exponential growth rates with no signs of slowdown. The 14 firms alone that participated in the recent survey by *Risk* magazine (Patel, 2002) had a notional volume of $1398 billion credit derivatives contracts outstanding in November 2001.

Traditionally, a bank could only manage its credit risks at origination. Once the risk was originated, it remained on the books until the loan was paid off or the obligor defaulted. There was no efficient and standardised way to transfer this risk to another party, to buy or sell protection, or to optimise the risk–return profile of the portfolio. Consequently, the pricing of credit risks was in its infancy, spreads on loans only had to be determined at origination and were often determined by non-credit considerations such as the hope of cross-selling additional business in the corporate finance sector. There was no need to become more efficient because the absence of a transparent market meant that the mode of operation was more like an oligopoly than an efficient competition. Whether a loan was mispriced or not was impossible to determine with certainty, it all depended on the individual subjective assessment of the obligor's default risk. The main "cost" of extending a loan was the cost of the regulatory risk capital as prescribed by the rules of the Basel I capital accord, and this is the point where credit derivatives came in.

Credit derivatives allow banks to transfer the credit risk (and thus a large part of the regulatory capital) off their books while keeping the loan business; the borrower would never need to know that the bank had hedged his exposure. They can also substitute "good" risks for "bad" risks (and some cash) while keeping the required capital constant, and can actively exploit many of the other loopholes that exist in the regulatory framework. Using creatively structured credit derivatives, some banks were able to reduce their regulatory capital requirements so far that these requirements almost lost their meaning. Ultimately this led to the collapse of the Basel I capital accord and to the development of the new Basel II rules designed to take these new possibilities into account.

It can be argued that the regulatory capital rules of Basel I fuelled the growth of the market for credit derivatives in its initial stages and helped these instruments to attain the critical mass of participants and liquidity. But credit derivatives had and still have other applications, even with changed regulatory capital rules they are here to stay.

In recent years, credit exposure on a large number of obligors has become a traded asset. And even if a particular credit exposure is not among these traded credits, it nevertheless is a *potentially* traded asset. It only requires filling another name in the ISDA standard confirmation to open up a new credit market. So, at least potentially, almost every important credit exposure has its market.

This gives us the most important reason why credit derivatives will remain a growing sector: *credit is now a traded asset*. While credit portfolios used to resemble an insurance portfolio, they are now closer to a portfolio of traded assets like equities. The management of equity portfolios involves marking-to-market, active trading, risk–return analysis and tradeoffs, active portfolio optimisation. All these activities have their credit analogue in the trading of credit derivatives.

The most common instrument by far is the credit default swap (CDS). A CDS is a swap contract in which one counterparty (the protection buyer) pays a regular fee (the CDS fee) and the other counterparty (the protection seller) must pay a *default payment* if a *credit event* should occur with respect to the *reference credit*. The default payment is designed to approximate the loss that a holder of a bond issued by the reference credit would suffer at the default event. (The exact specification of these terms will be described later on, they have been standardised by the ISDA.) In the course of time, other instruments have emerged, most notably portfolio credit derivatives which pose entirely new modelling problems, and credit derivatives with option features embedded in them.

The book begins with a presentation of the most important credit derivatives and their payoff structures in Chapter 2. There are other, more specialised books on the details of the documentation of credit derivatives so we focus on those features that are relevant for the pricing and risk management of credit derivatives. Thus we focus on the cash flows of the credit derivatives and describe some rough, but model-independent, hedging strategies. These strategies can be made more precise using the spread curve and bond-based pricing techniques presented in the following chapter. This chapter provides models that connect the markets for credit default swaps and defaultable bonds of the same issuer. Furthermore, the problem of pricing single-name credit default swaps is reduced to the pricing of a set of basic building block securities: defaultable zero-coupon bonds and payoffs at default.

For the more advanced models some mathematical background is necessary, which is given in Chapter 4. In particular, useful facts on point processes and stopping times are summarised.

Chapter 5 then picks up where Chapter 3 left off and provides an introduction to the *intensity-based* approach to the pricing of credit risk and credit derivatives. Intensity-based models are the most popular class of credit derivatives pricing models, they are easily calibrated to market prices and provide realistic dynamics of defaultable bond prices.

Chapter 6 treats the modelling of recovery risk, an important input variable of all credit derivatives pricing models. In the literature on intensity-based credit risk models, several different approaches to the modelling of positive recovery have been proposed. In this chapter, these approaches are compared and their implications for the prices of defaultable coupon bonds and credit default swaps are analysed. Recovery rate risk and default risk are frequently not separable using market data, therefore historical experience is often used to fix one of the two parameters and the last part of this chapter treats the results of some of the most recent studies on defaulted bond recoveries.

Based upon the analysis of the previous chapters, we can tackle the question of how to concretely specify and implement intensity-based models in Chapter 7. Here a variety of different approaches are presented: two concrete specifications with analytical tractability (a multifactor Gaussian model and a multifactor square-root-based model of the Cox *et al.*, 1985b type); a model for the full term structure of credit spreads based upon the Heath *et al.* (1992) approach; and a variety of numerical implementation methods, amongst them a tree-based implementation algorithm, and a discussion of p.d.e.-based methods and Monte Carlo methods that can be used to implement intensity-based default risk models.

The credit rating models of Chapter 8 can be viewed as an extension of the intensity-based models treated so far. Here, default intensities can also depend on the rating transition process.

In Chapter 9, the firm's value-based approach to credit risk modelling is explored. These models have much appeal as they provide a link between the equity and credit markets. The analogies between this approach and pricing models for equity derivatives are shown, and empirical evidence of the accuracy of the firm's value-based models is presented.

Finally, Chapter 10 treats the modelling of portfolio credit risk and default correlation. While single-name credit risk models often show great analogies to interest rate models (in the intensity-based approach) or exotic equity options (in the firm's value models), portfolio and basket credit derivatives pose entirely new modelling problems. Starting from an analysis of the nature of these problems, we investigate different approaches to these modelling issues. Starting from simple static one-time-step models like Moody's binomial expansion technique and the Vasicek (1987) model, we then analyse the possibilities to directly extend the firm's value models and the intensity-based models to the multi-obligor case. As these direct attempts to cover portfolio credit risk all have their problems and disadvantages, we then also introduce *copula-based models*, the most promising new approach in this area. To this end, basic facts about copula functions are introduced and the models are built up step-by-step from simple static copula default models to semi-dynamic models and finally fully dynamic models.

Many of the credit derivatives pricing models presented in this book are extensions or modifications of pricing models that were developed in other contexts, most frequently interest rate modelling or exotic equity options. Therefore, modelling credit risk can be a quite advanced subject in terms of the background knowledge that is presupposed. While I tried to avoid unnecessary mathematical complications and chose the simpler option whenever this was possible without losing realism, it was not possible to present the material without assuming some previous knowledge in mathematical finance.

On the finance side, I assume previous knowledge of the level of a typical introductory book on mathematical finance in continuous time, like the books by Hull (1989), Wilmott *et al.* (1993) or Nielsen (1999). On the mathematical side it is assumed that the reader is familiar with the basics of the theory of stochastic processes. In particular, I assume familiarity with probability spaces, measurability, filtrations, the stochastic integral with respect to Brownian motion and diffusion processes, quadratic variation for continuous processes and Itô's lemma for diffusion processes. Basic knowledge of concepts like adapted and predictable stochastic processes, martingales and the Doob–Meyer decomposition will also be helpful. There are now a number of good and not too difficult books on the subject, e.g. the books by Neftci (1996) or Lamberton and Lapeyre (1996). Mathematical concepts that cannot be found in these books will be explained here with as little technicality as possible. I will give references to the mathematical literature for those readers who would like to go into more depth on these issues.

Acknowledgements

This book would not have been possible without input and support from many sides. Special thanks are due to Professor Dr. Dieter Sondermann and all my colleagues at the Department of Statistics, Bonn University who created the environment in which a project such as this book could flourish; to my editor Samantha Whittaker at Wiley for her patience and support; to Martin Helm, Greg Gupton, Ebbe Rogge, Erik Schlögl, Lutz Schlögl and Paul Wilmott for carefully reading the whole or parts of the manuscript and providing valuable comments and guidelines for improvement. I am further indebted to all fellow researchers on credit risk modelling issues who helped push forward the frontiers of the area, and to many practitioners and participants at my training courses who helped me stay focused on the realism and applicability of the models I developed and who provided fascinating research questions.

Needless to say, while I am extremely grateful for all the support I received during the time it took to write this book, I still claim sole responsibility for any errors that occur.

Abbreviations

ANC	affine combination of non-central chi-squared random variables
bn	billion (American definition: 1 bn = 1000m)
bp	basis points (1 bp = 1/100 percentage points)
CBO	collateralised bond obligation
CDO	collateralised debt obligation
CDS	credit default swap
CIR	Cox, Ingersoll, Ross (1985) interest-rate model
CLN	credit-linked note
CLO	collateralised loan obligation
CSO	credit spread option
DDS	default digital swap
DtD	distance to default (KMV model)
E2C	'equity-to-credit' default-risk model
EDF	expected default frequency (KMV model)
EUR	euro
Euribor	European interbank offered rate
FR	fractional recovery model
FRA	forward rate agreement
FtD	first-to-default swap
HJM	Heath, Jarrow, Morton interest rate model
ISDA	International Swap Dealers Association
JLT	Jarrow, Lando, Turnbull rating transition model
JPY	Japanese yen
KMV model	default risk model marketed by Moody's KMV
LGD	loss given default
Libor	London interbank offered rate
LMM	Libor market model
m	million
MD	multiple defaults model
NPV	net present value
ntD	nth-to-default swap
OTC	over-the-counter (not traded on an organised exchange)
PDE	partial differential equation

repo	repurchase (referring to repurchase transactions)
RMV	recovery of market value model
RP	recovery of par value model
RT	recovery of treasury model
S&P	Standard and Poor's
SPV	special purpose vehicle
StD	second-to-default swap
t	thousand
TRS	total return swap
USD	US dollar
ZCB	zero-coupon bond
ZR	zero recovery model

Notation

Counterparties

A	protection buyer
B	protection seller
C	reference obligor

Loans and bonds

A	value of default-free annuity
c	coupon
$\bar{c}$	coupon (defaultable bond)
C	coupon-bearing bond, default-free
$\bar{C}$	coupon-bearing bond, defaultable
K	notional

Rates and spreads

L	Libor
r^{repo}	repo rate
s	interest-rate swap rate (fixed-for-floating)
s^A	asset swap rate
s^{par}	par spread of defaultable bonds
s^{TRS}	TRS rate
$\bar{s}$	CDS rate
$\bar{s}^{DDS}$	default digital swap rate
$\bar{s}^{FtD}$	FtD rate

Default-free term structure of bond prices

b	default-free continuously compounded bank account
B	zero-coupon bond price
β	discount factor
f	forward rate, continuous compounding

F	forward rate, effective compounding
r	instantaneous short rate, continuously compounded
R	short rate, effective compounding

Defaultable term structure of bond prices

$\overline{B}$	zero-coupon bond price, zero recovery
$\overline{\beta}$	discount factor
$\overline{f}$	forward rate, continuous compounding
$\overline{F}$	forward rate, effective compounding
$\overline{r}$	instantaneous short rate, continuously compounded
$\overline{R}$	short rate, effective compounding

Term structure dynamics

μ	drift, forward rates
$\overline{\mu}$	drift, defaultable forward rates
σ	volatility, forward rates
$\overline{\sigma}$	volatility, defaultable forward rates

Default model

I	survival indicator function
λ	default intensity
P	survival probability
$\tilde{P}$	pseudo-survival probability
P^{def}	default probability
τ	time of default

Recovery models

c	recovery rate, recovery of treasury
π	recovery rate, recovery of par
q	recovery rate, fractional recovery
Q	payoff quota, multiple defaults

Rating transition models

$\{1, \ldots, K\}$	credit rating classes
I	identity matrix
Λ	generator matrix
$Q(t, T)$	transition probability matrix
$R(t)$	rating at time t

Firm's value models

$\overline{K}$	default barrier
S	share price of the firm
V	firm's value

Other notation

$\Delta t > 0$	time step in discretisation
$(\Omega, (\mathcal{F}_t)_{t \geq 0}, \mathcal{F}, Q)$	filtered probability space

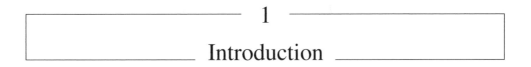

1

Introduction

1.1 THE WORLD OF CREDIT RISK

Credit risk[1] is the risk that an obligor does not honour his payment obligations.

Besides being an obvious topic for the introduction of a book on credit risk models, the proper definition of "credit risk" or "default risk" is also an important point in the documentation and definition of credit derivatives. Default risk is intrinsically linked to the payment obligation which the obligor ought to honour. An obligor who does not have any payment obligations, does not have any default risk either. (And no-one would be interested in his default risk anyway.) Therefore this definition only covers the default risk of a payment obligation, but not the default risk of the obligor himself. In principle, an obligor could not pay one of his obligations, but honour another.

This behaviour by the obligor is prevented by legal rules: the bankruptcy codes and contract law. Thanks to these, we can speak of the default risk of an obligor without specifying a particular payment obligation, because the obligor has to honour *all* his payment obligations as long as he is able to. If he is not able to do so, a workout procedure is entered, the obligor loses control of all of his assets and an independent agent tries to find ways to pay off the creditors using the obligor's assets. The bankruptcy code ensures that all creditors of the obligor are treated fairly and in accordance with a predetermined procedure. In particular, it is ensured that a default on one obligation entails a default on all other obligations, so the obligor cannot choose which claims he honours. Furthermore, because the workout procedure usually involves significant losses by the obligor, his incentives are such that he will try to ensure his solvency: a default only occurs if the obligor really cannot pay his obligations. But then it is no surprise that a default almost invariably entails a loss to the creditor.

It is usually very hard to predict these losses in default. They contain several unpredictable components: the question whether the obligor's business will be shut down and liquidated or sold to another investor, what assets there are to liquidate, the liquidation value or the sales price of the business, the vagaries of the legal proceedings, to name just a few.

Obligors who are not bound by bankruptcy codes, e.g. sovereign borrowers and borrowers in countries without a properly functioning legal system, frequently make use of the possibility to default only on selected of their obligations, sometimes without being in real financial distress. In these cases, the connection of default risk to the particular underlying payment obligation must not be ignored. Creditors often include cross-acceleration (or cross-default) clauses in the loan or bond contracts of such borrowers to ensure that a default on one obligation triggers an immediate repayment (or a default) of the debtor's other obligations. The severity of the losses in these cases is even more unpredictable than in the cases which are governed by a legal procedure. They depend almost entirely on the outcome of workout negotiations between the lenders and the obligor.

---

[1] Throughout the book, the terms "default risk" and "credit risk" will be used as synonyms.

This discussion already shows some important properties of default risk which make their quantitative modelling difficult:

- Default events are rare.
- They may occur unexpectedly.
- Default events involve significant losses.
- The size of these losses is unknown before default.

If default risk cannot be defined without a payment obligation, the converse is also true: there is no payment obligation that does not entail some credit risk.[2] Default risk is ubiquitous: firms might default on principal or interest payments on loans or bonds, on trade receivables, on tax obligations, on the wages of their employees, or on the invoices of their business partners, to name just a few. Basically, everything that represents a payment obligation carries default risk for exactly that reason.

In Section 2.3 we give a short overview of the most important defaultable payment obligations. They were selected for their relevance to credit risk modelling and credit derivatives. Thus we concentrate on large, financial obligations like loans and bonds which are usually of a long-term nature, while ignoring most of the others. These securities are used as underlying assets for credit derivatives, to define credit events, payoff times and payoffs of credit derivatives, and as hedge instruments to hedge the risks of uncovered credit derivatives positions.

1.2   THE COMPONENTS OF CREDIT RISK

We have already identified the most important components of credit risk.

Arrival risk is a term for the uncertainty whether a default will occur or not. To enable comparisons, it is specified with respect to a given time horizon, usually one year. The measure of arrival risk is the *probability of default*. The probability of default describes the distribution of the indicator variable *default before the time horizon*.

Timing risk refers to the uncertainty about the precise time of default. Knowledge about the time of default includes knowledge about the arrival risk for all possible time horizons, thus timing risk is more detailed and specific than arrival risk. The underlying unknown quantity (random variable) of timing risk is the *time of default*, and its risk is described by the *probability distribution function of the time of default*. If a default never happens, we set the time of default to infinity.

Recovery risk describes the uncertainty about the severity of the losses if a default has happened. In recovery risk, the uncertain quantity is the actual payoff that a creditor receives after a default. It can be expressed in several ways which will be discussed in a later chapter. Market convention is to express the recovery rate of a bond or loan as the fraction of the notional value of the claim that is actually paid to the creditor. Recovery risk is described by the *probability distribution of the recovery rate*, i.e. the probabilities that the recovery rate is of a given magnitude. This probability distribution is a conditional distribution, conditional upon default.

---

[2] Later on we will also speak of a *default-free* payoff but this is a convenient abstraction. Even the US government can default on its obligations (and many of the US states have indeed defaulted in history), we only assume that its default risk is negligible compared to the credit risk of some other obligor.

Market risk describes a different kind of risk, the risk of changes in the market price of a defaultable asset, even if no default occurs. Apart from other market factors that also affect the prices of default-free claims, market risk is also driven by *changes in timing and recovery risks*, or at least changes in the market's perception of these risks. This risk might be called **risk change risk**.

Market risk models are dynamic models, thus they add an additional layer of complexity. To avoid arbitrage opportunities in the model, market risk must be modelled in consistency with timing and recovery risk, and the changes in these risks, and in consistency with other market prices. For standard credit default swaps, changes in credit risk are in fact the dominant driver of market risk, while defaultable coupon bonds are also strongly influenced by changes in the default-free interest rates.

The impact of default risk can be affected by the behaviour of other market variables like movements in default-free interest rates, exchange rates, etc. These may influence the value of the defaultable claim, for instance if counterparty risk is considered in derivatives transactions. But it is also present in classical loans: for a given recovery rate, a default on a fixed-coupon loan in a high-interest-rate environment is less severe than a default on the same loan in a low-interest-rate environment, because the net present value of the lost claim is lower in the former case.

The term **market price correlation risk** covers this type of risk: the risk that defaults (and default likelihoods) are correlated with price movements of the defaultable asset.

While arrival risk and timing risk are usually specific to one defaultable obligor, recovery risk, market risk and market price correlation risk are specific to a particular payment obligation of a given obligor, or at least to a particular class of payment obligations.

If we consider the risk of joint defaults of several obligors, an additional risk component is introduced. **Default correlation risk** describes the risk that several obligors default together. Again here we have *joint arrival risk* which is described by the joint default probabilities over a given time horizon, and *joint timing risk* which is described by the joint probability distribution function of the times of default.

From a theoretical point of view, it is desirable to include as many of the different faces of default risk as possible. This comes at the cost of additional complexity in the model, implementation problems and slower runtime. Therefore, the first question a modeller has to ask himself is: Which risks do I need to include in the model, and which risks can I ignore without major losses in realism? For example, dynamic models of market risk are necessary to risk-manage and mark-to-model credit derivatives and tradeable defaultable bonds on a frequent basis. For a static book of loans this may be less important than having an accurate model of the default correlations. A second constraint is given by the available data. If there is no data to base a sophisticated model upon, one might as well choose a simpler version of the model which requires fewer inputs.

But this comes with a warning: every simplification involves implicit assumptions about the risks that are modelled, and these assumptions may have consequences that are not always obvious. One aim of this book is to give the quantitative modeller a good enough understanding of the properties of the different models, the risks that are modelled and the risks that are ignored, and the effects that changes in the inputs have on the model's outputs. This should enable him to make modelling decisions more confidently, and it should tell him which model is suitable to answer which question and in which circumstances to be wary of the model's outputs.

1.3   MARKET STRUCTURE

The market for credit derivatives was created in the early 1990s in London and New York. It is the market segment of derivative securities which is growing fastest at the moment. Table 1.1 shows estimates of the development of the market. The real size of the market will probably be even larger as both surveys only reached a subset of the market participants. Despite the downturn of most other markets, the credit derivatives market still exhibits strong growth rates. Nevertheless, viewed as a fraction of the total credit exposure in the world the market share of credit derivatives is minute – at least on this front the market is far from its limits.

According to the recent study by *Risk* magazine (Table 1.2; Patel, 2002), the largest share of the market is taken up by credit default swaps (CDSs). While the large majority of these will be "vanilla" CDSs based upon ISDA standards, there can still be significant variations and complications in the structures like cancellation or extension options or coupon stepups. First-to-default swaps (FtDs) also seemed to be grouped into this category. The second largest group are portfolio-related credit derivatives like collateralised loan obligations (CLOs), portfolio tranche protection, and synthetic collateralised debt obligations (CDOs). Finally, there are more exotic credit derivatives like credit spread options and hybrid instruments (i.e. instruments that combine features of other derivatives with a CDS) but – as mentioned before – many of the "exotic" features may already be present in a CDS.

Among newly traded CDSs, the most common specification has five years' maturity, a notional amount between 5m and 20m USD (or EUR), and is written on a large investment-grade reference credit at the lower end of the investment grade rating scale (A to BBB). Market share between European and US obligors is about equal, with 40% from Europe and 44% from the USA. Asian obligors had 12% market share in the Risk survey and emerging market obligors (excluding Asia) made up 5% of the market share. (As no Japanese bank took part in the Risk survey, the Asian market share may be misrepresented.) In many risks, the market for CDSs is already liquid enough to serve as a benchmark for marking-to-market or risk management.

Table 1.1   Size of the market for credit derivatives according to surveys by the British Bankers' Association and *Risk* (Patel, 2002)

Year	1997	1998	1999	2000	2001
Outstanding notional (USD bn)	170	350	586	893	1398

Table 1.2   Market share by instrument type (rounded numbers)

Instrument	Share (%)
Credit default swaps (including FtDs)	67
Synthetic balance sheet CLOs	12
Tranched portfolio default swaps	9
Credit-linked notes, asset repackaging, asset swaps	7
Credit spread options	2
Managed synthetic CDOs	2
Total return swaps	1
Hybrid credit derivatives	0.2

Source: Risk (Patel, 2002).

Examples are sovereign credit risk, most banks and financials, the large telecoms, and large industrial firms.

Participants in the market for credit derivatives are mostly banks (47%) who are motivated by regulatory capital arbitrage, funding arbitrage, or trading motives. Insurances and reinsurances (23%) and investment funds (5%) also have a large market share and often are the ultimate suppliers of credit protection to the market. They use credit derivatives as investments, or for the credit risk management of bond portfolios. Insurances feel comfortable with tranched portfolio transactions because many of the structures are designed to resemble reinsurance transactions. Hedge funds (8%) are entering the credit derivatives business in increasing numbers, motivated by the opportunities to gain on relative value trades between different markets (bonds and CDSs) and by the high leverage that many credit derivatives transactions allow. Not many industrials (4%) use credit derivatives up to this point, if they do they do it to hedge counterparty or country risk in isolated cases.

Trading takes place over-the-counter, but there are some virtual meeting places for buyers and sellers. The large investment banks routinely quote prices on their Bloomberg and internet pages, there are large specialised brokers (e.g. GFInet), and also two electronic exchanges for credit default swaps (creditex and credittrade). Nevertheless, these are only means to bring the counterparties together, in the end the contract is signed between the two counterparties and there is no central counterparty as there would be on an organised exchange.

2
Credit Derivatives: Overview and Hedge-Based Pricing

2.1 THE EMERGENCE OF A NEW CLASS OF DERIVATIVES

The market for credit derivatives is young, and the traded risks vary a lot in size, quality and structure. Trade takes place over-the-counter, after direct negotiations between buyers and sellers. Therefore the precise specification of credit derivatives is still in flux, and new structures appear on a regular basis.

The process of financial innovation starts from a given set of traded and liquid instruments. Investment banks use these instruments to offer their clients tailor-made risk-management solutions. Here, a more complete coverage of the end-users' risk means more business, but also fewer possibilities to hedge this exposure in the market using the standard instruments. A financial innovation may allow investment banks to offer their clients better risk-management solutions and to lay off these risks to other investors. If the innovation is successful its liquidity increases and eventually it will become a standard instrument itself.

Helpful factors for the success of a financial innovation are: the existence of a simple, robust hedging strategy (allowing to "borrow" liquidity from the hedging instrument), a similarity of the innovation with existing securities, at least some initial liquidity in the market, and the minimisation of legal risks within the structure which can be achieved by standardisation and the existence of precedence cases.

In the case of credit derivatives the cycle of innovation started from instruments like asset swap packages and total rate of return swaps, proceeded over credit default swaps and credit-linked notes, and has now reached exotic credit default swaps and basket and portfolio credit derivatives. For many obligors, credit default swaps have already the status of standard traded instruments.

The remainder of the chapter is organised as follows. After a short qualitative overview of the market and after introducing some notation, we have a closer look at the underlying assets that are needed to define credit derivatives. Then, the standard types of credit derivatives, asset swaps, total return swaps, and credit default swaps are introduced. The structures, motivations of buyer and seller, and important points to watch out for in the documentation are analysed. Next, simple, approximative hedging strategies are given for these credit derivatives. After that, some more recently developed, exotic credit derivatives are introduced and analysed. The chapter is concluded with a guide to the literature.

2.2 TERMINOLOGY

The term *credit derivative* is applied to a very broad class of derivative securities. Their common feature is the following:

Definition 2.1

(a) A credit derivative is a derivative security that is primarily used to transfer, hedge or manage credit risk.

(b) A credit derivative is a derivative security whose payoff is materially affected by credit risk.

According to the first definition above, the intended use of the derivative security determines whether the derivative is a credit derivative or not. A simple derivative contract like a forward contract on a defaultable bond may be a credit derivative to one counterparty (because he intends to use it to manage credit risk) and not a credit derivative to another. The second condition, that the payoff is materially affected by credit risk, is a necessary condition for the suitability of the derivative as a hedge instrument for credit risk. This broad definition covers instruments as varied as forwards and options on defaultable bonds, total return swaps on defaultable bonds, credit spread options, credit default swaps, and all other credit derivatives covered in this book.

The following definition is much narrower. It applies to derivatives that focus almost exclusively on credit risk, the credit risk is isolated. Amongst these are credit default swaps, basket credit derivatives, and similar products.

Definition 2.2   A credit derivative *is a derivative security that has a payoff which is conditioned on the occurrence of a* credit event. *The credit event is defined with respect to a* reference credit *(or several reference credits), and the* reference credit asset(s) *issued by the reference credit. If the credit event has occurred, the* default payment *has to be made by one of the counterparties.*

Besides the default payment a credit derivative can have further payoffs that are not default contingent.

This definition can be extended to include derivative securities whose payoffs are materially affected by credit events and derivatives on defaultable underlying securities. This would also cover asset swap packages, total rate of return swaps and options on defaultable bonds, which would not be classified as credit derivatives according to Definition 2.2.

Most credit derivatives have a default-insurance feature. In naming the counterparties we will use the convention that counterparty **A** will be the insured counterparty (i.e. the counterparty that receives a payoff if a default happens or the party that is long the credit derivative), and counterparty **B** will be the insurer (who has to pay or suffers a loss in default). Party **C** will be the reference credit.

One of the attractions of credit derivatives is the large degree of flexibility in their specification. Key terms of most credit derivatives are as follows.

Reference entity/reference credit: One (or several) issuer(s) whose defaults trigger the credit event. This can be one or several (a basket structure) defaultable issuers.

Reference obligations/reference credit asset: A set of assets issued by the reference credit. They are needed for the determination of the credit event and for the calculation of the recovery rate (which is used to calculate the default payment). Possible reference credit assets can range from "any financial obligation of the reference entity" to a specific list of some of the bonds issued by the reference entity. Loans and liquidly traded bonds are a common choice. The reference credit assets are clearly identified in the credit derivative's specification.

Frequently, different assets are used for the determination of the credit event and the recovery rate.[1]

Credit event: A precisely defined default event, which is usually defined with respect to the reference credit(s) and reference credit assets. Possible definitions include:

- bankruptcy,
- failure to pay (typically a certain materiality threshold must be exceeded and a grace period must have lapsed),
- obligation default,
- obligation acceleration,
- repudiation/moratorium,
- restructuring,[2]
- ratings downgrade below given threshold (only for ratings-triggered credit derivatives),
- changes in the credit spread (only for credit spread-triggered credit derivatives).

The definition of a credit event has by now been standardised by the ISDA (except for the possible inclusion of restructuring events). There may be cases when one of the counterparties would like to use a definition of the default event that differs from the standard ISDA definition, e.g. based upon the rating agencies' default definitions (which are narrower). The definitions are freely negotiable, so they can even include events going as far as "armed hostilities", "social unrest" or earthquakes (for sovereigns), or "merger or takeover" (for corporates). Furthermore, there are formal requirements for the default event to be triggered. Notice of the default event has to be given by one of the counterparties (usually the protection buyer), and it has to be based upon publicly available information.

Default payment: The payments which have to be made if a credit event has happened. This is the defining feature of most credit derivatives, and we will consider possible alternatives when discussing the individual credit derivatives. The technical modalities of the payment (cash or physical delivery, payment dates, determination of the payment amount) can also significantly affect the value of the default protection that the credit derivatives provides.

Example 2.1 *Default digital swap on the United States of Brazil. Counterparty **B** (the insurer) agrees to pay USD 1m to counterparty **A** if and when Brazil misses a coupon or principal payment on one of its Eurobonds. Here:*

- *The reference credit is the United States of Brazil;*
- *The reference credit assets are the Eurobonds issued by Brazil (in the credit derivative contract there would be an explicit list of these bonds);*
- *The credit event is a missed coupon or principal payment on one of the reference assets;*
- *The default payment is USD 1m.*

*In return for this, counterparty **A** pays a fee to **B**.*

---

[1] Assume a bank has a large loan exposure to **C**. To hedge this, a credit derivative could use a missed payment on the *loan* as credit event trigger and the post-default market price of a *bond* issued by **C** to determine the recovery rate. As the loan is not traded, its recovery rate cannot be determined from market prices.

[2] At the time of writing there was a dispute in the market whether "restructuring" should be included in the list of default events or not.

Recently, the ISDA has published a standard specification for credit default swaps. This contributed much to the transparency of the market. In the course of the 1997 Asian crisis and the ensuing Russian crisis many credit events were triggered, and these precedence cases helped to further resolve legal uncertainties. Nevertheless, there are still many open problems in the area of adequate documentation of credit derivatives. Despite the large degree of flexibility it is impossible to cover every contingency in the definition of the credit event, and – apart from digital payoffs – there will also be problems in matching the default payment exactly to the exposure that is to be hedged. Even with physical delivery there may be problems if the reference asset is very illiquid or not traded at all (e.g. a loan).

Ignoring the problems in the details of the specification, some credit derivatives have become quasi-standard credit derivative structures. In the following sections we will examine these structures and their applications in further detail.

2.3 UNDERLYING ASSETS

2.3.1 Loans

Historically, loans are the oldest type of payment obligation, and they are still one of the most important ways to raise investment capital.

Loans are bilateral contracts between the borrower and the lender (usually a bank). In its basic form, a loan consists of a sum (the principal or notional amount) which was originally lent by the creditor to the obligor and which the obligor has to repay to the creditor at the maturity date. In addition, the obligor has to make regular interest payments in the meantime. This results in the following promised payoff stream which is also shown in Table 2.1 (payoffs in default are treated in more detail in a later section):

- At origination, the lender pays the notional amount K to the borrower.
- At the maturity date T_N of the bond, the obligor pays back the notional amount K.
- At intermediate dates T_i, $i \leq N$, the obligor makes interest payments $\bar{c}_i$. ($0 < T_1 < T_2 < \cdots < T_N$).

There are many variations to this basic structure. Instead of repaying the whole principal amount at maturity (bullet repayment), the obligor might pay it back in regular instalments (an amortising loan). The borrower often has to provide collateral to secure the loan, and common

Table 2.1 Payoff streams to the lender in a loan or a defaultable bond. The initial investment is either the notional amount K lent to the borrower or the initial price $\overline{C}(0)$ paid for the bond. Payoffs marked with an asterisk are contingent on survival

Time	Loan/defaultable bond
$t = 0$	$-K$ or $-\overline{C}(0)$
$t = T_i$	$\bar{c}_i^*$
$t = T_N$	$(K + \bar{c}_N)^*$
Default	Recovery

forms of collateral are real estate (mortgages) or securities. There may be cancellation or continuation options on both sides of the loan. In a *credit facility* or *line of credit* the borrower can choose (within limits set by the lender) the timing and size of the loan himself, of course he must pay a fee for this flexibility. The interest payments can also vary. They can be a fixed fraction of the notional amount or floating, i.e. benchmarked to a market interest rate (usually Libor/Euribor), and if they are floating they can furthermore be capped and/or floored. There may also be periods when no interest has to be paid.

This flexibility in their specification is only possible because loans are bilaterally negotiated contracts, but this feature also makes loans difficult to trade or to transfer to other lenders.

2.3.2 Bonds

Bonds are the securitised version of loans, the major difference to loans is that they are tradeable in small denominations. Tradeability has several advantages. It opens access to a much larger number of potential lenders, the lenders can lend smaller amounts and do not need to remain invested for the whole borrowing period, they can easily sell the bond before its maturity. This adds value to the bonds, and therefore the borrower can sell them at better prices to the globally highest bidders, which usually results in better conditions than bilateral negotiations with just a few potential loan creditors. Furthermore, the prices of defaultable bonds contain extremely important information about the market's assessment of the issuer's credit risk. Defaultable bonds are natural hedge instruments against default risk exposures and the prices of defaultable bonds and credit default swaps are closely linked.

For marketability reasons, most bonds are more standardised than loans, but there are exceptions, e.g. structured notes which can have extremely complex payoffs. Bond issuance takes more time and resources than the preparation of a loan, and this is only worthwhile in the case of large issue sizes. If the amount of capital to be raised is small or time presses, loans are more popular.

The most important identifying properties of a bond are its issuer, the coupon size and frequency, and the date of maturity. The (promised) payoffs are very similar to those of loans (see also Table 2.1):

- At issuance, the lenders/investors buy the bonds from the borrower/issuer. The price is usually at par.
- At the coupon payment dates T_i the issuer pays the coupon payments $\bar{c}_i$ to the owners of the bonds.
- At the maturity date T_N, the issuer pays the final coupon payment $\bar{c}_N$ and the principal K.

After issuance, bonds are traded on a secondary market. Compared to equity markets, the market for corporate bonds is complex. Trade takes place through brokers and not exchanges, the number of tradeable securities is large because there are often several bonds per issuer, and the differences between the securities are subtle. Here, many conventions and rules have evolved to make the payoff streams of different bonds comparable and to avoid potential disputes. Such rules are e.g.:

Coupon payment conventions: *day count conventions* for the calculation of coupon payment amounts, *day shift conventions* for the determination of coupon payment dates if the original date falls on a holiday, or *common coupon frequencies*, e.g. semi-annual coupons for US corporate bonds, and annual coupons for European corporate bonds.

Price quotation conventions: *clean prices* (without accrued interest), *dirty prices* (with accrued interest), *yield-to-maturity* quotations which in turn depend on the discounting conventions used, or the fact that prices are given for a notional of 1000.

Furthermore, rating agencies have very successfully made a business out of providing credit risk analysis to the market participants.

Knowledge of the market conventions is important to precisely specify the prices and payoff streams of the bonds, and a good introduction to these and more details of the bond markets can be found in the books listed in Section 2.11 (Guide to the Literature). The following types of bonds are particularly important.

Fixed-coupon bonds are the most common type of bond. The coupon amounts are fixed in advance, and we also assume that the notional is only (and fully) repaid at maturity (bullet maturity).

Par floaters also have a full principal repayment at maturity but their coupon amounts are linked to a benchmark short-term interest rate (usually Libor) plus a constant spread. The spread is chosen such that the price of the par floater is initially at par.

Zero-coupon bonds do not have any coupon payments during the lifetime of the bonds and to compensate the investors they are issued at a deep discount from par. They are rarely seen in the corporate bond markets but they are very convenient building blocks for credit risk modelling.

Convertible bonds are discussed in the following subsection.

2.3.3   Convertible bonds

In addition to the conventional coupon and principal payments of a plain fixed-coupon bond, the holder of a convertible bond has the right to convert his bond into shares of the borrower. The precise conditions of this conversion right (conversion ratios, conversion dates, and other conditions for conversion) are specified in the bond's term sheet.

Convertible bonds are a popular financing instrument in particular for risky startup companies because they allow the creditor to participate in the upside of the venture while retaining the more preferable status of a creditor (rather than a shareholder) if things should go wrong. Convertible bonds also provide some protection against the asset substitution effect.

2.3.4   Counterparty risk

A more recent – but sometimes very important – type of defaultable payment obligation is created by counterparty risk in over-the-counter derivatives transactions. Given the long term and large notional amount of some of these transactions the default risks may be significant, even if netting procedures are in place. One major problem here is the complicated and volatile nature of the value of the underlying defaultable payment obligation.

2.4   ASSET SWAPS

An *asset swap package* is a combination of a defaultable bond (the asset) with an interest-rate swap contract that swaps the coupon of the bond into a payoff stream of Libor plus a spread. This spread is chosen such that the value of the whole package is the par value of the defaultable bond. Usually, the bond is a fixed-coupon bond and the interest-rate swap a fixed-for-floating interest-rate swap.

Example 2.2   *The payoffs of the asset swap package are as follows. **A** sells to **B** for 1 (the notional value of the **C**-bond):*

- *A fixed coupon bond issued by **C** with coupon $\bar{c}$ payable at coupon dates T_i, $i = 1, \ldots, N$;*
- *A fixed-for-floating swap (as below).*

As payments of the swap the following payments are made: at each coupon date T_i, $i \leq N$ of the bond

- ***B** pays to **A**: $\bar{c}$, the amount of the fixed coupon of the bond;*
- ***A** pays to **B**: Libor $+ s^A$.*

s^A is called the asset swap spread *and is adjusted to ensure that the asset swap package has indeed the initial value of 1.*

The asset swap is not a credit derivative in the strict sense, because the swap is unaffected by any credit events, so it is only a portfolio of a bond and a swap contract. Its main purpose is to transform the pre-default payoff streams of different defaultable bonds into the same form: *Libor + asset swap spread*. **B** still bears the full default risk and if a default should happen, the swap will still have to be serviced or to be unwound at market value.

Asset swap packages are popular and liquid instruments in the defaultable bonds market, and sometimes it is easier to trade an asset swap package than the underlying defaultable bond alone. A large fraction of traded asset swaps contain additional, more complex structural features that are either designed to strip out unwanted structural features from the underlying asset or to enhance yield. Asset swaps also serve frequently as underlying assets for other derivatives, e.g. options on asset swaps, so-called *asset swaptions*. An asset swaption gives **B** the right to enter an asset swap package at some future date T at a predetermined asset swap spread s^{A*}.

2.5   TOTAL RETURN SWAPS

An asset swap achieves the goal of transforming a payment of the *size* of the coupon of the defaultable bond into a floating-rate payment, but it is unaffected by changes in the market value of the defaultable bond or an actual default event. The total return swap on the other hand exchanges the *actual* return of the defaultable bond for a floating payment.

In a *total return swap* (**TRS**) (or *total rate of return swap*) **A** and **B** agree to *exchange all cash flows* that arise from two different investments. Usually one of these two investments is a defaultable investment, and the other is a default-free Libor investment. This structure allows an exchange of the assets' payoff profiles without legally transferring ownership of the assets.

The payoffs of a total rate of return swap are as follows. Counterparty **A** pays to counterparty **B** at regular payment dates T_i, $i \leq N$

- The coupon $\bar{c}$ of the bond issued by **C** (if there was one since the last payment date T_{i-1});
- The price appreciation $(\overline{C}(T_i) - \overline{C}(T_{i-1}))^+$ of bond **C** since the last payment;
- The principal repayment of bond **C** (at the final payment date);
- The recovery value of the bond (if there was a default).

B pays at the same intervals:

- A regular fee of Libor $+ s^{TRS}$;
- The price depreciation $(\overline{C}(T_{i-1}) - \overline{C}(T_i))^+$ of bond **C** since the last payment (if there was any);
- The par value of the bond (if there was a default in the meantime).

These payments are netted.

In the example above the two investments whose payoff streams are exchanged are: (a) an investment of a dollar amount of the face value of the **C**-bond at Libor and (b) the investment in the **C**-bond, adjusted by a spread on the Libor investment.

B has almost the same payoff stream as if he had invested in the bond **C** directly and funded this investment at $Libor + s^{TRS}$. The only difference is that the total rate of return swap is marked to market at regular intervals. Price changes in the bond **C** become cash flows for the TRS immediately, while for a direct investment in the bond they would only become cash flows when the bond matures or the position is unwound. This makes the TRS similar to a futures contract on the **C**-bond, while the direct investment is more similar to a forward. The TRS is not exactly equivalent to a futures contract because it is marked to market using the *spot* price of the underlying security, and not the *futures* price. The resulting price difference can be adjusted using the spread s^{TRS} on the floating payment of **B**.

The reference asset should be liquidly traded to ensure objective market prices for the marking to market. The prices are determined using a dealer poll mechanism. If there is no market for the asset (e.g. for bank loans), the total return swap cannot be marked to market. Then the term of the TRS must match the term of the underlying loan or another termination mechanism must be found (e.g. physical delivery).

Total rate of return swaps are among the most popular credit derivatives. They have several advantages to both counterparties:

- Counterparty **B** is long the reference asset without having to fund the investment up front. This allows counterparty **B** to leverage his position much higher than he would otherwise be able to. Usually, depending on his credit quality, **B** will have to post collateral, though.
- If the reference asset is a loan and **B** is not a bank then this may be the only way in which **B** can invest in the reference asset.
- Counterparty **A** has hedged his exposure to the reference credit if he owns the reference asset (but he still retains some counterparty risk).
- The transaction can be effected without the consent or knowledge of the reference credit **C**. **A** is still the lender to **C** and keeps the bank–customer relationship.
- If **A** does not own the reference asset he has created a short position in the asset. Because of its long maturity, a short position with a TRS is less vulnerable to short squeezes than a short repo position. Furthermore, directly shorting defaultable bonds or loans is often impossible.

Fundamentally, a TRS can be viewed as a synthetic form of funding the investment into the **C**-bond, where the **C**-bond is used as collateral. Thus, the TRS spread s^{TRS} should not only be driven by the default risk of the underlying asset but also by the credit quality of **B** as a counterparty.

If there is only one payment date, the TRS is equivalent to a forward contract on the **C**-bond.

2.6 CREDIT DEFAULT SWAPS

The total return swap achieves the goal of a transferral of the **C**-risk from **A** to **B**, but it has some disadvantages. The default risk of **C** is not isolated but mixed up with the market risk of the reference asset. Furthermore, basis risk may remain as the default risk of the obligor **C** is not transferred, only the risk of one bond issued by **C**. The obligor might not default on the reference asset of the TRS but on other obligations. A credit default swap on the other hand enables the investors to isolate the default risk of the obligor. The basic structure is as follows.

In a single-name *credit default swap* (**CDS**) (also known as a *credit swap*) **B** agrees to pay the default payment to **A** *if a default has happened*. The default payment is structured to replace the loss that a typical lender would incur upon a credit event of the reference entity. If there is no default of the reference security until the maturity of the default swap, counterparty **B** pays nothing.

A pays a fee for the default protection. The fee can be either a regular fee at intervals until default or maturity (the most common version, we speak of a default *swap*) or a lump-sum fee up front (less common, a default *put*). If a default occurs between two fee payment dates, **A** still has to pay the fraction of the next fee payment that has accrued until the time of default (Table 2.2).

Default swaps can differ in the specification of the default payment. Possible alternatives are:

- Physical delivery of one or several of the reference assets against repayment at par;
- Notional minus post-default market value[3] of the reference asset (cash settlement);
- A pre-agreed fixed payoff, irrespective of the recovery rate (default digital swap).

An example of a default swap with a fixed repayment at default was given in Example 2.1 (default digital swap on Brazil) but the fixed payment at default is a less common specification. The vast majority of credit default swaps specify physical delivery of one of the underlying securities against a payment of its par value as default payment. Sometimes substitute securities may be delivered, or a payoff that depends on other market variables may be specified (e.g. to hedge counterparty exposure in derivatives transactions).

Of the securities introduced so far, the credit default swap contains the cleanest isolation of obligor **C**'s default risk. If he has an underlying exposure to **C**, the protection buyer (**A**) retains the market risk but is hedged against the default risk, while the protection seller (**B**) can assume the credit risk alone. By changing the set of reference securities in the credit default swap, the counterparties can agree to focus more on the default risk of an individual bond issued by **C**, or they can widen the coverage to any of **C**'s obligations, thus covering the obligor's default risk completely.

Although the number of possible variations is large, the majority of traded credit default swaps follow a common specification which has been proposed by the ISDA. Because of their great importance, we now analyse the specification and payoffs of a typical credit default swap in more detail.

To identify a credit default swap, the following information has to be provided:

1. The reference obligor and his reference assets;
2. The definition of the credit event that is to be insured (default definition);
3. The notional of the CDS;

---

[3] The post-default market value is determined from dealer bid and ask quotes, averaged over a certain period of time and over several dealers and reference assets.

Table 2.2   Payoff streams of a credit default swap to protection seller **B** (the payoffs to the protection buyer **A** are the converse of these). Payoffs marked with an asterisk cease at default

Time	Defaultable bond	CDS
$t = 0$	$-\overline{C}(0)$	0
$t = T_i$	$\overline{c}^*$	$+\overline{s}^*$
$t = T_N$	$(1 + \overline{c})^*$	$+\overline{s}^*$
Default	Recovery	$-(1 - \text{Recovery})$ (minus the default payment)

4. The start of the CDS, the start of the protection;
5. The maturity date;
6. The credit default swap spread;
7. The frequency and day count convention for the spread payments;
8. The payment at the credit event and its settlement.

The reference obligor in our example is **C**, his default risk is the object of the CDS contract. In addition to the specification of the reference obligor, it is also necessary to specify a set of reference assets, usually a set of bonds of a given seniority class (e.g. senior unsecured) issued by the reference obligor. Reference assets are necessary to:

- Determine some default events (missed payments on the reference assets);
- Precisely specify the set of deliverable assets in default (for physical delivery);
- Determine a basis for the price and recovery determination mechanism in default (for cash settlement).

Different sets of reference assets are used for these different purposes. Usually, the set of deliverable obligations is smaller, while the set of reference obligations that determine the default event is very large.

It is unclear at the moment what happens if the reference obligor is taken over or merged with another company, or what happens if the reference obligor is split up into several individual companies. These events can significantly change the credit risk of the company. In the case of a takeover or merger, the protection should be transferred to the new company, but either of the parties may want to cancel the CDS for this reason. Splitting up the company will create different daughter firms whose credit risk will typically be higher than the mother's.

The event that is to be insured against is a default of the reference obligor, but because of the large payments involved the definition of what constitutes a default has to be made more precise, and a mechanism for the determination of the default event must be given. The standard definition of default includes:

- bankruptcy, filing for protection,
- failure to pay,
- obligation default, obligation acceleration,
- repudiation/moratorium,
- restructuring.[4]

---

[4] Restructuring is frequently omitted as a default event.

Of these, bankruptcy and filing for protection refer to the reference obligor himself, while failure to pay, obligation default and acceleration, repudiation/moratorium and restructuring are defined with respect to the reference obligations. For the latter to be triggered, the affected payments must exceed a materiality threshold and the event must prevail over a grace period of some days. These provisions have the purpose of ensuring that only real defaults trigger the CDS, and not technical glitches or minor legal disputes.

There is a debate whether restructuring should be included as a default event in the specification or not, and some market makers even quote different prices for CDSs with and without restructuring in the default definition. Sometimes (in particular in default definitions for CDOs), a slightly different default definition is used which is based upon rating agencies' definitions of default. Despite the growing standardisation of the default definition, one advantage of a CDS is that both parties can agree to an event definition that can be completely different from the standard ISDA specification.

Notional values of credit default swaps vary from one million USD up to several hundred million, with smaller sizes for lower credit quality. Typical trades for CDSs on investment-grade obligors have a notional size of 10–100m USD.

The starting date of most credit default swaps is three trading days after the trading date. A later starting date can be specified, and in this case one speaks of a *forward credit default swap*.

Most credit default swaps are quoted for a benchmark time-to-maturity of five years. For common reference credits, most dealers will also quote prices for other times to maturity, usual terms ranging from 1 to 10 years. For regulatory reasons' a 364-day (i.e. one year minus one day) CDS also had a place in the market some time ago.

The credit default swap spread constitutes the *price* of the default protection that has to be paid by the protection buyer to the protection seller. The cash payment amount is the CDS spread multiplied by the notional, adjusted for the day count fraction. Typical payment terms are quarterly or semi-annually with an actual/360 day count convention. The first fee is usually payable at the end of the first period, and if a default happens between two fee payment dates, the accrued fee up to the time of the default must be paid to the protection seller.

Depending on the credit quality of the protection seller, his counterparty may require him to post collateral on the contract which can range from 5% to 50% of the notional amount.

The possible payments in default have already been discussed above. Both counterparties can agree to appoint a *calculation agent* who supervises the price determination and settlement procedure of the CDS in default.

Example 2.3 *Credit default swap on Daimler Chrysler.*

The trade

At time t = 0, A and B enter a credit default swap on Daimler Chrysler, A as protection buyer and B as protection seller. They have agreed on:

  (i) The reference credit: Daimler Chrysler AG.
 (ii) The term of the credit default swap: 5 years.
(iii) The notional of the credit default swap: 20m USD.
(iv) The credit default swap fee: $\bar{s} = 116$ bp.

*These are the most important items in the specification. For the other details of the specification of the contract we assume that **A** and **B** follow the specifications proposed by the ISDA.*

The settlement period for the trade is three business days from the trade date, this is when the first fee payment period and the default protection begin.

The fee payments

*The credit default swap fee $\bar{s} = 116$ bp is quoted per annum as a fraction of the notional. **A** pays the fee in regular intervals, semi-annually. To make our life easier, we simplify the day count fractions to $1/2$ such that **A** pays to **B**:*

$$116 \, bp \times 20m/2 = 116\,000 \, USD \quad at \quad T_1 = 0.5, \; T_2 = 1, \ldots, T_{10} = 5$$

These payments are stopped and the CDS is unwound as soon as a default of Daimler Chrysler occurs.

Determining a credit event

The credit events (bankruptcy, failure to pay, obligation acceleration, repudiation/moratorium or restructuring) are defined in the CDS contract with respect to a large set of bonds issued by the reference entity, Daimler Chrysler. Let us assume these are all senior unsecured USD and EUR-denominated bonds issed by Daimler Chrysler with an issue size of at least 10m USD or 10m EUR.

Let us (hypothetically) assume that at date $t = \tau$, Daimler Chrysler has failed to pay a coupon that was due at this date on one of the bonds listed above. This could potentially constitute a credit event according to the CDS contract, if some conditions are met. First, the disputed amount must exceed a materiality threshold, and second, it must remain unpaid after a grace period of some days.

*If these conditions are satisfied then the protection buyer **A** will notify the protection seller **B** of the occurrence of a credit event and the credit default swap contract is unwound.*

The default payment

*First, **A** pays the remaining accrued fee. If the default occurred two months after the last fee payment, **A** will pay $116\,000 \times 2/6$. The next step is the determination of the default payment. If physical settlement has been agreed upon, **A** will deliver Daimler Chrysler bonds to **B** with a total notional of USD 20m (the notional of the CDS). The set of deliverable obligations has been specified in the documentation of the CDS. As liquidity in defaulted securities can be very low, this set usually contains more than one bond issue by the reference credit. Naturally **A** will choose to deliver the bond with the lowest market value, unless he has an underlying position of his own that he needs to unwind. (Even then he may prefer to sell his position in the market and buy the cheaper bonds to deliver them to **B**.) This* delivery option *enhances the value of his default protection. **B** must pay the full notional for these bonds, i.e. USD 20m in our example.*

If cash settlement has been agreed upon, a robust procedure is necessary to determine the market value of the bonds after default. If there were no liquidity problems, it would be sufficient to ask a dealer to give a price for these bonds, and use that price, but liquidity and manipulation are a very real concern in the market for distressed securities. Therefore not one, but several, dealers are asked to provide quotes, and an average is taken after eliminating the highest and lowest quotes. This is repeated, sometimes several times, in order to eliminate the influence of temporary liquidity holes. Thus the price of the defaulted bonds is determined, e.g. 430 USD for a bond of 1000 USD notional. Now, the protection seller pays the difference between this price and the par value for a notional of 20m USD, i.e.

$$(1000 - 430)/1000 \times 20m \ USD = 11.4m \ USD$$

Whichever settlement procedure is agreed upon, the CDS settles very quickly in a matter of only a few weeks (usually around six weeks) after the credit event notice. This is much quicker than the determination of the final recovery rate through the bankruptcy courts.

Because the price determination in cash settlement is so involved, most credit default swaps specify physical delivery in default. Cash settlement is only chosen when there may not be any physical assets to deliver (i.e. the reference entity has not issued enough bonds) or if the CDS is embedded in another structure where physical delivery would be inconvenient, e.g. a credit-linked note.

Physical delivery is not entirely without problems either. If many traders have speculated on the default of **C** by buying credit protection without having an underlying position in the bonds, these traders will all have to buy **C**-bonds after a default event in order to deliver them to their respective protection sellers. This demand may push up prices to an artificially high level which may damage the value of the default protection.

A word on terminology: the asset that is traded in a CDS is *default protection*. This means:

- A *long position* in a CDS is a position as protection buyer;
- A *short position* in a CDS is a position as protection seller;
- A *bid* of xx bp on a CDS means that the bidder is willing to enter a CDS as protection buyer at a spread of xx bp;
- An *offer* of yy bp on a CDS means that the offerer is willing to enter a CDS as protection seller at a spread of yy bp.

With this terminology, the bid quotes will always be below the offer quotes, as is usual in other markets. There is also a competing trader jargon where to "go long in defaults" can mean going long the credit, i.e. *selling* the protection. In this book we will not use that terminology but stick to the "protection" terminology.

2.7 HEDGE-BASED PRICING

For some of the basic credit derivatives there exist simple approximative hedge and replication strategies. These cash-and-carry valuation methods are often imprecise but very important and popular in practice. They provide upper and lower price bounds, provide hedge strategies that cover much of the risks involved in the credit derivatives, and these results are robust because they are independent of any specific pricing model.

2.7.1   Hedge instruments

For simplicity we assume that coupon payments of coupon bonds and swap payments occur on the same dates which are denoted by $0 = T_0, T_1, T_2, \ldots, T_N$. In reality this will not always be the case but the relevant adjustments should be obvious. We also abstract from the day count fractions that have to be used to adjust payments occurring at regular intervals.[5]

The following assets will be used in the hedge strategies.

Defaultable bonds: Defaultable coupon bonds issued by **C** with fixed and floating coupons. The fixed-coupon bond carries a coupon of $\overline{c}$ and has a price of $\overline{C}(t)$ at time t. We also consider defaultable floating coupon bonds with a coupon of Libor $+ s^{par}$ and a price of $\overline{C}'(t)$.

Default-free bonds: $C(t)$ denotes the time t price of a default-free coupon bond with a coupon of c. We also use $B(t, T)$, the time t price of a default-free zero-coupon bond with maturity T.

Interest-rate swaps: $s(t)$ denotes the swap rate at time t of a standard fixed-for-floating interest-rate swap. It is well known that the (forward) interest-rate swap rate contracted at t for the time interval $[T_n, T_N]$ is:

$$s(t) = \frac{B(t, T_n) - B(t, T_N)}{A(t; T_n, T_N)}, \qquad (2.1)$$

where $A(t; T_n, T_N) = \sum_{i=n+1}^{N} \delta_i B(t, T_i)$ is the value of an annuity[6] paying δ_i at each date T_i, starting from the first date T_{n+1} after T_n, and $\delta_i = T_i - T_{i-1}$ are the day count fractions for the time intervals. If the swap starts immediately, we have $T_n = t$.

Some of the hedge instruments may not always be available. Most obligors only issue fixed-coupon debt, if they issue traded debt at all. In many cases the only bonds available carry call provisions or are convertible into equity which again makes them unsuitable for the simple hedge strategies outlined here. On the other hand, we can safely assume the existence of default-free bonds and interest-rate swaps of all maturities. The floating rate (Libor) of the interest-rate swap and the swap payments are assumed to be default-free unless otherwise stated.

2.7.2   Short positions in defaultable bonds

Trading strategies that yield a positive payoff in the case of a default event are very important for the hedging of default risk. This can be achieved by implementing a short position in a defaultable bond. In the literature, short positions are often simply treated as "negative portfolio positions", without considering the sometimes rather complicated underlying trading strategies that have to be followed in reality. This can lead to confusion regarding the funding consequences of these positions and when counterparty risk is analysed.

2.7.2.1   Repo transactions

Repurchase (repo) transactions were first used in government bond markets where they are still an important instrument for funding and short sales of treasury bonds. Recently, a repo

---

[5] Thus, we write s for the payment of the fixed leg of an interest-rate swap at T_i, where it really should be $s\delta_i$ where δ_i is the day count fraction between T_{i-1} and T_i. We will explicitly incorporate day count fractions in the chapter on spread-based pricing and spread curve calibration.

[6] If it starts today at $t = T_n$ this annuity is also often referred to as "PV01" or "the value of one basis point".

market for corporate bonds has developed which can be used to implement short positions in corporate bonds.

A repurchase (repo) transaction consists of a sale part and a repurchase part:

- Before the transaction, **A** owns the defaultable bond $\overline{C}$;
- **B** buys the bond from **A** for the price $\overline{C}(0)$;
- At the same time, **A** and **B** enter a *repurchase* agreement: **B** agrees to sell the bond back to **A** at time $t = T$ for the forward price K. **A** agrees to buy the bond.

This agreement is binding to both sides.

The forward price K is the spot price $\overline{C}(0)$ of the bond, possibly adjusted for intermediate coupon payments, and increased by the *repo rate* r^{repo}:

$$K = (1 + Tr^{\text{repo}})\overline{C}(0)$$

(for a term of less than one year). To implement a short position, **B** does two more things:

- At time $t = 0$, **B** sells the bond in the market for $\overline{C}(0)$;
- At time $t = T$ (in order to deliver the bond to **A**), **B** has to buy the bond back in the market for the then current market price $\overline{C}(T)$.

B is now exposed to the risk of price changes in $\overline{C}$ between time $t = 0$ and time $t = T$. The price difference $K - \overline{C}(T)$ is his profit or loss. If the price increases above the forward price $\overline{C}(T) > \overline{C}(0)(1 + r^{\text{repo}}T)$, then **B** makes a loss because he must buy the bond at a higher price at time T. On the other hand, if the price falls $\overline{C}(T) < \overline{C}(0)(1 + r^{\text{repo}}T)$, then **B** makes a gain, because he can buy the bond back at a cheaper price. Thus, such a repo transaction is an efficient way for **B** to speculate on falling prices.

From **A**'s point of view, the transaction can be viewed as a collateralised lending transaction. Effectively, **A** has borrowed from **B** the amount of $\overline{C}(0)$ at the rate r^{repo}, and as collateral he has delivered the bond to **B**. At maturity of the agreement, he will receive his bond $\overline{C}$ back after payment of K, the borrowed amount plus interest. Thus, to owners of securities like **A**, a repo transaction offers the opportunity to refinance their position at the repo rate. Usually, the repo rate is lower than alternative funding rates for **A** which makes this transaction attractive to him. On the other hand **A** has given up the opportunity to get out of his position in the bond at an earlier time than T (except through another short sale in a second repo transaction). Repo lenders are therefore usually long-term investors who did not intend to sell the bond anyway.

To **B**, the repo transaction has achieved the aim of implementing a short position in the bond. This position is funding-neutral: he has to pay $\overline{C}(0)$ to **A**, but this amount he immediately gets from selling the bond in the market.

Counterparty risk in the transaction is generally rather small. The net value of the final exchange is only driven by the change in value of the bond $\overline{C}$ over $[0, T]$, its value is $K - \overline{C}(T)$, and the rest is collateralised by the underlying security. This final payment will only be large if there is a large price change in $\overline{C}$, for example if the issuer of the underlying bond should default. Then **B** will be exposed to the risk of **A**'s default on the payment of $K - \overline{C}(T)$ at time T. For default-free government bonds this risk can be neglected, for defaultable securities on the other hand it may be necessary to take into account the joint default risk of **A** and the underlying bond. From **A**'s point of view counterparty risk is even smaller, because **A** is only exposed to the risk of $\overline{C}(T) - K$ being large (i.e. a large rise in the price of the defaultable bond) *and* a default of **B** at the same time. For most bonds the upside is limited and large, sudden price rises do not occur.

The price of the implementation of a short position in a repo transaction is the repo rate that **B** must pay to **A**. As seen above, repo rates are not affected very much by counterparty risk considerations. More important drivers of repo rates are the supply of bonds by potential repo lenders and the demand of speculators who want to short this bond. In extreme cases, there is a large number of speculators who want to short the bond and only a limited number of possible lenders. Then repo rates decrease sharply, sometimes even below treasury rates. This allows the lenders **A** to refinance the position very cheaply, or even to earn an excess return by reinvesting the proceeds of the initial sale at a higher rate.

2.7.2.2 Forward contracts

Instead of making a repo transaction, **B** could have sold the bond $\overline{C}$ directly in a forward transaction, without buying it from **A** beforehand. This requires a counterparty **A** who would like to buy the defaultable bond $\overline{C}$ in a forward contract. It is usually easier to find an owner of a defaultable bond who wants to finance his position through a repo transaction than to find a forward buyer who wants to build up a new position.

2.7.2.3 Total rate of return swaps

A position as a total return payer in a TRS profits from decreases in the value of the underlying bond in a similar way to a short position. Compared to a repo transaction the TRS typically has a significantly longer time to maturity. This can be an advantage (no risk of lower repo rates or illiquidity when rolling the position over) or a disadvantage (less flexibility). Furthermore, if the final settlement of the TRS is done via cash settlement, the procedure by which the settlement prices are determined may generate additional risks of illiquidity and market manipulation, similar to the risks that occur in cash-settled credit default swaps. On the other hand, physical delivery as a settlement procedure is also open to the risk of a short squeeze.

A word of warning is necessary here. All versions of short selling require **B** to buy back the bond at some point. In particular in illiquid markets this exposes **B** to the risk of a *short squeeze*. If the potential sellers of the bonds know that **B** has no choice but to buy, they can dictate the price and force **B** into a very expensive purchase, sometimes with prices that are even above treasury bonds. This can be a very real risk that could ruin an otherwise sensible trading position.

2.7.3 Asset swap packages

As explained before, an asset swap package consists of a defaultable coupon bond $\overline{C}$ with coupon $\overline{c}$ and an interest-rate swap that swaps the bond's coupon into Libor plus the asset swap rate s^A. The payoff streams to **B**, the buyer of the asset swap package, are shown in Table 2.3.

Table 2.3 Payoff streams to **B** from an asset swap package. Payoffs marked with an asterisk are contingent on survival. Day count fractions are set to one $\delta_i = 1$

Time	Defaultable bond	Swap	Net
$t = 0$	$-\overline{C}(0)$	$-1 + \overline{C}(0)$	1
$t = T_i$	$\overline{c}^*$	$-\overline{c} + L_{i-1} + s^A$	$L_{i-1} + s^A + (\overline{c}^* - \overline{c})$
$t = T_N$	$(1 + \overline{c})^*$	$-\overline{c} + L_{i-1} + s^A$	$1^* + L_{i-1} + s^A + (\overline{c}^* - \overline{c})$
Default	Recovery	Unaffected	Recovery

To ensure that the value of the asset swap package to **B** is at par at time $t = 0$ we require:

$$\overline{C}(0) + A(0)s(0) + A(0)s^A(0) - A(0)\overline{c} = 1, \tag{2.2}$$

where $\overline{C}(0)$ is the initial price of the bond, $s(0)$ is the fixed-for-floating swap rate for the same maturity and payment dates T_i, and $A(0)$ is the value of an annuity paying $1 \cdot \delta_i$, one times the day count fraction of the previous interval[7] at all times T_i, $i = 1, \ldots, N$. All these quantities can be readily observed in the market at time T_0. $A(0)s^A(0)$ represents the value of receiving the asset swap rate s^A at each T_i until T_N and $-A(0)\overline{c}$ the value of having to pay the defaultable coupon at each T_i. The value of receiving Libor at each date is $A(0)s(0)$ by the definition of the market interest-rate swap rate.

To ensure that the value of the asset swap package is indeed 1, the asset swap rate must be:

$$s^A(0) = \frac{1}{A(0)}(1 - \overline{C}(0)) + \overline{c} - s(0). \tag{2.3}$$

Further insight can be gained from rearranging equation (2.2):

$$\overline{C}(0) + A(0)s^A(0) = \underbrace{[1 - A(0)s(0)] + A(0)\overline{c}}_{\text{default-free bond}}. \tag{2.4}$$

The right side of equation (2.4) is the value of a default-free bond with coupon $\overline{c}$, when the default-free rate is Libor. The term in square brackets $[1 - A(0)s(0)]$ is the value of receiving 1 at T_N (just substitute equation (2.1)), i.e. the value of the principal repayment, and $A(0)\overline{c}$ is the value of receiving $\overline{c}$ at all payment dates for sure. If we write $C(0) := [1 - A(0)s(0)] + A(0)\overline{c}$ for the value of this default-free bond, we reach

$$s^A(0) = \frac{1}{A(0)}(C(0) - \overline{C}(0)). \tag{2.5}$$

At later times $t > 0$ the asset swap rate for a contract initiated at time t becomes:

$$s^A(t) = \frac{1}{A(t)}(C(t) - \overline{C}(t)), \tag{2.6}$$

---

[7] In the tables I set $\delta_k = 1$ for notational simplicity.

Table 2.4 Payoff streams to **A** from a default-free coupon bond investment replicating his payment obligations from the interest-rate swap of an asset swap package. Day count fractions are set to one $\delta_i = 1$

Time	Default-free bond	Funding	Net
$t = 0$	$-C'(0)$	$+1$	$1 - C'(0)$
$t = T_i$	$\overline{c}_i - s^A$	$-L_{i-1}$	$\overline{c}_i - L_{i-1} - s^A$
$t = T_N$	$1 + \overline{c}_N - s^A$	$-L_{i-1} - 1$	$\overline{c}_i - L_{i-1} - s^A$
Default	Unaffected	Unaffected	Unaffected

where $A(t)$ denotes the value of the annuity over the remaining payment dates as seen from time t.

If at a later date $t > 0$ we want to revalue the whole asset swap package that was entered into at time $t = 0$ at the asset swap rate s^{A*}, we have to consider entering an offsetting asset swap transaction at time t. This will generate a default-free payoff difference of $s^{A*} - s^A(t)$ at each $T_i > t$, thus the value of the asset swap package is:

$$A(t)(s^{A*} - s^A(t)). \tag{2.7}$$

From equation (2.5) we can interpret the asset swap rate as a price difference in the numeraire asset[8] "annuity" $A(t)$:

The asset swap rate s^A of a defaultable coupon bond $\overline{C}$ with coupon $\overline{c}$ expresses the price difference between the defaultable coupon bond $\overline{C}$ and a default-free coupon bond with the same coupon $\overline{c}$, the same payment dates and the same maturity. This price difference is expressed in terms of units of the annuity A, i.e. the cash price difference is $s^A(t)A(t)$.

As mentioned before, a large number of asset swap transactions are driven by the desire to strip out unwanted structured features from the underlying asset. Therefore it is important to notice that this interpretation of the asset swap rate is not limited to fixed coupon bonds – the term $A(0)\overline{c}$ is just used to represent the net present value of a default-free payment stream of the size of the promised coupons of the bond. Instead of repeating the previous mathematical argument, we now give a replication-based argument from **A**'s point of view (see Table 2.4). Again we set $\delta_i = 1$.

At each T_i, **A** receives $\overline{c}_i$ for sure, but must pay $L_{i-1} + s^A$. To replicate this payoff stream, **A** buys a default-free coupon bond with coupon size $\overline{c}_i - s^A$, and borrows 1 at Libor and rolls this debt forward, paying: L_{i-1} at each T_i. At the final date T_N, **A** pays back his debt using the principal repayment of the default-free bond. Here, $\overline{c}_i$ need not be a fixed coupon payment. We only assume that it is possible to value a default-free bond with this coupon specification.

This replication generates a cash flow of $1 - C'$ initially, where $1 = $ proceeds from borrowing and $C' := $ price of the default-free coupon bond with coupons $\overline{c}_i - s^A$. All other cash flows are

---

[8] A numeraire asset defines the units in which prices are expressed. The default-free annuity $A(t)$ is a very useful numeraire asset for the analysis of prices in swap markets.

identical to the cash flows from the asset swap sale to **B**. Therefore, the initial cash flow of the replication must be equal to the value of selling the asset swap package to **B** which generates an initial cash flow of $1 - \overline{C}$.

Thus we can view the asset swap rate as the amount by which we could reduce the coupon of the defaultable bond $\overline{C}$ if it was *not* defaultable, and still keep the price at the original price level $\overline{C}(0)$.

This replication strategy from **A**'s point of view assumes that **A** can borrow money at Libor flat. It is easy to use other funding rates for **A**, either his borrowing rate or the repo rate for the default-free bond position. Furthermore it was assumed that no counterparty defaults on his payments from the interest-rate swap.

Equation (2.5) allows a further analysis of the asset swap rate around a default of **C**. First, at a default event, the price difference $(C(t) - \overline{C}(t))$ becomes $C(t) - recovery$, which will be a large number but not infinitely large, as recovery cannot be less than zero. This yields an upper bound on the asset swap rate of $C(t)/A(t)$ which is assumed when **C** defaults with zero recovery.

Furthermore, as time proceeds the price difference $C(t) - \overline{C}(t)$ in the numerator of equation (2.6) will tend to decrease to zero, *unless a default happens*. This is balanced by the denominator $A(t)$ which will also decrease because the annuity $A(t)$ will contain fewer and fewer payments.

2.7.4 Total return swaps

In this section we highlight the differences between entering a total return swap and an outright purchase. As before we assume that **B** is the total return receiver, and **A** the total return payer. Using the example in Table 2.5, we compare:

(a) An outright purchase of the **C**-bond at $t = 0$ with a sale at $t = T_N$. **B** finances this position with debt that is rolled over at Libor, maturing at T_N.
(b) A position as a total return receiver in a TRS with **A**.

First we note that **B** receives the coupon payments of the underlying security at the same time in both positions. Thus we need not consider these payments and we set $\overline{c} = 0$.

Second, the debt service payments in strategy (a) and the Libor part of the funding payment in the TRS (strategy (b)) coincide, too. Thus these payments cancel, too.

Table 2.5 Payoff streams of a total return swap to the total return receiver **B** (the payoffs to the total return payer **A** are the converse of these). The TRS is unwound upon default of the underlying bond. Day count fractions are set to one $\delta_i = 1$

Time	Defaultable bond	TRS payments		
		Funding	Returns	Marking to market
$t = 0$	$-\overline{C}(0)$	0	0	0
$t = T_i$	$\overline{c}$	$-\overline{C}(0)(L_{i-1} + s^{TRS})$	$+\overline{c}$	$+\overline{C}(T_i) - \overline{C}(T_{i-1})$
$t = T_N$	$(\overline{C}(T_N) + \overline{c})$	$-\overline{C}(0)(L_{N-1} + s^{TRS})$	$+\overline{c}$	$+\overline{C}(T_N) - \overline{C}(T_{N-1})$
Default	Recovery	$-\overline{C}(0)(L_{i-1} + s^{TRS})$	0	$-(\overline{C}(T_{i-1}) - \text{Recovery})$

Thus the source of value difference (if there is any at all) must lie in the marking-to-market of the TRS at the intermediate intervals. Let us look at the final payoff of strategy (a): **B** sells the bond in the market for $\overline{C}(T_N)$, and has to pay back his debt which costs him $\overline{C}(0)$. (The Libor coupon payment is already cancelled with the TRS.) This yields:

$$\overline{C}(T_N) - \overline{C}(0). \tag{2.8}$$

Equation (2.8) is the amount that **B** receives at time T_N from following strategy (a), net of intermediate interest and coupon payments. Now we decompose this total price difference between $t = 0$ and $t = T_N$ into the small, incremental differences that occur between the individual times T_i:

$$\overline{C}(T_N) - \overline{C}(0) = \sum_{i=1}^{N} \overline{C}(T_i) - \overline{C}(T_{i-1}).$$

It is easily seen that all except two terms in the summation above cancel. This representation allows us to distribute the final payoff of the strategy over the intermediate time intervals and to compare them to the payouts of the TRS position (b). Each time interval $[T_{i-1}, T_i]$ contributes an amount of

$$\overline{C}(T_i) - \overline{C}(T_{i-1})$$

to the final payoff, and this amount is directly observable at time T_i. This payoff contribution can be converted into a payoff that occurs at time T_i by discounting it back from T_N to T_i, reaching

$$(\overline{C}(T_i) - \overline{C}(T_{i-1}))B(T_i, T_N). \tag{2.9}$$

Conversely, if we paid **B** the amount given in equation (2.9) at each T_i, and if **B** reinvested this money at the default-free interest rate until T_N, then **B** would have exactly the same final payoff as in strategy (a), namely (2.8).

From the TRS position in strategy (b), **B** has a slightly different payoff:

$$\overline{C}(T_i) - \overline{C}(T_{i-1}) \tag{2.10}$$

at all times $T_i > T_0$, net of his funding expenses. The difference (b) − (a) is:

$$(\overline{C}(T_i) - \overline{C}(T_{i-1}))(1 - B(T_i, T_N)) =: \Delta\overline{C}(T_i)(1 - B(T_i, T_N)). \tag{2.11}$$

Equation (2.11) gives the excess payoff at time T_i of the TRS position over the outright purchase of the bond. This term will be positive if the change in value of the underlying bond $\Delta\overline{C}(T_i)$ is positive. It will be negative if the change in value of the underlying bond is negative, and zero if $\Delta\overline{C}(T_i)$ is zero.

If the underlying asset is a bond, the likely sign of its change in value $\Delta\overline{C}(T_i)$ can be inferred from the deviation of its initial value $\overline{C}(0)$ from par. If $\overline{C}(0) < 1$, i.e. the bond is initially below par, its price will have to increase to reach the final payoff $\overline{C}(T_N) = 1$. If $\overline{C}(0)$ is above par, the price changes will have to be negative on average.

The most extreme example of this kind would be a TRS on a default-free zero-coupon bond with maturity T_N. If we assume constant interest rates of R, this bond will always increase in value because it was issued at such a deep discount. A direct investor in the bond will only realise this increase in value at maturity of the bond, while the TRS receiver effectively receives prepayments. He can reinvest these prepayments and earn an additional return.

Thus, as a rule of thumb, bonds that initially trade at a discount to par should command a positive TRS spread s^{TRS}, while bonds that trade above par should have a negative TRS spread s^{TRS}. TRS spreads that are observed in the market do not always follow this rule, because investors in TRS are frequently motivated by other concerns that were ignored here (leverage, having an off-balance-sheet exposure, counterparty risk, alternative refinancing possibilities) and are willing to adjust the prices accordingly.

It should be noted from this analysis that the TRS rate s^{TRS} does *not* reflect the default risk of the underlying bond. If the underlying bond is issued at par and the coupon is chosen such that its price before default is always at par (assuming constant interest rates and spreads), then the TRS rate should be zero, irrespective of the default risk that the bond carries.

2.7.5 Credit default swaps

Assumption 2.1 *In order to derive the following results we need to make some simplifying assumptions on the payoff of a CDS in default:*

- *We assume that the payoff takes place* at the time of default. *The time delay through grace periods, dealer polls, etc. is ignored. In reality, this delay is not longer than six weeks in total, and often it can be much shorter (maybe two weeks). (Again this depends on the specification and the liquidity of the deliverable obligations.)*
- *We ignore the* delivery option *that is embedded in a CDS with physical delivery. We will frequently consider portfolios that contain a defaultable bond which is protected by a CDS, and in this case the defaultable bond is the only deliverable bond of the CDS.*
- *We assume that the CDS is triggered by all defaults of the reference obligor and only by defaults of the reference obligor. In particular we ignore the possibility of* technical defaults, *i.e. events that trigger the CDS default definition while they do not constitute a real default of the reference obligor. Furthermore we ignore the possibility of* legal, documentation and specification risk, *the risk that a real default does not trigger the CDS.*
- *In tabular representations of the payoff streams of a trading strategy we abstract from day count conventions and set $\delta_i = 1$ for all i. Otherwise we assume that the same day count conventions and payment dates apply to all the securities involved (this is not the case in reality).*

Unless otherwise stated, these assumptions apply throughout the rest of the book. They are common assumptions in the analysis of credit derivatives, although they are rarely explicitly stated. In most cases they just amount to a slight variation in the parameters (e.g. the recovery rate). Nevertheless the reader should be aware of them and at appropriate places we will discuss their implications.

A CDS is designed such that a combined position of a CDS with a defaultable bond issued by **C** is very well hedged against default risk, and should therefore trade close to the price of an otherwise equivalent default-free bond. This is the intuition behind the *cash-and-carry* arbitrage pricing of CDSs.

2.7.5.1 Cash-and-carry arbitrage with fixed-coupon bonds

Consider the following two portfolios:

Hedge strategy 1: *Fixed-coupon bonds.*

Portfolio I

- One defaultable coupon bond $\overline{C}$: coupon $\overline{c}$, maturity T_N.
- One CDS on this bond: CDS spread $\overline{s}$.
- The portfolio is unwound after a default.

Portfolio II

- One default-free coupon bond C: with the same payment dates as the defaultable coupon bond and coupon size $\overline{c} - \overline{s}$.
- The bond is sold after default.

The idea is that portfolio I can be viewed as something akin to a synthetical default-free bond, because it is protected from default risk.

As can be seen from Table 2.6, in survival the cash flows of both portfolios are identical. Thus, provided the payoffs in default also coincide, the initial prices of both portfolios should be the same. Otherwise, a risk-free profit could be generated by buying the cheaper portfolio of the two, and short-selling the more expensive one. Thus, provided the payoffs in default coincide, we must have

$$\overline{C}(0) = C(0) = B(0, T_N) + \overline{c} A(0) - \overline{s} A(0),$$

where the default-free bond price is expressed as the sum of the values of the final principal repayment ($B(0, T_N)$) and the regular coupon payments ($\overline{c} A(0)$ and $\overline{s} A(0)$). This equation can be solved for the fair CDS rate $\overline{s}$ for any given term structure of default-free interest rates (which

Table 2.6 Payoffs of the two portfolios of replication strategy 1

Time	Portfolio I		Portfolio II
	Defaultable bond	CDS	
$t = 0$	$-\overline{C}(0)$	0	$-C(0)$
$t = T_i$	$\overline{c}$	$-\overline{s}$	$\overline{c} - \overline{s}$
$t = T_N$	$(1 + \overline{c})$	$-\overline{s}$	$1 + \overline{c} - \overline{s}$
Default $t = \tau$	Recovery	$1 -$ Recovery	$C(\tau)$

will uniquely determine $B(0, T_N)$ and $A(0)$) in combination with the price of the defaultable coupon bond.

Unfortunately, the payoffs of both portfolios in default do not coincide exactly. In the event of a default, the value of a CDS-protected defaultable bond (portfolio I) will be the notional value of the bond, because the CDS gives us the right to put the bond to the protection seller at par. The value of the equivalent default-free bond on the other hand will depend on the then prevailing term structure of default-free interest rates, and almost certainly it will differ from par. The price difference at default (portfolio I − portfolio II) will be:

$$1 - C(\tau).$$

There are several reasons why $C(\tau)$, the value of the default-free bond, will differ from 1. First, it may have already been off par from the outset, i.e. $C(0) \neq 1$ already at time $t = 0$. Second, if the term structure of interest rates is stochastic, the value of $C(\tau)$ will move stochastically, too, and there is no reason to believe it will be close to par, except at its final maturity. Finally, there is the issue of accrued interest. At the coupon payment dates T_i, the (dirty) price of the bond will drop by the coupon payment amount $\overline{c} - \overline{s}$, then it will tend to increase again until the next coupon payment date. The resulting price path will have a typical sawtooth pattern that is common to all coupon-paying bonds.

All these effects make the simple cash-and-carry arbitrage not an exact, but only an approximate, arbitrage relationship. The problem lies in the unknown value of the default-free coupon bond at a random point in time later on.

2.7.5.2   Cash-and-carry arbitrage with par floaters

We can remove at least two of these sources of price uncertainty if we consider a *default-free floating-rate bond C'*. A default-free floater pays a regular coupon of Libor L_{i-1} at T_i. Because it can be replicated by a rolled investment at the default-free short-term interest rate (Libor), its initial value is 1, and so is its value immediately after each coupon payment date T_i.

If the default-free bond is a floating-coupon bond, we must have that the defaultable bond also pays a floating coupon in order to achieve matching payoffs in survival. Furthermore, we would like to match the initial value of 1. Such bonds are called *par floaters*:

A par floater $\overline{C}'$ is a defaultable bond with a floating-rate coupon of $\overline{c}_i = L_{i-1} + s^{par}$, where the par spread s^{par} is chosen such that at issuance the par floater is valued at par.

The modified hedging strategy now consists of:

Hedge strategy 2: *Par floaters.*

Portfolio I

- One defaultable par floater $\overline{C}'$ with spread s^{par} over Libor. The coupon is $\overline{c}_i = L_{i-1} + s^{par}$.
- One CDS on this bond: CDS spread $\overline{s}$.
- The portfolio is unwound after a default.

Table 2.7 Payoffs of the two portfolios of replication strategy 2

Time	Portfolio I		Portfolio II
	Defaultable bond	CDS	
$t = 0$	-1	0	-1
$t = T_i$	$L_{i-1} + s^{par}$	$-\bar{s}$	L_i
$t = T_N$	$1 + L_{N-1} + s^{par}$	$-\bar{s}$	$1 + L_{N-1}$
Default $t = \tau$	Recovery	$1 -$ Recovery	$C'(\tau)$

Portfolio II

- One default-free floating-coupon bond C': with the same payment dates as the defaultable par floater and coupon at Libor flat $c_i = L_{i-1}$.
- The bond is sold after default.

Let us now analyse if this portfolio gives us a better handle on the default swap spread $\bar{s}$.

First, the initial values of portfolio I and portfolio II in hedge strategy 2 are identical (Table 2.7). Next, the payoffs of the two strategies at default only differ by the accrued interest that the default-free floater will pay in excess of the notional value of 1. The value of the default-free par floater including the accrued interest is

$$C'(\tau) = 1 + L_i(\tau - T_i) \qquad (2.12)$$

if the time of default τ occurs in the interval $]T_i, T_{i+1}]$. The protected par floater on the other hand only pays off 1, because the CDS does not protect accrued interest payments but only the principal of the par floater.

Nevertheless, this payoff difference can be made rather small. First, defaults could occur anywhere in the interval $[T_i, T_{i+1}]$, so on average (if the time of default is uniformly distributed in this interval) the accrued interest will be $1/2 L_i(T_{i+1} - T_i)$. Second, we can increase the notional of the CDS in order to protect the accrued interest at least approximately. A rough rule of thumb would be to take additional protection on

$$x := \frac{1}{N} \sum_{i=0}^{N-1} \frac{1}{2} F_i(0)(T_{i+1} - T_i),$$

where $F_i(0)$ is the forward rate over $[T_i, T_{i+1}]$ as seen from $t = 0$. Here we approximated the spot Libor rates at times T_i with the respective forward interest rates. Alternatively one could use the swap rate which is also just a weighted average of forward interest rates. This adjustment will reduce the size of the error and the bias in the approximative hedging formula. Finally, if the frequency of the coupons is higher, the amount of interest accrual is reduced as well (because $(T_{i+1} - T_i)$ is reduced).

Overall, the hedge error in the payoff at default caused by accrued interest effects is small. For example, even without adjusting the protection size, for a Libor rate of 4% and semi-annual coupons, the error is at most 2%, and on average 1%. By adjusting the protection amount, the average error can be moved close to zero. Given the uncertainties that were introduced by Assumption 2.1, we can assume that we have matched the payoffs in default. In particular, the embedded delivery option of the CDS will make its payoff in default higher than we assumed here.

To sum up: we have matched the payoffs of both portfolios in default (approximately) and the initial costs (exactly). The payoffs before default differ only by the difference of the par spread to the credit default swap spread. But these payoffs must coincide, too, in order to remove any arbitrage opportunity. This means that the credit default swap spread must equal the par spread:

$$s^{par} = \bar{s}.$$

(2.13)

We can rearrange the portfolios in strategy 2 to replicate short and long positions in a credit default swap.

- Synthetic *long* position in the CDS:
  - buy the default-free floater,
  - short sell the defaultable floater.
- Synthetic *short* position in the CDS:
  - short sell the default-free floater,
  - buy the defaultable floater.

Provided a defaultable floater exists, a synthetic short position in the CDS (i.e. short protection) should not be very difficult to implement. A synthetic short position can be used to hedge a "real" long protection position in the CDS. In other words, we can run a roughly hedged position by buying the defaultable floater at $s^{par\ offer}$ (thus synthetically shorting protection) and buying the corresponding protection back in the form of a CDS at the price at which CDS protection is currently on offer in the market $\bar{s}^{offer}$. In order for this strategy not to make a profit we require:

$$\bar{s}^{offer} \geq s^{par\ offer}.$$

(2.14)

The synthetic long position in protection on the other hand requires a short sale of a defaultable bond, which can be difficult or even impossible to do. If the short sale is possible at the *bid* par spread $s^{par\ bid}$, we could do this (thus going synthetically long protection) and sell this protection in the CDS market at the current bid of $\bar{s}^{bid}$. This means that:

$$\bar{s}^{bid} \leq s^{par\ bid} \quad \text{if short sales are possible.}$$

(2.15)

If no short sale of the defaultable bond is possible (and this is frequently the case), the bid price of the credit default swaps can exceed the offered par spreads, and equation (2.15) does not hold.

The values of these synthetic positions have to be corrected for the fact that the short sales will generate costs at the relevant *repo rate* which may differ from the Libor interest earned on the long asset.

Table 2.8 Replication strategy 2 with asset swap package

Time	Portfolio I		Portfolio II
	Asset swap package	CDS	
$t = 0$	-1	0	-1
$t = T_i$	$L_{i-1} + s^A$	$-\bar{s}$	L_{i-1}
$t = T_N$	$1 + L_{N-1} + s^A$	$-\bar{s}$	$1 + L_{N-1}$
Default $t = \tau$	Recovery + value of swap	$1 -$ Recovery	$C'(\tau)$

2.7.5.3 Cash-and-carry arbitrage with asset swap packages

The biggest problem with strategy 2 is that in most cases defaultable par floaters do not exist in the market. An obvious alternative would be to use an asset swap package instead, as shown in Table 2.8. The asset swap package has at least some of the desired properties of the defaultable par floaters. It is initially priced at par (1), and before default it pays a coupon of Libor plus a spread.

Thus, the only payoff difference arises at default. While a par floater's value is just the recovery rate, the value of the asset swap package is the recovery *plus the market value of the interest rate swap*. The interest-rate swap derives its value from movements in the default-free term structure of interest rates, and from any initial value that the swap might have had (i.e. one minus the initial value of the underlying defaultable coupon bond).

If we assume that the initial value of the underlying coupon bond is close to par, and that the value movements of the default-free term structure of interest rates are largely independent of defaults, then we can view an asset swap package as a substitute to a defaultable par floater in the hedge strategies of the previous subsection. Thus, we have the following approximate relationship:

$$\boxed{\text{Default swap spread} \quad \bar{s} \approx s^A \quad \text{Asset swap spread.}} \tag{2.16}$$

The asset swap rate is a good indicator for a fair credit default swap spread. The accuracy of this relationship depends on the degree to which the following assumptions are fulfilled:

   (i) The initial value of the underlying bond is at par.
 (ii) Interest rate movements and defaults occur independently.
(iii) Short positions in the asset swap market are possible.
(iv) At default, the default-free floater trades at par.

Assumptions (i) and (ii) ensure that the value of the interest-rate swap does not introduce any bias in the analysis. In particular, from assumption (ii) it follows that the expected market value of the interest-rate swap at default is indeed zero. (That is just the *expected* value, though. The realised value can be completely different.) Assumption (iii) is necessary to reach a two-sided bound on the CDS rate, and assumption (iv) addresses the slight mismatch at default that arose in the hedge with a par floater.

If short sales of the asset swap package are impossible, then the equality of asset swap spread and default swap spread breaks down and we are left with an inequality similar to equation (2.14):

$$\text{CDS offer } \overline{s}^{\text{offer}} \geq s^{A \text{ offer}} \text{ Asset swap offer.} \tag{2.17}$$

If on the other hand short sales of the asset swap package are possible, then we have in addition the following inequality:

$$\overline{s}^{\text{bid}} \leq s^{A \text{ bid}} \quad \text{if short sales are possible.} \tag{2.18}$$

2.7.5.4 Fallen angels and distressed debt

An important special case arises when the underlying defaultable bond trades significantly below its par value. This is the case for bonds issued by "fallen angels": firms that had a good credit rating at the time of issuance of the bond, and that have been downgraded below investment grade at a later time. Now assumption (i) is strongly violated, and we cannot view the asset swap package as similar to a defaultable par floater. This will introduce a bias, and we now analyse the direction of this bias.

In order to apply equation (2.16), we would like to know the asset swap spread on a defaultable bond that *trades at par*. Imagine that the issuer of the bond, **C**, was friendly enough to help us out. He offers to raise the old coupon $\overline{c}$ on his bond by an amount $x > 0$, until his bond trades at par again. This new coupon is $\overline{c}' = \overline{c} + x$. (Of course we do not know x, and of course in reality **C** would never give away this much money for free.)

Next, the asset swap spread on this new par coupon bond is immediately clear. The interest-rate swap of the asset swap package swaps $\overline{c} + x$ into Libor $+ s^A$, and it must have an initial value of zero (the bond is already at par). Therefore the asset swap rate is now

$$s^{A\prime} = \overline{c} + x - s,$$

because equivalently to the asset swap package one can simply enter a plain interest-rate swap swapping the market swap rate s for Libor. Now assumption (i) is satisfied and we know from equation (2.16) that

$$\overline{s} \approx s^{A\prime} = \overline{c} + x - s.$$

In order to determine the "fallen angel" bias in (2.16) we need to know whether the asset swap rate s^A on the original bond with coupon $\overline{c}$ was smaller or larger than the asset swap rate $s^{A\prime}$ on the bond with the new, raised coupon $\overline{c}' = \overline{c} + x$. For this we use equation (2.5):

$$\overline{s} - s^A \approx s^{A\prime} - s^A$$
$$= \frac{1}{A(0)}[(C' - \overline{C}') - (C - \overline{C})]$$
$$= \frac{1}{A(0)}[(C' - C) - (\overline{C}' - \overline{C})] > 0,$$

where $\overset{.}{\overline{C}}{}'$ and C' are the prices of the defaultable and default-free bonds with coupon $\overline{c}'$, and $\overline{C}$ and C are the prices of the defaultable and default-free bonds with coupon $\overline{c}$. The price difference in the square brackets will always be positive, because $C' - C$ is the value of receiving x at all T_i *without default risk*, while $\overline{C}{}' - \overline{C}$ is the value of receiving x at all T_i *subject to C's default risk*. Thus we reach

$$\overline{s} > s^A \quad \text{if } \overline{C}(0) < 1. \tag{2.19}$$

Thus, the credit default swap rate for an obligor should be higher than the asset swap rate on his bonds if these bonds trade below par. As an extreme example, we can consider an obligor who will surely default at zero recovery the next day. His default swap rate will be infinite, but the asset swap rate will be finite (although very large).

If the "fallen angel" is downgraded even further and default seems imminent, we are faced with the problem of CDS on *distressed debt*. Recent examples of distressed debt were the defaults on Enron or Worldcom where for several months before the default event the market was clearly anticipating a very high probability of default in the very near future, and the bonds were trading around 30 cents to the dollar of par value.

In the case of distressed (but not yet defaulted) debt, a newly entered position in a CDS changes its risk characteristics significantly. The CDS becomes extremely sensitive to the *exact timing* of the default event. Consider the following example.

Example 2.4 (CDS on distressed debt)   *A few days ago, massive accounting irregularities have been uncovered at the large power supplier Norne.[9] Stockmarket investors and banks are losing confidence in the firm, the share price is in free fall, cash reserves are draining and banks have stopped extending new lines of credit. Yet Norne may still battle on for some time. The CDS spreads have reached 2400 bp. A default seems highly likely. Market consensus is that there is a 50% recovery to be expected from the Norne corporate bonds.*

Through careful research you are able to assess the cash reserves of Norne more accurately than the average market participant and you estimate that Norne will run out of cash in X months. Furthermore, you are 100% sure that Norne will default within the next 5 years. How do you trade?

Let us consider a long position in protection. The cash flows are (ignoring discounting):

- *Fee payments until default: $-2400\,bp \times \tau/12$, where τ is the number of months Norne still survives;*
- *Protection payment: $+50\% = 5000\,bp$.*

Thus, the long position in protection is worthwhile if and only if

$$0.5 > 0.24 \times \tau/12, \quad \tau < 25.$$

If you expect the default to happen within the next 25 months, you buy protection at 2400 bp. If you expect the cash to run out later, you sell protection, even though you are certain that the default will occur during the life of the CDS and that you will have to make the default payment.

---

[9] All names and events are entirely fictitious. Any resemblance to real events is purely coincidental.

Table 2.9 Example CDS and asset swap quotes with basis

	Default swap (bp) (bid/offer)	Asset swap (bp) (bid/offer)	Basis (bp) (CDS bid − AS bid)
Bank of America	48/55	46/43	2
Bank One	60/75	65/60	−5
Chase Corp.	40/48	35/30	5
Citigroup	38/45	30/27	8
First Union	68/85	66/63	2
Goldman Sachs	45/55	46/41	1
Lehman Brothers	70/80	68/63	2
Merrill Lynch	40/50	28/23	12
Morgan Stanley	45/55	28/23	17

Source: Deutsche Bank.

The point here is that the fee stream of the CDS is cancelled at default, too. Whether you earn the fee for another month more or less does make a big difference. If the obligor in the previous example had survived over the whole five years of the CDS, the protection seller would have earned more than the notional of the CDS in protection fee income alone. Thus, for distressed debt, CDS rates are mainly a play on the exact timing of default and of course also on the recovery rate.

2.7.5.5 Trading the basis

If one analyses quoted spreads in the markets, one can observe that default swap spreads differ from asset swap spreads even for defaultable bonds that trade close to par. This difference is called the *CDS/asset swap basis* or simply the *basis*. The inequality (2.17) for the offered CDS spreads will in most cases not be violated, but inequality (2.18) is regularly invalidated. This allows us to be more specific in the definition. *Basis* refers to the degree to which inequality (2.18) is violated:

$$\text{Basis} = \text{CDS bid} - \text{Asset swap bid} = \bar{s}^{\text{bid}} - s^{A\,\text{bid}}. \tag{2.20}$$

For an illustration see Table 2.9 with some selected real values. The basis can sometimes reach extremely high levels, e.g. 80 bp for Deutsche Telekom in February 2001. None of these firms was a fallen angel when these prices were observed.

A positive basis can be caused by the "fallen angels" bias which was analysed in the previous subsection. If this is not the case, a positive basis means that the default risk of a specific obligor (e.g. Deutsche Telekom) is priced significantly differently in the CDS market and in the bond market for Telekom bonds. The CDS market views the default risk of Deutsche Telekom to be much higher. It seems that potential protection sellers in the Telekom CDS market demand a high premium, while there are investors in the bond market who are willing to pay a rather high price (i.e. receive a low asset swap spread and a low compensation for the embedded default risk) for Telekom bonds. For these investors to take on Telekom risk in the bond market at such prices, they are either not aware of the investment opportunities in the CDS market, or they are not able to act as protection seller in the CDS market for other reasons (e.g. regulatory and supervisory reasons).

In perfect markets, such a situation would be exploited by an arbitrageur who could sell CDS default protection at a high price, and short the corresponding Telekom bond or asset swap package. If short sales of Telekom bonds are not possible, the arbitrageur has to find another way to transfer the default exposure from the CDS market to the bond market investors. This could be achieved by issuing credit-linked notes that are linked to the Telekom default risk, and selling these credit-linked notes to the investors in the asset swap market.

Issuance of credit-linked notes takes time and carries significant fixed costs which require a larger issue size than a typical CDS notional. Thus, this strategy will only be implemented if some conditions are satisfied. First, the bond investors who are restricted from selling CDS default protection must be allowed to invest in credit-linked notes. Second, the arbitrage opportunity must be large enough. The basis itself must be large and the aggregate notional of the quotes that violate the basis must be large enough. Finally, given the time delays involved, the arbitrage opportunity must be persistent over time.

These difficulties mean that the link between the underlying cash bond market and the CDS market is not always as efficient and close as, for example, the link between the cash and futures markets for share price index futures. Nevertheless, we can safely assume that the deviations from perfect market synchronicity will be limited in time and size (and if we are wrong, at least there will be a handsome compensation).

2.7.5.6 Problems with cash-and-carry arbitrage

Problems in implementing short positions in defaultable bonds form the main obstacle to an efficient cash-and-carry arbitrage link between the CDS market and the market for the corresponding defaultable bonds and asset swap packages. These problems are the reason for the phenomenon of a positive *basis* between these markets, in perfect markets a positive basis would not exist.

A second set of problems arises when the defaultable bond does not match the CDS in maturity and when coupon and CDS fee payment dates do not coincide. Then, even in survival, the arbitrageur is exposed to the risk of having to unwind the position in the defaultable bond at time T_N at a disadvantageous price.

Summing up the problems with cash-and-carry arbitrage:

- The implementation of a short position in a defaultable bond may be difficult or even impossible. Furthermore, the trader is exposed to short squeezes when he tries to roll over his short position, and he is exposed to the risk of changing repo rates.
- The arbitrage is imprecise at default events:
  - The default-free bond price will differ from par.
  - The interest-rate swap of an asset swap package will have a market value.
  - CDSs contain a delivery option for the protection buyer in the case of default. This increases the value of the protection offered by a CDS.
- There may be other peculiarities in the settlement of the CDS at default which make its value hard to predict.
- The default-free bond may not be available in the market. The trader may have to use a substitute bond.
- The only available defaultable bond may not match the CDS's maturity or its coupon payment dates may not coincide with the CDS fee payment dates.
- The method cannot be applied if the reference obligor has not issued any defaultable bonds.

All these problems widen the price bounds that can be imposed upon a CDS rate by using pure static arbitrage trading strategies. Nevertheless, besides being a good exercise to get acquainted with the most common instruments and their payoff peculiarities, the cash-and-carry arbitrage can still yield important insights.

First of all, analysis of potential arbitrage strategies enables us to better understand the links between the market for the underlying asset – the cash (bond) market – and the derivative market for CDS and other credit derivatives. Inefficiencies can occur in both markets but frequently there are more inefficiencies in the cash market than in the derivatives market. A liquid CDS market is often a more useful indicator for the price of the default risk of a particular obligor than the underlying cash market.

Second, cash-and-carry arbitrage is still a very useful instrument for spotting mispricing in the market and for finding advantageous prices, even if they do not constitute pure arbitrage strategies. The strategies only rely on payoff comparisons, therefore they are very robust and unaffected by the model and parameter risk of more complicated models.

Furthermore, the price bounds that can be derived from these strategies will necessarily reappear in the more formal mathematical arbitrage pricing models for credit derivatives. This clarifies the role of such models: their task is to tighten the arbitrage-based price bounds by imposing additional assumptions on the structure of the processes and the probabilities of default.

2.8 EXOTIC CREDIT DERIVATIVES

One of the advantages of single-name credit default swaps is the large flexibility in the detailed specification that these instruments give the trading counterparties. This flexibility is often used to specify default payments that differ from the usual "notional minus recovery" of a standard CDS. Or, alternative definitions of the default event may be used. We will discuss some popular specifications in the first part of this section. In the second part of this section we describe credit derivatives with optionalities.

2.8.1 Default digital swaps

A *default digital swap* (DDS) is a credit default swap with a particularly simple default payment. The default payment is a predetermined fixed cash payment, usually the notional amount of the DDS. In particular the recovery payment is independent from the loss in default of the reference assets. This specification avoids the complicated mechanisms that were necessary to determine the recovery rate of the defaulted bonds for default payment of a credit default swap.

A default digital swap is therefore less well suited for the hedging of defaultable bond and loan exposures, because the recovery risk remains unhedged. But there are other types of exposures that do not carry recovery risk, or exposures whose recovery in default will differ significantly from the loss and recovery of the reference bonds anyway. For these, a default digital swap may be a better hedge instrument than a plain vanilla credit default swap. The recovery-dependence of the payoff of the CDS would introduce additional risk here, instead of removing it. Such uncertainties can arise for counterparty exposures in other derivatives transactions, if the exposure is of a different seniority class than the underlying bonds, or if a market-based determination of recovery is made impossible because there are no traded bonds of this issuer.

A second application of a default digital swap is to trade expected recovery rates. For example, a portfolio of a long position in a CDS with notional of 1, and a short position in a DDS with payoff of 0.5 at default will have a positive payoff in default if and only if the recovery rate is below 50%. If the recovery rate is above 50%, the portfolio will have a negative payoff at default. Thus, by setting up this portfolio a trader can bet on recovery rates above 50%.

As a further application, a DDS is a useful building block for more complicated structured products because of its very simple payoff structure.

If quotes on default digital swaps and plain vanilla credit default swaps can be observed in the market, then these can be used to back out an implied recovery rate. Assume that the CDS is quoted at a spread of $\bar{s}$, and the DDS at a spread of $\bar{s}^{DDS}$ (now both have the same notional). Of course $\bar{s}^{DDS}$ will be higher than $\bar{s}$ because the DDS will always pay off more than the CDS (unless the recovery rate was zero, then the CDS and DDS will have identical payoffs).

In this situation, we can compare the following two portfolio positions:

1. A long position in a CDS with notional of 1.
   Fee: $\bar{s}$.
   Payoff in default: $1 - $ recovery.
2. A long position in a DDS with notional of $\bar{s}/\bar{s}^{DDS}$.
   Fee: $\bar{s}/\bar{s}^{DDS} \times \bar{s}^{DDS} = \bar{s}$.
   Payoff in default: $\bar{s}/\bar{s}^{DDS}$.

Both positions have the same fee payments before default. Therefore, in the market's view the payoffs in default must be equally valuable, too. This means that the implied recovery rate is:

$$\text{Recovery}^{\text{impl}} = 1 - \frac{\bar{s}}{\bar{s}^{DDS}}.$$

The implied information about the recovery rate is contained in the combination of both prices, the CDS rate and the DDS rate. But because default digital swaps are less frequently traded than credit default swaps, the usual view is that default digital swap rates contain the additional recovery information, not the credit default swaps. Default digital swaps are less frequently traded because they lack the cash-and-carry arbitrage connection to the underlying cash bond market, and most credit exposures are better hedged with CDS.

2.8.2 Exotic default payments in credit default swaps

Many traders in the CDS market use the asset swap basis as an indicator of the relative value of credit default swaps and trade the convergence of the basis back to values close to zero. Trading strategies with asset swap packages always involve the risk of having to unwind the interest-rate swap part of the asset swap package at default. To hedge this risk, some banks have begun to trade in credit default swaps that pay off the market value of other derivatives, e.g. an interest-rate swap, at default.

These swaps are an example of a credit default swap with an exotic default payment, it depends on market variables that have no connection with the underlying credit risk, and it can even be negative. Of course, the counterparties could also agree on other payments in default. Such payments could be used to hedge counterparty credit risk exposures, exposures that are denominated in different currencies or the residual exposure of a loan that is secured with collateral that has an uncertain value in default.

The pricing and risk management of such derivatives depends on the correlation of the default arrival risk of **C**, and the market value of the default payment. Any quantitative pricing model for these exotic credit default swaps will therefore have to jointly model the driving factors of the default payment and the default risk.

In the initial example for the interest-rate swap there is no need for such a quantitative pricing model because the underlying exposure is easily replicated. A portfolio of a long asset swap package, a long credit default swap and a short position in a default-free floater will pay off the interest-rate swap of the asset swap package at default.

The market-value risk of the interest-rate swap of the asset swap package at default could have been hedged with a Bermudan swaption. This would give the owner the right to cancel the interest-rate swap at any of the possible exercise dates. Such an option is significantly more expensive because the owner of this option can choose to exercise at a time which maximises the value of the option, and not necessarily the default time of **C**.[10]

Exotic credit default swaps can also be used to significantly reduce the counterparty credit risk charge in derivative transactions. Assume that **C** wanted to enter an FX swap with **A**. This swap has an initial value of zero, but subsequently its value will change, it can have a positive or a negative value to either counterparty at a later date. **C** will have to pay a counterparty credit risk charge to **A** because **A** can only lose money at defaults of **C**. Either the swap has a positive value to **C**, in which case **A** will have to continue to service the swap, or the swap has a negative value to **C**, in which case it will be treated as just another payment obligation of **C**, and **A** will have to try and recover what he can.

If on the other hand the FX swap is *cancelled at default of* **C**, then **A** will make a gain at least in those cases when the FX swap would otherwise have a negative value to **A**. This will allow **A** to reduce the counterparty credit risk charge. The potential losses of **A** in some default scenarios will be balanced by potential gains in other default scenarios.

If **A** *and* **C** gain with this scenario, who loses? The answer is: the other creditors of **C**. In effect, **C** has sold an FX swap that would otherwise increase the value of his assets in default. This does not hurt **C** because in the event of his default he does not own the FX swap anymore anyway.

2.8.3   Rating-triggered credit default swaps

Many issuers of debt are assigned a publicly available credit rating by rating agencies such as Standard and Poor's (S&P) or Moody's. These rating assignments, and in particular changes in these credit ratings, have important consequences. Many market participants have a lot of confidence in the rating agencies' research and their ability to correctly assess the default risk of an obligor or a debt issue. These investors will adjust their portfolios according to the rating agencies' new assessment of the bonds' risk. Even investors who do not believe in the accuracy of credit ratings use them as a first classification of the riskiness of the obligor. Furthermore, many institutional investors are subject to restrictions that only allow them to invest in investment-grade bonds (i.e. BBB/Baa or better in S&P and Moody's ratings respectively).

---

[10] If the default occurs before this optimal exercise date, the owner of the swaption can earn an additional premium by selling the swaption in the market rather than exercising it. If the optimal exercise date is reached earlier, the owner of the swaption can lock into a profit by exercising the swaption and buying a swaption with a cheaper value.

This causes large selling pressure on bonds that are downgraded below the investment-grade threshold. Almost invariably, a downgrade of a bond by a rating agency causes a significant drop in its market price.

As the actions of rating agencies are largely viewed as impartial and impervious to manipulation, they can be used to define the credit event of a credit default swap. For example, such a credit default swap would enable the manager of a portfolio of investment-grade bonds to sell a particular bond at a predetermined value as soon as it was downgraded below the investment-grade level.

Another occasionally voiced argument in favour of a rating-based specification of a credit default swap is that a rating-based default swap protects against market price movements while a plain vanilla CDS only provides protection against defaults. This argument is not correct because a plain vanilla CDS does indeed provide protection against intermediate credit-caused market price movements. If the market price of the underlying bond drops for credit reasons, then (because of the cash-and-carry arbitrage connection) the market CDS spread must increase simultaneously, and the mark-to-market value of a long CDS position must rise, too.

Similar ratings triggers are also embedded in some issues of corporate debt. For example, the coupons of some of the latest bond issues by European telecommunication companies (Vodafone-AirTouch or Deutsche Telekom) will be increased if the rating of the issuer is downgraded below a certain threshold. This coupon stepup is meant to compensate investors for the loss in value of the debt upon a downgrade. The drop in the bond's market value with such a coupon stepup should be smaller than without this provision. There is a flip side to this: the debt service payments of the firm will increase exactly when the firm's prospects are worsening, thus exacerbating the situation.

The credit event of a rating (downgrade)-triggered default swap has a much higher likelihood of occurring than the credit event of a plain vanilla CDS. The default payment on the other hand is typically much lower (unless the downgrade was caused by a default). This reduces counterparty risk because the payment at risk is smaller.

2.8.4 Options on defaultable bonds

A *call option* on a defaultable bond gives the owner of this option the right to buy the bond at a given date (the maturity date of the option) for a given price (the strike price of the option). A *put option* on the other hand gives the owner the right to sell the underlying bond for the strike price. These options can also contain early exercise rights of the type of American or Bermudan options.

When analysing the value of such an option, default risk must not be ignored. The option's value is composed of two parts:

- The value of the option if there is no default of the underlying bond, and
- The value of the option at default of the underlying bond.

The first component of the option's value is driven by normal price changes of the bond over the life of the option. The second component is either a default insurance (for a put option on the bond) or zero (for a call option on the bond). If the default risk of the underlying bond is significant, the specification of the option should be clear about what happens to the option at a default of the underlying bond.[11] They can specify a knockout at default or leave the option unchanged.

Put options on defaultable bonds can be effective instruments to hedge and transfer credit risk. Compared to a credit default swap, a put option on a bond has the advantage that it is a well-understood instrument whose payoff only depends on market prices and thus removes the specification uncertainty that may surround the formal definition of an abstract default event in a CDS. If the strike price is chosen sufficiently low (to remove the first component of the option's value), the put option will only be in-the-money if a default has happened. Then it is essentially equivalent to a CDS with a slightly changed default payment. In some cases, the sale of default protection in the form of bond put options has had regulatory capital advantages to a short position in a CDS, for example if the put option can be booked on the trading book while the CDS would have to be booked on the banking book.

Nevertheless, a put option on a defaultable bond also has disadvantages compared to a CDS. First, the default trigger mechanism and the default payment mechanism of a CDS have proven to be remarkably robust and to fulfil their function as intended in most cases, so documentation uncertainty in a CDS contract has lost importance. Second, the put option is only specified with respect to one particular bond and may therefore miss some default events, and it is also impossible to deliver substitute securities at default. Finally, in order to isolate default risk in a put option the strike price has to be chosen below the bond's par value. Then, the difference of the option's strike price and the bond's par value remains unhedged in default.

Therefore, options on defaultable bonds are less than perfect substitutes for credit default swaps. This leaves their original purpose: to lock into a price for a future purchase (call) or sale (put) of the underlying bond, while keeping the opportunity for additional gains.

2.8.5 Credit spread options

Credit spread options have the purpose to allow trading and hedging of credit spread movements alone. There are many different types of credit spreads, therefore there are equally many varieties of credit spread options.

- **Asset-swap spread**-based options:
  An **asset swaption** (call) gives the owner the right to buy an asset swap package with a given strike asset swap spread for par.
- **Default-swap spread**-based options:
  A **default swaption** (call) gives the owner the right to enter a long position in a credit default swap at the given default swap rate.
- **Yield-spread**-based options on defaultable bonds:
  A *yield-spread* call on a defaultable bond gives the owner of this option the right to buy the underlying bond at a prespecified strike yield spread over the yield of a given default-free benchmark bond.

The corresponding put options give their owners the right to *sell* the respective underlying securities (bond, asset swap package or CDS) to the seller of the option. The most common of

---

[11] For example, the bond may be reorganised or settled, which means that the underlying of the option ceases to exist before the maturity of the option.

these options are the asset swaptions, followed by default swaptions. Yield-spread options are less common because their payoff function is highly nonlinear and there is no direct underlying market for yield spreads. For asset swap packages and CDSs, though, there is a market for the underlying security.

The price of options of this type can consist of two parts: a one-off payment up front, and a regular commitment fee until the option is exercised. The exercise style of the option can be European (only at maturity of the option) or Bermudan (also at intermediate exercise dates). The treatment of the option at intermediate defaults should also be clearly specified. The option can be knocked out at default, or it can be unwound at market value.

A typical application for options on credit derivatives is the hedging of committed lines of credit. Consider the case of a bank that has extended a line of credit to **C**. As long as **C** does not use this line of credit, the bank will not need default insurance, but when **C** draws on it, the bank will want to hedge the exposure to **C**. Very often, **C** will draw only if he does not find better funding conditions elsewhere, i.e. if his credit quality has deteriorated. This means that the bank will have to buy a CDS exactly when it has become expensive. A call option on a CDS will hedge exactly this risk and it will be cheaper than buying default protection. For this reason, such options are also known as *synthetic lending facilities*.

Asset swaptions and default swaptions often come in the form of *extension or callability options* to an existing asset swap package or a CDS. In the case of embedded options the question whether the option is continued or knocked out at default is immediately clear: an option to extend or cancel an existing CDS always ceases to exist as soon as a default event occurs. The whole contract is unwound at default, therefore there will be nothing left to extend or cancel. Such options can be useful to hedge the default risk of callable debt or to satisfy regulatory requirements, as in the following example.

Example 2.5 *A has an exposure of a five-year loan to Daimler Chrysler. He would like to buy CDS default protection from **B** for the first two years of this loan but is happy to accept the next three years of Daimler Chrysler default risk.*

*The regulator of **A** will only give **A** regulatory capital relief if the default protection of the Daimler Chrysler risk matches the underlying exposure in maturity. Therefore, buying a two-year CDS from **B** will* not *give **A** the desired regulatory capital reduction.*

*In order to circumvent the maturity matching requirements of **A**'s regulator, **A** and **B** enter a cancellable stepup credit default swap (assume the CDS rates of Daimler Chrysler are at 116 bp for all maturities):*

- *The term of the contract is 5 years.*
- *A buys default protection from **B**, i.e. if a default of Daimler Chrysler happens at any time over the life of the contract, **B** pays to **A** the usual default payment of 1 − recovery.*
- *The CDS protection fee is $\bar{s} = 130\,bp$ for the first two years.*
- *After year two, the CDS protection fee increases by 100 bp every year (the stepup).*
- *A has the right to cancel the CDS after year two (the callability provision).*

*The regulator cannot complain now: **A** has secured his default protection over the full term. The only person who can remove this default protection is **A** himself if he chooses to call in the contract earlier, but no outsider can remove the protection. Therefore it fulfils the required maturity matching condition.*

Economically, things look different. Because of the stepup provision, the price of keeping the CDS after year two is extremely high: on average A will have to pay 330 bp over the next three years. A will only choose to continue the default protection after year two if the credit risk of Daimler Chrysler has worsened dramatically (to a three-year CDS spread of more than 330 bp), otherwise he will exercise his option and cancel the swap. Thus, there is a very high likelihood the protection will be cancelled after two years. This makes the embedded option cheaper to A.

We could have rephrased A's position as follows. He holds a two-year CDS on Daimler Chrysler at 116 bp, and a call option with maturity two years on a three-year CDS on Daimler Chrysler with a strike CDS spread of 230,330,430 bp over the three years of the CDS. The call option is knocked out at a default of Daimler Chrysler before the option's maturity. B is paid an additional fee of 14 bp over the next two years for this option that he has written to A.

2.9   DEFAULT CORRELATION PRODUCTS AND CDOs

The credit derivatives we have discussed so far are *single-name* credit derivatives, they are targeted on the default of one single obligor. These credit derivatives are very well suited for the management of individual exposure concentrations, but not for the management of default risk on a portfolio basis.

When viewed on a portfolio basis, a certain number of individual defaults is a completely natural phenomenon and should be covered by the excess returns of the other investments in the portfolio. Fully hedging all individual exposures with a portfolio of single-name CDSs is therefore not necessary. The real risk on a portfolio level is the risk of a *clustering* of defaults and of *joint defaults*, the risk that many more defaults occur than usual. In order to manage risks of this type, basket and portfolio credit derivatives have been innovated.

2.9.1   First-to-default swaps and basket default swaps

A first-to-default swap (FtD) is the extension of a credit default swap to portfolio credit risk. Its key characteristics are the following:

- Instead of referencing just a single reference credit, an FtD is specified with respect to a **basket of reference credits $C_1, C_2, \ldots, C_I$.**
- The set of reference credit assets (the assets that can trigger default events) contains assets by all reference credits.
- The protection buyer **A** pays a regular fee of $\overline{s}^{FtD}$ to the protection seller **B** until the default event occurs or the FtD matures.
- The default event is the **first default** of any of the reference credits.
- The FtD is terminated after the first default event.
- The default payment is "1 − recovery" on the defaulted obligor. If physical delivery is specified, the set of deliverable obligations contains only obligations of the defaulted reference credit.

The basket of a typical FtD can contain between four and 12 reference credits. If larger portfolios are referenced, first-loss structures (see next subsection) are more popular.

A natural extension of the first-to-default concept is the introduction of second-to-default (StD) and nth-to-default (ntD) basket credit derivatives. Such credit derivatives only differ in the specification of the default event, the basic structure remains the same. While FtD credit derivatives are a common structure, second- and higher-order ntD structures are rarer.

As will be seen in the chapter on default correlation modelling, a first-to-default protection on a basket of credits removes most of the default risk of the basket. As long as the probability of multiple defaults is low, the whole basket is well protected by an FtD. This risk structure will be reflected in the fee of $\bar{s}^{\text{FtD}}$ that must be paid to the protection seller.

An FtD can have advantages to both sides, the protection buyer **A** and the protection seller **B**. As argued before, the protection buyer **A** achieves good protection of a whole basket of reference credits at a cheaper price than the purchase of individual default protections on each of the reference credits.

The protection seller **B** has gained leveraged exposure to the basket of underlying credits. The risk that he will have to pay the default payment is significantly increased but so is also his premium income. The size of his exposure on the other hand is limited to one default. Many investors view the risk premia that are paid on high-grade credit risk as very attractive, and with an FtD they have the opportunity to gain a leveraged exposure to these risks.

A leveraged investment in an FtD can also have regulatory capital advantages, because **B**'s capital charge cannot be higher than his exposure size, and frequently the capital charge is equivalent to the charge on a single credit exposure. It can also enable investors to take on higher risks who might otherwise only be allowed to take on investment-grade exposures.

Sometimes FtDs are embedded in credit-linked notes. In the early stages of this market, some investors did not realise the full extent of the risk concentration in the FtD and were therefore willing to accept very low premiums. For example, an FtD-linked note on a basket of 10 AA-rated credits can have the default risk of a speculative-grade bond and should command a spread of at least eight times the AA spread, but a naive investor may view this as an AA investment.

2.9.2   First loss layers

Common motivations for the transfer of the credit risk of loan portfolios are portfolio credit risk management, regulatory capital management, or exploitation of arbitrage opportunities. For these purposes it is necessary to transfer a large fraction or the whole default risk exposure of the portfolio, and the portfolios under consideration are quite large.

If protection is sought on a larger portfolio numbering from 20 to several hundred loans or bonds, a credit derivative that just protects against the first default in the portfolio is impractical. A FtD protection will not significantly reduce the credit risk of the portfolio, and the exposures in the portfolio may not all be of the same size. When more of the default risk of a portfolio is to be transferred, things become very complicated very quickly.

A **loss layer protection** on the portfolio achieves a more flexible transfer of the portfolio's risks. Again this transaction can be viewed as a modification of the basic structure of a credit default swap.

- The reference credit is a *reference credit portfolio*. The reference credit portfolio consists of I credit default swaps on the reference credits $C_1, C_2, \ldots, C_I$ with notional amounts $K_1, K_2, \ldots, K_I$. The total notional amount of the reference credit portfolio is $K_{\text{tot}} = \sum_{i=1}^{I} K_i$.

- The *loss layer* is defined by its lower and upper notional bounds K_L and K_U respectively. The initial notional amount of the loss layer is $K = K_U - K_L$.
- The *credit events* are the default events of the reference credits of the portfolio.
- The *cumulative loss* calculation:
  - The initial cumulative loss is zero: $C_0 = 0$.
  - At the jth credit event ($1 \leq j \leq I$), the cumulative loss is increased by the loss at this default:

$$C_j = C_{j-1} + K_j(1 - \text{recovery}_j).$$

  - The *cumulative loss of the loss layer* C^L is the amount by which the cumulative loss has hit the loss layer:

$$C_j^L = \min(\max(C_j - K_L, 0),\ K_U - K_L).$$

- The **default payment** of **B** to **A** at a default event is the increase in the cumulative loss of the loss layer:

$$C_j^L - C_{j-1}^L.$$

- The notional of the loss layer is reduced by the default payments of **B**. If the notional reaches zero, the contract is unwound.
- The protection buyer **A** pays a periodic protection fee on the notional of the loss layer to **B**.

A very common variant of the loss layer protection are **first loss layers**. First loss layers have a lower notional bound of zero $K_L = 0$, so that they are hit by the first losses up to a cumulative loss amount of K_U.

First loss layers provide protection that is very similar to the protection provided by an FtD swap, but it is important to recognise the differences. Usually the first-loss protection covers the notional of several exposures in the basket, so that it will cover more than just a first default.

Example 2.6 (first loss vs. FtD) *Consider a reference portfolio of 10 reference credits with a notional of 20m USD each. At an* expected *recovery at default of 50%, do the following transactions provide the same default protection?*

(a) An FtD protection on the portfolio.
(b) A first-loss layer protection of 10m USD.

The answer is "no". The careful reader will have noticed that we spoke of an expected *recovery rate. If we knew* for sure *that the recovery of the first default would be 50%, then the answer would be "yes" but the recovery rate is a market price after an extremely important piece of news. The difference between the FtD and the first-loss protection here is similar to the difference between a CDS and a DDS.*

Comparing the two transactions, it is probably the FtD swap that provides the better protection. With the FtD, the residual risk in the portfolio is the risk of two or more defaults. The residual risk with a first-loss protection is:

- *The recovery risk on the first default (i.e. the risk that the recovery rate is below 50%).*
- *The risk of two or more defaults with a cumulative loss of more than 10m.*

Typically, the recovery risk *on the first default is much larger than the risk of having a second default after the first. If we assume that recovery rates are uniformly distributed between 0% and 100%, then there is a 0.5 probability that the recovery rate on the first default is below 50%. In contrast to this, the probability of a second default after the first default will be much lower.*

2.9.3   Collateralised debt obligations

Collateralised debt obligations (CDOs) are a financial innovation to securitise portfolios of defaultable assets: loans, bonds or credit default swaps. The assets are sold to a company that was set up exclusively for this purpose, and investors are offered the opportunity to invest in notes issued by this company. These *obligations* are *collateralised* by the underlying *debt* portfolio, hence the name CDO.

The financial innovation lies in the design of the payoff structure of the notes. They are structured in order to offer risk/return profiles that are specifically targeted to the risk appetite and investment restrictions of different investor groups. These risk/return profiles look very much like the loss layers introduced in the previous section.

In particular, even if the underlying portfolio is mostly unrated or speculative-grade, it is possible to enhance the credit rating of most of the notes to the high investment-grade ratings by concentrating the default risk in a small first loss layer. This enables investors to invest in these notes who otherwise would not be allowed to invest in the underlying assets themselves. The notes of a well-designed CDO can sometimes be sold for a cumulative price that is higher than the sum of the market value of the underlying assets.

CDO transactions can have several motivations. *Arbitrage CDOs* aim to arbitrage the price difference between the components of the underlying portfolio and the sale price of the CDO notes. Arbitrage CDOs have traded assets like bonds or CDS exposures as underlying securities.

By using *balance sheet CDOs*, banks aim to free up regulatory capital that is tied up in the underlying loan portfolio. Balance sheet CDOs usually reference a loan portfolio. Their size can be very large, it is estimated that about 35 balance sheet CDO transactions totalling over 70bn USD notional were completed in 1998 alone (Bowler and Tierney, 1999).

The classical motivation for securitisations is to gain funding for the underlying exposures while laying off the risks. Similar structures are also common for other types of claims, e.g. collateralised mortgage obligations, credit-card-backed debt obligations or car-loan-backed debt obligations. Of these, the market for collateralised mortgage obligations is the largest and oldest.

To demonstrate the basic structure, we first describe a very simple collateralised bond obligation (CBO). The components of this CBO are as follows.

- The underlying portfolio is composed of defaultable bonds issued by issuers C_i with notional amounts $K_i, i = 1, \ldots, I$. The total notional is $K = \sum_{i=1}^{I} K_i$.
- The portfolio is transferred into a specially created company, the special purpose vehicle (SPV).

- The SPV issues notes:
  - an equity (or first-loss) tranche with notional K_E,
  - several mezzanine tranches with notional K_{M1}, K_{M2}, K_{M3}, etc.,
  - a senior tranche with notional K_S.
- If during the existence of the CBO one of the bonds in the portfolio defaults, the recovery payments are reinvested in default-free securities.
- At maturity of the CBO, the portfolio is liquidated and the proceeds are distributed to the tranches, according to their seniority ranking.

The key point of the CBO is the final redistribution of the portfolio value according to the seniority of the notes. First, the senior tranche is served. If the senior tranche can be fully repaid, the most senior mezzanine tranche is repaid. If this tranche can also be fully repaid, then the next tranches are paid off in the order of their seniority, until finally the equity tranche is paid whatever is left of the portfolio's value.

Instead of viewing the payoffs of the different tranches as a function of the final value of the portfolio, for credit-risk-based structures it is more instructive to view the payoffs as a function of the *losses*.

1. The first losses hit the equity tranche alone. Until the cumulative loss amount has reached the equity's notional K_E, the other tranches are protected by the equity tranche.
2. Cumulative losses exceeding K_E affect the first mezzanine tranche, until its notional is used up.
3. After this, the subsequent mezzanine tranches are hit in the order of their seniority.
4. Only when all other tranches have absorbed their share of the losses will the senior tranche suffer any losses.

The owners of the tranches of this CDO have sold *loss layer protection* on a part of the potential losses of the portfolio, and these loss layers cover the whole portfolio. The tranches of lower seniority serve as a loss protection cushion for the tranches of higher seniority. The larger the degree of this subordination, the better the protection of the senior tranches and the higher their credit quality.

This basic structure is an idealised simplification of the real CDOs in the market. For these, the basic idea has been refined in several directions. In terms of the underlying portfolio:

- Instead of traded bonds, the portfolio can also consist of loans. In this case one speaks of a *collateralised loan obligation (CLO)*.
- A *synthetic CDO* is constructed using credit default swaps instead of bonds or loans in the underlying portfolio. This gives the structure a much larger degree of flexibility. Not all tranches must be sold off in the form of notes, protection can also be purchased in the form of pure derivatives transactions. The structure can be set up without the legally complicated transfer of the ownership of loans, and it is also not affected by peculiarities of the specification of the underlying loans or bonds.
- The underlying portfolio may be actively managed by a portfolio manager. In this case the portfolio manager has to observe several restrictions: concentration limits on individual exposures, industry groups and country concentration, minimum ratings and average rating restrictions of the portfolio. The investment now has features of an investment-fund investment. Actively managed CDOs are marked to market at regular intervals, and the payoffs of

the tranches of these CDOs are affected by the results of these markings to market. Therefore, such CDOs are also often called *market value CDOs*.

- If the underlying portfolio is not actively managed, the payoffs of the tranches are directly linked to the cash flows resulting from the portfolio. Then the CDO is called a *cash flow CDO*.
- If, for confidentiality reasons, the issuer cannot give the names of the obligors in the loan portfolio, the CLO is called a *black box* CLO. This is unusual and the investors will demand a large compensation for the additional uncertainty.

The maturity of the transaction is between 5 and 10 years. This means that the notes must pay regular coupons, which requires a modification of the distribution of the payoffs of the tranches.

At every coupon payment date, the cash flow (i.e. coupon payments minus default losses) from the collateral portfolio is distributed to serve the coupon payments and to fill up a reserve for future coupon payments. This is done according to a predetermined rank order, the *waterfall* structure. The nature of this payoff mechanism exposes mezzanine and senior tranches also to timing and clustering risk. If the times of defaults are clustered in the same coupon interval, a mezzanine or senior tranche could miss a coupon payment, although the same tranche would have had a full coupon payment if the defaults had been more evenly distributed over time.

In the majority of CDOs, tranches above equity level are rated by rating agencies such as Standard and Poor's or Moody's. The requirements of the rating agencies have a strong influence on the structuring of the tranches and the composition of the portfolio. The originators know the criteria of the agencies and try to adjust the composition of the portfolio and the subordination of the tranches in order to achieve the desired rating classification of the tranches of the CDO.

Example 2.7 (synthetic CDO)   *The underlying portfolio contains 100 CDSs with 5 years maturity on investment-grade reference credits with a notional amount of 10m USD each. An SPV is used to securitise an intermediate loss layer protection on this portfolio:*

- *The SPV sells loss layer protection to the issuer of the portfolio for losses between $K_L = 20m$ USD and $K_U = 120m$ USD.*
  - *The issuer pays a regular protection fee.*
  - *The SPV funds any default payments by selling collateral assets.*
- *The SPV issues notes:*
  - *20m   Mezzanine notes I   Rating BBB   Libor + 400*
  - *30m   Mezzanine notes II   Rating A   Libor + 180*
  - *30m   Mezzanine notes III   Rating AA   Libor + 110*
  - *20m   Senior notes   Rating AAA   Libor + 50*
  Interest on these notes is paid quarterly in arrears, maturity is 5 years.
- *The proceeds of the note issuance are invested in AAA-rated bonds or treasuries. These assets serve as a collateral pool for the loss layer protection that was sold to the issuer. The return on the collateral and the loss layer protection fees are paid into the "available funds" account.*
- *Initially, the final repayment amount of all notes is their notional amount.*
- *At default, the SPV may have to make protection payments to the issuer from the loss layer protection it has written. The cash for these payments comes from the liquidation of part of the collateral pool. Simultaneously, the payments are deducted from the final repayment amount*

of the mezzanine notes I, and if that repayment amount is reduced to zero, it is deducted from the final repayment amount of the mezzanine notes II, then from the mezzanine notes III and finally from the senior notes.

- *At coupon payment dates, the available funds are used to pay fees, taxes and expenses, and interest payments on the notes (in order of seniority).*
- *At maturity of the notes, the collateral pool is liquidated and the notes are paid off in order of their seniority. The payoff of each note is its final repayment amount.*

This leaves two exposures: equity exposure *for the first losses up to 20m USD and* super-senior exposure *for losses exceeding 120m USD. The issuer keeps the equity exposure and buys protection on the super-senior loss (losses above 120m) in the form of a loss layer protection from another highly rated counterparty.*

The issuer may decide to keep the equity exposure. Protection on equity exposure is very expensive and the issuer may feel that the risk premia demanded by the market are too high. Furthermore, the investors of the mezzanine tranches may want the issuer to retain the equity exposure to avoid asymmetric information problems in the composition of the portfolio.

Depending on market conditions, the offered coupons of the notes may vary significantly. Nevertheless, they are usually significantly higher than the coupons on classical corporate bonds with the same rating.

Synthetic arbitrage CDOs also have a significant effect on the underlying CDS markets, because they form an important channel through which outside investors can sell default protection in the CDS market on a diversified basis. If a reference credit is included in a synthetic arbitrage CDO, the CDO manager will be able to offer protection on this name relatively cheaply, in fact he may have to sell it for less than he expected to. The presence of protection sellers is of central importance to the functioning of the CDS market, and the volume of synthetic CDO issuance is an important indicator of the current supply of credit protection in the single-name CDS market.

2.10   CREDIT-LINKED NOTES

Credit-linked notes (CLNs) are a combination of a credit derivative with a medium-term note. The underlying note pays a coupon of Libor plus a spread and is issued by a high-quality issuer. The issuer of the note buys protection on the risk referenced in the credit derivative. In addition, having effectively sold protection on the underlying credit exposure, the investors also face the counterparty risk of the issuer.

Using a CLN makes the protection sale fully collateralised and splitting the note into smaller denominations enables the issuer to access other classes of investors. CLNs are an important vehicle to open the CDS market to bond and note investors who are not able to enter over-the-counter (OTC) derivatives transactions. Buying a CLN is nothing but a fully collateralised sale of credit protection, but it is usually treated as a fixed-income investment.

Example 2.8 (Wal-Mart credit-linked note)   *Issuer: JPMorgan, September 1996 (via an AAA trust). The buyers of the CLN receive:*

- *Coupon (fixed or floating);*
- *Principal if no default of reference credit (Wal-Mart) until maturity;*

- *Only the recovery rate on the reference obligation as final repayment if a default of reference credit occurs.*

The buyers of the note now have credit exposure to Wal-Mart which is largely equivalent to the direct purchase of a bond issued by Wal-Mart. They also have some residual exposure to the credit risk of the AAA-rated trust set up to manage the note. From JPMorgan's point of view the investors of the CLN have sold them a CDS and posted 100% collateral.

This example shows a CDS-linked note. In Section 2.9 we saw notes that were linked to the performance of loss layer protection, and there are also notes that are linked to the performance of a TRS. Sometimes CLNs have *principal protection*, i.e. only the coupon payments of the note are at risk during a credit event.

From a pricing and risk-management point of view, a CLN is not a complicated instrument. We can simply decompose it into its components and analyse the embedded credit derivatives separately. The only additional feature is that – as mentioned before – from the point of view of the issuer CLNs do not carry any counterparty risk.

2.11   GUIDE TO THE LITERATURE

By now there are a number of good books that describe the basic credit derivative structures and their applications, the market structure, and regulatory, legal and accounting issues involved with credit derivatives. Good examples are the books by Das (1998), Tavakoli (1998) and Nelken (1999), Burghof *et al.* (2000) (in German) and Mathieu and d'Herouville (1998) (in French). Besides these books there are also a number of quite good surveys and brochures published by the major investment banks to educate their investors.

The ISDA has made important contributions to standardise the documentation of credit derivatives, and the 1999 ISDA Credit Derivative Definitions are an essential reference on this topic. Nevertheless, not all documentation issues are resolved yet and new issues keep arising, so the documentation will certainly change or be supplemented in the future. The current version of the definitions and sample confirmations can be downloaded from the ISDA's website at `http://www.isda.org`.

The regulatory environment of Basel I is well described in the books given above, but the regulation for credit risk in general and credit derivatives in particular is in an even greater flux than the documentation. Much of the early growth of the CDS market was driven by regulatory capital motives, and after the finalisation of Basel II almost certainly new structures will evolve that aim to optimise the use of risk capital in the banking sector under this new set of rules. Information on Basel II must necessarily be temporary at this point, so we cannot give any more specific references other than the link to the Bank for International Settlements `http://www.bis.org`.

3
Credit Spreads and Bond
Price-Based Pricing

A very rich and useful source of information on the default risk of an obligor are the market prices of bonds and other defaultable securities that were issued by this obligor, and the prices of CDSs referencing this obligor's credit risk. Encoded in these prices we should find the market's assessment of the default risk of the obligor, adjusted for risk premia that may prevail in the market.

In this chapter we analyse the relationship between the prices of bonds issued by a defaultable obligor, the prices of similar default-free instruments and the default risk of the obligor. This will result in a method for the construction of a clean term structure of credit spreads from observed market prices. As we will show, such a term structure of credit spreads has a direct intuitive interpretation in terms of a simple default risk model and it can be used very profitably to price many simple credit derivatives, without any further modelling effort.

There are several reasons why we might like to recover this information and use it in our model. First, if we believe in some form of market efficiency, then there will be information aggregated in the market prices, and this may actually be more information than any of the market participants have individually. If we can recover this information, we can save a lot of work. Second, a model that is based upon and calibrated to the prices of traded assets is immune to simple arbitrage strategies using these traded assets.[1] Third, if we recover implied default probabilities from traded assets, we also directly recover the associated *risk premia* that are paid for this type of risk.

This is why a calibration capability of the model is regularly required by risk management guidelines. But the calibration of the model to market prices also precludes the applicability of the model in some other areas. In particular, a comparison of "model price" vs. "market price" in order to identify investment opportunities will only make sense for securities other than the calibration securities.

In the first section, we explore the basic case of default-free and defaultable zero-coupon bonds. This serves to illustrate the role that is played by zero-coupon credit spreads and their interpretation in terms of forward local default probabilities, furthermore many strengths and weaknesses of the approach can already be discussed.

It will be seen that the prices of defaultable and default-free bonds contain all the information on the distribution of the time of default that we need, provided the defaultable bonds default with zero recovery. Unfortunately, we cannot observe the prices of such a set of zero-recovery defaultable zero-coupon bonds in real markets, but we would like to somehow construct such a term structure from real traded assets in order to be able to recover the information that we reached previously.

In order to do so, we will go in the opposite direction: we will construct a simple method to calculate a model price for real traded assets such as defaultable coupon bonds or CDSs *for a*

---

[1] But beware, there may be arbitrage opportunities using other traded instruments.

given term structure of defaultable zerobonds. Then, we invert this pricing relationship in order to find the term structure of defaultable zerobonds that yields model prices which equal the observed market prices. This term structure is then the *implied term structure of default risk.*

The first step is the inclusion of positive recovery into the model, and this will be tackled in the second section. This, combined with the zero-coupon credit spreads of the first section will enable us to price the basic pricing building blocks that make up the payoffs of CDSs and defaultable bonds. These are the instruments we use to calibrate the spread curve. The second, closely connected step is the representation of the real-world defaultable securities in this framework, which is given in the next section. Finally, several issues in the calibration of the model have to be addressed before a successful calibration can be performed. In particular, some structural assumptions are needed in order to reduce the degrees of freedom that still reside in the model. These assumptions and their implications are discussed in detail at the end of this chapter.

The choice of a set of calibration securities is equivalent to the choice of a pricing benchmark. Ideally, this benchmark is based upon the prices of other defaultable securities issued by the obligor in question, but because of data scarcity, we sometimes must use substitute securities as proxies. If such a spread curve is constructed using securities issued by a diverse set of obligors (e.g. all obligors from a given rating class, industry or region), we should no longer require the calibration to perfectly replicate the prices of all defaultable bonds. This and similar problems will also be analysed at the end of this chapter.

3.1   CREDIT SPREADS AND IMPLIED DEFAULT PROBABILITIES

3.1.1   Risk-neutral probabilities

The analysis of this section takes place in a filtered probability space[2] $(\Omega, (\mathcal{F}_t)_{t \geq 0}, \mathcal{F}, Q)$ under the risk-neutral probability measure, the *spot martingale measure Q*, and all probabilities and expectations are taken under Q. This does not mean that we assume risk-neutrality. Rather, when we speak of *probabilities*, we are really speaking of *state prices*. If interest rates are constant, the discounted Q-probability of an event A at time T is really the price of a security that pays off 1 at time T if A occurs. If interest rates are stochastic, the price of this contingent claim is $\mathbf{E}[\beta(T)\mathbf{1}_{\{A\}}]$.

We will see in a later section that the difference between risk-neutral probabilities and historical (statistical, real-world) probabilities can be quite large when it comes to default risk, the risk of default usually carries a large risk premium for investment-grade obligors.

3.1.2   Setup

To set the framework of analysis, we need the following notation.

Definition 3.1

- *For $A \in \mathcal{F}$ we denote by $\mathbf{1}_{\{A\}}$ the indicator function of A, i.e. $\mathbf{1}_{\{A\}}(\omega) = 1$ if $\omega \in A$, and $\mathbf{1}_{\{A\}}(\omega) = 0$ otherwise.*
- *The time of default is denoted by τ, and the survival indicator function is $I(t)$:*

$$\tau = \text{time of default}, \qquad I(t) = \mathbf{1}_{\{\tau > t\}} = \begin{cases} 1 & \text{if} \quad \tau > t, \\ 0 & \text{if} \quad \tau \leq t. \end{cases}$$

---

[2] The filtration $(\mathcal{F}_t)_{t \geq 0}$ is assumed to satisfy the 'usual conditions'.

- *The default-free zero-coupon bond (ZCB) prices for all maturities $T > t$:*

$$B(t, T) = \text{Price at time } t \text{ of ZCB paying off } 1 \text{ at } T.$$

- *The defaultable zero-coupon bond prices for all maturities $T > t$, if $\tau > t$:*

$$\overline{B}(t, T) = \text{Price of defaultable ZCB if } \tau > t.$$

Later on we will show how to incorporate more commonly traded assets like coupon bonds or credit default swaps in the analysis, and we will discuss the modelling of positive recovery rates. When there is no danger of confusion, we will just speak of "bonds" when we mean "zero-coupon bonds".

To ensure absence of arbitrage we must require that defaultable bonds are always worth less than default-free bonds of the same maturity:

$$0 \leq \overline{B}(t, T) < B(t, T) \quad \forall\, t < T$$

and that the bond prices are a decreasing, non-negative function of maturity, starting at $\overline{B}(t, t) = 1 = B(t, t)$:

$$B(t, T_1) \geq B(t, T_2) > 0 \quad \text{and} \quad \overline{B}(t, T_1) \geq \overline{B}(t, T_2) \geq 0 \quad \forall\, t < T_1 < T_2, \quad \tau > t.$$

To set up the framework we need to make the assumptions below. The implications of these assumptions will be discussed at the points when we use them.

Assumption 3.1

- *Information: At time t, the defaultable and default-free zero-coupon bond prices of all maturities $T \geq t$ are known.*
- *Absence of arbitrage: The bond prices are arbitrage-free.*
- *Zero recovery: The defaultable zero-coupon bonds have no recovery at default. We write the price at time t of a defaultable bond with maturity T as:[3]*

$$I(t)\overline{B}(t, T) = \begin{cases} \overline{B}(t, T) & \text{if } \quad \tau > t, \\ 0 & \text{if } \quad \tau \leq t. \end{cases}$$

The survival indicator function is omitted in $I(t)\overline{B}(t, T)$ if it is clear that $\tau > t$.

Assumption 3.2 (independence)   *Under pricing probabilities (measure Q), the default-free interest-rate dynamics are independent of the default time. $\{B(t, T) \mid T \geq t\}$ and τ are independent under $(\Omega, \mathcal{F}, Q)$.*

The independence assumption 3.2 also implies independence of derived quantities, e.g. independence of: [default probability] and [default-free interest rates, short rate] under Q.

---

[3] This representation is convenient when we model the dynamics of these defaultable zero-coupon bonds, because we do not have to model a jump to zero in $\overline{B}(t, T)$ at $t = \tau$. Furthermore, we can divide by $\overline{B}$ without having to worry about divisions by zero.

3.1.3   The fundamental relationship

Under the spot martingale measure, the price of every contingent claim is given by the expected value of its discounted expected payoff. This means for the default-free zero-coupon bond

$$B(t, T) = \mathbf{E}\big[e^{-\int_t^T r(s)ds} \cdot 1\big], \tag{3.1}$$

where we used the default-free continuously compounded short rate $r(t)$ to discount the final payoff of 1.

For *defaultable* zero-coupon bonds, the payoff is 1 only if the obligor is still alive at T (in the following we assume that $\tau > t$):

$$\text{Payoff} = \mathbf{1}_{\{\tau > T\}} = \begin{cases} 1 & \text{if default after } T, \text{ i.e. } \tau > T, \\ 0 & \text{if default before } T, \text{ i.e. } \tau \leq T. \end{cases}$$

The price of the defaultable zero-coupon bond at time $t < \tau$ is therefore:

$$\overline{B}(t, T) = \mathbf{E}\big[e^{-\int_t^T r(s)ds} \cdot I(T)\big]. \tag{3.2}$$

Invoking Assumption 3.2 (independence) between defaults and the default-free interest rates, we can factor the expectation operator in (3.2) into a product of expectations:

$$\overline{B}(t, T) = \mathbf{E}\big[e^{-\int_t^T r(s)ds} \cdot I(T)\big] = \mathbf{E}\big[e^{-\int_t^T r(s)ds}\big]\mathbf{E}\,[I(T)]$$
$$= B(t, T)\mathbf{E}[I(T)] = B(t, T)P(t, T), \tag{3.3}$$

where $P(t, T)$ is the implied probability of survival in $[t, T]$.

3.1.4   The implied survival probability

Definition 3.2 (implied survival probability)   *Let $\tau > t$.*

(i) *The implied survival probability from t to $T \geq t$ as seen from time t is the ratio of the defaultable to the default-free ZCB prices:*

$$P(t, T) = \frac{\overline{B}(t, T)}{B(t, T)}. \tag{3.4}$$

(ii) *The* implied default probability *over $[t, T]$ is $P^{\text{def}}(t, T) := 1 - P(t, T)$.*

(iii) *If $P(t, T)$ has a right-sided derivative in T, the implied density of the default time is:*

$$\mathbf{Q}[\tau \in [T, T + dt] \mid \mathcal{F}_t] = -\frac{\partial}{\partial T}P(t, T)dt.$$

If we have zero-coupon bond prices for all maturities, we also have implied survival probabilities for all maturities. From this we can construct a term structure of survival probabilities – which is nothing but the complementary distribution function of the time of default. Viewed

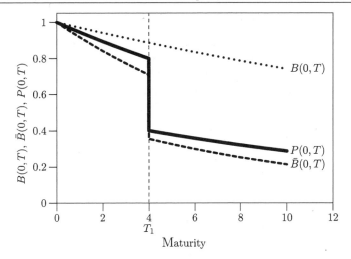

Figure 3.1   Implied survival probabilities $P(0, T)$ as a function of time horizon T, when there is an announcement at time T_1

as a function of the time horizon T, the implied survival probabilities have the following properties.

The implied survival probability $P(t, T)$ is initially at one $P(t, t) = 1$, it is non-negative and decreasing in T. It is also reasonable to assume that eventually there is a default (but this assumption is not necessary in the following):

$$P(t, \infty) = 0.$$

An example for a term structure of implied survival probabilities is given in Figure 3.1. As we will assume in the following that $P(t, T)$ is continuous in its second argument, we should analyse the point of discontinuity T_1 in Figure 3.1. At this point, the implied survival probabilities drop from 0.8 to 0.4, i.e. there is a 50% probability of default at precisely time T_1. This is known (and reflected in the prices) much earlier already, at time $t < T_1$. Such a discrete drop in the survival probabilities can only occur if there is an important event scheduled at T_1 that directly influences the default or survival of the obligor, e.g. a coupon payment date if it is unclear if the coupon will be paid.

Viewed as a function of its *first* argument t, the survival probability $P(t, T)$ will also change over time. There are two effects that change $P(t, T)$ over a small time step from t to $t + \Delta t$, even if no default occurs:

1. Updating for the non-arrival of a default in $[t, t + \Delta t]$. All survival probabilities $P(t, T)$ with $T > t + \Delta t$ contain the possibility that a default could occur in $[t, t + \Delta t]$. If this default has not occurred, this is good news and we must update the survival probabilities to reflect this information. All survival probabilities for fixed maturity dates will tend to increase.
2. Additional default-relevant information may arrive. This may be good or bad news on the obligor, the state of the industry he works in, or just some buy or sell orders that may contain information. The direction of the effect of new information is not predictable, otherwise the information would not be new and it should be already incorporated in the prices.

3.1.5   Conditional survival probabilities and implied hazard rates

The derivation of implied survival probabilities is an important step towards understanding the default risk implied in a term structure of defaultable bond prices, but they have disadvantages. First, implied survival probabilities overlap, i.e. if $t < T_1 < T_2$ then $P(t, T_1)$ and $P(t, T_2)$ both reference the risk of default in $[t, T_1]$. Furthermore, if a change in a survival probability is observed, one must first remove the deterministic "updating" effect described above from this change in order to assess whether the default risk has changed, and by how much it has changed. Finally, the implied survival probabilities are also affected by the length of the time interval that is referenced, such that longer maturity survival probabilities are more sensitive than short maturity survival probabilities.

For these reasons it is often easier to analyse *conditional survival probabilities* if we want to focus on the default risk over a given time interval in the future.

Definition 3.3 (conditional survival probability)   *The* conditional survival probability *over* $[T_1, T_2]$ *as seen from* t *is*

$$P(t, T_1, T_2) = \frac{P(t, T_2)}{P(t, T_1)}, \tag{3.5}$$

where $t \leq T_1 < T_2$.

The conditional survival probability is the probability of survival over $[T_1, T_2]$ as seen from t, *given that there was no default until* T_1. This is easily seen using Bayes' rule for conditional probabilities:

$$\mathbf{P}[A \mid B] = \frac{\mathbf{P}[A \cap B]}{\mathbf{P}[B]}.$$

Here the events are:

- $A =$ survival until T_2,
- $B =$ survival until T_1,
- $A \cap B =$ survival until T_1 and survival until T_2.

But $A \cap B = A$, because event B is contained in event A. If the obligor survives until T_2, he must also have survived until $T_1 < T_2$. Thus

$$P(t, T_1, T_2) = \frac{P(t, T_2)}{P(t, T_1)} = \frac{\overline{B}(t, T_2)}{B(t, T_2)} \frac{B(t, T_1)}{\overline{B}(t, T_1)},$$

which justifies equation (3.5). A very intuitive consequence of this is:

$$P(t, T_2) = P(t, T_1)P(t, T_1, T_2). \tag{3.6}$$

The probability of survival until T_2 is equal to the probability of survival until T_1 multiplied by the probability of survival from T_1 to T_2, given survival until T_1. Equation (3.6) holds for all intermediate time points T_1.

Table 3.1 A numerical example for implied survival probabilities

Mat.	Yield (%)		ZCB		Probabilities (%)		
	Gov.	Issuer	Gov.	Issuer	Surv.	CSurv.	CDef./T
0.5	5.75	7.00	0.9724	0.9667	99.41	99.41	1.17
1	6.10	7.85	0.9425	0.9272	98.38	98.96	2.09
3	6.25	8.25	0.8337	0.7883	94.56	96.12	1.94
5	6.40	8.65	0.7333	0.6605	90.07	95.25	2.38
7	6.78	9.08	0.6318	0.5442	86.14	95.64	2.18
10	6.95	9.70	0.5107	0.3962	77.58	90.06	3.31

The conditional survival probabilities isolate the view on the risk of a default event in a given future time interval. This enables us to directly compare the relative riskiness of different time intervals (e.g. the interval [1, 3] is less risky than the interval [5, 7] in Table 3.1). For a fair comparison the intervals should be of equal length. Furthermore, the conditional survival probabilities do not have to be updated for the non-occurrence of defaults as time proceeds. This makes conditional survival probabilities a more stable modelling variable than plain survival probabilities.

It is a good idea to reference conditional survival probabilities to future time intervals of *constant length*. The smaller the length of these time intervals, the finer the achieved resolution of the term structure of default risk will be, but the absolute value of the default probabilities will also decrease simply because the referenced time interval is reduced. To counteract this, we consider *default probabilities per time interval length*.

Definition 3.4 (implied hazard rates)

(i) *The* conditional probability of default per time unit Δt at time T *as seen from time* $t < T$ *is:*

$$\frac{1}{\Delta t} P^{\text{def}}(t, T, T + \Delta t) = \frac{1}{\Delta t}(1 - P(t, T, T + \Delta t)).$$

(ii) *The* discrete implied hazard rate of default *over* $[T, T + \Delta t]$ *as seen from time t is:*

$$H(t, T, T + \Delta t) := \frac{1}{\Delta t}\left(\frac{P(t, T)}{P(t, T + \Delta t)} - 1\right) = \frac{1}{\Delta t}\frac{P^{\text{def}}(t, T, T + \Delta t)}{P(t, T, T + \Delta t)}.$$

(iii) *The* continuous implied hazard rate of default *at time T is:*

$$h(t, T) := \lim_{\Delta t \searrow 0} \frac{1}{\Delta t} P^{\text{def}}(t, T, T + \Delta t) = \lim_{\Delta t \searrow 0} H(t, T, T + \Delta t), \tag{3.7}$$

$$= -\frac{\partial}{\partial T} \ln P(t, T) = -\frac{1}{P(t, T)}\frac{\partial}{\partial T} P(t, T), \tag{3.8}$$

provided that $\tau > t$ *and that the term structure of survival probabilities is differentiable with respect to T.*

The discrete implied hazard rates of default are defined in analogy to discretely compounded forward rates which will be defined in Definition 3.5. They will be useful modelling quantities later on because they are not restricted to be smaller than $1/\Delta t$. An intuitive interpretation of the discrete hazard rates is as an *odds ratio*. An odds ratio of an event is the (expected) number of events divided by the (expected) number of non-events. Here, $\Delta t H(t, T, T + \Delta t)$ is the ratio of the default probability over the survival probability over $[T, T + \Delta t]$, i.e. expected default events over expected survival events. So if you bet with your colleagues on the default or survival of the company and she says "1:3 that the company will default in July", she is saying that $P^{\mathrm{def}}(t, T, T + \Delta t) : P(t, T, T + \Delta t)$ is 1:3, or $H(t, T, T + \Delta t) = 12 \times 1/3 = 4$, a very negative statement on the company. (Real bookmakers' odds must be interpreted the other way around: events in which you lose over events in which you win.)

The continuous implied hazard rate of default gives the finest possible resolution of the likelihood of default in an infinitesimally small time interval $[T, T + dt]$. It contains the same information as the density of the default time defined in Definition 3.2, but presented in a different form.

The density of the default time at T gives the local probability that the default of the obligor happens at T, not earlier, not later. If the default risk of the obligor is very high, then the density will be small for times far in the future: not because there is no default risk but only because it is very likely that a default would have already happened earlier. The density must integrate to one, so it cannot remain positive in the limit. The hazard rate on the other hand can remain positive (until a default happens).

Again conditional survival probabilities and hazard rates can change stochastically as time proceeds. But given that no default happens from t to $t + \Delta t$, the only effect that changes the conditional survival probability over a future time interval $[T_1, T_2]$ is information that concerns the default risk in this time interval. If on the other hand a default occurs before T_1, conditional survival probabilities and future default hazard rates become meaningless.

3.1.6   Relation to forward spreads

Apart from their relative stability over time, conditional survival probabilities and implied hazard rates have another advantage as modelling variable: they are closely connected to forward credit spreads. Let us first define defaultable and default-free forward rates.

Definition 3.5 (forward rates)   *Let $t \leq T_1 < T_2$. The* simply compounded forward rate *over the period $[T_1, T_2]$ as seen from t is:*

$$F(t, T_1, T_2) = \frac{B(t, T_1)/B(t, T_2) - 1}{T_2 - T_1}.$$

The defaultable simply compounded forward rate *over the same period is:*

$$\overline{F}(t, T_1, T_2) = \frac{\overline{B}(t, T_1)/\overline{B}(t, T_2) - 1}{T_2 - T_1}.$$

The default-free *and* defaultable instantaneous *continuously compounded forward rates for T*

as seen from t are:

$$f(t, T) = \lim_{\Delta t \searrow 0} F(t, T, T + \Delta t) = -\frac{\partial}{\partial T} \ln B(t, T),$$

$$\overline{f}(t, T) = \lim_{\Delta t \searrow 0} \overline{F}(t, T, T + \Delta t) = -\frac{\partial}{\partial T} \ln \overline{B}(t, T).$$

The connection between these forward rates and the conditional probability of default and the implied hazard rates is given in the following proposition.

Proposition 3.1   *Seen from* $t < T_1 < T_2$, *for given defaultable and default-free forward rates, the conditional probability of default per time interval* $[T_1, T_2]$ *is the spread of defaultable over default-free forward rates, discounted by the defaultable forward rate:*

$$\frac{P^{\text{def}}(t, T_1, T_2)}{T_2 - T_1} = \frac{\overline{F}(t, T_1, T_2) - F(t, T_1, T_2)}{1 + (T_2 - T_1)\overline{F}(t, T_1, T_2)} = \frac{\overline{B}(0, T_2)}{\overline{B}(0, T_1)}(\overline{F}(t, T_1, T_2) - F(t, T_1, T_2)).$$

$$(3.9)$$

The discrete implied hazard rate of default is given by the spread of defaultable over default-free forward rates, discounted by the default-free forward rates:

$$H(t, T_1, T_2) = \frac{\overline{F}(t, T_1, T_2) - F(t, T_1, T_2)}{1 + (T_2 - T_1)F(t, T_1, T_2)} = \frac{\overline{B}(0, T_2)}{B(0, T_1)}(\overline{F}(t, T_1, T_2) - F(t, T_1, T_2)). \quad (3.10)$$

The implied hazard rate of default at time $T > t$ *as seen from time* t *is given by the spread of the defaultable over the default-free continuously compounded forward rates:*

$$h(t, T) = \overline{f}(t, T) - f(t, T).$$

Proof.   Substitute Definitions 3.4 and 3.5.   □

This is one of the key results of this chapter:

The probability of default in a short time interval $[T, T + \Delta t]$ is approximately **proportional** to the length Δt of the interval with proportionality factor $(\overline{f}(t, T) - f(t, T))$. In particular, the **local** default probability at time t over the next small time step Δt is approximately proportional to the length of the time step, with the short-term credit spread as proportionality factor:

$$\frac{1}{\Delta t}\mathbf{Q}[\tau \le t + \Delta t \mid \mathcal{F}_t \wedge \{\tau > t\}] \approx \overline{r}(t) - r(t) =: \lambda(t), \quad (3.11)$$

where $r(t) = f(t, t)$ and $\overline{r}(t) = \overline{f}(t, t)$.

There is a very close structural connection between the way in which a hazard rate can be used to model the uncertain arrival of a stopping time, and the continuous-time discounting that is used in classical interest-rate models. Mathematicians and finance practitioners have arrived at very similar concepts through quite different paths of reasoning. This is not surprising as we have already seen that the term structure of implied survival probabilities $P(t, T)$ looks very much like a zerobond curve: it is non-negative, decreasing and starting at $P(t, t) = 1$.

3.2   RECOVERY MODELLING

Extending the zero-recovery payoffs of the previous section, an asset with *positive* recovery can be viewed as an asset with an additional positive payoff *at* default.

This definition ignores the difficulties that are involved in the real-world determination of recovery in credit derivatives like time delays, dealer polls or delivery options. The recovery rate here is not the real CDS recovery rate (nor the legal recovery rate that will be determined in a bankruptcy court some months after the default), but rather is the expected value of the recovery shortly after the occurrence of a default.

We are modelling the recovery of a real defaultable asset, like a coupon bond or a loan. The recovery model presented here is just a building block for the pricing of such assets. Except in very rare cases defaultable zero-coupon bonds do not exist in reality, thus the concept of a recovery of the defaultable zero-coupon bond is meaningless, unless it leads to a recovery model for other defaultable assets such as coupon bonds and loans.

In the literature, many different setups have been proposed to model the recovery of defaultable assets. Here, we present one particular framework which is based upon the *recovery of par* model first presented by Duffie (1998). This and the other setups will be discussed in detail in the next chapter.

As a first step we analyse the value $e(t, T, T + \Delta t)$ at time $t < T$ of a deterministic payoff of 1 that is paid at time $T + \Delta t$ if and only if a default happens in the time interval $]T, T + \Delta t]$:

$$e(t, T, T + \Delta t) = \mathbf{E}^Q[\beta(t, T + \Delta t)(I(T) - I(T + \Delta t)) \mid \mathcal{F}_t]. \tag{3.12}$$

Writing the dependence on $\omega \in \Omega$ of the survival indicators explicitly, the random variable $I(T)(\omega) - I(T + \Delta t)(\omega)$ is 1 in all states of nature $\omega \in \Omega$ where a default occurs in $]T, T + \Delta t]$, in all other states of nature it is 0. Equation (3.12) can be easily solved using the results of the previous section:

$$
\begin{aligned}
e(t, T, T + \Delta t) &:= B(t, T + \Delta t)P(t, T) - \overline{B}(t, T + \Delta t) \\
&= \overline{B}(t, T + \Delta t)\left(\frac{P(t, T)}{P(t, T + \Delta t)} - 1\right) \\
&= \Delta t\, \overline{B}(t, T + \Delta t)H(t, T, T + \Delta t).
\end{aligned}
\tag{3.13}
$$

Here, we had to use the independence assumption again.

The next step is to let the time step size Δt converge to zero in equation (3.13) in order to reach a continuous coverage of the time axis. Dividing $e(t, T, T + \Delta t)$ by Δt in this process prevents the value from going to zero. We reach:

$$e(t, T) := \lim_{\Delta t \searrow 0} \frac{1}{\Delta t} e(t, T, T + \Delta t) = \overline{B}(t, T)h(t, T). \tag{3.14}$$

With equation (3.14) (and also already with (3.13)) we can give the value of a known payoff *at* default. The value of a security that pays $\pi(T)$ if a default occurs at time T for all $t < T \le T_1$ is:

$$\int_t^{T_1} \pi(s)e(t,s)ds = \int_t^{T_1} \pi(s)\overline{B}(t,s)h(t,s)ds.$$

This result holds for fixed recovery rates (or other payoffs at default) that are known in advance. But at least for pricing purposes the result also carries through for random recoveries. Assume the payoff at default is not $\pi(t)$, but a random variable π' which is drawn at the time of default[4] τ. We denote by $\pi^e(T)$ the expected value (under martingale measure Q-probabilities) of π' conditional on a default at time T, i.e.

$$\pi^e(t,T) = \mathbf{E}^Q[\pi' \mid \mathcal{F}_t \wedge \{\tau = T\}].$$

Almost full freedom in the distribution of π' is allowed here, only the conditional mean must exist. Then, conditional on a default occurring at time T we can still price a security that pays π' at default, its value is $B(t,T)\pi^e(t,T)$. If we do not know the time of default, we have to sum up (integrate) these values over all possible default times and weigh them with the respective probability of default occurring, i.e. the density of the time of default in the continuous-time case. This yields

$$\int_t^T \pi^e(t,s)B(t,s)P(t,s)h(t,s)ds \tag{3.15}$$

as the price at time t of a payoff of π' at τ if $\tau \in [t,T]$. Equation (3.15) allows us to use expected recovery rates in our calculations without losing any generality.

A similar result also holds if discrete points in time are considered. Assume π' is paid at $T + \Delta t$ if a default occurs in $]T, T + \Delta t]$. The value of this payoff is

$$\pi^e(t,T,T+\Delta t)e(t,T,T+\Delta t) \tag{3.16}$$

if we define $\pi^e(t,T,T+\Delta t)$ to be the conditional expectation of π' conditional on a default occurring in $]T, T + \Delta t]$.

3.3 BUILDING BLOCKS FOR CREDIT DERIVATIVES PRICING

We now have all ingredients to set up a simple credit "model". In order to make the numerical implementation feasible, we have to decide on a discrete grid of time points, the tenor structure:

$$0 = T_0, T_1, T_2, \ldots, T_K. \tag{3.17}$$

These dates should include the coupon and repayment dates for bonds or loans, fixing dates for rates, and payment and settlement dates for credit derivatives. The initial time is normalised to zero. Additional dates can be added in order to achieve a sufficiently fine resolution of the

---

[4] The mathematical structure is a *marked point process*.

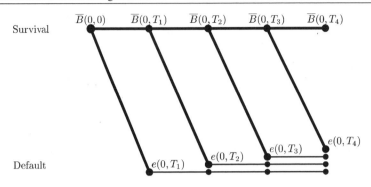

Figure 3.2   The building blocks and the nodes in which they pay off

time axis. The dates are indexed in increasing order ($T_k < T_{k+1}$) and the distance between two tenor dates is denoted by $\delta_k := T_{k+1} - T_k$ for all $0 \le k \le K$.

The default/survival structure of the simplified model is shown in Figure 3.2. At every date T_k a default can occur, or the obligor can continue until the next date T_{k+1}. After default, the default-free world goes on (indicated by the continuation of the tree) but the defaultable assets only earn their recovery payoff and cease to exist after default.

It is important to stress that we do **not** assume that defaults were actually driven by the tree model of Figure 3.2 with *constant probabilities*, nor do we assume that the tree model gives an adequate full picture of the price dynamics of any traded asset. Many price-relevant events are not represented in this tree diagram. For example, no interest-rate risk, rating transitions or other changes in the credit quality or credit spreads of the reference credit are shown; they are contained, but lumped together, in the nodes of the tree. The tree is only a representation of the basic building blocks and the states of nature, and the dates in which they have their payoffs.

This also means that the probabilities attached to the branches of the tree are only the conditional default and survival probabilities at this node *as seen from t = 0*. These probabilities can and will change over time as new information on the default risk of the obligor arrives – in reality as well as in the model. Thus, the tree does not give a full picture of the model, just a projection on the two-state world {*default, survival*}, with probabilities as they were seen at time $t = 0$.

Conversely, the tree can be supported by a more complicated model on the dynamics of defaults and survivals. In particular, the results of the calibration do not depend on any assumption of constant credit spreads, and the calibrated spread curve can be used in more detailed models including the dynamics of credit spreads and interest rates without contradiction.

The tree in Figure 3.2 is therefore a convenient representation of:

- The states of nature in which the different building block securities have their payoffs;
- The implied default and survival probabilities *as seen from time t = 0*;
- A method to represent the payoffs of calibration securities.

To price typical calibration securities (defaultable fixed- or floating-rate bonds, or CDSs) only one more thing is needed: an assumption on the recovery of the calibration securities. Apart from this, the calibration securities also have constant payoffs in the tree nodes (if the recovery payoff is replaced by its conditional expectation like in the previous section).

This observation leads us directly to the definition of the following basic assets, the *pricing building blocks* for all $0 \leq k \leq K$.

- $B(0, T_k)$: the prices of the default-free zero-coupon bonds

$$B(0, T_k) = \prod_{i=1}^{k} \frac{1}{1 + \delta_{i-1} F(0, T_{i-1}, T_i)}. \tag{3.18}$$

- $\overline{B}(0, T_k)$: the prices of the defaultable zero-coupon bonds with zero recovery

$$\overline{B}(0, T_k) = B(0, T_k) P(0, T_k) = B(0, T_k) \prod_{i=1}^{k} \frac{1}{1 + \delta_{i-1} H(0, T_{i-1}, T_i)}. \tag{3.19}$$

- $e(0, T_k, T_{k+1})$: the value of \$1 at T_{k+1} if a default occurred in $]T_k, T_{k+1}]$

$$e(0, T_k, T_{k+1}) = \delta_k H(0, T_k, T_{k+1}) \overline{B}(0, T_k). \tag{3.20}$$

The prices of these building blocks are expressed in terms of two fundamental modelling quantities: the term structure of default-free interest rates $F(0, T)$ and the term structure of implied hazard rates $H(0, T)$. Together with the expected recovery rate π, these will be the *fundamental quantities* of the model.

Forward hazard rates have several advantages over other choices of fundamental model quantities. They have a simple, intuitive meaning, both in the economic sense (via forward zerobond spreads) as well as in the probability sense (via local conditional default probabilities), the prices of the building blocks can be expressed in closed form, their structure is very close to well-understood interest rates and finally, their values are not restricted except for non-negativity.

We would like to stress that a solid intuition on the meaning and implications of the fundamental model quantities is not just "nice to have" but an essential property of any useful default-risk model. When a default-risk model is calibrated to real data on bond prices or CDS spreads, data scarcity will almost always force us to make assumptions on the shape or parametric form of the fundamental driving quantities of the model (unless the model structure has already imposed these assumptions implicitly). In order to choose the "right" assumptions (or at least to be quite confident on their implications) the meaning of these fundamental model quantities must be well understood. Precisely the uncertainty that is implicit in default-risk modelling calls for the best modelling structure.

We can also express the prices of the building blocks in continuously compounded instantaneous forward rates and hazard rates. This is the limit of the setup with simply compounded rates when the time intervals converge to zero $\delta_k \rightarrow 0$:

$$B(0, T_k) = \exp\left\{ -\int_0^{T_k} f(0, s) ds \right\},$$

$$\overline{B}(0, T_k) = \exp\left\{ -\int_0^{T_k} h(0, s) + f(0, s) ds \right\},$$

$$e(0, T_k) = h(0, T_k) \overline{B}(0, T_k).$$

In many cases, this setup is better suited for theoretical analysis, for the practical demonstration of the calibration process we use the discrete simply compounded rates.

The following assumption describes the recovery model for the calibration securities.

Assumption 3.3

(i) *If a defaultable coupon bond defaults in the time interval $]T_k, T_{k+1}]$ its recovery is paid off at time T_{k+1}. It is composed of the random recovery rate π' times the notional of the bond (here normalised to 1).*

(ii) *The Q-expectation of π' conditional on default at a given time $T > 0$ is π. It is between zero and one $\pi \in [0, 1]$ and does not depend on the time of default τ.*

(iii) *The conditionally expected recovery rate π is constant across all calibration securities.*

(iv) *If CDSs are among the calibration securities, the deliverable obligations of the CDSs all have the same recovery rate with conditional expectation π.*

All points in this assumption can be modified in order to make the model more realistic, for expositional purposes we start with the simplest version.

In (i) we ignored accrued interest, which should slightly increase the recovery in reality. If this is a concern, one can either recognise accrued interest explicitly, or it can be accounted for by increasing π by a factor of $(1 + \bar{c}/2)$, where $\bar{c}$ is the average coupon payment of the defaultable bond. Point (iii) is usually fulfilled if only assets of the same seniority class are used, otherwise different recovery rates for different seniority classes will have to be used. Point (iv) removes the delivery option problem from the CDS, and also ensures that the CDS is priced in accordance with the other bonds.

3.4   PRICING WITH THE BUILDING BLOCKS

The prices of typical calibration instruments in this setup can be given directly in terms of the building blocks. For this we index the calibration securities with $i = 1, \ldots, I$ and denote their model prices with $\overline{C}^{(i)}(t)$. The observed market prices are $\hat{C}^{(i)}$. All notionals are normalised to 1.

The number of (promised) payment dates of the ith calibration security is $N^{(i)}$, and the dates of these payments are indexed with $k_n^{(i)}$, i.e. $T_{k_n^{(i)}}, n = 1, \ldots, N^{(i)}$. The maturity date of the ith calibration security is $T_{k_{N^{(i)}}^{(i)}}$. In the final calibration algorithm we need to keep track of all these indices because not all coupon bonds will have payoffs at the same tenor dates, and tenor dates may be spaced much more closely than the payment frequencies of the different securities. For the pricing of individual calibration securities we omit the index i and write k_n for $k_n^{(i)}$, N for $N^{(i)}$ and $\delta_n' := T_{k_{n+1}} - T_{k_n}$ for the regular payment intervals in order to streamline notation.

3.4.1   Defaultable fixed-coupon bond

A defaultable fixed-coupon bond has coupon payments of $\bar{c}_n = \bar{c}\delta_{n-1}'$ at $T_{k_n}, n = 1, \ldots, N$. The individual fixed-coupon payments can differ slightly from each other depending on day count conventions and the bond's specification, but they are known in advance.[5]

---

[5] We are interested in very small price differences between defaultable and default-free bonds. Therefore it is important to correctly account even for such small details.

The model price of this bond is:

$$\overline{C}(0) = \sum_{n=1}^{N} \overline{c}_n \overline{B}(0, T_{k_n}) \qquad \text{[coupons]}$$

$$+ \overline{B}(0, T_{k_N}) \qquad \text{[principal]}$$

$$+ \pi \sum_{k=1}^{k_N} e(0, T_{k-1}, T_k) \quad \text{[recovery]}. \qquad (3.21)$$

The summation of the coupon payments only extends over the actual coupon payment dates T_{k_n}, while *all* dates T_k between T_0 and T_N are covered in the summation for the recovery payoffs. Thus, a default can happen in all time intervals, while a coupon payment only occurs at specific dates.

Using the representation of the prices of the $e(\cdot)$ building blocks, the recovery payment can be written as:

$$\pi \sum_{k=1}^{k_N} e(0, T_{k-1}, T_k) = \sum_{k=1}^{k_N} \pi \delta_{k-1} H(0, T_{k-1}, T_k) \cdot \overline{B}(0, T_k). \qquad (3.22)$$

We can view the recovery payments as an additional coupon payment stream of $\pi \delta_{k-1} H(0, T_{k-1}, T_k)$ which is paid at all dates until default.

3.4.2 Defaultable floater

Here, the coupon payments at T_{k_n} equal Libor plus a spread:

$$\delta'_{n-1}(L(T_{k_{n-1}}, T_{k_n}) + s^{par}) = \left(\frac{1}{B(T_{k_{n-1}}, T_{k_n})} - 1 \right) + s^{par} \delta'_{n-1}.$$

The term in large brackets represents the floating rate (Libor) over the preceding accrual period. Again, day count conventions can multiply a (known) factor by this payoff, which we will ignore for now.

We need to derive the price of a defaultable payment of Libor which we have not derived before. Without default risk, the value of a payoff of $1/B(T_{k_{n-1}}, T_{k_n})$ at T_{k_n} is equivalent to receiving 1 at $T_{k_{n-1}}$ and reinvesting it in $1/B(T_{k_{n-1}}, T_{k_n})$ default-free zero-coupon bonds with maturity T_{k_n}.

If the payoff is defaultable, then the value of $1/B(T_{k_{n-1}}, T_{k_n})$ at T_{k_n} is lower. At time $T_{k_{n-1}}$ (and given survival until then), the claim still carries the default risk from $T_{k_{n-1}}$ until T_{k_n}, thus it is equivalent to holding $1/B(T_{k_{n-1}}, T_{k_n})$ *defaultable* zero-coupon bonds with maturity T_{k_n}. The value of this position at $T_{k_{n-1}}$ is:

$$\frac{1}{B(T_{k_{n-1}}, T_{k_n})} \overline{B}(T_{k_{n-1}}, T_{k_n}) = P(T_{k_{n-1}}, T_{k_n}).$$

Seen from $t = 0$, the value of this position is

$$\mathbf{E}^Q[\beta(0, T_{k_{n-1}})I(T_{k_{n-1}})P(T_{k_{n-1}}, T_{k_n})]$$
$$= B(0, T_{k_{n-1}})\mathbf{E}^Q[I(T_{k_{n-1}})P(T_{k_{n-1}}, T_{k_n})]$$
$$= B(0, T_{k_{n-1}})P(0, T_{k_n}), \tag{3.23}$$

where we use independence of defaults (Assumption 3.2, survival indicators and survival probabilities) and interest rates again.

Combining this with the remaining, fixed part of the coupon payment yields the value of a defaultable payment of $[T_{k_{n-1}}, T_{k_n}]$-Libor at T_{k_n}:

$$(B(0, T_{k_{n-1}}) - B(0, T_{k_n}))P(0, T_{k_n}) = \delta'_{n-1}F(0, T_{k_{n-1}}, T_{k_n})\overline{B}(0, T_{k_n}). \tag{3.24}$$

The model price of the defaultable floating-rate bond is therefore:

$$\overline{C}(0) = \sum_{n=1}^{N} \delta'_{n-1}F(0, T_{k_{n-1}}, T_{k_n})\overline{B}(0, T_{k_n}) \quad \text{[default Libor]}$$

$$+ s^{par} \sum_{n=1}^{N} \delta'_{n-1}\overline{B}(0, T_{k_n}) \quad \text{[coupon spread]}$$

$$+ \overline{B}(0, T_{k_N}) \quad \text{[principal]}$$

$$+ \pi \sum_{k=1}^{k_N} e(0, T_{k-1}, T_k) \quad \text{[recovery].} \tag{3.25}$$

3.4.3 Variants of coupon bonds

In many cases, the incorporation of payment variants of coupon bonds is straightforward.

- Amortisation: Has several effects. First, the regular payments at the dates T_i are higher than they would be without amortisation. The additional payments reduce the outstanding principal according to a pre-agreed schedule. As final repayment only the then outstanding principal has to be repaid. Furthermore, in the case of default, the recovery payoff is reduced because recovery is only paid on a reduced principal amount. All these effects can be modelled by adjusting coupon payments, recoveries and principal repayments.
- Collateralisation: Leaves coupons and principal repayments unchanged, but reduces the notional amount that is at risk at default. In the model, the payoff at default must be adjusted.
- Atypical interest payments: Interest payment holidays and deterministic changes in coupon sizes require corresponding changes in the payoff streams.

3.4.4 Credit default swaps

A CDS consists of two payment legs: the fixed (fee-payment) leg and the floating (default-insurance) leg.

Fixed leg: Payment of $\delta'_{n-1}\bar{s}$ at T_{k_n} if no default until T_{k_n}. The value of the fixed leg is:

$$\bar{s}\sum_{n=1}^{N}\delta'_{n-1}\overline{B}(0, T_{k_n}).\tag{3.26}$$

Floating leg: Payment of $(1-\pi)$ at T_k if default in $]T_{k-1}, T_k]$. The value of the floating leg is:

$$(1-\pi)\sum_{k=1}^{k_N}e(0, T_{k-1}, T_k) = (1-\pi)\sum_{k=1}^{k_N}\delta_{k-1}H(0, T_{k-1}, T_k)\overline{B}(0, T_k).\tag{3.27}$$

Initially, the market CDS spread is chosen such that the fixed and floating leg of the CDS have the same value. Combining (3.26) and (3.27) yields the market CDS rate in the model:

$$\bar{s} = (1-\pi)\frac{\displaystyle\sum_{k=1}^{k_N}\delta_{k-1}H(0, T_{k-1}, T_k)\overline{B}(0, T_k)}{\displaystyle\sum_{n=1}^{N}\delta'_{n-1}\overline{B}(0, T_{k_n})}.\tag{3.28}$$

If tenor dates and payment dates coincide, i.e. $N = K$, $T_{k_n} = T_n$, $\delta_k = \delta'_k$, then we can write the CDS rate as a weighted sum of the implied hazard rates over the life of the CDS:

$$\bar{s} = (1-\pi)\sum_{n=1}^{N}w_n H(0, T_{n-1}, T_n),\tag{3.29}$$

where the weights are given by

$$w_n = \frac{\delta_{n-1}\overline{B}(0, T_n)}{\displaystyle\sum_{m=1}^{N}\delta_{m-1}\overline{B}(0, T_m)}\qquad\forall\, n \leq N.\tag{3.30}$$

The weights sum up to one $\sum_{n=1}^{N}w_n = 1$. Equation (3.29) is a useful tool to gain intuition on the size and dynamics of the implied hazard rates of default $H(\cdot)$. They should be of the same order of magnitude as a typical CDS rate divided by an expected loss rate in default, and the relative dynamics dH/H should accordingly resemble the relative dynamics $d\bar{s}/\bar{s}$ of the CDS rates in the market.

Representation (3.29) resembles closely a similar result for interest-rate swap rates (see e.g. Rebonato, 1998):

$$s = \sum_{n=1}^{N}w'_n F(0, T_{n-1}, T_n),\tag{3.31}$$

where

$$w'_n = \frac{\delta_{n-1} B(0, T_n)}{\sum\limits_{m=1}^{N} \delta_{m-1} B(0, T_m)} \quad \forall n \leq N.$$

After the initial date, the value of a CDS can (and will) change. The mark-to-market value of a CDS that was originally entered as protection *buyer* at a CDS spread of $\bar{s}'$ is:

$$(\bar{s} - \bar{s}') \left(\sum_{n=1}^{N} \overline{B}(0, T_{k_n}) \delta'_{n-1} \right). \tag{3.32}$$

Equation (3.32) can be explained as follows. If an offsetting trade (i.e. selling credit protection) is entered at the current market CDS rate $\bar{s}$, only the fee difference $(\bar{s} - \bar{s}')$ remains to be paid over the life of the CDS. Should a default happen, the protection payments will cancel out, and the fee difference payment will be cancelled, too. Thus, the fee difference stream is defaultable and must be discounted with defaultable zero-coupon bonds $\overline{B}(0, T)$. The sensitivity of the market value of a CDS position means that CDSs are useful instruments to gain exposure against spread movements, and not just against default arrival risks.

3.4.5 Forward start CDSs

A *forward start CDS* is a CDS which is contracted at time T_0, but fee payments and credit protection only begin at a later time, i.e. $T_{k_0} > T_0$. If a default occurs *before* T_{k_0}, the forward start CDS is cancelled without payments.

The pricing formulae for forward start CDSs are almost identical to the corresponding pricing formulae for plain vanilla CDSs, the only difference lies in the initial indices of the summation:

$$\bar{s} = (1 - \pi) \frac{\sum\limits_{k=k_1}^{k_N} \delta_{k-1} H(0, T_{k-1}, T_k) \overline{B}(0, T_k)}{\sum\limits_{n=1}^{N} \delta'_{n-1} \overline{B}(0, T_{k_n})}. \tag{3.33}$$

3.4.6 Default digital swaps

The value of the fee leg of a DDS equals the value of the fee leg of a vanilla CDS given in (3.26). The value of the credit protection leg is simply

$$\sum_{n=1}^{N} e(0, T_{k_{n-1}}, T_{k_n}), \tag{3.34}$$

because at default a fixed payoff of 1 is paid, independently of the actual recovery rate. The value of this payoff is $1/(1 - \pi)$ times the value of the protection payment of a CDS. The DDS rate is

$$\overline{s}^{DDS} = \frac{1}{1-\pi}\overline{s} \tag{3.35}$$

and the results on CDS rates carry through from the previous section.

3.4.7 Asset swap packages

To derive the fair asset swap rate on a defaultable coupon bond using equation (2.5), we also need the price of an equivalent default-free coupon bond. This is:

$$C(0) = \sum_{n=1}^{N} \delta_{n-1}\overline{c}B(0, T_{k_n}) + B(0, T_{k_N}). \tag{3.36}$$

Then, according to equation (2.5), the asset swap rate on this bond is:

$$s^A = \frac{C(0) - \overline{C}(0)}{\displaystyle\sum_{n=1}^{N} \delta'_{n-1}B(0, T_{k_n})}.$$

3.5 CONSTRUCTING AND CALIBRATING CREDIT SPREAD CURVES

The spread curve calibration problem consists of the following three steps.

1. Default-free calibration: Find $F = (F_1, \ldots, F_K)$ such that

$$\hat{C}^{(i)} = \overline{C}^{(i)}(F) \tag{3.37}$$

   for all default-free calibration securities $i \in I^{\text{def.free}}$.
2. Recovery calibration/estimation: Find an expected recovery rate π.
3. Spread calibration: Find $H = (H_1, \ldots, H_K)$ such that an optimal fit is achieved (in some suitable norm $\|\cdot\|$) for all defaultable calibration securities $i \in I^{\text{def}}$ with weights w_i

$$\sum_{i \in I^{\text{def}}} w_i \|\hat{C}^{(i)} - \overline{C}^{(i)}(F, H, \pi)\| \to \min. \tag{3.38}$$

In the rest of this chapter we will call the term structure of implied forward default hazard rates $H = (H_1, \ldots, H_K)$ the (*zerobond*) *spread curve*.

We propose to perform the calibration steps in the order given above. First, the default-free term structure of interest rates is calibrated separately. There is a wealth of liquidly traded default-free calibration securities with which a good and detailed fit can be achieved, and additional defaultable calibration securities are not necessary. A large literature discusses the calibration of the term structure of default-free interest rates (see Section 3.8) so that we do not need to go into very much detail here, except for the question *which* term structure of interest rates to consider default-free. This problem is discussed in the next section.

Then, the calibration of the term structure of default hazard rates (step 3) is separated from the estimation or calibration of the expected recovery rate in step 2. This separation is often made necessary by a fundamental problem of the whole calibration procedure: expected recoveries and default hazard rates have almost the same influence on the prices of defaultable bonds, so we have an identification problem. In some cases this problem can be solved by a joint calibration under inclusion of additional calibration securities (Merrick, 2001), but not always. Calibration securities are rare, and the effects of spread and recovery rate are almost parallel across different defaultable securities. A joint calibration procedure often produces unstable values.

For this reason, an expected recovery rate must be estimated (or calibrated) as a separate input to the calibration procedure, and the results of the calibration procedure must be checked for robustness against the recovery rate assumption. This set of problems is discussed in more detail in Section 3.2. In some special cases, a market implied recovery rate distribution can be recovered, e.g. if calibration prices for defaultable securities of different seniority classes are available, or prices for default digital swaps.

Once the default-free interest rates and a recovery rate have been found, step 3 contains the real fit of the (zero-recovery, zero-coupon) spread curve. Although this problem is structurally not much different from the calibration problem for a default-free term structure of interest rates, the practical implementation is faced with different problems because of data scarcity. Usually, only a small number of calibration securities is available for any given defaultable obligor, so that the remaining degrees of freedom in the term structure of credit spreads must be removed using other criteria. There are basically two approaches: either the term structure of hazard rates is parametrised using a functional form with very few parameters, or a non-parametric fit is attempted under addition of smoothness or regularity criteria which ensure a unique solution to the calibration problem. These approaches are discussed in the next subsections.

It can be useful to have aggregated term structures of credit spreads over several similar obligors, e.g. a spread curve for a given rating class, industry group or country (or combinations thereof). Here, a perfect fit to every given market price is not desirable. Outliers must be removed from the sample and different optimisation criteria must be used, which are discussed in the following subsection. For example, such aggregated spread curves can be used to fill in gaps in the spread curves for a specific defaultable obligor, or to spot mispriced securities in the market.

The section is concluded with some worked examples using real data.

3.5.1 Parametric forms for the spread curves

Calibrating a parametrised version of the spread curve has several advantages, for example the number of variables in the optimisation problem is greatly reduced and one has full control over the possible shapes of the resulting spread curve. In particular, regularity and smoothness of the resulting credit spread curve are automatically ensured.

The following popular choices for parametrised forward rate curves are well suited both for continuous as well as discretely compounded spread curves.

1. Constant (one parameter):

$$H(0, T) = \beta_0.$$

This is the simplest form of a spread curve. It can be used if no other information is available at all. Otherwise, the inclusion of a slope or hump parameter is advisable.

2. Constant offset to a given function (one parameter):

$$H(0, T) = \beta_0 + f(T).$$

This is a popular choice in situations with scarce data, the function $f(T)$ is some reference spread curve, e.g. the spread curve for the obligor's rating class, or his country's spread curve if he is based in an emerging economy. Then, only one offset parameter β_0 must be calibrated and the other shape (slope and curvature) of the spread curve is taken from $f(T)$.

3. Linear (two parameters):

$$H(0, T) = \beta_0 + \beta_1 T.$$

Spread curves often have a pronounced slope. The slope for highly rated credits is typically positive, while the slope for speculative credits is negative. The inclusion of a slope parameter is advisable in order to capture this feature.

4. Quadratic (three parameters):

$$H(0, T) = \beta_0 + \beta_1 T + \beta_2 T^2.$$

With a quadratic term, the curvature of the spread curve can also be captured.

5. Nelson and Siegel (1987) (four parameters):

$$H(\beta, \gamma; T) = \beta_0 + (\beta_1 + \beta_2)\frac{1 - e^{-T/\gamma}}{T/\gamma} + \beta_2 e^{-T/\gamma}$$

This family of spread curves has two hump parameters β_2 and γ in addition to level and slope. The limit as $T \to \infty$ is β_0, the short end is at $H(\cdot; 0) = \beta_0 + \beta_1$.

6. Model-based (various parameters): Most parametric credit risk models provide closed-form solutions $\overline{B}(\beta; 0, T)$ for the prices of defaultable zero-coupon bonds of all maturities as a function of the vector of model parameters β. This can be viewed as a parametric specification of a particular class of term structures of credit spreads.

For the calibration problem to be well-defined, the number of free parameters in the spread curve must not exceed the number of calibration instruments, otherwise, additional smoothness criteria (like (3.43) below) must be used.

The target function (3.38) that is optimised in the calibration penalises deviations of the model prices from market prices. A simple, useful choice is the mean-squared price deviation

$$\sum_{i \in I^{\text{def}}} w_i \left(\hat{C}^{(i)} - \overline{C}^{(i)}(F, H, \pi) \right)^2 \to \min. \tag{3.39}$$

The weights w_i can be used to specify a degree of confidence in the accuracy of the target price (e.g. 1/(bid–ask spread)). If $w_i = 1/\hat{C}^i$, relative (and not absolute) price deviations are minimised. For $w_i = 1/[$ modified duration$]_i^2$, (approximated) yield residuals in the calibration prices are minimised.

3.5.2   Semi-parametric and non-parametric calibration

Because they strongly restrict the set of possible shapes of the spread curve, parametric models may not be able to give an accurate picture of the real spreads observed in the market. Sometimes more flexibility is necessary. Here, semi- and non-parametric calibration methods can be used.

3.5.2.1   Bootstrap

The bootstrap method is a common method to strip default-free forward rate curves from observed coupon bond prices which can also be applied to spread curve construction. It produces a piecewise constant spread curve.

- The calibration securities are ordered by their maturity dates $t_1, \ldots, t_I$ from shortest to longest time to maturity.
- The spread curve is piecewise constant, with discontinuities at the maturity dates t_i:

$$H(0, T) = H_i \quad \text{if and only if} \quad t_{i-1} < T \leq t_i.$$

- Start: $i = 1$
  Find H_1 such that the first bond price is calibrated:

$$\overline{C}^{(1)}(H_1) = \hat{C}^{(1)}.$$

- Step: $i - 1 \to i$
  Given $H_1, \ldots, H_{i-1}$, find H_i such that:

$$\overline{C}^{(i)}(H_1, \ldots, H_{i-1}; H_i) = \hat{C}^{(i)}.$$

The model prices of the calibration securities $\overline{C}^{(i)}$ do not depend on values of H at later dates than the maturity date t_i of the security, therefore the solutions of the problems above are well-defined.

The bootstrap does not require the solution of a minimisation problem, and the spread curve can be built up iteratively from the shortest maturity. Furthermore, it imposes less structure on the shape of the spread curve than a parametric function, only that the spread curve can be approximated with a step function.

The size of the steps in the resulting spread curve depends on the number of available calibration securities and on the spacing of their maturity dates. In government bond markets or the swap/FRA market, the steps are comparatively small and the maturity dates are closely spaced, hence the resulting curve also only has small steps. It can be viewed as a good approximation of a "true" underlying continuous curve.

The situation can be different in the credit markets. There are rarely more than three calibration securities, and of these, some frequently have very close maturities. The calibrated spread curve then has only few steps at the shorter maturity dates, thus the steps can be quite large. This shape can be implausible.

3.5.2.2 Full free specification

The largest degree of flexibility is achieved if all values $H(0, T_k)$ can be freely chosen for all tenor dates T_k, $k \leq K$. This method is not always advisable because it requires an optimisation over a very large number of free parameters.

3.5.2.3 Spline functions

Spline functions represent a compromise between full flexibility and the imposition of a smooth structure. They are more robust to small changes in input prices than most classes of global parametric functions, in particular they have much better stability properties than polynomial functions of degrees larger than two.

An nth-order spline is a piecewise polynomial, a curve consisting of polynomial segments of order n that are joined together at the *node points* x_m, $m \leq M$ under certain smoothness conditions. The step functions of the bootstrap method are a special case of a spline: zeroth-order polynomials with node points at the maturities of the calibration securities.

The most commonly used splines are linear splines ("straight-line interpolation": piece-wise linear, continuous functions) and cubic splines (piecewise third-order polynomials with continuous first derivatives at the node points).

Spline functions of a given degree form a vector space. They can be represented as linear combinations of a set of basis functions. One particularly stable and convenient set of basis functions are the B-splines (where B stands for "basis"). B-splines of order n are most simply implemented by the following recursion relations for the spline functions themselves:

$$B_{i,n}(x) = \frac{x - x_i}{x_{i+n-1} - x_i} B_{i,n-1}(x) + \frac{x_{i+1} - x}{x_{i+n} - x_{i+1}} B_{i+1,n-1}(x) \tag{3.40}$$

and for their derivatives:

$$B'_{i,n}(x) = n \left(\frac{B_{i,n-1}(x)}{x_{i+n} - x_i} - \frac{B_{i+1,n-1}(x)}{x_{i+n+1} - x_{i+1}} \right) \tag{3.41}$$

with $B_{i,0}(x) = 1$ if $x_i \leq x < x_{i+1}$ and $B_{i,0} = 0$ otherwise. B-splines are non-negative, integrate to 1[6] and $B_{i,n}(x)$ has support on $[x_i, x_{i+n+1}]$. To interpolate a function between node points $x_0, \ldots, x_M$ with a spline function of nth degree, a basis of B-splines $B_{i,n}(x)$ with $i = -n, \ldots, M - 1$ must be used. To define the B-splines, additional node points $x_{-n}, \ldots, x_{-1}$ to the left of x_0 and $x_{M+1}, \ldots, x_{m+n}$ to the right of x_M must be defined.

When placing the node points on the time axis, more closely spaced node points imply more flexibility, but also more sensitivity to outliers and data errors. Several strategies have been proposed for the placement of nodes (apart from the obvious choices at $x_0 = 0$ and $x_M = T_{\max}$): to place at the maturity dates of the calibration assets; or to place the nodes at 1, 5 and 10 years[7] (corresponding to short, medium and long end). Houweling *et al.* (2001) propose to use just one node at 9 years which they claim to be sufficient for most rating classes. The curve will have a tendency to linear extrapolation under the smoothness criterion (3.43) and (3.45) below.

---

[6] Therefore B-splines can also be viewed as probability density functions. If the node points are the integers $x_i = i$ $\forall i$, then $B_{0,n}(x)$ is the density of a sum of $n + 1$ random variables which are i.i.d. uniformly distributed on $[0, 1]$.
[7] These recommendations refer to the choice of nodes on default-free yield curves, not spread curves.

Apart from B-splines, other sets of basis functions $\phi_m(t)$, $m = 1, \ldots, M$ can also be used. In all these cases, the spread curve can be written as:

$$H(\beta;\, t) = \sum_{m=1}^{M} \beta_m \phi_m(t). \tag{3.42}$$

3.5.2.4 Smoothness as optimisation target

If splines or other semi- or non-parametric methods with a large number of parameters are used, not all degrees of freedom will be determined by the calibration to market prices. By imposing additional optimality criteria, these degrees of freedom can be used to achieve additional smoothness and regularity on the spread curve.

A good smoothness criterion is the minimisation of the second derivative

$$S(H) := \int_0^T \left(\frac{\partial^2}{\partial T^2} H(0, t) \right)^2 \alpha(t) dt \to \min. \tag{3.43}$$

The second derivative term in large brackets measures approximately the curvature of the spread curve at maturity t, the weight function $\alpha(t) \geq 0$ allows us to impose more smoothness (and less flexibility) in some sections (e.g. for longer maturities), and less smoothness in other sections. A zero second derivative implies a linear structure.

In a discrete-time setting this criterion can be implemented by approximating the second derivative with finite differences:

$$S(H) := \sum_{k=1}^{K-1} \alpha(T_k) \frac{1}{4(T_{k+1} - T_{k-1})^2} \left(\frac{1}{T_{k+1} - T_k} (H(0, T_{k+1}) - H(0, T_k)) \right.$$
$$\left. - \frac{1}{T_k - T_{k-1}} (H(0, T_k) - H(0, T_{k-1})) \right)^2. \tag{3.44}$$

Adding the smoothness criterion to the original optimisation problem (3.38) gives the complete optimisation problem:

$$w S(H(\beta)) + (1 - w) \sum_{i \in I^{\text{def}}} w_i \left(\hat{C}^{(i)} - \overline{C}^{(i)}(F, H(\beta), \pi) \right)^2 \to \min_{\beta}. \tag{3.45}$$

There are two competing optimisation goals in (3.45): smoothness and closeness of fit to the market prices of cailbration instruments. By choice of the weight w the relative importance of these two goals can be adjusted. With w very small (but positive), closeness of fit can be given first-order importance. Using the weights w_i and $\alpha(t)$, we can also adjust which prices should be fitted more closely than others, and in which areas we require more smoothness.

3.5.3 Approximative and aggregate fits

A common practical problem is the calibration of a spread curve to a whole set of different obligors (e.g. a rating class or industry group) in order to isolate the common risk structure of this set of obligors. A precise fit to all given calibration securities would defeat this purpose, as the idiosyncracies in the individual obligors should be smoothed out, not replicated.

Except for the bootstrap, all parametric and semi-parametric fit methods introduced above can also be used in approximative fitting, under the following modifications. The weight w of the smoothness criterion in the complete optimisation target function (3.45) should be increased in order to achieve more regularity, and the weights of the individual calibration securities can be adjusted according to the degree of confidence in the price or the degree to which the corresponding obligor belongs to the rating class considered.

When defaultable bonds of different obligors are used to derive an aggregate spread curve, new problems arise. The first and most important problem is the choice of an adequate set of bonds to calibrate the spread curve to. Often this set is given by a rough classification (e.g. rating class or country) of the obligors. In other cases, one is looking to analyse the default risk of one particular obligor. Then it will pay off to take more care in selecting the benchmark set of bonds. They should be as similar as possible to the obligor in question, and in particular also have a similar degree of indebtedness and profitability.

In the choice of the sample of bonds, selection bias must be avoided. Even within a fairly homogeneous sample the credit quality of the obligors will vary. If obligors with better credit quality tend to issue longer maturity debt than obligors with worse credit quality, one may mistakenly reach a downward-sloping spread curve, even if all the individual obligors' spread curves are upward sloping. This phenomenon was first observed by Helwege and Turner (1999).

Another problem which arises frequently is the removal of outliers. Outliers are obligors whose spreads deviate very much from the average spreads of the other obligors. Including them into the sample would distort the whole calibrated curve. Typically these are obligors who have not been downgraded by the rating agencies although the market trades them at downgraded spread levels.

A common strategy to remove outliers is as follows:

1. Calibrate a spread curve for the current set of calibration securities.
2. Calculate the pricing errors of all calibration securities.
3. Remove those securities from the set of calibration securities whose pricing error exceeds some threshold, e.g. three times the average root mean-squared relative pricing error.
4. If no securities have been removed, exit the algorithm. Else, repeat at 1.
5. Get a list of the removed outliers and do a quick plausibility check.

This algorithm will end with a spread curve that misprices the underlying calibration instruments by less than the error margin, but it can happen that too many calibration securities are excluded. Therefore, the number of excluded calibration securities should be recorded in order to check the quality of the results. It may be possible that there is a particular characteristic that is common to all outliers which may be useful to know for risk management and trading.

3.5.4 Calibration example

In this section, the spread curve for Royal KPN N.V. (KPN) is calibrated using the prices of the bonds given in Table 3.2. At the time the prices were taken (4th September 2000), KPN was rated AA. As relevant risk-free curve the swap curve was chosen. It is shown in Figure 3.3.

Figure 3.4 shows the result of the calibration using the bootstrap method. For all assumed recovery rates, an almost perfect fit to the observed bond prices is possible. As expected, the

Table 3.2   Calibration securities: corporate bonds issued by Royal KPN
N.V. Rating: AA (S&P); prices and rating at 4th September 2000.
Seniority: senior unsecured, currency EUR

No.	Coupon	Maturity	Vol.	Mid	Yield	Gov.	Swap
1	5.75	13/06/2003	1500	99.71	5.85	57.9	26.1
2	4.00	30/06/2004	1250	93.52	5.94	65.4	29.4
3	6.50	03/07/2006	590	100.98	6.29	96.2	52.2
4	4.75	05/11/2008	1500	88.83	6.56	121.3	68.7

Source: Data from Reuters.

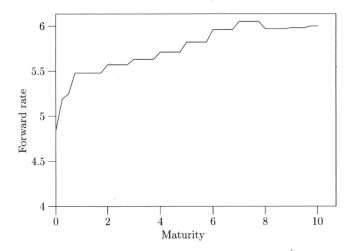

Figure 3.3   Forward rates curve stripped from the EUR swap curve on 4th September 2000

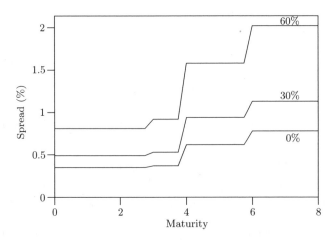

Figure 3.4   Royal KPN N.V.: forward zero-coupon bond spreads/default intensities for different assumed recovery rates $\pi = 0, 30\%, 60\%$. Calibration using the bootstrap method

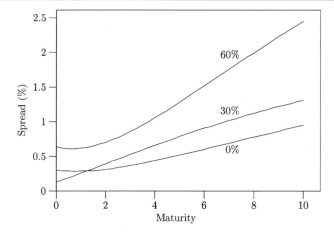

Figure 3.5   Royal KPN N.V.: forward zero-coupon bond spreads/default intensities for different ass-umed recovery rates $\pi = 0, 30\%, 60\%$. Calibration to the Nelson–Siegel parametric form

calibrated credit spreads exhibit discontinuities at the maturity dates of the bonds used for calibration. The implied default intensities depend positively on the assumed recovery rate: for $\pi = 100\%$, the spreads go to infinity; for $\pi = 0$, the spreads are very close to the spreads over swap in Table 3.2 (the differences result from the calibration to a term structure, and not just a single swap rate). Thus, these spreads are a good starting point for minimisation-based calibration routines.

Figure 3.5 shows the result of a calibration to the Nelson and Siegel (1987) parametric form for the credit spread curve. The resulting curve is much smoother, for an assumed recovery rate of 30%, it is almost linear. Nevertheless, although the number of calibration parameters equals the number of calibration securities, mispricing remains. For $\pi = 0$, the 04 bond is mispriced by 0.15 and the 06 bond by 0.22; for $\pi = 30\%$, the 04 bond is mispriced by 0.23; for $\pi = 60\%$, the 04 bond is mispriced by 0.13. It seems that the Nelson–Siegel parametric form has difficulties adjusting to the change in slope of the spread curve at the 04-maturity.

The spline-calibrated spread curves are shown in Figure 3.6. They can be viewed as smoothed versions of the bootstrap spread curves. The pricing errors of the bonds are below 0.01 for each bond.

3.6   SPREAD CURVES: ISSUES IN IMPLEMENTATION

3.6.1   Which default-free interest rates should one use?

The question of the proper choice of risk free interest rate curve was left unanswered in the previous section. This is actually a more complicated issue than one might think, and still an open discussion. So far, two candidates have been proposed in the literature and by practitioners: a government bond (treasuries, bunds or gilts)-based interest rate curve, the *government curve* and a Libor and swap market-based curve, the *Libor curve*. Some academic authors tend to favour the government curve, while practitioners usually choose the Libor curve (at least for obligors who are rated below AAA). The spread between treasuries and Libor can be as large as 100 bp, so this is an important question.

At first glance, government bonds would seem to be the best approximation to a risk-free investment opportunity in reality (at least if the issuing government is trusted not to default),

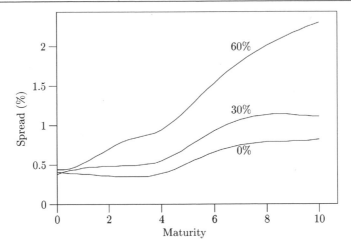

Figure 3.6   Royal KPN N.V.: forward zero-coupon bond spreads/default intensities for different assumed recovery rates $\pi = 0, 30\%, 60\%$. Calibration using cubic splines with nodes at 0, the maturity dates of the bonds, and 10

but there are problems with the results that are reached when government bonds are used as benchmark default-free assets. The spread from government bonds to AAA-rated, almost default risk-free non-government obligations is much too large to be explained by default risk alone, even if risk premia are included. Liquidity premia, taxation effects and various other explanations have been put forward to explain this phenomenon, and some authors have claimed the existence of a "real" default-free interest rate somewhere above the treasury rate.

For the practical implementation of a spread-curve calibration this means that the spread of a defaultable corporate bond over the corresponding government bond may not be an appropriate measure of the implied default risk: it will be too high (and it frequently is!).

The Libor curve on the other hand is problematic, too. Most importantly, Libor is not default-free, it is the interbank offered refinancing rate of AA-rated banks in London. There are bonds with a *negative* spread to Libor (e.g. Italian government bonds) which would seem to imply a *negative* default risk. Nevertheless, in many cases, spreads over Libor seem to work much better than spreads over government when CDS spreads are to be explained.

This problem is resolved when we take a step back and consider the static replication portfolios of the hedge-based pricing strategies of Section 2.7.5, which is where the idea of "implied" probabilities originated from. In order to replicate a short position in a CDS we had to buy the corresponding defaultable bond and short sell the default-free bond, for a long position in a CDS we needed to short sell the defaultable bond and buy a default-free bond.

The function of the positions in the defaultable bond are clear: we need them to produce the desired payoffs in default. But the only function of the positions in the default-free bonds is *to provide funding for the positions in the defaultable bonds or to invest excess cash*. This was correct in Section 2.7.5, because we made the seemingly innocuous assumption that the trader who implements the replication strategy is not defaultable himself and therefore able to fund himself at the "true" default-free rate.

If we look at real data and real markets, traders do not have access to funding at default-free rates because they are defaultable themselves. This means that:

- To replicate a short position in a CDS, the trader must buy the defaultable bond and *borrow the money for it as cheaply as he can.*
- To replicate a long position in a CDS, the trader must (somehow) short sell the defaultable bond and *invest any proceeds as profitably as possible, without incurring additional risks.*

For different types of reference credits there are different funding opportunities. Long positions in Italian government bonds and highly rated industrials can be funded by using them as collateral on the repo market. This enables the buyer of the bond to borrow money at r^{repo}. Long positions in speculative-grade bonds on the other hand must be funded using the investor's own refinancing rate, which seems to be Libor flat (or close to it) for most market participants – or at least for those who can quote the best prices.

Similar results hold for the short position in defaultable bonds. If it can be implemented on the repo market, the short seller must first produce the cash for the initial purchase of the bond. He immediately recovers that cash from the sale of the bond in the market.[8] At the repurchase date, the loan to the repo counterparty has accrued the repo rate, but the repayment must be used to buy the bond back in the market. Thus, the repo short sale is equivalent to a "negative" position in the defaultable bond and a long position in a default-free bond yielding the repo rate.

Alternatively, the short is implemented by securities lending, i.e. by borrowing the bond from an investor, and selling it in the market. But the lender of the bond will require compensation for the borrower's (counterparty) default risk: he will ask for collateral (which must be funded), or at least for a risk premium. This again leads us back to the borrower's refinancing rate.

The market CDS bid price will be such that the marginal market participant (i.e. the market participant who gives the best price) is indifferent between earning the CDS spread and earning the spread of the defaultable bond over his funding rate, and this is what we are really trying to extract when we construct a spread curve. The market CDS offer will be such that the marginal market participant is indifferent between paying the CDS offer spread and funding a short position in the underlying bond.

Although we tried to keep it simple, this analysis already led us to problems involving counterparty risk (the funding rates of market participants), the nature of the risk-neutral pricing paradigm and its foundations and equilibrium theory (the marginal investor). Nevertheless, the following advice regarding the choice of the default-free curve seems to be appropriate:

> For the default-free rate, use the relevant funding rates for investments in the defaultable obligor's assets. For highly rated obligors, this will be the repo rates, for lower rated obligors, it will be the swap curve.

3.6.2 Recovery uncertainty

There are several concerns regarding the recovery rate π. First, it is an important parameter in the calibration of a spread curve. An error in π will translate into a corresponding error in the calibrated spreads and implied default and survival probabilities. Second, one of the main

---

[8] This is the positive cash flow that seems to arise in a theoretical model when a "negative" portfolio position is entered – but in practice this positive cash flow has already been lent to the repo counterparty. For this reason it is impossible in practice to fund at treasury rates by short selling treasury bonds.

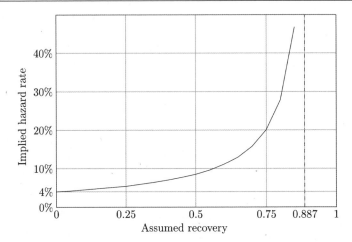

Figure 3.7 The implied default hazard rate h of a defaultable zero-coupon bond as a function of the assumed average recovery rate π. Parameters: observed market price 0.887 (i.e. a spread of 4% at a maturity of $T = 3$), default-free rates $= 0$

uses of the calibrated spread curve is the pricing of CDSs. The recovery rate also enters the CDS pricing formula (3.28), which represents another opportunity where an error in π could affect the resulting CDS rate. Finally, there will be errors in the recovery rate. In some cases the recovery rate can be estimated jointly from the observed market prices (see e.g. Merrick, 2001), but in many cases this will not be possible or the results will be too unstable. Then one will have to resort to a historical estimate, which will contain estimation errors, and it will not be a risk-adjusted expectation either.

To analyse the first error, Figure 3.7 shows the effect of the level of the expected recovery rate π on the resulting implied default hazard rate. Although this figure was derived for a defaultable zero-coupon bond, the picture for coupon bonds is qualitatively the same, see e.g. the calibration example for KPN bonds in Figures 3.4, 3.5 and 3.6. If a high recovery rate is expected, a higher default hazard rate (and default probability) is necessary to reproduce the observed bond price of 0.887. No expected recovery rate above 0.887 can be consistent with the observed bond price, and for $\pi = 0$ the hazard rate converges to the level of the credit spread 4%. Thus, if the used recovery rate π is larger than the "true" recovery rate π^*, the implied default hazard rate h will also be larger than the corresponding "true" value h^*.

The relationship between h and π can also be inverted. Figure 3.7 also shows the recovery rate π that one has to assume in order to reproduce the observed market price for a particular hazard rate of defaults. If one is willing to make an assumption on a plausible range for the default hazard rate, e.g. $h \in [0.05, 0.10]$, then a corresponding range for the recovery rate can be derived: $\pi \in [0.20, 0.55]$.

The second error occurs in the CDS pricing formula (3.28) or (3.29):

$$\bar{s} = (1 - \pi) \sum_{n=1}^{N} w_n H(0, T_{n-1}, T_n)$$

where the weights are given by:

$$w_n = \frac{\delta_{n-1}\overline{B}(0, T_n)}{\sum\limits_{m=1}^{N} \delta_{m-1}\overline{B}(0, T_m)} \quad \forall\, n \leq N.$$

In a first approximation we can assume that H is constant across maturity dates, then the CDS rate is $\bar{s} \approx (1 - \pi)H$. Hence, the direct effect of a positive error in π (i.e. $\pi > \pi^*$) is a *lower* CDS rate.

The recovery rate has a strong influence on the results of the calibration procedure – in fact it enters *twice*, once when the spread curve is calibrated and a second time when it is substituted in the CDS pricing formula. Fortunately, both errors go in opposite directions (one biases the CDS rate high, the other low), and they tend to cancel to a large extent. This is also true in real-world applications.

On second thoughts, this result is not surprising. The simple spread-curve pricing methodology must result in *market consistent prices*, and we have already derived rather tight pricing bounds on a CDS rate in Section 2.7.5. These bounds must (and do) reappear in the spread model, in fact they have been sharpened by assuming some structure on the shape of the H-curve.

Another important consequence of this robustness result is the following:

The same recovery rate should be used in calibration and in pricing with the spread curve.

Otherwise, the resulting prices may be outside the hedge-based price bounds of Section 2.7.5.

For a default digital swap (DDS) there are no tight hedge-based price bounds. Therefore, its value is much more sensitive to an error in the specification of the assumed recovery rate. On the other hand, as explained in Chapter 2, DDSs can be viewed as direct speculation on the recovery rate, therefore their prices can provide the missing information on π (if they are available).

3.6.3 Bucket hedging

The spread curve can also be used to derive rough "bucket" hedge ratios for credit derivatives that have been priced using this instrument. From every given (hypothetical) price change in one of the hedge (and calibration) instruments follows a new spread curve and a new value of the investment portfolio. If a portfolio manager wants to be hedged against this price change risk, he should adjust the weights of the hedge instruments until the portfolio is neutral to the assumed price change. Frequently, just parallel moves in the spread curve are assumed and the hedge is calibrated against these. Then the computer-intensive recalibration of the spread curve is avoided.

This hedging strategy is simple and popular, but it should be used with caution. In particular, a hedge against small spread moves is not sufficient. The possibility of sudden default or downgrade events must not be overlooked, and at default events, recovery risk must be explicitly recognised.

3.7   SPREAD CURVES: DISCUSSION

The credit spread curve (based upon forward default intensities) has proven to be a versatile instrument in the analysis of the default risk of an obligor. It allows us to price CDSs, DDSs, forward-start CDSs and a variety of other instruments. It is a very robust procedure (we made almost no critical assumptions), and it is very popular in practice.

There are many different types of spreads and spread curves in credit markets. There are the yield spreads of the defaultable bonds over government, Libor or some other defaultable benchmark bond; there are par coupon spreads, asset swap spreads, total return swap spreads and CDS spreads; there are average spread curves of rating classes; and finally, there are the implied forward default hazard rates which we call simply "spreads" and "spread curves".

All these spreads are related and of a similar order of magnitude, but the setup presented in Section 3.3 has the advantage of an underlying simple pricing model. This model allows the consistent pricing of several different important classes of defaultable securities, and it yields values for implied default probabilities which may be useful for more complicated credit derivatives.

Houweling and Vorst (2001) have performed a careful and encompassing study on the pricing performance of an implied hazard rate pricing method that is very similar to the one presented in this chapter. Using a large data set of CDS quotes, swap and repo rates, and government and corporate bond prices from 1999 and 2000, they find the following.

- Default-free reference curve: Repo or swap rates outperform government rates as risk-free reference curve. This effect is particularly pronounced for highly rated obligors. Repo rates seem to be slightly better than swap rates.
- Parametric form of the hazard curve: A linear or quadratic hazard curve[9] is sufficient for a good fit of the given corporate bond prices.
- Recovery uncertainty: For CDS pricing, the model is robust against misspecification in the recovery rate.
- Pricing performance vs. hedge-based pricing: Calibrating a hazard curve to observed bond prices reduces the average CDS pricing error by 35% to 55% for investment-grade issuers and by 15% to 20% for speculative-grade issuers. The comparison was made against two types of "spread comparison" methods where the CDS spread is assumed to be equal to the spread of the corresponding bonds over repo rates.
- Pricing performance (absolute): For highly rated bonds (AAA to BBB), hazard rate-based CDS rates are slightly above their market equivalents but pricing performance is generally good. For lower rated bonds (BB to B) on the other hand, model CDS spreads are substantially (140 bp and more) below the market CDS spreads. The error is slightly smaller for (bond bid/CDS ask) pairs than for (bond ask/CDS bid) pairs. Pricing errors depend also on the maturity of the CDS, with market prices for short maturities being lower than the corresponding model prices.

Most of these results confirm the theoretical arguments made previously. The case for repo as default-free rates is now confirmed. The "spread comparison methods" are very similar to the cash-and-carry arbitrage pricing methods with asset swap rates, so we would expect a similar

---

[9] Houweling and Vorst (2001) only consider polynomials as candidates for the hazard curve. In their paper they parametrise the integral of the hazard rate, thus the degrees of the polynomials reported there are higher by one.

improvement over asset swap spread pricing, too. The relatively poor pricing performance for subinvestment-grade obligors shows that the markets for subinvestment-grade bonds and CDSs are imperfectly linked. If short positions in these bonds were possible, this systematic bias could be arbitraged away.

Thus, for investment-grade obligors a spread-based CDS pricing model seems to be a significant improvement on the simple cash-and-carry arbitrage. For speculative-grade obligors there is still a significant improvement, but the pricing errors remain large, and a systematic bias is present.

It cannot be denied that the construction of spread curves involves judgement, there are degrees of freedom and "slack" in the model. The most important consequence of this is the existence of several spread curves, all of which are consistent with a given set of prices of the calibration instruments. This freedom was removed by assuming some form of additional structure on the spread curve: smoothness or particular parametric forms.

From a modelling point of view, every possible spread curve corresponds to a particular distribution of default times which is consistent with market prices, i.e. a particular martingale measure. Credit markets are incomplete as there is more than one martingale measure. Thus, the main source of the "slack" and excess degrees of freedom of the spread curve pricing method is not caused by implausible assumptions in the spread curve modelling approach but by the presence of risks in the credit market itself which cannot be perfectly hedged.

By choosing one particular spread curve for pricing, the martingale measure is selected, and here the modeller's judgement must enter. Fortunately (or rather by design of the method), this choice is made in terms of picking plausible conditional default intensities and recovery rates: quantities over which it is relatively simple to form an intuition. Thus, many theoretically possible spread curves can be ruled out immediately, and the difference between the remaining spread curves will not be large. Market incompleteness is a constant companion in credit risk models, but the problem is not as large as it may seem at first.

Another weak point of the approach is Assumption 3.2 of independence between defaults and default-free interest rates. Empirical evidence seems to indicate a negative correlation between the movements of interest rates and spreads (= implied default likelihoods). This assumption will be removed in the following sections. Its influence on implied default probabilities is rather small for realistic parameter values, so that it is often kept in order to retain much more analytical tractability.

The procedure of calibration to market prices itself can have disadvantages. There is the danger of overfitting if the prices of the calibration instruments are wrong, stale or manipulated, or if no calibration instruments are available at all. The model can only detect mispricing in securities that were not used for calibration. Some securities cannot be priced in this framework at all (e.g. equity shares, convertible bonds), and some only after major extensions of the framework (basket CDS or credit derivatives with option character).

3.8 GUIDE TO THE LITERATURE

Many of the ideas presented in this chapter (implied default probabilities, recovery of par, pricing building blocks) have been used for quite some time by practitioners and academics, and they can often be found as remarks and asides in larger papers. The earliest references to a defaultable bond pricing model setup very similar to the one presented here are Jonkhart (1979), Bierman and Haas (1975), Yawitz (1977) and Yawitz and Maloney (1985). These authors use a setup with survival probabilities (and not default intensities), but the recovery as a fraction of the par value of the bond and the resulting coupon bond pricing equations are structurally equivalent to equation (3.21).

The fundamental relationship between defaultable zero-coupon bond prices and implied default probabilities appears in several places, for example Das (1998), Mathieu and d'Herouville (1998), Duffie (1999), most papers on intensity-based credit risk models, and the early references above. Similar spread curve calibration methods for the pricing of CDSs have been proposed by Scott (1998), Duffie (1999), Schmidt (2001) and Das (1998). The method presented here is based upon Schönbucher and Sommer (2000). Lando (1998a) introduces building blocks similar to the ones defined in Section 3.3. The recovery of par model setup can be found in Duffie (1998). Duration and convexity-based hedging in a similar framework are discussed in Skinner (1998) and Fooladi et al. (1997).

The proposed numerical and parametric methods for the calibration of spread curves are direct adaptations of similar methods for the calibration of default-free forward rates and yield curves. In particular, the papers by Nelson and Siegel (1987) and Svensson (1994, 1995), for parametric forms of forward rate curves and of McCulloch (1971), McCulloch (1975), Adams and van Deventer (1994), Waggoner (1997) and Vasicek and Fong (1982) for spline-based methods should be mentioned here, as well as the book by Anderson et al. (1996). The kernel regression methods of Linton et al. (2001) are another possibility to estimate a smooth yield curve.

Almost no empirical papers use actual CDS quotes, mostly defaultable bond prices are analysed. The paper by Houweling and Vorst (2001) and the paper by Cossin and Hricko (2001) are exceptions. Houweling and Vorst (2001) is an empirical study of the performance of this chapter's pricing model. This paper was discussed in detail above. Cossin and Hricko (2001) analyse which exogenous factors (rating, leverage, etc.) have an influence on CDS rates.

For the defaultable bond market, levels and term structures of credit spreads are empirically calibrated and estimated in several papers, e.g. Sarig and Warga (1989), Litterman and Iben (1991), Flesaker et al. (1994), Duffie and Huang (1996), Duffie and Singleton (1997), Duffee (1998), Schwartz (1998), Nickell et al. (1998), Düllmann et al. (2000), Tauren (1999), Schönbucher and Sommer (2000), Helwege and Turner (1999), Merrick (2001) and Cumby and Pastinte (2001). Most of these papers either concern the testing and estimation of intensity-based credit risk models, or they test the firm's value setup of Chapter 9. Thus, the underlying models may be slightly different from the setup presented here, but the qualitative results on level and shape of the resulting spread curves are robust. More references to empirical results can be found at the end of later chapters. Litterman and Iben (1991) consider spread curve calibration in emerging markets and advocate using a country-specific spread curve with an issuer-specific offset to overcome data scarcity. Cumby and Pastinte (2001) estimate implied default probabilities for Brady debt. Houweling et al. (2001) estimate rating-class spread curves using splines. Merrick (2001) is a case study on Russian and Argentinian Eurobond debt during the Russian crisis of 1998. He uses a linearly parametrised spread curve and jointly calibrates level, slope and recovery rate to the observed bond prices. Duffie et al. (2003) also investigate the Russian default using a different modelling approach which will be presented in Chapter 5.

The question of the correct specification of the risk-free rate has been addressed by Pimbley (2000). Liu et al. (2000) and Longstaff (2000) also recognise the importance of repo rates and use them to separate liquidity premia from credit risk premia in swap spreads.

4
Mathematical Background

The formalism of the stochastic analysis of point and jump processes can be daunting to the uninitiated. This is unfortunate because the basic concepts are no more difficult to understand than stochastic analysis for continuous stochastic processes, frequently they are even simpler and more intuitive. In this chapter we provide the mathematical notation and tools that we will need to use in the rest of the book. These concepts are also essential to follow, assess and understand large parts of the recent literature on quantitative credit risk models.

Readers who have a sufficient background in stochastic processes and mathematical finance (or readers who are simply impatient) can safely skip most of this chapter and return later if they should encounter a concept that is new to them. Nevertheless, even these readers are advised to have a look at the section on jump and compensator measures to familiarise themselves with this notation for a marked point process.

In order to make the presentation as accessible as possible without sacrificing mathematical correctness, we sometimes avoid generality in favour of simplicity. For the same reason, this chapter can only provide the basic intuition behind the mathematical concepts that are presented. It cannot replace the careful study of a good, more general and more rigorous book on stochastic processes. Thus, to fully understand the mathematics behind the models, the reader should also consult books like Jacod and Shiryaev (1988), Protter (1990) or the survey by Liptser and Shiryaev (1998) (for general stochastic processes), or Last and Brandt (1995) (for marked point processes in particular).

It is assumed that the reader is familiar with the basics of the theory of stochastic processes. In particular, probability spaces, measurability, filtrations, the stochastic integral with respect to Brownian motion and diffusion processes, quadratic variation for continuous processes and Itô's lemma for diffusion processes will not be explained. Knowledge of concepts like adapted and predictable stochastic processes, martingales and the Doob–Meyer decomposition will also be helpful. There are a number of good and not too difficult books on the subject, e.g. the books by Neftci (1996) (for an intuitive introduction) or Lamberton and Lapeyre (1996) (intermediate) or the book by Nielsen (1999) (very nice balance between rigour and intuition). Many textbooks on mathematical finance also cover these topics with varying degrees of detail and rigour. Further reading pointers will be given in the last section of this chapter.

All processes and random variables that we introduce are defined on a complete filtered probability space $(\Omega, (\mathcal{F}_t)_{(t \geq 0)}, P)$, where Ω is the set of possible states of nature, the filtration $(\mathcal{F}_t)_{(t \geq 0)}$ represents the information structure of the setup, and P is the probability measure that attaches probabilities to the events in Ω. In particular, $\mathcal{F}_t$ is the information available at time t, and random variables whose realisation is known at time t are said to be measurable with respect to $\mathcal{F}_t$. We assume that $(\mathcal{F}_t)_{(t \geq 0)}$ satisfies the usual conditions (see Jacod and Shiryaev, 1988, p. 2). Throughout the book we assume that all processes are special semi-martingales, in particular they are continuous from the right with left limits. We will also gloss over the difference between martingales and local martingales in several places.

4.1 STOPPING TIMES

To model the *arrival risk* of a credit event we need to model an unknown, random point in time $\tau \in \mathbb{R}_+$. It is convenient to extend the possible set of realisations of τ to include ∞ in order to model events that may never occur. Thus τ is a random variable with values in $\mathbb{R}_+ \cup \{\infty\}$.

But this is not enough: we have to link τ to the way information is revealed in the filtration $(\mathcal{F}_t)_{(t \geq 0)}$. In particular, if τ is the time of some event, we want that *at the time of the event it is known that this event has occurred.* Mathematically this means that at every time t we know if τ has already occurred or not:

$$\{\tau \leq t\} \in \mathcal{F}_t \quad \forall t \geq 0. \tag{4.1}$$

This property defines the random time τ as a *stopping time.*

Requiring equation (4.1) seems so obvious that one starts to wonder if it is really a necessary requirement. In fact it is, because there are many examples for random times that do *not* satisfy this requirement. For example, consider a Brownian motion $W(t)$ on a fixed time interval $[0, T]$, and let τ be the time at which $W(t)$ attains its maximum. This τ is a random point in time but we will only be able to decide at time T – after we have observed the whole path of W over $[0, T]$ – when the maximum really was attained. At the time of the maximum we do not know yet if it was the global maximum because we do not know the future development of the path of W.

Equation (4.1) says that we can observe the event at the time it occurs. But it does not require that the event comes as a surprise. The value of the stopping time may be known a long time before time $t = \tau$. The simplest example is a fixed stopping time that always takes the same value $\tau = t^*$. The value t^* is known from time zero onwards, but still τ is a stopping time.

The maximum and minimum of a set of stopping times is again a stopping time, and the sum of two stopping times is also a stopping time. In order to represent a stopping time with a stochastic process, we define its *indicator process* that jumps from zero to one at the stopping time:

$$N_\tau(t) := \mathbf{1}_{\{\tau \leq t\}}. \tag{4.2}$$

For default risk modelling we use *default indicator functions* (the indicator function of the default event) and *survival indicator functions* (one minus the default indicator function).

Another concept that will be used later on is the idea of a *predictable stopping time* τ. The indicator process of a predictable stopping time is a predictable process. A predictable stopping time has an *announcing sequence* of stopping times $\tau_1 \leq \tau_2 \leq \cdots$ with

$$\tau_n < \tau \quad \text{and} \quad \lim_{n \to \infty} \tau_n = \tau \quad \text{for all } \omega \in \Omega \text{ with } \{\tau(\omega) > 0\}.$$

This means there is a sequence of early warning signals τ_n that occur before τ and that announce the predictable stopping time. An example of a predictable stopping time is the first hitting time of a continuous stochastic process $X(t)$, i.e. the first time when $X(t)$ hits a barrier $\overline{K}$. If the process starts above the barrier $X(0) > \overline{K}$, then one possible announcing sequence is given by the following times $\tau_n = \inf\{t \mid X(t) \leq \overline{K} + 1/n\}$. The announcing sequence gives the times when $X(t)$ hits barriers that are closer and closer to the final barrier $\overline{K}$.

One important consequence for modelling should be mentioned here already: No market price of an asset can have a *predictable* jump with known jump size in an arbitrage-free market. (Unless the asset has a payoff at this time of exactly the opposite of the jump.[1]) Let us assume that the price of some corporate bond jumps from $x(t) = c > 0$ to $x(\tau) = 0$ at the predictable jump time τ. Then a smart trader would short sell the bond just before the jump down to zero and make a large profit. He can do this because the default time is announced by the announcing sequence, so by choosing a very late time in the sequence he can make the probability of missing the default time arbitrarily small. Such a predictable time can only be consistent with absence of arbitrage if the profit of the trader would go to zero, too. This means that the price must converge to its value at the predictable time $x(\tau_n) \to 0 = x(\tau)$.

If the size and direction of the jump in price are not known, then the model can still be arbitrage-free. A simple example is the binomial share price model where the share price jumps up *or* down at times that are known in advance.

The opposite of a predictable stopping time is a *totally inaccessible* stopping time. A totally inaccessible stopping time is a stopping time τ for which no predictable stopping time can give any information, i.e. for all predictable stopping times τ' we have:

$$\mathbf{P}[\tau = \tau' < \infty] = 0.$$

That means, we cannot find a predictable stopping time that coincides with τ, nor can we find one that coincides with τ with some positive probability.

Many stopping times are neither predictable nor totally inaccessible: they can have both features, predictability and total inaccessibility are just two extreme cases. Nevertheless, it can be shown (see Liptser and Shiryaev, 1998, theorem 3.3) that every stopping time can be decomposed into a totally inaccessible stopping time and an accessible time.

4.2   THE HAZARD RATE

The implied hazard rate already appeared in Chapter 3, Definition 3.4, now it is time to give a formal definition of the hazard rate in the mathematical sense.

Definition 4.1 *Let τ be a stopping time and $F(T) := \mathbf{P}[\tau \leq T]$ its distribution function. Assume that $F(T) < 1$ for all T, and that $F(T)$ has a density $f(T)$. The* hazard rate function *h of τ is defined as:*

$$h(T) := \frac{f(T)}{1 - F(T)}. \tag{4.3}$$

At later points in time $t > 0$ with $\tau > t$, the conditional hazard rate *is defined as:*

$$h(t, T) := \frac{f(t, T)}{1 - F(t, T)}, \tag{4.4}$$

where $F(t, T) := \mathbf{P}[\tau \leq T \mid \mathcal{F}_t]$ is the conditional distribution of τ given the information at time t, and $f(t, T)$ is the corresponding density.

---

[1] Share prices drop by the dividend amount at the ex-dividend date, and the (dirty) price of a bond drops by the coupon amount at the coupon payment date.

The interpretation of the hazard rate was already given in Section 3.1.5. The hazard rate $h(t)$ is the local arrival probability of the stopping time per time:

$$h(t) = \lim_{\Delta t \to 0} \frac{1}{\Delta t} \mathbf{P}[\tau \le t + \Delta t \mid \tau > t].$$

Knowledge of the hazard rate function allows a reconstruction of $F(t)$ and $F(t, T)$:

$$F(T) = 1 - e^{-\int_0^t h(s)ds} \quad \text{and} \quad F(t, T) = 1 - e^{-\int_t^T h(t,s)ds}.$$

4.3   POINT PROCESSES

A stopping time is the mathematical description of *one* event, a point process is a generalisation to multiple events. The term *point process* may lead to confusion because a point process is not really a stochastic process, rather it is a collection of *points in time*:

$$\{\tau_i, \, i \in \mathbb{N}\} = \{\tau_1, \, \tau_2, \ldots\}$$

We assume that we have indexed these points in time in ascending order ($\tau_i < \tau_{i+1}$), that they are all stopping times, that they are all different, and that there are only a finite number of such points over any finite time horizon almost surely. (This allows us to avoid much of the mathematical technicality that would obscure the presentation otherwise.) The reader will immediately observe that point processes should provide a good mathematical framework to analyse timing risk of several events, e.g. rating transitions, or multiple defaults of a single obligor, or defaults of several obligors.

We can turn this collection of time points into a stochastic process using the associated *counting process*:

$$N(t) := \sum_i \mathbf{1}_{\{\tau_i \le t\}}.$$

$N(t)$ counts the number of time points of the point process that lie before t. If all τ_i are greater than zero, a sample path of $N(t)$ would be a step function that starts at zero and increases by one at each τ_i. $N(t)$ contains all the information that is contained in the point process $\{\tau_i, \, i \in \mathbb{N}\}$ and vice versa. The advantage of using $N(t)$ is that we now do have a *stochastic process* and we can use the whole machinery of stochastic analysis to model and analyse N.

4.4   THE INTENSITY

For counting processes the predictable compensator process $A(t)$ is an increasing process, because $N(t)$ is also increasing. The compensated process is a local martingale:

$$M(t) = N(t) - A(t).$$

The compensator gives a lot of information about the *probabilities* of jumps over the next time step. We have:

$$\mathbf{E}[N(t + \Delta t) - N(t) \mid \mathcal{F}_t] = \mathbf{E}[A(t + \Delta t) - A(t) \mid \mathcal{F}_t].$$

Over small time steps we can assume that $N(t + \Delta t) - N(t)$ can only take values 1 or 0. Then:

$$
\begin{aligned}
\mathbf{E}[A(t + \Delta t) - A(t) \mid \mathcal{F}_t] \\
= 1 \cdot \mathbf{P}[N(t + \Delta t) - N(t) = 1 \mid \mathcal{F}_t] + 0 \cdot \mathbf{P}[N(t + \Delta t) - N(t) = 0 \mid \mathcal{F}_t] \\
= \mathbf{P}[N(t + \Delta t) - N(t) = 1 \mid \mathcal{F}_t].
\end{aligned}
\tag{4.5}
$$

If at time t we have a jump of size $\Delta A \in [0, 1]$ in the predictable compensator of $N(t)$, then this means that *the local jump probability over the next instance is* ΔA. Because the compensator is predictable, its increments over the next time step are known. Thus, the compensator is a running measure of the local jump probabilities of the counting process $N(t)$.

If A does not have discrete jumps, the probability of a jump in the next instance is infinitesimally small. If A is differentiable,[2] this leads to the concept of the jump intensity.

Definition 4.2   *The non-negative, progressively measurable process* $\lambda(t)$ *is the intensity of the counting process* $N(t)$ *if and only if*

$$A(t) := \int_0^t \lambda(s)ds$$

is the predictable compensator of $N(t)$, *i.e.* $N(t) - A(t)$ *is a local martingale.*

We assume that A is not only increasing, but is also differentiable with derivative $\lambda(t)$. This is not an innocuous assumption, a finite intensity only exists in a particular class of models, aptly named *intensity models*. Most of the firm's value-based credit risk models discussed in Chapter 9 do *not* have a differentiable predictable compensator for the default indicator process.

Intensity, hazard rate and the survival probability of the process N are closely linked. Under suitable regularity conditions:

$$\lambda(t) = h(t, t).
\tag{4.6}$$

Both views, intensity and local conditional hazard rate, coincide for all applications that we consider in this book. If the intensity $\lambda(t)$ of the process is a deterministic function of time, then the future path of the intensity is given by the forward hazard rates, i.e. $\lambda(t) = h(0, t)$. The formal theorem to equation (4.6) is the following.

---

[2] There are cases when A is increasing, continuous, but does *not* admit an intensity, for example the running maximum of a Brownian motion $A(t) := \max_{0 \le s \le t} W(s)$.

Theorem 4.1 (Aven, 1985) *Let* $\{\epsilon_n\}_{n=1}^{\infty}$ *be a sequence which decreases to zero and let* $Y_n(t)$, $t \in \mathbb{R}_+$ *be a measurable version of the process*

$$Y_n(t) := \frac{1}{\epsilon_n} \mathbf{E}[N(t + \epsilon_n) - N(t) \mid \mathcal{F}_t].$$

Assume there are non-negative and measurable processes $g(t)$ *and* $y(t)$, $t \in \mathbb{R}_+$ *such that:*

(i) for each t

$$\lim_{n \to \infty} Y_n(t) = g(t) \quad a.s.$$

(ii) for each t there exists for almost all $\omega \in \Omega$ *an* $n_0 = n_0(t, \omega)$ *such that*

$$|Y_n(s, \omega) - g(s, \omega)| \le y(s, \omega) \quad \forall\, s \le t, \, n \ge n_0$$

(iii)

$$\int_0^t y(s)ds < \infty \quad a.s. \quad t \in \mathbb{R}_+$$

then $N(t) - \int_0^t g(s)ds$ *is a local martingale, and* $\int_0^t g(s)ds$ *is the compensator of* $N(t)$.

From this follows directly our recipe for deriving the default intensities if the conditional survival probabilities are known.

Lemma 4.2   *Let* $N(t) := \mathbf{1}_{\{\tau \le t\}}$ *be the default indicator function,* $A(t)$ *its predictable compensator, and let*

$$P(t, T) := \mathbf{P}[\tau > T \mid \mathcal{F}_t]$$

denote the probability given $\mathcal{F}_t$ *that the jump has not occurred until* T. *Furthermore let* $P(t, T)$ *be differentiable from the right with respect to* T *at* $T = t$, *and let the difference quotients that approximate the derivative satisfy the assumptions of Theorem 4.1. Then the intensity* $N(t)$ *is given by:*

$$\frac{dA(t)}{dt} = g(t) = -\left.\frac{\partial}{\partial T}\right|_{T=t} P(t, T) = h(t, t). \tag{4.7}$$

Basically, there are two different ways of viewing a counting process, first from the point of view of stochastic processes and predictable compensators (including intensities), and second by analysing the distribution of the next jump time (including hazard rates).

Under some regularity conditions, the arrival intensity $\lambda(t)$ coincides with the (conditional) hazard rate $h(t, t)$ for the next time step, thus the intensity is the local arrival rate of the stopping time τ. At the same time, the intensity defines the compensator of the default indicator function. Thus, it is an important tool to express the *dynamics* (not just the probabilities) of the model variables. This explains why the intensity of the default time is at the core of many default risk models.

Using Lemma 4.2, we can directly derive the default intensity if we have the conditional survival probabilities. Unfortunately, the converse direction (from intensities to survival probabilities) is not always so straightforward. Much of the analysis in the rest of this chapter is devoted to the problem of finding realistic specifications for the default intensity that still allow analytical tractability for survival probabilities and other basic pricing problems.

Because of the relationship described in Lemma 4.2, many authors use the terms "hazard rate of default" and "default intensity" synonymously. The only difference (apart from the original definition) is that hazard rates are also defined for future dates: $h(t, T)$ is defined for $T > t$, while there is only one $\lambda(t)$.

4.5   MARKED POINT PROCESSES AND THE JUMP MEASURE

The next step of generalisation from a point process is a *marked point process*.[3] If we want to incorporate *magnitude risk* into the point process framework, we need to attach a second variable, a *marker*, to each event τ_i. Thus we have a double sequence

$$\{(\tau_i, Y_i), \ i \in \mathbb{N}\}$$

of points in time τ_i with marker Y_i. The marker can be any type of random variable, we only assume that it is drawn from a measurable probability space $(E, \ \mathcal{E})$. For default risk modelling, τ_i will represent the time of either a default event or a rating transition event. Then, Y_i will either be a recovery rate (then E is the unit interval $[0, 1]$ and the σ-algebra $\mathcal{E}$ will be the Borel sets on E), or Y_i will be the new rating class (so E will be the set of possible rating classes and $\mathcal{E}$ will be the set of all subsets of E).

We now have a small problem when we want to find a canonical way of transforming the marked point process into a "standard" stochastic process without losing information. For example, one possibility would be to define the sum process of all Y_i that occurred before t:

$$X(t) := \sum_i Y_i \, \mathbf{1}_{\{\tau_i \le t\}}.$$

There may be problems with this, though: first, the Y_i may not be summable at all. For instance, we could have taken E to be the set of the names of the obligors in a portfolio, and Y_i the name of the obligor who defaulted at τ_i. How would we sum up the names?[4] The other problem occurs when a marker can take the value zero $Y_i = 0$. Then some information is lost if we only look at $X(t)$: some events may slip through unnoticed. Finally, we would like to be able to represent those stochastic processes that are driven by this marked point process as stochastic integrals, similar to the way all diffusion processes can be written as stochastic integrals with respect to a driving Brownian motion.

There are fudges to solve these problems but they are fudges and there is a better way of representing marked point processes: the jump measure. The jump measure is a method of

---

[3] Sections 4.5–4.7 are rather technical and can be skipped at first reading.
[4] We could of course index all names and sum up the index numbers.

representing the information contained in a marked point process in a concise and general way which also opens the marked point process for stochastic analysis.

The jump measure is a particular case of a random measure. A *random measure* v is a measure on the marker space and time, which also depends on the particular state of nature.

Definition 4.3 $v : \Omega \times \mathcal{E} \times \mathcal{B}(\mathbb{R}_+) \to \mathbb{R}_+$ *is a* random measure *if for every* $\omega \in \Omega$, $v(\omega, \cdot, \cdot)$ *is a measure on* $((E \times \mathbb{R}_+), \mathcal{E} \otimes \mathcal{B}(\mathbb{R}_+))$ *and* $v(\omega, E, \{0\}) = 0$ *identically.*

Because it depends on ω, the random measure v is stochastic (hence *random* measure), but it is not a stochastic process because it does not depend explicitly on the time t. Time is present only in the form of the second measure dimension. Nevertheless, random measures can be used to *construct* stochastic processes by integrating some random function up to the current time t. (A number of examples follow below.)

The first example of a random measure is the *jump measure* of a marked point process.

Definition 4.4   *The jump measure of a marked point process* $\{(T_i, Y_i)\}_{i \in \mathbb{N}}$ *is a random measure on* $E \times \mathbb{R}_+$ *such that for all* $E' \in \mathcal{E}$:

$$\mu(\omega, E', [0, t]) = \int_0^t \int_{E'} \mu(\omega, de, ds) := \sum_{i=1}^{\infty} \mathbf{1}_{\{\tau_i(\omega) \leq t\}} \mathbf{1}_{\{Y_i(\omega) \in E'\}} \quad \forall \omega \in \Omega. \quad (4.8)$$

Here we write the dependence on $\omega \in \Omega$ explicitly to make the point that the jump measure is a *random* measure. (We will omit this dependence in the following if it is not necessary for the understanding.) The jump measure $\mu(E', [0, t])$ of a set $E' \in \mathcal{E}$ and a time interval $[0, t]$ counts the number of events (τ_i, Y_i) with a marker from E' during the time interval $[0, t]$. (Such measures are also often called *counting measures*.)

As a measure, the jump measure places a unit mass (like a Dirac delta function) at all the realisations (τ_i, Y_i) of the marked point process in the product space $[0, T] \times E$. This means that the jump measure does indeed contain all information that is contained in the marked point process.

By integrating with respect to the jump measure, functionals of the marked point process can be represented.

- The number of jumps until a given time t:

$$N(t) = \int_0^t \int_E 1 \cdot \mu(de, ds).$$

- The sum of the markers of all events until t:

$$X(t) = \sum_{i \mid \tau_i \leq t} Y_i = \int_0^t \int_E e \cdot \mu(de, ds).$$

- The product of the markers of all events until t:

$$X(0) := 1 \quad \text{and} \quad X(t) = \prod_{i|\tau_i \leq t} Y_i = \int_0^t \int_E X(s-)(e-1)\mu(de, ds).$$

- The sum of a function $f(\cdot)$ of the markers Y_i:

$$Z(t) = \sum_{i|\tau_i \leq t} f(Y_i) = \int_0^t \int_E f(e)\mu(de, ds).$$

- The function f can also depend on time or it can be stochastic. In general, f is a function from the state space, time and marker space into the real numbers $f : \Omega \times \mathbb{R}_+ \times E \to \mathbb{R}$. For such functions we can define the most general form of an integral process with respect to the random measure μ:

$$Z_f(\omega, t) = \sum_{\{i \in \mathbb{N}|\tau_i \leq t\}} f(\omega, \tau_i, Y_i) = \int_0^t \int_E f(\omega, s, e)\mu(\omega, de, ds). \tag{4.9}$$

With the jump measure we can describe the realisations of the marked point process, and with the integral process we can also describe the effects of the realisation of the marked point process on other state variables of our model.

4.6   THE COMPENSATOR MEASURE

To complete the model, we need to specify the probabilities of the realisations of the marked point process. For this we use another random measure: the predictable compensator measure $\nu(de, dt)$. But first we must define what predictability means in the context of random measures. (There is a discrete-time explanation of these concepts right after the definitions.)

Definition 4.5

(i) A predictable stochastic function $f : \Omega \times E \times \mathbb{R}_+ \to \mathbb{R}$ is *a function that is measurable with respect to the σ-algebra $\mathcal{P} \otimes \mathcal{E}$, where $\mathcal{P}$ is the σ-algebra which is generated by the predictable processes on $(\Omega, (\mathcal{F}_t)_{(t \geq 0)}, P)$.*

(ii) A random measure ν is called predictable *if for every predictable stochastic function f, the integral process*

$$X(\omega, t) := \int_0^t \int_E f(\omega, e, s)\nu(\omega, de, ds) \tag{4.10}$$

is again a predictable process.

Essentially, for every given $e \in E$, we have a process $f(\omega, e, t)$. If this process is predictable (in the classical sense) for every $e \in E$, then $f(\cdot, \cdot, \cdot)$ is a predictable stochastic function (provided that we have sufficient regularity[5] of f). In particular, the indicator function of any set $E' \in \mathcal{E}$ is a predictable function, and all the functions used as integrands in the examples for the jump measure are predictable functions.

A predictable random measure preserves predictability of the integrated functions. If "predictability" can be interpreted as "having no surprises", then a predictable random measure does not have any surprises. In particular, the jump measure of a totally inaccessible stopping time will *not* be a predictable measure, because it transforms a predictable function ($f \equiv 1$) to a process that is not predictable: the default indicator function.

Now we can define the *compensator measure* using the following defining result (Liptser and Shiryaev, 1998, theorem 3.13).

Definition 4.6 (compensator measure)   *The compensator measure of $\mu(\omega, de, dt)$ is the unique (a.s.) predictable random measure $v(\omega, de, dt)$ with the following property.*

Let $f(\omega, e, t)$ be a predictable stochastic function. Let $M(\omega, t)$ be defined as follows:

$$M(\omega, t) := \int_0^t \int_E f(\omega, e, s)\mu(\omega, de, ds) - \int_0^t \int_E f(\omega, e, s)v(\omega, de, ds), \quad (4.11)$$

then $M(t)$ is a local martingale. The compensator measure $v(\omega, de, ds)$ is the unique predictable measure for which (4.11) holds for all predictable functions f as above.

Thus, if we define a stochastic process $X(t)$ as integral $X(t) = \int_0^t \int_E f(e, s)\mu(de, ds)$, then the predictable compensator of $X(t)$ will be the integral of the same predictable function f with respect to the compensator measure v:

$$A(t) = \int_0^t \int_E f(e, s)v(de, ds).$$

Thus, by specifying one random measure (v), we have defined the predictable compensator of all stochastic processes that arise as integrals w.r.t. μ.

Very often, we can separate the probability *that an event occurs* from the conditional distribution of the marker *given that an event has occurred*. In the continuous-time case, we assumed enough regularity[6] to ensure $\int_t^{t+\Delta t} \int_E v(de, dt) < \infty$ for all $\Delta t > 0$. Thus if we can write the compensator measure as

$$v(de, dt) = K(t, de)dA(t), \quad \text{with} \int_E K(t, de) = 1 \quad (4.12)$$

then $K(t, de)$ is the conditional distribution of the marker at time t, and $dA(t)$ gives the probability of having a jump in the next small time step. Of course, K and A can both also depend on the state of nature $\omega \in \Omega$. In general, a decomposition like (4.12) is not always possible.

---

[5] For example, f must be integrable over E.
[6] We assumed a finite number of jumps over finite time intervals a.s.

The process A in equation (4.12) is the predictable compensator of the event counting process $N(t)$ of the marked point process

$$N(t) = \sum_{\{i \mid \tau_i \le t\}} 1 = \int_0^t \int_E \mu(de, dt).$$

Equation (4.12) gives the best intuition on what the marked point process does. It gives the compensator of the arrival counting process, i.e. how often and with what probability or intensity the events arrive, and it also gives the conditional distribution $K(t, de)$ of the marker, given that an event happens at time t. These quantities must be present in every model with jumps or defaults anyway. Random measures are just the correct notation in such situations, and they allow a solid mathematical foundation of the model.

4.6.1 Random measures in discrete time

The concept of the compensator measure is best understood in a discrete-time setting. We divide the interval $[0, T]$ into N intervals of equal length $\Delta t = T/N$, and let $0 = t_0, t_1, \ldots, t_N = T$ be the points on our time grid. We move all jump events to the next grid time, i.e. $\tau_i = t_n$ if $\tau_i \in]t_{n-1}, t_n]$. Then the jump measure will only have mass at grid times t_n and we can write $\mu_n(de) := \mu(\{t_n\}, de)$ for the jump measure at time t_n.

The first question to answer is: Why do we need *predictable functions*? We saw that all quantities $X(t)$ we were interested in could be represented as integrals of functions f from $\Omega \times [0, T] \times E$ to $\mathbb{R}$ with respect to the jump measure $\mu(de, dt)$:

$$X(\omega, t) = \int_0^t \int_E f(s, e)\mu(de, ds).$$

In particular, in the discrete-time setup, we can write the increments of X as:

$$X(t_n) - X(t_{n-1}) = \int_E f(t_n, e)\mu_n(de). \tag{4.13}$$

So far, the function f can be fully stochastic. First, it must be measurable with respect to $\mathcal{F}_{t_n}$, otherwise $X(t_n)$ would not be adapted. It can depend on other state variables of the model, and in fact it could even depend on the realisation of the marker Y itself. But if we admit every kind of stochastic development for f, we do not need the marker any more. Just modelling the arrival times would be sufficient, because we could artificially create the marker by defining $f(\tau_i, 1) = Y_i$. (Remember, we had complete freedom in the definition of f.) Any other stochastic function $g(t, e)$ of the marker can then be rewritten as a function $h(t, 1) = g(t, f(t, 1))$ which again does not depend on the marker value. Thus, all randomness in the realisation of the marker could be absorbed in the randomness in the development of function f.

In a clean modelling method we want to take the opposite approach: instead of absorbing all randomness of the marker Y into the function f, we want to absorb as much randomness of the function f into the marker Y as we possibly can. The realisation of the marker represents the "innovation" in the model, the nature of the random event that takes place at the associated stopping time τ, while the function f represents the effect that this innovation has on some dependent variable. We want the marker to represent the nature of the random event *completely*, and f to be *only* the reaction, given the event. This pins down the freedom that we had in the specification of the model. Mathematically, we must restrict the possible random variation of the function f to *predictable functions*: for all marker values $e \in E$ and all time points t_n, the value $f(t_n, e)$ is measurable with respect to the filtration $\mathcal{F}_{t_{n-1}}$. At t_{n-1}, we already know the value of the function f, *conditional on the realisation of Y*.

In a model of a financial market this makes sense: $f(t_n, e)$ describes the reaction of a state variable to a marked point event, *given that* the marker takes the value $Y_i = e$ at the time t_n. The qualitative nature of this reaction is encoded in $f(t_n, \cdot)$, and this can be known one time step earlier, but the precise value of the marker Y is only revealed at time t_n.

Thus, we can view the function $f(t_n, e)$ in equation (4.13) as the *conditional increment of X between time t_{n-1} and time t_n*, conditional on an event occurring at time t_n and the marker taking value e:

$$X(t_n) = X(t_{n-1}) + f(t_n, e) \quad \text{if } \tau_i = t_n \text{ and } Y_i = e \text{ for some } i \in \mathbb{N}. \tag{4.14}$$

From the concept of a predictable function it is only a small step to the idea of a compensator measure. Just like a predictable function f gives the conditional *realisations* of a functional of a marked point process, the compensator measure gives the corresponding *conditional probabilities*.

$v_n(de)$ is the probability of a jump at time t_n with marker $Y \in de$, as seen from t_{n-1}:

$$v_n(de) := \mathbf{P}[Y \in de \wedge \tau = t_n \mid \mathcal{F}_{t_{n-1}}]. \tag{4.15}$$

Being conditioned on information at t_{n-1}, it is clear that $v_n(\cdot)$ is *predictable* if we view it as a stochastic process in time t_n. It can indeed be stochastic, as the examples below will show.

Using the compensator process v_n, we can now write down the *expected* increment of the process $X(t)$ over $]t_{n-1}, t_n]$:

$$\mathbf{E}[X(t_n) - X(t_{n-1}) \mid \mathcal{F}_{t_{n-1}}] = \int_E f(t_n, e)v_n(de). \tag{4.16}$$

Using this conditional expectation we can construct the predictable compensator of the process $X(t)$. Just define $A(0) = 0$ and for later times:

$$A(t_n) - A(t_{n-1}) := \int_E f(t_n, e)v_n(de).$$

Then A will be predictable and $M(t_n) = X(t_n) - A(t_n)$ will be a martingale. This proves the discrete-time version of equation (4.11).

Very often, we can even separate the probability *that an event occurs* from the conditional distribution of the marker *given that an event has occurred*. In the discrete-time example the conditional distribution $K_n(de)$ of the markers is just a normalisation of v_n:

$$K_n(de) := \frac{1}{\int\limits_E v_n(de)} v_n(de),$$

provided that the denominator is not zero or infinity. This concludes our excursion to discrete time.

4.7 EXAMPLES FOR COMPENSATOR MEASURES

When we set up a stochastic credit risk model our task is always the description of a suitable compensator measure. The jump measure is only a description of the *realisations* of the jump times and sizes, while the compensator measure encodes the *distribution* of the jump times and sizes. When we design a model we want to produce a realistic distribution, thus we have to be very careful and precise when defining the compensator measure. The realisations on the other hand can be drawn by simple Monte Carlo simulation according to the initial distribution, and can be viewed as an output of the distribution that was the input.

In order to build the intuition for the continuous-time case, we now give some examples of marked point processes with their associated compensator measures.

Poisson process $N(t)$ with intensity λ

- Arrival times: $\tau_i =$ time of the ith jump of N.
- Marker: jump size $= 1$. Thus the mark space is trivial: $E = \{1\}$.
- Compensator measure:

$$\nu(de, dt) = \delta_{Y=1}(de)\lambda dt.$$

- Conditional distribution:

$$dA(t) = \lambda dt, \qquad K(de) = \delta_{Y=1}(de).$$

Cox process with stochastic intensity $\lambda(t)$

- Compensator measure:

$$\nu(de, dt) = \delta_{Y=1}(de)\lambda(t)dt.$$

- Conditional distribution:

$$dA(t) = \lambda(t)dt, \qquad K(de) = \delta_{Y=1}(de).$$

Marked inhomogeneous Poisson process I

- Marker: Y is drawn from a standard normal distribution at jump times.
- The realisation of the marker is only known at the time of the jump, it is *not* predictable.
- Compensator measure:

$$\nu(de, dt) = \frac{1}{\sqrt{2\pi}} \exp\left\{-\frac{1}{2}e^2\right\} \lambda(t)de dt.$$

- Conditional distribution:

$$dA(t) = \lambda(t)dt \qquad K(de) = \frac{1}{\sqrt{2\pi}} \exp\left\{-\frac{1}{2}e^2\right\}(de).$$

Marked Poisson process II

- Marker: Y is the value of another stochastic process $S(t)$ at the time of the jump. $S(t)$ follows a lognormal Brownian motion and $S(t)$ is observable at time t:

$$\frac{dS}{S} = \alpha dt + \sigma dW.$$

- Compensator measure:

$$v(de, dt) = \delta_{Y=S(t-)}(de)\lambda(t)dt.$$

Note that the compensator measure is not really different from the Poisson process case. This is because the value of the marker is predictable (it follows a predictable process).
- Conditional distribution:

$$dA(t) = \lambda(t)dt \qquad K(de) = \delta_{Y=S(t-)}(de).$$

Lognormal jump diffusion process

- Jump times triggered by Poisson process with intensity λ.
- Marker: Y, the log of the jump size, standard normally distributed, density:

$$\frac{1}{\sqrt{2\pi}} \exp\left\{-\frac{1}{2}e^2\right\}.$$

- $S(t)$ follows a lognormal diffusion process when no jumps occur. At jump times, S is multiplied with a lognormal increment. The s.d.e. for the development of S is:

$$dS(t) = \sigma S(t-)dW(t) + \int_{\mathbb{R}} S(t-)(\exp(e) - 1)(\mu(de, dt) - v(de, dt)). \qquad (4.17)$$

- The compensator measure is:

$$v(de, dt) = \frac{1}{\sqrt{2\pi}} \exp\left\{-\frac{1}{2}e^2\right\}\lambda(t)dedt.$$

First hitting time process

- The arrival time is the first time the lognormal diffusion process $S(t)$ hits a barrier $\overline{K}$. Here:

$$dS(t) = \alpha dt + \sigma S(t-)dW(t). \qquad (4.18)$$

- No marker.
- Compensator measure:

$$v(dt) = dA(t) \quad \text{where} \quad \begin{cases} dA(t) = 1 & \text{if the barrier is hit } S(t) = \overline{K}, \\ dA(t) = 0 & \text{otherwise.} \end{cases}$$

Obviously, here the compensator measure only describes what was known anyway, the event of the default arrival. Because the default arrival is predictable, its predictable compensator will be the process itself.

A (maybe not so) unusual process

- The compensator measure is:

$$v(de, dt) = \frac{1}{|e|} \, dedt \quad \text{for } 0 \notin de. \tag{4.19}$$

Note that we cannot form the conditional distribution of the jump sizes as the integral over $E = \mathbb{R}$ will not converge.
- This process has an infinite number of extremely small jumps, and a few larger jumps, a property that is shared by many so-called *Levy processes*. They are useful in the modelling of share price and share index movements.
- Let $[a, b]$ be an interval not containing zero. Then jumps of a size in $[a, b]$ occur with an intensity of:

$$\lambda_{[a,b]} = \int_a^b \frac{1}{|e|} de.$$

Thus we can view this process as being triggered by a number of Poisson processes: one Poisson process for each small interval on the mark space $\mathbb{R}$. The intensity will converge to infinity the closer we get to the marker value zero.
- Examples like this one make the stochastic analysis of marked point processes very complicated. We exclude such examples by assuming that our marked point process only has a finite number of jumps in a finite interval.

A very simple process

- Jumps occur at $\tau_1 = 2$, $\tau_2 = 4$, $\tau_3 = 8, \ldots$
- This is known at the beginning.
- Compensator measure: everything is totally predictable, so the compensator will be the jump measure

$$v(de, dt) = \delta_{t=\tau_i}(dt),$$

where δ denotes the Dirac delta function.

4.8   ITÔ'S LEMMA FOR JUMP PROCESSES

First, in order to handle the jumps correctly, we need the following notation. The processes $X(t)$ considered here are right-continuous with left limits (RCLL), and they have only a finite number of jumps over finite time intervals a.s. For every path of the process $X(t)$ we define:

- the left limit $X_-(t) := \lim_{h \searrow 0} X(t - h)$, $X_-(0) = X(0)$ (we also write $X(t-) := X_-(t)$ for the left limit),
- the jumps $\Delta X(t) := X(t) - X_-(t)$,
- the discontinuous part $X^d(t) := \sum_{s \le t} \Delta X(s)$,
- the continuous part $X^c(t) := X(t) - X^d(t)$.

At jump times of X, the process X jumps by the amount $\Delta X(t)$. These jumps are collected in the process X^d, at all other times X^d is constant. The process X^c on the other hand represents the continuous part of the path of X.

Itô's lemma is a very powerful tool to derive pricing equations for derivative securities. Because it does not add any additional complexity, we give Itô's lemma for an extremely general class of stochastic processes, the semi-martingales with a finite number of jumps over finite time intervals a.s. All processes that we will consider in this book are members of this class of processes but there are exceptions to this class in the literature.[7]

Theorem 4.3 (Itô's lemma)   *Let $X = (X^1, \ldots, X^n)$ be an n-dimensional semi-martingale with a finite number of jumps, and f a twice continuously differentiable function on $\mathbb{R}^d$. Then $f(X)$ is also a semi-martingale, and we have:*

$$
f(X(t)) - f(X(0)) = \sum_{i=1}^n \int_0^t \frac{\partial f(X_-(s))}{\partial x_i} dX^{c,i}(s) + \frac{1}{2} \sum_{i,j=1}^n \int_0^t \frac{\partial^2 f(X_-(s))}{\partial x_i \, \partial x_j} d\langle X^{c,i}, X^{c,j} \rangle(s)
$$
$$
+ \sum_{s \le t} \Delta f(X(s)). \tag{4.20}
$$

Proof.   A formal proof of this theorem can be found in Jacod and Shiryaev (1988).   □

In order to account for jumps, we only have to add a jump term $\Delta f = \lim_{h \to 0} f(X(t)) - f(X(t - h))$ to the familiar form of Itô's lemma for continuous processes which we recognise in the first line. There is no additional complication, unlike the transition from standard calculus to stochastic calculus which introduced the cross-variation terms and the second derivatives.

The jump times τ_i and the jump sizes $\Delta X(\tau_i)$ of X together define a marked point process. This marked point process has an associated jump measure μ_X. This measure puts a Dirac

---

[7] There are processes that have an infinite number of jumps over a finite time interval, for example most Levy processes are of this type, but we will not consider them here.

measure of 1 on the times of the jumps and the sizes of the jumps $(\tau_i, \Delta X(\tau_i))$ in the space $\mathbb{R}_+ \times \mathbb{R}^n$, and it will also have a compensator measure ν_X. Using these measures, we can re-express the dynamics of X as:

$$dX(t) = dX^c(t) + \int_{\mathbb{R}^n} x \mu_X(dx, dt). \tag{4.21}$$

Itô's lemma takes the following form.

Theorem 4.4 (Itô's lemma with random measures) *Let X and f be defined as in Theorem 4.3. Then $f(X)$ is also a semi-martingale, and we have:*

$$
\begin{aligned}
f(X(t)) - f(X(0)) &= \sum_{i=1}^{n} \int_0^t \frac{\partial f(X_-(s))}{\partial x_i} dX^{c,i}(s) \\
&+ \frac{1}{2} \sum_{i,j=1}^{n} \frac{\partial^2 f(X_-(s))}{\partial x_i \partial x_j} d\langle X^{c,i}, X^{c,j}\rangle(s) \\
&+ \int_0^t \int_{\mathbb{R}^n} f(X_-(s) + x) - f(X_-(s))\mu_X(dx, ds).
\end{aligned} \tag{4.22}
$$

These versions of Itô's lemma only hold under the assumption of "finite number of jumps in finite intervals". There is a more general version (again to be found in Jacod and Shiryaev, 1988) which is valid for general semi-martingales but is a bit more complicated.

4.9   APPLICATIONS OF ITÔ'S LEMMA

In most applications, the dynamics of X can be written as a jump diffusion process of the form

$$dX^i = \alpha_i dt + \sum_{k=1}^{K} \sigma_{ik} dW_k + \int_{\mathbb{R}^n} h_i(x)\mu_X(dx, dt), \tag{4.23}$$

for $i = 1, \ldots, n$. The process is driven by a K-dimensional Brownian motion W and the jump measure μ_X. Drift α_i, volatilities σ_i and jump sizes h_i can all be predictable stochastic processes.

Furthermore, the jump measure μ_X of X has a compensator measure ν_X which can be decomposed according to (4.12):

$$\nu_X(dx, dt) = K(t, dx)dA(t).$$

We call $\overline{\Delta}(t) := \int_{\mathbb{R}^n} x K(t, dx)$ the average jump size, conditional on a jump at time t. Then Itô's lemma takes the following form.

Theorem 4.5 (Itô's lemma for jump diffusion processes) *Let f be defined as in Theorem 4.3, and let X have the dynamics (4.23). Then $f(X)$ is also a semi-martingale, and we have:*

$$
f(X(t)) - f(X(0)) = \sum_{i=1}^{n} \int_0^t \frac{\partial f(X_-(s))}{\partial x_i} \alpha_i dt + \sum_{i=1}^{n} \sum_{k=1}^{K} \int_0^t \frac{\partial f(X_-(s))}{\partial x_i} \sigma_{ik} dW_k
$$

$$
+ \frac{1}{2} \sum_{i,j=1}^{n} \frac{\partial^2 f(X_-(s))}{\partial x_i \partial x_j} (\sigma \sigma^T)_{ij} dt
$$

$$
+ \int_0^t \int_{\mathbb{R}^n} f(X_-(s) + x) - f(X_-(s)) \mu_X(dx, ds). \tag{4.24}
$$

4.9.1 Predictable compensators for jump processes

It is often important to derive the predictable compensator of $f(X)$, for example to impose a risk-neutral drift on a derivative price. In matrix and vector form the process X can be written as

$$
X(t) = X(0) + \int_0^t \alpha ds + \int_0^t \sigma dW(s) + \int_0^t \int_{\mathbb{R}^n} x \mu_X(dx, ds) \tag{4.25}
$$

and also

$$
X(t) = X(0) + \int_0^t \alpha ds + \int_0^t \overline{\Delta}(s) dA(s) + M(t). \tag{4.26}
$$

Equation (4.26) is the decomposition of the process X into a predictable finite variation process $\int_0^t \alpha ds + \int_0^t \overline{\Delta}(s) dA(s)$, and a local martingale $M(t)$. The local martingale has the form

$$
M(t) = \int_0^t \sigma dW(s) + \int_0^t \int_{\mathbb{R}^n} x \mu_X(dx, ds) - \int_0^t \int_{\mathbb{R}^n} x \nu_X(dx, ds). \tag{4.27}
$$

The predictable compensator of $f(X)$ follows in a similar way from Itô's lemma 4.5:

$$
f(X(t)) - f(X(0)) = \sum_{i=1}^{n} \int_0^t \frac{\partial f(X_-(s))}{\partial x_i} \alpha ds + \frac{1}{2} \sum_{i,j=1}^{n} \frac{\partial^2 f(X_-(s))}{\partial x_i \partial x_j} (\sigma \sigma^T)_{ij} ds
$$

$$
+ \int_0^t \left[\int_{\mathbb{R}^n} f(X_-(s) + x) K(s, dx) - f(X_-(s)) \right] dA(s)
$$

$$
+ \int_0^t f(X_-(s) + x) - f(X_-(s))(\mu_X(dx, ds) - K(t, dx) dA(s))
$$

$$
+ \sum_{i=1}^{n} \int_0^t \frac{\partial f(X_-(s))}{\partial x_i} \sigma dW(s). \tag{4.28}
$$

The drift (and predictable compensator) of $f(X)$ can be found in the first two lines of (4.28).

It consists of the well-known drift components from Itô's lemma: the first derivative with drift X^c and the cross-derivative Itô terms. In addition to this, there is a term

$$\int_0^t \left[\int_{\mathbb{R}^n} f(X_-(s) + x)K(s, dx) - f(X_-(s)) \right] dA(s)$$

which compensates for the influence of the jumps. The integral $\int_{\mathbb{R}^n} f(X_-(s) + x)K(s, dx)$ represents the expected value of f after a jump at time s.

Equations like (4.28) are used in finance whenever a jump process with finite number of jumps is present. The use of jump and compensator measures allows a clean derivation of these equations and interpretation of the terms.

4.9.2 Itô product rule and Itô quotient rule

The Itô product and quotient rules are two very useful equations that give the dynamics of products and fractions of processes driven by jump diffusion processes. They can be derived directly from Itô's lemma. Let the dynamics of Y and Z be given by:

$$\frac{dY}{Y_-} = \alpha^y ds + \sum_{k=1}^K \sigma_k^y dW_k(s) + \int_{\mathbb{R}^n} h^y(x)\mu_X(dx, dt), \tag{4.29}$$

$$\frac{dZ}{Z_-} = \alpha^z ds + \sum_{k=1}^K \sigma_k^z dW_k(s) + \int_{\mathbb{R}^n} h^z(x)\mu_X(dx, dt). \tag{4.30}$$

Y and Z are both driven by the jumps in X (through μ_X), but react differently to them. The functions $h^y(x)$ and $h^z(x)$ give the relative jump sizes of Y and Z as a function of the jump in x, therefore they map $\mathbb{R}^n \to \mathbb{R}$. Because we want Y and Z to remain positive, the jumps must satisfy $h^y > -1$ and $h^z > -1$. We assume $Y > 0$ and $Z > 0$ a.s. and that all drift and diffusion coefficients and the functions h^y and h^z are predictable and sufficiently regular.

The product YZ has the following dynamics:

$$\frac{d(YZ)}{Y_-Z_-} = (\alpha^y + \alpha^z)dt + \frac{1}{2} \sum_{k=1}^K \sigma_k^y \sigma_k^z dt + \sum_{k=1}^K (\sigma_k^y + \sigma_k^z)dW_k$$

$$+ \int_{\mathbb{R}^n} (h^y(x)h^z(x) - 1)\mu_X(dx, dt). \tag{4.31}$$

The ratio Y/Z has the following dynamics:

$$\frac{d(Y/Z)}{Y_-/Z_-} = (\alpha^y - \alpha^z)dt - \sum_{k=1}^K (\sigma_k^y - \sigma_k^z)\sigma_k^z dt + \sum_{k=1}^K (\sigma_k^y - \sigma_k^z)dW_k$$

$$+ \int_{\mathbb{R}^n} \frac{h^y(x) - h^z(x)}{1 + h^z(x)} \mu_X(dx, dt). \tag{4.32}$$

For illustration, here is the derivation of the new jump influence function $h^{y/z}$:

$$\Delta\left(\frac{Y}{Z}\right) = \frac{Y_- + \Delta Y}{Z_- + \Delta Z} - \frac{Y_-}{Z_-} = \frac{Y_-}{Z_-} \frac{\dfrac{\Delta Y}{Y_-} - \dfrac{\Delta Z}{Z_-}}{1 + \dfrac{\Delta Z}{Z_-}}$$

$$= \frac{Y_-}{Z_-} \int_{\mathbb{R}^n} \frac{h^y(x) - h^z(x)}{1 + h^z(x)} \mu_X(dx, ds). \tag{4.33}$$

4.9.3 The stochastic exponential

The stochastic exponential $\mathcal{E}(X)$ is defined for stochastic processes X with $\Delta X \geq -1$. It is a generalisation of the "exp" function from classical analysis, and like the "exp" function it describes growth processes. Stochastic growth processes occur in many places in mathematical finance and knowledge of the solution of this stochastic differential equation is extremely useful in a large number of applications.

Definition 4.7 (stochastic exponential) *Let X be a stochastic process with $\Delta X \geq -1$. Then $Y(t)$ is called the stochastic exponential of X iff $Y(0) = 1$ and Y solves the stochastic differential equation*

$$dY(t) = Y_-(t)dX(t). \tag{4.34}$$

We write $\mathcal{E}(X)$ for the stochastic exponential of X.

Theorem 4.6 *The solution of (4.34) is (for X with finitely many jumps):*

$$\mathcal{E}(X)(t) = Y(t) = \exp\left\{X^c(t) - X^c(0) - \frac{1}{2}\langle X^c\rangle(t)\right\} \prod_{s \leq t}(1 + \Delta X(s)). \tag{4.35}$$

Furthermore, if X is a local martingale, then Y will also be a local martingale.

Proof. Theorem 4.6 is easily verified using Itô's lemma (see e.g. Jacod and Shiryaev, 1988). □

From the general solution formula (4.35) we see the following. The jumps in X contribute a product of discrete factors to the process Y, while the continuous movements of X contribute an exponential term that will be familiar to many readers from stochastic analysis for continuous processes. If $\Delta X = -1$, the process Y jumps to zero. This is no surprise because dX is the growth rate of Y. If this growth rate is -100%, then the process falls to zero. A very useful property of the stochastic exponential is also the fact that the martingale property is preserved.

4.10   MARTINGALE MEASURE, FUNDAMENTAL PRICING RULE AND INCOMPLETENESS

Definition 4.8 (martingale measure)   *Let Q be a probability measure. If for every dividend-free traded asset with price process $p(t)$, the discounted price process $p(t)/b(t)$ is a martingale under Q, then Q is called a martingale measure (or spot-martingale measure). Here $b(t) = \exp\{\int_0^t r(s)ds\}$ is the value of the default-free continuously compounded bank account at time t, and the default-free continuously compounded discount factor from t to T is defined as $\beta(t) = 1/b(t)$.*

The central importance of the martingale measure in mathematical finance is based upon the fact that under some technical conditions the existence of an equivalent martingale measure is equivalent to absence of arbitrage in the underlying market (see Harrison and Pliska, 1981).

If we add another security to the assets in the market, we must ensure that the discounted price process of this new security is again a martingale. Then we have found an arbitrage-free price for this asset. The method by which this can be achieved is known as the fundamental pricing rule.

Theorem 4.7 (fundamental pricing rule)   *Let X be an $\mathcal{F}_T$-measurable random variable that is bounded from below, and let Q be a martingale measure on the market for the underlying assets. An arbitrage-free price of a new contingent claim paying off X at $T > t$ is:*

$$p_X(t) = \mathbf{E}^Q \left[\frac{b(t)}{b(T)} X \,\middle|\, \mathcal{F}_t \right].$$ (4.36)

The following local condition is necessary for equation (4.36) to hold:

$$\mathbf{E}^Q[dp_X \mid \mathcal{F}_t] = p_X(t-)r(t)dt.$$ (4.37)

The fundamental pricing rule achieves two aims. First, the new discounted price process $p_X \beta$ is a uniformly integrable martingale (hence the market with the added asset will still be arbitrage-free) and second, the price process p_X has the final value X.

If the dynamics of $p_X(t)$ remain regular at all times, condition (4.37) is also sufficient. In this case we have ensured absence of arbitrage in the model as long as all prices p of traded assets in the model have a local drift of rp.

As an illustration let us derive the drift of an asset price with jumps under the spot martingale measure Q. Assume Y is the price process of a traded asset with Q-dynamics given in equation (4.29). Let $Z := b$ be the continuously compounded bank account with $db = rbdt$, and take the compensator $\nu_X(dx, dt) =: K(dx)\lambda dt$ for the jumps. Then by the Itô quotient rule (4.32) and criterion (4.37) we must have:

$$\alpha^y(t) = r(t) - \int_{\mathbb{R}^n} h^y(x)K(dx)\lambda(t),$$ (4.38)

i.e. the diffusion drift of the asset price process Y must be corrected by the average influence of the jumps that this asset may have.

These results suggest the following model building strategy in order to derive an arbitrage-free model of a financial market. First, a set of fundamental securities is chosen. The prices of these securities are either modelled directly or as a function of a set of fundamental state variables. Then, using equation (4.37) the dynamics of the state variables are modelled such that the discounted price processes are martingales. Finally, derivatives and contingent claims can be valued using the fundamental pricing rule.

Unfortunately, equation (4.37) only enforces the martingale property locally. If the final value of the price process is already fixed (e.g. a bond's final payoff), this condition must also be satisfied by the price process. In a good modelling framework this additional condition can be satisfied very easily, in other modelling frameworks this may be complicated or even impossible.

Another quite opposite problem arises if there are many possible choices for the dynamics of the prices of the fundamental securities that all satisfy the martingale property. This situation can only occur if at least some contingent claims cannot be priced uniquely by absence of arbitrage, it is known as *market incompleteness*.

If the martingale measure is not unique one will get different prices for a contingent claim depending on which martingale measure is used. This is obviously not a very satisfactory situation, and unfortunately in credit risk in particular incomplete markets arise very often. Nevertheless, even in incomplete markets the martingale pricing approach does not lose all of its power. Prices may not be unique any more, but for any given martingale measure the resulting price system still satisfies absence of arbitrage. In particular, all arbitrage price bounds will be automatically satisfied. Furthermore, many potential martingale measures imply extremely unrealistic (but not impossible) behaviour of the state variables. If such extreme martingale measures are ruled out, one can further narrow the resulting price bounds.

Market incompleteness cannot be avoided in credit risk modelling, it is there in the markets and it should also be reflected in the model. It is not a fault of the martingale modelling approach, in fact one can view it as an advantage of the martingale modelling approach that this problem is highlighted clearly. Market incompleteness adds to the responsibilities of the modeller and to the requirements of the model.

The modeller will have to make choices in order to arrive at a unique price or at narrow price bounds for the credit derivative under consideration. Such choices could be to only model linear credit spread curves, or the choice of an assumed recovery rate or a particular distribution of a recovery rate. The modeller and the user must understand the implications of these choices, and they should check the results for robustness.

The model should be set up in such a way that the modeller's choices can be made in a setup where it is easier to build an intuition. Thus it may be very hard to make an assumption on the dynamics of an unobservable firm's value, but easier to decide whether there should be a large difference between the conditional survival probabilities between years 9 and 10 and years 10 and 11. Or it may be easier to build an intuition on the correlation of the value of two firms' assets than on the correlation between the default indicator functions of these firms.

In some models, assumptions that remove market incompleteness are well hidden in seemingly innocuous points of the model's setup (e.g. by assuming that the recovery rate at default is predictable). We consider this not to be a good strategy[8] and try to highlight these assumptions and their implications. Finally, it should be easy to change such assumptions that remove market incompleteness in order to check their effect on the final price of the credit derivative.

---

[8] Although it may be a very good strategy to sell the model to an unsuspecting audience.

4.11 CHANGE OF NUMERAIRE AND PRICING MEASURE

The change of numeraire/change of measure technique is a very useful tool to price derivative securities. It exploits the fact that many pricing problems become much simpler when the prices are redefined relative to another basic "price unit asset", the new *numeraire* asset. If we change the definition of the prices, we will also have to change the corresponding state prices, and thus there will be another pricing probability measure. The following theorem will describe how this can be achieved.

4.11.1 The Radon–Nikodym theorem

A fundamental result of measure theory (the theorem of Radon–Nikodym; see Jacod and Shiryaev, 1988) states that the change of probability measure from a measure Q to another measure $P \ll Q$ is uniquely characterised by the corresponding Radon–Nikodym density L. This density is a non-negative random variable with expectation one: $\mathbf{E}^Q[L] = 1$ and $L \geq 0$. Then, expected values under the new measure P can be expressed as follows:

$$\mathbf{E}^P[X] = \mathbf{E}^Q[LX] \quad \text{for all measurable } X. \tag{4.39}$$

Intuitively speaking, if a state of nature $\omega \in \Omega$ had probability $\mathbf{Q}[\omega]$ under the probability measure Q, it now has probability $\mathbf{P}[\omega] := L(\omega)\mathbf{Q}[\omega]$ under the new probability measure P. This relationship is also written as:

$$\frac{d\mathbf{P}}{d\mathbf{Q}} = L.$$

For this reason, L is also interpreted as a *likelihood ratio* between the two probability measures. The restriction $L \geq 0$ ensures that the probabilities under P are non-negative, and $\mathbf{E}^Q[L] = 1$ ensures that they sum up to one.

In a dynamic model, we also want to analyse stochastic processes. For this we define the *Radon–Nikodym density process*

$$L(t) := \mathbf{E}^Q[L \mid \mathcal{F}_t]. \tag{4.40}$$

If X is $\mathcal{F}_T$-measurable, the law of iterated expectations yields the following result:

$$
\begin{aligned}
\mathbf{E}^P[X \mid \mathcal{F}_t] &= \mathbf{E}^Q[LX \mid \mathcal{F}_t] \\
&= \mathbf{E}^Q[\mathbf{E}^Q[LX \mid \mathcal{F}_T] \mid \mathcal{F}_t] = \mathbf{E}^Q[\mathbf{E}^Q[L \mid \mathcal{F}_T]X \mid \mathcal{F}_t] \\
&= \mathbf{E}^Q[L(T)X \mid \mathcal{F}_t] = L(t)\mathbf{E}^Q\left[\frac{L(T)}{L(t)}X \,\middle|\, \mathcal{F}_t\right].
\end{aligned}
\tag{4.41}
$$

The Radon–Nikodym density process is reached by conditioning L on the information at time t, by projection on the $\mathcal{F}_t$-measurable random variables. This projection construction ensures that $L(t)$ is a martingale (in fact, a uniformly integrable martingale). The expectation property $\mathbf{E}^Q[L] = 1$ translates into the initial value of $L(0) = 1$.

4.11.2   The Girsanov theorem

A change of measure is a change of probabilities, but not of *realisations*. Therefore, the paths of the random variables remain unchanged, but all probabilistic properties are changed. In particular, a process W_Q which was a Brownian motion under Q need not be a Brownian motion under P. Its paths will be the same, but the increment over $[t, t + \Delta t]$ will not have a normal *probability distribution* with mean zero and variance Δt – we changed the probabilities. For marked point processes the situation is similar. The jump measure $\mu(\cdot)$ will be unchanged (the realisations did not change), but the compensator measure $\nu(\cdot)$ will change, because the compensator measure describes the probabilities.

Girsanov's theorem answers several questions in this context. It describes how the Radon–Nikodym density L of a change of probability measure from one probability measure Q to an equivalent measure P determines which processes are Brownian motions under the new measure, what happens to the old Brownian motions, and which form the compensator of a jump process takes under the new measure. It also shows how these changes are connected to the representation of the dynamics of the Radon–Nikodym *density process $L(t)$* as a stochastic process.

We give a general form of this theorem which is valid for probability spaces that support marked point processes and diffusions. For a proof see Jacod and Shiryaev (1988).

Theorem 4.8 (Girsanov theorem: marked point processes)   *Let $(\Omega, (\mathcal{F}_t)_{(t \geq 0)}, Q)$ be a filtered probability space which supports an n-dimensional Q-Brownian motion $W_Q(t)$ and a marked point process $\mu(de, dt)$. The marker e of the marked point process is drawn from the mark space $(E, \mathcal{E})$. The compensator of $\mu(de, dt)$ is assumed to take the form $\nu_Q(de, dt) = K_Q(de)\lambda_Q(t)dt$ under Q. Here $\lambda_Q(t)$ is the Q-intensity of the arrivals of the point process, and $K_Q(t, de)$ is the Q-conditional distribution of the marker on $(E, \mathcal{E})$.*

Let φ be an n-dimensional predictable process and $\Phi(e, t)$ a non-negative predictable function with

$$\int_0^t \|\varphi(s)\|^2 ds < \infty \quad and \quad \int_0^t \int_E |\Phi(e, s)| K_Q(s, de)\lambda_Q(s)ds < \infty$$

for finite t. Define the process $L(t)$ by $L(0) = 1$ and

$$\frac{dL(t)}{L(t-)} = \varphi(t)dW_Q(t) + \int_E (\Phi(e, t) - 1)(\mu(de, dt) - \nu_Q(de, dt)). \qquad (4.42)$$

Assume that $\mathbf{E}^Q[L(t)] = 1$ for finite t. Define the probability measure P with

$$\frac{dP}{dQ}\bigg|_{\mathcal{F}_t} = L(t) \quad \forall t > 0. \qquad (4.43)$$

It holds that:

(i) The process W_P is a P-Brownian motion, where $W_P(0) = 0$ and

$$dW_P(t) := dW_Q(t) - \varphi(t)dt. \qquad (4.44)$$

(ii) *The predictable compensator of μ under P is*

$$\nu_P(de, dt) = \Phi(t, e)\nu_Q(de, dt). \tag{4.45}$$

(iii) *Define* $\psi(t) := \int_E \Phi(e, t)K_Q(t, de)$ *and* $L_E(e, t) := \Phi(e, t)/\psi(t)$ *for* $\psi(t) > 0$, $L_E(e, t) = 1$ *otherwise. The intensity of the counting process of the arrivals of the marked point process under P is*

$$\lambda_P(t) = \psi(t)\lambda_Q(t). \tag{4.46}$$

(iv) *The conditional distribution of the marker under P is*

$$K_P(t, de) = L_E(e, t)K_Q(de). \tag{4.47}$$

4.12   THE CHANGE OF MEASURE/CHANGE OF NUMERAIRE TECHNIQUE

Any given spot price $p(t)$ (using discounting with the bank account $b(t)$) can be transformed to a price $p'(t)$ under a different numeraire $A(t)$ via $p'(t) := p(t)/A(t)$. For example, many traders are used to thinking in forward prices (i.e. dollars at a future date T) instead of spot prices (dollars today), or expressing option payoffs in a foreign currency.

We assume that the Q-price process $A(t)$ of the new numeraire asset is non-negative and that A has no intermediate payoffs. Using equation (4.36) the price under the new numeraire is

$$
\begin{aligned}
p'(t) = \frac{p(t)}{A(t)} &= \frac{b(t)}{A(t)}\mathbf{E}^Q\left[\frac{A(T)}{b(T)}X' \,\middle|\, \mathcal{F}_t\right] \\
&= \mathbf{E}^Q\left[\frac{L_A(T)}{L_A(t)}X' \,\middle|\, \mathcal{F}_t\right] = \mathbf{E}^{P_A}[X' \mid \mathcal{F}_t],
\end{aligned}
\tag{4.48}
$$

where $X' = X/A(T)$ is the payoff (final value) X of the contingent claim in terms of the new numeraire asset A. In equation (4.48) a new pricing measure P_A is defined by the Radon–Nikodym density process $L_A(t)$:

$$\left.\frac{dP_A}{dQ}\right|_{\mathcal{F}_t} = L_A(t) := \frac{1}{A(0)}\frac{A(t)}{b(t)}. \tag{4.49}$$

Because $A(t)$ is the b-price of a traded asset, the discounted price process $L_A(t)$ is a non-negative Q-martingale with initial value $L_A(0) = 1$. $L_A(t)$ is therefore a valid Radon–Nikodym density process and P_A is a well-defined probability measure.

By equation (4.48), prices p' in the numeraire A are P_A-martingales. Thus the calculation of the initial price p' can be reduced to the calculation of the expected final value X' under a changed probability measure P_A. This new probability measure arises directly from the change of numeraire; the new numeraire A and probability measure P_A are inseparably linked.

This change of measure technique would not be useful if there was no way to calculate the new expectation $\mathbf{E}^{P_A}[X]$ in (4.48) other than going back and evaluating $\mathbf{E}^Q[L_A(T)X]$. Here, Girsanov's theorem allows us to derive the dynamics of all stochastic processes under the new measure and thus to directly evaluate expectations under P_A. For this we need to analyse the dynamics of L_A, write them in the form of equation (4.42), and then read off the results from Theorem 4.8.

Advanced Credit Spread Models

In this chapter, we return to credit risk modelling. A more formal, mathematical foundation is given for the spread-based model of Chapter 3 which will naturally lead to the important class of *intensity-based credit risk models*. The mathematical foundation will also give us the ability to extend the model to include stochastic dynamics of implied default probabilities, it will build the bridge to the published literature on intensity-based default risk models, and it will enable us to apply known numerical solution methods for more exotic credit derivative specifications.

The chapter consists of a sequence of sections building up to stochastic-intensity default risk models. On the way, we discuss Poisson processes, inhomogeneous and marked Poisson processes, Cox processes and general intensity-based point processes. Picking up the thread from Chapter 3, we will also analyse if and how the pricing of the "building block" securities is changed in the different default-arrival setups.

5.1 POISSON PROCESSES

One of the insights from Chapter 3 was the following: over small time steps, the local implied default probability is proportional to the length of the time step. The proportionality factor is the short-term credit spread under zero recovery.

In this section we will introduce a mathematical framework for modelling default times which has exactly this property: the local probability of a jump of a Poisson process over a small time step is approximately proportional to the length of this time interval. The processes introduced will gradually increase in complexity, but also in realism and in their capability to reproduce realistic default dynamics, starting from plain constant-intensity Poisson processes, via inhomogeneous and compound Poisson processes to Poisson processes with stochastic intensities, the Cox processes.

5.1.1 A model for default arrival risk

The following assumption describes the way in which default arrival risk is modelled in all intensity-based default risk models:

Assumption 5.1 (intensity model default arrivals) *Let $N(t)$ be a counting process[1] with (possibly stochastic) intensity $\lambda(t)$. The time of default τ is the time of the first jump of N, i.e.*

$$\tau = \inf\{t \in \mathbb{R}_+ \mid N(t) > 0\}. \tag{5.1}$$

The survival probabilities in this setup are given by:

$$P(0, T) = \mathbf{P}[N(T) = 0 | \mathcal{F}_0]. \tag{5.2}$$

---

[1] A counting process is a non-decreasing, integer-valued process $N(t)$ with $N(0) = 0$. See Section 4.3.

In this chapter we will see many different specifications of the counting process $N(t)$, and many different specifications for the probabilities of the jumps of $N(t)$.

5.1.2 Intuitive construction of a Poisson process

A Poisson process $N(t)$ is an increasing process in the integers $0, 1, 2, 3, \ldots$. More important than its unexciting set of values are the *times of the jumps* $\tau_1, \tau_2, \tau_3, \ldots$ and the probability of a jump in the next instant.

We assume that the probability of a jump in the next small time interval Δt is proportional to Δt:

$$\mathbf{P}[N(t + \Delta t) - N(t) = 1] = \lambda \Delta t, \tag{5.3}$$

that jumps by more than 1 do not occur, and that jumps in disjoint time intervals happen independently of each other. This means, conversely, that the probability of the process remaining constant is

$$\mathbf{P}[N(t + \Delta t) - N(t) = 0] = 1 - \lambda \Delta t,$$

and over the interval $[t, 2\Delta t]$ this probability is

$$\begin{aligned} \mathbf{P}[N(t + 2\Delta t) - N(t) = 0] \\ = \mathbf{P}[N(t + \Delta t) - N(t) = 0] \cdot \mathbf{P}[N(t + 2\Delta t) - N(t + \Delta t) = 0] = (1 - \lambda \Delta t)^2. \end{aligned}$$

Now we can start to construct a Poisson process. We subdivide the interval $[t, T]$ into n subintervals of length $\Delta t = (T - t)/n$. In each of these subintervals the process N has a jump with probability $\Delta t \lambda$. We conduct n independent binomial experiments each with a probability of $\Delta t \lambda$ for a "jump" outcome.

The probability of *no* jump at all in $[t, T]$ is given by:

$$\mathbf{P}[N(T) = N(t)] = (1 - \Delta t \lambda)^n = \left(1 - \frac{1}{n}(T - t)\lambda\right)^n.$$

Because $(1 + x/n)^n \to e^x$ as $n \to \infty$, this converges to:

$$\mathbf{P}[N(T) = N(t)] \to \exp\{-(T - t)\lambda\}.$$

Next we look at the probability of exactly *one* jump in $[t, T]$. There are n possibilities of having exactly one jump, giving a total probability of

$$\begin{aligned} \mathbf{P}[N(T) - N(t) = 1] &= n \cdot \Delta t \lambda (1 - \Delta t \lambda)^{n-1} \\ &= n \cdot \frac{(T - t)}{n} \lambda \left(1 - \frac{1}{n}(T - t)\lambda\right)^n \Big/ \left(1 - \frac{1}{n}(T - t)\lambda\right) \\ &= \frac{(T - t)\lambda}{1 - \frac{1}{n}(T - t)\lambda} \left(1 - \frac{1}{n}(T - t)\lambda\right)^n \\ &\to (T - t)\lambda \exp\{-(T - t)\lambda\} \quad \text{as } n \to \infty, \end{aligned}$$

again using the limit result for the exponential function. The term in the denominator converges to 1 and therefore drops out in the limit.

Similarly one can reach the limit probabilities of *two* jumps:

$$\mathbf{P}[N(T) - N(t) = 2] = \frac{1}{2}(T - t)^2 \lambda^2 \exp\{-(T - t)\lambda\}$$

or n jumps:

$$\mathbf{P}[N(T) - N(t) = n] = \frac{1}{n!}(T - t)^n \lambda^n \exp\{-(T - t)\lambda\}.$$

We have now derived the equation that is usually used to formally define a Poisson process.

Definition 5.1 (Poisson process)   *A Poisson process with intensity $\lambda > 0$ is a non-decreasing, integer-valued process with initial value $N(0) = 0$ whose increments are independent and satisfy, for all $0 \leq t < T$*

$$\mathbf{P}[N(T) - N(t) = n] = \frac{1}{n!}(T - t)^n \lambda^n \exp\{-(T - t)\lambda\}. \tag{5.4}$$

The discrete-time approximation of the Poisson process resembles the binomial approximation of a Brownian motion. In both constructions we take a number of binomially distributed random variables with only two possible values and add them up to get the process. In the Poisson case above we take the individual jumps in the time interval Δt, for the Brownian motion we take the "up" and "down" movements at the individual nodes.

The difference lies in what we do in the limit. For the Brownian motion we *decrease the jump size* (proportional to $1/\sqrt{n}$) and *keep the probabilities constant*. Here for the Poisson process we do the opposite. We *keep the jump size constant* (at 1) and *decrease the probability* (proportional to $1/n$). Both limiting procedures ensure that the variance of the final value of the process remains finite, but the resulting behaviour of the process is completely different.

Equation (5.3) points to a good way to check the plausibility of the results we will get later on: the *large portfolio approximation*. Instead of assuming that we have just one defaultable security to price that is driven by just one Poisson process, just assume that *we have a large portfolio of defaultable securities that are all driven by independent Poisson processes*. Then we can assume that Poisson events happen almost continuously at a rate of λdt to our whole portfolio. This trick allows one to transform the unwieldy discrete jumps to a continuous rate of events.

5.1.3   Properties of Poisson processes

Poisson processes are usually used to model either rare events (as for example in insurance mathematics) or discretely countable events (e.g. radioactive decay, the number of customers in a queue, the number of calls through a telephone exchange, the number of soldiers in the Prussian cavalry that die because they were kicked by a horse[2] ...). Both properties also apply to defaults. They are rare (hopefully) and they are discrete. Usually one models the time of default of a firm as *the time of the first jump of a Poisson process*.

---

[2] Reportedly, this was the first statistical application of Poisson processes.

The parameter λ in the construction of the Poisson process is called the *intensity* of the process. We already saw that the Poisson process is discontinuous and the distribution of the jump heights was given in equation (5.4). Here are some further properties:

- The Poisson process has no memory. The probability of n jumps in $[t, t + s]$ is independent of $N(t)$ and the history of N before t. In particular a jump is not more likely just because the last jump occurred a long time ago and "it's about time".
- The inter-arrival times of a Poisson process $(\tau_{n+1} - \tau_n)$ are exponentially distributed with density

$$\mathbf{P}[(\tau_{n+1} - \tau_n) \in t dt] = \lambda e^{-\lambda t} dt.$$

This is the density of the time of the next jump of N.
- Two or more jumps at exactly the same time have probability zero.

For financial modelling we need to know how to handle Poisson-type jump processes in stochastic differential equations. From the construction we have obviously

$$\mathbf{E}[dN] = \lambda dt. \tag{5.5}$$

The predictable compensator of $N(t)$ is λt, i.e. the following process is a martingale:

$$N(t) - \lambda t. \tag{5.6}$$

Furthermore the following covariations follow directly from the construction:

$$dN dN = dN, \qquad \mathbf{E}[dN^2] = \lambda dt.$$

Furthermore we have

$$[N, W] = \langle N, W \rangle = 0$$

where W is any Brownian motion. This may require some more explanation. Remember that on any time interval $[0, T]$ almost surely $dN = 0$ except for a finite number of points in time $T_1, \ldots, T_K$. But then $\int_0^T dN(t) dW(t) = \sum_{k=1}^K dW(T_k)$. But the last sum is zero because the increments of the Brownian motion are infinitesimally small.

Similarly, this can be used to show that for any (differentiable) functions f and g at all times we have

$$d(f(N(t))g(W(t))) = f(N(t))dg(W(t)) + g(W(t))df(N(t))$$

and all martingales generated by $N(t)$ are uncorrelated with all martingales generated by any Brownian motion, as will be shown in Proposition 5.1.

5.1.4   Spreads with Poisson processes

If we use the default-arrival model of Assumption 5.1 (default at the first jump of $N(t)$) with a Poisson process with intensity λ, the survival probabilities can be read off equation (5.4):

$$P(0, T) = e^{-\lambda T}.$$

Now, assuming independence of defaults and interest rate movements (Assumption 3.2), the analysis of Chapter 3 can be repeated using these survival probabilities. Following Definition 3.4, the hazard rates of default are (assuming $\tau > t$ and $T > t$):

$$H(t, T, T + \Delta t) = \frac{1}{\Delta t}(e^{\lambda \Delta t} - 1),$$

$$h(t, T) = \lambda.$$

Note that neither default hazard rates H nor h depend on the current time t or the future point in time T. Thus, when a Poisson process with constant intensity λ is used as default triggering process, the term structure of spreads will be flat (i.e. not change if T is changed) and it will not change over time (as t is changed).

5.2   INHOMOGENEOUS POISSON PROCESSES

Credit spread curves are not flat in reality, although a constant-intensity Poisson process implies this. In order to reach a more realistic shape of the spread curve we must allow the default intensity (and thus the hazard rates) to change over time. If we let the intensity λ of the Poisson process be a function of time $\lambda(t)$, we reach an *inhomogeneous* Poisson process. Its properties are very similar to the properties of a homogeneous Poisson process. Starting from the local jump probability

$$\mathbf{P}[N(t + \Delta t) - N(t) = 1] = \lambda(t)\Delta t$$

we can calculate the probability of *no* jump in the interval $[t, T]$ (using the fact that $\ln(1 - x) = -x + O(x^2)$ for small x):

$$\mathbf{P}[N(T) - N(t) = 0] = \prod_{i=1}^{n}(1 - \lambda(t + i\Delta t)\Delta t),$$

$$\ln \mathbf{P}[N(T) - N(t) = 0] = \sum_{i=1}^{n} \ln(1 - \lambda(t + i\Delta t)\Delta t)$$

$$\approx \sum_{i=1}^{n} -\lambda(t + i\Delta t)\Delta t$$

$$\rightarrow -\int_{t}^{T} \lambda(s)ds \quad \text{as } \Delta t \rightarrow 0,$$

$$\mathbf{P}[N(T) - N(t) = 0] \rightarrow \exp\left\{-\int_{t}^{T} \lambda(s)ds\right\} \quad \text{as } \Delta t \rightarrow 0.$$

Similarly one can derive the general formula for the probability of n jumps of an inhomogeneous Poisson process in $[t, T]$ which is given in the following definition.

Definition 5.2 (inhomogeneous Poisson process)   *An inhomogeneous Poisson process with intensity function $\lambda(t) > 0$ is a non-decreasing, integer-valued process with initial value $N(0) = 0$ whose increments are independent and satisfy*

$$\mathbf{P}[N(T) - N(t) = n] = \frac{1}{n!} \left(\int_t^T \lambda(s)ds \right)^n \exp \left\{ - \int_t^T \lambda(s)ds \right\}. \tag{5.7}$$

The intensity $\lambda(t)$ is a non-negative function of time only.

Again the only difference from (5.4) is that $\lambda(T - t)$ has been replaced by the integral of $\lambda(s)$ over the respective time span. If a constant intensity function was used in Definition 5.2, then we would recover a homogeneous Poisson process.

An inhomogeneous Poisson process resembles a homogeneous Poisson process in many ways, in particular the compensators are similar:

$$\mathbf{E}[dN(t)|\mathcal{F}_t] = \lambda(t)dt \qquad dNdW = 0, \tag{5.8}$$

$$M(t) := N(t) - \int_0^t \lambda(s)ds. \tag{5.9}$$

$M(t)$ is a martingale, the compensator of the inhomogeneous Poisson process is $\int_0^t \lambda(s)ds$.

Here is the promised proposition on the absence of correlation between jump martingales and diffusion martingales.

Proposition 5.1   *Consider the following martingales: $X(0) = 0$, $Y(0) = 0$ and*

$$dX(t) = \alpha(t)(dN(t) - \lambda(t)dt),$$
$$dY(t) = \sigma(t)dW(t),$$

where $\alpha(t)$ and $\sigma(t)$ are predictable stochastic processes, $W(t)$ is a Brownian motion, and $N(t)$ is an inhomogeneous Poisson process with intensity $\lambda(t)$. Then $X(T)$ and $Y(T)$ are uncorrelated for all T.

Proof.   By Itô's product rule: (4.31), or heuristically as follows

$$d(XY) = X_-dY + Y_-dX + dXdY.$$

Now

$$X(T)Y(T) = \int_0^T d(XY) = \int_0^T X_-dY + \int_0^T Y_-dX + \int_0^T dXdY$$

and thus

$$\mathbf{E}[X(T)Y(T)] = \mathbf{E} \left[\int_0^T X_-dY \right] + \mathbf{E} \left[\int_0^T Y_-dX \right] + \mathbf{E} \left[\int_0^T dXdY \right].$$

Using the fact that $dNdW = 0$ and $dtdW = 0$ means that the last summand is zero. Furthermore, as X and Y are martingales, the integrals $\int_0^T X_- dY$ and $\int_0^T Y_- dX$ will be (local) martingales and (under suitable regularity on α and σ) their expectation will also be zero. Thus, $X(T)$ and $Y(T)$ are uncorrelated.   □

This proposition holds for even more general point processes, in particular it holds for all intensity-based point processes. It is even used to characterise a particular class of martingales: the *purely discontinuous martingales*. These are those martingales which have zero covariation with all continuous martingales, i.e. the ones for which an equivalent proposition to 5.1 holds (see Jacod and Shiryaev (1988)).

The integrands α and σ in the preceding proposition can be stochastic, in particular they can depend on N and on W. If α is independent of Y, and σ is independent of X, then X and Y are not just uncorrelated, they are independent.

Like the above, we can derive survival probabilities for an inhomogeneous Poisson process using equation (5.7):

$$P(0, T) = e^{-\int_0^T \lambda(s)ds},$$

the density of the time of the first jump, given that no jump has occurred until t:

$$\lambda(s)e^{-\int_t^s \lambda(u)du}$$

and analyse the corresponding hazard rates of default (assuming $\tau > t$ and $T > t$):

$$H(t, T, T + \Delta t) = \frac{1}{\Delta t}\left(e^{\int_T^{T+\Delta t} \lambda(s)ds} - 1\right),$$

$$h(t, T) = \lambda(T).$$

Now, the default hazard rates *do* depend on the time horizon T. This means that the term structure of spreads and hazard rates is not flat, but given by $\lambda(T)$. By suitable choice of the function $\lambda(\cdot)$, we can reach every term structure of hazard rates we desire.

5.2.1   Pricing the building blocks

If the time of default is the time of the first jump of an inhomogeneous Poisson process $N(t)$, the pricing building blocks have the following prices.

5.2.1.1   *Defaultable zero-coupon bonds*

We have to evaluate the following expression:

$$\overline{B}(0, T) = \mathbf{E}\left[e^{-\int_0^T r(s)ds} \mathbf{1}_{\{N(T)=0\}}\right].$$

If we assume that the default-free rate $r(t)$ does not depend on the *arrival* of the default of the obligor:

$$\overline{B}(0, T) = \mathbf{E}\big[e^{-\int_0^T r(s)ds}\big]\mathbf{E}\big[\mathbf{1}_{\{N(T)=0\}}\big],$$

$$\overline{B}(0, T) = B(0, T)e^{-\int_0^T \lambda(s)ds}. \tag{5.10}$$

5.2.1.2 Payoffs at default (discrete)

A payoff of 1 at T_{k+1}, if and only if a default happens in $[T_k, T_{k+1}]$, has the value

$$e(0, T_k, T_{k+1}) = \mathbf{E}\big[e^{-\int_0^{T_{k+1}} r(s)ds}\big(\mathbf{1}_{\{N(T_k)=0\}} - \mathbf{1}_{\{N(T_{k+1})=0\}}\big)\big].$$

Using the same assumption as above:

$$= \mathbf{E}\big[e^{-\int_0^{T_{k+1}} r(s)ds}\big]\big(\mathbf{E}\big[\mathbf{1}_{\{N(T_k)=0\}}\big] - \mathbf{E}\big[\mathbf{1}_{\{N(T_{k+1})=0\}}\big]\big)$$

$$= B(0, T_{k+1})e^{-\int_0^{T_k} \lambda(s)ds}\big(1 - e^{-\int_{T_k}^{T_{k+1}} \lambda(s)ds}\big), \tag{5.11}$$

$$e(0, T_k, T_{k+1}) = \overline{B}(0, T_{k+1})\big(1 - e^{-\int_{T_k}^{T_{k+1}} \lambda(s)ds}\big). \tag{5.12}$$

5.2.1.3 Payoffs at default (continuous)

The limit of (5.12) as $T_{k+1} \to T_k = T$ is:

$$e(0, T) = \lim_{\Delta t \to 0} \frac{1}{\Delta t} e(0, T, T + \Delta t) = \overline{B}(0, T)\lambda(T). \tag{5.13}$$

Using these building blocks, defaultable coupon bonds and credit default swaps can be priced as demonstrated in Chapter 3.

5.3 STOCHASTIC CREDIT SPREADS

In the previous sections we saw that, if defaults are triggered by an inhomogeneous Poisson process, we can exactly fit a given term structure of defaultable bond prices by choosing a time-dependent default intensity/hazard rate function. In this setup, the prices of the defaultable zero-coupon bonds with zero recovery are given by

$$\overline{B}(t, T) = B(t, T)e^{-\int_t^T \lambda(s)ds},$$

given that $\tau > t$. Here $\lambda(t)$ is the time-dependent default arrival intensity. The continuously compounded yield spread of this bond over the equivalent default-free bond is:

$$\frac{1}{T-t} \int_t^T \lambda(s)ds.$$

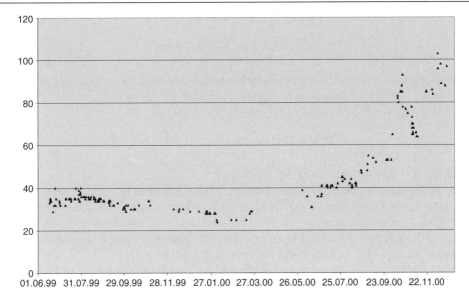

Figure 5.1   Market quotes (offer) (bp) for five-year CDS protection on Ford Motor Co.

This yield spread only depends on the current time t, it is not stochastic. Its value for every given future date $t' > t$ is already determined by the function $\lambda(t)$ that we found when we initially calibrated the initial hazard rate function. Because we calibrated smooth hazard rate functions, the resulting dynamics of the yield spreads will also be smooth and very regular.

Figure 5.1 shows market quotes for five-year CDS protection on Ford Motor Co. Constant or smoothly changing credit spreads are obviously not what we observe in the market, we need a more flexible model to be able to model *dynamics* of defaultable bond prices and credit spreads.

Stochastic dynamics in the credit spreads are necessary for several reasons. We need them if we want to price credit derivatives whose payoff is directly affected by volatility (e.g. credit spread options), if the credit derivative has a payoff which might be correlated with the spread movements (e.g. an option on the currency of an emerging market), and in general if we want to have a model which enables us to measure, manage and hedge this type of risk.

These stochastic intensity dynamics can be modelled with a generalisation of the Poisson process $N(t)$, the *Cox process*.

5.3.1   Cox processes

Roughly speaking, Cox processes are Poisson processes with stochastic intensity. Going back to the discrete-time approximation of the Poisson process in Section 5.1.2, we again consider the jump probability of the process $N(t)$ over a small time interval Δt:

$$\mathbf{P}[N(t + \Delta t) - N(t) = 1] = \lambda(t)dt, \tag{5.14}$$

where $\lambda(t)$ is now a *stochastic process*. Let us assume it follows a diffusion process of the form

$$d\lambda(t) = \mu_\lambda(t)dt + \sigma_\lambda(t)dW(t). \tag{5.15}$$

In the choice of drift and volatility processes we must ensure that $\lambda(t)$ is never negative.

Again we conduct n binomial experiments to simulate the jumps of N, one for each time interval Δt, but now the probability of a jump in $[t, t + \Delta t]$ is

$$\mathbf{P}[N(t + \Delta t) - N(t) = 1] = \lambda(t)\Delta t,$$

proportional to the *realised value of* $\lambda(t)$ *at time* t.

The jumps are now correlated via the path taken by $\lambda(t)$. If there is a jump at some time T_1, that makes it more likely that $\lambda(t)$ is large around T_1, which in turn means that the next jump is more likely to happen sooner than later. This correlation is only indirect, via the default intensity. There is no connection like "the probability of the next jump is proportional to the number of jumps so far", which would constitute a direct connection.

If we knew the full realisation of $\lambda(t)$ in advance (i.e. the *whole path* $\{\lambda(t); t \geq 0\}$), then we would have an inhomogeneous Poisson process like in Section 5.2. The only difference is that the intensity function $\lambda(t)$ is quite irregular but apart from that, Definition 5.2 would still hold.

This is also the basic idea of a formal definition of a Cox process. Conditional on knowing everything else about the future development of the economy (except the process $N(t)$ itself), the process $N(t)$ should be an inhomogeneous Poisson process with intensity $\lambda(t)$.

For a formal definition we must first define what is meant by "knowing everything else". This is done using a background driving process $X(t)$. Knowledge of this process is equivalent to knowing the whole future development of the economy, except for the times of default.

Assumption 5.2 (background driving process)

- *There is a d-dimensional* background driving process $X(t)$. *We call the filtration generated by* $X(t)$ *the* background filtration $(\mathcal{G}_t)_{(t\geq0)}$, *and* $\mathcal{G} = \cup_{t\geq0}\mathcal{G}_t$ *is the information set containing all future and past background information.*
- *All default-free processes (in particular the default-free interest rates) are adapted to* $(\mathcal{G}_t)_{(t\geq0)}$.
- *The intensity process* $\lambda(t)$ *is adapted to* $(\mathcal{G}_t)_{(t\geq0)}$.
- *The full filtration is reached by combining* $(\mathcal{G}_t)_{(t\geq0)}$ *and the filtration* $(\mathcal{F}_t^N)_{t\geq0}$ *which is generated by* $N(t)$:

$$(\mathcal{F}_t)_{(t\geq0)} = (\mathcal{G}_t)_{(t\geq0)} \vee (\mathcal{F}_t^N)_{t\geq0}.$$

A simple example is the following.

Example 5.1 *The default-free interest rates have the dynamics* [3]

$$dr = \kappa(\alpha - r(t))dt + \sigma\sqrt{r}dW_1(t) \tag{5.16}$$

---

[3] These dynamics are of a class introduced in Cox *et al.* (1985a). This specification still has a large degree of tractability, and non-negativity of rates and intensities is ensured if $k, \alpha, k', \alpha' > 0$.

and the default intensity follows

$$d\lambda = \kappa'(\alpha' - \lambda(t))dt + \sigma'\sqrt{\lambda}dW_2(t), \tag{5.17}$$

where W_1 and W_2 are two independent Brownian motions. The default counting process $N(t)$ has intensity $\lambda(t)$. Then the background process is $X = (W_1(t), W_2(t))$ (or $(r(t), \lambda(t))$).

It is not essential that the background filtration is generated by a stochastic process $X(t)$, but often it is more convenient to think of it that way. $X(t)$ can be viewed as an (incomplete) state vector of the economy, where the complete state vector would be $(X(t), N(t))$.

The filtration $(\mathcal{G}_t)_{(t \geq 0)}$ is the filtration that would be present in the equivalent default-free model, i.e. a model in which all the same stochastic processes (interest rates, exchange rates, share prices, etc.) are modelled, with the exception of the default arrivals and the recovery rates. In particular, the default-free interest rates $r(t)$ and the intensity process $\lambda(t)$ are part of this "equivalent default-free model" (although $\lambda(t)$ cannot have the meaning of an intensity process then because there is no associated point process).

Note that, although $(\mathcal{G}_t)_{(t \geq 0)}$ was generated without using $N(t)$, it may still be possible that $N(t)$ is measurable with respect to $(\mathcal{G}_t)_{(t \geq 0)}$ or that knowledge of the background information gives us some information on the realisation of $N(t)$. There are two ways in which this can happen in a modelling environment:

• Either, the jumps in $N(t)$ are *caused* by a background process, e.g. $N(t)$ jumps whenever a background process hits a prespecified barrier;
• Or, the arrivals of $N(t)$ themselves influence in an unmistakeable way one of the background processes. For example, if $N(t)$ jumps, one of the background processes jumps, too.

The first situation is the case in all firms' value models, which will be analysed in a later chapter. As an example of the second situation assume that the background filtration contains the USD/EUR exchange rate, and that this exchange rate will jump significantly at a default of Russia, say. Then the jump in the path of the USD/EUR exchange rate will reveal the time of the default.

Definition 5.3 (Cox process)   *A point process $N(t)$ with intensity process $\lambda(t)$ is a Cox process if, conditional on the background information $\mathcal{G}$, $N(t)$ is an inhomogeneous Poisson process with intensity $\lambda(t)$.*

Thus, a Cox process $N(t)$ cannot be measurable with respect to $\mathcal{G}$. No background process can be caused directly by $N(t)$, nor can a jump in $N(t)$ be triggered by a background process. The only influence of the background on $N(t)$ is the determination of the local jump probabilities via $\lambda(t)$.

In Definition 5.3, much more information (all of $\mathcal{G}$) was assumed than just knowledge of $\lambda(t)$. The additional information does not hurt, and using $\mathcal{G}$ will simplify the calculations later on.

Sometimes, Cox processes are defined differently. First, in some definitions (e.g. Brémaud, 1981) it is required that $\lambda(t)$ is $\mathcal{F}_{0+}$-measurable. This means that – although we do not know the path of $\lambda(t)$ at time $t = 0$ – we will know the full path one instant later. This is a common assumption in actuarial calculations where it does not matter when the information is revealed as long as the initial distribution is realistic. In finance, it is essential to model the *dynamics* of $\lambda(t)$ in order to analyse hedging and risk management properly, so we cannot reveal the full future path of the intensity directly after $t = 0$.

While it would undoubtedly be nice to have a process with the convenient properties described in Definition 5.3, we still have to prove that such a process actually exists. Therefore, many authors take the opposite route and first construct a Cox process to a given intensity process, and then prove that it satisfies the "conditioning property".

A common way to enlarge the "equivalent default-free model" to incorporate defaults is as follows:

1. Start with the equivalent default-free model $(\Omega, (\mathcal{G}_t)_{(t \geq 0)}, Q)$.
2. Add a unit random variable U to the model with:
   - U uniformly distributed on $[0, 1]$ (i.e. the density is $f(x) \equiv 1$ constant to one on $[0, 1]$);
   - U independent of the default-free model; (i.e. if $\mathcal{G}$)
3. Define the time of default as the first time when the countdown process $e^{-\int_0^t \lambda(s)ds}$ hits the level U:

$$\tau = \min\left\{ t > 0 \mid e^{-\int_0^t \lambda(s)ds} \leq U \right\}. \tag{5.18}$$

4. Reveal τ at the time of default.

This is only the construction of the time of the first jump of the Cox process, for later jump times this construction will have to be repeated after each jump. We will return to this construction when we discuss the numerical implementation of these models and when we build a model for default dependencies. For the analysis we only need the "conditional Poisson process" property.

Cox processes form a very large class of processes, almost all implementations of intensity-based default risk models belong to this class. In a way, the intuitive construction of the Cox process above can be viewed as an existence proof. Still, it is instructive to find out which point processes $N(t)$ have an intensity process $\lambda(t)$ but are *not* Cox processes.

Here is one example of such a process which is not a Cox process:

- Until the first jump, $N(t)$ is a Poisson process with constant intensity $\lambda(t) = \lambda^*$.
- After the first jump, $N(t)$ is a Poisson process with constant intensity $\lambda(t) = 2\lambda^*$.

The intensity of $N'(t)$ jumps at the time of the first jump of N. Therefore, *conditional on knowing the path of the local intensity $\lambda(t)$, the process $N(t)$ is not an inhomogeneous Poisson process*. By knowing $\lambda(t)$ we can already see the first jump time of $N(t)$.

Thus, if we restrict ourselves to Cox processes, *we rule out all processes whose intensity path reveals too much information on the jump times*.

Definition 5.3 allows us to directly calculate some properties of Cox processes. From the Poisson-type construction we can directly see the form of the predictable compensator of $N(t)$. Locally, the expected increment is

$$\mathbf{E}[dN(t)|\mathcal{F}_t] = \lambda(t)dt$$

and globally, the compensated process

$$M(t) := N(t) - \int_0^t \lambda(s)ds \tag{5.19}$$

is a local martingale. Apart from the fact that $\lambda(t)$ is now stochastic, these results are identical to equations (5.8) and (5.9) for inhomogeneous Poisson processes.

For jump probabilities we reach new results. Given $\mathcal{G}$ which includes knowledge of the realisation of λ, we know by (5.7) that the probability of n jumps for an inhomogeneous Poisson process is:

$$\mathbf{P}[N(T) - N(t) = n] = \frac{1}{n!} \left(\int_t^T \lambda(s)ds \right)^n \exp\left\{ -\int_t^T \lambda(s)ds \right\}.$$

For a Cox process we have to take the expectation over the possible paths λ could take:

$$\mathbf{P}[N(T) - N(t) = n] = \mathbf{E}[\mathbf{P}[N(T) - N(t) = n|\lambda]]$$

$$= \mathbf{E}\left[\frac{1}{n!} \left(\int_t^T \lambda(s)ds \right)^n \exp\left\{ -\int_t^T \lambda(s)ds \right\} \right].$$

The *survival probabilities* under Cox processes are:

$$P'(0, T) = \mathbf{E}\left[e^{-\int_0^T \lambda(s)ds} \right]. \tag{5.20}$$

The prime indicates that now there can be a difference between the survival probability and the ratio of defaultable and default-free zerobond prices $P'(0, T) \neq P(0, T) = \overline{B}(0, T)/B(0, T)$. The difference is zero if default intensities $\lambda(t)$ and interest rates $r(t)$ are independent.

The *density of the time of the first default* is the conditional expectation of the corresponding result for inhomogeneous Poisson processes:

$$\mathbf{P}[\tau \in [t, t + dt]] = \mathbf{E}\left[\lambda(t)e^{-\int_0^t \lambda(s)ds} \right]dt. \tag{5.21}$$

From the analysis of inhomogeneous Poisson processes we know how to handle the pricing problems given the path of λ. This suggests the following general recipe:

1. First, solve the pricing problem conditional on knowledge of $\mathcal{G}$ for a given realisation of a path of $\lambda(t)$;
2. Then, take expectations over all possible paths of $\lambda(t)$.

In the first step one is usually able to eliminate all direct reference to the jump process $N(t)$ and replace with terms in $\lambda(t)$ and the other state variables.

Mathematically, this is justified by the *law of the iterated expectation*, a basic fact of probability theory.

Theorem 5.2 (iterated expectations)   *Let $\mathcal{G} \subset \mathcal{F}_\infty$ be a sub-σ-algebra of $\mathcal{F}_\infty$, and let X be an integrable random variable. Then $Z := \mathbf{E}[X|\mathcal{G}]$ is an integrable random variable and*

$$\mathbf{E}[X] = \mathbf{E}[\mathbf{E}[X|\mathcal{G}]] = \mathbf{E}[Z]. \tag{5.22}$$

If all background processes follow continuous paths, $Z = \mathbf{E}[X|\mathcal{G}]$ will also only depend on these continuous processes. Thus, we are back in the known fields of continuous-time finance when evaluating $\mathbf{E}[Z]$. If we have modelled the dynamics of $\lambda(t)$ with a tractable process, this will enable us to derive solutions or apply known numerical techniques. The jumps of $N(t)$ were eliminated in the first step, in the evaluation of $\mathbf{E}[X|\mathcal{G}]$. But this step can be done pretending $N(t)$ was an inhomogeneous Poisson process.

To illustrate the pricing technique using iterated expectations let us consider some generic pricing problems. An integral with respect to $N(t)$, an expectation of a function of $N(t)$, and a function of the first jump time:

$$p_1 = \mathbf{E}\left[\int_0^T x(t)dN(t)\right],$$

$$p_2 = \mathbf{E}[f(N(T))],$$

$$p_3 = \mathbf{E}[g(\tau)],$$

where τ is the time of the first jump of $N(t)$.

The first problem can be solved using the predictable compensator of N:

$$p_1 = \mathbf{E}\left[\int_0^T x(t)dN(t)\right] = \mathbf{E}\left[\int_0^T x(t)\lambda(t)dt\right].$$

For the second problem we use iterated expectations:

$$p_2 = \mathbf{E}[f(N(T))] = \mathbf{E}[\mathbf{E}[f(N(T))|\mathcal{G}]].$$

Now use the inhomogeneous Poisson process properties. The inner expectation is the sum over all possible jump numbers weighted with the respective probabilities:

$$\mathbf{E}[f(N(T))|\mathcal{G}] = \sum_{n=0}^{\infty} f(n)\frac{1}{n!}\left(\int_0^T \lambda(s)ds\right)^n e^{-\int_0^T \lambda(s)ds}.$$

Thus:

$$p_2 = \mathbf{E}\left[\sum_{n=0}^{\infty} f(n)\frac{1}{n!}\left(\int_0^T \lambda(s)ds\right)^n e^{-\int_0^T \lambda(s)ds}\right].$$

For the third problem we also use iterated expectations, and then the density of the first arrival time of an inhomogeneous Poisson process:

$$p_3 = \mathbf{E}[g(\tau)] = \mathbf{E}[\mathbf{E}[g(\tau)|\mathcal{G}]]$$

$$= \mathbf{E}\left[\int_0^T g(t)\lambda(t)e^{-\int_0^t \lambda(s)ds}dt\right].$$

In all three cases we end up with expressions where the point process $N(t)$ has been eliminated and which therefore can be attacked with "conventional" methods.

5.3.2   Pricing the building blocks

5.3.2.1   *Defaultable zero-coupon bonds*

The pricing problem is

$$\overline{B}(0, T) = \mathbf{E}\Big[e^{-\int_0^T r(s)ds} \mathbf{1}_{\{\tau > T\}}\Big].$$

Conditioning:

$$= \mathbf{E}\Big[\mathbf{E}\big[e^{-\int_0^T r(s)ds} \mathbf{1}_{\{\tau > T\}}\big|\mathcal{G}\big]\Big].$$

Now it is useful that $r(t)$ is measurable with respect to $\mathcal{G}$. The inner expectation is

$$\mathbf{E}\big[e^{-\int_0^T r(s)ds} \mathbf{1}_{\{\tau > T\}}\big|\mathcal{G}\big] = e^{-\int_0^T r(s)ds} \mathbf{E}\big[\mathbf{1}_{\{\tau > T\}}\big|\mathcal{G}\big]$$
$$= e^{-\int_0^T r(s) + \lambda(s)ds},$$

and finally wrapping the outer expectation around this expression yields

$$\overline{B}(0, T) = \mathbf{E}\Big[e^{-\int_0^T r(s) + \lambda(s)ds}\Big]. \tag{5.23}$$

Note that now it is *no longer possible* to factor out the default-free bond price: $\lambda(t)$ and $r(t)$ might be correlated. Without any further assumptions, equation (5.23) cannot be simplified any further. In particular:

$$\overline{B}(0, T) \neq B(0, T)\mathbf{E}\Big[e^{-\int_0^T \lambda(s)ds}\Big]$$

unless $r(t)$ and $\lambda(t)$ are independent.

5.3.2.2   *Stochastic payoff in survival*

Along similar lines, the following pricing problem is reduced. A payoff of X (X is stochastic, but $\mathcal{G}$-measurable) at T if no default occurs before T:

$$p = \mathbf{E}\Big[e^{-\int_0^T r(s)ds} \mathbf{1}_{\{\tau > T\}} X\Big] = \mathbf{E}\Big[e^{-\int_0^T r(s) + \lambda(s)ds} X\Big]. \tag{5.24}$$

5.3.2.3   *Payoffs at default (discrete)*

A payoff of 1 at T_{k+1}, if and only if a default happens in $[T_k, T_{k+1}]$, has the value

$$e(0, T_k, T_{k+1}) = \mathbf{E}\Big[e^{-\int_0^{T_{k+1}} r(s)ds} \big(\mathbf{1}_{\{N(T_k)=0\}} - \mathbf{1}_{\{N(T_{k+1})=0\}}\big)\Big]$$
$$= \mathbf{E}\Big[\mathbf{E}\big[e^{-\int_0^{T_{k+1}} r(s)ds} \big(\mathbf{1}_{\{N(T_k)=0\}} - \mathbf{1}_{\{N(T_{k+1})=0\}}\big)\big|\mathcal{G}\big]\Big].$$

The inner expectation is

$$\mathbf{E}\left[e^{-\int_0^{T_{k+1}} r(s)ds}\left(\mathbf{1}_{\{N(T_k)=0\}} - \mathbf{1}_{\{N(T_{k+1})=0\}}\right)\Big|\mathcal{G}\right]$$
$$= e^{-\int_0^{T_{k+1}} r(s)ds}\left(e^{-\int_0^{T_k} \lambda(s)ds} - e^{-\int_0^{T_{k+1}} r(s)ds}\right).$$

Combining the two yields:

$$e(0, T_k, T_{k+1}) = \mathbf{E}\left[e^{-\int_0^{T_{k+1}} r(s)ds} e^{-\int_0^{T_k} \lambda(s)ds}\right] - \overline{B}(0, T_{k+1}). \tag{5.25}$$

5.3.2.4   Payoffs at default (continuous)

The limit of (5.25) as $T_{k+1} \to T_k = T$ is:

$$e(0, T) = \lim_{\Delta t \to 0} \frac{1}{\Delta t} e(0, T, T + \Delta t) = \mathbf{E}\left[\lambda(T)e^{-\int_0^T r(s)+\lambda(s)ds}\right]. \tag{5.26}$$

Again, we can use these building blocks to price defaultable coupon bonds and credit default swaps as demonstrated in Chapter 3.

Nevertheless, now we cannot claim to have completely solved the pricing problem. Because the default intensity is stochastic, it may be correlated with the default-free short-term interest rate. This again means that we can no longer factor the prices of defaultable claims into "survival probability times default-free price", and we are left with expectations over expressions involving both $r(t)$ and $\lambda(t)$.

Nevertheless, we could still make much progress in the simplification of the pricing equations. The law of iterated expectations allows us to remove all references to the point process $N(t)$ itself from the pricing equations. The resulting pricing problems are structurally identical to the pricing problems encountered in two-factor models for the default-free short rate $r(t)$. They reside in the "equivalent default-free" model which was introduced in the construction of the Cox process.

5.3.2.5   Compound Cox processes

If we want to model stochastic markers to the arrival times of a Cox process, we reach a *compound Cox process*. A compound Cox process is essentially the same thing as a compound Poisson process. The conditioning property will now yield that, conditional on the background filtration $\mathcal{G}$, we are faced with an inhomogeneous *marked* Poisson process.

5.3.3   General point processes

Cox processes provide a rich framework to model stochastic default intensities, and usually the flexibility of this class of models is entirely sufficient to capture all salient features of the model. For completeness, we consider the fully general case of an intensity-based model. We only assume that the time of default τ is triggered by the first jump of a counting process $N(t)$ with a *stochastic* intensity $\lambda(t)$.

The prices of defaultable zero-coupon bonds and other defaultable payoffs in this general setup follow from Proposition 6.4, when the loss quota is set to one $q = 1$. We just repeat the result.

Proposition 5.3 (general intensity-based setup) *Let $p(t)$ be the price of a defaultable promised payoff of X at T, where X is $\mathcal{F}_T$-measurable. Let the time of default be the time of the first jump of a point process $N(t)$ with intensity process $\lambda(t)$. Assume that the process $m(t) = \mathbf{E}[e^{-\int_0^T r(s)+\lambda(s)ds} X \mid \mathcal{F}_t]$ does not jump at τ. Then*

$$p(t) = \mathbf{1}_{\{\tau > t\}} \mathbf{E}\big[e^{-\int_t^T r(s)ds} X \, \mathbf{1}_{\{\tau > T\}} \big| \mathcal{F}_t\big] = \mathbf{1}_{\{\tau > t\}} \mathbf{E}\big[e^{-\int_t^T r(s)+\lambda(s)ds} X \big| \mathcal{F}_t\big]. \tag{5.27}$$

(For $t > \tau$, the price $p(t) = 0$.)

Proof. Set $q = 1$ in Proposition 6.4.   □

This gives us the prices of our building blocks.

5.3.3.1 Defaultable zero-coupon bonds

$$\overline{B}(0, T) = \mathbf{E}\big[e^{-\int_0^T r(s)ds} \mathbf{1}_{\{\tau > T\}}\big] = \mathbf{E}\big[e^{-\int_0^T r(s)+\lambda(s)ds}\big]. \tag{5.28}$$

The pricing of defaultable zero-coupon bonds in the general setup follows the same equation as in the Cox process setup (5.23).

5.3.3.2 Stochastic payoff in survival

This is the statement of Proposition 5.3. A stochastic, defaultable payoff of X at T if no default occurs before T:

$$p = \mathbf{E}\big[e^{-\int_0^T r(s)ds} \mathbf{1}_{\{\tau > T\}} X\big] = \mathbf{E}\big[e^{-\int_0^T r(s)+\lambda(s)ds} X\big]. \tag{5.29}$$

5.3.3.3 Payoffs at default (discrete)

A payoff of 1 at T_{k+1}, if and only if a default happens in $[T_k, T_{k+1}]$, has the value

$$e(0, T_k, T_{k+1}) = \mathbf{E}\big[e^{-\int_0^{T_{k+1}} r(s)ds} \big(\mathbf{1}_{\{N(T_k)=0\}} - \mathbf{1}_{\{N(T_{k+1})=0\}}\big)\big]$$

$$= \mathbf{E}\big[e^{-\int_0^{T_{k+1}} r(s)ds} \mathbf{1}_{\{N(T_k)=0\}}\big] - \mathbf{E}\big[e^{-\int_0^{T_{k+1}} r(s)ds} \mathbf{1}_{\{N(T_{k+1})=0\}}\big]. \tag{5.30}$$

The second expectation is $\overline{B}(0, T_{k+1})$. The first expectation is

$$\mathbf{E}\big[e^{-\int_0^{T_{k+1}} r(s)ds} \mathbf{1}_{\{N(T_k)=0\}}\big] = \mathbf{E}\big[\mathbf{E}\big[e^{-\int_0^{T_{k+1}} r(s)ds} \mathbf{1}_{\{N(T_k)=0\}} \big| \mathcal{F}_{T_k}\big]\big]$$

$$= \mathbf{E}\big[e^{-\int_0^{T_k} r(s)ds} \mathbf{1}_{\{N(T_k)=0\}} \mathbf{E}\big[e^{-\int_{T_k}^{T_{k+1}} r(s)ds} \big| \mathcal{F}_{T_k}\big]\big]$$

$$= \mathbf{E}\big[e^{-\int_0^{T_k} r(s)ds} \mathbf{1}_{\{N(T_k)=0\}} B(T_k, T_{k+1})\big]$$

$$= \mathbf{E}\big[e^{-\int_0^{T_k} r(s)+\lambda(s)ds} B(T_k, T_{k+1})\big].$$

This decomposition has an economic interpretation: e is the value of \$1 at T_{k+1} if and only if a default occurred in $[T_k, T_{k+1}]$. This is equivalent to receiving a default-free zerobond with maturity T_{k+1} at time T_k, if no default has occurred until then (this will generate $1 at T_{k+1}) *and* being short a defaultable zerobond with maturity T_{k+1} (this means we will have to return the $1 at T_{k+1} if there was no default in the interval).

Without any further assumptions on the default dynamics, this cannot be simplified any further and we reach:

$$e(0, T_k, T_{k+1}) = \mathbf{E}\big[e^{-\int_0^{T_k} r(s)+\lambda(s)ds} B(T_k, T_{k+1})\big] - \overline{B}(0, T_{k+1}). \tag{5.31}$$

5.3.3.4 Payoffs at default (continuous)

A payment of $1 directly at default can be valued with simple martingale theory. The payoff can be written as:

$$e^{-\int_0^\tau r(s)ds}\mathbf{1}_{\{\tau<T\}} = \int_0^T e^{-\int_0^t r(s)ds}\mathbf{1}_{\{\tau\geq t\}}dN(t). \tag{5.32}$$

$\int_0^t \lambda(s)ds$ is the predictable compensator of $N(t)$, so the expectation of any integral with respect to $dN(t)$ equals the expectation of the same integrand with respect to $\lambda(t)dt$. This yields:

$$\mathbf{E}\big[e^{-\int_0^\tau r(s)ds}\mathbf{1}_{\{\tau<T\}}\big] = \mathbf{E}\left[\int_0^T e^{-\int_0^t r(s)ds}\mathbf{1}_{\{\tau\geq t\}}\lambda(t)dt\right]$$

$$= \int_0^T \mathbf{E}\big[e^{-\int_0^t r(s)ds}\mathbf{1}_{\{\tau\geq t\}}\lambda(t)\big]dt.$$

The term in the expectation has the form of Proposition 5.3. The "local" $1-at-default has the price:

$$e(0, t) = \mathbf{E}\big[e^{-\int_0^t \lambda(s)+r(s)ds}\lambda(t)\big]. \tag{5.33}$$

Again, we can use these building blocks to price defaultable coupon bonds and credit default swaps as demonstrated in Chapter 3.

5.3.4 Compound Poisson processes

A Poisson arrival is used to model the arrival of a specific event. But what happens at this event? So far we can only model *when* something happens, but we obviously also want to model *what* will happen.

For example in default risk modelling we not only want to model when the default occurs, but also how large this default will be, or in a model of jumping stock prices one would have to model the size of the jump, not only the time of the jump. The appropriate mathematical model for this is a *compound Poisson process*.

In a *compound Poisson process* at each time τ_i of a jump of the Poisson process a random variable Y_i is drawn from a distribution $K(dY)$. Y_i is called the *marker* to the point of jump τ_i, the whole set $\{(\tau_i, Y_i)\}_{i\in\mathbb{N}}$ of points in time and markers is called a *marked point process* (see Section 4.5).

The formal way to handle marked point processes is explained in Chapter 4, here it is sufficient to consider a simple example to show how the mathematical analysis proceeds. Let us consider the cumulative sum of the Y_i:

$$X_t = \sum_{\tau_i \leq t} Y_i.$$

A function $f(X)$ then has the following properties:

$$
\begin{aligned}
dX &= \Delta X = Y dN, \\
df &= \Delta f = (f(X+Y) - f(X)) dN, \\
\mathbf{E}[dX] &= \int y K(dy) \lambda dt =: y^e \lambda dt, \\
\mathbf{E}[df(X)] &= \int (f(X+y) - f(X)) K(dy) \lambda dt,
\end{aligned}
\tag{5.34}
$$

where y^e is the local expectation of Y. Note that the expected change of f upon a jump is *not* equal to the value of f at the expected jump size: $\mathbf{E}[df(X)] \neq f(\mathbf{E}[dX])$. (This is an obvious but common mistake.) Itô's lemma for this case is given in Theorem 4.3. The compensator measure for a compound inhomogeneous Poisson process with intensity $\lambda(t)$ is:

$$\nu(de, dt) = K(t, de) \lambda(t) dt. \tag{5.35}$$

6
Recovery Modelling

With the (inhomogeneous) Poisson process we now have a first mathematical model to model the arrival time of a default event which has the advantage that it is very similar to the model presented in Chapter 3. In order to apply this model to credit derivatives pricing, the model must be extended at two connected points: the recovery mechanism must be modelled and it must be shown how to price credit-sensitive payoffs in this framework. This is done in this chapter.

The inhomogeneous Poisson process is not the last word on how default arrival risk should be modelled. More realistic (and more complex) models for the default arrival exhibit stochastic default intensities. Nevertheless, we address the modelling of recovery risk in the framework of inhomogeneous Poisson processes because the modelling of arrival risk is quite complex with stochastic intensities. With an inhomogeneous Poisson process, the salient features of the recovery models can be analysed with a minimum of distraction through stochastic intensity arrivals processes. Finally, any results in a setup with an inhomogeneous Poisson process triggering the default arrival can be re-used in a stochastic-intensity Cox process setup using the familiar conditioning technique.

A variety of ways to model the recovery of defaultable claims have been proposed in the literature: *recovery of treasury (RT)*, *multiple defaults (MD)* and *recovery of market value (RMV)* (also known as *fractional recovery*), *recovery of par (RP)* and *zero recovery (ZR)*. These approaches and their extension to stochastic recovery rates will be introduced, explained and discussed in the next sections.

These recovery models do not attempt to model the *real-world outcome* of the bankruptcy process or the terms of payment, all we model is the *value* of the settlement. Thus, if a recovery rate is specified in terms of a certain number of default-free bonds (as in RT), this does not mean that the defaulted obligor really pays off the creditors in default-free bonds, but only that the *value* of the settlement is approximately equal to the value of the aforementioned number of default-free bonds. This is consistent with the recovery treatment of credit derivatives: the recovery rate in a credit default swap is a market price, the market's expectation of the value of the settlement.

The modelling approaches differ in the *units* in which this value is expressed: cash, default-free bonds, defaultable bonds. Within limits, we can transform the models into each other if a different recovery rate is assumed for every defaultable asset. In this sense, the models are mathematically equivalent. Nevertheless, we would like to assume one identical recovery rate across different securities (of the same seniority class). Then, some models are more convenient or have more realistic outcomes than others. In particular, empirical testing is possible by comparing the prices of several defaultable assets of the same defaultable obligor after a default event.

We consider the following pricing problems:

- A defaultable zero-coupon bond with payoff 1 at its maturity T (as benchmark case);

- A defaultable payment of X at T, where X is stochastic but independent of default events (e.g. an exposure from an OTC derivatives contract);
- A defaultable coupon bond with coupons $\bar{c}$ at T_i, $i = 1, \ldots, N$.

The default arrival risk is modelled as follows.

Assumption 6.1 (inhomogeneous Poisson process arrival risk) *Defaults are triggered by the jumps of an inhomogeneous Poisson process $N(t)$ with intensity $\lambda(t)$. The Poisson arrivals are independent of all other modelling variables. Stochastic recovery parameters are markers to the Poisson process.*

The general framework for all recovery models the following.

Assumption 6.2 (general recovery framework) *Let $\bar{p}(t)$ be the price process of a defaultable asset, given that no default has occurred until time t. If a default occurs at time τ, the asset has a recovery of $\phi(\tau)$ units of account (e.g. USD) at the time of default τ. The recovery $\phi(\tau)$ is stochastic, it is known at the time of default (it is $\mathcal{F}_\tau$-measurable) but not necessarily before default (not necessarily $\mathcal{F}_{\tau-}$-measurable).*

Under the general recovery modelling framework, the pricing problems above can be restated as follows (all expectations are under the martingale measure Q).

- Defaultable zero-coupon bond:

$$\mathbf{E}\left[\beta(\tau)\phi(\tau)\mathbf{1}_{\{\tau \le T\}} + \beta(T)\mathbf{1}_{\{\tau > T\}}\right]. \tag{6.1}$$

- Defaultable stochastic payoff X:

$$\mathbf{E}\left[\beta(\tau)\phi(\tau)\mathbf{1}_{\{\tau \le T\}} + \beta(T)\mathbf{1}_{\{\tau > T\}}X\right]. \tag{6.2}$$

- Defaultable coupon bond:

$$\mathbf{E}\left[\beta(\tau)\phi(\tau)\mathbf{1}_{\{\tau \le T\}} + \sum_{i=1}^{N}\bar{c}\beta(T_i)\mathbf{1}_{\{\tau > T_i\}} + \beta(T_N)\mathbf{1}_{\{\tau > T_N\}}\right]. \tag{6.3}$$

The different possibilities for the parametrisation of the recovery payoff $\phi(\tau)$ in the following subsections aim to make the pricing problems above analytically tractable while capturing salient features and risks of real-world recovery payoffs. At the same time the models also aim to give a consistent rule for the specification of recovery rates across different securities issued by the same obligor. The recovery payoff ϕ may take different values for different pricing problems.

6.1 PRESENTATION OF THE DIFFERENT RECOVERY MODELS

6.1.1 Zero recovery

Zero recovery is the simplest specification of a recovery mechanism, and in almost all cases also the most unrealistic. Still, pricing formulae under zero recovery are useful for other reasons.

Zero recovery is an important benchmark, and in the solution of pricing problems in other recovery setups, zero recovery prices are frequently used.

Assumption 6.3 (zero recovery) *All claims have a zero recovery at default:*

$$\phi(t) = 0 \quad \forall\, t \geq 0.$$

The pricing problems are easily solved.

• Defaultable zero-coupon bonds (see equation (3.3)):

$$\overline{B}(0, T) = P(0, T)B(0, T) = B(0, T)e^{-\int_0^T \lambda(s)ds}. \tag{6.4}$$

• Stochastic payoff:

$$\mathbf{E}\big[\beta(T)X\,\mathbf{1}_{\{\tau > T\}}\big] = \mathbf{E}[\beta(T)X]\mathbf{E}\big[\mathbf{1}_{\{\tau > T\}}\big]$$
$$= \mathbf{E}[\beta(T)X]P(0, T) = \mathbf{E}[\beta(T)X]e^{-\int_0^T \lambda(s)ds}. \tag{6.5}$$

• Defaultable coupon bond: The defaultable coupon bond is decomposed into a sum of defaultable zero-coupon bonds. The sum of the prices of these zero-coupon bonds makes up the price of the defaultable coupon bond

$$\overline{C} := \sum_{i=1}^{N} \overline{c}\overline{B}(0, T_i) + \overline{B}(0, T_N). \tag{6.6}$$

6.1.2   Recovery of treasury

In the *recovery of treasury (RT)* setup, the recovery of defaulted claims is expressed in terms of the market value of equivalent default-free assets.

Assumption 6.4 (recovery of treasury)

 (i) *There exists an equivalent default-free asset to every defaultable claim. This equivalent default-free claim pays off for sure the payoffs that were promised in the defaultable asset. Its price process is denoted p(t).*
 (ii) *At default, the recovery of every defaulted claim is c times the value of the equivalent default-free asset:*

$$\phi(\tau) = cp(\tau). \tag{6.7}$$

The equivalent default-free asset does not necessarily have to be an actively traded asset, it is sufficient if its price at the time of default can be determined. There are defaultable assets for which such an equivalent asset might not exist, e.g. defaultable shares or the options on defaultable shares that are embedded in convertible bonds. On the other hand, for coupon bonds and derivatives transactions the definition of an equivalent default-free asset is usually straightforward.

The main point of the RT model is the payoff in terms of c default-free assets. If these default-free assets are held until maturity, then the final payoff of the asset is:

$$
[\text{Final payoff}] = \begin{cases} [\text{Promised payoff}] & \text{if no default before maturity,} \\ c \times [\text{Promised payoff}] & \text{otherwise.} \end{cases}
$$

Thus, in all cases, at least c of the promised payoff is actually paid. The rest (a fraction of $(1-c)$) is only paid in survival. Thus – without any further assumptions – we reach the following proposition.

Proposition 6.1 (prices under recovery of treasury) *Let* $\overline{p}_{\text{RT}}$ *be the price of a defaultable asset with maturity T under RT (Assumption 6.4),* $\overline{p}$ *the price of this defaultable asset under zero recovery, and p the price of the equivalent default-free asset. If the recovery rate c is constant, then:*

$$
\overline{p}_{\text{RT}} = (1-c)\overline{p} + c\,p. \tag{6.8}
$$

Proposition 6.1 gives the reason why the RT model is often chosen. It is a good first step to incorporate positive recovery in a model without incurring additional complexity in the pricing problem. Irrespective of other modelling assumptions, the solution of a pricing problem under RT with fixed recovery rate can be reduced to one pricing problem under zero recovery and one default-free pricing problem. In many cases, a solution to the default-free pricing problem will already be available, so that one only has to derive a price under zero recovery in order to be able to apply the RT model.

With this result, we can solve the pricing problems.

- Defaultable zero-coupon bonds (see equation (3.3)):

$$
\overline{B}_{\text{RT}}(0, T) = (1-c)\overline{B}(0, T) + cB(0, T). \tag{6.9}
$$

- Stochastic payoff:

$$
c\mathbf{E}[\beta(T)X] + (1-c)P(0, T)\mathbf{E}[\beta(T)X]. \tag{6.10}
$$

- Defaultable coupon bond: The defaultable coupon bond is decomposed into a sum of defaultable zero-coupon bonds. The sum of the prices of these zero-coupon bonds makes up the price of the defaultable coupon bond

$$
\begin{aligned}
\overline{C}_{\text{RT}} &= (1-c)\overline{C} + cC \\
&= (1-c)\sum_{i=1}^{N}\overline{c}\overline{B}(0, T_i) + c\sum_{i=1}^{N}\overline{c}B(0, T_i) + (1-c)\overline{B}(0, T_N) + cB(0, T_N).
\end{aligned}
$$

$$\tag{6.11}$$

The decomposition in Proposition 6.1 must be modified if the recovery rate changes over time. Then it does matter when the default happens, even if the recovery is invested in the equivalent asset and held until maturity. As an example we consider the second pricing problem (stochastic payoff X) with $c(t)$ time-dependent. The value of the payoff at default is:

$$\mathbf{E}\left[\beta(\tau)c(\tau)p(\tau)\mathbf{1}_{\{\tau \leq T\}}\right]$$
$$= \int_0^T \mathbf{E}[\beta(\tau)c(\tau)p(\tau) \mid \tau = t]\lambda(t)e^{-\int_0^t \lambda(s)ds}dt.$$

Under independence of $\beta(t)p(t)$ and the defaults, this is:

$$= \int_0^T \mathbf{E}\left[\beta(t)c(t)p(t)\right]\lambda(t)e^{-\int_0^t \lambda(s)ds}dt$$

$$= \int_0^T p(0)c(t)\lambda(t)e^{-\int_0^t \lambda(s)ds}dt$$

$$= p(0)\int_0^T c(t)\lambda(t)e^{-\int_0^t \lambda(s)ds}dt$$

$$= p(0)P^{\mathrm{def}}(0, T)\mathbf{E}[c(\tau) \mid \tau \leq T]. \tag{6.12}$$

The derivation of equation (6.12) also carries through for other specifications of the density of the default time than the density of an inhomogeneous Poisson process. The important assumption here was the assumption of independence of the time of default τ and p and β.

Proposition 6.2 (prices under recovery of treasury: time-dependence) *Let $\overline{p}_{\mathrm{RT}}$ be the price of a defaultable asset with maturity T under RT (Assumption 6.4), $\overline{p}$ the price of this defaultable asset under zero recovery, and p the price of the equivalent default-free asset. If the recovery rate $c(t)$ is time-dependent, then:*

$$\overline{p}_{\mathrm{RT}} = (1 - c')\overline{p} + c'p, \tag{6.13}$$

where $c' = \mathbf{E}[c(\tau) \mid \tau \leq T]$ is the expected recovery rate over $[0, T]$ conditional on default in $[0, T]$.

6.1.3 Multiple defaults and recovery of market value

Although they start from slightly different points, the multiple defaults (MD) model and the recovery of market value (RMV) (fractional recovery) model both yield the same pricing relationships.

The multiple defaults model is based upon the following empirical intuition. In many defaults, the defaulted obligor's business is not liquidated but a reorganisation takes place. In the course of such a reorganisation, the bondholders lose a fraction q of the face value of their claims, but the claims continue to live and the issuer continues to operate. After the first default and reorganisation, subsequent defaults are possible, and we can have multiple defaults, which can cause a reduction of the face value of the claims, again. This is the basic idea of the multiple defaults model.

This model mimicks the effect of a rescue plan as it is described in many bankruptcy codes. The old claimants have to give up some of their claims in order to allow for rescue capital to be invested in the defaulted firm. They are *not* paid out in cash[1] (this would drain the defaulted firm of valuable liquidity) but in "new" defaultable bonds of the same maturity. In reality, the new bonds often have a longer term to maturity than the original bonds, and sometimes, part of the payoff is made in shares of the reorganised firm.

Assumption 6.5 (multiple defaults)   *Consider a defaultable claim of X payable at T:*

- *Defaults occur at the stopping times $\tau_1 < \tau_2 < \cdots$, where τ_i is the time of the ith jump of $N(t)$.*
- *At each time τ_i of default, the promised final payoff of the defaultable claim is reduced by the loss quota q.*
- *At time T, the payoff is*

$$X \cdot Q(T) := X \cdot (1-q)^{N(T)}, \tag{6.14}$$

where $Q(T)$ denotes the remaining fraction of the face value of the claim[2] after all reductions through defaults between $t = 0$ and $t = T$.
- *Claims that have multiple payoffs at intermediate times (e.g. defaultable coupon bonds) are treated as a portfolio of individual claims, each suffering payoff reductions until its maturity.*

Because it involves more than one time of default, the MD model leaves the framework set in the outset. Nevertheless, it will be seen that the RMV model yields essentially identical results within the general framework.

Although it involves a possibly infinite number of defaults, the multiple defaults model is constructed in such a way that the pricing of defaultable claims is not complicated. If there are n defaults each with a loss quota of q the final payoff will be:

$$(1-q)^n X.$$

At each default the payoff is reduced to $(1-q)$ times its previous value. Then the price of a general (random) payoff of X at T is

$$p_{\text{MD}} = \mathbf{E}\big[\beta(T)(1-q)^{N(T)}X\big]$$

$$= \mathbf{E}\big[(1-q)^{N(T)}\big]\mathbf{E}\,[\beta(T)X] = \mathbf{E}\big[(1-q)^{N(T)}\big]p,$$

where we used the independence between defaults and X and β. The expectation of the reduced $\mathbf{E}[(1-q)^{N(T)}]$ can be calculated by summing up over all possible realisations of

---

[1] The holder of a defaulted bond is free to sell this bond on the market, though.
[2] It will be clear from the context whether Q denotes the martingale measure or the accumulated fractional default losses.

$N(T)$, weighted with the corresponding probabilities:

$$\mathbf{E}\left[(1-q)^{N(T)}\right] = \sum_{n=0}^{\infty}(1-q)^n \mathbf{P}[N(T)=n]$$

$$= \sum_{n=0}^{\infty}(1-q)^n \frac{1}{n!}\left(\int_0^T \lambda(s)ds\right)^n e^{-\int_0^T \lambda(s)ds}$$

$$= e^{-\int_0^T \lambda(s)ds} \sum_{n=0}^{\infty}\frac{1}{n!}\left((1-q)\int_0^T \lambda(s)ds\right)^n.$$

Now we use the defining property of the exponential function $e^x = \sum_{n=0}^{\infty}\frac{1}{n!}x^n$:

$$= e^{-\int_0^T \lambda(s)ds} e^{(1-q)\int_0^T \lambda(s)ds}$$

$$= e^{-\int_0^T q\lambda(s)ds}.$$

Combining these results yields

$$p_{\mathrm{MD}} = e^{-\int_0^T q\lambda(s)ds} p = \mathbf{E}\left[e^{-\int_0^T r(s)+q\lambda(s)ds} X\right]. \tag{6.15}$$

The pricing problems are solved as follows.

- Defaultable zero-coupon bonds:

$$\overline{B}_{\mathrm{MD}}(0, T) = \mathbf{E}\left[e^{-\int_0^T r(s)+q\lambda(s)ds}\right]. \tag{6.16}$$

- Defaultable random payoff:

$$p_{\mathrm{MD}} = e^{-\int_0^T q\lambda(s)ds} p = \mathbf{E}\left[e^{-\int_0^T r(s)+q\lambda(s)ds} X\right].$$

- Defaultable coupon bond:

$$\overline{C}_{\mathrm{MD}} = \sum_{i=1}^{N}\overline{c}\overline{B}_{\mathrm{MD}}(0, T_i) + \overline{B}_{\mathrm{MD}}(0, T_N). \tag{6.17}$$

The result of the MD model can be summarised in a simple rule.

Proposition 6.3 (multiple defaults) *The prices of defaultable payoffs with MD recovery are reached by discounting the promised payoff with the defaultable short-term interest rate $\overline{r}(t) := r(t) + q\lambda(t)$. The price of a defaultable promised payoff of X at time T is, under Assumptions 6.1, 6.2 and 6.5:*

$$p_{\mathrm{MD}}(t) = Q(t)\mathbf{E}\left[e^{-\int_t^T r(s)+q\lambda(s)ds} X\right] = Q(t)\mathbf{E}\left[e^{-\int_t^T \overline{r}(s)ds} X\right].$$

The factor $Q(t)$ captures the effects of defaults that have already occurred before t. If there was no previous default, it will be $Q(t) = 1$.

Let us now turn our attention to the RMV model.

Assumption 6.6 (recovery of market value)   *Let $p_{RMV}(t)$ be the price of a defaultable asset. If a default happens at $t = \tau$, then the recovery of the defaultable asset is $(1 - q)$ times its pre-default value:*

$$\phi(\tau) = (1 - q)p_{RMV}(\tau-). \tag{6.18}$$

The RMV model is inspired by the recovery rules of OTC derivatives. The ISDA master agreement for swap contracts specifies that at default of one counterparty, the other counterparty's claim is the *market value of a non-defaulted, but otherwise equivalent security* (if this is positive). He is paid a fraction $(1 - q)$ of this claim.

The recovery specification of the RMV model seems to be circular. The recovery is proportional to the pre-default value of the asset, but the pre-default value itself must again depend on the recovery payoff. This does not lead to an inconsistency but to an equation that determines the price of the defaultable asset.

This can be illustrated in discrete time. Assume the following setup:

- We consider the time step from t to $t + \Delta t$.
- The price of the defaultable asset at time t is $p_{RMV}(t)$. The *expected* price of the defaultable asset at time $t + \Delta t$ *given survival* is $p'_{RMV}(t + \Delta t)$.
- The default-free interest rate over $[t, t + \Delta t]$ is R.
- At time t, the obligor has not defaulted yet, but there is a positive probability of default over $[t, t + \Delta t]$ which is P^{def}. The default hazard rate over $[t, t + \Delta t]$ is defined as:

$$\Delta t \cdot H = \frac{P^{def}}{1 - P^{def}}.$$

The price of an asset at time t must be the expected discounted value of its value at time $t + \Delta t$. For a defaultable asset with fractional recovery this means:

$$p_{RMV}(t) = \frac{1}{1 + R\Delta t}((1 - P^{def})p'_{RMV}(t + \Delta t) + P^{def}(1 - q)p_{RMV}(t)). \tag{6.19}$$

Given the price $p_{RMV}(t + \Delta t)$ at time $t + \Delta t$, this equation can be solved recursively for the price $p_{RMV}(t)$ one time step earlier, yielding:

$$p_{RMV}(t) = \frac{1}{1 + \dfrac{\Delta t R + q P^{def}}{1 - P^{def}}} p'_{RMV}(t + \Delta t). \tag{6.20}$$

Equation (6.20) can be expressed in terms of the hazard rate H as:

$$p_{RMV}(t) = \frac{1}{(1 + \Delta t R)(1 + \Delta t q H) + (\Delta t)^2(1 - q)RH} p'_{RMV}(t + \Delta t) \tag{6.21}$$

or

$$\frac{p'_{\text{RMV}}(t + \Delta t) - p_{\text{RMV}}(t)}{p_{\text{RMV}}(t)} = (R + qH)\Delta t + RH(\Delta t)^2. \tag{6.22}$$

In the limit as $\Delta t \to 0$, this turns into a stochastic differential equation that describes the expected development of p_{RMV}. In the limit we ignore terms of order Δt^2 and replace interest and hazard rates with their continuously compounded equivalents. The resulting pricing rule for the price given survival is:

$$\mathbf{E}\left[\frac{dp_{\text{RMV}}(t)}{p_{\text{RMV}}(t-)} \,\middle|\, \mathcal{F}_t\right] = (r + qh)dt. \tag{6.23}$$

This leads us to the following conjecture. Under RMV, the price $p_{\text{RMV}}(t)$ of a defaultable asset at time t is reached by discounting the expected price in survival $p_{\text{RMV}}(t + \Delta t)$ at time $t + \Delta t$ twice: once with the default-free interest rates, and then again with the loss quota q times the default hazard rate over $[t, t + \Delta t]$. The full result is as follows.

Proposition 6.4 (recovery of market value) *Let $p_{\text{RMV}}(t)$ be the price of a defaultable promised payoff of X at T under RMV. Let the time of default be the time of the first jump of a point process $N(t)$ with intensity process $\lambda(t)$. Assume that the process $m(t) = \mathbf{E}[e^{-\int_0^T r(s)+q\lambda(s)ds} X | \mathcal{F}_t]$ (introduced in the proof below) does not jump at τ. Then:*

$$p_{\text{RMV}}(t) = \mathbf{1}_{\{\tau > t\}} \mathbf{E}\left[e^{-\int_t^T r(s)+q\lambda(s)ds} X \,\middle|\, \mathcal{F}_t\right] + \mathbf{1}_{\{\tau = t\}}(1 - q)p_{\text{RMV}}(t-). \tag{6.24}$$

(For $t > \tau$, the price $p_{\text{RMV}}(t)$ is not defined.)

Proof. To prove Proposition 6.4 we must show that the discounted price process $\beta(t)p_{\text{RMV}}(t)$ is a martingale and that it attains the final payoffs: the promised payoff X at T in survival and the recovery payoff at τ as specified by the RMV model.

1. $p_{\text{RMV}}(T) = X$ if $\tau > T$,
2. $p_{\text{RMV}}(\tau) = (1 - q)p_{\text{RMV}}(\tau-)$,
3. $\beta(t)p_{\text{RMV}}(t)$ is a martingale (if stopped at $t = \tau$).

The first two points can be seen directly. For $t = T$, the discounting disappears, and the value at τ was specified precisely so that the second property is ensured. For the last property we must show that the expected increments of βp_{RMV} are zero. Consider the martingale

$$m(t) := e^{-\int_0^t q\lambda(s)ds} \beta(t) \mathbf{E}\left[e^{-\int_t^T r(s)+q\lambda(s)ds} X \,\middle|\, \mathcal{F}_t\right].$$

$m(t)$ is a martingale because it is just the expectation of the random variable $\exp\{-\int_0^T r(s) + q\lambda(s)ds\}X$ given the information at time t. It coincides with $\exp\{-\int_0^t q\lambda(s)ds\}\beta(t)p_{\text{RMV}}(t)$ on $t < \tau$. Thus, the dynamics of $\beta(t)p_{\text{RMV}}(t)$ on $t \leq \tau$ are:

$$d(\beta p_{\text{RMV}})(t) = d\left(e^{\int_0^t q\lambda(s)ds} m\right) - \beta(t-)p_{\text{RMV}}(t-)q\,dN(t).$$

The second term in these dynamics uses the jump process dN in order to achieve the proportional jump downwards in p_{RMV} at the time of default (because then $dN = 1$). We did not need to consider the covariation of the jumps in dN and in dm because we assumed that m and N never have jumps at the same time.

Using Itô's lemma (product rule), the first increment can be evaluated:

$$d(\beta p_{RMV})(t) = m(t-)\lambda(t)q e^{\int_0^t q\lambda(s)ds} dt + e^{\int_0^t q\lambda(s)ds} dm - \beta(t-)p_{RMV}(t-)q\,dN(t),$$

and taking expectations yields the expected increment of (βp_{RMV}):

$$\mathbf{E}\,[d(\beta p_{RMV})(t)] = m(t-)q\lambda(t)e^{\int_0^t q\lambda(s)ds} dt - \beta(t-)p_{RMV}(t-)q\lambda(t)dt$$
$$= \beta(t-)p_{RMV}(t-)q\lambda(t)dt - \beta(t-)p_{RMV}(t-)q\lambda(t)dt = 0.$$

Here we used the fact that $\mathbf{E}\,[dm] = 0$, because m is a martingale. Thus, the expected increments of the discounted price βp_{RMV} are zero, and the proposed price p_{RMV} attains the correct final values at $t = T$ and $t = \tau$. Thus, p_{RMV} is indeed the price of an asset paying off X at T in survival, and which has a recovery according to RMV Assumption 6.6 at τ if $\tau \leq T$. □

The proof above is slightly more complicated than the proofs of the other propositions so far but it also covers a much wider range of possible situations. The default is triggered by a general point process with an intensity that can be stochastic and correlated with all other modelling variables. Furthermore, if the loss quota q was time-dependent or if it followed a predictable stochastic process, the result would still remain unchanged. The payoff time T of the defaultable claim can be a stopping time.

It should not be too surprising that the basic result of the RMV model is the same as for the MD model. In the MD model, the final payoff of the claim is reduced to $(1 - q)$ times the previous final payoff. This means that – other things unchanged – if we had 100 defaultable claims in the portfolio before the default event, after reduction of the claim amount we are in the same position as if the original number of securities was reduced to $100 \times (1 - q)$, without any other default effects. The value of the portfolio after the default event is therefore $(1 - q)$ times what it was before. And this is exactly what the RMV model tells us.

Because they yield essentially the same pricing results and have a similar interpretation, we will consider MD and RMV as equivalent from now on.

Viewed across different defaultable securities, the pricing rule (discounting with $\bar{r} = r + q\lambda$) should apply to all defaultable claims of the same seniority class in the same way. Thus, there is no way of separating the parameters q and λ by observing prices of this form. The same set of prices that is produced by a default intensity of $\lambda = 2\%$ and a loss quota of $q = 50\%$ will be produced by a default intensity of $\lambda' = 1\%$ and a loss quota of $q' = 100\%$. In principle, if only the product

$$x := \lambda q$$

is observed, any value of the default intensity λ in $[x, \infty)$ can be made consistent with this observation (just choose $q = x/\lambda$).

In econometric estimations this disadvantage can be turned into a virtue. It is sufficient to estimate a stochastic process/the term structure of the *product* λq of default intensity and loss quota. If this product is viewed as a fundamental variable, one can still make meaningful statements about the dynamics, distribution and term structure of λq. Even in some pricing problems knowledge of the product λq may be sufficient to derive a solution, sidestepping the question of the size of the recovery rate.

Unfortunately, while perfectly admissible for some econometric studies, avoiding the question of the relative sizes of recovery rate and default intensity will be impossible in other situations. The fee streams of most credit derivatives are cancelled at default, and thus the value of this fee stream does depend on λ alone, not on q. Options and other derivatives with nonlinear payoffs in the underlying defaultable bond are affected by default *arrivals*, but their loss at default will not be a fraction q of the pre-default value. For risk management one needs the probabilities and distributions of both quantities, recovery q *and* intensity λ separately, in order to derive the distribution of the payoffs of the instrument that is to be priced. The same applies to hedging problems.

6.1.4 Recovery of par

The recovery of par model was already introduced in Section 3.2 and Assumption 3.3. Here we rephrase it in a continous-time default setup.

Assumption 6.7 (recovery of par)

- *If a defaultable coupon bond defaults at time t, its recovery payoff is composed of the recovery rate π times the notional of the bond (here normalised to 1):*

$$\phi(t) = \pi. \tag{6.25}$$

- *The coupons of the coupon bond have zero recovery.*[3]
- *For other defaultable securities, a* legal claim amount *V can be defined at all times. If a default should occur, the recovery of the defaultable security is $\pi \times V$.*

While the idea of the MD/RMV model was the renegotiation of the defaulted obligor's debt, the fundamental idea of the RP model is a liquidation under the supervision of a bankruptcy court. In most cases, a bankruptcy court will distribute the proceeds in proportion to the legal claim amount. Claimants of the same seniority class will receive the same proportion of their claim as payoff. If additionally junior claims are not paid off until all claims of higher seniority are paid off in full, one speaks of *absolute priority* being observed. In reality, absolute priority is rarely observed, but claims of the same seniority class are usually treated equally.

For most defaultable claims, the legal claim amount is well-defined. It can be found in the documentation of the bond/obligation in question. Here are some typical specifications:

- For defaultable coupon bonds and loans it is the principal (par) amount plus any accrued interest and missed interest payments.
- For defaultable zero-coupon bonds (rare, but they do exist) an accrual schedule is determined at issuance. This schedule determines by how much the claim amount increases over a given

---

[3] One may add outstanding accrued interest to the notional amount.

time period. The claim amount will increase with the yield to maturity at the issuance price.

- Similarly, for defaultable amortising bonds, a notional reduction schedule is given in the prospectus. This schedule determines which part of the regular payments are deemed interest payments and which part is a principal repayment. Here, the principal (and thus the legal claim amount) will be reduced over time.
- If the loans or bonds are secured with collateral, the collateral is liquidated at the time of default to pay the legal claim amount to the secured loans or bonds. If the value of the collateral is insufficient to do this, then the remaining portion of the legal claim amount enters the normal recovery proceedings. If the loan or bond was guaranteed by a third party, the third party has to pay the legal claim amount to the creditor.[4]
- For OTC derivatives exposures, the claim amount is determined using special rules, e.g. the ISDA rules if a master agreement is in place. Under ISDA rules, the claim amount is the market value of an otherwise equivalent, but not defaulted, derivative. Effectively, this is the RMV model.

As in Section 3.2, the value of a defaultable claim can be decomposed into the sum of the value in survival, and the value of the payoff at default. Unlike in the other recovery models, the claim amounts for coupon bonds are known in advance and do not depend on other variables. Hence, the value of the payoff in survival can be determined by summing up (or integrating) the values of the payments over the different possible default dates. A default at time $t > 0$ would yield a recovery payment of

$$\pi(t)V(t).$$

This payoff is only reached if the default has *not* occurred before, hence we must discount it with the zero-recovery defaultable bond $\overline{B}(0, t)$:

$$\pi(t)V(t)\overline{B}(0, t),$$

and we must also weigh it with the conditional probability of default in $[t, t + dt]$, conditional on survival until t. Seen from $t = 0$, this probability is the default hazard rate $h(0, t)$ for t multiplied by dt. The result is:

$$\pi(t)V(t)\overline{B}(0, t)h(0, t)dt.$$

Integrating over all payment dates yields the following proposition.

Proposition 6.5 (recovery of par)   *Let $V(t)$, $0 \leq t \leq T$ be the claim amount of a defaultable claim with maturity T if a default occurs at time t. Let $\pi(t)$ be the corresponding recovery rate. Assume that the RP model holds, and defaults and default-free interest rates are independent (Assumption 3.2) and that $V(t')$ is known at $t = 0$ for all $t' \geq 0$.*

---

[4] Depending on the specification of the guarantee, the guarantor may enter the loan as borrower and pay interest and principal as agreed with the lender.

(i) The value at time $t = 0$ of the payoff at default is:

$$\int_0^T \pi(t)V(t)h(0, t)\overline{B}(0, t)dt. \tag{6.26}$$

(ii) Let $\overline{p}$ be the value of the claim under zero recovery. Then the value of the claim under RP is:

$$p_{RP} = \overline{p} + \int_0^T \pi(t)V(t)h(0, t)\overline{B}(0, t)dt. \tag{6.27}$$

(iii) The (infinitesimal) value of a payoff of 1 at t if a default occurs at time t, is:

$$e(0, t)dt := h(0, t)\overline{B}(0, t)dt. \tag{6.28}$$

Then, the value of the defaultable claim is:

$$p_{RP} = \overline{p} + \int_0^T \pi(t)V(t)e(0, t)dt. \tag{6.29}$$

Equation (6.28) is the continuous-time version of equation (3.20).

6.1.5   Stochastic recovery and recovery risk

In the previous subsections we assumed that the value of the recovery parameter is constant or time-dependent. This assumption simplified the analysis, but completely ignored the *recovery risk* component. Recovery risk is an important risk factor that can have a significant effect on the prices of credit derivatives (e.g. default digital swaps relative to CDSs, or CDOs). It is therefore desirable to make the parameters π, c and q stochastic.

Mathematically, the correct framework to handle stochastic recovery rates is the general marked point process framework.

Assumption 6.8   *We modify the setup of Assumption 6.2 such that the recovery rate Φ is a random variable that is drawn from E at the time of default τ. Then the time of default τ and the recovery rate $\Phi \in E$ form a marked point process. The compensator measure of this marked point process is:*

$$v(d\varphi, dt) = K(d\varphi)\lambda(t)dt. \tag{6.30}$$

$K(d\varphi)$ is the conditional distribution of Φ, given that a default happens in the next instance. $K(d\varphi)$ and the intensity $\lambda(t)$ can be predictable stochastic processes themselves. The locally expected recovery payoff

$$\mathbf{E}[\Phi \mid \mathcal{F}_{t-} \wedge \{\tau = t\}] = \int_E \varphi K(d\varphi) =: \varphi^e(t) \tag{6.31}$$

follows a predictable stochastic process, too.

For RT, RMV and RP, the compensator of the marked point process describing stochastic recovery is defined analogously:

- *In the RT model, c in equation (6.7) is the stochastic marker at default. We denote the jump measure of the defaults by $\mu_{RT}(dc, dt)$, and its compensator measure by $v_{RT}(dc, dt) = K_{RT}(dc)\lambda(t)dt$, with conditional distribution $K_{RT}(dc)$ and local expectation $c^e(t)$.*
- *In the RMV model, the loss quota q in equation (6.18) is the marker at default with conditional distribution $K_{RMV}(dq)$ and local expectation $q^e(t)$.*
- *In the RP model, π in equation (6.25) is the marker at default with conditional distribution $K_{RP}(d\pi)$ and the local expectation $\pi^e(t)$.*
- *In the MD model, there is a marker[5] q_i to each time of default τ_i. The conditional distribution of these markers is $K_{MD}(q)$, and the local expectation $q^e(t)$.*

In the second part of this assumption, we denoted the random recovery rates and the integrand in the conditional distribution by the same letters.

For pricing purposes, one can replace the stochastic recovery rate almost always with its local expected value as follows.

We assume an asset with maturity T, and general stochastic recovery as in Assumption 6.8. Using the jump measure of the marked point process, the payoff at default can be written as follows:

$$\int_0^T \int_E \beta(t)\phi\mu(d\phi, dt) = \begin{cases} \beta(\tau)\Phi & \text{if } \tau < T, \\ 0 & \text{otherwise.} \end{cases}$$

The integral will evaluate to the discounted value of the realised recovery rate Φ if a default happens in $[0, T]$, otherwise it will be zero. Thus, recovery pricing is the evaluation of the following expectation:

$$\mathbf{E}\left[\int_0^T \int_E \beta(t)\phi\mu(d\phi, dt)\right]. \tag{6.32}$$

By the definition of the compensator measure, an integral with respect to the jump measure has the same expected value as an integral of the same integrand with respect to the compensator measure. This means here:

$$\mathbf{E}\left[\int_0^T \int_E \beta(t)\phi\mu(d\phi, dt)\right] = \mathbf{E}\left[\int_0^T \int_E \beta(t)\phi K(d\phi)\lambda(t)dt\right]$$

$$= \mathbf{E}\left[\int_0^T \beta(t)\left(\int_E \phi K(d\phi)\right)\lambda(t)dt\right]$$

$$= \mathbf{E}\left[\int_0^T \beta(t)\varphi^e(t)\lambda(t)dt\right]. \tag{6.33}$$

The pricing problem (6.32) with a stochastic marker as recovery payoff Φ can be reduced to a pricing problem (6.33) with a predictable process $\varphi^e(t)$ as recovery payoff. This is a major

---

[5] The equivalence between MD and RMV also holds for stochastic recovery, therefore we use the same notation for both models.

improvement, as it allows us to move back from a *marked* point process framework to an *unmarked* point process. We just substitute the locally expected recovery payoff φ^e for the stochastic recovery rate Φ.

The same applies to the multiple recovery rates in the MD model. Fundamentally, the pricing problem is the evaluation of expressions like

$$\mathbf{E}\left[\beta(T)\prod_{\tau_i \leq T}(1-q_i)X\right] =: \mathbf{E}\left[\beta(T)Q(T)X\right].\tag{6.34}$$

At each default τ_i, the final claim amount is reduced by a loss quota q_i to $(1-q_i)$ times what it was before. Here, q_i is the stochastic marker to the default time τ_i. At maturity T, the cumulative effect of all intermediate defaults until T is represented by the product $\prod_{\tau_i \leq T}(1-q_i)$.

From the solution formula (4.35) of stochastic exponentials we see, furthermore, that the product $Q(t)$ can be represented by the following stochastic differential equation:

$$dQ(t) = -Q_-(t)q_i dN(t),$$

or equivalently:

$$Q(T) = \int_0^T\int_E -Q_-(t)q\mu(dq, dt),$$

with initial condition $Q(0) = 1$.

We already showed that for the single-default models the stochastic marker can be replaced with its local expectation. The MD pricing problem (6.34) with multiple defaults can also be reduced to one involving only the locally expected loss quota $q^e(t)$ (and no longer a marked point process). We start from the s.d.e. for $Q(T)$:

$$\mathbf{E}\left[\beta(T)XQ(T)\right] = \mathbf{E}\left[\beta(T)X\int_0^T\int_E -qQ_-(t)\mu(dq, dt)\right].$$

Using the compensator measure this is:

$$= \mathbf{E}\left[\beta(T)X\int_0^T Q_-(t)\left(\int_E -qK(dq)\right)\lambda(t)dt\right]$$

$$= \mathbf{E}\left[\beta(T)X\int_0^T -Q_-(t)q^e(t)\lambda(t)dt\right].$$

Now we change back from integrating with respect to $\lambda(t)dt$ to integration with respect to $dN(t)$. This is allowed because $\int_0^T \lambda(t)dt$ is the compensator of $N(T)$:

$$= \mathbf{E}\left[\beta(T)X\int_0^T -Q_-(t)q^e(t)dN(t)\right].$$

Finally, the integral in the expectation is a stochastic exponential. Therefore we can use the solution formula (4.35) to reach:

$$E[\beta(T)Q(T)X] = E\left[\beta(T)\prod_{\tau_i \leq T}(1 - q^e(\tau_i))X\right].$$
(6.35)

But equation (6.35) is the pricing problem if the loss quota was given by the predictable process $q^e(t)$. Summarising the results so far we have following proposition.

Proposition 6.6 (stochastic recovery)   *Under stochastic recovery (Assumption 6.8), the prices of defaultable bonds can be calculated by assuming predictable recovery rates* $\varphi^e(t)$ *($c^e(t)$, $\pi^e(t)$ or loss quota $(1 - q)^e(t)$), where:*

$$\varphi^e(t) = \int_E \varphi K(d\varphi), \qquad c^e(t) = \int_E c K_{RT}(dc),$$

$$\pi^e(t) = \int_E \pi K_{RP}(d\pi), \qquad (1 - q)^e(t) = \int_E (1 - q) K_{RMV}(d(1 - q)).$$

The simple rule of thumb "Always use the locally expected recovery rate" is true for the pricing of defaultable bonds, but sometimes it does not yield the right results. It is correct, as long as the payoff or the value of the defaultable instrument depends *linearly* on the recovery rate. As soon as nonlinearities enter, the problem becomes more complicated. Consider for example the following modification of a default digital swap (DDS):

The payoff at default is 1 *if the recovery rate is below 50%*. Otherwise the payoff at default is zero.

This is a special case of a *recovery contingent claim*. In general, the payoff of a credit derivative can be some nonlinear function $f(\cdot)$ of the recovery rate π, if a default happens before the maturity of the contract T. (For convenience we use the RP model.)
   To price this contract, we need to evaluate the following expression:

$$E\left[\int_0^T\int_E \beta(t)f(\pi)\mu(d\pi, dt)\right].$$
(6.36)

The same arguments as above lead to the pricing relationship

$$E\left[\int_0^T\int_E \beta(t)f(\pi)\mu(d\pi, dt)\right] = E\left[\int_0^T \beta(t)\int_E f(\pi)K(d\pi)\lambda dt\right].$$
(6.37)

Thus, for the example above, $f(e) = \mathbf{1}_{\{e \leq 1/2\}}$ and $\int_E f(\pi)K(d\pi) = \int_0^{\frac{1}{2}} f(\pi)K(d\pi) = K([0, \frac{1}{2}])$, the "recovery" value to be used is the probability that the recovery is less than $1/2$. Of course this result could have been guessed directly from the specification above, but in more complicated cases the result will not be so obvious.

Furthermore, the "expected value" rule of thumb is incorrect and dangerous when it comes to risk management and hedging. Almost always, stochastic recovery changes a complete markets model in which perfect hedging is at least theoretically possible to an incomplete markets model, where no perfect hedging strategies exist and residual uncertainty must be taken.

To illustrate this point, a model with stochastic recovery can be approximated with a tree model like the tree in Figure 3.2, only we now have not just one branch to default at every node but 100 branches: one for a default with 0% recovery, one for a default with 1% recovery, ... To span this uncertainty, we would need 101 securities with linearly independent payoffs at default, i.e. 101 different seniority classes.

6.1.6 Common parametric distribution functions for recoveries

So far, nothing has been said about the distribution function $K(dx)$ of the recovery rate that can be used in a credit risk model. We need a flexible class of distributions on the unit interval $[0, 1]$ that does not depend on many parameters. The standard choices here are either the class of *beta distributions* or transformations of "standard" distributions on $\mathbb{R}$ to $[0, 1]$, e.g. the logit- or probit-transformed normal distribution.

Definition 6.1 (beta distribution)   *The density of the beta distribution with parameters p and q is*

$$f(x) = \frac{1}{B(p, q)} x^{p-1}(1 - x)^{q-1}, \quad x \in [0, 1] \tag{6.38}$$

where p and q are non-negative parameters. Outside $[0, 1]$, the beta distribution has zero mass. The beta function $B(\alpha, \beta)$ *is defined as*

$$B(\alpha, \beta) = \int_0^1 t^{\alpha-1}(1 - t)^{\beta-1} dt \tag{6.39}$$

for $\alpha > 0$ and $\beta > 0$.

If the gamma function $\Gamma(\cdot)$ is implemented, it can be used to evaluate the beta function as follows:

$$B(\alpha, \beta) = \frac{\Gamma(\alpha)\Gamma(\beta)}{\Gamma(\alpha + \beta)},$$

and if α and β are integers, we can use factorials:

$$B(\alpha, \beta) = \frac{(\alpha - 1)!(\beta - 1)!}{(\alpha + \beta - 1)!}.$$

The moments of a beta-(p, q) distributed random variable X are:

$$\mathbf{E}[X] = \frac{p}{p+q}, \tag{6.40}$$

$$\text{var}(X) = pq(p+q)^{-2}(p+q+1)^{-1}, \tag{6.41}$$

$$\mathbf{E}[X^r] = \frac{B(p+r, q)}{B(p, q)} = \frac{p^{[r]}}{(p+q)^{[r]}}, \tag{6.42}$$

where $r \in \mathbb{N}$ and $y^{[r]} := y(y+1)\cdots(y+r-1)$ is the ascending factorial (see Johnson and Kotz, 1970).

If p and q are increased while keeping the ratio q/p constant, the distribution will keep its mean at $1/(1 + q/p)$ and the variance will decrease; the distribution will be more centred.

Some possible shapes of the density function of the beta distribution are shown in Figure 6.1. These include the special cases of uniform and linear density functions, but also hump-shaped densities with arbitrary location of the hump.

As an alternative to using the family of beta distributions, one can also use a transformed normally distributed random variable. The logit transformation

$$\pi(X) := F(X) = \frac{e^X}{1 + e^X} \tag{6.43}$$

transforms any random variable X from $\mathbb{R}$ to the unit interval $[0, 1]$. The converse transformation is:

$$X = F^{-1}(\pi) = \ln\left(\frac{\pi}{1-\pi}\right). \tag{6.44}$$

Thus, given a set of observations $\pi_1, \ldots, \pi_N$, a standard maximum likelihood estimation can be performed on the transformed variables $X_1 := F^{-1}(\pi_1), \ldots$ using the transformation (6.44). This transformation is used in Unal et al. (2001).

6.1.7   Valuation of the delivery option in a CDS

In a standard CDS, the protection buyer has the right to choose which defaultable obligation he delivers to the protection seller in a credit event. Whenever possible, he will choose to deliver the cheapest deliverable security. If the set of deliverable obligations is large and the post-default market prices of the deliverable obligations are not perfectly correlated, this right can be of significant value.

We consider $k = 1, \ldots, K$ deliverable obligations, all issued by the same obligor, with prices $\pi_1, \ldots, \pi_K$ after the credit event. The post-default prices π_k are modelled as markers to the default arrival time τ. Thus the mark space is actually $E = [0, 1]^K$.

We are interested in the distribution of $\pi^* := \min_k \pi_k$, because that is the recovery of the obligation that will be delivered. For the distribution function of the minimum we have:

$$\mathbf{P}[\min_k \pi_k \leq x] = 1 - \mathbf{P}[\pi_k > x \; \forall \, k = 1, \ldots, K].$$

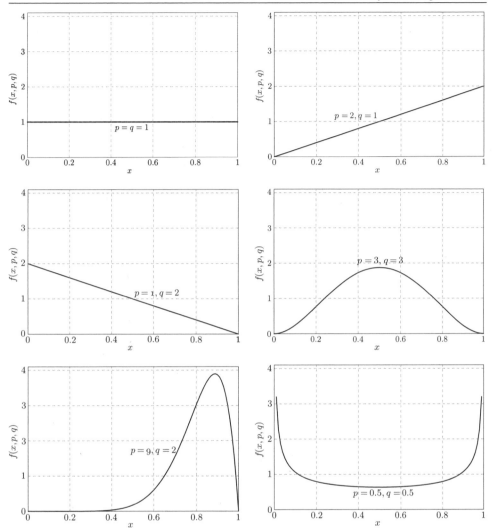

Figure 6.1 Densities of beta distributions for different parameter values

To further analyse this distribution we need a specific model for the different recovery rates of the deliverable obligations. Let us assume that the recovery rates are generated from normally distributed random variables using the following recipe.

First, we generate normally distributed random variables X_k, $k = 1, \ldots, K$ with mean μ_k, standard deviation σ_k and correlation ρ as follows:

$$X_k = \mu_k + \sigma_k\left(\sqrt{\rho}Y + \sqrt{1 - \rho}\epsilon_k\right), \tag{6.45}$$

where ϵ_k and Y are identically independently distributed standard normal $N(0, 1)$ random numbers. The correlation is induced by having a common driving factor Y, and some idiosyncratic variation is caused by the noise terms ϵ_k. The kth recovery rate is then given by the logit transformation (6.43) of this number:

$$\pi_k = F(X_k) = \frac{e^{X_k}}{1 + e^{X_k}}. \tag{6.46}$$

It is now straightforward to calculate the conditional probability distribution, conditioned on the realisation of the systematic factor Y:

$$\mathbf{P}[F(X_k) \geq x \mid Y = y] = N\left(\frac{\sqrt{\rho}\sigma_k y + \mu_k - F^{-1}(x)}{\sqrt{1 - \rho}\sigma_k}\right),$$

where $N(\cdot)$ is the cumulative normal distribution function. (This and similar calculations will be derived in detail in the chapter on correlation modelling.)

6.2 COMPARING THE RECOVERY MODELS

6.2.1 Theoretical comparison of the recovery models

In the previous sections, three different ways of modelling the recovery of defaultable claims have been introduced: recovery of treasury (RT), recovery of market value and multiple defaults (RMV/MD), and recovery of par value (RP). There is one free, unspecified parameter in each of the models. Thus, if we are free to choose this parameter for every defaultable security, we can (in principle) reach every possible payoff at default in each of the recovery models. In this sense, the recovery models are mathematically equivalent to each other. Unfortunately, this equivalence does not help much because all it tells us is that the models lack structure unless we impose additional restrictions.

One natural restriction is that we would like to use the *same* recovery parameter for *all* defaultable instruments of equal seniority that were issued by the same obligor. This parameter may be stochastic and time-dependent, but we do not want to have to specify a separate recovery parameter for each and every individual bond. Such a restriction is sensible if either through bankruptcy courts or through cross-default provisions an equal treatment of these defaultable instruments can be expected. As the recovery models parametrise the payoff at default in different ways, different recovery models will affect the bonds in different ways, e.g. different maturities or differences in the size of their coupons. This gives us a handle to identify and discuss the differences between the recovery models.

In addition to this stability across different securities, we would also like to have some degree of stability over time. The recovery parameter (or its distribution if it is stochastic) should remain relatively stable over time, in particular as the security approaches its maturity date. This requirement is meant to preclude artificial variations that are caused by the modelling approach, and not empirical regularities like the variation of average recovery rates over the business cycle.

An important application of the recovery model is the derivation of a term structure of implied default hazard rates. Typically, we have several (e.g. three to five) defaultable instruments of the same seniority class and the same obligor to which we want to calibrate a spread curve. These could be defaultable coupon bonds and/or CDSs. If we assume a time-invariant distribution of the recovery parameter, and assume that the same parameter value applies to all instruments at default, how "realistic" is the resulting spread curve for different recovery models? (Of course the term "realistic" involves judgement.) We will consider the following test cases to (theoretically) analyse the influence of the recovery part of the model on the output of the model itself. Ideally, the analysis of these cases will lead to data-based tests of the models.

(i) For a given default mechanism (Poisson arrival with constant intensity) and a given constant recovery rate, what form do the resulting zero-coupon spread curves and the par spread curves have?

(ii) For a given zero-coupon spread curve or par spread curve (flat) and a given value for the recovery parameter, what form will the calibrated default hazard rate curve have?

(iii) What does the price difference of two bonds with the same maturity but different coupon sizes mean for the implied default probabilities?

(iv) How does the model perform for high-yield bonds and for distressed bonds that trade at a large discount from their par value?

Furthermore, the "story" behind the model should be convincing. Given the lack of reliable information on recovery rates, it is necessary to be able to form an intuition on realistic parameter sizes (plausibility checks). It should be possible to calibrate to historical data[6] on recovery rates. The model should also not show any unrealistic behaviour (e.g. recoveries of more than 100%).

6.2.1.1 Recovery of treasury

Let us first discuss the RT model, because it is the weakest candidate of the three. The weaknesses of the RT model are:

- Coupon bonds can recover more than their par value.

This occurs for example if the defaultable coupon bond has a high default risk, a long time to maturity, and trades close to par. Then, the equivalent default-free coupon bond will have a value that is significantly above par (because of the larger coupon). If the recovery rate is large, this can result in a recovery payoff that is larger than the par value of the bond.

As a numeric example consider the following situation:

- Continuously compounded default-free interest rates $r = 4\%$ at all times.
- Default intensity $\lambda = 5\%$ constant, average RT recovery rate $c^e = 40\%$.
- Defaultable coupon bonds of 5 and 10 years to maturity annual coupons $\bar{c}_5 = 7.0967\%$ and $\bar{c}_{10} = 6.9584\%$. The bonds trade at par ($= 100$) at these coupons.

The equivalent default-free coupon bonds with 5 and 10 years to maturity have a value of $c_5 = 113.39$ and $c_{10} = 123.24$ respectively. In the case of the 10-year bond, a recovery rate of $c = 82\%$ or more would result in a payoff $c\bar{C}$ at default of more than 100. We assume that the *average* recovery rate is 40%, but in situations with stochastic recovery rates there can still be events when the realised recovery rate is much larger.

---

[6] Strictly speaking, the use of historical data in expectations-based pricing is only valid if the risk does not carry any systematic risks or risk premia. The recourse to historical data is a sign of the lack of market data and of the large degree of uncertainty surrounding recovery risk.

To remove such a situation from the model, an upper bound below 100% must be imposed on the recovery rate parameter c. This upper bound will be tighter the longer the term to maturity of the bond: for a 30-year defaultable par bond it will be 66%. If the same recovery rate is to be used for defaultable bonds of all maturities, then it is not clear at which maturity to draw the line.

- For every value of $c > 0$, there is an upper bound for market-observed credit spreads. RT is inconsistent with any spreads that are higher than this upper bound.

Consider the yield spread $s_{RT}^y(0, T)$ of a defaultable zero-coupon bond $\overline{B}_{RT}(0, T)$, which is defined by:

$$\overline{B}_{RT}(0, T) = B(0, T)e^{-s_{RT}^y(0,T)T}.$$

In RT, the price of the defaultable zero-coupon bond is given by $\overline{B}_{RT}(0, T) = (1 - c)\overline{B}(0, T) + cB(0, T)$. Thus:

$$e^{-s_{RT}^y(0,T)T} = \frac{\overline{B}_{RT}(0, T)}{B(0, T)} = (1 - c)P(0, T) + c > c.$$

Taking logarithms and dividing both sides by $-T$ leads to the bound

$$s_{RT}^y(0, T) < -\frac{1}{T}\ln c. \tag{6.47}$$

(The logarithm of c will be negative.) This bound is significant, particularly as it does *not* depend on the default intensity. If $c = 0.4$, then $-\ln c \approx 0.916$. For $T = 10$ this means that $s_{RT}^y < 9.16\%$ *whatever the actual default risk of the obligor.* In particular, for high-risk bonds this can be a significant restriction.

These points highlight a fundamental problem of the RT model:

A constant RT recovery rate means different loss severities for bonds of different maturities and different loss severities for bonds of different coupon sizes.

With increasing maturity or increasing coupons the "equivalent" default-free coupon bonds become more valuable (provided the coupon is larger than the risk-free rate). Thus, the recovery payoff of a defaultable bond is higher for bonds with longer maturities.

To analyse the test cases we need the par spreads of defaultable coupon bonds under the RT model setup. Equation (6.11) gives the price $\overline{c}_{RT}$ of a defaultable coupon bond in the RT recovery model. To derive the par coupon we set this price equal to 1 (par) and solve for the coupon $\overline{c}$:

$$\overline{c}_{RT}^{par} = \frac{1 - cB(0, T_N) - (1 - c)\overline{B}(0, T_N)}{c\sum_{i=1}^{N} B(0, T_i) + (1 - c)\sum_{i=1}^{N} \overline{B}(0, T_i)}.$$

Subtracting the default-free par coupon amount from this gives the par coupon spread s_{RT}^{par} in the RT model:

$$s_{RT}^{par} = \frac{(1 - \overline{B}(0, T_N)) \sum_{i=1}^{N} B(0, T_i) - (1 - B(0, T_N)) \sum_{i=1}^{N} \overline{B}(0, T_i)}{\sum_{i=1}^{N} B(0, T_i) \left(c \sum_{i=1}^{N} B(0, T_i) + (1 - c) \sum_{i=1}^{N} \overline{B}(0, T_i) \right)}. \tag{6.48}$$

There is also an upper bound for par spreads. This is reached by letting the default intensity approach infinity, or setting $\overline{B}(0, T_i) = 0$ for all $i \leq N$. This will increase the numerator and decrease the denominator. The bound is:

$$s_{RT}^{par} \leq \frac{1}{c \sum_{i=1}^{N} B(0, T_i)}. \tag{6.49}$$

In the RT model the par spread is bounded from above very much like the zero-coupon bond yield spreads. This upper bound is again independent of the default intensity.

Using the numbers given above (recovery $c = 40\%$, default-free interest rates $r = 4\%$, annual coupons) we reach the following results.

(i) Par spreads for a given term structure of default intensities: If defaults are triggered by a constant intensity Poisson process with intensity $\lambda = 5\%$, the par spreads of the defaultable coupon bonds range from 3.14% (for maturity $T = 1$) to 2.48% (for maturity $T = 30$). The par spread curve is monotonically decreasing (see Figure 6.2). The zero-coupon bond yield spreads exhibit the same behaviour, but they are a little bit below the par spreads. From Figure 6.2 one can also see that the upper bound for the zero-coupon bond spreads can become a significantly binding restraint.

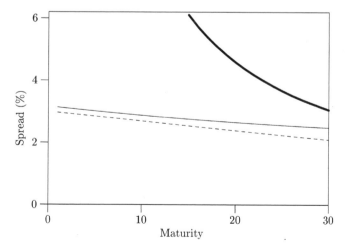

Figure 6.2 Spreads in the recovery of treasury (RT) model. Par coupon spreads (straight line), zero-coupon spreads (dashed), upper bound for zero-coupon spreads (bold). Parameters: default-free interest rate $r = 4\%$, default intensity $\lambda = 5\%$, recovery rate $c = 40\%$, annual coupons

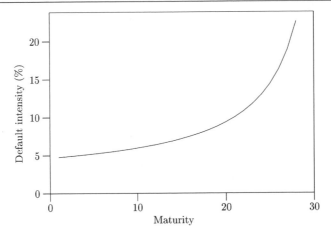

Figure 6.3 Forward default intensities corresponding to a flat 3% par spread curve in the recovery of treasury (RT) model. Parameters: default-free interest rate $r = 4\%$, given par spread $s_{RT}^{par} = 3\%$, recovery rate $c = 40\%$, annual coupons

(ii) Implied intensities for a given par spread curve: If a term structure of par spreads is given, the corresponding term structure of implied default intensities is influenced by the upper bounds on the par spreads. The closer the par spread curve comes to this upper bound, the higher the resulting implied default intensity. If the upper bound is touched, the implied default intensity approaches infinity. This effect is shown in Figure 6.3 for a flat initial par spread curve of 3%. Furthermore, the RT model is inconsistent with any empirically observed par spreads that violate the spread bounds (6.47) or (6.49). Similar upper bounds can be derived for time-dependent or stochastic interest rates and default intensities.

(iii) Coupon differences: Because the recovery in the RT model is specified in terms of all defaultable claims, a different coupon amount will result in a different recovery payoff for the bond in question, even if all other terms (principal amount, maturity, payment dates) are unchanged.

(iv) Behaviour for high-yield bonds: The high coupons and default intensities of high-yield bonds exacerbate the problems of the RT model. In the example above, a flat par spread curve of $s_{RT}^{par} = 7\%$ cannot be fitted beyond a maturity of 14 years. This is caused by the upper bounds on par- and zero-bound yield spreads. The higher the default intensity, the closer we get to these bounds, and there are cases when the model is inconsistent with market prices. The likelihood of recovery rates over 100% is also increased by the large coupon. (If the par coupon spread is 7%, the equivalent four-year default-free bond is worth 125.34).

The biggest strength of the RT model is computational convenience. If a price for the corresponding default-free payoff is already available, and a model for the zero-recovery case has also already been built, then the RT model does not require anything but forming a weighted average of the default-free and the zero-recovery price.

Unfortunately, this strength is not sufficient to cover the significant shortcomings of this modelling approach. In particular for low credit qualities the RT model can lead to unrealistic shapes of spread curves and intensities, and precluding recoveries above 100% requires some complicated adjustments to the model.

Thus, the verdict on RT is: RT is convenient as a quick fix to add some kind of recovery to models that previously only had zero recovery, but otherwise it cannot be recommended for credit derivatives pricing.

6.2.1.2 Recovery of market value and recovery of par value

As opposed to the RT model, RMV (and therefore also MD) does not impose unrealistic bounds on spreads. By definition, the par coupon of a defaultable coupon bond with default intensity λ, loss quota q and default-free interest rate r must ensure that the price of the defaultable bond is at par after the payment of the coupon (given survival and given no change in interest rates and default intensities). If coupons are paid at intervals of Δt, the par coupon amount is

$$e^{(r+q\lambda)\Delta t} - 1 \tag{6.50}$$

and the corresponding par coupon spread is

$$s_{\text{RMV}}^{par} = e^{(r+q\lambda)\Delta t} - e^{r\Delta t}. \tag{6.51}$$

This par coupon amount is independent of the maturity of the bond, and there is no upper bound to the par spreads s_{RMV}^{par}, nor is there an upper bound to the zero-coupon bond spreads $q\lambda$. This means that the problems of the RT model are avoided. Thus we can immediately answer some test questions.

(i) Shape of par spreads for given default intensities: For constant default intensities, the par spread curves are also constant over maturity, and the par spread is given by (6.51). It is approximately equal to the product $q\lambda\Delta t$ of the corresponding default intensity curve.

(ii) Shape of default intensities for given par spreads: For the same reason as in (i), there will be no distortion in the implied default hazard rates that are derived from a par spread curve under the RMV model. The default intensity curve that corresponds to a given flat par spread curve is again flat.

(iii) ...

(iv) Different coupon sizes and bonds below par: If two defaultable bonds are identical except for the sizes of their respective coupons, they will have different pre-default prices. Thus, according to the specification of the RMV model, they will have different payoffs at default. Similarly, if they have the same RMV recovery rate, bonds that trade far below par will also have recovery payoffs far below the recovery of bonds of the same issuer and seniority that trade at par.

For par coupon bonds, the RMV and RP models imply the same payoffs at default. The pre-default market value and the par value of this bond coincide in this case. Therefore we expect the RP model to exhibit qualitatively similar properties to the RMV model.

The par coupon amount in the RP model is the zero-recovery par coupon $e^{(r+\lambda)\Delta t} - 1$, but reduced by the value of the expected payoff at default, if a default happens over the next coupon interval. A short calculation yields the following par coupon amount in the RP model:

$$\frac{r + \lambda(1 - \pi)}{r + \lambda}\left(e^{(r+\lambda)\Delta t} - 1\right), \tag{6.52}$$

assuming no recovery on accrued interest and a par value of 1. The corresponding par spread is:

$$s_{RP}^{par} = \frac{r + \lambda(1 - \pi)}{r + \lambda}\left(e^{(r+\lambda)\Delta t} - 1\right) - \left(e^{r\Delta t} - 1\right). \tag{6.53}$$

Again (given a flat term structure of interest rates and default intensities), the par coupon spreads do not depend on the maturity of the bond considered. Conversely, the implied default intensity curve that results from a constant par spread curve will also be constant, and there are no distortions in the shape of the spread curve through the RP model. To derive zero-coupon bond spreads in the RP model, the principal accrual schedule of the zerobond must be known, therefore we do not analyse these spreads here.

For small Δt, the par coupon amount is approximately $r\Delta t + (1 - \pi)\lambda\Delta t$. This is equivalent to the par coupon of the RMV model: $r\Delta t + q\lambda\Delta t$. (Note that q is a *loss* quota.) This confirms that RMV and RP are equivalent for all securities whose market price is close to the corresponding par value.

Differences between RP and RMV occur if the prices of the bonds are far away from par, e.g. for "fallen angels" and bonds close to default. Assume a bond with one year to maturity trades at 50, although its par value is 100. This situation can be consistent with any RMV recovery rate, if the default intensity is chosen large enough (the product must be larger than $-\ln 0.5 \approx 69.3\%$). For the RP model on the other hand, the assumed recovery parameter π must be less than 50%, otherwise there would be no losses at default. This restricts the RP model.

Now assume that (due to lack of data and manpower) we are forced to estimate one recovery parameter (and maybe also its distribution) for a whole industry, and we do not want to change this parameter too often. Let us say it is $\pi = 40\%$ or $q = 60\%$, depending on the model we use. If we only consider bonds at par, we should be indifferent as to which model we use.

But what if one obligor is downgraded to CCC, trades at 50 for two weeks, and eventually defaults? Here, RP and RMV imply different payoffs at default. RP implies that the payoff at default will be 40, irrespective of the path the bond took into default. RMV on the other hand implies that the payoff will be 20, because the pre-default market value is only 50, and not 100. If the bond had defaulted directly, RMV would imply a recovery of 40. Thus, RMV depends on the path the bond takes into default. This also applies to the multiple-defaults interpretation of the RMV model. The firm is reorganised, but emerges from the reorganisation with the same default risk that it had just before default, a CCC risk.

The coupon bond prices resulting from the different recovery assumptions in a distressed situation are shown in Figure 6.4. The default intensity was chosen very high at $\lambda = 50\%$, the one-year survival probability is just 60%, and the five-year survival probability is 8%. The various recovery parameters (except DF and ZR) were all set to 40%. Not surprisingly, in all models bonds trade far below their par value.

With increasing maturity, bond prices under RP approach very quickly a limiting value (47.5). This limit represents the value of the next coupons and the value of the expected recovery payoff at default. For a five-year bond, the value of the recovery payment alone is 35.18 and makes up 69% of the value of the bond. In the case with 5% default intensity it only contributed 8% of the value of the bond.

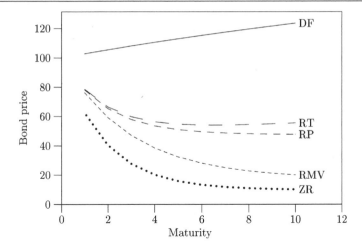

Figure 6.4 Distressed coupon bond prices in different recovery models. (DF = default-free, RT = recovery of treasury, RP = recovery of par, RMV = recovery of market value, ZR = zero recovery.) Parameters: 7% annual coupon, 100 par value, default intensity $\lambda = 50\%$, recovery rate parameter 40%, default-free interest rate $r = 4\%$

Bond prices under RT can even increase with increasing time to maturity (55.54 for a 10-year bond, and 65.85 for a 30-year bond). This is caused by the increase in value of the equivalent default-free bond.

In the RMV model, all payoffs are discounted with $r + \lambda q$. If the default intensity λ is very large and maturity is far away, the principal repayment will have almost no contribution to the initial bond price, and most of the value is contributed by early coupon payments. In the RP model on the other hand, the cash recovery payment *at* default does carry more value.

The RMV bond prices are generally much lower than the RP bond prices for the same default intensity and recovery parameter values, and they also converge to a much lower level (around 17.3). Conversely, for a given bond price and recovery parameter value, both models imply strongly different default intensities. In the setup of Figure 6.4 a five-year bond price of 50 implies a default intensity of $\lambda = 53.1\%$ under the RP model. In the RMV model, the same bond price is reached with a much lower intensity of $\lambda = 31.8\%$. This contrasts strongly with the situation for par coupon bonds, where the par coupon spreads (and thus the implied default intensities) were approximately equal between the RMV and RP models.

The recovery payoff of a bond in the RMV model depends on the path that the bond's price has taken before default. To some extent this is validated by empirical observations on the connection between recovery rates and pre-default ratings (see next subsection), but there is no *a priori* reason why this relationship should have precisely the form given in RMV. The price-dependence of recoveries can also be a problem when credit crises occur that force large price drops over whole market segments, before the actual defaults happen. To avoid this effect, one can adjust the RMV recovery rate to the current rating class of the bond. In the example above we could set the loss quota in CCC q_{CCC} to 20%, then the bond would recover 40 (in cash) at default. This amounts to mimicking the RP setup. Furthermore, we now reach very different implied default intensities. To reach a price of 50 for a five-year bond with $q = 20\%$, the default intensity must be extremely high: $\lambda = 95.4\%$.

Alternatively, one can already view the downgrade to CCC as the default event, and consider the price drop from the pre-*downgrade* price as the loss in default. In this approach it is hard to decide where to draw the line. The obligor can spend a long time in a CCC rating state, until he finally defaults. Furthermore, redefining the default event for modelling convenience is not a good idea in the pricing of credit derivatives. "Default" is a term that is precisely specified in the documentation of credit derivatives, and ultimately we want to model the uncertainty of the arrival of exactly this event. Having to handle the distinction between "model default events" and "CDS default events" will introduce additional uncertainty into the model. A clear model for the timing of CDS default events is particularly important because CDSs only have a finite maturity. It makes all the difference if a CDS default event occurs before or after the maturity of the CDS.

These problems are avoided if defaults come as *complete surprises*. Then the pre-default price will be close to par, and the recovery will have the usual meaning, without any need to tamper with loss quotas or recovery rates. And not surprisingly, defaults in all intensity-based models *do* come as complete surprises, including the hazard-rate-based spread model of Chapter 3 and the Poisson models. For these modelling approaches, RMV is indeed a good and very elegant way to describe losses at default.

We can sum up the pros and cons of RMV and RP as follows.

- Pricing of par bonds/securities close to par:
  RMV similar to RP.
  RP similar to RMV.
- Pricing of recovery of OTC derivatives:
  RMV very good.
  RP must mimic RMV.
- Downgraded and distressed debt:
  RMV recovery assumption must be adjusted.
  RP recovery assumption can remain unchanged as long as the market price is above the recovery rates.
- Differing coupon sizes, same par value:
  RMV different recovery rates – price difference is the value of the coupon difference *under RMV recovery.*
  RP same recovery rates – price difference is the value of the coupon difference *under zero recovery.*
- Pricing formulae:
  RMV elegant, simply discount with adjusted "defaultable" rate.
  RP more complicated, need to integrate/sum over all possible times of default.
- Estimation and calibration:
  RMV no artificial distortion in the calibration of implied hazard rates from par bond spreads, simple consistent estimation (of product process $q\lambda$) possible, no separate calibration of λ and q possible.
  RP no artificial distortion in the calibration of implied hazard rates from par bond spreads, may be able to calibrate implied recovery rate *and* default intensity (but unstable because of closeness to RMV), historical data on recovery rates is almost always given as fraction of par.
- Modelling issues:
  RMV only need to model dynamics of product process for pricing, OK if used with intensity-based models, cannot be used in firm's value-based models.
  RP model closer to default payoff definition in CDS documentation, can also be used in models where default is gradually approached (firm's value models, price deterioration).

- "Story":

  RMV reorganisation, renegotiation of debt.

  RP bankruptcy proceedings under an authority ensuring strict *relative* priority (same seniority claims have same recovery payoff).

Both RP and RMV have their strengths and weaknesses, and given the uncertainty surrounding the value or distribution of recovery rates, small theoretical differences will not make much difference in many application scenarios.

RMV is mathematically more elegant and is a good model for counterparty risk in OTC derivatives transactions, but in particular for debt trading far below par it has conceptual and modelling problems.

RP seems to do better here. Its setup is closely related to the way historical recovery data is collected, and it is supported by a convincing story (but so is RMV). This is reached at the expense of a slightly more complicated pricing relationship for the recovery payoff. Because the recovery definition of RP equals the recovery definition in the payoff specification of a CDS, having priced the recovery payoff will help us in the pricing of CDSs.

Thus, RP wins the race by a small margin. RT dropped out early on, and the role of RMV is unclear for crisis scenarios, although it is a good model in other respects. The additional work that RP requires in order to determine the value of the recovery payoffs will have to be done anyway if a CDS is to be priced.

6.2.2   Empirical analysis of recovery rates

6.2.2.1   *Market implied recovery rates*

In general, recovery rates are difficult to imply from observed market prices. In the RMV model, backing out recovery rates from prices of bonds of the same seniority is impossible (because only the product λq enters the prices), and the recovery rate is not identifiable. The RP model is very close to RMV for bonds that trade at par, thus the relationship between prices and implied recovery rates will be quite unstable. Small price changes can trigger large variations in implied parameters. For these reasons, implicit recovery rates will often be unreliable, unless they were recovered from instruments whose payoffs at default are significantly different (e.g. CDS and DDS).

Nevertheless, basing the recovery-rate input on market prices (instead of historical observations) is desirable. The resulting values will be given under risk-neutral probabilities and can be used directly in a pricing model. Bakshi *et al.* (2001) (and also Merrick (2001) for RP) have used market prices of corporate bonds to imply the recovery parameters of RP and RT', and to compare the models' relative pricing power. RT' is a variant of the RT model where the recovery payoff is a fraction of the discounted (with default-free interest rates) value of the *final par payoff, without recovery* on the coupons. Thus, for a given recovery parameter c' the recovery payoff for bonds with longer time to maturity is smaller than the recovery payoff for bonds with shorter time to maturity.

In order to be able to imply recovery rate parameters from market prices, the number of free parameters in the pricing model must be less than or equal to the number of market prices of different defaultable bonds that are available. Bakshi *et al.* (2001) choose four model parameters. They model the default intensity as $\lambda = \Lambda_0 + \Lambda_1 r(t)$ and the recovery parameter as $w_0 + w_1 e^{-\lambda}$. These four parameters $w_0, w_1, \Lambda_0, \Lambda_1$ allow us to capture the dependencies between default intensity and recovery rates (via w_1), and between default intensities and interest rates (via Λ_1), but do not allow a term structure of default intensities, in particular they do not allow upward-sloping forward default hazard rate curves. Furthermore, they model a stochastic default-free short-term interest rate using the model by Cox *et al.* 1985b.

Bakshi *et al.* (2001) now calibrate the model to the term structures of bond prices for 25 BBB-rated bond prices for every month between June 1989 and March 1998. Their results are:

- The calibration procedure is possible and gives meaningful results.
- The RT' model has lower pricing errors than RP.[7]
- w_1, the parameter that captures the connection between default intensities and hazard rates, is fairly small (0.245).
- RT' has on average lower default intensities and higher expected recovery payoffs.

These results seem to support the RT' model, but they may also be caused by the presence of an upward-sloping default hazard rate curve in the market. Assume an upward-sloping hazard rate curve was present in the market and RP was correct. If an RP model with a *flat* hazard rate curve is fitted to these prices, it will not be able to capture the relative price differences over the bonds' maturities; bonds with shorter maturities will be underpriced and bonds with longer maturities will be overpriced. If, on the other hand, an RT' model with flat hazard rate is fitted to the same prices, it will fit better, because RT' implies lower recovery payoffs for bonds with longer maturities. (RT' says that the payoff is discounted to the original maturity of the bond.) Thus, RT' will reach lower prices for bonds with long maturities, and higher prices for bonds with shorter maturities.

Most of the bonds in the sample had yields below their coupon size, thus they traded above par. As bonds approach their par value as they approach maturity, an early default in the RP model will hurt a bondholder with long maturity more than a bondholder with short maturity. Thus, if the default intensity is increased with a compensating increase in the recovery rate, bonds with long maturities will lose and bonds with short maturities will gain in value. This explains why RP has on average higher default intensities and recovery rates than RT'.

Instead of trying to imply recovery rates from debt prices of the same seniority class, Unal *et al.* (2001) use the price differentials between senior- and junior-rated debt of the same obligor to imply expected recovery rates. The basic idea is the following. Suppose that the recovery payoffs are functionally related to some underlying value A for the "assets in default", the total amount that is paid to creditors. For example, the specification

$$\pi^S(A) = \frac{1}{K^S} \min\{K^S, A\}$$

stands for absolute priority. The recovery payoff π^S of the senior debt is the whole value of the assets in default A, until the notional K^S of senior debt is fully paid off. (The division by K^S converts the cumulative payoff to a per-bond payoff.) The corresponding payoff to junior debt is

$$\pi^J(A) = \frac{1}{K^J} \max\{A - K^S, 0\},$$

assuming that there are no other claimants. With this specification $K^J \pi^J + K^S \pi^S = A$. Of course, deviations from absolute priority can be modelled by specifying other functions $\pi^S(A)$

---

[7] Mean absolute error of $1.65 per $100 par amount for RP, and $1.43 for RT'. The difference is statistically significant.

and $\pi^J(A)$, where the payoff of junior debt is positive, even if the recovery rate of senior debt is not 100%.

Stochastic recovery is modelled by modelling A as a random variable, a marker that is realised at default. The conditional distribution of A must be given with only few degrees of freedom. Let us assume that we choose a beta distribution with fixed variance but unknown mean μ, and call its density function $f(\mu, \cdot)$. Then, the expected recovery payoffs are:

$$\pi^{Se}(\mu) := \int \pi^S(a) f_A(\mu, a) da \quad \text{and} \quad \pi^{Je}(\mu) := \int \pi^J(a) f_A(\mu, a) da.$$

The model prices for the defaultable bonds are given by substituting these expected recovery values in the corresponding bond pricing formula. Setting model prices equal to market prices yields two equations for two unknowns: mean asset-in-default value μ and default hazard rate h. This method is robust because we use defaultable securities that react very much differently to realisations of A. This calibration algorithm also works for other default recovery models, and a term structure of hazard rates can also be calibrated if a sufficient number of defaultable calibration instruments is available. The calibration to the relative prices of DDS and CDS presented in Chapter 3 follows a similar intuition.

6.2.2.2 Historical recovery rates

If market implied recovery rates are not available, historical recovery rates can give a valuable benchmark for appropriate values. Before they can be used in a pricing model, historical distributions or averages must be adjusted for risk premia. Recently, research interest in this topic has increased, and academics and practitioners alike have been trying to find empirical regularities in the recovery rates of defaulted debt in order to reduce the uncertainty around this parameter.

Recovery rates show extremely high variability across different default events. Some empirical indicators have been found that explain some of this variability, but much uncertainty remains. Table 6.1 shows mean, median and standard deviations of the recovery rates for different debt classes over the years 1981–2000. The large standard deviations are an indicator for the uncertainty surrounding real-world recovery rates.

Table 6.1 Historical recovery rates (percentages of par, market quotes one month after default) by seniority classes, 1981–2000

Seniority/security	Median	Average	St. Dev.	1st Quartile	3rd Quartile
Senior/secured bank loans	72.0	64.0	24.4	45.3	85.0
Senior/unsecured bank loans	45.0	49.0	28.4	25.0	75.8
Senior/secured bonds	53.8	52.6	24.6	34.8	68.6
Senior/unsecured bonds	44.0	46.9	28.0	25.0	66.8
Senior/subordinated bonds	29.0	34.7	24.6	15.1	50.0
Subordinated bonds	28.5	31.6	21.2	15.0	44.1
Junior/subordinated bonds	15.1	22.5	18.7	11.3	33.0
Preferred stock	11.1	18.1	17.2	6.4	24.9

Source: Hamilton *et al.* (2001).

Table 6.2   Recovery rates by type of collateral. Collateral codes: all assets and current
assets = 5; most assets = 4; secured transactions, real estate, PP&E, oil and gas reserves
and equipment = 3; capital stock of operating units, intellectual property and
intercompany debt = 2; second lien = 1; unsecured = 0

Collateral	Recovery	St. Dev.	95% Conf.	Count
(1–5)	79.6	26.7	35.5	327
(2–5)	80.6	25.9	37.8	312
(3–5)	82.9	25.3	41.2	254
(4–5)	86.3	23.7	47.2	174
(5)	89.8	19.8	57.2	157

Source: van De Castle and Keisman (1999).

Hamilton *et al.* (2001) study the recovery rates and losses given default (LGD) of defaulted
public debt 1981–2000. Their principal findings[8] are:

- Seniority and instrument type is the most important determinant of recovery rates at default:
  higher seniority ⇒ higher recovery at default.
- Secondary, but strong influences are the level of subordination and security.
- Ratings can also be used as predictor of likely recovery rates: better rating ⇒ higher recovery.
- Default losses are correlated with the leverage (liabilities over assets) of the defaulting firm
  with higher leverage implying higher losses.
- This relationship (loss–leverage) is stronger in business cycle downturns yielding very low
  recoveries for highly leveraged firms in recessions. In the Moody's Loss-Calc model this
  is modelled as a multiplicative combination of the two indicators leverage and business
  cycle.
- Neither long-term averages nor moving averages of loss given default are good predictors of
  current losses given default. This is caused by the cyclical nature of LGD. In fact, sometimes
  the averages may be moving in one direction while the realised values move in the opposite
  direction.
- Secured debt is less sensitive to the general state of the economy than unsecured debt. This
  applies to most asset classes, including loans, bonds and mortgage-backed debt.
- LGD is (positively) correlated with the aggregate default rate.

The results for defaulted loans are qualitatively similar, as Gupton *et al.* (2000) find.

van De Castle and Keisman (1999) investigate the effect of the *debt cushion* on the recovery
rate of defaulted loans and bonds. The debt cushion is the proportion of debt in the capital
structure that ranks below the loan or bond considered. They find that the debt cushion is an
extremely significant indicator for the likely recovery value at default. For the 58 loans with a
debt cushion of 75% or more, 89% had recoveries of 90% or more. For the 43 loans with an
unsecured debt cushion of less than 20%, just 28% had recoveries of 90% or more. They also
find that the recovery is strongly affected by the definition of the class of assets that creditors
can liquidate in the case of default. The wider the definition of this collateral class, the higher
the recovery rate. This is shown in Table 6.2.

Note that this type of collateral is different from pledged assets as in mortgages, collateral
for derivatives transactions or project finance loans. The value of such physically collateralised

---

[8] I am grateful to Greg Gupton for clarifying some of these findings for me.

claims obviously depends very much on the value of the collateral and its correlation with the default likelihood of the obligor.

While these studies try to explain recovery rates using variables that are endogenous to the defaulted obligor or the defaulted bond issue, Altman *et al.* (2001) considered a different and important issue: systematic dependence of recovery rates *across* different defaults. They find that average recovery rates in the USA are significantly affected by the aggregate number of defaults that have happened in the corresponding year. They explain this by the limited size of demand for defaulted bonds. If the supply is too high (because many defaults have occurred), then post-default prices are depressed.

Demand and supply for defaulted bonds are also very important for the determination of CDS payoffs. This not only covers the market for defaulted bonds in general, but also the market for the particular defaulted issue. When cash settlement is chosen in a CDS, the default payment itself depends on the depth of the market at the polling dates. Furthermore, if default protection was bought without owning a deliverable security (a negative speculation on the credit quality of the reference credit), then a deliverable obligation must be bought in a short time span after default. This can lead to artificially inflated prices.

Systematic dependencies in default recovery rates can be an important, but often overlooked risk component in portfolio and CDO risk analysis. The large variation in recovery rates reported in Table 6.1 should not be too much of a cause for worry if the variation is unsystematic and will diversify out in a large portfolio. But the presence of systematic dependencies in recovery rates means that this diversification is not possible. This increases the probability of large losses in the portfolio. This point was first stressed and analysed by Frye (2000a–c).

Further studies of historical default recovery rates have been performed by Eberhart *et al.* (1990), James (1991), Eberhart and Sweeney (1992), Altman (1993), Altman and Eberhart (1994), Asquith *et al.* (1994), Franks and Torous (1994), Asarnow and Edwards (1995), Altman and Kishore (1996), and many other authors. Moody's is even offering a commercial tool to predict recovery rates based upon a statistical model of firm-specific variables that have been found to explain recovery rates. The explanatory power of these models is generally not too high, and typical values for the proportion of explained variance (adjusted R^2) are around 40–60%.

When using these or similar studies one must check if the data set is comparable to the modelling problem. Is it the same or a similar legislation, are loans or bonds considered, what time period is covered? The definition of recovery (discounted value of settlement or market value after default) is also important; for credit derivatives, studies using market prices should be more relevant.

7

Implementation of Intensity-Based Models

This chapter covers the implementation of stochastic intensity-based models for the default risk of a single obligor. We do not cover the implementation of deterministic intensity models, as these are equivalent to the spread-based models which were extensively covered in Chapter 3.

There are several aspects to the implementation of intensity-based models. The first is the choice of the precise model specification, and the second is its numerical implementation.

The model must be calibrated to market data. For this closed-form solutions (or at least good approximations) to the prices of the building blocks must be available in the model, and the specification of the model should be flexible enough to allow a good fit to the prices that were prescribed by the market. Fitting the term structure of default-free interest rates is an additional requirement. If there are closed-form solutions for other securities, this is an additional advantage, but it is not essential. Second, the dynamics of the model parameters should be realistic, i.e. they should replicate the risks and qualitative behaviour that is observed in real markets. Finally, there must be a numerical methodology to price more complicated payoffs in this model.

There are two fundamentally different approaches to the first problem (model specification). In the first approach, the stochastic dynamics of the short-term interest rate r and the short-term default intensity λ are specified in such a way that the necessary closed-form solutions for calibration can be derived analytically. This is a rather strong requirement on the analytical tractability of the models. The advantage is that the analytical tractability is not restricted to the calibration pricing problems but also extends to other pricing problems. Furthermore, these model specifications can help us to understand the influence of various model parameters (in particular the correlation between r and λ) which would otherwise only be accessible to numerical experiments. Finally, such models are able to identify price constellations which can only be arbitrage-free under extreme assumptions on the dynamics of the short rate and default intensity: potential trading opportunities.

The second approach is to take directly the prices of the calibration instruments taking them as given (instead of deriving them analytically), and specify the dynamics of these prices such that the resulting dynamic model is arbitrage-free. Here, this means that we take the whole term structures of default-free and defaultable zerobond prices as given, and specify their arbitrage-free dynamics. The obvious advantage of these models is that the calibration problem is automatically solved. On the other hand, these models cannot identify mispricing in the calibration instruments as these are now automatically priced perfectly.

The two approaches imply different numerical solution techniques. Models specifying the dynamics of spot intensities are Markovian in nature so that tree-based numerical implementations and analysis using partial differential equations (and the corresponding finite-difference solution schemes) is possible. The term-structure-based models exhibit path-dependent dynamics so that Monte Carlo simulation is the numerical solution method of choice.

7.1   TRACTABLE MODELS OF THE SPOT INTENSITY

The introduction of stochastic default intensities allows us to capture an important risk component: the risk of a *change in the credit quality* of the obligor. This additional realism comes at the price of additional complexity in the model.

First, default intensities may be correlated with the default-free interest rates (most empirical studies find a negative correlation around 20%). This correlation means that the independence assumption 3.2 does not hold any more. We cannot interpret the ratio of a defaultable over a default-free zerobond price of the same maturity as implied survival probabilities under Q.

Furthermore, to price defaultable zero-coupon bonds we now need to evaluate expressions of the form

$$\overline{B}(0, T) = \mathbf{E}\big[e^{-\int_0^T r(s)+\lambda(s)ds}\big],$$

where both $r(t)$ and $\lambda(t)$ are stochastic. Expressions of this form closely resemble the pricing expressions that are encountered in multifactor interest rate models, so there is hope that we may be able to borrow solutions from this literature (and indeed we can). Nevertheless, zerobond pricing in a two-factor interest rate model is almost always a non-trivial problem. The pricing of the other building blocks is also complicated, for the pricing of $e(0, T)$ expressions of the form $\mathbf{E}[\lambda(T) \exp\{-\int_0^T r(s) + \lambda(s)ds\}]$ must be evaluated.

The second set of problems concerns the specification of the dynamics of the default intensities. Naturally, to ease the calibration of the model, one would like to choose a specification which allows an easy solution of the pricing problems for the building blocks, but some of these specifications run into other problems. Most importantly, specification of Gaussian dynamics could mean negative default intensities in a large number of cases.[1] Other models may restrict the correlation between interest rates and intensities in an unrealistic manner, or they may simply be analytically intractable.

When it comes to concrete pricing of specific derivatives, we must leave the level of generality assumed in the previous chapters and we need a full specification of the dynamics of the default-free interest rate r and the intensity of the default process λ. A suitable specification should have the following properties:

- Both r and λ are stochastic. Stochastic default-free interest rates are indispensable for fixed-income analysis, and a stochastic default intensity is required to reach stochastic credit spreads, necessary for meaningful prices for credit spread options and to capture spread change risks.
- The dynamics of r and λ are rich enough to allow for a realistic description of the real-world prices. Duffie and Singleton (1997) and Duffee (1999) come to the conclusion that in many cases a multifactor model for the credit spreads is necessary.
- There should be scope to include correlation between credit spreads and default-free interest rates.
- It is desirable to have processes for interest rates and credit spreads that remain positive at all times. Although negative credit spreads or interest rates represent an arbitrage opportunity, relaxing this requirement in favour of a Gaussian specification is still acceptable because of

---

[1] The same problem exists for Gaussian default-free interest rate models, but the volatilities of default intensities are generally much higher than the corresponding interest rate volatilities, and the levels of default intensities are lower. Both make negative intensities much more likely than negative interest rates.

the analytical tractability that is gained. The Gaussian specification should then be viewed as a local approximation to the real-world dynamics rather than as a fully closed model. Furthermore, many important effects are more easily understood in the Gaussian setup.

- It should be possible to price the pricing building blocks in closed form, in order to be able to easily calibrate the model.

Here, we demonstrate three alternative setups:

1. A two-factor *Gaussian short rate/intensity* setup. This setup suffers from the possibility of reaching negative credit spreads and interest rates with positive probability, but a high degree of analytical tractability is retained. The model can be calibrated to full term structures of bond prices and spreads, and the correlations between interest rates and default intensities are unconstrained.
2. A *multifactor Gaussian* setup. This setup is very similar to the two-factor Gaussian setup, but now the model is specified directly in terms of the initial term structures of defaultable and default-free zerobonds and their volatilities. This setup has a similar degree of tractability, and some of the formulae are even more intuitively accessible than the formulae of the Gaussian short-rate model.
3. A *multifactor Cox–Ingersoll–Ross (CIR)* (Cox *et al.*, 1985b) setup, following mainly Jamshidian (1996).[2] This model setup gives us the required properties of non-negativity and ease of calibration while still retaining a large degree of analytical tractability. Furthermore, models of credit spreads of the CIR square root type have been estimated by Duffie and Singleton (1997) and Duffee (1999). Unfortunately, the correlation between interest rates and intensities in this model is restricted to essentially non-negative correlations.

Defaultable zero-coupon bond prices are given for the RMV model, and prices for the pricing building blocks for the RP model. The results are straightforward to transfer to the other recovery models. By assuming full loss in default $q = 1$, the specification can be viewed as a specification of the dynamics of zero-recovery defaultable bond prices $\overline{B}(t, T)$. Combining these dynamics of the zero-recovery defaultable bond prices with an assumption on the equivalent recovery rate c will yield a specification in terms of the RT recovery model where defaultable bond prices are given by $\overline{B}(t, T) = cB(t, T) + (1 - c)\overline{B}(t, T)$.

7.1.1   The two-factor Gaussian model

In this section we present very briefly a specification of the dynamics of default-free short rate and default intensities which is popular for its analytical tractability and its flexibility: the Gaussian specification. The dynamics are also known as the (extended) Vasicek (1977) model in the interest-rate-modelling literature.

This specification allows credit spreads and interest rates to become negative with positive probability. This problem is well known from default-free Gaussian interest rate models and is partly compensated by the analytical tractability gained, provided the probability of these events remains low. This setup should therefore be viewed as an approximation to more realistic

---

[2] Related models can also be found in Jamshidian (1995, 1997b), Duffie and Kan (1996), Chen and Scott (1995) and Longstaff and Schwartz (1992).

models of credit spread and interest rates, and despite this drawback it will yield some valuable insights.

Assumption 7.1 (two-factor Gaussian model)

(i) The dynamics of the default-free short rate are given by the extended Vasicek (1977) model:

$$dr(t) = (k(t) - ar)dt + \sigma(t)dW(t). \tag{7.1}$$

(ii) Similarly, the dynamics of the default intensity λ are:

$$d\lambda(t) = (\bar{k}(t) - \bar{a}\lambda)dt + \bar{\sigma}(t)d\overline{W}(t). \tag{7.2}$$

(iii) $W(t)$ and $\overline{W}(t)$ are Brownian motions with correlation:

$$dWd\overline{W} = \rho dt. \tag{7.3}$$

The dynamics (7.1) (and analogously (7.2)) have the following interpretation: interest rates move stochastically with an absolute volatility of $\sigma(t)$. The drift term is positive if $r(t)$ is below $k(t)$ at time t, otherwise it is negative. The drift always has a tendency to move r towards k. This effect is known as *mean reversion*, and $k(t)$ is the *level of mean reversion*. The strength of this effect is measured by the parameter $a \geq 0$ which is known as the *speed of mean reversion*.

The levels of mean reversion $k(t)$ and $\bar{k}(t)$ can be used to fit the model dynamics to the initial term structure of bond prices and are therefore already implicitly defined if an initial term structure is known. The spot volatility function $\sigma(t)$ can be used to fit an initial term structure of volatilities. We make provisions for the fitting of the volatility $\bar{\sigma}(t)$ of the default intensity to an initial term structure of volatilities for the defaultable bonds, although in typical applications there will not be sufficient data to support this fitting. In this case one can set the volatility to a constant: $\bar{\sigma}(t) = \bar{\sigma} = \text{const.}$

The specification of a time-dependent interest rate volatility $\sigma(t)$ translates into time-dependent bond price volatilities via the resulting zerobond dynamics (cf. the closed-form solutions below)

$$\frac{dB(t, T)}{B(t, T)} = r(t)dt - \sigma(t)\frac{1}{a}\left(1 - e^{-a(T-t)}\right)dW(t) \tag{7.4}$$

and forward rate volatilities

$$df(t, T) = \frac{\sigma(t)^2}{a}e^{-a(T-t)}\left(1 - e^{-a(T-t)}\right)dt + \sigma(t)e^{-a(T-t)}dW(t) \tag{7.5}$$

where the drift of the forward rates follows from the Heath *et al.* (1992) drift restriction (this will also be derived later on). We see that – although it enters into the drift term of the short rate – the speed of mean reversion a is actually a *volatility parameter* which affects bond volatility. The two parameters a and $\sigma(0)$ can be used to fit a given initial volatility term structure of bond prices or forward rates. $\sigma(t)$ can be used to make this fit time-dependent, but as it does not depend on the maturity date T, the shape of the volatility structure will always remain exponential.

The following lemma shows why we can expect this model setup to yield nicely tractable solutions. We can remove the mean-reversion property and end up with normally distributed state variables that simply follow Brownian motions with drift.

Lemma 7.1 *If x follows the dynamics*

$$dx(t) = [\kappa(t) - \alpha(t)x(t)]dt + \sigma(t)dW(t), \tag{7.6}$$

then the value of $x(T)$ is given by:

$$x(T) = x(t)e^{-\int_t^T \alpha(s)ds} + \int_t^T e^{-\int_s^T \alpha(u)du}\kappa(s)ds + \int_t^T e^{-\int_s^T \alpha(u)du}\sigma(s)dW(s). \tag{7.7}$$

Thus, $x(T)$ given $x(t)$ is normally distributed with mean and variance

$$x(t)e^{-\int_t^T \alpha(s)ds} + \int_t^T e^{-\int_s^T \alpha(u)du}\kappa(s)ds \quad and \quad \int_t^T e^{-2\int_s^T \alpha(u)du}\sigma^2(s)ds.$$

Furthermore, if $\alpha(t) = \alpha = const.$

$$\mathbf{E}\left[e^{-\int_t^T x(s)ds} \mid \mathcal{F}_t\right] = e^{\mathcal{A}(t,T)-\mathcal{B}(t,T;\alpha)x(t)} \tag{7.8}$$

where

$$\mathcal{B}(t,T;\alpha) = \frac{1}{\alpha}\left(1 - e^{-\alpha(T-t)}\right), \tag{7.9}$$

$$\mathcal{A}(t,T;\alpha,\kappa,\sigma) = \frac{1}{2}\int_t^T \sigma^2(s)\mathcal{B}(t,s;\alpha)^2 ds - \int_t^T \mathcal{B}(t,s;\alpha)\kappa(s)ds. \tag{7.10}$$

Proof. Let $y(t) := x(t)e^{\int_0^t \alpha(s)ds}$. Then using Itô's lemma:

$$dy(t) = e^{\int_0^t \alpha(s)ds}[\kappa(t)dt + \sigma(t)dW(t)]. \tag{7.11}$$

Integrate from t to T to reach $y(T)$ and substitute back for $x(T)$.

The final claim is well known in the interest-rate-modelling literature. We refer the reader to good textbooks like Duffie (2001) or Björk (1998). □

The prices of the building block securities are given in the following proposition.

Proposition 7.2 *At time t for short rate $r(t)$, default intensity $\lambda(t)$ and the dynamics given in Assumption 7.1 we have the following prices.*

(i) The price of a default-free zero-coupon bond with maturity T:

$$B(t, T) = e^{A(t,T;a,k,\sigma)-B(t,T;a)r(t)}. \tag{7.12}$$

(ii) The survival probability from t until T:

$$P(t, T) = e^{A(t,T;\overline{a},\overline{k},\overline{\sigma})-B(t,T;\overline{a})\lambda(t)}. \tag{7.13}$$

(iii) The price of a defaultable zero-coupon bond under zero recovery with maturity T, given survival until t:

$$\overline{B}(t, T) = B(t, T)e^{A(t,T;\overline{a},\widetilde{k},\overline{\sigma})-B(t,T;\overline{a})\lambda(t)} \tag{7.14}$$

where

$$\widetilde{k}(t) = \overline{k}(t) - \rho\overline{\sigma}(t)\sigma(t)B(t, T). \tag{7.15}$$

(iv) The price of a defaultable zero-coupon bond under RMV/MD with maturity T, given survival until t:

$$\overline{B}_{\text{RMV}}(t, T) = B(t, T)e^{\mathcal{A}'(t,T)-B(t,T;\overline{a})q\lambda(t)} \tag{7.16}$$

where

$$\overline{\mathcal{A}}'(t, T) = \frac{1}{2}\int_t^T q^2\overline{\sigma}^2(s)B(t, s;\overline{a})^2 ds - \int_t^T B(t, s;\overline{a})q\widetilde{k}(s)ds. \tag{7.17}$$

(v) The value of \$1 at T if a default happens at T:

$$e(t, T) = \overline{B}(t, T)\left[\lambda(t)e^{-\overline{a}(T-t)} + \int_t^T e^{-a(T-s)}\widetilde{k}'(s)ds\right]$$

where

$$\widetilde{k}'(t) = \overline{k}(t) - \rho\overline{\sigma}(t)\sigma(t)B(t, T;a) - \overline{\sigma}^2 B(t, T;\overline{a}).$$

Proof. (i) and (ii) follow directly from Lemma 7.1.
   (iii) The pricing problem is the evaluation of:

$$\overline{B}(t, T) = \mathbf{E}\left[e^{-\int_t^T r(s)+\lambda(s)ds}\right] = \mathbf{E}\left[e^{-\int_t^T r(s)ds}e^{-\int_t^T \lambda(s)ds}\right].$$

Changing measure (see Girsanov's theorem 4.8) to the T-forward measure yields:

$$\overline{B}(t, T) = B(t, T)\mathbf{E}^{P_T}\left[e^{-\int_t^T \lambda(s)ds}\right]$$

and the dynamics of the default intensity under the T-forward measure are:

$$d\lambda(t) = (\widetilde{k}(t) - \overline{a}\lambda)dt + \overline{\sigma}(t)d\overline{W}^T(t),$$

where $\overline{W}^T$ is a Brownian motion under the T-forward measure and $\widetilde{k}$ is given in the proposition. The expectation can now be evaluated using the solution given in Lemma 7.1.

(iv) is proved analogously to (iii).

(v) Again a change of measure yields the result. We have to evaluate

$$e(t, T) = \mathbf{E}\left[\lambda(T)e^{-\int_t^T r(s)+\lambda(s)ds}\right].$$

If we use $L(u) := e^{-\int_t^u r(s)+\lambda(s)ds}\overline{B}(u, T)/\overline{B}(t, T)$ as Radon–Nikodym density to a new measure $\overline{P}'$, we reach

$$e(t, T) = \overline{B}(t, T)\mathbf{E}^{\overline{P}'}[\lambda(T)]$$

and the dynamics of $\lambda(t)$ under the new measure are:

$$d\lambda(t) = \left\{\overline{k}(t) + \sigma(t)\overline{\sigma}(t)\rho B(t, T) - \overline{\sigma}^2(t)\overline{B}(t, T) - \overline{a}(t)\lambda(t)\right\}dt + \overline{\sigma}(t)d\overline{W}^{\overline{P}'}(t).$$

Using Lemma 7.1 the claim follows.   □

The two-factor Gaussian model setup can be viewed as the simplest stochastic-intensity credit risk model which can have non-zero correlations between the default intensity λ and the short-term interest rate r. The time-dependence in the model parameters can be used to calibrate the model to observed term structures of default-free zero-coupon bonds $B(0, T)$ and a spread curve of defaultable bonds $\overline{B}(t, T)$. An algorithm for this will be presented later on.

7.1.2   The multifactor Gaussian model

The two-factor Gaussian model is easily generalise to include multiple driving factors. In a way, this generalisation highlights even more clearly the new features introduced through stochastic intensities. The starting point of the model are the dynamics of default-free and defaultable zerobond prices.

Assumption 7.2   *The following asset price dynamics under the martingale measure are given:*

- *default-free bond prices $B(t, T)$*

$$\frac{dB(t, T)}{B(t, T)} = r(t)dt + a(t, T)dW,$$

- *defaultable bond prices $\overline{B}(t, T)$*

$$\frac{d\overline{B}(t, T)}{\overline{B}(t-, T)} = (r(t) + q\lambda(t))dt + \overline{a}(t, T)dW - qdN(t).$$

The Brownian motion dW is d-dimensional, the volatilities $a(t, T)$ and $\bar{a}(t, T)$ are d-dimensional deterministic functions of time t and time to maturity T only, and at $t = 0$ there has been no default: $\tau > 0$ and $Q(0) = 1$.

Assumption 7.2 implicitly specifies the RMV recovery model for the zerobond prices. (At a jump of N, the bond prices are only reduced by a factor $(1 - q)$.) This setup was chosen because by setting the loss fraction to one $q = 1$, it encompasses zero recovery and RT, and RP is reached if we also give the prices of the $e(t, T)$ building block securities. Therefore, this specification does not restrict the generality of the results. Furthermore, the drift of the defaultable bond prices was directly specified in the form it must have under the spot martingale measure: r plus the default correction term λq.

How should one read the bond price dynamics of Assumption 7.2? The drifts of the bond prices are not predetermined by the fact that we are modelling these prices under the spot martingale measure Q, under which the prices of all traded securities must have expected increment $r dt$. Thus, the distinguishing feature of this model is the *volatility* $a(t, T)$ (or $\bar{a}(t, T)$) of the bond prices. This volatility is assumed to be only *time-dependent*. Thus, the bond price dynamics are essentially lognormal. Nothing prevents an extreme realisation of dW from carrying the zerobond prices above one, $B(t, T) > 1$ and $\bar{B}(t, T) > 1$ have positive probabilities. This situation corresponds to negative interest rates as can occur in Gaussian models. It is not hard to prove that the setup really does correspond to normally distributed short-term interest rates and instantaneous forward rates, and the reader is referred to Musiela and Rutkowski (1997) or Björk (1998) for a proof.

From a modelling point of view the important feature is that this setup can be used to model any degree of correlation between different bond prices that is desired, because we have a *multidimensional* Brownian motion and vector volatilities driving the dynamics. Multiplication of the volatilities is defined by the scalar product in $\mathbb{R}^d$: $a\bar{a} = \sum_{i=1}^{d} a_i \bar{a}_i$. If for two bonds $B(t, T)$ and $\bar{B}(t, T')$ we have that the volatility vectors are orthogonal (i.e. $a(t, T)\bar{a}(t, T') = 0$), then the dynamics of the prices of these two bonds are (locally) independent. If $a(t, T)\bar{a}(t, T') > 0$, then we have positive correlation, and $a(t, T)\bar{a}(t, T') < 0$ corresponds to negative correlation. Of course the degree of correlation between bonds of the same class (defaultable or default-free) can be modelled in the same way.

7.1.3 Implied survival probabilities

In the Gaussian setup we can derive the implied survival probability from t to T in closed form. Given $\tau > t$ the survival probability is defined as:

$$P(t, T) = \mathbf{E}\left[e^{-\int_t^T \lambda(s)ds} \mid \mathcal{F}_t\right].$$

Lemma 7.3

(i) *For zero-recovery, zero-coupon bonds (full loss $q = 1$ in default), the survival probability is:*

$$P(0, T) = \frac{\bar{B}(0, T)}{B(0, T)} \exp\left\{-\int_0^T a^p(s, T)a(s, T)ds\right\}. \tag{7.18}$$

(ii) In the RMV setup (q < 1), the survival probabilities $P(0, T)$ are given by:

$$P(0, T) = \left(\frac{\overline{B}(0, T)}{B(0, T)}\right)^{\frac{1}{q}} \exp\left\{-\frac{1}{2}\int_0^T a^P(s, T)[a(s, T) + \overline{a}(s, T) - a^P(s, T)]ds\right\}.$$

$$(7.19)$$

(iii) In the RMV setup, the dynamics of the survival probabilities are:

$$\frac{dP(t, T)}{P(t, T)} = \lambda(t)dt + a^P(t, T)dW, \tag{7.20}$$

$$a^P(t, T) = \frac{1}{q}(\overline{a}(t, T) - a(t, T)). \tag{7.21}$$

(iv) The dynamics of the survival probabilities under zero recovery follow from setting $q = 1$ in (7.20) and (7.21).

Proof.   See Section 7.3.2 (p. 180).   □

The key determining difference between models with and without correlation between spreads and intensities lies in the expression:

$$a^P(s, T)a(s, T).$$

This term is the local covariation between $B(s, T)$ and $P(s, T)$. Under independence of credit spreads and interest rates the scalar product of the volatilities is zero $a^P(s, T)a(s, T) = 0$. The implied survival probability would then reduce to $\overline{B}(0, T)/B(0, T)$ as we know it from constant (or time-dependent) intensities. Hence the factor

$$e^{-\int_0^T a^P(s,T)a(s,T)ds}$$

represents the influence of correlation between spreads and interest rates on the implied default probabilities. There is an intuitive explanation of the direction of the effect.

If interest rates and credit spreads are positively correlated ($a^P a > 0$), this means that defaults are slightly more likely in states of nature when interest rates are high. Because of the higher interest rates these states are discounted more strongly when they enter the price of the defaultable bond, and conversely states with low interest rates enter with less discounting and simultaneously fewer defaults. To reach a *given* price for a defaultable bond, the absolute default likelihood must therefore be higher. This implies a lower survival probability which is also what equation (7.18) yields for $a^P a > 0$. The argument runs conversely for negative correlation $a^P a < 0$.

The reader should be aware that – while still retaining its intuitive significance – the pure survival probability has lost its importance when it comes to pricing issues. Any payoff that is paid in survival must be discounted, and discounting introduces the effects of correlation with interest rates. For this reason we introduced the building block securities which already contain the effects of correlated interest rates in their prices.

Using Lemma 7.3 we can now derive the values of some credit derivatives.

7.1.4   Payoffs at default

A default digital put with maturity T is the protection leg of a default digital swap. It has a payoff of 1 at default, if the default is before T. Its value is, according to equation (5.26):

$$\int_0^T e(0, t)dt = \int_0^T \mathbf{E}\Big[\lambda(t)e^{-\int_0^t \lambda(s)ds}e^{-\int_0^t r(s)ds}\Big]dt.$$

The resulting price for the default digital put is given in the following proposition.

Proposition 7.4   *Based upon survival probabilities, the price of a default digital put with maturity T and payoff 1 at default is, in the multifactor Gaussian model framework:*

$$D = \int_0^T P(0, t)B(0, t)e^{\int_0^t a(s,t)a^P(s,t)ds}\left[\lambda(0, t) + \int_0^t a(s, t)\sigma^P(s, t)ds\right]dt \qquad (7.22)$$

where $\lambda(0, t) := -\partial \ln P(0, t)/\partial t$ and $\sigma^P(s, t) := -\partial a^P(s, t)/\partial t$ are given in Lemma 7.3.
  Based upon defaultable bond prices, the price of a default digital put is:

$$D = \int_0^T \overline{B}(0, t)\left[\overline{f}(0, t) - f(0, t) - \int_0^t \overline{a}(s, t)\sigma(s, t)ds\right]dt. \qquad (7.23)$$

The price of $e(t, T)$ is:

$$e(t, T) = \overline{B}(t, T)\left[\overline{f}(t, T) - f(t, T) - \int_t^T a^P(s, T)\sigma(s, T)ds\right]. \qquad (7.24)$$

Proof.   See Section 7.3.2 (p. 183).   □

7.2   THE MULTIFACTOR CIR MODEL

The multifactor CIR model is set up as follows.

Assumption 7.3   *Interest rates and default intensities are driven by n independent factors x_i, $i = 1, \ldots, n$ with dynamics of the CIR square root type:*

$$dx_i = (\alpha_i - \beta_i x_i)dt + \sigma_i \sqrt{x_i}dW_i. \qquad (7.25)$$

The coefficients satisfy $\alpha_i > \frac{1}{2}\sigma_i^2$ to ensure strict positivity of the factors, and the Brownian motions W_i are mutually independent.
  The default-free short rate r and the default intensity λ are positive linear combinations of the factors x_i with weights $w_i \geq 0$ and $\overline{w}_i$ $(0 \leq i \leq n)$ respectively:

$$r(t) = \sum_{i=1}^n w_i x_i(t), \qquad (7.26)$$

$$\lambda(t) = \sum_{i=1}^n \overline{w}_i x_i(t). \qquad (7.27)$$

With all coefficients $w_i \geq 0$ and $\overline{w}_i \geq 0$ non-negative we have ensured that $r > 0$ and $\lambda > 0$ almost surely. Unfortunately, this specification can only generate *positive* correlation between r and λ. If negative correlation is needed one could define modified factors x_i' that are negatively correlated to the x_i by $dx_i' = (\alpha_i - \beta_i x_i')dt - \sigma_i \sqrt{x_i'} dW_i$ (note the minus in front of the Brownian motion). This would complicate the analysis. Alternatively one could restrict the specification to a squared Gaussian model.

Typically only the first $m < n$ factors would describe the dynamics of the default-free term structure (i.e. $w_i = 0$ for $i > m$), and the full set of state variables would be used to describe the spreads. The additional $n - m$ factors for the spreads ensure that the dynamics of the credit spreads have components that are independent of the default-free interest rate dynamics. The simplest example would be independence between r and λ, where $r = x_1$ and $\lambda = x_2$; one factor driving each rate:

$$
\begin{aligned}
n = 2 & \quad m = 1, \\
w_1 = 1 & \quad w_2 = 0, \\
\overline{w}_1 = 0 & \quad \overline{w}_2 = 1.
\end{aligned}
$$

7.2.1 Bond prices

For a linear multiple cx_i ($c > 0$ is a positive constant) of the factor x_i the following equation gives the corresponding "bond price" (see Cox et al., 1985b):

$$
\mathbf{E}\left[\exp\left\{-\int_t^T cx_i(s)ds\right\} \Bigg| \mathcal{F}_t\right] = H_{1i}(T - t, c)e^{-H_{2i}(T-t,c)cx_i} \tag{7.28}
$$

where

$$
H_{1i}(T - t, c) = \left[\frac{2\gamma_i e^{\frac{1}{2}(\gamma_i+\beta_i)(T-t)}}{(\gamma_i + \beta_i)(e^{\gamma_i(T-t)} - 1) + 2\gamma_i}\right]^{2\alpha_i/\sigma_i^2}, \tag{7.29}
$$

$$
H_{2i}(T - t, c) = \frac{2(e^{\gamma_i(T-t)} - 1)}{(\gamma_i + \beta_i)(e^{\gamma_i(T-t)} - 1) + 2\gamma_i}, \tag{7.30}
$$

$$
\gamma_i = \sqrt{\beta_i^2 + 2c\sigma_i^2}. \tag{7.31}
$$

The default-free bond prices are given by

$$
B(t, T) = \mathbf{E}\left[e^{-\int_t^T r(s)ds} \Big| \mathcal{F}_t\right] = \mathbf{E}\left[e^{-\sum_i \int_t^T w_i x_i(s)ds} \Big| \mathcal{F}_t\right]
$$

$$
= \mathbf{E}\left[\prod_i e^{-\int_t^T w_i x_i(s)ds} \Big| \mathcal{F}_t\right] = \prod_i \mathbf{E}\left[e^{-\int_t^T w_i x_i(s)ds} \Big| \mathcal{F}_t\right]
$$

because the factors are independent. The bond price is thus a product of one-factor bond prices

$$
B(t, T) = \prod_{i=1}^n H_{1i}(T - t, w_i)e^{-H_{2i}(T-t,w_i)w_i x_i(t)}. \tag{7.32}
$$

Similarly, the defaultable bond prices under fractional recovery are given by

$$\overline{B}(t, T) = Q(t) \prod_{i=1}^{n} H_{1i}(T - t, w_i + q\overline{w}_i)e^{-H_{2i}(T-t, w_i + q\overline{w}_i)(w_i + q\overline{w}_i)x_i}. \qquad (7.33)$$

Because $\overline{B}(t, T) = Q(t)\mathbf{E}[\exp\{-\int_t^T r(s) + q\lambda(s)ds\} \mid \mathcal{F}_t]$, zero recovery bond prices can be derived from (7.33) by setting $q = 1$.

7.2.2   Affine combinations of independent non-central chi-squared distributed random variables

The mathematical tools for the analysis of the model have been provided by Jamshidian (1996), who used them to price interest rate derivatives in a default-free interest rate environment. Of these tools we need the expressions for the evaluation of the expectations that will arise in the pricing equations, and the methodology of a change of measure to remove discount factors from these expectations.

First the distribution function of an affine combination of non-central chi-squared random variables is presented. Most of the following expressions are based upon this distribution function. Then we consider the expressions for the expectations of non-central chi-squared random variables, and finally the change-of-measure technique that has to be applied in this context.

Definition 7.1   *Let* z_i, $1 \leq i \leq n$ *be* n *independent, non-central, chi-square distributed random variables with* v_i *degrees of freedom and non-centrality parameter*[3] $\widetilde{\lambda}_i$. *Let* Y *be an affine combination of the random variables* z_i, $1 \leq i \leq n$ *with weights* η_i *and offset* ϵ:

$$Y = \epsilon + \sum_{i=1}^{n} \eta_i z_i. \qquad (7.34)$$

We call Y *an* affine combination of non-central chi-squared random variables (ANC) *and denote its distribution function by* χ_n^2:

$$\mathbf{P}[Y \leq y] =: \chi_n^2(y; v, \widetilde{\lambda}, \eta, \epsilon),$$

where η, v *and* $\widetilde{\lambda}$ *are vectors giving weight, degrees of freedom and non-centrality of the* z_i, *and for* $\epsilon = 0$ *we will omit the last argument.*[4]

The evaluation of this distribution function can be efficiently implemented via a fast Fourier transform of its characteristic function (see e.g. Chen and Scott, 1995). Alternatively, Jamshidian gives the following formula (which is basically the transform integral of the characteristic function for $\eta > -\frac{1}{2}$):

$$\chi^2(y; v, \widetilde{\lambda}, \eta, 0) = \frac{1}{2} + \frac{1}{\pi} \int_0^{\infty} \Psi\left(\frac{v}{2}, \widetilde{\lambda}, 2\xi^2\eta^2\right) \sin(\xi y - \Phi(v, \widetilde{\lambda}, \xi\eta))\frac{d\xi}{\xi}, \qquad (7.35)$$

---

[3] The non-centrality parameter $\widetilde{\lambda}$ is not to be confused with the intensity λ of the defaults.
[4] This is justified by equation (7.38).

where $\Psi(v, \widetilde{\lambda}, \eta) = \mathbf{E}[e^{-Y}]$ will be given in equation (7.39) and

$$\Phi(v, \widetilde{\lambda}, \gamma) = \sum_{i=1}^{n} \left(\frac{v_i}{2} \arctan(2\gamma_i) + \frac{\gamma_i \widetilde{\lambda}_i}{1 + 4\gamma_i^2} \right).$$

The integral in (7.35) is numerically well-behaved in that the limit of the integrand as $\xi \to 0$ is finite and the integrand is absolutely integrable. Using equation (7.38) this can be extended for the case of $\epsilon \neq 0$.

One advantage of this setup is that – although we are working with an n-factor model – most valuation problems can be reduced to the evaluation of this one-dimensional integral. The evaluation of the non-central chi-squared distribution function which one encounters in the one-factor case also requires a numerical approximation, and the implementation effort of the multifactor model therefore does not seem to be very much higher than the effort required for a model with one independent factor each for interest rates and spreads.

The following lemma by Jamshidian (1996) provides most of the expressions we need.

Lemma 7.5 *Let Y and Y' be ANC distributed with the same z_i, but Y with weights η and offset ϵ, and Y' with weights η' and offset ϵ':*

$$Y \sim \chi_n^2(\, \cdot \, ; \, v, \widetilde{\lambda}, \eta, \epsilon) \qquad Y' \sim \chi_n^2(\, \cdot \, ; \, v, \widetilde{\lambda}, \eta', \epsilon'). \tag{7.36}$$

Let y be a constant. Then the expectation of Y is:

$$\mathbf{E}[Y] = \epsilon + \sum_{i=1}^{n} \eta_i(\widetilde{\lambda}_i + v_i). \tag{7.37}$$

The distribution of Y is:

$$\mathbf{P}[Y \leq y] = \chi_n^2(y - \epsilon; \, v, \widetilde{\lambda}, \eta). \tag{7.38}$$

The expectation of e^{-Y} is:

$$\mathbf{E}[e^{-Y}] = e^{-\epsilon} \prod_{i=1}^{n} \frac{1}{(1 + 2\eta_i)^{v_i/2}} \exp\left\{ -\frac{\eta_i \widetilde{\lambda}_i}{1 + 2\eta_i} \right\}. \tag{7.39}$$

The value of a call option on e^{-Y} with strike e^{-y} is:

$$\mathbf{E}[(e^{-Y} - e^{-y})^+] = \mathbf{E}[e^{-Y}]\chi_n^2 \left(y - \epsilon; v, \frac{\widetilde{\lambda}}{1 + 2\eta}, \frac{\eta}{1 + 2\eta} \right)$$
$$- e^{-y}\chi_n^2(y - \epsilon; v, \widetilde{\lambda}, \eta). \tag{7.40}$$

The value of an exchange option on e^{-Y} and $e^{-Y'}$ is:

$$\mathbf{E}[(e^{-Y} - e^{-Y'})^+] = \mathbf{E}[e^{-Y}]\chi_n^2\left(\epsilon' - \epsilon; \nu, \frac{\tilde{\lambda}}{1+2\eta}, \frac{\eta-\eta'}{1+2\eta}\right)$$

$$-\mathbf{E}[e^{-Y'}]\chi_n^2\left(\epsilon' - \epsilon; \nu, \frac{\tilde{\lambda}}{1+2\eta'}, \frac{\eta-\eta'}{1+2\eta'}\right). \tag{7.41}$$

Proof. The expectation (7.37) and the moment generating function (7.39) are well known (see e.g. Johnson and Kotz, 1970). The statement (7.38) follows directly from the definition of the probability distribution function. For a proof of (7.40) and (7.41), see Jamshidian (1996). $\square$

7.2.3 Factor distributions

As observed by Cox *et al.* (1985a,b), the square root dynamics of the factors x_i give rise to non-central chi-squared distributed final values.

Lemma 7.6 *Let x be given by*

$$dx = (\alpha - \beta x)dt + \sigma\sqrt{x}dW. \tag{7.42}$$

Then $x(T)$ given $x(t)$ is ANC distributed with weight

$$\eta = \frac{\sigma^2}{4\beta}\left(1 - e^{-\beta(T-t)}\right)$$

and non-centrality $\tilde{\lambda}$ and degrees of freedom ν:

$$\tilde{\lambda} = x(t)\frac{4\beta e^{-\beta(T-t)}}{\sigma^2\left(1 - e^{-\beta(T-t)}\right)} \qquad \nu = \frac{4\alpha}{\sigma^2}.$$

The distribution of the factors $x_i(T)$ remains of the ANC type even under a change of measure to a T-forward measure. This change of measure will be necessary to eliminate discounting with the factors later on. It is defined in Lemma 7.7 which is Girsanov's theorem (points (i) and (ii)) combined with a slight extension of results by Jamshidian (1996, 1997b) (points (iii) and (iv)).

Lemma 7.7 *Let x follow a CIR-type square root process under the measure P:*

$$dx = (\alpha - \beta x)dt + \sigma\sqrt{x}\,dW, \tag{7.43}$$

such that $x = 0$ is an unattainable boundary ($\alpha > \frac{1}{2}\sigma^2$) and let $c > 0$ be a positive real number.

(i) *Then there is an equivalent probability measure $\tilde{P}_c$, whose restriction on $\mathcal{F}_t$ has the following Radon–Nikodym density w.r.t. P:*

$$\frac{d\tilde{P}_{c_t}}{dP_t} := Z(t) = \mathcal{E}\left(-\int_0^t \sigma(s)c\sqrt{x(s)}H_{2x}(T-s,c)dW(s)\right)$$

and under which the process $\widetilde{W}_t^c$:

$$dW_t = d\widetilde{W}_t^c - H_{2x}(T - t, c)c\sigma\sqrt{x}dt$$

is a $\widetilde{P}_c$-Brownian motion.

(ii) Expectations under P are transformed to expectations under $\widetilde{P}_c$ via

$$\mathbf{E}^P\left[e^{-\int_t^T cx(s)ds}F(x(T))\,\middle|\,\mathcal{F}_t\right] = G(x(t), t, T, c)\mathbf{E}^{\widetilde{P}_c}[F(x(T)) \mid \mathcal{F}_t] \qquad (7.44)$$

where

$$G(x, t, T, c) = \mathbf{E}\left[e^{-\int_t^T cx(s)ds}\,\middle|\,\mathcal{F}_t\right] = H_{1x}(T - t, c)e^{-H_{2x}(T-t,c)cx}. \qquad (7.45)$$

(iii) Under $\widetilde{P}_c$ the process x has the dynamics

$$dx = [\alpha - (\beta + H_{2x}(T - t, c)c\sigma^2)x]dt + \sigma\sqrt{x}\,d\widetilde{W}^c, \qquad (7.46)$$

and $x(T)$ given $x(t)$ is ANC distributed under $\widetilde{P}_c$ with weight

$$\eta_T = \frac{c\sigma^2}{4}H_{2x}(T - t, c) \qquad (7.47)$$

and degrees of freedom ν_T and non-centrality $\widetilde{\lambda}_T$:

$$\nu_T = \frac{4\alpha}{\sigma^2}, \qquad (7.48)$$

$$\widetilde{\lambda}_T = \frac{4}{\sigma^2}\frac{\frac{\partial}{\partial T}H_{2x}(T - t, c)}{H_{2x}(T - t, c)}x(t). \qquad (7.49)$$

(iv) The dynamics of the other factors are unaffected.

Proof.   See Section 7.3.3.   □

The lemma also holds for time-dependent parameters with $\alpha(t)/\sigma^2(t) > 1/2$, but here we only need the time-independent case.

   The change of measure to P_c^Z removes the discounting with $\exp\{-\int_0^T cx(t)dt\}$, while changing the distribution of $x(T)$ to an ANC distribution with parameters given in equations (7.47) to (7.49).

7.3   CREDIT DERIVATIVES IN THE CIR MODEL

Using the results from Section 7.2 we are now able to give solutions for the general pricing formulae for credit derivatives that were derived previously.

7.3.1 Default digital payoffs

In general, the price for a default digital put is:

$$D = \int_0^T \mathbf{E}\big[\lambda(t)e^{-\int_0^t \lambda(s)ds} e^{-\int_0^t r(s)ds}\big]dt.$$

In this setup, the resulting price for the default digital put is given in the following proposition.

Proposition 7.8   *The price of a default digital put with maturity T and payoff 1 at default is, in the CIR model framework:*

$$D = \int_0^T \mathbf{E}\big[\lambda(t)e^{-\int_0^t \lambda(s)ds} e^{-\int_0^t r(s)ds}\big]dt \tag{7.50}$$

$$= \int_0^T \left(\sum_{i=1}^n \overline{w}_i(w_i + \overline{w}_i)\left(\alpha_i H_{2i}(t, w_i + \overline{w}_i) + \frac{\partial H_{2i}(t, w_i + \overline{w}_i)}{\partial t}x_i(0)\right)\right)\prod_{j=1}^n \overline{B}_{j0}(0, t)dt \tag{7.51}$$

where for $1 \le j \le n$

$$\overline{B}_{j0}(0, t) = H_{1j}(t, w_j + \overline{w}_j)e^{-H_{2j}(t, w_j + \overline{w}_j)(w_j + \overline{w}_j)x_j}. \tag{7.52}$$

Proof.   See Section 7.3.3 (p. 185).   □

7.3.2 Calculations to the Gaussian model

The survival contingent measure: The following lemma describes the change of measure that is necessary to value survival contingent payoffs in this framework.

Lemma 7.9   *Let $X \ge 0$ be an $\mathcal{F}_T$-measurable random variable and $\tau > t$. In the Gaussian model framework, the time t value of receiving X at T given no default has happened before T is:*

$$\mathbf{E}^Q\big[\beta_{t,T}\mathbf{1}_{\{\tau>T\}}X \,\big|\, \mathcal{F}_t\big] = \overline{B}_0(t, T)\mathbf{E}^{P_S}[X \,|\, \mathcal{F}_t], \tag{7.53}$$

where

$$\overline{B}_0(t, T) = B(t, T)P(t, T)\exp\left\{\int_t^T a^P(s, T)a(s, T)ds\right\} \tag{7.54}$$

$$= \left(\frac{\overline{B}(t, T)}{B(t, T)^{1-q}}\right)^{\frac{1}{q}}\exp\left\{\frac{1-q}{2q}\int_t^T (\overline{a}(s, T) - a(s, T))^2 ds\right\}. \tag{7.55}$$

The measure P_S is called the survival contingent measure. *It is defined by the Radon–Nikodym density*

$$dP_{ST} = M_T dQ_T \tag{7.56}$$

where $dP_{ST} = dP_S | \mathcal{F}_T$ and $dQ_T = dQ | \mathcal{F}_T$, and

$$M_u = \mathcal{E}\left(\int_t^u (a^P(s, T) + a(s, T))dW_s\right), \quad u \geq t. \tag{7.57}$$

The Q-Brownian motion W_s is transformed into a P_S-Brownian motion via

$$dW_s = dW_s^{P_S} + (a^P(s, T) + a(s, T))ds. \tag{7.58}$$

Proof.   See p. 183.   □

If the survival contingent measure is known, the valuation of the payoff X can be decoupled from the default valuation which is represented by $\overline{B}_0(t, T)$. The numeraire used in this change of measure is

$$\mathbf{E}\left[e^{-\int_t^T r(s)+\lambda(s)ds} \mid \mathcal{F}_t\right],$$

which is almost exactly the price of a zero-recovery defaultable bond:

$$\overline{B}_0(t, T) = \mathbf{1}_{\{\tau > t\}}\mathbf{E}\left[e^{-\int_t^T r(s)+\lambda(s)ds} \mid \mathcal{F}_t\right].$$

For no previous defaults $(\tau > t)$ both expressions coincide. In equations (7.54) and (7.55) the lemma also gives the value of a zero-recovery defaultable bond with maturity T in the fractional recovery setup.

Proof of Lemma 7.3

The survival probability is defined as:

$$P(0, T) = \mathbf{E}[\mathbf{1}_{\{\tau > T\}}]. \tag{7.59}$$

Using iterated expectations and the Cox process properties this can be expanded to:

$$P(0, T) = \mathbf{E}\left[\mathbf{E}\left[\mathbf{1}_{\{\tau > T\}} \mid \lambda(t), t \geq 0\right]\right]$$
$$= \mathbf{E}\left[\exp\left\{-\int_0^T \lambda(t)dt\right\}\right]. \tag{7.60}$$

From Assumption 7.2 we know the dynamics of the defaultable and default-free bond prices:

$$\frac{dB(t, T)}{B(t, T)} = r(t)dt + a(t, T)dW,$$
$$\frac{d\overline{B}(t, T)}{\overline{B}(t, T)} = (r(t) + q\lambda(t))dt + \overline{a}(t, T)dW.$$

Thus the bond prices satisfy for all $t \leq T_1 \leq T$ (conditional on survival):

$$B(T_1, T) = B(t, T) \exp\left\{ \int_t^{T_1} r(s)ds - \frac{1}{2} \int_t^{T_1} a^2(s, T)ds + \int_t^{T_1} a(s, T)dW_s \right\}, \quad (7.61)$$

$$\overline{B}(T_1, T) = \overline{B}(t, T) \exp\left\{ \int_t^{T_1} r(s) + q\lambda(s)ds - \frac{1}{2} \int_t^{T_1} \overline{a}(s, T)^2 ds + \int_t^{T_1} \overline{a}(s, T)dW_s \right\}.$$
$$(7.62)$$

Using the previous equations with $T_1 = T$, $t = 0$ and $B(T, T) = \overline{B}(T, T) = 1$ we reach

$$1 = B(0, T) \exp\left\{ \int_0^T r(s)ds - \frac{1}{2} \int_0^T a^2(s, T)ds + \int_0^T a(s, T)dW_s \right\},$$

$$1 = \overline{B}(0, T) \exp\left\{ \int_0^T r(s) + q\lambda(s)ds - \frac{1}{2} \int_0^T \overline{a}(s, T)^2 ds + \int_0^T \overline{a}(s, T)dW_s \right\},$$

which can be solved for the integral of λ to yield:

$$\exp\left\{ -\int_0^T \lambda(s)ds \right\} = \left(\frac{\overline{B}(0, T)}{B(0, T)} \right)^{\frac{1}{q}} \mathcal{E}\left(\int_0^T \frac{1}{q}(\overline{a}(s, T) - a(s, T))dW_s \right)$$

$$\times \exp\left\{ -\frac{1}{2q^2} \int_0^T (\overline{a}(s, T) - a(s, T))[(1 + q)a(s, T) - (1 - q)\overline{a}(s, T)]ds \right\}. \quad (7.63)$$

Taking expectations of (7.63) yields the first part of the claim.

It remains to show the dynamics (7.20) and (7.21) of the survival probability. From representation (7.60) it follows that

$$M_t := P(t, T)e^{-\int_0^t \lambda(s)ds}$$

is a martingale. Thus $\mathbf{E}\left[dM\right] = 0$ and combined with Itô's lemma this means that

$$\mathbf{E}\left[dP(t, T)\right] = \lambda(t)P(t, T)dt. \quad (7.64)$$

The volatility of $P(t, T)$ can be derived from (7.63) by substituting for the bond prices $B(t, T)$ and $\overline{B}(t, T)$ from equations (7.61) and (7.62) respectively, and using Itô's lemma again. Finally, similar to equations (7.61) and (7.62), the survival probability can be represented as follows for all $t \leq T_1 \leq T$:

$$P(T_1, T) = P(t, T) \exp\left\{ \int_t^{T_1} \lambda(s)ds - \frac{1}{2} \int_t^{T_1} a^P(s, T)^2 ds + \int_t^{T_1} a^P(s, T)dW_s \right\}. \quad (7.65)$$

$\square$

Proof of Lemma 7.9

The proof of this lemma is an application of Girsanov's theorem. First, the expectation has to be converted using iterated expectations and the Cox process properties of the default process:

$$\mathbf{E}^Q \left[\beta_{t,T} \mathbf{1}_{\{\tau > T\}} X \right] = \mathbf{E}^Q \left[\mathbf{E}^Q \left[e^{-\int_t^T r(s)ds} \mathbf{1}_{\{\tau > T\}} X \mid \lambda(s), \; s \geq 0 \right] \right]$$

$$= \mathbf{E}^Q \left[e^{-\int_t^T r(s) + \lambda(s)ds} X \right].$$

Now we use the representation of the default-free bond price (7.61) and the survival probability in (7.65) to substitute for $\exp\{\int r(s)ds\}$ and $\exp\{\int \lambda(s)ds\}$:

$$\mathbf{E}^Q \left[\beta_{t,T} \mathbf{1}_{\{\tau > T\}} X \right] = B(t, T) P(t, T) \exp\left\{ -\frac{1}{2} \int_t^T a(s, T)^2 + a^P(s, T)^2 ds \right\}$$

$$\times \mathbf{E}^Q \left[\exp\left\{ \int_t^T (a(s, T) + a^P(s, T)) dW_s \right\} X \right]$$

$$= B(t, T) P(t, T) \exp\left\{ \int_t^T a(s, T) a^P(s, T) ds \right\}$$

$$\times \mathbf{E}^Q \left[\mathcal{E} \left(\int_t^T (a(s, T) + a^P(s, T)) dW_s \right) X \right].$$

The rest of the lemma follows directly from Girsanov's theorem. The representation of the zero-recovery defaultable bond price follows by setting $X = 1$. □

Proof of Proposition 7.4

We have to calculate

$$x(t) := \mathbf{E} \left[\lambda(t) e^{-\int_0^t \lambda(s)ds} e^{-\int_0^t r(s)ds} \right].$$

The change of measure to the survival contingent measure P_S (see Lemma 7.9, the measure is contingent on survival until t) reduces the problem to finding

$$x(t) = B(0, t) P(0, t) \exp\left\{ \int_0^t a(s, t) a^P(s, t) ds \right\} \mathbf{E}^{P_S} [\lambda(t)] \qquad (7.66)$$

where under P_S

$$dW_s^{P_S} = dW_s - (a(s, t) + a^P(s, t)) ds$$

is a P_S-Brownian motion.

To evaluate equation (7.66) we need to find the dynamics of λ. Define the forward default intensity

$$\lambda(t, T) := -\frac{\partial}{\partial T} \ln P(t, T)$$

and denote its dynamics by

$$d\lambda(t, T) = \alpha^P(t, T)dt + \sigma^P(t, T)dW_t.$$

The spot default intensity is $\lambda(t) = \lambda(t, t)$. The volatility $\sigma^P(t, T)$ and the drift $\alpha^P(t, T)$ of $\lambda(t, T)$ can be derived directly from equation (7.65):

$$\sigma^P(t, T) = -\frac{\partial}{\partial T} a^P(t, T),$$
$$\alpha^P(t, T) = -\sigma^P(t, T)a^P(t, T).$$

This yields

$$\lambda(t) = \lambda(t, t) = \lambda(0, t) + \int_0^t \alpha^P(s, t)ds + \int_0^t \sigma^P(s, t)dW_s$$

$$= \lambda(0, t) + \int_0^t \alpha^P(s, t)ds + \int_0^t \sigma^P(s, t)dW_s^{Ps}$$

$$+ \int_0^t (a(s, t) + a^P(s, t))\sigma^P(s, t)ds$$

$$= \lambda(0, t) + \int_0^t a(s, t)\sigma^P(s, t)ds + \int_0^t \sigma^P(s, t)dW_s^{Ps}$$

and therefore

$$\mathbf{E}^{Ps}[\lambda(t)] = \lambda(0, t) + \int_0^t a(s, t)\sigma^P(s, t)ds.$$

$\square$

7.3.3   Calculations to the CIR model

Proof of Lemma 7.7

Consider the process x with P-dynamics

$$dx = (\alpha - \beta x)dt + \sigma \sqrt{x}\, dW$$

and the process $y = cx$. Note that y has dynamics

$$dy = d(cx) = (c\alpha - \beta y)dt + \sigma \sqrt{c}\, \sqrt{y}\, dW$$
$$=: (\widehat{\alpha} - \widehat{\beta}y)dt + \widehat{\sigma}\sqrt{y}\, dW, \tag{7.67}$$

which is still of the CIR square root form.

The proof of points (i) and (ii) of Lemma 7.7 is an application of the Girsanov theorem and the change of measure technique. Define

$$g(0, t) = e^{-\int_0^t y(s)ds}. \tag{7.68}$$

Then

$$Z(t) := \frac{1}{G(y(0), 0, T)} g(0, t)G(y(t), t, T) \tag{7.69}$$

is a positive martingale with initial value $Z(0) = 1$ and can therefore be used as a Radon–Nikodym density for a change of measure from P to $\widetilde{P}_c$ defined by $d\widetilde{P}_c/dP = Z$, and

$$Z(t) = \mathcal{E}\left(-\int_0^t \sigma c \sqrt{x(s)} H_{2x}(T - s, c)dW(s)\right).$$

Then

$$Z(t)\mathbf{E}^{\widetilde{P}_c}[F(x(T)) \mid \mathcal{F}_t] = \mathbf{E}^P[Z(T)F(x(T)) \mid \mathcal{F}_t] = \mathbf{E}^P\left[e^{-\int_t^T cx(s)ds} F(x(T)) \mid \mathcal{F}_t\right].$$

(iii) The P dynamics of x are

$$dx = (\alpha - \beta x)dt + \sigma \sqrt{x}\, dW$$

where W is a P-Brownian motion. By Girsanov's theorem

$$dW = d\widetilde{W}^c - H_{2x}(T - t, c)c\sigma \sqrt{x}dt$$

where $\widetilde{W}^c$ is a $\widetilde{P}_c$-Brownian motion. Thus

$$dx = (\alpha - \beta x)dt - H_{2x}(T - t, c)c\sigma^2 xdt + \sigma \sqrt{x}\, d\widetilde{W}^c. \tag{7.70}$$

The distribution of $x(T)$ under $\widetilde{P}_c$ can be found, for example, in Jamshidian (1996) or Schlögl (1997). There the distribution is only given for $c = 1$, but by applying these results to y equations (7.46)–(7.49) follow directly.

(iv) The dynamics of the other factors remains unchanged because the change of measure here does not affect them. (Z does not depend on any of the other factors.) □

Proof of Proposition 7.8

We have to evaluate

$$\mathbf{E}\left[\lambda(t)e^{-\int_0^t \lambda(s)ds}e^{-\int_0^t r(s)ds}\right].$$

First, simplify the expression in the expectation operator:

$$\lambda(t)e^{-\int_0^t \lambda(s)+r(s)ds} = \left(\sum_{i=1}^n \overline{w}_i x_i(t)\right) e^{\sum_{j=1}^n -\int_0^t (w_j+\overline{w}_j)x_j(s)ds}$$

$$= \sum_{i=1}^n \left(\overline{w}_i x_i(t)e^{\sum_{j=1}^n -\int_0^t (w_j+\overline{w}_j)x_j(s)ds}\right).$$

Looking at the ith summand:

$$\mathbf{E}\left[\overline{w}_i x_i(t)e^{\sum_{j=1}^n -\int_0^t (w_j+\overline{w}_j)x_j(s)ds}\right] = \mathbf{E}\left[\overline{w}_i x_i(t)e^{-\int_0^t (w_i+\overline{w}_i)x_i(s)ds}\right]$$

$$\times \mathbf{E}\left[e^{\sum_{j\neq i} -\int_0^t (w_j+\overline{w}_j)x_j(s)ds}\right]$$

$$= \mathbf{E}\left[\overline{w}_i x_i(t)e^{-\int_0^t (w_i+\overline{w}_i)x_i(s)ds}\right]$$

$$\times \prod_{j\neq i} \mathbf{E}\left[e^{-\int_0^t (w_j+\overline{w}_j)x_j(s)ds}\right]$$

$$= \overline{w}_i \mathbf{E}\left[x_i(t)e^{-\int_0^t (w_i+\overline{w}_i)x_i(s)ds}\right]$$

$$\times \prod_{j\neq i} \overline{B}_{j0}(0, t),$$

where $\overline{B}_{j0}(0, t)$ is defined as in the proposition.

It remains to evaluate $\mathbf{E}[\overline{w}_i x_i(t) \exp\{-\int_0^t (w_i + \overline{w}_i)x_i(s)ds\}]$. For this we change the measure according to Lemma 7.7 choosing $c = w_i + \overline{w}_i$. Then

$$\mathbf{E}\left[x_i(t)e^{-\int_0^t cx_i(s)ds}\right] = \overline{B}_{i0}(0, t)\mathbf{E}^{\widetilde{P}_c}[x_i(t)].$$

By Lemma 7.7 (iii) and Lemma 7.5 equation (7.37) the expectation of $x_i(t)$ under $\widetilde{P}_c$ is

$$\mathbf{E}^{\widetilde{P}_c}[x_i(t)] = \eta_t(\nu_t + \widetilde{\lambda}_t)$$

$$= c\frac{\sigma_i^2}{4} H_{2i}(t, c)\left(\frac{4\alpha_i}{\sigma_i^2} + \frac{4}{\sigma_i^2}\frac{\frac{\partial}{\partial T}H_{2i}(t, c)}{H_{2i}(t, c)}x_i(0)\right)$$

$$= c\alpha_i H_{2i}(t, c) + c\frac{\partial}{\partial T}H_{2i}(t, c)x_i(0).$$

Thus, combining all yields

$$\mathbf{E}\left[\lambda(t)e^{-\int_0^t \lambda(s)ds}e^{-\int_0^t r(s)ds}\right] = \left(\sum_{i=1}^n \overline{w}_i(\overline{w}_i + w_i)(\alpha_i H_{2i}(t, w_i + \overline{w}_i)\right.$$

$$\left. + \frac{\partial}{\partial T}H_{2i}(t, w_i + \overline{w}_i)x_i(0))\right)\prod_{j=1}^n \overline{B}_{j0}(0, t).$$

$\square$

7.4   TREE MODELS

In the previous sections two (out of many possible) specifications of the dynamics of default intensities and default-free interest rates were analysed, and we were able to derive closed-form solutions for the prices of the basic building block securities. The availability of these closed-form solutions simplifies the calibration of the model significantly, but to price more complicated, exotic credit derivatives we need a numerical solution scheme for the model.

In this section, we present a tree-based numerical solution method for the Gaussian model specification and related specifications. Tree models for assets with diffusion-type dynamics are well known, models like the Cox *et al.* (1979) binomial tree approximating share prices following a lognormal Brownian motion feature in the first lessons of any course on option pricing. In interest rate modelling, a prominent place is taken by the Hull and White (1994a,b, 1996) trinomial tree and the binomial tree models by Black *et al.* (1990) and also Sandmann and Sondermann (1995). Tree models have the advantage that their mechanics are very intuitive, and that the hedge ratios are automatically found in the derivation of the price. For some pricing problems (e.g. American or Bermudan options) they also dominate Monte Carlo methods.

The model is based upon the two-factor Hull and White (1994b) model for default-free interest rates, but we extend this tree to include default risk following Schönbucher (2002). We refer the reader to Schönbucher (2002) for further details. The method for the extension of the tree is not specific to the Hull and White (1994b) model, it can also be applied to other tree models.

The Hull and White (1994b) tree has two factors. We will use one of the two factors to model default-free interest rates, and the other to model default intensities. The model can be fitted to any given term structures of default-free and defaultable bond prices, and it is shown how this fit can be achieved. The Gaussian setup of the model can easily be extended to non-Gaussian processes (e.g. lognormal spreads and volatilities) that avoid negative interest rates or credit spreads.

7.4.1   The tree implementation: inputs

We need the following inputs for the tree implementation.

- $B(0, T)$: an initial term structure of default-free zero-coupon bond prices for all maturities T. We will calibrate the model to exactly reproduce this term structure of interest rates.
- The parameters of the dynamics of the default-free short rate. We use the extended Vasicek (1977) model

$$dr(t) = (k(t) - ar)dt + \sigma dW(t).$$

  We will use the level of mean reversion $k(t)$ to calibrate the model to the initial term structure of default-free interest rates. The local volatility σ and the speed of mean reversion a are usually calibrated to the prices of liquid derivatives on default-free interest rates such as caps, floors and swaptions.
- $\overline{B}(0, T)$: an initial term structure of defaultable zero-coupon bond prices. Depending on the choice of recovery model, these zero-coupon bonds can be either zero-recovery zero-coupon bonds or zero-coupon bonds with positive recovery according to the RMV model. The model will also be calibrated to this term structure of these defaultable bond prices.

- $\bar{a}$, $\bar{k}(T)$ and $\bar{\sigma}(T)$: the parameters of the dynamics of the default intensity λ. Similarly to the default-free interest rate model we choose the extended Vasicek (1977) model

$$d\lambda(t) = (\bar{k}(t) - \bar{a}\lambda)dt + \bar{\sigma}d\overline{W}(t).$$

The parameter for the level of mean reversion $\bar{k}(t)$ will be used to calibrate the dynamics of the default intensity to the initial term structure of defaultable bond prices. For the other parameters $\bar{\sigma}$ and $\bar{a}$, there are usually not enough liquid securities with volatility information on default intensities (e.g. options on defaultable bonds or options on CDSs). Thus, the volatility parameters $\bar{a}$ and $\bar{\sigma}$ will have to be chosen either based upon historical data or based upon a forward-looking assessment of the likely development of the default risk of the obligor.
- ρ: the correlation between the Brownian motions W and $\overline{W}$.
- π or q: the recovery rate for the recovery model in use.
- Numerical parameters: time step size Δt.

7.4.2 Default branching

Figure 7.1 shows how defaults and diffusion dynamics are combined in the tree using a basic tree element. (The full tree using the combination of these basic elements is shown in Figure 7.2.)

There is a "standard" survival-based part of the tree in the dashed box. The standard part of the tree contains the branches which model the continuous, diffusion-based dynamics of the default-free interest rate and the default intensity. *Before* this standard part, a branch to default is attached.

There is only one branch to default over the time step $[t, t + \Delta t]$, i.e. we discretise the time of default, and the default intensity is the value of the default intensity process at t, the

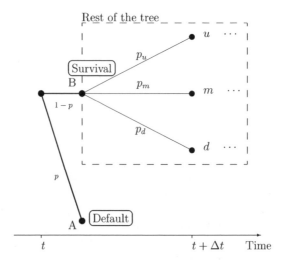

Figure 7.1 The basic tree element with the branch to default

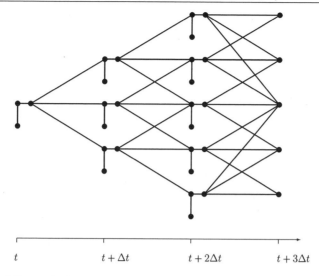

Figure 7.2   The full tree with branches to default

beginning of the time interval. (This is consistent with the modelling of a *predictable* default intensity process.) Thus, the survival probability from t to $t + \Delta t$ is:

$$1 - p = e^{-\lambda(t)\Delta t}.$$

In the tree element, this is the probability with which the survival branch is taken. For small time steps Δt we can assume that default happens at the left end of the interval. This allows us to locally separate the default branching from the continuous interest rate and intensity dynamics. If more precision is needed one can use the expected time of default, given that there is a default in $[t, t + \Delta t[$. This expectation is:

$$\tau^e = \mathbf{E}[\tau \mid \tau \in [t, t + \Delta t]] = t + \frac{1}{\lambda} - \Delta t \frac{e^{-\lambda \Delta t}}{1 - e^{-\lambda \Delta t}}.$$

To reach the total probabilities of a particular end node, the probabilities for the survival movements must now be multiplied by the survival probability $(1 - p)$:

$$p_u \to p_u(1 - p), \qquad p_m \to p_m(1 - p), \qquad p_d \to p_d(1 - p).$$

In this implementation, the tree *ends* at a default. Although it would be possible, a continuation of the tree is usually not necessary. The default payoffs of most credit derivatives can either be specified directly, or their values can be given in closed form as simple functions of the current short-term interest rate r and its dynamics.

A note of caution: The separation of the default branch from the dynamics in survival was made for numerical and expositional convenience only, to derive hedge strategies we have to be hedged against all movements simultaneously, i.e. against defaults and interest rate and intensity dynamics at the same time. It would be incorrect to hedge against the default branch first, and then reshuffle the hedge in the survival node to hedge against the u, m and d moves in the "rest of the tree".

7.4.3 The implementation steps

The implementation proceeds in the following steps:

1. Build a tree for the default-free short rate r.
2. Fit this tree to the default-free bond prices $B(0, T)$.
3. Build a tree for the default intensity λ. If $\rho \neq 0$ do not fit the tree yet.
4. Combine the two trees and incorporate the correlation.
5. Incorporate default branches into the tree.
6. Fit the combined tree to the defaultable bond prices $\overline{B}(0, T)$, while preserving the fit to the default-free bond prices.
7. The tree can now be used to price credit derivatives.

We will now explain each step in more detail.

7.4.4 Building trees: the Hull–White algorithm

There are two steps that require the building of a tree: the building of a tree for the default-free interest rates and the building of a tree for the default intensity. Here, we use the method of Hull and White (1994a,b, 1996) to build a recombining, trinomial tree for a process with Gaussian mean-reverting dynamics of the form

$$dr(t) = (k(t) - ar(t))dt + \sigma dW(t).$$

(We illustrate the method for the interest rate tree.) As $k(t)$ will be used to calibrate the tree after it has been built, Hull and White propose to first build a tree for the following auxiliary process: $r^*(0) = 0$ and

$$dr^* = -ar^*dt + \sigma dW. \tag{7.71}$$

By Lemma 7.1, we have that

$$r(T) - r^*(T) = r(0)e^{-aT} + \int_0^T e^{-(T-s)a}k(s)ds, \tag{7.72}$$

i.e. the interest rate process $r(T)$ and the auxiliary process $r^*(T)$ differ only by a deterministic, time-dependent function, but nothing more. Thus, if we have modelled the *dynamics* of r^* correctly, we will also have modelled the dynamics of r correctly except for a time-dependent offset. This offset will be determined in the calibration step, so there is no necessity to model it now, we can concentrate on the volatility dynamics encoded in r^*.

The tree for r^* (without branches to default) will qualitatively look as shown in Figure 7.3. Building the tree proceeds as follows.

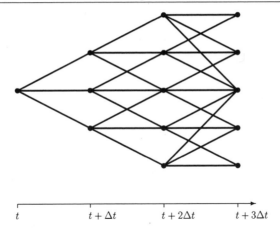

Figure 7.3   The one-dimensional tree without default branches

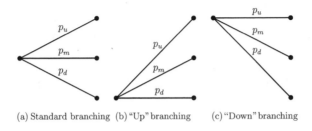

(a) Standard branching (b) "Up" branching   (c) "Down" branching

Figure 7.4   The different one-dimensional branching methods

1. Fix time step Δt. The same time step must be used to build both the interest rate *and* the intensity trees.
2. Determine the interest rate step:

$$\Delta r = \sigma \sqrt{3} \sqrt{\Delta t}. \tag{7.73}$$

3. Determine the maximum and minimum node index j_{max} and j_{min}:

$$j_{\text{max}} \geq \frac{0.184}{a \Delta t} \quad \text{and} \quad j_{\text{min}} = -j_{\text{max}}. \tag{7.74}$$

4. Determine which branching method to use (see Figure 7.4):
   (c) at the top node j_{max},
   (a) at intermediate nodes,
   (b) at the bottom node j_{min}.
5. Calculate the probabilities such that the first two moments of the continuous-time dynamics are fitted.

To identify the nodes in the tree we use the following notation: node (n, j) is at time $n \Delta t$ and interest rate $j \Delta r$. As $j_{\text{min}} < 0$, j can be *negative*.

The interest rate step Δr in equation (7.73) is larger than the time step Δt because $\sqrt{\Delta t} \gg \Delta t$ for small Δt. There are other ways to choose the interest rate step size but whichever choice is made, one must ensure that the branching probabilities remain non-negative. For this it is necessary that Δr is of order $\sqrt{\Delta t}$ as $\Delta t \to 0$, but other choices of the constant factors are possible.

The mean reversion in the drift of r^* in (7.71) pulls it towards $r^* = 0$, the centre of the tree. The strength of this effect is proportional to $|r^*|$, thus it is stronger the further the process is away from the centre. One consequence of this in a discrete tree is that the expected increment of r^* over the next time step Δt can become arbitrarily large (or negative) if only r^* is negative (positive) enough:

$$\mathbf{E}[r^*(t + \Delta t) - r^*(t) \mid \mathcal{F}_t] \approx -ar^*(t)\Delta t.$$

If we want to model this increment in a "classical" trinomial branch like (a) in Figure 7.4, the expected value of $r^*(t + \Delta t)$ will be below the lower branch of the trinomial branch, if $r^*(t)$ is large enough (i.e. j is large enough). In this case, the tree cannot replicate the first moment of the dynamics of r^* any more, because the expected value of the *tree* increment must lie between $r^*(t) + \Delta r$ and $r^*(t) - \Delta T$ if branching probabilities are to remain non-negative.

To solve this problem, Hull and White proposed to use a modified branching method at the top ((c) in Figure 7.4) and bottom nodes ((b) in Figure 7.4) which only has movements across and downwards (or upwards respectively). This has two advantages: first, the original problem of matching the first moment in the tree has been resolved, and second, the tree does not expand in this direction any more. This reduces the number of nodes and ensures that the same problem only occurs once every time step. Equation (7.74) tells us at which node index we have to switch to downward and upward branching respectively, it was derived by checking at which node index we cannot properly match the first moment of r^* any more using standard branching (a).

Finally, we have to calculate the branching probabilities in each node. This is done by fitting the first and second moments of the tree dynamics to the first and second moments of the continuous-time dynamics. This yields two equations for the three probabilities, the third equation is given by ensuring that the probabilities sum up to one. The equations are:

$$\mathbf{E}[r^{*n+1} - r^{*n}] = p_u \Delta r_u + p_m \Delta r_m + p_d \Delta r_d = -ar_j^{*n} \Delta t, \tag{7.75}$$

$$\mathbf{E}[(r^{*n+1} - r^{*n})^2] = p_u \Delta r_u^2 + p_m \Delta r_m^2 + p_d \Delta r_d^2 = \sigma^2 \Delta t + a^2 (r_j^{*n})^2 \Delta t^2, \tag{7.76}$$

$$p_u + p_m + p_d = 1. \tag{7.77}$$

The branching probabilities are given by the following solution of equations (7.75) to (7.77).

At node (a):

$$p_u = \frac{1}{6} + \frac{a^2 j^2 \Delta t^2 - aj\Delta t}{2}, \tag{7.78}$$

$$p_m = \frac{2}{3} - a^2 j^2 \Delta t^2, \tag{7.79}$$

$$p_d = \frac{1}{6} + \frac{a^2 j^2 \Delta t^2 + aj\Delta t}{2}. \tag{7.80}$$

At node (b):

$$p_u = \frac{1}{6} + \frac{a^{2}{}^{*}j^2 \Delta t^2 + aj\,\Delta t}{2}, \tag{7.81}$$

$$p_m = -\frac{1}{3} - a^2 j^2 \Delta t^2 - 2aj\,\Delta t, \tag{7.82}$$

$$p_d = \frac{7}{6} + \frac{a^2 j^2 \Delta t^2 + 3aj\,\Delta t}{2}. \tag{7.83}$$

At node (c):

$$p_u = \frac{7}{6} + \frac{a^2 j^2 \Delta t^2 - 3aj\,\Delta t}{2}, \tag{7.84}$$

$$p_m = -\frac{1}{3} - a^2 j^2 \Delta t^2 + 2aj\,\Delta t, \tag{7.85}$$

$$p_d = \frac{1}{6} + \frac{a^2 j^2 \Delta t^2 - aj\,\Delta t}{2}. \tag{7.86}$$

Here we used the fact that $\Delta r^2 = 3\sigma^2 \Delta t$ (another reason why (7.73) is a convenient choice of constants). This is only true for constant σ. If $\sigma(t)$ is time-dependent, the tree can nevertheless be built, and we refer the reader to Schönbucher (2002) for details.

For the implementation of the tree it is convenient to note that the branching probabilities (7.78) to (7.86) only depend on the node index j and the direction of the branching (u, m or d), but *not* on the time index n. Thus, the branching probabilities can be saved once in three one-dimensional arrays indexed from $j_{\min}$ to $j_{\max}$.

7.4.5 Fitting the tree: default-free interest rates

The basic idea in the fitting procedure stems from equation (7.72). r^* and r only differ by a time-dependent constant. Thus, the *trees* for r and r^* also only differ by a constant α_n, which only depends on the time index n. Effectively, we shift the r^*-tree by α_n:

$$r^n_j = r^{*n}_j + \alpha_n. \tag{7.87}$$

Fitting the r-tree involves the iterative determination of these shifts, such that the bond prices $B_n := B(0, n\Delta t)$ are fitted perfectly. In principle, we could use the closed-form solutions for $B(t, T)$ in the continuous-time model to determine the parameter $k(t)$ which would replicate exactly these bond prices in continuous time. But this would mean that in the discrete tree model, the bond prices will not be perfectly fitted because of the discretisation errors in the transition from continuous to discrete time. Furthermore, this procedure would not work if an additional transformation of the rate is used to ensure non-negativity. Thus we calibrate in discrete time.

The calibration procedure is done iteratively using *forward induction*, starting from $n = 0$.

It is convenient to use *state prices* π^n_j in the calibration procedure (and later also to price payoffs). π^n_j is the state price of node (n, j), i.e. the time 0 value of a payoff of \$1 payable at time $t = n\Delta t$ if node (n, j) is reached. Its value is given by

$$\pi^n_j := \mathbf{E}\left[\mathbf{1}_{\{r(n\Delta t)=r^n_j\}} \prod_{m=0}^{n-1} e^{-r^m \Delta t} \right]. \tag{7.88}$$

Now we can state the calibration algorithm (which will incidentally also produce a complete set of state prices in the interest rate dimension).

$n = 0$:
- Initialise the first state price $\pi_0^0 = 1$.
- Determine $r(0) = \alpha_0$ such that B_1 is priced correctly:

$$e^{-r_0 \Delta t} = B_1. \tag{7.89}$$

$(n-1) \to n$:
- Determine the state prices at level n:

$$\pi_j^n = \sum_{k \in \text{Pre}(n,j)} p_{kj}^{n-1} \pi_k^{n-1} e^{-r_k^{n-1} \Delta t}. \tag{7.90}$$

Pre(n, j) denotes the set of all immediate predecessor nodes of node (n, j). Thus, the state price of (n, j) is the sum of all state prices of the predecessor nodes $(n-1, k)$ of (n, j), weighted by the probability p_{kj}^{n-1} of going from $(n-1, k)$ to (n, j) and discounted by the rate r_k^{n-1} at $(n-1, k)$ over the next Δt.

- Using these state prices, we can determine the offset α_n at time $t = n\Delta t$ such that $B(n+1)$ is priced correctly:

$$B_{n+1} = \sum_j \pi_j^n e^{-r_j^{n+1} \Delta t} = \sum_j \pi_j^n e^{-r_j^{*n} \Delta t} e^{-\alpha_n \Delta t}. \tag{7.91}$$

- Repeat until all zero-coupon bonds are fitted.

The interest rate tree is now fitted, and we can already use it to price default-free interest rate derivatives.

To use the tree for defaultable bonds and credit derivatives, we now have to extend it to include:

(a) default intensity dynamics,
(b) branches to default.

As a first step, we build a tree for λ^*. As the procedure is identical to the building of the tree for r^*, it is not repeated here. We index the nodes in the intensity tree with $i_{\min} \leq i \leq i_{\max}$, and call the transition probabilities in this intensity tree p_u', p_m', p_d'.

The next step is to combine the two trees, then we will incorporate the branches to default, and finally, the combined tree will be fitted to a term structure of defaultable bond prices $\overline{B}(0, T)$.

7.4.6 Combining the trees

The combined tree will extend in *three* dimensions, the interest rate dimension, the intensity dimension and time. We denote by (n, i, j) the node in the tree at time $t = n\Delta t$, intensity $\lambda^* = i\Delta\lambda$ and interest rate $r = j\Delta r + \alpha_n$. (We do not know the offset α_n' for the intensity

Table 7.1 The combined tree transition probabilities under independence. To reach the full transition probabilities including the survival probability, multiply the joint probabilities in the table by the survival probability p

λ-Move	r-Move			Marginal
	Down	Middle	Up	
Up	$p'_u p_d$	$p'_u p_m$	$p'_u p_u$	p'_u
Middle	$p'_m p_d$	$p'_m p_m$	$p'_m p_u$	p'_m
Down	$p'_d p_d$	$p'_d p_m$	$p'_d p_u$	p'_d
Marginal	p_u	p_m	p_d	1

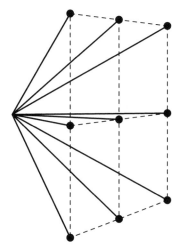

Figure 7.5 An element of the combined tree with trinomial branching in two dimensions

calibration yet, thus the combined tree is still in terms of λ^*.) The tree node indices will range from $n = 0, \ldots, N$, $j_{min} \leq j \leq j_{max}$ and $i_{min} \leq i \leq i_{max}$.

Figure 7.5 shows one tree element of the combination (i.e. the product) of two trinomial branches. The combined tree will have nine branches, three possible movements in the interest rate dimension combined with three more possible moves in the intensity:

$$(r_u, r_m, r_d) \times (\lambda_u, \lambda_m, \lambda_d).$$

If we add the branch to default to this, we have one additional branch.

Table 7.1 shows the transition probabilities in the combined tree as a function of the original one-dimensional transition probabilities p_u, p_m, p_d (interest rate transition probabilities) and p'_u, p'_m, p'_d (intensity transition probabilities) *if independence between r and λ is assumed*, i.e. $\rho = 0$. We see that the combined tree recovers the correct marginal transition probabilities.

Table 7.2 The probabilities of the indicated combined movements of r and λ in the combined tree for a given positive correlation $\rho = 36\varepsilon$. To reach the full transition probabilities including the survival probability, multiply the joint probabilities in the table by the survival probability p

λ-Move	r-Move			Marginal
	Down	Middle	Up	
Up	$p_u' p_d - \varepsilon$	$p_u' p_m - 4\varepsilon$	$p_u' p_u + 5\varepsilon$	p_u'
Middle	$p_m' p_d - 4\varepsilon$	$p_m' p_m + 8\varepsilon$	$p_m' p_u - 4\varepsilon$	p_m'
Down	$p_d' p_d + 5\varepsilon$	$p_d' p_m - 4\varepsilon$	$p_d' p_u - \varepsilon$	p_d'
Marginal	p_u	p_m	p_d	

Table 7.3 The probabilities of the indicated combined movements of r and λ in the combined tree for a given negative correlation of $\rho = -36\varepsilon$. To reach the full transition probabilities including the survival probability, multiply the joint probabilities in the table by the survival probability p

λ-Move	r-Move			Marginal
	Down	Middle	Up	
Up	$p_u' p_d + 5\varepsilon$	$p_u' p_m - 4\varepsilon$	$p_u' p_u - \varepsilon$	p_u'
Middle	$p_m' p_d - 4\varepsilon$	$p_m' p_m + 8\varepsilon$	$p_m' p_u - 4\varepsilon$	p_m'
Down	$p_d' p_d - \varepsilon$	$p_d' p_m - 4\varepsilon$	$p_d' p_u + 5\varepsilon$	p_d'
Marginal	p_u	p_m	p_d	

If the correlation ρ is non-zero, we must modify the transition probabilities of Table 7.1. To recover the correct univariate moments, we must still recover the same marginal probabilities, but to reach the correlation coefficient, the distribution of the probability mass within the marginal events must be modified. Viewing this as a system of equations, we have $3 \times 3 = 9$ unknowns (the joint transition probabilities) to satisfy $3 + 3 + 1 = 7$ restrictions (two times three from the marginal probabilities and one for the correlation coefficient), under the additional restriction of non-negativity.

One possible way the joint fit can be achieved is shown in Tables 7.2 (for positive correlation) and 7.3 (for negative correlation). This method proposes to transfer probability weight from the off-diagonal elements to the diagonal elements if ρ is positive, and vice versa if ρ is negative. This is done using the parameter ε which is given by:

$$\varepsilon = \begin{cases} \dfrac{\rho}{36} & \text{if} \quad \rho > 0, \\[2mm] -\dfrac{\rho}{36} & \text{if} \quad \rho < 0. \end{cases}$$

There is a bound on the size of correlation that can be achieved with this specification, essentially the joint transition probabilities must not become negative. This bound converges to ± 1 as the time step size is refined $\Delta t \to 0$.

To reach the complete transition probabilities in the combined tree, we then still need to incorporate the survival probability p, i.e. multiply each transition probability by the survival probability, as indicated in Figure 7.1.

7.4.7 Fitting the combined tree

Now we have built a combined tree for λ^* and r. The r-tree is already fitted to the default-free term structure of interest rates. The final step is to calibrate this tree to λ (or $\overline{B}_k$) without upsetting the calibration to r.

This calibration is achieved by shifting the tree *only* in the λ-direction. Mathematically:

$$\lambda_i^n = \lambda^{*n}{}_i + \overline{\alpha}_n. \tag{7.92}$$

Equation (7.92) only affects the realisations of the intensity λ_i^n at node (n, i, j), the interest rate realisation r_j^n remains unchanged. Furthermore, the dynamics and transition probabilities in the tree are not affected either, so the tree remains calibrated to the default-free bond prices B_k. The calibration to $\overline{B}_k$ can only be achieved at this time *after* the default-free interest rates have already been incorporated and calibrated because the defaultable bond prices $\overline{B}_k$ include discounting with the default-free interest rates.

The calibration algorithm is very similar to the calibration algorithm for default-free interest rates, the only difference is that we now have to take the full tree into account. The algorithm will again produce a complete set of state prices for the full tree.

$n = 0$:
- Initialise the first survival state price $\overline{\pi}_{00}^0 = 1$.
- Determine $\lambda_0^0 = \overline{\alpha}_0$ such that $\overline{B}_1$ is priced correctly:

$$e^{-r_0^0 \Delta t} e^{-\lambda_0^0 \Delta t} = \overline{B}_1. \tag{7.93}$$

- Initialise the first default state price $\overline{\overline{\pi}}_{00}^0 = 1 - e^{-\lambda_0^0 \Delta t}$.

$(n - 1) \to n$:
- Determine the state prices at level n:

$$\overline{\pi}_{ij}^n = \sum_{(n-1,k,l) \in \mathrm{Pre}(n,i,j)} p_{kl,ij}^{n-1} \overline{\pi}_{kl}^{n-1} e^{-r_l^{n-1} \Delta t} e^{-\lambda_k^{n-1} \Delta t}. \tag{7.94}$$

$\mathrm{Pre}(n, i, j)$ denotes the set of all immediate predecessor nodes of node (n, i, j). Thus, the state price of (n, i, j) is again the weighted sum of all state prices of the predecessor nodes $(n - 1, k, l)$ of (n, i, j). The probability $p_{kl,ij}^{n-1}$ is the probability of going from $(n - 1, k, l)$ to (n, i, j) *given survival*, therefore we need to additionally include the survival probability via $e^{-\lambda_k^{n-1} \Delta t}$.

- Determine the default state prices at level n via

$$\overline{\overline{\pi}}_{ij}^{n} = \pi_{ij}^{n}\left(1 - e^{-\lambda_{k}^{n}\Delta t}\right). \tag{7.95}$$

- Using these state prices, we can determine the offset $\overline{\alpha}_n$ at time $t = n\Delta t$ such that $\overline{B}_{n+1}$ is priced correctly:

$$\overline{B}_{n+1} = \sum_{i,j} \overline{\pi}_{i,j}^{n} e^{-r_{j}^{n}\Delta t} e^{-\lambda_{i}^{*n}\Delta t} e^{-\overline{\alpha}_{n}\Delta t}. \tag{7.96}$$

- Repeat until all defaultable zero-coupon bonds are fitted.

On our way forward inducing the calibration through the tree, we also derive two sets of state prices which require further explanation.

$\overline{\pi}_{ij}^{n}$: The survival state price of node (n, i, j) is the value at time $t = 0$ of \$1 payable at time $n\Delta t$ if node (n, i, j) is reached at this time.

$\overline{\overline{\pi}}_{ij}^{n}$: The default state price of node (n, i, j) is the value at time $t = 0$ of \$1 payable at time $n\Delta t$ if node (n, i, j) is reached at time $n\Delta t$ *and a default happens in the next instant.*

Going back to Figure 7.1, $\overline{\pi}$ would be the value of \$1 at the *root* of this tree element, and $\overline{\overline{\pi}}$ the value of \$1 at the default branch of this tree element.[5]

7.4.8 Applying the tree

The tree can now be used to price credit derivatives in the usual backwards-induction fashion. Specify payoffs at the tree "leaves" and nodes, incorporate early exercise rights where applicable, and roll the values backwards through the tree.

The following payoffs can be specified.

- f_{ij}^{n}: The payoff of the credit derivative if a default happens in node (n, i, j).
- F_{ij}^{n}: The payoff of the derivative if node (n, i, j) is reached (without defaulting previously). This can be coupons, CDS fees, dividends or other intermediate payments.
- G_{ij}^{n}: The early exercise payoff in node (n, i, j). This only applies if the credit derivative can be exercised early at node (n, i, j), otherwise we set G_{ij}^{n} to $-\infty$ (or do not implement the early exercise right).

If possible, it is advisable to use the closed-form solutions to express the payoffs of the credit derivative. For example for a bond option, this will allow us to end the tree at maturity of the option and not at maturity of the underlying bond. If this is not possible, one can change the tree step size Δt to larger time steps if the underlying security must be valued in the tree.

The backward induction follows the following algorithm (let V_{ij}^{n} be the value of the credit derivative in node (n, i, j)).

---

[5] We assume that *if* a default happens, it happens at the beginning of the time interval $[t, t + \Delta t]$. Equivalently we could also assume that the default occurs some time between t and $t + \Delta t$, or at the end of the interval (this would involve additional discounting). In the limit (as $\Delta t \to 0$) the results will not differ.

Initialisation: $n = N$
Initialise at the final nodes of the tree:

$$V_{ij}^N := F_{ij}^N.$$

Iteration: $n + 1 \rightarrow n$
The value at the survival node (B in Figure 7.1) of the default branch is given by:

$$V''^n_{ij} = \sum_{k,l \in \text{Succ}(n,i,j)} p_{ij,kl}^n e^{-r_j^n \Delta t} V_{kl}^{n+1}. \tag{7.97}$$

If there is no early exercise, the value at node (n, i, j) is:

$$V'^n_{ij} = e^{-\lambda_i^n \Delta t} V''^n_{ij} + \left(1 - e^{-\lambda_i^n \Delta t}\right) f_{ij}^n + F_{ij}^n. \tag{7.98}$$

With early exercise the value is:

$$V_{ij}^n = \max\left(V'^n_{ij}, G_{ij}^n\right). \tag{7.99}$$

Repeat until: $n = 0$
$V_{0,0}^0$ is then the value of the credit derivative.

The "Greeks" are also directly given from the solution of the algorithm.

Interest rate sensitivity:

$$\frac{V_{0,1}^1 - V_{0,-1}^1}{2\Delta r}.$$

Intensity sensitivity:

$$\frac{V_{1,0}^1 - V_{-1,0}^1}{2\Delta \lambda}.$$

Default sensitivity:

$$V_{0,0}^0 - f_{0,0}^0.$$

These sensitivities are all quite standard in tree-based models, the only new sensitivity parameter is the default sensitivity. It is important to recognise that in order to achieve a good hedge, the position must also be hedged against defaults; some practitioners tend to hedge against spread movements and assume that is sufficient for a default hedge.

7.4.9 Extensions and conclusion

The tree implementation in this section serves several points. First, it is a viable implementation of an intensity-based credit derivatives pricing model which can be used in practice. Second, by example we demonstrated how *other* tree-based models for a short-term interest rate may be extended to incorporate default risk in an intensity-based setup. The steps are again:

- Build and calibrate a one-factor model for the default-free short rate;
- Build a similar tree for the default intensity;
- Combine the trees (in two dimensions). Incorporate correlation at this step;
- Calibrate the combined tree to defaultable zero-coupon bonds.

For example, this method would also work for the popular Black *et al.* (1990) binomial interest rate tree.

Finally, there are some extensions to this setup which will be worthwhile implementing if the model is used in practice. First, intensities and interest rates can become negative in the tree model as it is presented here. A simple and effective remedy for this problem is the specification of a positive transformation of the original interest rates and intensities at each node (n, i, j), e.g.

$$\widehat{r}_{ij}^n := e^{r_{ij}^n}$$

and

$$\widehat{\lambda}_{ij}^n := e^{\lambda_{ij}^n}.$$

Thus, the tree is now effectively only a tree for the *logarithm* of interest rate and intensity, so negative values of the logs will still translate into positive interest rates and intensities. The disadvantage of this specification is that now the calibration procedure can only be done numerically because, for example, equation (7.91) can no longer be solved in closed form. Nevertheless, a Newton root-search procedure starting from the forward rate or the previous value for α should converge in very few steps.

The second possible modification concerns the calibration to the defaultable bond prices $\overline{B}_k$. If we assume non-zero correlation between interest rates and default intensities, we cannot exactly recover $\overline{B}_k$ and e_k from observed defaultable coupon bond prices or CDS spreads any more, because there are no closed-form solutions to the prices of the e_k building blocks any more. It may be better to directly calibrate the whole tree to the few defaultable coupon bonds or CDSs which are going to be used as calibration instruments. This means that now we have to specify the intensity offset $\overline{\alpha}_n$ parametrically, e.g. as $\overline{\alpha}_n = a + bn\Delta t$ (or any other parametric specification presented in Section 3.5.1). Then we find the parameters a and b such that the prices of the calibration instruments in the tree are reproduced as closely as possible. Again, with a reasonable initial value, this procedure should converge quickly, and it is ensured that the hedge instruments are priced correctly in the tree, even if $\rho \neq 0$.

7.5 PDE-BASED IMPLEMENTATION

The tree-based implementation of the previous section can be viewed as a particular form of an explicit finite difference scheme to solve a partial differential equation. Besides the explicit finite difference scheme, there are other numerical solution schemes for partial differential equations, e.g. implicit and semi-implicit finite differences, finite elements, method of lines, Fourier series, and many others.

Most of these schemes have been tested and used in other problems of mathematical finance, mostly in the pricing of exotic equity and FX options. This book is not directly concerned with these numerical solution techniques, and we can safely refer the reader to Wilmott *et al.* (1993), Wilmott (1998) and references cited therein for an introduction. Here, we rather show how to *derive* the partial differential equation which must be satisfied by the price of all derivative securities whose payoffs are not (or only weakly) path-dependent. The numerical solution of this p.d.e. can then be tackled with these numerical techniques.

Let us consider a defaultable payoff claim whose value depends on interest rate risk r, spread risk λ, defaults, and time t.

To describe the dynamics of the model, we assume the following stochastic processes:

$$dr = \mu_r dt + \sigma_r dW_1 \tag{7.100}$$

for the risk-free interest rate, and

$$d\lambda = \mu_\lambda dt + \sigma_\lambda\left(\rho dW_1 + \sqrt{1 - \rho^2}\, dW_2\right) \tag{7.101}$$

for the intensity of defaults. We assume that the time of default is the time of the first jump of a Cox process. Drifts μ_r and μ_λ and volatilities σ_r and σ_λ can themselves be functions of r, λ and t. We include the possibility of correlation ρ between λ and r by representing the Brownian motion of the intensity λ as a weighted average of W_1 and a second, independent Brownian motion W_2. Defaults are described with a marked point process with indicator measure

$$m(dt, d\pi)$$

and compensator measure

$$v(dt, d\pi) = \lambda(t)K(d\pi)dt,$$

where $K(d\pi)$ is the conditional distribution of the recovery rate π at default. We assume that all dynamics are specified under the spot martingale measure.

For the credit-sensitive security that we want to price in this setup, we assume the following payoff structure.

- Final payoff: At time T, the security has a final payoff

$$V(T) = F(r(T), \lambda(T)) \tag{7.102}$$

  which can be represented as a function $F(\cdot)$ of the then current short-term interest rate and default intensity. This payoff is only paid if no default has occurred until T.
- Continuous payoffs: At all times $t \le T$, the security pays at a rate of $f(\cdot)$, where $f = f(t, r, \lambda)$. This is only paid before default, i.e. for $t \le \tau$.
- Payoff at default: If a default happens at time t, we assume that we can represent the payoff at default as a function

$$g(t, r, \lambda, \pi) \tag{7.103}$$

  which depends, besides r, λ and t, also on the (stochastic) recovery rate π.

We assume that the price V of the default-sensitive security can be represented as a function $v : \mathbb{R}_+^3 \to \mathbb{R}$ of time t, short rate r and intensity λ:

$$V(t) = v(t, r(t), \lambda(t)) \quad \text{for} \quad t \leq \tau. \tag{7.104}$$

We furthermore assume that v is twice continuously differentiable in r and λ, and once in t.

To derive the partial differential equation satisfied by v we proceed as follows. First we calculate dv by Itô's lemma:

$$dv = \frac{\partial v}{\partial t}dt + \frac{\partial v}{\partial r}dr + \frac{1}{2}\sigma_r^2\frac{\partial^2 v}{\partial r^2}dt + \frac{\partial v}{\partial \lambda}d\lambda + \frac{1}{2}\sigma_\lambda^2\frac{\partial^2 v}{\partial \lambda^2}dt + \rho\sigma_r\sigma_\lambda\frac{\partial^2 v}{\partial \lambda \partial r}dt$$

$$+ \int_0^1 g(t, r, \lambda, \pi) - v(t, r, \lambda)\, m(dt, d\pi).$$

The final integral term represents the payoff of the credit derivative at default. At a default with recovery π^*, the increment in v will be $+g(t, r, \lambda, \pi^*) - v(t, r, \lambda)$ which will take the value v to the payoff function g at default. The payoff at default is therefore already contained in the dynamics of v, while most other payoffs enter the boundary conditions only.

To reach the *full return* of holding one unit of this credit derivative we have to add $f(\cdot)dt$ to dv. By the fundamental pricing rule, the expected rate of return from holding any security under the martingale measure Q must be the default-free short-term interest rate, i.e.

$$\mathbf{E}^Q[dv + f dt] = rv dt. \tag{7.105}$$

Substitution of the full dynamics of dv yields:

$$rv dt = \mathbf{E}^Q[dv + f dt]$$

$$= f dt + \frac{\partial v}{\partial t}dt + \frac{\partial v}{\partial r}\mu_r dt + \frac{1}{2}\sigma_r^2\frac{\partial^2 v}{\partial r^2}dt + \frac{\partial v}{\partial \lambda}\mu_\lambda dt + \frac{1}{2}\sigma_\lambda^2\frac{\partial^2 v}{\partial \lambda^2}dt$$

$$+ \rho\sigma_r\sigma_\lambda\frac{\partial^2 v}{\partial \lambda \partial r}dt + \int_0^1 g(t, r, \lambda, \pi) - v(t, r, \lambda)\, K(d\pi)\lambda dt.$$

Note how in the last line the jump measure was replaced by the compensator measure. This is allowed (in fact necessary) because we are taking a local expectation. Equating all terms in dt and using $\int_0^1 K(d\pi) = 1$ results in the fundamental pricing partial differential equation (p.d.e.):

$$0 = \frac{\partial v}{\partial t} + \frac{\partial v}{\partial r}\mu_r + \frac{1}{2}\sigma_r^2\frac{\partial^2 v}{\partial r^2} + \frac{\partial v}{\partial \lambda}\mu_\lambda + \frac{1}{2}\sigma_\lambda^2\frac{\partial^2 v}{\partial \lambda^2} + \rho\sigma_r\sigma_\lambda\frac{\partial^2 v}{\partial \lambda \partial r}$$

$$- v(\lambda + r) + g^e\lambda + f, \tag{7.106}$$

where we define the locally expected default payoff

$$g^e(t, r, \lambda) := \int_0^1 g(t, r, \lambda, \pi)K(d\pi). \tag{7.107}$$

To put this result in a more general framework, we recall the fact that to every diffusion process there is an associated linear operator $\mathcal{L}$, which in this case takes the form

$$\mathcal{L} = \mu_r \frac{\partial}{\partial r} + \frac{1}{2}\sigma_r^2 \frac{\partial^2}{\partial r^2} + \mu_\lambda \frac{\partial}{\partial \lambda} + \frac{1}{2}\sigma_\lambda^2 \frac{\partial^2}{\partial \lambda^2} + \rho\sigma_r\sigma_\lambda \frac{\partial^2}{\partial\lambda\partial r} \qquad (7.108)$$

for the dynamics (7.100) and (7.101) specified above. Using this linear operator, we can rewrite the fundamental pricing equation (7.106) as:

$$\frac{\partial v}{\partial t} + \mathcal{L}v - (\lambda + r)v = -g^e\lambda - f. \qquad (7.109)$$

The partial differential equation (7.109) must be equipped with appropriate boundary conditions in order to uniquely determine the solution of the equation. The final condition to impose follows from (7.102):

$$v(T, r, \lambda) = F(r, \lambda). \qquad (7.110)$$

In addition to this we need boundary conditions as $r \to 0, r \to \infty, \lambda \to 0$ and $\lambda \to \infty$. These boundary conditions must be specified in such a way that v remains finite (or at least square-integrable). If the credit derivative has a barrier feature, this can also be incorporated in the form of a boundary condition at the barrier. Similarly, American and Bermudan early exercise features can be incorporated (see Wilmott *et al.*, 1993 and Wilmott, 1998 for details on how exotic options can be priced in a p.d.e. framework).

It is instructive to analyse equation (7.109) in more detail, and to contrast it with the corresponding pricing p.d.e. (7.111) for a default-free security v':

$$\frac{\partial v'}{\partial t} + \mathcal{L}v' - rv' = -f. \qquad (7.111)$$

v' will not depend on λ, therefore the derivatives with respect to λ in $\mathcal{L}v'$ will be equal to zero.

The pricing equations (7.109) and (7.111) have the same common structure with some modifications:

- The dividend rate f of the default-free security is replaced by a modified dividend rate $f + g^e$ for the defaultable security. The payoff at default enters the equation like a continuous dividend stream. Imagine you were holding a large number of these securities issued by different issuers: every time step a few issuers would default and generate exactly this dividend stream.
- The default-free security is discounted by r, and the defaultable security is discounted by $r + \lambda$.
- v only represents the value process up to default. Thus, $v(t, r, \lambda)$ is the price at time t *given that $\tau > t$.*

Both of the first two modifications were derived by a different route in Chapters 5 and 6.

The fact that the pricing equation for a credit derivative security is only slightly different from the pricing equation for a "classical" security is very good news for the numerical solvability of the problem. All methods that have been developed to solve partial differential equations of the form (7.111) can be transferred with only very small modifications to solve (7.109). Furthermore, methods and modifications of the pricing equations that were developed in order to capture barrier payoffs, American or Bermudan early exercise rights, or other exotic options features can be applied to the defaultable pricing equation in the same way.

We described the model setup using only r and λ as state variables. Sometimes it can become necessary to incorporate other, additional state variables to the model, e.g. the share price of the firm if a defaultable convertible bond is to be modelled, or an exogenous variable when counterparty default risk in OTC derivatives transactions is to be priced.

The pricing problem does not change qualitatively if the state vector is extended. To demonstrate this, consider a model with a general n-dimensional Markovian state vector $\mathbf{x} = (x_1, \dots, x_n)$ with dynamics

$$d\mathbf{x} = \mu_x(\mathbf{x})dt + \Sigma_x(\mathbf{x})dW, \qquad (7.112)$$

where $\mu_x : \mathbb{R}^n \to \mathbb{R}^n$ is the drift vector, $\Sigma_x : \mathbb{R}^n \to \mathbb{R}^{n \times n}$ is the volatility matrix of $\mathbf{x}$, and W is an n-dimensional Brownian motion. μ_x and Σ_x must satisfy certain regularity conditions. The complete state of the model (except for default events) is summarised in this state vector. In particular, the short-term interest rate r and the default intensity λ are functions of this state vector:

$$r = r(\mathbf{x}) \qquad \lambda = \lambda(\mathbf{x}). \qquad (7.113)$$

The generator operator of the diffusion process $\mathbf{x}$ is:

$$\mathcal{L}_x = \sum_{i=1}^{n} \mu_{x,i} \frac{\partial}{\partial x_i} + \frac{1}{2} \sum_{i,j=1}^{n} \left(\Sigma_x \Sigma_x^T \right)_{ij} \frac{\partial^2}{\partial x_i^2} x_j. \qquad (7.114)$$

The pricing p.d.e. in this extended setup is still equivalent to equation (7.109), the only difference is that we now use the operator associated with $\mathbf{x}$:

$$\frac{\partial v}{\partial t} + \mathcal{L}_x v - (\lambda(\mathbf{x}) + r(\mathbf{x}))v = -g^e(\mathbf{x})\lambda(\mathbf{x}) - f(\mathbf{x}), \qquad (7.115)$$

where we wrote the dependence of some of the state variables on $\mathbf{x}$ explicitly. Equation (7.115) must be solved subject to the appropriate boundary conditions defining the payoff of the derivative.

7.6 MODELLING TERM STRUCTURES OF CREDIT SPREADS

So far, we have used the connection between intensity-based default risk models and interest rate models to apply well-known *short-term interest rate* models to the modelling of default intensities. In the following subsections we will show that *forward-rate*-based approaches can also be extended to incorporate default risk in a straightforward and convenient way.

In forward-rate-based models not only the short-term interest rate r is evolved stochastically, but the whole term structure of forward rates is taken as state variable and is directly equipped with stochastic dynamics. The term structure is either expressed in terms of continuously compounded forward rates $f(t, T)$ as in Heath, Jarrow and Morton (HJM) (1992) or in discretely compounded forward rates $F_k(t)$ as in the Libor market models (LMMs) by Miltersen *et al.* (1997), Brace *et al.* (1997) and Jamshidian (1997a).

Forward-rate-based models have the advantage that – by definition – they are automatically calibrated to the initial term structures of default-free and defaultable interest rates. In the LMMs, volatility calibration is also significantly simplified. In Schönbucher (2000c), the adaptation of this framework to credit risk is described.

As the number of traded securities is very large (basically to every maturity date there is a zerobond in the model), forward-rate-based models are overdetermined: the number of traded securities exceeds the number of risk factors to span. To avoid arbitrage opportunities in this setup, the dynamics of the forward rates must satisfy certain *no-arbitrage conditions* which have become known as drift restrictions on the dynamics of the rates.

In the following subsections, we will show how the HJM modelling framework can be extended to incorporate default risk. The exposition follows closely Schönbucher (1998, 2000a). As a reference to the default-free HJM model we can recommend Björk (1998), but many other good textbooks also treat this model in detail.

The main goal is the derivation of a so-called *HJM drift restriction* on the drifts of the defaultable and default-free forward rates of different maturities. The drift restriction has two functions. First, it will allow us to express the drifts of the forward rates $f(t, T)$ and $\overline{f}(t, T)$ as functions of the forward rate volatilities (under the spot martingale measure). Second, it will ensure that the model remains arbitrage-free. Given these results, an implementation of the HJM model would proceed in the following steps:

1. Specify an initial term structure of *default-free* forward rates $f(t = 0, T)$ of all maturities T.
2. Specify an initial term structure of *defaultable* forward rates $\overline{f}(t = 0, T)$ of all maturities T.
3. Specify the volatilities of all default-free forward rates $f(t, T)$. Do the same for the defaultable forward rates.
4. Calculate the drifts of the default-free and defaultable forward rates.
5. Using these dynamics, simulate one (or 100 000) scenarios (sample developments of the full forward rate curves). Appropriate Monte Carlo simulation techniques are described in the next section.
   - Associated with each scenario there is a development of the default intensity.[6] Use this intensity to generate default times.
   - Evaluate the final payoffs of the credit derivative under investigation. (This should be relatively easy because we can price bonds off the forward rate curve.)
   - Average the final payoffs.

It is advisable to model the spread of the defaultable to the default-free forward rates instead of the defaultable forward rates, we therefore also give the corresponding drift restrictions for spreads.

---

[6] This is also a result of the next sections.

7.6.1   Intensity models in a Heath, Jarrow, Morton framework

In this section an extension of the HJM modelling framework to default risk is presented. In the HJM modelling framework, continuously compounded forward rates are used to model default-free bond prices. In the context of default risk, defaultable forward rates and forward credit spreads are used to represent the defaultable bond prices.

The focus of the section lies on modelling the development of this term structure of defaultable bond prices, and we give conditions under which these dynamics are arbitrage-free. These conditions are a drift restriction that is closely related to the HJM drift restriction for default-free bonds, and the restriction that the defaultable short rate must always be not below the default-free short rate. Reassuringly, it will turn out that the difference between the defaultable and the default-free short-term interest rates must equal the default intensity under the spot martingale measure Q – a key result which was derived using different arguments earlier on.

In the next chapter, we will extend the model setup to a general ratings transition framework which can incorporate stochastic dynamics for the credit spreads in all ratings classes and also stochastic transition intensities.

The model in this section is based upon Schönbucher (1998a). The reader should refer to this paper for a detailed derivation of the results and extensions to the MD/RMV model and to include jumps in the intensities at defaults in the MD model.

7.6.1.1   Model setup

First, we recall the definition of the defaultable and the default-free continuously compounded forward rates, Definition 3.5, because these will be the fundamental quantities of the model.

- The *instantaneous risk-free forward rate* at time t for date $T > t$ is defined as:

$$f(t, T) = -\frac{\partial}{\partial T} \ln B(t, T). \tag{7.116}$$

- The *instantaneous defaultable forward rate* at time t for date $T > t$ is defined as:

$$\overline{f}(t, T) = -\frac{\partial}{\partial T} \ln \overline{B}(t, T). \tag{7.117}$$

- The implied hazard rate of default at time $T > t$ as seen from time t is given by the spread of the defaultable over the default-free continuously compounded forward rates:

$$h(t, T) = \overline{f}(t, T) - f(t, T). \tag{7.118}$$

Defaultable forward rates and hazard rates are only defined up to the time of default. As usual, we assume that the time of default is the time of the first jump of a Cox process N with stochastic intensity process $\lambda(t)$ under the spot martingale measure Q. Here, we do not impose that $\lambda(t) = h(t, t)$ because it will follow directly from no-arbitrage conditions.

The dynamics of the forward rates and spreads are given in the following assumption.

Assumption 7.4

1. *The dynamics of the default free forward rates are given by:*

$$df(t, T) = \alpha(t, T) \, dt + \sum_{i=1}^{n} \sigma_i(t, T) \, dW^i(t). \tag{7.119}$$

2. *The dynamics of the defaultable forward rates are given by:*

$$d\overline{f}(t, T) = \overline{\alpha}(t, T) \, dt + \sum_{i=1}^{n} \overline{\sigma}_i(t, T) \, dW^i(t). \tag{7.120}$$

The drift and diffusion parameters in the forward rate dynamics (7.119) and (7.120) can be arbitrary predictable stochastic processes satisfying certain regularity conditions. The Brownian motion W is an n-dimensional vector Brownian motion with independent components.[7]

We start by analysing the consequences of the specification (Assumption 7.4) of the default-free and defaultable forward rates. From Definition 3.5 of the defaultable forward rates the prices of default-free and defaultable zero-coupon bonds are given by:

$$B(t, T) = \exp\left\{-\int_t^T f(t, s) \, ds\right\}. \tag{7.121}$$

$$\overline{B}(t, T) = (1 - N(t)) \exp\left\{-\int_t^T \overline{f}(t, s) \, ds\right\}. \tag{7.122}$$

The factor of $(1 - N(t))$ in the defaultable bond price ensures that the defaultable bond price drops to zero at times of default: $\overline{B}(t, T) = 0$ for $t \geq \tau$. Given this representation, it is a straightforward exercise to derive the *dynamics* of the defaultable and default-free bond prices by applying Itô's lemma.

Proposition 7.10

1. *Given the dynamics of the risk-free forward rates (7.119):*
   (i) The dynamics of the risk-free bond prices are given by

$$\frac{dB(t, T)}{B(t-, T)} = \left[-\gamma(t, T) + r(t) + \frac{1}{2} \sum_{i=1}^{n} a_i^2(t, T)\right] dt$$

$$+ \sum_{i=1}^{n} a_i(t, T) \, dW^i(t) \tag{7.123}$$

---

[7] Dynamics of defaultable interest rates are always meant as dynamics *before* default $t < \tau$.

where $a_i(t, T)$ and $\gamma(t, T)$ are

$$a_i(t, T) = -\int_t^T \sigma_i(t, v)\, dv, \tag{7.124}$$

$$\gamma(t, T) = \int_t^T \alpha(t, v)\, dv. \tag{7.125}$$

(ii) The dynamics of the risk-free short rate are given by

$$r(t) = f(t, t) = f(0, t) + \int_0^t \alpha(s, t)ds$$

$$+ \sum_{i=1}^n \int_0^t \sigma_i(s, t)dW^i(s). \tag{7.126}$$

2. *Given the dynamics of the defaultable forward rates (7.120):*
   (i) The dynamics of the defaultable bond prices are given by

$$\frac{d\overline{B}(t, T)}{\overline{B}(t-, T)} = \left[-\overline{\gamma}(t, T) + \overline{r}(t) + \frac{1}{2}\sum_{i=1}^n \overline{a}_i^2(t, T) \right] dt$$

$$+ \sum_{i=1}^n \overline{a}_i(t, T)\, dW^i(t) - dN(t) \tag{7.127}$$

where $\overline{a}_i(t, T)$ and $\overline{\gamma}(t, T)$ are defined by

$$\overline{a}_i(t, T) = -\int_t^T \overline{\sigma}_i(t, v)\, dv, \tag{7.128}$$

$$\overline{\gamma}(t, T) = \int_t^T \overline{\alpha}(t, v)\, dv. \tag{7.129}$$

(ii) The dynamics of the defaultable short rate are given by

$$\overline{r}(t) = \overline{f}(t, t) = \overline{f}(0, t) + \int_0^t \overline{\alpha}(s, t)ds$$

$$+ \sum_{i=1}^n \int_0^t \overline{\sigma}_i(s, t)dW^i(s). \tag{7.130}$$

Proposition 7.10 shows the bond price dynamics which are implied by the forward rate dynamics given in Assumption 7.4. If $\overline{\sigma}$ and σ are deterministic functions of time t and maturity T only, then by (7.124) and (7.128) the bond price volatilities a and $\overline{a}$ will also be deterministic functions of time t and maturity T only. This setup is called the *Gaussian* HJM model because forward rates are normally distributed in this setup. We have analysed the Gaussian setup in Section 7.1.2. The bond volatilities in Assumption 7.2 can be viewed as bond price volatilities stemming from equations (7.124) and (7.128) above.

Although we would gain much analytical tractability by assuming Gaussian dynamics, we do not assume that forward rates are normally distributed here. The forward rate volatility processes σ_i and $\overline{\sigma}_i$ can be *arbitrary* stochastic processes (as long as the existence of solutions to the s.d.e.s is ensured). One popular alternative specification are square root dynamics for forward rates $\sigma_i(t, T) = \sigma_i' \sqrt{f(t, T)}$. Unfortunately, one cannot use lognormal dynamics for the *continuously compounded* forward rates because for this specification no solutions would exist for the s.d.e.s (7.119) and (7.120) under the spot martingale measure. (To alleviate this problem, LMMs were introduced which use *simply compounded* forward rates.)

The HJM model family encompasses all short rate models, it is a modelling *framework* rather than a particular specification of the dynamics of some state variables. It is possible to rewrite any short rate/intensity model as a HJM forward rate model as follows. Calculate bond prices $B(t, T)$ and $\overline{B}(t, T)$ in the short rate model, calculate the corresponding forward rates $f(t, T)$ and $\overline{f}(t, T)$, and finally derive the dynamics of the forward rates $df(t, T)$ and $d\overline{f}(t, T)$. Then substitute these dynamics in Assumption 7.4 to define the forward rate dynamics of the corresponding HJM model.

In order to ensure absence of arbitrage, the fundamental theorem of asset pricing tells us that we must require (under the spot martingale measure Q) all bond price processes to have drift r, i.e.

$$\mathbf{E}^Q[dB(t, T)\,|\,\mathcal{F}_t] = r(t)B(t-, T)dt,$$
$$\mathbf{E}^Q[d\overline{B}(t, T)\,|\,\mathcal{F}_t] = r(t)\overline{B}(t-, T)dt.$$

From equation (7.123) this yields, for the default-free term structure of interest rates:

$$\gamma(t, T) = \frac{1}{2} \sum_{i=1}^{n} a_i^2(t, T),$$

$$\int_t^T \alpha(t, v)dv = \frac{1}{2} \sum_{i=1}^{n} \left(\int_t^T \sigma_i(t, v)dv \right)^2,$$

and taking the derivative with respect to T:

$$\alpha(t, T) = \sum_{i=1}^{n} \sigma_i(t, T) \left(\int_t^T \sigma_i(t, v)dv \right) = \sum_{i=1}^{n} -\sigma_i(t, T)a_i(t, T). \qquad (7.131)$$

From (7.127) we reach a similar expression for the defaultable bond prices, where we use the fact that $\mathbf{E}[dN(t)] = \lambda(t)dt$:

$$\overline{\gamma}(t, T) = \overline{r}(t) - r(t) - \lambda(t) + \frac{1}{2} \sum_{i=1}^{n} \overline{a}_i^2(t, T),$$

$$\int_t^T \overline{\alpha}(t, v)dv = \overline{r}(t) - r(t) - \lambda(t) + \frac{1}{2} \sum_{i=1}^{n} \left(\int_t^T \overline{\sigma}_i(t, v)dv \right)^2.$$

This equation has to hold for all t and for all maturities T. In particular, it must still remain valid as $T \searrow t$. In this limit, the integrals on both sides disappear, and we are left with

$$\bar{r}(t) = r(t) + \lambda(t). \tag{7.132}$$

The difference $\bar{r}(t) - r(t)$ between the defaultable and the default-free short rate is exactly the default intensity λ.

Substituting (7.132) back into the original equation and taking the derivative with respect to T yields the second no-arbitrage condition on the dynamics of the defaultable forward rates

$$\bar{\alpha}(t, T) = \frac{1}{2} \sum_{i=1}^{n} \bar{\sigma}_i(t, T) \int_t^T \bar{\sigma}_i(t, v) dv. \tag{7.133}$$

Summing up we reach the following proposition.

Proposition 7.11 *To ensure absence of arbitrage, the drift of the forward rates under the martingale measure Q must be of the following form for all $t \leq T$:*

$$\alpha(t, T) = \sum_{i=1}^{n} \sigma_i(t, T) \left(\int_t^T \sigma_i(t, v) dv \right) = \sum_{i=1}^{n} -\sigma_i(t, T) a_i(t, T), \tag{7.134}$$

$$\bar{\alpha}(t, T) = \frac{1}{2} \sum_{i=1}^{n} \bar{\sigma}_i(t, T) \int_t^T \bar{\sigma}_i(t, v) dv = \sum_{i=1}^{n} -\bar{\sigma}_i(t, T) \bar{a}_i(t, T). \tag{7.135}$$

Furthermore, the short-term interest rate spread must be the Q-default intensity

$$\bar{f}(t, t) - f(t, t) = \lambda(t). \tag{7.136}$$

If defaultable zerobond prices under the MD/RMV recovery specification are modelled, the short-term forward rate spread is

$$\bar{f}_{\text{RMV}}(t, t) - f(t, t) = q\lambda(t), \tag{7.137}$$

and the drift of $\bar{f}_{\text{RMV}}$ must also satisfy equation (7.135).

The result for RMV follows from $d\bar{B}_{\text{RMV}}(t, T)/\bar{B}_{\text{RMV}}(t, T) = \cdots dt + \cdots dW - qdN(t)$ and following the argument for zero recovery.

The three conditions (7.134), (7.135) and (7.136) are all we have to observe when we are building a HJM model of defaultable forward rates. The most important result of this section is equation (7.135), the defaultable bond equivalent of the well-known HJM drift restriction (7.134). This restriction has been derived for default risk-free bonds in Heath *et al.* (1992) and, as we see here, it is also an important part of the modelling of the defaultable bonds' dynamics.

Using this result, we could now proceed to specify volatilities for the defaultable and default-free forward rates and define the drifts as they are given in Proposition 7.11. But in addition to this, we must also ensure that the implied default intensity $\lambda(t, t) := \bar{f}(t, t) - f(t, t)$ remains non-negative, and this can be quite difficult. Therefore, it is more convenient to model the *spread* between defaultable and default-free forward rates. The advantage of modelling $h(t, T)$ instead of $\overline{f}(t, T)$ is that (7.136) reduces to the well-known problem of ensuring that $h(t, t) > 0$, and we can hope to use some of the extensive literature on interest rate models with positive short rates.

For the spreads, a similar drift restriction to (7.135) can be found. First, from (7.136) we have

$$\lambda(t) = h(t, t).$$

We use the following dynamics for h:

$$h(t, T) - h(0, T) = \int_0^t \alpha^h(v, T)dv + \sum_{i=1}^n \sigma_i^h(v, T)dW^i(v). \tag{7.138}$$

In place of the drift restrictions on $\overline{f}(t, T)$ we reach:

$$\begin{aligned}
\alpha^h(t, T) = \sum_{i=1}^n \Bigg[&\sigma_i(t, T) \int_t^T \sigma_i^h(t, v)dv \\
&+ \sigma_i^h(t, T) \int_t^T \sigma_i(t, v)dv \\
&+ \sigma_i^h(t, T) \int_t^T \sigma_i^h(t, v)dv \Bigg].
\end{aligned} \tag{7.139}$$

Independence between spread and risk-free interest rate dynamics means in this modelling setup that the volatility vectors $(\sigma_1(t, T_1), \ldots, \sigma_n(t, T_1))^T$ and $(\sigma_1^h(t, T_2), \ldots, \sigma_n^h(t, T_2))^T$ are orthogonal to each other for all $t \leq T_1$ and $T_2 \geq t$.

Under independence, (7.139) simplifies to:

$$\alpha^h(t, T) = \sum_{i=1}^n \sigma_i^h(t, T) \int_t^T \sigma_i^h(t, v)dv. \tag{7.140}$$

Satisfying the positivity requirement (7.136) on $h(t, t)$ becomes very easy in the setup of credit spread modelling. One can use any interest rate model for $h(t, T)$ that is known to generate positive short rates, e.g. the square root model of Cox *et al.* (1985a,b), a positive affine rate model, or the model with lognormal interest rates by Sandmann and Sondermann (1997).

7.7   MONTE CARLO SIMULATION

Most specifications of forward-rate-based models of the evolution of the term structure of interest rates and forward rates require the use of Monte Carlo simulation methods to find the values of all but the most basic payoffs. The recourse to Monte Carlo methods is made necessary because the state-space of forward-rate-based models is very large or even infinite (every forward rate essentially forms an additional dimension), and the dynamics of the forward rates are path-dependent. Finite difference and tree methods can only be applied efficiently in models with a low-dimensional ($d \leq 3$) Markovian state vector.

Monte Carlo methods and the various modifications and tricks to achieve improved speed of convergence have been (and still are) an area of active research. In this respect Monte Carlo methods resemble the p.d.e.-based pricing approaches very much, yet there are still some new problems in the simulation of credit risk models.

The fundamental principle of the Monte Carlo simulation is the generation of a large number N of independent samples $x_1 = X(\omega_1), \ldots, x_N = X(\omega_N)$ of a random variable $X(\omega)$, for example the discounted value of the payoff of a credit derivative. The fair price of the credit derivative is

$$ p_X = \mathbf{E}^Q [X(\omega)] $$

and we use the unbiased estimator

$$ \widehat{p}_X := \frac{1}{N} \sum_{n=1}^{N} x_n $$

as an approximation of the "true" value of the expectation p_X. Because we can ensure that we generate *independent* samples x_n, we can apply the central limit theorem which tells us that in the limit as $N \to \infty$ the simulation error

$$ p_X - \widehat{p}_X $$

is normally distributed with mean zero and standard deviation $\sigma_X / \sqrt{N}$, where σ_X is the standard deviation of X. σ_X can be approximated by the sample standard deviation s, where

$$ s^2 = \frac{1}{N-1} \sum_{n=1}^{N} (x_n - \widehat{p}_X)^2. $$

It does not require much additional work to keep track of s^2 when generating the x_n, and thus one can very easily form a confidence interval for the price, e.g.

$$ \left[\widehat{p}_X - 2s N^{-1/2}, \widehat{p}_X + 2s N^{-1/2} \right] $$

is a two standard deviations confidence interval for the price corresponding to approximately 95% certainty that the true value p_X is in this interval.

One advantage of the Monte Carlo method is that one can always generate additional samples and increase the accuracy of the estimate, should the error bound at the end of one set of simulation runs be unsatisfactory.

While the basic principle is very simple, convergence can be slow: to double the accuracy, we have to simulate four times as many samples. A number of advanced techniques have been developed in order to increase the speed of convergence and reduce the variance of the simulation, so-called variance-reduction techniques. Popular techniques are antithetic variables, stratified sampling, importance sampling, usage of control variates or quasi-Monte Carlo methods. Jaeckel (2002) gives a comprehensive introduction to these methods. From now on we only concentrate on the generation of *one* sample, the averaging will have to proceed according to the method given above.

We assume that we simulate in the following model setup:

- Defaults are triggered by the first jump of a Cox process N with intensity process $\lambda(t)$.
- Recovery rates are distributed according to the distribution function $K(d\pi)$, a beta-(a, b) distribution.
- Default-free interest rates $f(t, T)$, the default intensity $\lambda(t) = h(t, t)$, and forward credit spreads $h(t, T)$ follow "standard" diffusion processes.
- There may be other payoff-relevant state variables and price processes which also follow diffusion processes.

The discretisation occurs with a time step size of Δt on a time interval of $[0, \overline{T}]$. Time t_m is defined as $t_m := m\Delta t$, the final time $\overline{T} = t_M$. Unless a dependency is explicitly stated, all random variables used in simulation algorithms are assumed to be independent.

Similar to the credit derivative priced in the section on p.d.e.-based methods, we assume the following payoff structure.[8]

- Final payoff: At time T, the security has a final payoff

$$F(\omega). \tag{7.141}$$

This payoff is only paid if no default has occurred until T.
- Continuous payoffs: At all times $t \leq T$, the security pays at a rate of $\widetilde{f}(t, \omega)$. These payments stop at default, i.e. $\widetilde{f}(t, \omega) = 0$ for $t \geq \tau$.
- Payoff at default: If a default happens at time t, the payoff at default is

$$g(t, \pi(\omega), \omega), \tag{7.142}$$

which depends besides also on the (stochastic) recovery rate $\pi(\omega)$.

By the fundamental pricing rule, the value of a security with this payoff structure is:

$$
\begin{aligned}
p = {} & \mathbf{E}^Q \left[\beta(0, T)(\omega) I(T)(\omega) F(\omega) \right] \\
& + \mathbf{E}^Q \left[\beta(0, T)(\omega) \mathbf{1}_{\{\tau \leq T\}}(\omega) g(\tau(\omega)\pi(\omega), \omega) \right] \\
& + \mathbf{E}^Q \left[\int_0^T \beta(0, t)(\omega) I(t)(\omega) \widetilde{f}(t, \omega) dt \right].
\end{aligned}
\tag{7.143}
$$

Note that *all* random variables/processes depend on the state of nature $\omega \in \Omega$, i.e. the whole expression inside the expectation operators in (7.143) is the random variable $X(\omega)$ that we used in the stylised representation of the Monte Carlo method above. One state of nature $\omega \in \Omega$ determines a full realisation of one simulation run, including the whole paths of all stochastic processes, the default times, recovery rates, and realisations of marked point processes.

---

[8] We explicitly denote the dependence on the state of nature $\omega \in \Omega$ to highlight the stochastic nature of the payoffs.

7.7.1   Pathwise simulation of diffusion processes

Diffusion processes are used to describe the stochastic development of state variables which have continuous paths, e.g. interest rates, share prices, exchange rates, and also credit spreads and default intensities in the context of our models. There are many different ways to simulate a sample path of a diffusion process of the form

$$dx(t) = \mu_x(x, t)dt + \sigma_x(x, t)dW, \tag{7.144}$$

where μ_x and σ_x can themselves be stochastic processes, and the initial value of the process is $x(0) = X_0$. Kloeden and Platen (1992) give an extensive treatment of a large number of approximation schemes that can be used to simulate sample paths of such diffusion processes. The simplest (and still quite adequate) method of simulating paths is known as the *Euler method*:

$$x_{m+1} = x_m + \mu_x(x_m, t_m)\Delta t + \sigma_x(x_m, t_m)\sqrt{\Delta t}\,\epsilon_m. \tag{7.145}$$

In order to ensure convergence of the solution of (7.145) towards the solution of (7.144) (as $\Delta t \to 0$), the ϵ_m must be independent random variables with mean 0 and variance 1. Usually one uses standard normally distributed random variables here because this would approximate the increment of the Brownian motion more closely and results in higher accuracy, but for example one could also use (with a certain loss of accuracy) random variables which take the values ± 1 with equal probability. The key to the Euler scheme is the fact that drift $\mu_x(\cdot)$ and diffusion $\sigma_x(\cdot)$ are kept constant at their values at t_m over the next small time interval $[t_m, t_{m+1}]$. The Euler scheme can be stated as follows.

Euler scheme for diffusion processes

- Initialisation: $x_0 := X_0$
- Iteration: $m \to m + 1$
  1. Calculate $\mu_x(x_m, t_m)$, $\sigma_x(x_m, t_m)$.
  2. Calculate x_{m+1} according to (7.144).
  3. If $t_m < \overline{T}$ go to 1.

This basic simulation scheme can also be applied to a diffusion process of the HJM type. The Euler scheme for (7.119) and (7.138) is

$$\Delta f(t_m, T) = \alpha(t_m, T)\Delta t + \sum_{i=1}^{n} \sigma_i(t_m, T)\epsilon_m^i \sqrt{\Delta t}, \tag{7.146}$$

$$\Delta h(t_m, T) = \alpha^h(t_m, T)\Delta t + \sum_{i=1}^{n} \sigma_i^h(t_m, T)\epsilon_m^i \sqrt{\Delta t}, \tag{7.147}$$

where all ϵ_m^i are standard normally distributed random variates.

7.7.1.1   Simulation of default arrival times

When intensity-based default risk models are implemented via Monte Carlo simulation, there are three different ways of simulating the default arrival risk. The first is a simulation in a fixed time grid with default/survival sampling at each grid time, the second is the direct simulation of the time of default, and the third is not to *simulate* the default arrival but to price it directly in a tree very similar to the basic tree model of Figure 3.2. Of these, the first is intuitively closest to our construction of a Cox process, but it is also the slowest algorithm. Therefore this approach is not recommended.

Fixed time grid

One simulation run in the fixed time grid setup is performed as follows.

Default time with fixed time grid

- Set up the initial forward rates $f(0, T)$, hazard rates $h(0, T)$ and default intensity $\lambda(0)$; $t \leftarrow 0, m \leftarrow 0$.
- Repeat:
  1. Draw U_m, where U_m is uniformly distributed on $[0, 1]$.
  2. If

$$U_m \geq e^{-\lambda(t_m)\Delta t}$$

  then a default occurs in $[t_m, t_m + \Delta t]$. Draw the recovery rate π (see later), record the payoffs.
  End of this simulation run.
  3. Else (no default): Evolve the rest of the state variables according to the Euler scheme (7.146) and (7.147).
  4. $t \leftarrow t + \Delta t, m \leftarrow m + 1$.
  Until the final date is reached $t_m = \overline{T}$, or a default has occurred.
- Record the payoffs.

This algorithm is numerically expensive because typically (unless a default occurs early on) we must simulate M uniform random variates in every sample path just to determine the time of default τ.

Direct simulation of the time of default

We can improve on the grid-based algorithm for the simulation of the time of default. The basic idea is based upon the conditioning property of a Cox process and goes back to an observation by Lando (1998): If we knew the path of the default intensity $\lambda(t)$, the Cox process would simply be an inhomogeneous Poisson process with that intensity, and the distribution of the time of the first jump of N would be essentially (inhomogeneously) exponential. But for *every* given simulation run we *do* know the path of the default intensity in this run. This suggests the following algorithm.

Direct simulation of the time of default

- Set up the initial forward rates $f(0, T)$, hazard rates $h(0, T)$ and default intensity $\lambda(0)$; $m := 0, t := 0$.
- Draw one uniformly distributed random variate U, the *trigger level*.
- Initialise the *default countdown process*

$$\gamma(0) := 1. \tag{7.148}$$

- Repeat:
  1. Decrease the default countdown process to

$$\gamma(t_{m+1}) = \gamma(t_m)e^{-\lambda(t_m)\Delta t}. \tag{7.149}$$

  2. Compare $\gamma(t_{m+1})$ to U. If

$$U \geq \gamma(t_{m+1})$$

  then a default occurs in $[t_m, t_+\Delta t]$. (The default is deemed to occur exactly at the time τ when $U = \gamma(\tau)$.) Draw the recovery rate π (see later).
  3. Else (no default): Evolve the rest of the state variables according to the Euler scheme (7.146) and (7.147).
  4. $m \leftarrow m + 1, \quad t \leftarrow t + 1$.
  Until the final date is reached $t_m = \overline{T}$, or a default has occurred.
- Record the payoffs.

In this modified algorithm, only one uniform random variate must be drawn to determine the time of default. Instead, we must keep track of the *default countdown process* which is in continuous time

$$\gamma(t) := e^{-\int_0^t \lambda(s)ds}, \tag{7.150}$$

i.e. $d\gamma(t) = -\gamma(t)\lambda(t)dt$. The $\gamma(t_m)$ in the algorithm above is only a discretisation of these continuous-time dynamics.

The algorithm can be further improved if $\ln \gamma$ is simulated and compared to $\ln U$. The logarithm of U can be calculated once initially, and the logarithm of γ starts at $\ln \gamma(0) = 0$ and is then decreased by $\lambda(t_m)\Delta t$ at every time step t_m. Thus, the numerically expensive evaluation of the exponential function can be avoided.

We now show that this algorithm does indeed produce the correct distribution of default times. First, we note that the distribution of the "true" default time τ can be found as

$$\mathbf{P}[\tau \geq T] = \mathbf{E}\left[e^{-\int_0^T \lambda(s)ds}\right] = \mathbf{E}[\gamma(T)]. \tag{7.151}$$

Let U now be an independent uniform random variate on $[0, 1]$ and denote by τ' the time at which

$$\gamma(\tau') = U.$$

The probability distribution of τ' is given by

$$P[\tau' \geq T] = P[\gamma(T) \geq U]$$
$$= E[P[U \leq \gamma(T) \mid \gamma(T)]] = E[\gamma(T)] = P[\tau \geq T],$$

where we used the law of iterated expectations in the key step of the equation. The equation above shows that τ', the time (approximately) simulated in the algorithm above and τ, the time of the first jump of the Cox process with intensity λ have the same distribution.

This simulation algorithm is particularly efficient if the other state variables (interest rates and intensities) are not stochastic. In this case, one can directly simulate the time of the default in one step.

If multiple defaults are to be simulated (e.g. the MD recovery model), then we reset the default countdown function $\gamma(\tau_k) = 1$ at each time of default, and draw a new trigger level U_k.

Simulation with branching to default

Both of the algorithms proposed above provide a *simulation* of the time of default. Unfortunately, such simulations converge very slowly, because usually the *probability* of a default event is very low, while the *payoff effect* of a default event can be quite drastic.

As an illustration let us consider the simulation of a simple binary random variable X which can take the values

$$X = \begin{cases} 1 & \text{with probability} \quad p, \\ 0 & \text{with probability} \quad 1 - p, \end{cases}$$

where we assume that p is very small, but the payoff effect 1 is very important. We want to find $E[x]$ by MC simulation, the true value is p. (Think of p as a default probability or a fair CDS spread.) The variance of X is $\sigma_X^2 = p(1 - p)$, thus after N the sample average $\bar{x}$ will be approximately normally distributed around p with a standard error of

$$\epsilon_{\text{abs}} = \frac{1}{\sqrt{N}} \sqrt{p(1 - p)}.$$

The *relative* standard error measures the accuracy of the estimation $\bar{x}$ relative to the value that we are looking for. That is, if we want to find the fair CDS spread with an accuracy of 95% this is the number we are looking for. The relative standard error is reached by dividing the absolute standard error by the value we are looking for, here this is p:

$$\epsilon_{\text{rel}} = \frac{1}{\sqrt{N}} \frac{1}{\sqrt{p}} \sqrt{1 - p} \approx \frac{1}{\sqrt{N}} \frac{1}{\sqrt{p}}, \tag{7.152}$$

for small p. In equation (7.152) the small probability p appears in the denominator as a factor to the number of iterations N needed for a given accuracy. This means that – in order to reach a given relative error of 1% – we must perform $N = 100\,000$ simulation runs at $p = 10\%$, but $N = 1\,000\,000$ simulation runs if $p = 1\%$. The smaller p, the worse the relative error, and the worse the performance of a direct, unmodified MC simulation of these rare events.

This analysis shows that it is advisable to try to avoid simulating very low probability events wherever possible. Fortunately, the Cox process properties of N allow us to do exactly this by relegating default events to a simple tree of the form of the original tree in Figure 3.2, but using the *simulated* realisation of the default intensity as determinant of the default probability.

Simulation with branching to default

- Initialisation: Initialise the term structures of $f(0, T), h(0, T); t = 0, \beta \leftarrow 1, \gamma \leftarrow 1, c \leftarrow 0,$ $c_{loc} \leftarrow 0.$
- Repeat ($t_m \rightarrow t_{m+1}$):
  1. Calculate the default probability over $[t_m, t_{m+1}]$:

  $$p \leftarrow 1 - e^{-h(t_m, t_m)\Delta t}.$$

  2. Update the discount factor:

  $$\beta \leftarrow \beta \cdot e^{-f(t_m, t_m)\Delta t}.$$

  3. Update forward rates and forward hazard rates for all maturities:

  $$f(t_{m+1}, T) \leftarrow f(t_m, T) + \Delta f(t_m, T),$$
  $$h(t_{m+1}, T) \leftarrow h(t_m, T) + \Delta h(t_m, T).$$

  Also evolve all other state variables that follow diffusion processes one time step further.
  4. Calculate the local payoffs in $[t_m, t_{m+1}]$:

  $$c_{loc} \leftarrow \tilde{f}(t_m) + p \cdot g(t_m).$$

  (At $t = T$, the final payoff F must be used in addition to $\tilde{f}$.)
  5. Update the payoffs along this sample path:

  $$c \leftarrow c + \beta \cdot \gamma \cdot c_{loc}.$$

  6. Update the survival probability along this path:

  $$\gamma \leftarrow \gamma \cdot e^{-h(t_m, t_m)\Delta t}.$$

  7. $t \leftarrow t_{m+1}$.
- Until $t \geq T$.
- The results of this simulation run are the following.
  c: The present value of the payoff of the credit derivative along this simulation run.
  $1 - \gamma$: The default probability at this simulation run.

In the algorithm above, we effectively walk along the tree starting from $t = 0$. At each time step t_m, we "collect" the payoffs c_{loc} that we can receive at this time: payoffs if a default occurs in the next time step (g), and payoffs now if no default occurs ($\tilde{f}$). These payoffs are discounted by the continuously compounded discount factor β, weighted by the probability γ that we arrive at this node (and have not defaulted before), and weighted by the local probability of default p for the payoff at default. This is then added to the cumulative payoff c of the credit derivative, and we proceed along the survival branch of the tree in Figure 3.2 to the next time step.

Mathematically, this algorithm implements the conditioning trick of the Cox processes. Instead of evaluating the full expectation (7.143), we use

$$\mathbf{E}^{Q}[X] = \mathbf{E}^{Q} \left[\underbrace{\mathbf{E}^{Q}[X \mid \mathcal{G}]}_{\text{use a tree here}} \right],$$

where $\mathcal{G}$ contains the realisations of all diffusion processes (in particular also the realisation of the default intensity), except the times of default. In the algorithm, $\mathcal{G}$ represents the realisation of one sample path of the forward rates and hazard rates and all other diffusion-type state variables. *Given* this realisation we are in a very simple setup and we can use the simple tree of Figure 3.2 to evaluate the expectation of some random variable depending on the Cox process $N(t)$, which is now only an inhomogeneous Poisson process.

Thus, if we call

$$Y(\omega) := \mathbf{E}^{Q}[X \mid \mathcal{G}](\omega), \tag{7.153}$$

then Y is also a random variable (hence the dependence on ω). It is a conditional expectation, and if the information that we condition on changes (in the next simulation run), then the value of the conditional expectation changes, too. Furthermore, we have

$$p_X = \mathbf{E}^{Q}[Y(\omega)]. \tag{7.154}$$

The simulation algorithm with branching to default uses MC simulation only to evaluate (7.154), equation (7.153) is evaluated using a simple tree. Because Y has a much smaller standard deviation than X, and because it does not involve any of the nasty low-probability events any more, the convergence of the Monte Carlo simulation of (7.154) is much faster than methods involving a direct simulation of defaults.

7.7.2   Simulation of recovery rates

Very often, a distribution from the family of beta distributions is used to model recovery rates, and it may become necessary to draw random samples from this distribution. The beta distribution was defined in Definition 6.1, and the beta distribution with parameters p and q has the density function (6.38):

$$f(x) = \frac{1}{B(p, q)} x^{p-1}(1 - x)^{q-1}, \quad x \in [0, 1]$$

where $B(\alpha, \beta)$ is the beta function.

The following algorithm (Johnk's beta generator, see Devroye, 1986, p. 418) generates a beta-(a, b)-distributed random variate. It is not very efficient for large a, b (the expected number of iterations is $\Gamma(a + b + 1)/(\Gamma(a + 1)\Gamma(b + 1))$), but for moderate values of a and *b* it is quite convenient and faster than numerically inverting the beta function. This and other (more efficient) algorithms can be found in the standard reference on the generation of random variates of all sorts of distributions: Devroye (1986).

Generation of beta-(a, b) random variates

- Repeat:
  1. Generate U, V uniform on $[0, 1]$.
  2. Let

$$X \leftarrow U^{1/a}, \qquad Y \leftarrow V^{1/b}.$$

  Until $X + Y \leq 1$.
- Return:

$$Z \leftarrow \frac{X}{X + Y} \quad \text{is beta-}(a, b)\text{-distributed.}$$

In many applications, the structure of the payoff at default is simple enough to allow a closed-form evaluation of the conditional expected payoff, *given default* and *given the state of the rest of the economy* (e.g. the term structure of interest rates). For example, consider the case of a credit derivative to hedge an FX forward counterparty exposure which pays off

$$\pi \cdot X(\tau)$$

at the time of default. Here $X(\tau)$ is the UDS/EUR exchange rate, and π is a beta-(a, b)-distributed random variable. It may seem that – because of the FX rate – we need to simulate, but this is not the case, because $X(\tau)$ can be observed at the time of default; for the determination of the payoff at default it is locally constant. Thus the locally expected payoff at default reduces to

$$\mathbf{E}^{Q}[\pi \cdot X(\tau) \,|\, \widetilde{f}_{\tau}] = \pi^{e} X(\tau).$$

In particular, if the simulation algorithm with branching to default is used, it is advisable not to use a simulation for the recovery rate as this would destroy much of the speed improvement gained.

7.8 GUIDE TO THE LITERATURE

The analogy between the survival probability of a Poisson process and the risk-free discounting with continuously compounded interest rates has been known for a long time, and we therefore concentrate on models where the intensity of the default process is stochastic.

The first model of this type was developed by Madan and Unal (1998). In this model the intensity of the default is driven by an underlying stochastic process that is interpreted as the firm's value process, and the payoff in default is a random variable drawn at default; it is not predictable before default. Madan and Unal estimate the parameters of their process using rates for certificates of deposit in the Savings and Loan Industry.

Duffie and Singleton (1997) developed a similar model where the payoff in default is also cash, but denoted as a fraction $(1 - q)$ of the value of the defaultable security just before default. This model was applied to a variety of problems including swap credit risk, estimation and two-sided credit risk, by a group around Duffie (Duffie and Singleton, 1997; Duffie et al., 1996; Duffie and Huang, 1996; Duffie, 1994).

Lando (1994) developed the Cox process methodology with iterated conditional expectations. His model has a default payoff in terms of a certain number of default-free bonds and he applies his results to a Markov chain model (see the following chapter).

In the Schönbucher (1998) model multiple defaults can occur and instead of liquidation with cash payoffs a restructuring with random recovery rate takes place. The model is set in a Heath–Jarrow–Morton framework and a rich variety of credit spread dynamics is allowed. For many pricing purposes the model can be reduced to the similar form of Duffie and Singleton, and in Schönbucher (1997) it is applied to the pricing of several credit risk derivatives.

There is a variety of other models that fall into the class of intensity-based models, we only mention Flesaker et al. (1994), Artzner and Delbaen (1992, 1995) and Jarrow et al. (1997). On the empirical side the papers by Duffee (1999) and Duffie and Singleton (1997) have to be mentioned. In both papers the authors estimate the parameters for the stochastic process of the credit spread for the Duffie–Singleton model.

As a good reference for the mathematical requirements, we have already recommended the books by Jacod and Shiryaev (1988) (first part) and Protter (1990). Jacod and Shiryaev is not an easy read but well worth the effort.

There are a number of books on point processes and on marked point processes like Brémaud (1981), but most of them consider point processes in isolation, without linking them to general stochastic processes. This means that important ideas like jump diffusion processes or point processes with stochastic intensities are rarely discussed in detail in these books.

Credit Rating Models

8.1 INTRODUCTION

Many issuers of defaultable debt are assigned a publicly available credit rating by rating agencies such as Standard and Poor's, Moody's KMV or Fitch.

Besides the large rating agencies there are also other sources of credit rating classifications like ratings by other rating agencies, internal credit scoring models or Moody's KMV EDF-based ratings. Yet the rating assignments by the large public rating agencies have a particular influence in the market. Many market participants place a lot of trust in the rating agencies' analysis, and the majority of institutional investors are restricted to investments in certain rating classes. Even investors who do not believe in the accuracy of credit ratings use them as a first classification of the riskiness of the obligor. Furthermore, the payoffs of a number of securities are defined as a function of the credit rating of the obligor. For example, the coupons of some of the latest bond issues by European telecoms companies (Vodafone-AirTouch or Deutsche Telekom) will be increased if the rating of the issuer is downgraded below a certain threshold. Another example is the recent December 2008 issue by Continental Tyres, which is equipped with a coupon of 6.875% increased by 175 bp if the company's rating from Moody's or S&P has fallen below investment grade on an interest payment date.[1] This provision is meant to protect investors against the loss in value of the debt upon a downgrade.

Both the initial credit rating of newly issued debt as well as changes in credit ratings have a significant price effect on the bonds and debt of the rated issuer. This is partly due to the extent to which new credit ratings confer information to the market, and partly due to other market participants who anticipate and front-run these price effects. In particular downgrades cause credit spreads to jump up, while the price effect of upgrades is less significant.

Furthermore, classification of debt into different rating classes allows the derivation of benchmark credit curves for each rating class. If the risk of a large number of obligors must be modelled, this can greatly reduce the complexity of the problem; now only eight (instead of maybe hundreds) of credit curves must be derived, possibly equipped with an obligor-specific offset.

There is a large and – in the light of Basel II – rapidly growing literature on the problem how to *assign* a rating to a given obligor and how to build up an internal rating system. We do *not* consider this problem here. Rather, we are interested in the following questions:

- Given that rating changes have a price impact, how can we model the *price* risks of rating changes?
- Given that ratings imply default risk assessments, how can we build default risk models that are based upon rating transitions?
- How can we consistently calibrate such a model to historical data?

---

[1] At issuance in November 2001 Continental's rating was Baa2 with negative outlook (Moody's) and BBB with stable outlook (S&P) respectively. (*Source: Financial Times*, Nov 27, 2001, p. 39.)

- Using only the *classification* of obligors into rating classes (but not historical transition data), how can we calibrate a model to market average credit spreads for each rating class?
- How can we price credit derivatives whose payoffs are affected by the change of a publicly assigned rating?

Thus, we take the rating and the changes in the rating of an obligor as given (instead of trying to assign a rating), and model the *risk* of rating change (including default).

The intensity models that were described in the previous chapter are usually implemented using continuous diffusion processes for the short-term credit spreads and are therefore not able to reproduce the jumps in credit spreads that accompany rating changes.[2] These models have to be extended to take rating information into account and to realistically reproduce the dynamics of rating changes and credit spreads.

The mathematical framework commonly chosen to model rating transition dynamics is a continuous-time Markov chain which is introduced in the next section. After reviewing some properties, different approaches of pricing models taking into account rating migrations are presented.[3]

8.1.1 Empirical observations

There are several empirical regularities that have to be taken into account for a realistic rating transition model. Most models take historical rating transition matrices as a starting point. This requires a later calibration step to market-observed spreads, if the model is to be used for the *pricing* of credit derivatives.

First, there are problems with the inference from empirically observed rating events. Particularly the frequencies for low-probability events (e.g. distant rating transitions) are usually based upon very few observations and therefore the estimates of their probabilities are not very significant. Furthermore, in most empirical transition matrices one can find entries where rating transition frequencies are not monotonous, e.g. for a given reference rating class, a transition to (or from) a more distant class has occurred more often than a transition to (or from) a closer rating class. Also, in most transition matrices some rating transitions do not occur at all, which of course does not mean that the corresponding transition probabilities are zero.

Second, historical rating adjustments exhibit *ratings momentum* and *ratings delay* (Altman and Kao, 1992; Lando and Skodeberg, 2002). A firm that has been up/downgraded in the previous year is more likely to be up/downgraded again than a firm whose rating has remained unchanged for a longer time, and rating agencies tend to lag market prices in the adjustment of their credit ratings upon the arrival of new credit-relevant information; in some cases this lag may be several months. It seems that the transition matrix of obligors that have been recently *upgraded* is very quiet with high probabilities of remaining in the same rating class, while transition matrices for recently *downgraded* obligors show a tendency towards further downgrades.

Third, empirical default probabilities from rating transitions do not justify the credit spreads that are observed in the markets, they are past observations and contain neither forward-looking

---

[2] It should be pointed out that the general results of Chapter 5 on intensity-based models remain valid even if the default intensity process has jumps.

[3] Another approach extending the models to more frequent jumps in prices is to model certain components of the default event via jump diffusions. Further details about using jump processes in default models can be found in Duffie (1998), Lando (1998) and Schönbucher (2000b, c).

information nor risk premia. In particular, investment-grade bond prices exhibit large risk (or liquidity) premia such that the market spreads are several times larger than the historically observed default rates. Additional problems arise if the rating transition model is to be calibrated to the *term structures* of credit spreads for all rating classes.

Fourth, credit spreads within a given rating class are not constant. On a portfolio-wide level it is probably a viable approximation to assume one spread curve for all bonds of a given rating and industry class, but assuming that this spread curve is constant over time would neglect a large systematic risk factor in credit markets.

In particular, the third and fourth points pose major modelling problems.

8.1.2   An example

The following example highlights many of the problems that are encountered when one tries to build a mathematical model of the real-world phenomenon of rating transition.

Firm ABC is currently rated A, but obviously this rating can change. We assume that there are only three possible ratings, A, B and D, the rating for defaulted debt. For simplicity we set the recovery rate of defaulted debt to zero.

The rating agency publishes the following rating migration data:

	A	B	D
A	$p_{AA} = 0.80$	$p_{AB} = 0.15$	$p_{AD} = 0.05$
B	$p_{BA} = 0.10$	$p_{BB} = 0.80$	$p_{BD} = 0.10$
D	$p_{DA} = 0.00$	$p_{DB} = 0.00$	$p_{DD} = 1.00$

For example, of the companies rated A at the beginning of a year:

- $p_{AA} = 80\%$ were still rated A after one year,
- $p_{AB} = 15\%$ were rated B after that year, and
- $p_{AD} = 5\%$ were rated D, they had defaulted within the year.

We assumed that no firm can recover from default, the state D is called *absorbing*.

What is the probability of a default of the A-rated ABC debt within the next two years? There is an obvious, but wrong, answer.

One could say, we have two events of default each with a probability of $p_{AD} = 0.05$ or a survival probability of $(1 - p_{AD}) = 0.95$, giving a total survival probability of $(1 - p_{AD})^2 = 0.9025$ and a default probability of 0.0975. But this answer does not take *rating migration* into account. In the next two years a default can also occur via a transition to the B rating. Default can be reached via the following transitions:

$$A \rightarrow A \rightarrow D \quad \text{with probability} \quad p_{AA}p_{AD} = 0.85 \times 0.05 = 0.0425,$$
$$A \rightarrow B \rightarrow D \quad \text{with probability} \quad p_{AB}p_{BD} = 0.15 \times 0.10 = 0.015,$$
$$A \rightarrow D(\rightarrow D) \quad \text{with probability} \quad p_{AD}p_{DD} = 0.05 \times 1 = 0.05.$$

This gives a total default probability of 0.1075, which is a full percentage point larger than before. This effect is even stronger with real-world ratings. Here the credit risk for investment-grade bonds lies mainly in the risk of downgrading (with subsequently very much higher risk of default), and not in the risk of direct default.

To sum up, the two-period probability of default given initial rating A, i.e. the *two-period transition probability from A to D* is:

$$p_{AD}^{(2)} = p_{AA}p_{AD} + p_{AB}p_{BD} + p_{AD}p_{DD} = \begin{pmatrix} p_{AA} & p_{AB} & p_{AD} \end{pmatrix} \begin{pmatrix} p_{AD} \\ p_{BD} \\ p_{DD} \end{pmatrix}.$$

If one takes the transition matrix

$$A = \begin{pmatrix} p_{AA} & p_{AB} & p_{AD} \\ p_{BA} & p_{BB} & p_{BD} \\ p_{DA} & p_{DB} & p_{DD} \end{pmatrix}$$

then it is easily seen that the two-period transition probability $p_{AD}^{(2)}$ is exactly the (A, D) component of the square A^2 of A. This also holds for the other two-period transition probabilities, and we reach the two-period transition probability matrix as:

$$A^{(2)} = A \cdot A = A^2.$$

8.2   THE RATING PROCESS AND TRANSITION PROBABILITIES

Assumption 8.1

- *There are K rating classes. The set of rating classes is denoted by $S = \{1, \ldots, K\}$. We will call S the* state space.
- *The rating classes are ordered by their credit risk. Rating class 1 represents the best possible credit quality, class $K - 1$ the worst non-defaulted credit quality, and class K represents the state of default.*[4]
- *The rating of a firm at time t is denoted by:*

$$R(\omega, t) \quad where \quad R : \Omega \times [0, T] \rightarrow S.$$

$R(\omega, t)$ is an adapted stochastic process. We suppress the dependence on $\omega \in \Omega$ from now on.

The numeric notation for the rating classes was only chosen for notational convenience. In S&P/Moody's rating classes, we would set $K = 8$, and class $R = 1$ corresponds to AAA/Aaa, $R = 2$ to AA/Aa, etc. until $R = 7$ (CCC/Caa) and $R = 8$ (default, D).

It has become common to describe the behaviour of the rating process with the *transition probabilities* of this process which are arranged in a transition matrix like the transition matrix shown in Table 8.1. A wealth of such empirical rating transition matrices are regularly published

---

[4] This classification must be supported by the corresponding default probabilities.

Table 8.1 Historical average one-year rating transition frequencies. (a) Standard and Poor's 1981–1991, "no rating" eliminated. (b) Moody's 1971–2001 (Hamilton *et al.*, 2002). In percentages

(a)

	AAA	AA	A	BBB	BB	B	CCC	D
AAA	89.10	9.63	0.78	0.19	0.30	0	0	0
AA	0.86	90.10	7.47	0.99	0.29	0.29	0	0
A	0.09	2.91	88.94	6.49	1.01	0.45	0	0.09
BBB	0.06	0.43	6.56	84.27	6.44	1.60	0.18	0.45
BB	0.04	0.22	0.79	7.19	77.64	10.43	1.27	2.41
B	0	0.19	0.31	0.66	5.17	82.46	4.35	6.85
CCC	0	0	1.16	1.16	2.03	7.54	64.93	23.19
D	0	0	0	0	0	0	0	100

(b)

	Aaa	Aa	A	Baa	Ba	B	Caa-C	Default	WR
Aaa	89.09	7.15	0.79	0.00	0.02	0.00	0.00	0.00	2.94
Aa	1.17	88.00	7.44	0.27	0.08	0.01	0.00	0.02	3.01
A	0.05	2.41	89.01	4.68	0.49	0.12	0.01	0.01	3.21
Baa	0.05	0.25	5.20	84.55	4.51	0.69	0.09	0.15	4.51
Ba	0.02	0.04	0.47	5.17	79.35	6.23	0.42	1.19	7.11
B	0.01	0.02	0.13	0.38	6.24	77.82	2.40	6.34	6.67
Caa-C	0.00	0.00	0.00	0.57	1.47	3.81	62.90	23.69	7.56
D	0	0	0	0	0	0	0	100	

by all major rating agencies for time horizons up to 10 years, see e.g. Hamilton *et al.* (2002). This data serves as main input for most rating-based models.

Definition 8.1 *Formally, the* transition probability matrix $Q(t, T)$ *for the time interval* $[t, T]$ *is written as:*

$$
Q(t, T) = \begin{pmatrix} q_{11}(t, T) & q_{12}(t, T) & \cdots & q_{1K}(t, T) \\ q_{21}(t, T) & q_{22}(t, T) & \cdots & q_{2K}(t, T) \\ \vdots & \vdots & \ddots & \vdots \\ q_{K1}(t, T) & q_{K2}(t, T) & \cdots & q_{KK}(t, T) \end{pmatrix}.
\tag{8.1}
$$

For all $i, j \in S$*, the component* $q_{ij}(t, T) \geq 0$ *is the probability that the rating process changes to state* j *at time* T*, given that it was in state* i *at time* t*:*

$$
q_{ij}(t, T) = \mathbf{P}[R(T) = j \mid R(t) = i] \quad \forall \, i, j \in S, \, t \leq T.
\tag{8.2}
$$

For conservation of probability $\sum_{j=1}^{K} q_{ij}(t, T) = 1$ must hold for all $i \in S$, and over zero time no transition takes place: $Q(t, t) = I$, where I is the identity matrix.

As they are defined in Definition 8.1, the transition probabilities are the transition probabilities *as seen from time* $t_0 = 0$. For example, $q_{1K}(2, 3)$ is the probability that an obligor who was rated AAA at time $t = 2$ will default by time $t = 3$, *as seen from $t = 0$*. This probability may change over time, for example if we enter a recession at $t = 1$, the default probability of such an obligor may actually rise. Therefore, to be precise, we should give the transition probability a third argument t_0, the time on which information these transition probabilities are based:

$$q_{ij}(t_0, \omega; t, T) = \mathbf{P}[R(T) = j \mid R(t) = i \wedge \mathcal{F}_{t_0}] \quad \forall\, i, j \in S,\ t_0 \leq t \leq T,$$

where we have also added the dependence on the state of nature $\omega \in \Omega$, because the conditional probability conditional on $\mathcal{F}_{t_0}$ is random – it depends on the information that we have at time t_0.

This level of generality contradicts in a way the intention with which we set out to model rating transitions. The idea was that the current rating class $R(t)$ of the obligor contains a lot – ideally *all* – information that we need to know to assess the default risk of this obligor. Thus, conditioning on further information besides the current rating $R(t)$ at time t should not improve the risk assessment. This idea is contained in the following assumption.

Assumption 8.2 *The rating transition process $R(\omega, t)$ has the following properties.*

(i) *Markov property: At any time t, the probability of transition to another state until time $T > t$ only depends on the current state $R(t)$ of the process*

$$\mathbf{P}[R(T) = r \mid \mathcal{F}_t] = \mathbf{P}[R(T) = r \mid R(t)] \quad \forall\, r \in S. \tag{8.3}$$

Equivalently, $Q(t_0, t, T) = Q(t, T)$ for all $t_0 < t \leq T$.

(ii) *Time homogeneity: The transition probabilities only depend on the time interval over which the transitions take place*

$$Q(t, T) = Q(T - t) \quad \forall\, t \leq T. \tag{8.4}$$

A stochastic process satisfying the Markov property is called a *Markov process*, and if the state space of this process is countable, the process is called a *Markov chain*.

The Markov property (i) is in conflict with the empirical phenomenon of ratings momentum, and it also precludes stochastic changes in transition probabilities that are driven by other factors. Yet for the moment it is kept because it allows a complete description of the dynamics of the rating process, with matrices of transition probabilities that only depend on two points in time: the point t at which the state of the Markov process is observed, and the time horizon T.

Time homogeneity (ii) is an even stronger restriction on the rating transition process. While we naturally want to impose some regularity on the transition process, it can also be argued that rating transition probabilities should indeed vary over time according to business cycle variations. We will not need this assumption except to simplify the demonstration of the basic features of the model, and in most estimation procedures one needs to make some sort of homogeneity assumption.

In principle it is possible to model the rating transition process of an obligor via a direct specification of all transition probabilities $Q(t, T)$ for all $t < T$. This approach is not practical because certain consistency requirements have to be observed. The transition probability $q_{ij}(t, T)$ from state i at time t to state j at time T can be conditioned on the state k of the Markov chain at any intermediate time s, $t \leq s \leq T$. Summing up these conditional probabilities over all states the process can possibly visit yields

$$q_{ij}(t, T) = \sum_{k=1}^{K} q_{ik}(t, s) q_{kj}(s, T) \quad \forall t < s < T, \quad \forall i, j \in S. \tag{8.5}$$

Equations (8.5) are known as the *Chapman–Kolmogorov* equations, they must be satisfied for any Markov chain model. In matrix notation they take the form

$$Q(t, T) = Q(t, s) Q(s, T) \quad \forall t < s < T. \tag{8.6}$$

The Chapman–Kolmogorov equations tell us that the transition probability matrix $Q(t, T)$ over a longer time interval $[t, T]$ is already uniquely determined once the transition probability matrices $Q(t, s)$ and $Q(s, T)$ are given. If several transition probability matrices over different time intervals are given, consistency problems can only be avoided if the time intervals never overlap.

8.2.1 Discrete-time Markov chains

Let us assume that the rating transitions take place at discrete times $0 = t_0 < t_1 \cdots < t_N$. In this case there is a set of smallest possible time intervals $[t_n, t_{n+1}]$ for which we can specify rating transition matrices. These intervals are non-overlapping (so the specification is consistent) and cover the whole time axis (so the specification is complete). Let

$$Q_n := Q(t_n, t_{n+1})$$

denote the transition matrix from time t_n to time t_{n+1}. Given these, equation (8.6) uniquely determines the transition probability matrices for all larger time intervals:

$$Q(t_n, t_m) = \prod_{k=n}^{m-1} Q_k \quad \forall n < m. \tag{8.7}$$

If the Markov chain is also time-homogeneous, then all one-period transition matrices must coincide to $Q = Q(t_n, t_{n+1}) \quad \forall n < N$. The transition matrix for larger time intervals is then given by taking Q to the power of the length of the time interval:

$$Q(t_n, t_m) = Q^{m-n} \quad \forall n \le m \le N. \tag{8.8}$$

8.2.2 Continuous-time Markov chains

A continuous-time modelling framework is very useful because it permits the exact determination of survival probabilities and prices of payoffs at arbitrary points in time.

For the continuous-time setup we assume that the transition probabilities $Q(t, T)$ are continuous in T at $T = t$. This amounts to assuming that rating transitions come as surprises, there are no scheduled dates at which a transition will happen with positive probability. (At such a point in time a discontinuity would occur in $Q(t, T)$.)

It can be shown (e.g. Rogers and Williams, 1994) that in this case $Q(t, T)$ is not only continuous but also differentiable with respect to T at $T = t$. For small time intervals Δt the transition probability matrix can be approximated with a Taylor series. Similarly to the construction of the Poisson process we assume that the transition probability from state k to state l in the small time interval Δt is approximately proportional to Δt:

$$\mathbf{P}[R(t + \Delta t) = l \mid R(t) = k] = \lambda_{kl} \Delta t \quad \text{for } k \neq l.$$

The probability of a transition of the rating process $R(t)$ of the firm from class k at time t to $R(t + \Delta t) = l$ at time $t + \Delta t$ is $\lambda_{kl} \Delta t$. Conservation of probability (the transition probabilities must sum up to 1) means that the off-diagonal elements of Λ are given by

$$\mathbf{P}[R(t + \Delta t) = k \mid R(t) = k] = 1 - \sum_{l \neq k} \lambda_{kl} \Delta t =: 1 + \lambda_{kk} \Delta t.$$

We define $\lambda_{kk} = -\sum_{l \neq k} \lambda_{kl}$.

Then the matrix of transition probabilities for the time interval $[t, t + \Delta t]$ is

$$Q(t, t + \Delta t) = I + \Delta t \Lambda(t) + \text{terms of order } \Delta t^2, \tag{8.9}$$

where I is the unit matrix and $\Lambda = (\lambda_{kl})_{1 \leq k, l \leq K}$ is the matrix of transition intensities. Now we can go and derive the matrix of transition probabilities for a larger interval $[t, s]$. Exactly as in the Poisson case we subdivide $[t, s]$ into i subintervals of length Δt. From the previous section we know that the two-period transition matrix is reached by multiplying the one-period transition matrix by itself:

$$Q(t, t + 2\Delta t) = Q(t, t + \Delta t) Q(t + \Delta t, t + 2\Delta t)$$
$$= (I + \Delta t \Lambda)(I + \Delta t \Lambda) = (I + \Delta t \Lambda)^2.$$

Similarly we have for the i-period transition matrix:

$$Q(t, t + i\Delta t) = Q(t, s) = (I + \Delta t \Lambda)^i = \left(I + \frac{(s - t)}{i} \Lambda\right)^i, \tag{8.10}$$

and again in the limit:

$$Q(t, s) = \exp\{(s - t)\Lambda\}, \tag{8.11}$$

where the exponential function for matrices is defined by the series expansion of the exponential function:

$$\exp\{(s - t)\Lambda\} = \sum_{n=0}^{\infty} \frac{((s - t)\Lambda)^n}{n!}.$$

Definition 8.2 *Let $Q(0, 1)$ be the one-period transition probability matrix of a time-homogeneous Markov chain. If there exists a matrix Λ with the properties stated below then* *this matrix is called the* generator matrix of Q:

(i) *The matrix Λ is the matrix logarithm of $Q(0, 1)$*

$$Q(0, 1) = e^{\Lambda}. \tag{8.12}$$

(ii) *The off-diagonal elements of Λ are non-negative*

$$\lambda_{ij} \geq 0 \quad \forall i, j \in S, i \neq j. \tag{8.13}$$

(iii) *The diagonal elements of Λ satisfy*

$$\lambda_{kk} = -\sum_{l \neq k} \lambda_{kl} \quad \forall k \in S. \tag{8.14}$$

Definition 8.2 is deliberately phrased as "*if* there exists ..." since in many cases a generator matrix does *not* exist. This problem is addressed in the next section.

Besides this representation of the transition probabilities, the limiting process has another consequence. Substituting equation (8.9) in the Chapman–Kolmogorov equations (8.6) and taking the limit as $\Delta t \to 0$ yields the *Kolmogorov forward differential equations* and the *Kolmogorov backward differential equations*

$$\frac{\partial}{\partial t} Q(t, T) = -\Lambda(t) Q(t, T), \tag{8.15}$$

$$\frac{\partial}{\partial T} Q(t, T) = Q(t, T) \Lambda(T) \quad \text{and} \quad Q(t, t) = I. \tag{8.16}$$

If the generator matrix is constant $\Lambda(t) = \Lambda = $ const., these differential equations have the solution

$$Q(t, T) = \exp\{(T - t)\Lambda\} := \sum_{n=0}^{\infty} \frac{1}{n!} ((T - t)\Lambda)^n, \tag{8.17}$$

where the matrix exponential is defined using the power series.

If the generator matrices $\Lambda(t)$ and $\Lambda(s)$ commute[5] for all $t \neq s$, then solution (8.17) generalises to the time-inhomogeneous case:

$$Q(t, T) = \exp\left\{ \int_t^T \Lambda(s) ds \right\}. \tag{8.18}$$

8.2.3 Connection to Poisson processes

A continuous-time Markov chain with generator matrix Λ can be viewed as a collection of K compound Poisson processes. For every class $k \in S$, the Poisson process $N_k(t)$ that triggers a transition away from this class has an intensity $\lambda_k = -\lambda_{kk}$. Whenever a jump occurs, a marker

---

[5] Matrices A and B commute iff $AB = BA$. A sufficient condition is that A and B have the same eigenvectors.

$V \in S$ is drawn that indicates the state the chain is migrating to; the conditional probability of a transition to class j is λ_{kj}/λ_k. The stochastic differential equation for the rating process $R(t)$ is then

$$dR(t) = (V - R(t))dN_{R(t)}(t),\tag{8.19}$$

where $N_k(t)$ is a Poisson process with intensity $-\lambda_{kk}$. The relative probabilities of the different rating classes are given by the relative magnitudes of the λ_{kl}. The conditional distribution of the marker V of the transition is

$$\mathbf{P}[V = j \mid dN_k(t) = 1] = -\lambda_{kj}/\lambda_{kk}.\tag{8.20}$$

(Remember that λ_{kk} is negative.)

Alternatively, the rating transition Markov chain can be viewed as a collection of $K \times (K-1)$ Poisson processes, each driving the transition to a different rating class. The intensity of the process that triggers the transition from class n to class k is given by λ_{nk}, and the resulting stochastic differential equation is

$$dR(t) = \sum_{k=1, k \neq R(t)}^{K} (k - R(t))dN_{R(t),k}(t),$$

where N_{jk} is a Poisson process with intensity λ_{jk}. This also holds for the time-inhomogeneous case, then the transition intensities are given by $-\lambda_{kk}(t)$ and $\lambda_{jk}(t)$ respectively.

Finally, returning to the marked point process setup, we can describe the rating transition process as a marked point process. The points in time are the times of rating transitions, we call $N(t)$ the counting process counting the number of rating transitions up to time t. The marker space is the set of rating classes S. At each time of a rating transition, a marker C is drawn from S which indicates the number of the new rating class. The marker measure of the rating transition process is

$$m(k, dt) = \mathbf{1}_{\{C=k\}}dN(t) \quad \forall k \in S.\tag{8.21}$$

The rating process $R(t)$ can then be represented as an integral with respect to $m(k, dt)$:

$$R(t) = \int_0^t \sum_{k \in S}(k - R_-(t))m(k, dt),\tag{8.22}$$

where $R_-(t)$ is the rating one instance before time t (the left limit at time t). The compensator measure is

$$\nu(k, dt) = \lambda_{R_-(t),k}dt \quad \forall k \neq R_-(t).\tag{8.23}$$

As the marker space is now the finite set S, integration over the marker space reduces to a summation over all possible states except $R(t)$. A function $f(R)$ of the credit rating R of a firm has the increments

$$df(R) = \sum_{k \neq R_-} (f(k) - f(R_-))m(k, dt), \tag{8.24}$$

$$\mathbf{E}[df(R)] = \left(\sum_{k \neq R_-} (f(k) - f(R_-))\lambda_{R_- k}\right) dt = \sum_{k=1}^{K} f(k)\lambda_{Rk}dt, \tag{8.25}$$

$$\lambda_{Rk}dt \doteq \mathbf{P}[df(R) = f(k) - f(R)]. \tag{8.26}$$

We see that the treatment of f is exactly as in the case of a compound Poisson process.

8.3   ESTIMATION OF TRANSITION INTENSITIES

8.3.1   The cohort method

Usually rating agencies do not publish the generating matrix Λ of the rating migration process, but only the transition probabilities Q for a given time period, usually one year. The most common method for the estimation of this discrete transition probability matrix from empirical observations is based upon the observed behaviour of groups of firms with the same initial rating, the cohorts. Denote by $n_i(t)$ the total number of firms in class i at time t, and by $n_{ij}(0, t)$ the number of observed transitions of the firms rated in class i at time 0 to class j at time t. Assuming Markov chain dynamics for the rating transitions, the transition events from each class i can be viewed as the outcomes of $n_i(0)$ independent multinomial trials. Then the maximum likelihood estimator of q_{ij} is:

$$\widehat{q}_{ij} = n_{ij}(0, T)/n_i(0) \quad i \neq j. \tag{8.27}$$

This estimator uses the information of the transition behaviour of the cohort of the $n_i(0)$ initially i-rated firms. Confidence intervals for this estimator can be found in many places, e.g. in Johnson and Kotz (1969).

The one-year time horizon of the rating agencies' data publications is too rigid and coarse, we cannot base a model solely on one-year time steps. To have full flexibility to be able to price payoffs occurring at arbitrary points in time we need a continuous-time rating transition model.

Thus, based upon this estimator, the next step is the derivation of an infinitesimal generator matrix $\widehat{\Lambda}$ that is consistent with the given (empirical) transition matrix $\widehat{Q}$ over a discrete (e.g. one-year) time horizon, i.e. find $\widehat{\Lambda}$ such that:

$$\widehat{Q} = e^{\widehat{\Lambda}}, \tag{8.28}$$

where $\widehat{\Lambda}$ is a generator matrix. This problem is known as the *embedding problem* for continuous-time Markov chains. Kreinin and Sidelnikova (2001) give a good survey over analytical and numerical methods to attack this problem, in the following we just point out some key observations.

Besides the embedding problem, there are other caveats to the cohort method of estimating transition probabilities. The cohort method does not use all available information, only the *first* transition of any rated firm during the interval enters the estimator. Transitions to the "not rated" category are removed from the sample, although they are usually not caused by credit events. This can introduce a significant bias to the cohort estimator. Furthermore, it is hard to rigorously test for the influence of external covariates or ratings drift in this framework.

8.3.2   The embedding problem: finding a generator matrix

From equation (8.11) we know that (in the time-homogeneous case):

$$Q(t) = e^{\Lambda t}.$$

If Q were a scalar and not a matrix we would simply solve this to:

$$\Lambda = \frac{1}{t} \ln Q.$$

This is in fact the solution of (8.11) for Λ, when we define the logarithm of a matrix by its power series:

$$\ln(I + X) = X - X^2 + X^3 \cdots$$

and use $X := Q - I$. This power series can be used in practice to calculate the logarithm of Q, and it will converge reasonably fast if the original transition matrix Q is *diagonally dominated*, i.e. $q_{ii} > \frac{1}{2}$ for all $i \in S$. The closer the values of the diagonal elements are to 1, the faster the convergence. This condition also ensures that – if a generator matrix exists – it will be unique. (Yes, a transition matrix can have several possible generators.) In order to ensure existence of the matrix logarithm we must also demand that the eigenvalues of Q are distinct, that the determinant of Q is positive, and that there is exactly one absorbing state (i.e. default) of the chain which can be reached from all other states (see Kreinin and Sidelnikova, 2001 for details).

Not every matrix has a logarithm, for example matrices with one of the following properties do *not* have a logarithm: $\det Q < 0$, or $\det Q > \prod_{i \in S} q_{ii}$, or one or more elements are zero $q_{ij} = 0$ if the state j is accessible from i.

In particular the positivity requirement is regularly violated by historical transition frequency matrices, for example the one-year default frequency of AAA is usually zero, although default can be reached from AAA if previous downgrades are taken into account. This problem disappears if we realise that the transition frequency matrices are *observations* and not probabilities. Everybody will agree that the true one-year default probability is not zero, it is just extremely small so that the observed one-year frequencies are usually zero.

Note that the existence of a matrix logarithm is only one of the conditions in Definition 8.2. We must also have non-negativity of off-diagonal elements and the sum property for diagonal elements.

The cumbersome calculation of the matrix logarithm or the matrix exponential via the corresponding power series can be avoided if the matrix $\widehat{Q}$ or $\widehat{\Lambda}$ can be *diagonalised*. If there exist a non-singular transformation matrix M and a diagonal matrix $D_Q = \text{diag}\{d_1, \ldots, d_K\}$ such that

$$\widehat{Q} = M^{-1} D_Q M,$$

then the matrix $\widehat{\Lambda}$ with $\widehat{Q} = e^{\widehat{\Lambda}}$ can also be diagonalised with the same transformation matrix M, and is given by

$$\widehat{\Lambda} = M^{-1} D_{\Lambda} M, \tag{8.29}$$

where the diagonal matrices are

$$D_Q = \text{diag}\{d_1, \ldots, d_K\}, \qquad D_{\Lambda} = \text{diag}\{\ln d_1, \ldots, \ln d_K\}.$$

A diagonalisation of $\widehat{Q}$ is possible if $\widehat{Q}$ has a complete set of distinct eigenvalues (possibly in the complex numbers). This is not a restrictive assumption because multiple eigenvalues correspond to multiple zeroes in the characteristic polynomial of $\widehat{Q}$, and this situation is not robust to small perturbations of the input data.

Yet, even if the matrix $\widehat{Q}$ can be diagonalised, the matrix $\widehat{\Lambda}$ from equation (8.29) may not satisfy the conditions $\widehat{\Lambda}_{ii} = -\sum_{j \neq i} \widehat{\Lambda}_{ij}$ and $\widehat{\Lambda}_{ij} \geq 0$ for $i \neq j$. In this case $\widehat{\Lambda}$ will not be a continuous-time generator matrix to the Markov chain. This problem will certainly occur if $\widehat{Q}$ contains cyclical components or zero entries. For a discussion of necessary and sufficient conditions for the existence of generator matrices, see e.g. Carette (1995) or Israel et al. (2001). A simple example of a cyclical transition matrix is

$$\widehat{Q}(0, 1) = \begin{pmatrix} 0 & 1 \\ 1 & 0 \end{pmatrix}.$$

This transition matrix can be diagonalised because it has two distinct eigenvalues $+1$ and -1. Thus (at least in complex numbers) there exists a matrix $\widehat{\Lambda}$ such that $\widehat{Q}(0, 1) = e^{\widehat{\Lambda}}$, but there is no time-homogeneous generator matrix that could give rise to $\widehat{Q}(0, 1)$ as one-period transition probabilities. A process with this transition probability matrix switches between states with probability 1 (it has a cycle). If a valid generator matrix existed, then this process would be a time-homogenenous Markov chain and there would be a well-defined transition probability $\widehat{Q}(0, 1/2)$ for $t = 1/2$ with $\widehat{Q}(0, 1/2)^2 = \widehat{Q}(0, 1)$. But if $\widehat{Q}(0, 1/2)_{11} > 0$, then we would also have $\widehat{Q}(0, 1)_{11} > 0$, but this is not true. Therefore we must have $\widehat{Q}(0, 1/2)_{11} = 0$, with certainty the process does not remain in state 1 even until $t = 1/2$. By conservation of probability, we must then have $\widehat{Q}(0, 1/2)_{12} = 1$. Similar arguments apply to the second row and we finally reach $\widehat{Q}(0, 1/2) = \widehat{Q}(0, 1)$ as the only possible solution. But $\widehat{Q}(0, 1)^2 = I \neq \widehat{Q}(0, 1)$, so this solution is ruled out, too. Therefore, the problem cannot be solved, there is no generator matrix from which this transition matrix could have arisen.

Another common problem already mentioned above arises if $\widehat{Q}$ contains a zero entry $\widehat{q}_{ij} = 0$. This zero can only be consistent with the existence of a continuous-time generator matrix if it is not possible to reach state j from state i, not even via intermediate states $k \neq j$ at an intermediate time s, $t \leq s \leq T$. This implies for instance that for every state $k \in S$, either $\lambda_{ik} = 0$ or $\lambda_{kj} = 0$ must hold, and this argument can be repeated. Ultimately, the only way in which a zero could arise in a transition probability matrix is if it must be possible to decompose the state space into two groups of rating states, and one of these groups cannot be reached from the other. One of these groups contains state i and the other contains state j.

Clearly the only such separation of the state space for rating transition matrices is the separation of the default state from the rest of the rating classes. Nevertheless, zero transition *frequencies* do occur for distant rating transitions, e.g. from AAA to D.

Table 8.2 Approximative generator matrix to the previously stated transition matrix by Standard and Poor's

	AAA	AA	A	BBB	BB	B	CCC	D
AAA	−11.59	10.75	0.42	0.13	0.29	0.00	0.00	0.00
AA	0.95	−10.61	8.32	0.81	0.26	0.27	0.00	0.00
A	0.08	3.24	−12.14	7.46	0.90	0.40	0.00	0.06
BBB	0.06	0.36	7.56	−17.75	7.91	1.40	0.13	0.33
BB	0.04	0.22	0.58	8.85	−26.12	12.95	1.36	2.08
B	0	0.21	0.27	0.47	6.40	−19.98	5.90	6.73
CCC	0	0.04	1.44	1.36	2.46	10.13	−43.53	28.10
D	0	0.00	0.00	0.00	0.00	0.00	0.00	0.00

The pragmatic remedy to these problems is to try to perform the fitting of the generator matrix only approximately, i.e. to minimise

$$\|\widehat{Q} - e^{\widehat{\Lambda}}\| \to \min_{\Lambda} \qquad (8.30)$$

in a suitable matrix norm (see e.g. Arvanitis *et al.*, 1999), which will yield a numerically robust approximation to the observed dynamics, even if the exact algebraic problem (8.28) does not have a solution.

Table 8.2 shows the result of such an approximative fit to the rating transition matrix of Table 8.1. First, an approximative diagonalisation of the transition matrix was performed by minimising[6]

$$\|\widehat{Q} - M^{-1} D_Q M\|_2 \to \min_{M, D_Q}, \qquad (8.31)$$

where the $\| \cdot \|_2$-norm is defined as the square root of the sum of the squared matrix elements. Such an approximative diagonalisation is numerically more stable than the exact analytical approach of trying to solve the characteristic polynomial for the eigenvalues, which cannot be recommended.

In the next step, the logarithms of the diagonal elements were taken and the generator matrix was reassembled. Finally, we checked that all conditions of Definition 8.2 were satisfied.

So far, we only considered the problem of the matrix logarithm of Q. The second set of problems arises when this logarithm does not satisfy the other requirements of Definition 8.2. Here, we must again modify and adjust the matrix entries of the logarithm matrix. Kreinin and Sidelnikova (2001) compare some algorithms with which this task can be performed without perturbing the original matrix too much.

8.3.2.1 General solution to matrix decomposition

A general method of solving the problem of taking an exponential or a logarithm of a given matrix Q uses the Jordan normal form of the matrix. The Jordan decomposition always exists

---

[6] There are better algorithms to diagonalise a matrix than this minimisation, which can be found in good reference books on numerical linear algebra.

and has the following form:

$$Q = MJM^{-1},$$

where J is a block diagonal matrix:

$$J = \begin{pmatrix} B_1 & \Theta & \cdots & \Theta \\ \Theta & B_2 & \cdots & \Theta \\ \vdots & & \ddots & \vdots \\ \Theta & \cdots & \Theta & B_N \end{pmatrix}.$$

Here Θ denotes zero block matrices and the block matrices on the diagonal have the form

$$B_k = \lambda_k I + N_k.$$

Here λ is the kth eigenvalue of the matrix Q and N_k has the following form:

$$\begin{pmatrix} 0 & 1 & 0 & \cdots & 0 \\ \vdots & \ddots & \ddots & \ddots & \vdots \\ \vdots & & \ddots & \ddots & 0 \\ \vdots & & & \ddots & 1 \\ 0 & \cdots & \cdots & \cdots & 0 \end{pmatrix}.$$

If this decomposition is achieved, the matrix exponential is

$$e^Q = Me^J M^{-1}$$

and the exponential of the Jordan matrix J is given by the block diagonal matrix with e_k^B on the diagonal blocks. We have

$$e^{B_k t} = e^{\lambda t} e^{N_k t}$$

and if l is the dimension of N_k, $e^{N_k t}$ is given by

$$\begin{pmatrix} 1 & \dfrac{t}{1!} & \dfrac{t^2}{2!} & \cdots & \dfrac{t^{l-1}}{(l-1)!} \\ 0 & \ddots & \ddots & \ddots & \vdots \\ \vdots & \ddots & \ddots & \ddots & \dfrac{t^2}{2!} \\ \vdots & & \ddots & \ddots & \dfrac{t}{1!} \\ 0 & \cdots & \cdots & 0 & 1 \end{pmatrix}.$$

Similarly, to reach the logarithm of Q we must take logarithms of the diagonal blocks of J. This logarithm is defined by

$$\ln(B_k) = (\ln \lambda)I + L$$

where L is given by

$$
\begin{pmatrix}
0 & \dfrac{1}{\lambda} & -\dfrac{1}{2\lambda} & \cdots & \dfrac{(-1)^{l-2}}{(l-1)\lambda^{l-1}} \\
\vdots & \ddots & \ddots & \ddots & \vdots \\
\vdots & & \ddots & \ddots & -\dfrac{1}{2\lambda} \\
& & & \ddots & \dfrac{1}{\lambda} \\
\vdots & & & \ddots & \\
0 & \cdots & \cdots & \cdots & 0
\end{pmatrix}.
$$

If the Jordan decomposition can be achieved without error, this gives an exact method to calculate matrix logarithms and matrix exponentials.

8.4   DIRECT ESTIMATION OF TRANSITION INTENSITIES

To avoid the embedding problem, Lando and Skodeberg (2002) propose the direct maximum likelihood estimator of the generator matrix: either constant $\widehat{\Lambda}$ in the time-homogeneous case or $\widehat{\Lambda}(t)$ in the time-inhomogeneous case. In addition to the cumulative rating transition data, these estimators also require a knowledge of the precise points in time at which the rating transitions take place.

The estimator under the assumption of constant transition intensities is

$$
\widehat{\lambda}_{ij} = \frac{m_{ij}(T)}{\displaystyle\int_0^T n_i(s)\,ds}, \quad i \neq j \tag{8.32}
$$

where $m_{ij}(0, T)$ is the *total* number of transitions from class i to class $j \neq i$ over the interval $[0, T]$. We have $m_{ij}(0, T) \geq n_{ij}(0, T)$ because m_{ij} also includes transitions of firms that entered class i after $t = 0$.

If a fully non-parametric, time-inhomogeneous transition intensity is to be estimated, Lando and Skodeberg (2002) propose to use the Nelson–Aalen estimator

$$
\widehat{A}_{ij}(t) = \sum_{T_{ij}(k) \leq t} \frac{1}{n_i(T_{ij}(k)-)}, \tag{8.33}
$$

where $T_{ij}(k)$ is the time of the kth transition from class i to class j in the sample, and $n_i(t-)$ is the number of i-rated firms, evaluated just before time t. $A_{ij}(t) = \int_0^t \lambda_{ij}(s)\,ds$ is the intensity measure of the process. Lando and Skodeberg also provide a framework for estimating parametric dependencies of the transition intensities on systematic (e.g. macroeconomic) variables which is based upon the Cox semi-parametric regression model. For more details on this and other areas of the statistical theory of point processes we refer the reader to Andersen *et al.* (1992).

8.5 PRICING WITH DETERMINISTIC GENERATOR MATRIX

In this section we assume that ratings transitions under the martingale measure follow a Markov chain. The dynamics are assumed to be specified under the martingale measure.

8.5.1 Pricing zero-coupon bonds

The price of a defaultable zero-coupon bond will now be a function of the issuer's credit rating $R(t)$ at time t:

$$\overline{B} = \overline{B}(t, T, R(t)),$$

and it will also depend on time and the risk-free interest rates. By construction of the model it is impossible to price a bond for a single rating class without simultaneously pricing the bonds for the other rating classes, too. As transitions are possible at any time we always need to know the price that the bond will have after a transition, i.e. we need to know the price of the bond for all other ratings.

Because R can only take K different values it is convenient to write the defaultable bond price as a vector

$$\overline{B}(t, T) = \begin{pmatrix} \overline{B}(t, T, R = 1) \\ \overline{B}(t, T, R = 2) \\ \vdots \\ \overline{B}(t, T, R = K) \end{pmatrix},$$

with the kth component $\overline{B}_k(t, T)$ denoting the price of the defaultable bond if the current rating is $R(t) = k$. The price for a given rating can then be read directly from the vector $\overline{B}(t, T)$.

If we assume zero recovery, the payoffs at maturity are:

$$\overline{B}(T, T) = (1, 1, \ldots, 1, 0)'.$$

The payoff in maturity is 1 for all rating classes, except in the last class (the default) where it is zero. The price of the defaultable bond is the risk-neutral expectation of its discounted payoff, given an initial rating of $R(0)$:

$$\overline{B}_{R(0)}(0, T) = \mathbf{E}\left[\exp\left\{ -\int_0^T r(s)ds \right\} \overline{B}_{R(T)}(T, T) \,\middle|\, R(0) \right]$$

$$= \mathbf{E}\left[\exp\left\{ -\int_0^T r(s)ds \right\} \right] \mathbf{E}\left[\overline{B}_{R(T)}(T, T) \,\middle|\, R(0) \right]$$

$$= B(0, T)\mathbf{E}\left[\overline{B}_{R(T)}(T, T) \,\middle|\, R(0) \right]$$

$$= B(0, T)(Q(0, T)\overline{B}(T, T))_{R(0)}$$

$$= B(0, T) \sum_{k=1}^{K-1} q_{R(0)k}(0, T)$$

$$= B(0, T)(1 - q_{R(0)K}(0, T)).$$

In this simple case the defaultable bond prices are given by the default-free bond prices times the survival probability (i.e. one minus the transition probability to default).

There are several observations to be made here. First, for a given credit class R and maturity T, the transition probability to default is $q_{RK}(0, T)$, where T is the time to maturity. This remains constant for a given time to maturity $T - t$ if we are using a time-homogeneous Markov chain, and therefore the credit spreads remain constant *within* every credit class, too. Even if a time-inhomogeneous Markov chain is used, changes in the spreads within rating classes will only be time-dependent but not stochastic. Thus, the only way in which a bond can change its spread in a Markov chain setup is through rating transitions.

Second, we assumed zero recovery at default. This can be relaxed to the RT model, which is the most common recovery specification for rating transition models for its mathematical convenience.

If RP is assumed, we must price the value of a cash payment at default. Given the default probabilities $q_{RK}(T)$, we can derive the density of the time of default as follows:

$$\mathbf{P}[\tau \in [t, t + dt]] = \frac{\partial}{\partial t} q_{RK}(t) dt.$$

From there follows directly the price $e_R(0, T)$ of a payoff of 1 at default of an obligor with initial rating R:

$$e_R(0, T) = \int_0^T B(0, t) \frac{\partial}{\partial t} q_{RK}(t) dt. \tag{8.34}$$

Here our life was made very easy by the fact that default-free interest rates are independent from rating transitions R in this setup.

Third, we assumed that the generator matrix used already reflected the risk-neutral probabilities of rating transitions and defaults. This is usually not the case either, and the pricing generator matrix must be found by calibrating the model as shown in the next section.

8.5.2 Pricing derivatives on the credit rating

Again we use vector notation for the price of a derivative security whose payoff depends on the credit rating of an underlying bond and the interest rate r. Let

$$F(t, r) = (F_1(t, r), F_2(t, r), \ldots, F_K(t, r))'$$

be the price of this derivative. $F_R(\cdot)$ is this price given an initial rating of R.

8.5.2.1 European-style payoffs

If F has a European payoff at T, which is given by

$$F(T, r) = (F_1^*(r), \ldots, F_K^*(r))',$$

we can apply the methods we used for the defaultable zero-coupon bonds to this situation. Again we have that $F(t)$ is the risk-neutral expectation of its discounted payoff. If F^* does not depend on r we have for the expectation of the final payoff (without discounting and given an initial rating of R):

$$\mathbf{E}[F_R(T)] = F_1^* q_{R1} + F_2^* q_{R2} + \cdots + F_K^* q_{RK},$$

the sum of the payoffs weighted by the transition probabilities. In vector notation this is

$$\mathbf{E}[F(T)] = Q(T)F^*.$$

With interest rate dependence and discounting this extends to (remember the definition of the discount factor $\beta_{tT} = \exp\{-\int_0^T r(s)ds\}$):

$$\mathbf{E}[F(r, T)] = Q(T)\mathbf{E}[\beta_{tT} F^*(T)] = Q(T)F(t),$$

where $F_k(t)$ is the (default-free) price of a security paying off $F_k^*(r)$ at time T for sure.

This can be seen if the equation is written for the Rth rating class and conditioning on the final class is used:

$$
\begin{aligned}
F_R(t) &= \mathbf{E}[\beta_{t,T} F_{R(T)}(T, r)] \\
&= \mathbf{E}\big[\beta_{t,T} F_{R(T)}(T, r) \mid R(T) = 1\big] q_{R1}(T) \\
&\quad + \mathbf{E}\big[\beta_{t,T} F_{R(T)}(T, r) \mid R(T) = 2\big] q_{R2}(T) \\
&\quad + \cdots + \mathbf{E}\big[\beta_{t,T} F_{R(T)}(T, r) \mid R(T) = K\big] q_{RK}(T) \\
&= \mathbf{E}[\beta_{t,T} F_1^*(r)] q_{R1} + \mathbf{E}[\beta_{t,T} F_2^*(r)] q_{R2} + \cdots + \mathbf{E}[\beta_{t,T} F_K^*(r)] q_{RK} \\
&= F_1(t) q_{R1} + F_2(t) q_{R2} + \cdots + F_K(t) q_{RK} \\
&= \sum_{k=1}^{K} F_k(t, r) q_{Rk}(T).
\end{aligned}
$$

The value of the European-style payoff is just the value of the individual risk-free payoffs times the transition probabilities of actually receiving this payoff.

8.5.3 General payoffs

One possible approach to price more general payoffs is the p.d.e. approach. For this we again need an Itô lemma representation of the price process of the derivative and use a general diffusion process for the short-rate dynamics:

$$
\begin{aligned}
dF_R(t, r) &= \frac{\partial}{\partial t} F_R dt + \frac{1}{2} \sigma_r^2 \frac{\partial^2}{\partial r^2} F_R dt \\
&\quad + \frac{\partial}{\partial r} F_R dr + (F_{R+\Delta R}(t, r) - F_R(t, r)).
\end{aligned}
$$

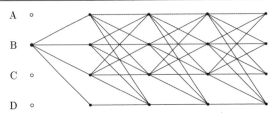

Figure 8.1   The dynamics of a rating transition process in discrete time. The initial rating is B, branching probabilities are given by the probabilities of the transition matrix over the time step of the tree

Here the last term represents the changes in the value of the derivative due to the change ΔR in the credit rating of the underlying instrument.[7] The expectation of dF is given by

$$\mathbf{E}[dF_R(t, r)] = \frac{\partial}{\partial t} F_R dt + \frac{1}{2}\sigma_r^2 \frac{\partial^2}{\partial r^2} F_R dt$$

$$+ \mu_r \frac{\partial}{\partial r} F_R dt + \sum_{k=1}^{K} \lambda_{Rk} F_k dt.$$

As usual, by the fundamental pricing rule this must equal $rF dt$ which yields the pricing equation

$$0 = \frac{\partial}{\partial t} F_R + \frac{1}{2}\sigma_r^2 \frac{\partial^2}{\partial r^2} F_R + \mu_r \frac{\partial}{\partial r} F_R + \sum_{k=1}^{K} \lambda_{Rk} F_k.$$

Similar equations must be satisfied for all R, so we can write this set of equations in compact matrix notation:

$$0 = \frac{\partial}{\partial t} F + \frac{1}{2}\sigma_r^2 \frac{\partial^2}{\partial r^2} F + \mu_r \frac{\partial}{\partial r} F + \Lambda F - rF. \tag{8.35}$$

Without any further knowledge about the structure of the problem we have to stop here and solve the pricing equation numerically subject to the appropriate boundary and final conditions.

The solution is complicated by the fact that we are dealing with K coupled partial differential equations, one for each rating class. Because the prices in the different classes will interact in general, we have to solve these equations simultaneously. The good news is that this situation is no worse than having an additional dimension in the partial differential equation.

8.5.4   Rating trees

Alternatively, one can use the tree shown in Figure 8.1 to implement a tree-based rating transition model. Setting up this tree model does not require much additional work as all branching probabilities are given in the (risk-neutral) transition matrix. Of course, the transition probabilities must be the transition probabilities for the time step size of the tree.

---

[7] All partial derivatives apply to every component if applied to a vector function.

If in addition there is already a tree for the default-free interest rates, the tree model can be implemented in the following steps:

1. Choose a time step size Δt.
2. Build a tree for the default-free interest rate r and calibrate that tree (see Section 7.4 for a description).
3. Find a generator matrix for the rating transition process.
4. Calibrate this generator matrix to the term structure of defaultable bond prices in all rating classes (see Section 8.6).
5. From the generator matrix, find the Δt one-period transition matrices $Q_i := Q(t_i, t_{i+1})$ for all time intervals $[t_i, t_{i+1}]$.
6. Build a rating transition tree of the form shown in Figure 8.1.
7. The branching probabilities in the rating transition tree over the interval $[t_i, t_{i+1}]$ are the transition probabilities of the transition matrix Q_i.
8. Combine the interest rate and the rating trees. If we have a trinomial tree for the interest rate and a tree with K branches for the ratings, the combined tree will have $3 \times K$ branches, one for each joint movement.
9. The joint movement probabilities are given by the product of the individual transition probabilities.

Remarks: The rating transition probabilities are only time-dependent. Therefore, they cannot be realistically correlated with interest rate movements. The only possible sources of correlation stem from dependencies between default-free interest rates and actual rating transitions. It is unlikely that an (infinitesimal) interest rate move can trigger a rating transition, or vice versa that a rating transition has an effect on the dynamics of default-free interest rates. Dependency can realistically exist between interest rate moves and the *likelihood* of a rating transition, but not between interest rates and *actual* rating transitions. For this reason, independence relieved us from the problem of specifying correlated joint movement probabilities.

As opposed to the calibration in the tree model of Section 7.4, here we performed the calibration of the transition probability matrix outside of the tree. This method was chosen because most calibration methods only provide approximative fits to the average spreads of the rating classes anyway, and because we are not forced to do a joint calibration by correlation effects as in Section 7.4. Separate calibration involves a slight loss in accuracy because the tree is a discretisation of the continuous-time process that was approximated; for this we gain a simpler implementation.

As usual, the tree can be used for pricing by backwards induction.

8.5.5   Downgrade triggers

A common specification of credit derivatives triggers some payment or a knockout at a specific change of rating (e.g. the stepup provisions described in the introduction). As an example we consider here a downgrade insurance, which would have a payoff of

$$F = \overline{B}_A - \overline{B}$$

if the rating of the bond $\overline{B}$ with maturity T_2 drops to less than A. Here $\overline{B}_A$ is the price of an equivalent A-rated defaultable bond, so as soon as the bond $\overline{B}$ is downgraded the buyer of the insurance can exchange it for an equivalent A-rated bond.[8] We assume that the insurance is valid until time $T_1 \le T_2$.

For the pricing of F this means that we already know F_k for all $k > 3$ (where $k = 3$ represents the rating A and $k > 3$ represents ratings worse than A):

$$F_k(r, t) = \overline{B}_3(t, T) - \overline{B}_k(t, T)$$

$$= B(t, T_2)[1 - cq_{3K}(t, T_2) - (1 - cq_{kK}(t, T_2))]$$

$$= cB(t, T_2)[-q_{3K}(t, T_2) + q_{kK}(t, T_2)]$$

where we used the bond pricing formula from the previous section. Note that we used the default transition probabilities until T_2 in the bond prices. For clarity we included T_2 in the arguments where appropriate.

The final payoff for F at T_1 is zero. (If the insurance has a payoff, it is earlier.) Thus we have a final payoff, and the payoffs at certain rating transitions. Then we must substitute these values for F_4 to F_8 in (8.35), and solve equation (8.35) numerically for the three remaining components F_1, F_2 and F_3.

Often it is interesting to calculate *hitting probabilities* for the rating transition process: What is the probability of a transition to a rating of k in the period $[0, T]$? This is a different problem from asking for the probability of being at k at time T. If we only condition on the final moment we ignore the possibility that the rating may have changed to k and then away from it. We would underestimate the hitting probability.

To frame this problem as a final state problem we only have to make the state k an *absorbing* state. The kth row of the generating matrix Λ contained the intensities of the Poisson processes triggering the transitions to other classes. λ_{kl} for instance is the intensity of a transition from k to l. If we thus set the kth row of Λ to zero we make transitions away from k impossible: if the process hits k once, it will remain there. The matrix Λ is thus changed from

$$\Lambda = \begin{pmatrix} \lambda_{11} & \lambda_{12} & \cdots & \cdots & \cdots & \lambda_{1K} \\ \lambda_{21} & \lambda_{22} & \cdots & \cdots & \cdots & \lambda_{2K} \\ \vdots & \vdots & \ddots & & & \vdots \\ \lambda_{k1} & \lambda_{k2} & \cdots & \cdots & \cdots & \lambda_{kK} \\ \vdots & \vdots & & & \ddots & \vdots \\ \lambda_{K1} & \lambda_{K2} & \cdots & \cdots & \cdots & \lambda_{KK} \end{pmatrix}$$

to

$$\Lambda_k = \begin{pmatrix} \lambda_{11} & \lambda_{12} & \cdots & \cdots & \cdots & \lambda_{1K} \\ \lambda_{21} & \lambda_{22} & \cdots & \cdots & \cdots & \lambda_{2K} \\ \vdots & \vdots & \ddots & & & \vdots \\ 0 & 0 & \cdots & \cdots & \cdots & 0 \\ \vdots & \vdots & & & \ddots & \vdots \\ \lambda_{K1} & \lambda_{K2} & \cdots & \cdots & \cdots & \lambda_{KK} \end{pmatrix}.$$

---

[8] This payoff is obviously always positive.

With this change of the generating matrix we can see that the probability of hitting k until T is equal to the probability of being at k at T, the transition probability to k. We have already derived the expression for the transition probabilities, it is

$$Q_k(t) = e^{\Lambda_k t}. \tag{8.36}$$

Q_k will have zeroes in the kth row except on the diagonal where $p_{kk} = 1$. There are two types of information we can gain from Q_k. For $j \neq k$ the (ij)th element p_{ij} of Q_k denotes the *probability of a transition from class i to class j without going through k in the meantime*. And in the kth column we have the hitting probabilities of class k: the element p_{ik} is the probability of hitting k if the rating process started at i.

Obviously we can also modify several rows of the matrix Λ, for instance if we wanted the probability of a downgrade to k or worse we would set the last rows of Λ, starting from row k, to zero. The rating transition process is then stopped as soon as one of the classes that have been set to zero is reached.

In all these cases we have to recalculate the diagonal decomposition of the modified matrix Λ_k.

8.5.6 Hedging rating transitions

Assuming we have K rating classes we need K different hedge instruments F_k to hedge the rating transitions. The hedge weights α_k to hedge a security V have to satisfy

$$V(r, R) - V(r, R_0) = \sum_{k=1}^{K} \alpha_k (F_k(r, R) - F_k(r, R_0)), \quad \forall 1 \leq R \leq K$$

where R_0 is the rating class we are starting from. This equation means that for every possible rating class R we need the change in value of the hedge portfolio (on the right-hand side) to equal the change in value of the security to hedge (on the left-hand side), if there is a transition to this class R. This yields $(K - 1)$ equations[9] that are to be satisfied by the K hedge instruments. The Kth equation to make the solution unique comes from the hedging of the continuous interest rate risk. We need that

$$\frac{\partial}{\partial r} V(r, R_0) = \sum_{k=1}^{K} \alpha_k \frac{\partial}{\partial r} F_k(r, R_0).$$

In practice, such a hedging strategy will be hard to implement and its performance will be unreliable. First, it relies on the assumption that we can predict the price change in the instrument V that is caused by every given rating change. Second, we must also be able to predict with similar certainty the price changes that are caused by the same rating transition in the other hedge instrument. Furthermore, these price changes must be sufficiently different so that we can hedge different rating transitions at the same time. Bonds of the same seniority class would have almost proportional reactions to different rating changes, so they will not allow us

---

[9] Note that the equation for $R = R_0$ drops out trivially.

to span more rating events. Finally, we still have not hedged against the risk of spread changes that are not caused by a rating change.

All these arguments speak against putting too much trust in a rating-based hedge strategy. But the analysis of what might happen to the value of a traded instrument upon a rating change is important because this forces the focus onto large changes in spreads and in the credit quality, and these may cause more risk than the normal day-by-day spread volatility.

8.6   THE CALIBRATION OF RATING TRANSITION MODELS

An important requirement for a credit risk pricing model is the calibration of the model to benchmark market prices, or equivalently that it is specified under the martingale measure, and not under historical probabilities. The adjustment of historical probabilities to martingale probabilities is necessary because of the presence of large risk premia in credit markets, historically estimated rating transition frequencies cannot be used directly.

For the calibration of rating transition models one usually specifies term structures of defaultable zero-coupon bond prices for each rating class, and a default-free term structure of zero-coupon bond prices. These should be jointly reproduced by the model.

In a finite state Markov chain setup, the class of equivalent probability measures is very large. If Λ^P is the matrix of transition intensities (generator matrix) of a rating transition process under the probability measure P, then an equivalent probability measure Q is characterised by its matrix Λ^Q of transition intensities.[10] Assuming suitable regularity, the new transition intensities λ^Q under Q are the original transition intensities λ^P modified by a predictable, positive multiplier process ϕ:

$$\lambda_{ij}^P = \phi_{ij} \lambda_{ij}^Q, \quad i \neq j \tag{8.37}$$

where as usual we set $\lambda_{ii}^Q = -\sum_{j \neq i} \lambda_{ij}^Q$.

There are $(K-1)^2$ intensity adjustment processes ϕ_{ij} to choose.[11] As there are only $K-1$ term structures of credit spreads to fit, the calibration problem is *ex ante* underspecified if only spread *levels* are used to calibrate the model. The remaining degrees of freedom are used to also fit the shape (term structure) of credit spreads within the rating classes. Alternatively one can try to stay as close as possible to the historical transition frequencies, to reach transition rates that do not vary too much over time, or to achieve some analytical tractability (e.g. the Markov property or an affine factor structure) of the resulting model.

8.6.1   Deterministic intensity approaches

In the models of this subsection, rating transitions are modelled using a Markov chain whose transition intensities may be time-dependent, but not stochastic. Members of this class are the models of Lando (1994), Jarrow *et al.* (1997) (JLT) (who were the first to model credit rating transition in a continuous-time Markov chain setup), Das and Tufano (1996), Kijima and Komoribayashi (1998) and Lando (2000). The basic model of this section is JLT.

Interest rate risk is modelled using a diffusion-based interest rate model, with a stochastic short-term interest rate $r(t)$. If we assume that default-free interest rate movements are not

---

[10] This is a consequence of the Girsanov theorem for marked point processes.
[11] The transition intensities from the default class K are all zero.

affected by individual rating transitions, this implies that interest rate movements and rating transitions are independent.

Recovery risk is modelled with the recovery of treasury (RT) model, in the case of Das and Tufano (1994) with a stochastic process for the recovery rate. As seen earlier, the prices of defaultable zero-coupon bonds $\overline{B}_{RT}(t, T)$ in this setup are:

$$\overline{B}_{RT}(t, T) = cB(t, T) + (1 - c)\overline{B}(t, T), \tag{8.38}$$

where c is the RT recovery rate, $B(t, T)$ is the default-free zero-coupon bond price, and $\tau > t$ is assumed. The price of the zero-recovery defaultable zerobond $\overline{B}(t, T)$ is

$$\overline{B}(t, T) = P(t, T)B(t, T), \tag{8.39}$$

where $P(t, T)$ is the survival probability over $[t, T]$ under the martingale measure. Defaults and rating transitions are modelled as the transitions of a continuous-time Markov chain; the time of default is the first time the rating process of the obligor hits the rating class K. Using the martingale measure transition probabilities $\widetilde{Q}$ the survival probabilities of an obligor with rating i at time t are:

$$P_i(t, T) = 1 - \widetilde{q}_{iK}(t, T). \tag{8.40}$$

The generator matrix of the Markov chain under the historical probability measure is the constant matrix Λ, which we assume to be diagonalisable:[12]

$$\Lambda = MD_\Lambda M^{-1}. \tag{8.41}$$

The modelling problem at this point is the specification of a generator matrix $\widetilde{\Lambda}$ under the martingale measure. This will necessarily involve a modification of the historical transition rates, but it is desirable to stay as close to them as possible. Several parametric modifications of the generator matrix have been proposed in the literature.

Method 1

In Lando (1994) the transition intensities under the martingale measure are parametrised with one time-dependent adjustment factor $\mu(t)$:

$$\widetilde{\Lambda}(t) = \mu(t)\Lambda. \tag{8.42}$$

This method is very simple to implement but it can only achieve a fit to one term structure of defaultable bond prices.

Method 2

The rating transitions are left unchanged, except for the transition intensities to default (Lando, 2000):

$$\widetilde{\lambda}_{ij}(t) = \lambda_{ij}(t), \quad \text{for } i, j < K, \ i \neq j \tag{8.43}$$

$$\widetilde{\lambda}_{iK}(t) = \mu_i(t)\lambda_{iK}(t) \quad \text{and} \quad \widetilde{\lambda}_{ii}(t) = -\sum_{j \neq i} \widetilde{\lambda}_{ij}(t). \tag{8.44}$$

---

[12] This assumption is not made in all papers, but as mentioned before, it is not restrictive.

Method 3 (JLT, Das and Tufano)
The generator matrix under the equivalent martingale measure is given by

$$\widetilde{\Lambda} = U(t)\Lambda, \tag{8.45}$$

where $U(t) = \mathrm{diag}\{\mu_1(t), \ldots, \mu_{K-1}(t), 1\}$ is a diagonal matrix of time-dependent risk adjustment factors with $\int_0^T \mu_i(t)dt < \infty$. The historical transition rates of each rating class i are multiplied by the time-dependent adjustment factor $\mu_i(t)$ to reach the transition rates under the martingale measure. Thus, if $\mu_i > 1$ *all* transitions from class i occur more frequently under the martingale measure. Usually downgrades are more likely than upgrades so that for $\mu_i(t) > 1$ an increase in risk results.

Method 4 (Lando, 2000; Arvanitis *et al.*, 1999)
Modifying equation (8.41), the generator matrix under the martingale measure is

$$\widetilde{\Lambda} = MU(t)D_\Lambda M^{-1}, \tag{8.46}$$

i.e. the generator matrix $\widetilde{\Lambda}$ under the martingale measure has the same eigenvectors M as the historical generator matrix Λ, but different eigenvalues. The advantage of this specification is that now the generator matrices commute and the solution of the Kolmogorov equations can be written down in closed form:

$$\widetilde{Q}(t, T) = MD_{\widetilde{Q}}(t, T)M^{-1}, \tag{8.47}$$

$$D_{\widetilde{Q}}(t, T) = \mathrm{diag}\left\{e^{\int_t^T d_1\mu_1(s)ds}, \ldots, e^{\int_t^T d_K\mu_K(s)ds}\right\}, \tag{8.48}$$

where $d_1, \ldots, d_k$ are the diagonal elements of D_Λ. The disadvantage is that we cannot give an easy interpretation to the effect these adjustment factors have on the martingale measure probabilities.

In all these approaches, when the generator matrix $\widetilde{\Lambda}(t)$ under the martingale measure is given, survival probabilities of defaultable zero-coupon bonds in the different rating classes can be derived either using the Kolmogorov equations (8.16) or directly (in the case of methods 1 and 4).

In Lando (2000) an iterative calibration procedure is proposed to determine the adjustment factors $U(t)$ by using the information contained in the whole term structures of forward rates for all rating classes. The procedure can be based upon the following representation of the instantaneous forward credit spread in rating class $i < K$:

$$-\frac{\partial}{\partial T} \ln \overline{B}_i(t, T) - f(t, T) = \frac{1}{1 - \widetilde{Q}_{iK}(t, T)} \sum_{n=1}^K \widetilde{Q}_{in}(t, T)\widetilde{\Lambda}_{nK}(T).$$

If $\widetilde{\Lambda}(T)$ depends on $K - 1$ parameters (like the diagonal elements of $U(T)$ above), letting i vary from 1 to $K - 1$ will yield $K - 1$ equations to determine these parameters at this point in time. Because the diagonalisations of the matrices are explicitly given, the solution of these equations is trivial. Now we can proceed a small time step Δt in the future using an Euler step to the Kolmogorov forward equation to reach the new $\widetilde{Q}(t, T + \Delta t)$-matrix:

$$\widetilde{Q}(t, T + \Delta t) = \widetilde{Q}(t, T)(I + \widetilde{\Lambda}(T)\Delta t),$$

and repeat the procedure with the determination of $\widetilde{\Lambda}(T + \Delta t)$. The process is started from the initial condition $\widetilde{Q}(0, 0) = I$.

Arvanitis et al. (1999) propose a slightly different calibration procedure where – instead of time-stepping a time-dependent intensity matrix like Lando (2000) – a time-invariant intensity matrix is sought which reproduces a set of prespecified bond prices as accurately as possible while keeping close to the historical transition intensities.

All calibration procedures are subject to certain consistency conditions to ensure that transitions to more distant rating classes are less likely than transitions to closer rating grades. Kijima (1998) investigated this question and provided sufficient conditions on the one-period transition probabilities that ensure such monotonicities over all future time horizons.

Stochastic recoveries: Das and Tufano
In the models presented above, credit spreads within the rating classes are deterministic, because both transition intensities and expected recovery rates are deterministic. The model of Das and Tufano (1994) represents a first attempt to make spreads within the rating classes stochastic by making recovery rates stochastic. They specify a stochastic process of the form $1/(1 + X(t))$, where $X(t)$ is a lognormal random walk for the recovery rate in the RT framework.

8.6.2 Incorporating rating momentum

The models considered so far did not incorporate rating momentum. Arvanitis et al. (1999) propose to incorporate rating momentum via an extension of the state space. Each rating class $k \in S$ is split into three subclasses.

- Class k_+: obligors who were recently upgraded to k.
- Class $k_=$: obligors who have been in k for a long time.
- Class k_-: obligors who were recently downgraded to k.

This enables us to specify different transition rates for recently up/downgraded obligors and for stable obligors, while retaining the Markov structure in the extended state space. The specification of the transition intensities will have to be modified as follows. First, transitions to different rating classes will now go to the + (recently upgraded) or − (recently downgraded) classes respectively. Second, within the subclasses there are transitions from the +, − classes to the stable class. These transition intensities must be chosen such that the expected holding times in the +, − classes match the time for which the rating momentum effect is present.

Lando and Skodeberg directly estimate the effects of rating momentum on the transition intensities. In their setup, the transition intensities not only depend on the current rating class, but also on a vector Z of external covariates, in particular the time since the last transition, the direction of the last transition, and macroeconomic variables. Their model is an extension of the Cox intensity regression model and takes the form

$$\lambda_{ij}^n(t) = \alpha_{ij}(t) \exp\{\beta_{ij} Z_n(t)\}, \tag{8.49}$$

where $\lambda_{ij}^n(t)$ is the transition intensity of a transition of firm n from class i to class j. The firm-specific covariates are in the vector $Z_n(t)$ and the regression weights of the influence of these covariates are β_{ij}. Because the covariates can vary stochastically over time, this model can be viewed as a specification of a stochastic intensity model.

8.6.3 Stochastic rating transition intensities

While stochastic spreads within classes are a desirable feature of a model, it is questionable whether in reality spreads are really exclusively driven by market expectations of the *recovery rate*, as Das and Tufano suggest. Anecdotal evidence from the markets seems to suggest that spreads are driven by changing perceptions of the *probability* of default; only for obligors close to default do changes in the expected recovery rate have a significant impact.

If the transition intensities $\widetilde{\Lambda}$ are stochastic, the resulting rating transition process is not Markovian any more, but the transition probability matrix and the infinitesimal generator matrix of the process are still well-defined.

Second, the calibration of the model may become very complicated; the problem is akin to calibrating K stochastic interest rate models (which may be correlated) simultaneously. A tractable representation of the transition probabilities is essential.

Lando 1998 proposes the following framework. The transition intensity matrices are diagonalisable with a common transformation matrix M (see method 4 above), and the eigenvalues are driven by a multidimensional stochastic process $X(t)$. The transition intensity matrix is now

$$\widetilde{\Lambda} = MU(X(t))M^{-1} \quad \text{where} \quad U(X(t)) = \text{diag}\{\mu_1(X(t)), \ldots, \mu_K(X(t))\}. \quad (8.50)$$

The advantage of this representation is the following, still tractable representation of the resulting transition probability matrix over $[t, T]$ as seen from t:

$$\widetilde{Q}(t, T) = M E_X(t, T) M^{-1} \quad (8.51)$$

where

$$E_X(t, T) = \text{diag}\{\mathbf{E}[e^{\int_t^T \mu_1(X(s))ds} \mid \mathcal{F}_t], \ldots, \mathbf{E}[e^{\int_t^T \mu_K(X(s))ds} \mid \mathcal{F}_t]\}. \quad (8.52)$$

The dynamics of $X(t)$ and the functions $\mu_i(X(t))$ must now be specified in a form which allows a simple evaluation of expressions of the form $\mathbf{E}[\exp\{\int_t^T \mu_K(X(s))ds\}|\mathcal{F}_t]$. Lando proposes an exponentially affine specification of X and affine functions $\mu_i(X)$, according to the specifications in Duffie *et al.* (2000).

Arvanitis *et al.* (1999) propose to model X as a one-dimensional Ornstein–Uhlenbeck process, and the functions are multiplications with constants $\mu_i(X(t)) := d_i X(t)$. This simplifies the model structure, but makes the credit spread dynamics of all rating classes perfectly correlated. Using an Ornstein–Uhlenbeck process may be problematic because it must be ensured that $\mu_i(X) \leq 0$ at all times. Given the high volatility and low level of credit spreads another specification may be preferable.

8.7   A GENERAL HJM FRAMEWORK

In Schönbucher (2000a) the calibration problem is avoided by directly modelling the dynamics of the term structures of credit spreads in the different rating classes, based upon the approach pioneered by Heath *et al.* (1992) (HJM). The model is automatically calibrated to all term structures of credit spreads in all rating classes. Furthermore, it is not necessary to assume that all intensity matrices at all times and states have the same eigenvectors.

The fundamental quantities of the model are:

- The transition intensities λ_{ij} between all states $i, j \in \{1, \ldots, K-1\}$ (except the default state).
- The initial term structures of default-free and defaultable forward rates for each rating class.[13]
- The volatilities of these forward rates.

The modeller is free to choose these quantities from market data and historical experience. The drifts of the forward rates and the default intensities on the other hand are fixed by the no-arbitrage restrictions (8.58) and (8.59).

In this model one differentiates between the defaultable bond prices $\overline{B}(t, T)$ of the zerobonds issued by the defaultable obligor, and "benchmark" bond prices $\overline{B}_k(t, T)$. For each rating class $k \in S$, there is a set of "benchmark" bond prices $\overline{B}_k(t, T)$. The benchmark bond prices never change their rating, nor are they affected by defaults; they describe the term structure of credit spreads within the rating class k. The benchmark term structure of defaultable zero-coupon bond prices $\overline{B}_k(t, T)$ is described by the defaultable forward rates $\overline{f}_k(t, T)$:

$$\overline{B}_k(t, T) = \exp\left\{-\int_t^T \overline{f}_k(t, s)ds\right\}. \tag{8.53}$$

The defaultable bond prices $\overline{B}_k(t, T)$ and forward rates $\overline{f}_k(t, T)$ for all classes can be observed at all times.

To every defaultable obligor there is a ratings process $R(t)$ which gives the rating of the bond at time t. If the rating of the obligor at time t is $R(t)$, the prices of his zerobonds are given by the prices of the benchmark bonds:

$$\overline{B}(t, T) = \overline{B}_{R(t)}(t, T).$$

The dynamics of the model are as follows:

(i) At a rating transition the defaultable bond price jumps to the equivalent (same maturity and face value) defaultable bond price of the new rating class. The rating transition of a defaultable bond from class $i \in S$ to class $j \neq i \in S$ is driven by a point process N_{ij} with intensity λ_{ij}. The transition intensities are arranged in a transition matrix $\Lambda = (\lambda_{kl})_{1 \le k, l \le K}$. The elements λ_{kl} of Λ can be predictable stochastic processes.

---

[13] It is advisable to specify the defaultable forward rates as spreads over default-free rates or as spreads over the next better rating class.

(ii) The dynamics of the defaultable forward rates *within class k* are:

$$d\overline{f}_k(t, T) = \overline{\alpha}_k(t, T)dt + \sum_{i=1}^{n} \overline{\sigma}_{i,k}(t, T)dW^i(t),$$ (8.54)

where again the volatilities can be arbitrary predictable stochastic processes.

(iii) From this follow the dynamics of the benchmark bond price $\overline{B}_k(t, T) :=$ $\exp\{-\int_t^T \overline{f}_k(t, s)ds\}$ in rating class k:

$$\frac{d\overline{B}_k(t, T)}{\overline{B}_k(t-, T)} = m_k(t, T)dt + \sum_{i=1}^{n} \overline{a}_{i,k}(t, T)dW^i(t),$$ (8.55)

where $m_k(t, T)$ and $\overline{a}(t, T)$ can be expressed in terms of $\overline{f}_k$, $\overline{\alpha}_k$ and $\overline{\sigma}$.

(iv) Defaults and recoveries of the defaultable bond are driven by the multiple default/fractional recovery model as in Schönbucher (1998). At a default event, a reorganisation takes place, the face value of the defaulted bond is reduced (multiplied by $1 - q < 1$), and the obligor continues his life in the pre-default rating class. Thus the price of a defaultable bond, taking previous defaults into account, is:

$$\overline{B}(t, T) = Q(t)\overline{B}_{R(t)}(t, T),$$ (8.56)

where $Q(t) = (1 - q)^{N(t)}$ is the cumulative face value reduction of the bond due to the $N(t)$ defaults until time t. Setting $q = 1$ reduces the model to zero recovery.

(v) The resulting dynamics of the defaultable bond prices are:

$$\frac{d\overline{B}(t, T)}{\overline{B}(t-, T)} = m(t, T)dt + \sum_{i=1}^{n} \overline{a}_i(t, T) dW^i(t) - q\left(dN_{R(t),K}(t) - \lambda(t)dt\right)$$

$$+ \sum_{k=1}^{K-1} \left(\frac{\overline{B}_k(t, T)}{\overline{B}_{R(t)}(t, T)} - 1\right)\left(dN_{R(t),k} - \lambda_{R(t),k}dt\right),$$ (8.57)

where the drift coefficient $m(t, T)$ can be expressed in terms of the other model variables.

The following restrictions close the dynamics of the model under the martingale measure and ensure absence of arbitrage.

(i) The short rate spread in rating class i ($i \in \{1, \ldots, K - 1\}$) is determined by the default intensity of this class and the recovery rate:

$$\lambda_{iK}(t)q(t) = \overline{f}_i(t, t) - f(t, t).$$ (8.58)

(ii) The drift of the defaultable forward rates is restricted by:

$$\overline{\alpha}_k(t, T) = \sum_{i=1}^{n} \overline{\sigma}_{i,k}(t, T) \left(\int_t^T \overline{\sigma}_{i,k}(t, s) \, ds \right)$$

$$+ \sum_{l=1}^{K-1} \frac{\overline{B}_l(t, T)}{\overline{B}_k(t, T)} (\overline{f}_k(t, T) - \overline{f}_l(t, T)) \lambda_{k,l}. \tag{8.59}$$

(iii) If the conditions above hold, the drifts of the defaultable bond prices are $m(t, T) = f(t, t)$, i.e. discounted defaultable bond prices are local martingales.

These results hold without assuming Markovian dynamics for the rating transition process or special assumptions on the eigenvectors of the transition intensity matrix, and can easily be generalised to stochastic recovery rates, different recovery models and joint jumps of ratings and defaults. The drift restrictions (8.59) are versions of the drift restriction found by Björk *et al.* (1997) in the context of default-free term structures of interest rates. To close the model, the default-free forward rates have to satisfy the classical HJM drift restrictions, too.

It is interesting to note that the short-term credit spread $\overline{f}_i(t, t) - f(t, t)$ is exclusively driven by the default intensity of this rating class. This is due to the fact that very short-term investments will be repaid in the next time step, even after downgrades. Only if the next transition goes directly to default will the short-term investment suffer a loss.

Bielecki and Rutkowski (2000) analysed a similar model in the recovery of treasury setup. Their consistency restrictions are (for all $i \neq j$):

$$\lambda_{ij}(\overline{B}_j(t, T) - \overline{B}_i(t, T)) + \lambda_{iK}(\delta_i B(t, T) - \overline{B}_i(t, T)) + \lambda_{ii} \overline{B}(t, T) = 0.$$

This restriction is more difficult to implement as it is a joint system of equations in the transition intensities λ_{ij}, λ_{iK} and λ_{ii} and the bond prices, and it is not clear which elements of the model can be taken as primitives and which are determined by the no-arbitrage conditions. Restrictions (8.58) and (8.59) on the other hand can be directly implemented.

8.8 CONCLUSION

The largest advantage and the largest disadvantage of rating-based models lies in the data they are based upon. There is a wealth of historical data and empirical analysis on credit ratings and rating transitions. This data is from a trustworthy and independent source and is readily available, and rating-based models can make the best use of it. The model is (in its simplest version) relatively straightforward and can be adapted to other areas of application like internal risk-scoring models.

On the other hand, historical data has only limited use for the pricing of credit derivatives. By definition, historical data is backward-looking, i.e. it is only valid insofar as history has not changed in the meantime. In all fairness it must be acknowledged that the analysis that rating agencies perform when initially assigning a new rating is *not* backward-looking but a forward-looking analysis of the future payment capabilities of the obligor in question. The problem lies not in the rating itself, but rather in the way historical transition data is used in the quantitative model.

Another problem with ratings information is that real-world rating adjustments often occur with delays, i.e. frequently the rating adjustments can lag behind market price movements, sometimes by several weeks if not months. Given the impact that rating downgrades can have on the survival prospects of an obligor, it is understandable that the rating agencies do not want to be the cause (rather than the signaller) of a default, but unfortunately this slows down the adjustment process. Things would be easier if ratings were not assigned on a cardinal scale of eight (or 12) classes, but on a continuous scale like Moody's KMV EDF-measures. Then, the rating agency could make "small" adjustments that would be recognised as small by the market and therefore would not have the massive impact of a full downgrade. Furthermore, a more detailed differentiation of the credit assessment would be possible.

A minor technical point is also that the rating agencies define default events differently from the default event specification in a credit default swap, or that many (in particular distant) reported rating transition frequencies are based upon very few observations, or (more seriously in some cases) that the data is mostly on US corporates – data on other regions is usually very scarce.

But the largest and most difficult problem is the calibration problem: How should one adjust the historical transition probabilities in order to reach the spread curves observed in the market? The necessary adjustments are usually quite large and the last word has not been spoken as to which of the various adjustment methods performs best.

9

Firm Value and Share Price-Based Models

9.1 THE APPROACH

9.1.1 Modelling philosophy

In the intensity and spread-based models for default risk, the focus was on *consistent* pricing, i.e. finding a not too complicated formal model of the stochastic arrival of a default which can easily be calibrated to existing debt instruments like traded bonds. Using this calibrated model we could gain a better understanding of the distribution of default times and price more complicated credit instruments in a consistent manner. An intensity-based model does not give any fundamental reason for the arrival of the defaults, only a consistent description of the market-implied distribution of the default arrival times.

Compared to this, models that are based upon a stochastic process for the firm's value take a much more fundamental approach to valuing defaultable debt with a more ambitious aim: to provide a link between the prices of equity and all debt instruments issued by one particular firm – basically to price every single item on the liabilities side of the balance sheet of the firm in question. A particular focus lies on finding a link between the values of equity and debt of the firm. This is an important question which has many applications, some very practical and others of academic (but still highly relevant) interest. A model which provides this link allows:

- Relative value trading between shares and debt of one particular issuer (or between equity and credit derivatives);
- Default risk assessment of a firm based upon its share price and fundamental (balance sheet) data alone;
- Capital structure optimisation – the firm's CFO can now identify the capital structure which optimises the total market value of the firm;
- The pricing of convertible bonds;
- The identification and analysis of potential conflicts of interest between owners of different assets issued by the firm.

In the following we will focus on the default risk modelling questions. Firm's value models are built on the premise that there is a fundamental process V, usually interpreted as the total value of the assets of the firm that has issued the bonds in question (hence the name "firm's value models"). The value of the firm V is assumed to move around stochastically. It is the driving force behind the dynamics of the prices of all securities issued by the firm, and all claims on the firm's value are modelled as *derivative securities with the firm's value as underlying*.

Default can be triggered in two ways. In the pioneering papers by Black and Scholes (1973)[1] and Merton (1974) which started the literature on firm's value models, V is used to pay off the

---

[1] It is often overlooked that the famous Black and Scholes (1973) paper was entitled "The pricing of options and *corporate liabilities*" (my emphasis). Already in its title it was also a credit risk paper. Nevertheless, Merton (1974) is usually credited with properly expanding on the credit risk theme in the new option pricing literature.

debt *at maturity* of the contract. A default occurs at maturity if V is insufficient to pay back the outstanding debt but during the lifetime of the contract a default cannot be triggered.

Alternatively (and more realistically) one can assume that a default is already triggered as soon as the value of the collateral V falls below a barrier $\overline{K}$. This feature is exactly identical to a standard knockout barrier in equity options, and was first used in Black and Cox (1976), therefore we will call models with this feature Black–Cox-type models.

9.1.2   An example

Assume firm XYZ has issued zero-coupon bonds of maturity $T = 2$ years with a total face value $\overline{D}$ of $100m. The value V of the firm's assets is currently $150m and follows a geometric Brownian motion

$$dV = \mu V dt + \sigma V dW.$$

We can observe the value of the firm's assets but are unable to intervene before the maturity of the debt. Both bonds and shares issued by the firm are actively traded. The firm has issued $\overline{S}$ shares. Interest rates are constant r. From this setup, the following questions arise naturally:

- What should be the value of the firm's debt?
- What should be the value of the firm's shares?
- Can we hedge one with the other?

The state variable is the firm's value V. We write the prices of both debt $\overline{B}(V, t)$ and shares $S(V, t)$ as functions of firm's value V and time t. For ease of notation, from now on S denotes the price of *all* shares and $\overline{B}$ of *all* bonds. For the prices of the individual securities we will have to divide these by the respective numbers $\overline{D}$ and $\overline{S}$. Alternatively we could consider only *per share* units. This has the advantage that many model parameters are already given in this form in many places. Debt per share is a common key accounting figure and share prices are by definition "per share".

The capital structure of the firm ABC is shown in Table 9.1. The accounting identity of the balance sheet states that the value of the firm's assets must equal the sum of the values of equity and liabilities:

$$\text{Assets} = \text{Equity} + \text{Liabilities}$$
$$V = S + \overline{B}.$$

Table 9.1   The balance sheet of the firm ABC

Assets		Liabilities	
Assets (value of firm)	$V = 150$	Equity (shares)	S
		Debt (bonds)	$\overline{B}$
	$V = 150$		$S + \overline{B} = 150$

We know the *face* value of the firm's debt but not the present value $\overline{B}$, so the accounting identity alone does not allow us to derive the value of the firm's equity.

The firm ABC is a limited liability firm. At time T, the firm's managers (equity) will be faced with a payment obligation of $\overline{D}$. If the value $V(T)$ of the firm at this time is less than the payment obligation, equity will declare bankruptcy of the firm, effectively putting the firm to the debtholders. This is better to equity than the alternative: liquidation of the assets (proceeds $= V(T)$), injection of $\overline{D} - V(T)$ new cash and full repayment of the debt. This would leave the equityholders with $\overline{D} - V(T)$ less cash than before, and a firm of value zero. This argument also works in the reverse direction. If we observe that equityholders "save" the firm by issuing new shares and using the proceeds to pay off the debt, this means that (at least in the view of the new investors) the value of the firm's assets is higher than the debt of the firm.

The key observation of Black and Scholes (1973) and Merton (1974) was that both equity and debt can be viewed as *derivative securities on the value V of the firm's assets*. The payoffs of these derivatives at time T (the maturity of the debt) are:

$$\overline{B}(V, t) = \min(\overline{D}, V), \tag{9.1}$$
$$S(V, t) = \max(V - \overline{D}, 0). \tag{9.2}$$

The payoff of the shares is exactly the payoff of a European call option on the firm's value; the payoff of the bond is either its face value (if the firm's value is above $\overline{D}$ at T), or whatever is left of the firm's value V if it is below the face value of the debt. The payoffs are shown in Figure 9.1.

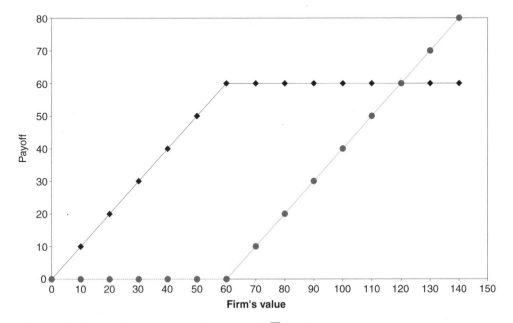

Figure 9.1 Payoffs of shares and bonds at $t = T$ for $\overline{D} = 60$

Shares and bonds together must give the total value of the firm, we get directly

$$V = \overline{B}(V, t) + S(V, t) \quad \Leftrightarrow \quad \overline{B}(V, t) = V - S(V, t).$$

Otherwise there would be an arbitrage opportunity.

As we have two securities with only one underlying source of uncertainty, we are able to hedge the bond with the share or vice versa. Let us consider the case of hedging the bond with the share. We set up a portfolio Π consisting of one bond and Δ shares. Its value is:

$$\Pi = \overline{B}(V, t) + \Delta S(V, t)$$

and by Itô's lemma its change in value over a short interval is:

$$d\Pi = d\overline{B} + \Delta dS \tag{9.3}$$

$$= \left(\frac{\partial \overline{B}}{\partial t} + \frac{1}{2} \frac{\partial^2 \overline{B}}{\partial V^2} + \Delta \frac{\partial S'}{\partial t} + \frac{1}{2} \Delta \frac{\partial^2 S'}{\partial V^2} \right) dt \tag{9.4}$$

$$+ \left(\frac{\partial \overline{B}}{\partial V} + \Delta \frac{\partial S}{\partial V} \right) dV. \tag{9.5}$$

To eliminate the stochastic dV term from the portfolio we only have to choose

$$\Delta = -\frac{\partial \overline{B}/\partial V}{\partial S/\partial V},$$

then the portfolio is fully hedged and its return is predictable. It must therefore earn the risk-free rate of interest r to locally eliminate any arbitrage opportunities. This will yield the following pricing partial differential equation:

$$\frac{\partial}{\partial t} F + \frac{1}{2} \sigma^2 V^2 \frac{\partial^2}{\partial V^2} F + rV \frac{\partial}{\partial V} F - rF = 0, \tag{9.6}$$

the well-known Black–Scholes partial differential equation. This enables us to directly price the share. Its value is given by the Black–Scholes formula for a European call option:

$$S(V, t) = C^{BS}(V, t; T, \overline{D}, \sigma, r),$$

where $C^{BS}(V, t; T, \overline{D}, \sigma, r)$ denotes the Black–Scholes price of a European call option on V with expiry date T and exercise price $\overline{D}$, where the underlying volatility is σ and the interest rate is r:

$$C^{BS}(V, t; T, \overline{D}, \sigma, r) = V N(d_1) - e^{-r(T-t)} \overline{D} N(d_2),$$

where

$$d_1 = \frac{\ln V/\overline{D} + (r - \frac{1}{2}\sigma^2(T - t))}{\sigma\sqrt{T - t}}$$

and $d_2 = d_1 - \sigma\sqrt{T - t}$.

Alternatively, although hedging in the classical sense directly with V is not possible, we can use the relation $S + \overline{B} = V$ to synthesise V from a portfolio of one share and one bond to replicate the firm's value and use the firm's value as hedge instrument.

This example already demonstrates the salient features of a firm's value model as originally proposed by Black and Scholes (1973) and Merton (1974). The point of view is more fundamental: one tries to model the *whole* obligor and his business in one, consistent model. Particularly attractive is the hedge-based connection between equity and debt prices. If this link was solid, it would enable us to hedge credit exposure in the much more liquid equity markets. This would be a major breakthrough for the risk management of obligors who do not have actively traded bond issues that can be used to build a term structure of credit spreads. A disadvantage of the model is the fact that it is based upon an essentially unobservable quantity: the firm's value process V, and the parameters of its dynamics, in particular its volatility.

9.1.3 State variables and modelling

In a more general setup, the inputs to a firm's value model are the following.

- First we have to model the dynamics of the underlying security, the value V of the firm's assets. Let us assume it follows a geometrical Brownian motion under the martingale measure Q:

$$\frac{dV}{V} = r dt + \sigma dW.$$

  If we assume that the firm's value can be constructed from traded securities we can set its risk-neutral drift to r. The risk-neutral dynamics are all we need for pricing.
- Given the value of the firm's assets we need to know all claims on these assets. For simplicity it is usually assumed that there is only a single issue of debt (zero-coupon bonds of total face value $\overline{D}$), but multiple issues with a seniority structure are also possible.
- The way in which a default is triggered is determined by the capital structure. Here there are several alternatives:
  - The firm continues to operate until it has to pay back its debt. Here a default can only occur at the maturity of the outstanding debt or at coupon dates before that. This was the case in the fundamental Merton (1974) model.
  - Following Black and Cox (1976), we can model *safety covenants* in the issued debt that allow the creditors to close down and liquidate the firm if the value of its assets should fall below a certain level $K(t) = K^*$. Default occurs as soon as

$$\tau = \inf\{t \geq 0 \mid V(t) \leq K^*\}.$$

  - The level $K(t)$ is not constant but time-dependent. For example, the covenant may be such that a default is only triggered if the firm's value falls below the *discounted* value of the assets outstanding, i.e. when the firm's value is worth less than a similar but default-free investment. Then default occurs as soon as

$$V(t) \leq \overline{K} B(t, T) = K(t),$$

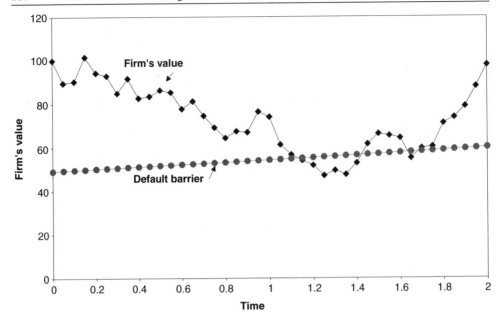

Figure 9.2   Default is triggered when the firm's value hits the barrier

where $B(t, T)$ is the value of a default-free bond of the same specification as the debt outstanding.
- In a practical implementation one could go and implement exactly *to the word* the covenants of the debt contract and firm that one wants to model. This is not done very often because the accuracy gained here is swamped by other cruder approximations one has to make in other parts of the model. (See the critique of the model.)
From now on we will assume the third case: default occurs at the barrier $K(t) = \overline{K} B(t, T)$. The state space (or its firm's value section) is shown in Figure 9.2.
• The capital structure of the firm has another consequence, it determines the payoffs to the different securities:
- The bonds pay off their face value $\overline{D}$ if there is no default, and their fraction of the value of the firm minus some bankruptcy costs c in the case of a default. The payoff function is

$$\overline{B}(V, t = T) = \min\{\overline{D}, V\}$$

at the final payoff date, and

$$\overline{B}(V = K(t), t) = V - c = K(t) - c$$

if a default is triggered in the meantime.
- The shares pay off $S(V, t = T) = (V - \overline{D})^+$ at maturity of the debt, and nothing if a default is triggered $S(V = K(t), t) = 0$. This means we model strict absolute priority. Deviations from priority can be incorporated with a different payoff distribution at $V = K(t)$. For

instance we could say that the bankruptcy costs c to the bondholders result from deviations from strict absolute priority.[2] Then $S(V = K(t), t) = c$.

– If there is debt of different seniority classes this can be reflected in an appropriate modification of the payoffs at the default barrier.

• Finally we might want to incorporate interest rate uncertainty. Here we have two alternatives. If we assume correlation between the dynamics of the firm's value and the interest rate dynamics, we will have to add at least one other state variable to our model, the short-term risk-free interest rate r. Assuming a general one-factor model

$$dr = \mu_r(r, t)dt + \sigma_r(r, t)d\widetilde{W},$$

we have instantaneous correlation between dW (the Brownian motion driving the firm's value) and $d\widetilde{W}$ (the Brownian motion driving the interest rates) of ρ, i.e. $dW d\widetilde{W} = \rho dt$. Alternatively, under some assumptions the firm's value process can be independent of the risk-free interest rate dynamics and all interest rate dependence can be eliminated. Thus there is a tradeoff between accuracy (modelling correlation explicitly) and efficiency in the choice of the model. Even if in most practical applications the interest rate correlation is set to zero, it is important to analyse the implications of this assumption in a more general setup to see if an important risk has been ignored.

Bankruptcy costs (or deviation from absolute priority) had to be introduced for a reason: without these costs, the defaultable bonds would not suffer any loss at all at default (if $\overline{D} \leq K(t)$). The creditors can force a liquidation exactly at the time when they would start suffering a loss.

9.1.4 The time of default

In the simplest version of the default model, the time of default τ is the first hitting time of a diffusion process at a fixed barrier. This type of stopping time has some special qualitative properties that affect the shape of the credit spread curves implied by the models.

For simplicity we now consider the case of a standard Brownian motion W started at $W_0 = 1$ and with a barrier $\overline{K} = 0$ at zero. Let $P(t, W)$ be the probability that W has *not* hit the barrier until time T, given that the Brownian motion is at W at time t and that it has not hit the barrier before t.

We know that $P(T, W) = 1$, at $t = T$ there is no time left to hit the barrier and the survival probability is one. We also know that $P(t, 0) = 0$, at $W = 0$ the barrier is already reached and the probability of evading it is zero. On the other hand, $P(t, W) \to 1$ as $W \to \infty$: as W becomes very large the survival probability approaches one.

In the meantime, for $0 < W < \infty$ and $t < T$ we know that P, being a function of W, has to satisfy Itô's lemma:

$$dP = \left(\frac{\partial P}{\partial t} + \frac{1}{2} \frac{\partial^2 P}{\partial W^2} \right) dt + \frac{\partial P}{\partial W} dW.$$

But P cannot have a drift as a stochastic process. P is the best estimate of the survival indicator function $\mathbf{1}_{\{\tau > T\}}$, therefore *all* changes in P have to be purely stochastic and unpredictable. If

---

[2] Empirical studies by Franks and Torous (1994) show that in most bankruptcies and distressed reorganisations some deviation from absolute priority occurs.

there were a positive drift term in dP, we would know that the survival probability tomorrow will be higher than it is today, but this knowledge should already be incorporated in today's probability. Mathematically speaking, if $\tau > t$ we have for all $s > 0$:

$$P(t, W(t)) = \mathbf{E}\big[\mathbf{1}_{\{\tau > T\}}\big] = \mathbf{E}\,[P(t + s, W(t + s))],$$

P has the property that it is its own future expectation, it is a martingale. Here we can use this to set $\mathbf{E}\,[dP] = 0$, and hence the dt term in P must be equal to zero:

$$0 = \frac{\partial P}{\partial t} + \frac{1}{2}\frac{\partial^2 P}{\partial W^2}. \tag{9.7}$$

Equation (9.7) is called the *forward heat equation*. P must satisfy this equation with the final and boundary conditions given above. The solution to this equation is:

$$P(t, W) = N\left(\frac{x}{\sqrt{t}}\right) - N\left(-\frac{x}{\sqrt{t}}\right).$$

Typical credit spreads that result from this survival probability are plotted in Figure 9.3.

We can see that the credit spreads become very low for short times to maturity. This is caused by the very flat shape of the survival probability P as $T - t \to 0$. (Remember that the spreads at the short end are determined by the slope of the survival probabilities.)

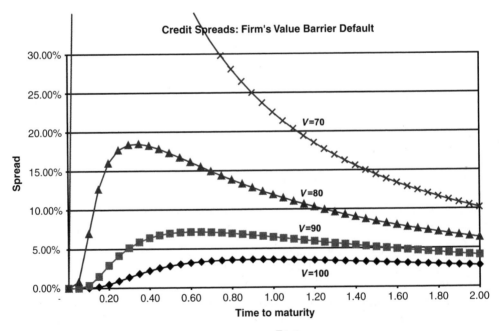

Figure 9.3   Spreads for barrier defaults, $\left(s(T) = -\frac{1}{T}\ln\frac{\bar{B}(0, T)}{B(0, T)} = -\frac{1}{T}\ln P(T, V)\right)$

In firm's value models the probability of a default in a very short time interval $[t, t + \Delta t]$ from t is very small, it is smaller than of order Δt. Even if we divide the default probability by Δt the result goes to zero as $\Delta t \to 0$:

$$\frac{1}{\Delta t}(1 - P(t, t + \Delta t)) \to 0.$$

Intuitively speaking, we know that the firm's value follows a diffusion, that it has continuous paths and cannot jump. So if we know that we are away from the knockout barrier, we also know that the firm's value *cannot* reach it at once – it cannot jump. Therefore the short-term default probability goes to zero very quickly.

This qualitative behaviour of the spread curves will be encountered in *all* diffusion-based models where a default is triggered by the first hitting time of a diffusion process, and it cannot be changed by a different choice of parameters, only by introducing qualitatively different dynamics for the firm's value process.

For more realistic applications we need to know the probability that a Brownian motion with drift (e.g. the log of the firm's value) remains above a certain threshold level at all times in a given time interval. Let

$$dX(t) = \mu_x dt + \sigma_x dW(t),$$

where μ_x and σ_x are constant. Then the probability that $X(s)$ remains above a level $k < X(t)$ at all times $s \in [t, T]$ is

$$P(t, T; X(t) - k) = \mathbf{P}[X(s) > k \; \forall s \in [t, T]]$$
$$= \Phi\left(\frac{\mu_x(T - t) + (X(t) - k)}{\sigma_x\sqrt{T - t}}\right)$$
$$- \exp\left\{-2\frac{(X(t) - k)\mu_x}{\sigma_x^2}\right\}\Phi\left(\frac{\mu_x(T - t) - (X(t) - k)}{\sigma_x\sqrt{T - t}}\right). \quad (9.8)$$

In the Black and Cox (1976) model we have (in logs):

$$d \ln V(t) = \left(r - \tfrac{1}{2}\sigma_V^2\right)dt + \sigma_V dW(t)$$

and the log of the barrier is $\ln K^*$. Then the survival probability is given by (9.8), setting $X(0) := \ln V(0)$, $k = \ln K^*$ and $\mu_X = r - \tfrac{1}{2}\sigma_V^2$.

9.2 PRICING EQUATIONS

9.2.1 The firm's value model

We assume a firm's value process V with

$$\frac{dV}{V} = rdt + \sigma dW, \quad (9.9)$$

an interest rate process r with

$$dr = \mu_r(r, t)dt + \sigma_r(r, t)d\widetilde{W}, \tag{9.10}$$

where $d\widetilde{W}dW = \rho dt$, and a default time τ which is defined as

$$\tau = \min\{t \mid V(t) \leq \overline{K}B(t, T)\},$$

i.e. τ is the first time at which the firm's value V hits the barrier $\overline{K}B(t, T)$.

Traded securities are a share S and a defaultable bond $\overline{B}$ with maturity T. The total numbers of shares $\overline{S}$ and bonds $\overline{D}$, and the constant in the knockout barrier $\overline{K}$, are all normalised to 1. The share pays off

$$S(V, T) = (V - 1)^+$$

at maturity and the bond pays off

$$\overline{B}(V, T) = 1 - (1 - V)^+,$$

assuming there was no default before. If there is a default the defaultable bond pays off

$$\overline{B}(V = \overline{K}B(t, r, T), t) = V - c = B(t, r, T)(\overline{K} - \widetilde{c})$$

and the shares pay off

$$S(V = \overline{K}B(t, r, T), t) = B(t, r, T)\widetilde{c}$$

in default, assuming a deviation from absolute priority by $c = \widetilde{c}B(t, r, T)$ in favour of the shareholders.[3]

Furthermore we have a full term structure of traded default-risk-free bonds $B(t, T)$.

9.2.2   The pricing equation

Like in the introductory example we now consider all securities as derivatives on the firm's value V. There is a knockout barrier at $\overline{K}B(t, T) = B(t, T)$ where the default payoffs are triggered. Otherwise we only have the contractually specified payoffs.

The share and the bond added together have the firm's value as payoff in all states, thus we can consider the firm's value as a traded security. We know that under risk-neutral valuation traded securities have a drift term of rdt, thus

$$dV = rVdt + \sigma VdW. \tag{9.11}$$

We assume that the risk-neutral dynamics of the interest rate is already given by (9.10) so that now everything is ready for the derivation of the pricing equation.

---

[3] Writing the deviation from absolute priority as a proportion $\widetilde{c}$ of the default-free bond price will facilitate the analysis later on.

Bonds and shares are functions of firm's value V, interest rate r and time t. Itô's lemma gives us their dynamics:

$$d\overline{B} = \left(\frac{\partial \overline{B}}{\partial t} + \frac{1}{2}\sigma^2 V^2 \frac{\partial^2 \overline{B}}{\partial V^2} + \rho\sigma\sigma_r V \frac{\partial^2 \overline{B}}{\partial V \partial r} + \frac{1}{2}\sigma_r^2 \frac{\partial^2 \overline{B}}{\partial r^2}\right)dt$$

$$+ \frac{\partial \overline{B}}{\partial V}dV + \frac{\partial \overline{B}}{\partial r}dr, \tag{9.12}$$

the share price dynamics dS are analogous. Now we apply again the fact that the risk-neutral drift must be $r\overline{B}dt$ to reach:

$$r\overline{B}dt = \left(\frac{\partial \overline{B}}{\partial t} + \frac{1}{2}\sigma^2 V^2 \frac{\partial^2 \overline{B}}{\partial V^2} + \rho\sigma\sigma_r V \frac{\partial^2 \overline{B}}{\partial V \partial r} + \frac{1}{2}\sigma_r^2 \frac{\partial^2 \overline{B}}{\partial r^2}\right)dt$$

$$+ rV\frac{\partial \overline{B}}{\partial V}dt + \mu_r \frac{\partial \overline{B}}{\partial r}dt,$$

and hence $\overline{B}$ has to satisfy the partial differential equation

$$0 = \frac{\partial \overline{B}}{\partial t} + \frac{1}{2}\sigma^2 V^2 \frac{\partial^2 \overline{B}}{\partial V^2} + \rho\sigma\sigma_r V \frac{\partial^2 \overline{B}}{\partial V \partial r} + \frac{1}{2}\sigma_r^2 \frac{\partial^2 \overline{B}}{\partial r^2}$$

$$+ rV\frac{\partial \overline{B}}{\partial V} + \mu_r \frac{\partial \overline{B}}{\partial r} - r\overline{B}. \tag{9.13}$$

Equation (9.13) is the fundamental partial differential equation every security has to satisfy. Bonds, shares and all other securities on the firm's value have to satisfy this partial differential equation, they only differ in the final and boundary conditions that apply.

The final condition for the bond is its payoff given no default (as discussed before):

$$\overline{B}(T, V, r) = \min\{1, V\}, \tag{9.14}$$

with boundary conditions:

$$\begin{aligned}
\overline{B} &= B(t, T)(1 - \tilde{c}) & \text{at} \quad & V = \overline{K}B(t, T), \\
\overline{B} &\to B(t, T) & \text{as} \quad & V \to \infty, \\
\overline{B} &\to 0 & \text{as} \quad & r \to \infty, \\
\overline{B} &< \infty & \text{at} \quad & r = 0.
\end{aligned} \tag{9.15}$$

Most of these conditions have an obvious intuitive interpretation except for the condition at $r = 0$, which had to be included to preclude a possible singularity of the solution.

9.2.3 Some other securities

As mentioned before, by applying different boundary and final conditions to (9.13) we can price a variety of other securities.

9.2.3.1   Coupon payments

For *coupon bonds* we need to add the coupon payments to the dynamics of V and the bond price $\overline{B}_c$. At a coupon date T_i the coupon C is paid from the firm's value. Thus the firm's value has to decrease by this amount: $V(T_i+) = V(T_i-) - C$, where $V(T_i-)$ is the firm's value shortly before T_i and $V(T_i+)$ shortly after the coupon payment at T_i.

The bond price has to make the same jump downwards. If a coupon payment is due at T_i, the price shortly *before* the payment, i.e. $\overline{B}_c(T_i-, V(T_i-), r)$ is higher by the amount of the coupon C than the price *after* the coupon payment $\overline{B}_c(T_i+, V(T_i+), r)$. Again we see the similarity to equity options where we have a similar effect at dividend days with discrete dividends. We reach the condition

$$\overline{B}_c(T_i-, V, r) = \overline{B}_c(T_i+, V - C, r) + C. \tag{9.16}$$

Condition (9.16) is easily incorporated in a numerical time-stepping scheme to solve the pricing equation (9.13). The situation does not change for floating-rate coupons except that then C is a function of r: $C = C(r)$.

9.2.3.2   Convertible bonds

A particular strength of the firm's value model is the naturally arising connection between share and bond prices. This can be exploited to price convertible bonds. A convertible bond can be converted into a certain number α of shares of the issuing firm. This conversion can take place either at certain fixed times or at any time. Whenever a conversion is allowed we must have

$$\overline{B}(t, V, r) \geq \alpha S(t, V, r),$$

because we can always convert the bond and secure a payoff of $\alpha S(t, V, r)$. Equality only holds in the above equation when conversion is optimal. Using the relation $V = \overline{B} + S$ this condition becomes

$$\overline{B}(t, V, r) \geq \frac{\alpha}{1 + \alpha} V. \tag{9.17}$$

This condition is similar to the early exercise conditions in American options. In the numerical solution, when stepping backwards in time, condition (9.17) has to be checked whenever conversion is allowed. If the price from the backward-stepping scheme does not satisfy the inequality it has to be adjusted to satisfy (9.17) with equality. At these points one should convert.[4] The optimal exercise boundary is then at the values of the firm's value where conversion just became optimal.

Rule (9.17) takes *dilution* into account. If new shares are issued for the conversion the share price after conversion will be lower than before. After conversion of all bonds we have α

---

[4] It may seem that by adjusting the price upwards by a large amount an arbitrage opportunity is introduced. This is not so: if the price has to be adjusted by a large amount, this means that we have been going backwards in time from a region where conversion was not allowed to a region where conversion is allowed and optimal. Or forward looking: the conversion opportunity is about to end. When it ends and you still hold a bond you have missed the opportunity and lose the value of the conversion, but you should have converted already anyway. You cannot profit from this drop in value as all bonds will have been converted and they would not be available to short for the subsequent drop in value.

additional shares, but no bonds left. Thus $1 + \alpha$ shares own the firm's value V, and one share is worth $S = V/(1 + \alpha)$. Thus, after conversion of the bonds you get $V\alpha/(1 + \alpha)$ exactly as given in equation (9.17).

9.2.3.3 Callable bonds

A callable bond can be bought back by the issuer at prespecified times for a prespecified price B^*. Again this feature has some similarity to American options. Now the issuer has an American call on the bond, and the bondholders are short this call; they have to deliver if their bond is called. Thus there is another inequality the bond price has to satisfy at call dates:

$$\overline{B}(t, V, r) \le B^*.$$

The bond price must be less than the call price (otherwise it will be called).

9.2.3.4 Derivatives on defaultable bonds

A derivative on a defaultable bond is priced in conjunction with the pricing of the underlying bond. Let's assume the derivative has a payoff at time T_1 which is given by the function

$$F(\overline{B}, V, r),$$

which has the price of the defaultable bond $\overline{B}$ with maturity $T_2 > T_1$, the firm's value and the risk-free interest rate as argument.[5]

We could have an option on the defaultable bond, e.g. an exchange option to exchange the defaultable bond $\overline{B}$ for α default-free bonds B of otherwise equivalent specification. Its payoff is

$$F(\overline{B}, V, r) = (\alpha B(T_1, r) - \overline{B}(T_1, V, r))^+.$$

The yield spread of the defaultable bond $\overline{B}$ over the default-free bond B is given by:

$$s(\overline{B}, V, r) = -\frac{\ln \overline{B}(T_1, V, r) - \ln B(T_1, r)}{T_2 - T_1}.$$

We can imagine a large variety of derivatives conditioning on the size of the spread. A caplet for instance would have a payoff like

$$F(\overline{B}, V, r) = L\Delta T(s - \overline{s})^+,$$

where L is the principal and ΔT the time interval.

Besides the regular payoff at T_1, the expiry date of the derivative, we also have to specify the payoff the derivative will have if there is a default before T_1. This depends on the specification of the contract.

---

[5] Strictly speaking the defaultable bond's price $\overline{B}$ is not really needed as an argument of F because it can be represented in terms of V and r itself.

As derivative and underlying both have to satisfy (9.13), they can be priced simultaneously. At each step of the backward induction we now calculate *two* prices, the price of the underlying bond and the price of the derivative. Starting from the maturity T_2 of the underlying bond, equation (9.13) is solved for the price of the underlying until the expiry date T_1 of the derivative. Then the derivative's final condition F can be applied and backwards from there we can solve for both prices simultaneously.

9.2.4 Hedging

In principle and within the model, there is nothing special about delta hedging. Given a price process $C(t, V, r)$ of the security to be hedged, and $\overline{B}(t, V, r)$ and $B(t, r)$ the prices of two hedge instruments, a defaultable bond and a default-risk-free bond, we need two hedge instruments because we have two underlying sources of risk: V and r.

We are looking for values of Δ' and Δ that make the hedged portfolio

$$\Pi = C(t, V, r) + \Delta'\overline{B}(t, V, r) + \Delta B(t, r)$$

locally risk-free. Applying Itô's lemma we see that Δ' and Δ must satisfy

$$-\frac{\partial C}{\partial V} = \Delta'\frac{\partial \overline{B}}{\partial V}, \tag{9.18}$$

$$-\frac{\partial C}{\partial r} = \Delta'\frac{\partial \overline{B}}{\partial r} + \Delta\frac{\partial B}{\partial r}, \tag{9.19}$$

which solves to

$$\Delta' = -\frac{\partial C/\partial V}{\partial \overline{B}/\partial V}, \tag{9.20}$$

$$\Delta = -\frac{1}{\partial B/\partial r}\left(\frac{\partial C}{\partial r} + \Delta'\frac{\partial \overline{B}}{\partial r}\right). \tag{9.21}$$

Obviously, reality is not going to be so kind to us and dynamic risk management of a credit position using shares and equity derivatives can be extremely hard. First of all, there are all the unknown model parameters. Firm's value, firm's value volatility, default barrier and recovery rates are all unknowns, and the strategy must be made robust against errors in the specification of these. This can be achieved by stressing these values and ensuring that the hedged position is not too sensitive to these variations, but frequently there will not be enough hedge instruments available to achieve this.

Second, even if we got all the parameters right initially there can be unexpected events that were not foreseen in the model and that change the parameters again. A large change in the capital structure, for example, caused by a merger or takeover, or a large new issue of debt or convertibles, or even just the expiration and exercise of the management's stock options could all fundamentally change the model's parameters.

Third, even within the model, close to the default barrier we can expect to encounter large gammas. This problem is well known from equity or FX barrier options, but even in these comparatively well-behaved markets it is difficult to hedge.

Fourth, and finally, the assumption of a lognormal random walk for the value of the firm's assets is not to be expected to be true in reality. Almost certainly there will be jumps and other irregularities which will make the hedger's life hard. Given all these fundamental problems which will arise in all firm's value models when they are used for hedging, it is no surprise that the market has a preference for extremely simple models – the simpler the model, the easier it is to understand. And then we at least know exactly *which* mistakes we are making.

9.3 SOLUTIONS TO THE PRICING EQUATION

The results of this section are a special case of the results of Briys and de Varenne (1997). For details and extensions we refer to this reference.

We will assume a one-factor Gaussian term structure model of the Ho and Lee (1986) type for the initial term structure of defaultable bonds. This means that the risk-neutral dynamics of the default-free zero-coupon bond with maturity T are given by:

$$\frac{dB}{B} = rdt + \sigma_r(T - t)dW_1. \tag{9.22}$$

Furthermore we rewrite the dynamics of the firm's value process as:

$$\frac{dV}{V} = rdt + \sigma_V\left(\rho dW_1 + \sqrt{1 - \rho^2}\,dW_2\right). \tag{9.23}$$

In equation (9.23) we have explicitly represented the correlation between firm's value and interest rates with ρ and two orthogonal (= uncorrelated) Brownian motions W_1 and W_2.

9.3.1 The T-forward measure

The price of a defaultable zero-coupon bond can be represented as

$$\overline{B} = B(1 - cP^T[\tau < T]) = B(1 - c(1 - P^T[\tau \geq T])), \tag{9.24}$$

where P^T denotes the probability under the T-forward measure and B is the price of a default-free zerobond with maturity T.

The event $\{\tau \geq T\}$ is equivalent to

$$\{\tau \geq T\} \Leftrightarrow \{\tilde{V} \geq \overline{K}\ \forall t \leq T\} \tag{9.25}$$

where $\tilde{V} = V/B$ has the following dynamics under P^T:

$$\frac{d\tilde{V}}{\tilde{V}} = (\rho\sigma_V - \sigma_r(T - t))dW_1^T + \sigma_V\sqrt{1 - \rho^2}dW_2^T$$
$$=: \sigma(t)d\widehat{W}, \tag{9.26}$$

where

$$\sigma(t) = \left[\sigma_V^2 - 2\rho\sigma_V\sigma_r(T - t) + \sigma_r^2(T - t)^2\right]^{1/2} \tag{9.27}$$

and $\widehat{W}$ is a Brownian motion constructed from W_1^T and W_2^T. Now we have reduced the problem to calculating the probability of the event given in (9.25), the hitting probability of the process $\tilde{V}$ which follows a geometric Brownian motion (9.26) with time-dependent volatility (9.27).

9.3.2 Time change

To eliminate the time dependence in the volatility $\sigma(t)$ we perform the following time change. Consider the process M given by:

$$dM = \sigma(t)d\widehat{W}.$$

Its quadratic variation is given by:

$$\langle M \rangle_t =: Q(t) = \int_0^t \sigma(s)^2 ds$$
$$= -\sigma_V^2(T-t) + \rho\sigma_V\sigma_r(T-t)^2 - \tfrac{1}{3}\sigma_r^2(T-t)^3$$
$$+ \sigma_V^2 T - \rho\sigma_V\sigma_r T^2 + \tfrac{1}{3}\sigma_r^2 T^3,$$

and the value of this process M_t at time t can be represented as the value of a Brownian motion $W_{Q(t)}$ at time $Q(t)$. M is a time-changed Brownian motion (see Karatzas and Shreve, 1991, theorem 3.4.6, p. 174):

$$M_t = W_{Q(t)}.$$

Also (and equally important to us) we can define the same time change for $\tilde{V}$:

$$Y_{Q(t)} = \tilde{V}_t.$$

Then (Karatzas and Shreve, 1991, theorem 3.4.8, p. 176):

$$\tilde{V}_t = \int_0^t \tilde{V}_v dM_v = \int_0^{Q(t)} Y_u dW_u = Y_{Q(t)}. \tag{9.28}$$

The right-hand side of (9.28) means nothing but that Y satisfies the stochastic differential equation

$$dY = Y dW. \tag{9.29}$$

Y follows a lognormal random walk itself and it does not have any time-dependent volatility.

9.3.3 The hitting probability

Next we look back at the event given in (9.25) whose probability we need to calculate:

$$\{\tilde{V} \geq \overline{K} \; \forall t \leq T\}$$
$$\Leftrightarrow \{Y \geq \overline{K} \; \forall t \leq Q(T)\}$$
$$\Leftrightarrow \left\{ \ln \frac{Y}{Y_0} \geq \ln \frac{\overline{K}}{Y_0} \; \forall t \leq Q(T) \right\}. \tag{9.30}$$

We know that $x := \ln Y$ follows the diffusion

$$dx = -\tfrac{1}{2}dt + dW,$$

and its barrier hitting probability is well known (see e.g. Musiela and Rutkowski, 1997, corollary B.3.4, p. 340 or (9.8)). The probability of the event given in (9.30) is

$$N\left(\frac{k + \tfrac{1}{2}Q(T)}{\sqrt{Q(T)}}\right) - e^{-2k} N\left(\frac{-k + \tfrac{1}{2}Q(T)}{\sqrt{Q(T)}}\right),$$

where $k = \ln Y_0 - \ln \overline{K}$ is the barrier.

9.3.4 Putting it together

Now we can substitute our results in equation (9.24):

$$\overline{B} = B(1 - c(1 - P)), \tag{9.31}$$

where P is given by

$$P = N\left(\frac{k + \tfrac{1}{2}Q(T)}{\sqrt{Q(T)}}\right) - e^{-2k} N\left(\frac{-k + \tfrac{1}{2}Q(T)}{\sqrt{Q(T)}}\right) \tag{9.32}$$

with k and $Q(T)$ given by

$$k = \ln \frac{V_0}{B_0 \overline{K}}, \tag{9.33}$$

$$Q(T) = \sigma_V^2 T - \rho \sigma_V \sigma_r T^2 + \tfrac{1}{3}\sigma_r^2 T^3. \tag{9.34}$$

In this pricing formula we still have scope to fit the risk-free term structure to an initial term structure.

9.3.5 The Longstaff–Schwartz results

Longstaff and Schwartz (1995) use a slight modification of the model proposed above to reach semi-closed-form solutions for defaultable zero-coupon bonds and floating-rate bonds.

In their model the risk-free interest rate follows the Vasicek process

$$dr = (\zeta - \beta r)dt + \sigma_r d\widetilde{W}$$

with instantaneous correlation of ρ between W and $\widetilde{W}$. The firm's value follows the same lognormal diffusion process as given in (9.9), and a default is triggered when V reaches a threshold value K^*. In default the bondholders are paid $(1 - c)$ default-risk-free bonds of the same specification. The partial differential equation they solve is exactly equivalent to (9.13). In this framework the price of a defaultable zero-coupon bond is

$$\overline{B}(T, X, r) = B(r, T)(1 - cQ(X, r, T)), \tag{9.35}$$

where $X = V/K^*$ and $B(r, t)$ is the value of a default-free zerobond of the same maturity. The function Q is given by

$$Q(X, r, T) = \lim_{n \to \infty} Q(X, r, T, n),$$

where

$$Q(X, r, T, n) = \sum_{i=1}^{n} q_i$$

and the q_i are defined recursively by

$$q_1 = N(a_1),$$

$$q_i = N(a_i) - \sum_{j=1}^{i-1} q_j N(b_{ij}).$$

The parameters a_i and b_{ij} are now given by:

$$a_i = \frac{-\ln X - M(iT/n, T)}{\sqrt{S(iT/n)}},$$

$$b_{ij} = \frac{M(jT/n, T) - M(iT/n, T)}{\sqrt{S(iT/n) - S(jT/n)}}.$$

Here we used the functions M and S, which are

$$M(t, T) = \left(\frac{\zeta - \rho\sigma\sigma_r}{\beta} - \frac{\eta^2}{\beta^2} - \frac{\sigma^2}{2} \right) t$$

$$+ \left(\frac{\rho\sigma\sigma_r}{\beta^2} + \frac{\eta^2}{2\beta^3} \right) \exp(-\beta T)(\exp(\beta t) - 1)$$

$$+ \left(\frac{r}{\beta} - \frac{\alpha}{\beta^2} + \frac{\sigma_r^2}{\beta^3} \right)(1 - \exp(-\beta t))$$

$$- \frac{\sigma_r^2}{2\beta^3} \exp(-\beta T)(1 - \exp(-\beta t))$$

and

$$S(t) = \left(\frac{\rho\sigma\sigma_r}{\beta} + \frac{\eta^2}{\beta^2} + \sigma^2 \right) t$$

$$- \left(\frac{\rho\sigma\sigma_r}{\beta^2} + \frac{2\eta^2}{\beta^3} \right)(1 - \exp(-\beta t))$$

$$+ \frac{\sigma_r^2}{2\beta^3}(1 - \exp(-2\beta t)).$$

This is a rather long and involved expression which only qualifies as a semi-closed form because of the limit $n \rightarrow \infty$ that has to be taken. In fact the expression is nothing but a numerical approximation scheme to an integral equation that is encountered when solving the problem. Longstaff and Schwartz propose using $n = 200$ as an approximation to the infinite sum. This would imply $\frac{1}{2} \times 200(200 - 1) = 19\,900$ evaluations of the cumulative standard normal distribution function, and the number of other time-intensive operations like square roots, logarithms and exponentials is of the same order of magnitude. Thus the formula given by Longstaff and Schwartz will not necessarily be quicker to use than a fast finite-difference approximation to the pricing equation (9.13) which only uses fast multiplications and additions.[6]

Another problem is that the model as it stands does not allow for fitting of the interest rate model to an initial term structure or any other modification of the model, which makes it highly inflexible. Nevertheless the formula above has been successfully used in practice.

9.3.6 Strategic default

Recently (Leland, 1994; Leland and Toft, 1996; Mella-Barral and Perraudin, 1997), a new class of firm's value-based models have been put forward in the literature on continuous-time corporate finance with the aim of removing some empirical inconsistencies of the classical Black/Scholes/Merton-based models. These models are characterised by:

- Endogenous capital structure and default barrier;
- Time-independent capital structure – large degree of analytical tractability;
- The ability to study the effects of different bankruptcy regimes and fundamental questions like the asset substitution effect or incentive problems.

Although much of this literature addresses more fundamental questions, we present these models here because of their large degree of analytical tractability.

One of the first models of this class was developed by Leland (1994). In this model, the value of firm's *assets* follows a geometrical Brownian motion:

$$dV = rV\,dt + \sigma V\,dW.$$

In order to reach a time-invariant problem, the debt is assumed to have an infinite maturity, with an aggregate coupon of C, and a market price of $\overline{B}$. Debt generates a *tax benefit* of $\tau^* C\,dt$ (this is necessary to give the firm's owners an incentive in the model to issue debt).

Default occurs at a barrier V_B of V. At default, debt recovers $(1 - \alpha)V_B$ and there are bankruptcy costs of αV_B. This constitutes a disadvantage of debt which must balance the tax advantage of debt in the optimum.

The model has *endogenous bankruptcies*: the firm's management (i.e. the equity holders) can choose the bankruptcy level V_B, provided they ensure that the coupon will always be paid. This gives equity the option to postpone bankruptcy and pay the coupon from their own pocket if they consider the upside in the firm attractive enough.

---

[6] Even if it is not directly apparent to the user, advanced functions (like square roots or exponentials) are several hundred times slower than basic multiplications or additions. The cumulative normal distribution function is again very much slower to evaluate.

9.3.6.1 Debt valuation

Every time step dt, a coupon of $C dt$ is paid to the debtholders. This is financed by issuance of new equity, while the dynamics of V remain unchanged.

The standard arguments allow us to derive a pricing ordinary differential equation for all claims on V, in particular also for debt:

$$0 = \frac{1}{2}\sigma^2 V^2 \frac{\partial^2}{\partial V^2}\overline{B} + rV\frac{\partial}{\partial V}\overline{B} - r\overline{B} + C$$

with boundary conditions $\overline{B} \to C/r$ as $V \to \infty$ and $\overline{B} = (1 - \alpha)V_B$ at $V = V_B$.

The solution to the bond pricing equation is

$$\overline{B} = (1 - p_B)\frac{C}{r} + p_B(1 - \alpha)V_B$$

where

$$p_B = \left(\frac{V}{V_B}\right)^{-X}, \quad X = 2r/\sigma^2$$

p_B is the present value of receiving 1 at default.

Then $p_B(1 - \alpha)V_B$ represents the value of recoveries for the default strategy V_B, and $(1 - p_B)\tau^* C$ represents the value of the tax benefits of debt. From this, the total value of the firm can be derived:

$$
\begin{aligned}
\text{[Market value of the firm]} &= \text{[Value of equity]} \\
&\quad + \text{[Value of debt]} \\
&= \text{[Value of assets]} \\
&\quad + \text{[Value of tax break]} \\
&\quad - \text{[Value of bankruptcy costs]}.
\end{aligned}
$$

We can solve this for the value of equity

$$E = V - (1 - \tau^*)C/r + ((1 - \tau^*)C/r - V_B)p_B.$$

As equity can choose the default barrier V_B at any time, they will choose V_B in order to maximise this expression, *not* to maximise the total value of the firm. Once the debt has been successfully issued, equity does not care about the value of its debt.

The optimal choice of bankruptcy barrier will have the following properties:

- Equityholders will *hold off* bankruptcy. . . .
- until the value of the *gamble for resurrection* is less than the cash needed to keep the firm alive.
- Bankruptcy occurs at asset levels significantly *below* the outstanding debt level.

Empirical tests seem to indicate that this model setup performs as well (or as badly) as the classical Merton (1974) or Black and Cox (1976) setups.

9.4   A PRACTICAL IMPLEMENTATION: KMV

When one tries to implement even a very simple firm's value-based model like the Merton (1974) model, the largest obstacle is the fact that most of the fundamental model quantities are *not* readily observable, let alone their dynamics. In this section we show how these problems may be overcome in practice, and which compromises must be taken, e.g. in the implementation of the model marketed by Moody's (KMV).[7]

9.4.1   The default point

According to the KMV model, the default point is the "asset value at which the firm will default". As real-world balance sheets are not as simple as Table 9.1, the problem is to draw the borderline between equity and debt, in particular as there can be a large variety of liabilities: senior, junior, junior subordinated, preferred shares, convertible bonds, pension obligations, long-term and short-term debt, and so on.

The KMV model proposes to put the default point somewhere between the face value of total (including long-term) liabilities and the face value of short-term liabilities. As the firm must regularly refinance its short-term liabilities it will not be able to continue operating if these are not fully covered. With long-term liabilities on the other hand the firm may very well survive a temporary dip into the negative, as for these liabilities the refinancing need does not arise. Implicitly, a barrier model assumption is made in this setup.

9.4.2   The time horizon

The time horizon T is an innocent-looking parameter that is usually set to one or five years, depending on the problem to be solved. The reader should be warned that – although it *looks* innocent – the time horizon T can have a significant effect on the results of the model. We have seen that the default probabilities (and credit spreads) in firm's value models start at zero for very short time horizons and have a hump-shaped form after that. By choosing the time horizon we choose how far we are moving towards (or beyond) the peak of that hump: this can have a significant effect on the results. The only model-consistent way of choosing the time horizon is to adapt it to the pricing model encountered, i.e. to the maturity of the defaultable security that one wants to price. Another alternative is to choose a time-invariant model like the Leland (1994) model presented before. But still, when the survival probabilities are calculated, a time horizon must be chosen.

9.4.3   The initial value of the firm's assets and its volatility

The large degree of freedom in the choice of asset valuation methods for accounting purposes makes it impossible to infer the value V of the firm's assets from the firm's balance sheet. It

---

[7] KMV (named after the founders Kealhover, McQuown and Vasicek) was taken over by Moody's in February 2002 and is now named "Moody's KMV". Nevertheless, their modelling approach had become known as the "KMV model" before the takeover and (when referring to the model rather than the firm) we will just speak of "the KMV model".

is therefore common to infer this value and its volatility from market-based information: the market capitalisation of the firm and the volatility of its shares.

Call S' the observed value of the firm's market capitalisation (i.e. the share price multiplied by the number of shares outstanding). In the Merton model, we can represent S as a function of the following variables:

$$S' = C^{\mathrm{BS}}(V, \sigma_V; \, r, T, \overline{D}), \qquad (9.36)$$

where C^{BS} is the Black-Scholes call option pricing formula.

Secondly, we assume that we can observe a volatility σ_S of the equity price process. This can either be a historical volatility, or an option-implied volatility. The observation tells us that

$$dS' \approx S' \sigma_S dW. \qquad (9.37)$$

On the other hand, we can directly apply Itô's lemma to (9.36) to reach the *theoretical* dynamics of the share prices

$$dS' = (\ldots)dt + C_V^{\mathrm{BS}}(V, \sigma_V, \ldots)V\sigma_V dW, \qquad (9.38)$$

where $C_V^{\mathrm{BS}}(\cdot)$ denotes the first derivative of the call option formula (9.36) with respect to V. We can now equate the dW terms in equations (9.37) and (9.38) to reach

$$S'\sigma_S = V\sigma_V C_V^{\mathrm{BS}}. \qquad (9.39)$$

Strictly speaking, equation (9.39) is not valid, because in the estimation of σ_S in equation (9.37) it was implicitly assumed that the *share price* volatility of the firm is constant, while equation (9.38) clearly implies that the volatility is *not* constant but a nonlinear function of V and σ_V. Nevertheless, the estimation error in equation (9.37) is probably larger, and it would be hard to distinguish between the two specifications. Thus we can view (9.39) as a first approximation and not an exact relationship, but it will give largely realistic values.

If equation (9.39) is still too nonlinear, it can be approximated further by setting the partial derivative C_V^{BS} of the share to 1. If the option is deep in-the-money (i.e. the firm is far from default) this will be a good approximation. We therefore reach the following set of equations:

$$S' = C^{\mathrm{BS}}(V, \sigma_V; \, r, T, \overline{D}), \qquad (9.40)$$
$$S'\sigma_S = V\sigma_V C_V^{\mathrm{BS}}, \qquad (9.41)$$

where we have only observable quantities on the left-hand side, and two unknowns V and σ_V on the right-hand side. Although these two equations are nonlinear, a numerical root searcher usually quickly finds a solution (V, σ_V) this is consistent with (S', σ_S).

9.4.4 The distance to default

The KMV model does *not* follow the Merton model to its logical conclusion, which would be to *price and imply the default probabilities within the model.* Instead of this, they only use the Black and Scholes (1973)/Merton (1974) setup as motivation for a summary statistic for the credit quality of the obligor in question (something like a new accounting ratio, but based upon market data and not only accounting data).

The *distance to default* (DtD) is the d_2 of the Black–Scholes formula, if smaller terms (like r or $\frac{1}{2}\sigma^2$) are ignored[8] and $T = 1$ it is

$$[\text{Distance to default}] = \frac{\ln[\text{Market value of assets}] - \ln[\text{Default point}]}{[\text{Asset volatility}]}$$

The name "distance to default" was chosen because d_2 gives the standardised distance (i.e. distance in standard deviations) of the initial value of V from $\overline{D}$.

This new "key accounting ratio" of the firm is assumed to contain all default-relevant information, and is used in table lookup/univariate scoring models to compare with the default experience of other firms that had the same DtD using the Moody's KMV proprietary defaults database.

This yields the **expected default frequency**, the frequency with which firms of the same distance to default have defaulted in history. In the calibration to historical data the KMV model leaves the modelling framework of a firm's value model. It should rather be viewed as a (probably good) statistical scoring model with a large historical database and a very specific definition of the key model quantity.

9.5   UNOBSERVABLE FIRM'S VALUES AND CREDITGRADES

Let us now return to the basic Black and Cox (1976) barrier defaults model as described at the beginning of this chapter.

- The firm's value follows a lognormal Brownian motion with zero drift (this is assumed for simplicity):

$$dV = \sigma V dW.$$

- Defaults occur as soon as the firm's value hits a constant barrier $\overline{K}$:

$$\tau = \inf\{t\, V(t) \le \overline{K}\}.$$

- Interest rates are set to zero for simplicity.

The survival probability until T in this setup is given by

$$P(0, T; V(0) = V) = \Phi\left(\frac{-\frac{1}{2}\sigma^2 T + \ln(V/\overline{K})}{\sigma\sqrt{T}}\right) - \left(\frac{V}{\overline{K}}\right)\Phi\left(\frac{-\frac{1}{2}\sigma^2 T - \ln(V/\overline{K})}{\sigma_x\sqrt{T-t}}\right). \quad (9.42)$$

As demonstrated before, one particular property of this model (and all firm's value models considered so far) is the fact that they produce *zero* credit spreads for very short maturities. Fundamentally, this problem is caused by the fact that if there is a *finite distance* to the barrier,

---

[8] Moody's KMV are very secretive about the internals of their model, and in some publications slightly different definitions of the distance to default are used.

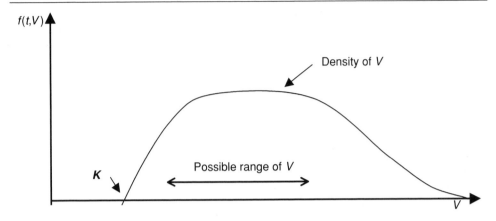

Figure 9.4 The conditional density of the true location of V in the Duffie–Lando model

a *continuous process* cannot reach it in the next instance. Now, the question is how to avoid zero short-term spreads. There are two fundamental ideas that can be followed here:

- Introduce jumps in the firm's value V. Then the firm's value can move a large distance in one step. (This idea was, for example, implemented in Zhou, 2001.)
- Maybe the default barrier is indeed closer than we thought. Then it will not have to move very far after all. This approach goes back to Duffie and Lando (1997) and was later also partially used in Giesecke (2001) and the CreditGrades E2C model of Finger *et al.* (2002).

The idea of Duffie and Lando (1997) is the following: defaults happen when the firm's value $V(t)$ hits a lower barrier $\overline{K}(t)$ *but we do not know the true value of the firm.* What we do know at time t is the following (see Figure 9.4).

- $V(t) > \overline{K}(t)$: There is no default right now.
- $f(t, v)$: We have some prior probability density function for our guess (at time t) where $V(t)$ actually is. This density has the following properties.
  - $f(t, \overline{K}) = 0$: We know that the firm's value is above the barrier.
  - $\mathbf{P}[V(t) \in [v, v + dv]] = f(t, v)dv.$
  - We also assume $f(t, \cdot)$ is continuous in $\overline{K}$ and that f has a derivative from the right in $\overline{K}$.
- We also know the dynamics of V (μ_V and σ_V can even be stochastic).

Given this information, we must now analyse how a default can happen over the next small time step $[t, t + dt]$ in this setup. Naturally, it must be through the movement of the firm's value, and to assess the potential movements of the firm's value over one small time step we use the following mathematical result (see Karatzas and Shreve, 1991 for more details and proofs). The *law of the iterated logarithm* gives the size of the local fluctuations of a Brownian motion:

Over a small time interval $[t, t + \Delta t]$ the Brownian motion will fluctuate up and down by $\pm\sqrt{\Delta t}$ with probability 1. Not more, not less.

This holds in the limit as $\Delta t \to 0$. In fact, the statement of the law of the iterated logarithm[9] is even slightly stronger. The Brownian motion will almost surely hit

$$\pm\sqrt{\Delta t} \, \ln\left(\ln\left(\frac{1}{\Delta t}\right)\right),$$

but it will not exceed these values.

Thus, over a small time interval $[t, t + \Delta t]$ the worst movement for V is therefore:[10]

$$\Delta V^{\text{bad}} = \mu_V \Delta t - \sigma_V \sqrt{\Delta t}.$$

If we can observe V with certainty, there are two cases.

(i) $V(t) > \overline{K} + \sigma_V \sqrt{\Delta t}$: V is too far away from the barrier. No default will happen, even for the worst-case movement. (This is why we usually have zero spreads in all diffusion-based models.)

(ii) $\overline{K} < V(t) \leq \overline{K} + \sigma_V \sqrt{\Delta t}$: V is very close to the barrier. Here a default can happen over the next time step. As $\Delta t \to 0$ we know that it will indeed happen because the barrier is hit almost surely in the law of the iterated logarithm.

In the setup with an unknown default barrier, we must calculate the probability of being in case (ii) in order to reach the probability of default over the next Δt. This is where we need the conditional density:

$$\mathbf{P}\big[\overline{K} < V(t) \leq \overline{K} + \sigma_V \sqrt{\Delta t}\big] = \int_{\overline{K}}^{\overline{K}+\sigma_V \sqrt{\Delta t}} f(t, v)dv.$$

As we are only interested in the area very close to the default barrier, we make a Taylor approximation around $\overline{K}$. By assumption on f we know that $f(t, \overline{K}) = 0$ and f is approximately linear over small intervals:

$$f(t, x) \approx f(t, \overline{K}) + f'(t, \overline{K})(x - \overline{K}) = f'(t, \overline{K})(x - \overline{K})$$

for $x - \overline{K}$ small. Figure 9.5 shows this critical area.

Thus the probability of being close to a default is:

$$\mathbf{P}[\overline{K} < V(t) \leq \overline{K} + \sigma_V \sqrt{\Delta t}] = \int_{\overline{K}}^{\overline{K}+\sigma_V \sqrt{\Delta t}} f(t, v)dv$$

$$= f'(t, \overline{K}) \int_{\overline{K}}^{\overline{K}+\sigma_V \sqrt{\Delta t}} (v - \overline{K})dv$$

$$= f'(t, \overline{K}) \int_0^{\sigma_V \sqrt{\Delta t}} v\,dv = f'(t, \overline{K}) \, \tfrac{1}{2} \sigma_V^2 \, \Delta t.$$

---

[9] Formally, the statement is: $\lim\sup_{h\to 0} W(h)/(\sqrt{h}\,\ln(\ln(1/h))) = 1$, and the same for $\lim\inf$ with -1.

[10] We will ignore the $\ln\ln(1/\Delta t)$ term because it grows far too slowly to have an effect. Its greatest effect was probably to give the name to this theorem.

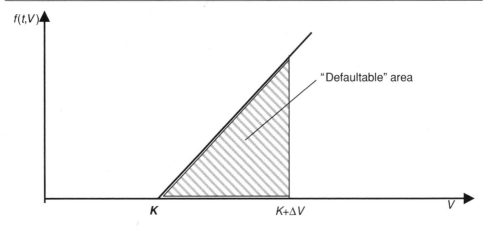

Figure 9.5   The critical area of the conditional density of V close to $\overline{K}$ in the Duffie–Lando model

Summing up – over a small time interval $[t, t + \Delta t]$ from the point of view of the uninformed investor, the probability of default is proportional to the length of that time interval:

$$\lim_{\Delta t \to 0} \frac{1}{\Delta t} \mathbf{P}[\text{default in } [t, t + \Delta t]] = \tfrac{1}{2}\sigma_V^2 f'(t, \overline{K}).$$

This defines the defaults as a process with an intensity

$$\lambda = \lim_{\Delta t \to 0} \frac{1}{\Delta t}\left[\tfrac{1}{2}\sigma_V^2 f'(t, \overline{K})\Delta t\right] = \tfrac{1}{2}\sigma_V^2 f'(t, \overline{K}).$$

Summing up – from the point of view of the investor, defaults are triggered by a jump process with intensity

$$\tfrac{1}{2}\sigma_V^2 f'(t, \overline{K}).$$

The "steeper" the conditional density f is at $\overline{K}$, the more probability mass is close to $\overline{K}$ and the higher the likelihood of a default. As time proceeds, we need to update f after the next time step. This can get very complicated, but there is a simple special case.

9.5.1   A simple special case: delayed observation

Consider the following setup:

- At time t, we do not observe $V(t)$ but only $V(t - \Delta) = v$ where $\Delta > 0$ is a positive number, the *observation delay*. For example, we may only get the accounting numbers of one quarter/one year ago.
- We also observe if there was a default in $[t - \Delta, t]$.

Our conditional distribution of the firm's value given this information is therefore:

$$\mathbf{P}[V(t) \leq H \mid \mathcal{F}_t] = \mathbf{P}[V(t) \leq H \mid \{V(t-\Delta) = v\} \wedge \{V(s) > \overline{K} \; \forall s \in [t-\Delta, t]\}].$$

This is known in closed form. Let $dV/V = \mu dt + \sigma dW$, $V(0) = V_0$ and $m_V(T) := \min_{t \leq T} V(t)$. Then:

$$\mathbf{P}[V(T) \geq H \; \wedge \; m_V(T) \geq \overline{K}] = N(d_3) - \left(\frac{\overline{K}}{V_0}\right)^{(2\mu/\sigma^2)-1} N(d_4),$$

where

$$d_3 = \frac{\ln(V_0/H) + (\mu - \frac{1}{2}\sigma^2)T}{\sigma\sqrt{T}},$$

$$d_4 = \frac{\ln(\overline{K}^2/(V_0 H)) + (\mu - \frac{1}{2}\sigma^2)T}{\sigma\sqrt{T}}.$$

The conditional density is useful if we want to value equity of the firm. For *debt* of the firm (i.e. survival probabilities), on the other hand, we have an elegant shortcut. The probability of survival from t to T given a delayed observation of the firm's value $V_0 = SV(t-\Delta)$ and the information that we have not had a default in $[t-\Delta, t]$ equals (by definition) the *conditional survival probability from* $t' + \Delta$ *to* $T' + \Delta$ in a model without delay where the current firm's value is V_0 and we condition on survival.

In Section 3.1.5 we have already analysed in detail how to reach a conditional survival probability from a set of unconditional survival probabilities: we divide. Thus we directly reach the term structure of survival probabilities under delayed observation as a simple ratio of undelayed observed survival probabilities $P'(t, T)$:

$$P^{\Delta \text{delayed}}(t, T, V_0) = \frac{P'(t, T + \Delta, V_0)}{P'(t, \Delta, V_0)}. \tag{9.43}$$

Summing up – assuming a delayed observation of the firm's value which is delayed by Δ moves us Δ forward on the original spread curve. But the firm's value models only had zero spreads at the (undelayed) very short end, so with a bit of delay we will move into the positive area and have much more realistic term structures of credit spreads without having to make the model any more complicated. Only one new parameter Δ was introduced and the survival probability calculations can be re-used from the undelayed case using (9.43).

9.5.2 The idea of Lardy and Finkelstein: CreditGrades and E2C

The idea of Finger *et al.* (2002)[11] was slightly different. In their model setup, again defaults happen when the firm's value $V(t)$ hits a lower barrier $\overline{K}$ but *we do not know the true value of the lower barrier.* The lower barrier is random and drawn once at the beginning at $t = 0$, after

---

[11] CreditGrades and E2C (equity to credit) are essentially the same model under different names. Giesecke (2001) very carefully analyses an essentially similar model in the multivariate case.

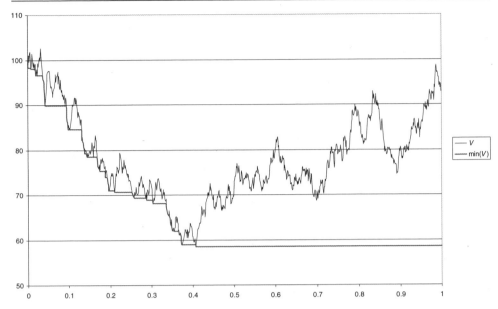

Figure 9.6 A typical firm's value process and its running minimum in the CreditGrades/E2C model

that it is constant. This is *almost* the same as Duffie/Lando, but unfortunately not exactly. The consequences for the dynamics of the model are quite drastic. To see this let us analyse the new information now:

- We know today's (time t) firm's value.
- We know that no default has occurred yet.
- Hence, the barrier must be *less than the running minimum of the firm's value up to now*.

If the barrier was anywhere above the current running minimum, we would have defaulted when we reached that minimum point (or even earlier). But we are still alive, so this cannot be the case. Figure 9.6 shows a sample path of the firm's value process and its running minimum.

The consequence is that for any $t > 0$, as long as we are above the running minimum, the local default probability is zero because we are a positive distance away from the current running minimum level. And that is just the point where the risk starts: It does not mean that we really must default if we hit the running minimum. The credit spread curves will be zero at the short end and should be even flatter at the short end than for a "normal" barrier model like the Black–Cox model.

In his analysis of this model setup Giesecke (2001) finds the following:

- The default compensator behaves like the running maximum of a diffusion process. That is, it is constant up to a small set of points of increase, non-decreasing and not differentiable at points of increase.
- The time of default is totally inaccessible but a default intensity does not exist.
- Unless $V(t)$ happens to equal its current running minimum, we again have zero short-term credit spreads for any $t > 0$.

Concretely, the CreditGrades model is specified as follows:

- The firm's value follows the usual lognormal random walk.
- At $t = 0$, a *random default threshold* L is drawn. L is lognormally distributed with

$$LD = \overline{L}De^{\lambda Z - \frac{1}{2}\lambda^2},$$

where $\overline{L}$ is the mean of L, λ the standard deviation of $\log L$ and Z is a $\Phi(0, 1)$ standard normal random variable. D is the debt per share of the firm (all quantities are set up in per share units).

- Defaults occur as soon as $V(\tau) \le LD$.

The stochastic barrier L is interpreted as a *stochastic recovery*, and it is assumed that the recovery of a defaultable bond is indeed L. Accordingly, $\overline{L}$ is interpreted as *average recovery* and λ as *recovery rate volatility*.

After some algebra, the CreditGrades authors reach the following approximation for the survival probability: (It is not exact, only an approximation.)

$$P(t) = \Phi\left(-\frac{A_t}{2} + \frac{\log(d)}{A_t}\right) - d \cdot \Phi\left(-\frac{A_t}{2} - \frac{\log(d)}{A_t}\right), \qquad (9.44)$$

where

$$A_t^2 = \sigma^2 t + \lambda^2,$$

$$d = \frac{V_0 e^{\lambda^2}}{\overline{L}D}.$$

Part of the CreditGrades package is a calibration procedure. For this, it is essentially assumed that

$$S = V - \overline{L}D,$$

i.e. the "option" of the share price is reduced to its intrinsic value. Under this (very strong) assumption, the calibration is straightforward. Firm's value and firm's value volatility are:

$$V = S + \overline{L}D, \qquad \sigma_V = \sigma_S \frac{S}{S + \overline{L}D}.$$

Furthermore, $\overline{L}$ is set to a historical average recovery rate (0.5), and λ to a historically plausible recovery rate volatility (0.3). The debt per share D is taken from balance sheet data. S is the current share price, and for σ_S a 750–1000-day historical average volatility is used.

The model setup has the following consequences. In the CreditGrades model, there is a discrete, positive probability of default at $t = 0$. This can be seen by substituting $t = 0$ in (9.44). The reason is that – when the barrier is drawn initially at $t = 0$ – nothing stops the barrier from being above the initial firm's value V_0. So, if we are unlucky, we die even before we started. Second, at $t = 0$ there will be positive short-term credit spreads. But we already saw that for $t > 0$ the short-term credit spreads will be zero almost surely. Being at the new running minimum has probability zero for any given time, and that is the only place where short-term spreads will be positive. Thus the short-term credit spreads will jump to zero immediately after $t = 0$. These are quite unrealistic dynamics, and if the dynamics are unrealistic, using the model for hedging is dangerous because hedge ratios should usually be calculated on the basis of the model's dynamics. For simple credit pricing at $t = 0$ (i.e. without using the model's dynamics), the model may be acceptable and give sensible results. But whatever model one uses, one should always be aware of the shortcomings and implications of the model.

9.6   ADVANTAGES AND DISADVANTAGES

9.6.1   Empirical evidence

The firm's value models make strong predictions on the dynamics of share and debt prices of firms, which have been tested against empirical data.

9.6.1.1   Shape of credit spreads

The Merton model (and most other firm's value models) predict a humped shape for the term structure of credit spreads. While this seems to be the case for bad rating classes, at least in investment-grade credits there is some evidence against humps and for increasing credit spreads. The empirical investigations are the following.

- Litterman and Iben (1991): Anecdotal evidence for increasing spread structures.
- Sarig and Warga (1989): Negative slope.
- Helwege and Turner (1999): Positive slope for speculative grade (<BB) debt for each issuer. The negative slope in Sarig and Warga is due to a selection bias: better quality issuers tend to be able to issue longer dated debt.

9.6.1.2   Ranking of issuers

The next set of tests investigates whether firm's value-based approaches are able to reproduce the risk ranking of obligors that is found in the market. It is admitted that there may be (rather large) pricing errors, but this test checks whether the firm's value models are able to distinguish between riskier and less risky issuers.

Lardic and Rouzeau (1999) performed a study on this using corporate bonds issued by French firms. They compared the theoretical (model) prices of the bonds (using balance sheet and share prices) with the observed market prices of these bonds. It turned out that the theoretical prices did *not* reproduce the risk ranking in the market, i.e. the model classified a significant number of issuers as less risky than others even though the bond market indicated the converse. Nevertheless, the *movements* of theoretical and empirical spreads seemed cointegrated, which means that the firm's value models were able to pick up changes in the credit quality of the same obligor.

9.6.1.3   Credit spread movements

If credit spread movements could be accurately predicted (independent of share price movements), this would enable us to use the firm's value models for hedging purposes.

Longstaff and Schwartz (1995) analysed this question on the aggregate using Moody's corporate bond yield averages (monthly observations, by sector and rating class). They regressed yield spread changes on treasuries and sector share indices and found the following results:

- Negative correlation: spreads–rates.
- Negative correlation: spreads–share index.
- The influence of the share index was less important than the influence of interest rates.
- The coefficient was larger (i.e. stronger connection) for lower credit quality.
- $R^2 \approx 0.5$ for industrials.
  R^2 increases with lower credit quality.

9.6.1.4 Pricing accuracy

This point needs no motivation. Eom *et al.* (2000) performed the following study.

- The models were tested on a one-shot pricing problem of a cross-section of corporate bonds with asset-based models. On one given day, the corporate bonds in the sample were priced using the current share prices and balance sheet data of the issuing firms. (Thus, the dynamics of the spreads were *not* included in the study.)
- They found substantial pricing errors in all models, in particular the following:
- Merton: The Merton model generally underestimated the spreads by a significant amount (80% of the spread). Parameter variations did not help much to improve the pricing accuracy.
- Geske: The Geske model performed similarly to the Merton model, again a severe underestimation of spreads.
- Longstaff–Schwartz: This model tended to *overestimate* the spreads severely for risky bonds, but could not raise spreads enough for good-quality credits, so here it underestimated. Still, its performance was slightly better than the Merton model.
- Leland–Toft: In this model the coupon size (a model parameter) drove much of the variation in predicted spreads. It was hard to give a realistic value for this parameter from outside the model (i.e. without trying to calibrate the model and thus to "cheat").

In particular, all models had problems for short maturities or high quality, and the predictive power of the models was very poor in all cases. Mean absolute errors in spreads were more than 70% of the true spread. Thus, if the true spread was 100 bp, the model-predicted spreads were either above 170 bp or below 30 bp, but not closer. Jones *et al.* (1984) come to similar results.

These *academic* empirical studies form a very strict test of the firm's value modelling approach. In particular, all parameters must be given from sources outside the model: the default point was taken from the balance sheets and asset volatilities were calibrated from historical share price volatilities (or otherwise estimated). As we saw in the KMV implementation, practitioners' implementations take some shortcuts here which are more pragmatic and in the end result in better pricing performance. Therefore, it would be rash to throw asset-based models out of the window just based upon these studies. They only show that there is a lot of work yet to be done until a proper, reliable and robust model is found which somehow describes the link between equity and debt prices which *must* be there – somewhere.

9.6.2 Discussion

Most of the advantages and disadvantages of firm's value models for defaultable bonds have already been mentioned. These models are well suited if the relationship between the prices of different securities issued by the firm is of importance, as in convertible bonds or callable bonds that can be converted into shares when called by the issuer. Furthermore the model allows us to price defaultable bonds directly from fundamentals, from the firm's value.

The foundation on sound fundamentals makes models of this type also very well suited for the analysis of questions from corporate finance, like the relative powers of shareholders and creditors or questions of optimal capital structure design. This strength, the orientation towards fundamentals, is also one of the model's weaknesses: often it is hard to define a meaningful process for the firm's value, let alone observe it continuously. It can be very hard to calibrate such a firm's value process to market prices, and for some issuers, like sovereign debt, it may not exist at all. Furthermore the model may very quickly become too complex to analyse in a real-world application. If one were to model the full set of claims on the value of the assets of a medium-sized corporation one may very well have to price 20 or more classes of claims: from banks, shareholders and private creditors down to workers' wages, taxes and suppliers' demands. This obviously becomes quickly unfeasible. On the other hand, it seems that firm's value models are tailor-made for collateralised loans with traded collateral.

For the above-mentioned reasons, practical implementations of the firm's value approach tend not to stick too closely to the model but just take it as a rough guideline. For example, the model by KMV uses the firm's value model only to give an intuitive justification of the key summary statistic that is used in the model: the *distance to default*. Default predictions and risk classifications are then based on an extensive database of historical defaults, and not on any implications from the firm's value model.

Nevertheless, much work remains to be done until firm's value models achieve the degree of accuracy and reliability that we would like to see in these models. Judging by the empirical studies above, the pricing performance is extremely unsatisfactory. Nevertheless, if a firm's value model with good (or at least fair) pricing and hedging performance could be found, this would constitute a major breakthrough linking debt and equity markets which still are largely segregated.

An advantage of the firm's value approach which has not become apparent here is that it provides an easy and intuitive way to incorporate correlations in a portfolio framework. The correlation structure of a multifactor firm's value model is used by JPMorgan in their CreditMetrics model.

A weakness of the firm's value models is the unrealistic nature of the short-term credit spreads implied by the model. As mentioned before, these spreads are very low and tend towards zero as the maturity of the debt considered approaches zero.

Finally, for the pricing of credit risk derivatives one would like to have a model where the prices of defaultable bonds can be taken as *fundamentals* and do not have to be calculated (which then necessarily means a calibration process). In this respect the intensity-based models are to be preferred.

9.7 GUIDE TO THE LITERATURE

The firm's value approach is historically the oldest to the pricing of credit-risky securities in modern continuous-time finance. It was first proposed by Black and Scholes (1973) in their pathbreaking article "The pricing of options *and corporate liabilities*", which already explicitly refers to corporate bond pricing in its title. Merton (1974) expands on this idea. In these models a default can only occur at maturity of the debt, the payoff is like a European option.

In Black and Cox (1976) this approach is extended to allow for intermediate defaults when the firm's value hits a lower boundary. Now the model has more similarity with a barrier option model. Black and Cox (1976) show how to value a variety of corporate bonds and bond covenants in this framework. Further papers using this approach in a risk-free interest rate setup are Merton (1977), Geske (1977), Hull and White (1995), Nielsen *et al.* (1993), Schönbucher (1996b) and Zhou (1997).

Geske (1977) models defaultable coupon debt as a compound option on the firm's value, where defaults can occur at the coupon dates when the firm's value is insufficient to pay off the coupon. He gives a closed-form solution for a defaultable bond with one intermediate coupon. For a higher number of coupons the compound options become of a too high order to be represented in simple integrals of the normal density.

Hull and White (1995) consider the problem of counterparty risk in derivatives transactions within the classical firm's value framework. They argue rightly that the interpretation as a firm's value is not necessary for the validity of the model, all that matters is that there is a process which can trigger a default. This allows them to avoid the difficulties in explaining bankruptcy costs consistently within the model.

In Nielsen *et al.* (1993) the Black and Cox model is extended by the introduction of a stochastic default barrier. For pricing purposes it can be argued that this unnecessarily complicates the model because the only important quantity of the model is the distance of the firm's value from the barrier. If the firm's value is stochastic already, introducing a stochastic barrier would not introduce any new quality.

In Schönbucher (1996b) and Zhou (1997) the problem of the low credit spreads for short times to maturity is addressed. As the low credit spreads are caused because it is impossible for a continuous diffusion process to reach the default barrier in a very short time span, the obvious remedy is to introduce jumps into the process of the firm's value. Zhou (1997) proposes to solve the resulting equation with Monte Carlo simulations, while Schönbucher (1996b) gives a numerical finite difference algorithm to solve the resulting pricing equation.

Application of the firm's value approach to the pricing of credit derivatives can be found in Das (1995b) and Pierides (1997). Because of the inflexibility of the firm's value approach and the simplifying assumptions regarding the payoffs of the credit derivatives, these applications are only of limited practical value, their merit is more to give a benchmark for model comparison and calibration.

In the paper of Bensoussan *et al.* (1995) the problem of implying the volatility of the firm's value from the volatility of the firm's equity (and vice versa) is addressed and the relationship between both volatilities is analysed in detail, including the leverage effect that applies to equity.

Longstaff and Schwartz (1993) have managed to reach semi-closed-form solutions (an infinite series) for defaultable bonds in a firm's value model with stochastic interest rates that can be correlated with the firm's value process. They use the Vasicek (1977) model for the risk-free interest rates and have to assume a constant initial risk-free term structure. The closed-form solution for stochastic Gaussian interest rates, correlated with the firm's value given here in Section 1.3, is a special case of the results of Briys and de Varenne (1997). Briys and de Varenne give closed-form solutions using the discounted default barrier for defaultable bonds within the Vasicek model for default-free interest rates.

Lehrbass (1999) extends the firm's value approach to the modelling of country risk. In this paper the country's stock price index (in international currency) is used as a proxy for the price of the country's "assets". Lehrbass tests the pricing and hedging performance of this model on DM Eurobonds of several emerging countries.

Because of their more explanative approach firm's value models have been popular in more theoretical areas, too. For example, in an approach initiated by Leland (1994), Leland and Toft (1996) and Mella-Barral and Perraudin (1997), the firm's value framework is used to analyse strategic interaction between debtors and creditors. The bankruptcy barrier is endogenously determined from the optimal behaviour of the debtors and with these models it is possible to satisfactorily explain bankruptcy costs at the default barrier.

Related to this more theoretical class of papers is the paper by Duffie and Lando (1997), who show in a setup with asymmetric information that there is a close link between firm's value models and the intensity models. They show that a firm's value model with barrier à la Leland (1994) will appear as an intensity model to a creditor who is unable to accurately observe the firm's value process. With this (realistic) extension of the model the problem of the low short credit spread is also resolved without having to resort to jump diffusions.

The best known commercial implementation of the firm's value models is certainly the KMV (Kealhover, McQuown, Vasicek) model. Almost all literature on this model is based upon the information released by Moody's KMV who are (understandably) reluctant to release all details of the model, as they are trying to sell it. Nevertheless, a good picture of the principal ideas behind the model can be found in the papers by Crosbie (an employee of Moody's KMV) or Das (1998). As mentioned before, the KMV model uses the firm's value approach to define the key indicator for credit quality, the distance to default, but leaves the model framework after that to imply default likelihoods from historical data.

Unfortunately, apart from the studies mentioned earlier, there are hardly any empirical studies of the performance of the firm's value models in pricing and hedging of defaultable bonds. Crosbie analyses in his papers the performance of the KMV model and finds that it gives better results than using the firm's ratings for default prediction. Kwan (1996) empirically investigates the relationship between stock returns and yield changes of bonds by the same firm (controlling for default-free interest rate changes). He finds negative correlation between the two, both on a pooled and on an individual level, with a stronger connection for low ratings. Further empirical studies are by Jones et al. (1984) and Sarig and Warga (1989). In general the result seems to be that there is a connection between share prices and defaultable bond prices, but it only exists for lower credit ratings and it is not stable enough to implement a successful hedging strategy based on it.

10

Models for Default Correlation

Default correlation and default dependency modelling is probably the most interesting and also the most demanding open problem in the pricing of credit derivatives. While many single-name credit derivatives are very similar to other, non-credit-related derivatives in the default-free interest rate world (e.g. interest-rate swaps, options), basket and portfolio credit derivatives have entirely new risks and features.

When it comes to portfolio credit risk modelling for credit derivatives, a good model should have the following properties.

- **Default dependence:** The model must be able to produce default correlations (default dependency) of a realistic magnitude.
- **Estimation/parsimony:** The number of parameters needed to describe the dependence structure of the defaults in the model should be limited, in particular it should not grow exponentially in the number of obligors.
- **Timing risk/clustering:** Ultimately, the model must be a dynamic model, not a fixed-time-horizon model with just one step. To the payoffs of a CDO or the performance of a hedging strategy for a first-to-default swap, the *timing* of defaults can be as important as the number of defaults. The model should be capable of producing "clusters" of defaults in time, several defaults that occur close to each other (but not at the same time). This feature can also be viewed as *serial correlation* in the defaults.
- **Calibration:** There are two types of information that we would like to calibrate the model to. First, there are the *individual term structures of default (or survival) probabilities*, and second there is *joint defaults and correlation information* which is given for a *fixed time horizon*, usually one year.
- **Implementation:** There should be a viable implementation mechanism, usually we will have to use Monte Carlo simulation.

The chapter begins with a section on the basics of default dependency modelling. Many old habits, like thinking in linear correlation coefficients (instead of dependency structures) or common estimates for orders of magnitude, can be misleading and dangerous in portfolio credit risk modelling. These traps are shown in the first section, and a motivation is given for later sections.

After this, the chapter can be separated into two parts. The first part treats models for portfolio credit risk *on a fixed time horizon*. This allows us to concentrate on the problems in the modelling and calibration of the default dependencies. The basic Moody's binomial model is presented in this section, but the main focus lies on the factor models (or conditionally independent models) which can be viewed as a special, analytically tractable case of the CreditMetrics modelling framework. Parts of this half of the chapter are based upon Schönbucher (2000b, 2001).

The second part of the chapter treats models for dependent default risks which extend to continuous time. Here, we place particular emphasis on the resolution of *timing risk* and on calibration issues which now become relevant as these models seriously aim to fulfil the criteria stated above. We present methods for the modelling of default dependency in both intensity-based and firm's value-based modelling frameworks.

Finally, we show how the advantages of both modelling approaches can be combined (and significantly generalised) in a modelling framework using copula functions. The model presented in the last section can be calibrated to individual term structures of credit spreads, while full generality is retained in the specification of the default dependency. In particular, default dependency can be modelled using a factor-based approach based upon asset correlations in a firm's value modelling framework.

The factor-based copula model is probably the best model to price portfolio-based credit derivatives such as first-to-default swaps and tranches of CDOs, as it strikes a good balance between freedom and parsimony, flexibility and calibration. Due to the potentially very large number of obligors, the model must be implemented using Monte Carlo simulation, and we present efficient algorithms for the generation of dependent default times in the portfolio.

10.1 DEFAULT CORRELATION BASICS

10.1.1 Empirical evidence

Historically, defaults tended to cluster as the following examples from the USA show.

- Oil industry: 22 companies defaulted in 1982–1986.
- Railroad conglomerates: 1 default each year 1970–1977.
- Airlines: 3 defaults in 1970–1971, 5 defaults in 1989–1990.
- Thrifts (savings and loan crisis): 19 defaults in 1989–1990.
- Casinos/hotel chains: 10 defaults in 1990.
- Retailers: >20 defaults in 1990–1992.
- Construction/real estate: 4 defaults in 1992.

If defaults were indeed independent, such clusters of defaults should not occur.

This anecdotal evidence is supported by historical data on average default rates. The top panel of Figure 10.1 shows the actual average 12-month default rates of US corporate bonds from 1970 to 2000. The bottom panel shows the result of the simulation of a hypothetical portfolio which has a similar composition to the one in the top panel (number and default probability), but *independent* defaults.

Even without a rigorous statistical test it is clear that the historical time series exhibits much higher variation than the simulated time series: while all default rates of the simulated series lie well within the 1–2% band, the majority of the historical series is well outside it. It is highly unlikely that a series of default rates like the one on the top panel was generated by obligors who default independently from each other, therefore there must be a systematic influence which causes either many joint defaults (like in 1991–1992) or – the other side of the coin – very few joint defaults (like in 1972–1982).

Secondly, there also seems to be serial dependence in the default rates of subsequent years. A year with high default rates is more likely to be followed by another year with an above average default rate than to be followed by a low default rate. The same applies to low default rates.

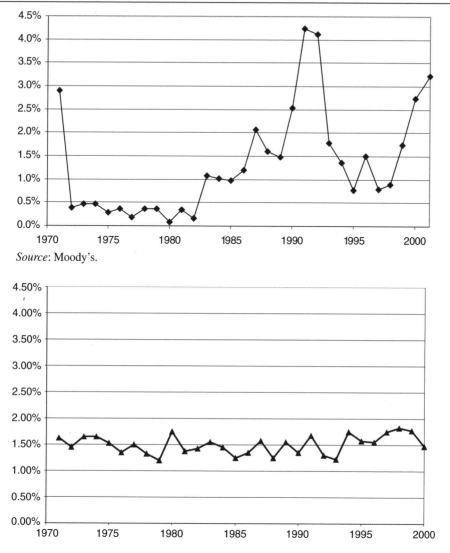

Figure 10.1   Top: Average 12-month default rates, US corporate bonds 1970–2000. Bottom: A simulated path of the default rates of 4000 obligors with individual default probability 1.5% and *independent* defaults

Thus, aggregate default rate data can give us information about default dependencies. A realistic model of default correlation should – when compared to historical data – yield a similar degree of variation between default rates and similar serial dependence over subsequent years.

10.1.2   Terminology

Although it has become common to talk about default *correlation*, the term *correlation* is misleading. The classical linear correlation coefficient that we know from the analysis of share prices, exchange rates and interest rates is an inadequate measure of dependence between defaults in a portfolio. This is implicitly recognised by many portfolio managers and risk managers who use different concepts to measure the total credit risk in a portfolio of credit exposures. The conclusive measure of the risk of the portfolio is the full distribution of its returns which is also the quantity that we are mostly concerned with. Nevertheless, many risk-relevant features of this distribution can be summarised in a few key numbers like the expected loss and VaR numbers at various levels.

Despite its shortcomings, the term *default correlation* has become so common that we will use it also. But here, *default correlation* will be used as a generic term for interdependent defaults. Otherwise the specific term *linear correlation* will be used.

10.1.3 Linear default correlation, conditional default probabilities, joint default probabilities

As it is difficult to gain an intuitive feeling for the size and effect of the linear default correlation coefficient we set it in context with two more accessible quantities: the conditional default probability and the joint default probability.

We consider two obligors A and B and a fixed time horizon T. The probability of a default of A before T is denoted by p_A, the default probability of B by p_B. We assume that these probabilities are exogenously given.

Knowledge of these quantities is not yet sufficient to determine the following:

- The probability that A *and* B default before T: the joint default probability p_{AB}.
- That is, the probability that A defaults before T, *given that B has defaulted before T*, or the probability that B defaults given that A has defaulted: the conditional default probabilities $p_{A|B}$ and $p_{B|A}$.
- The linear correlation coefficient ϱ_{AB} between the default events $\mathbf{1}_{\{A\}}$ and $\mathbf{1}_{\{B\}}$. (The default indicator function equals one $\mathbf{1}_{\{A\}} = 1$ if A defaults before T, and $\mathbf{1}_{\{A\}} = 0$ if A does *not* default.)

We need at least one of the quantities above to calculate the others. The connection is given by Bayes' rule:

$$p_{A|B} = \frac{p_{AB}}{p_B}, \qquad p_{B|A} = \frac{p_{AB}}{p_A} \tag{10.1}$$

and by the definition of the linear correlation coefficient:

$$\varrho_{AB} = \frac{p_{AB} - p_A p_B}{\sqrt{p_A(1 - p_A)p_B(1 - p_B)}}. \tag{10.2}$$

In the case of two obligors, we can reach the probabilities of all elementary events by using the linear correlation coefficient. If we had more than two obligors, though, this would not be possible. With three obligors, we have eight elementary events (no default, three times a single default, three pairs of two joint defaults, and one event of three defaults), but only seven restrictions (the fact that probabilities must add up to one, three individual default probabilities and three pairwise correlation coefficients). Thus, the probability of the joint default of all three obligors is not determined by the specification of only the linear correlations between pairs of obligors. The larger the portfolio, the more significant this problem becomes. For

N obligors, we have $N(N-1)/2$ correlations, N individual default probabilities (and one restriction that the probabilities must sum up to one). Yet we have 2^N possible joint default events. Mathematically, the correlation matrix only gives us the bivariate marginal distributions, but the full distribution remains undetermined.

Furthermore, this is relevant in practice. The risks of larger portfolios are caused by the possibility of several (more than two) joint defaults, and these are exactly the events that we cannot directly reach with pairwise correlations.

10.1.4   The size of the impact of default correlation

Because default probabilities are very small, the correlation ϱ_{AB} can have a much larger effect on the joint risk of a position than the effect that we are used to from other markets (e.g. equities or FX).

The joint default probability is given by:

$$p_{AB} = p_A p_B + \varrho_{AB}\sqrt{p_A(1-p_A)p_B(1-p_B)} \tag{10.3}$$

and the conditional default probabilities are:

$$p_{A|B} = p_A + \varrho_{AB}\sqrt{\frac{p_A}{p_B}(1-p_A)(1-p_B)}. \tag{10.4}$$

To illustrate the significance of the size of the default correlation let us assume the following orders of magnitude: $\varrho_{AB} = \varrho = O(1)$ is not very small and $p_A = p_B = p \ll 1$ is small. In accordance with the results of later sections on US corporate bonds[1] we choose the values $\varrho_{AB} = 6\%$ and $p = 1\%$:

$$p_{AB} = 0.01 \times 0.01 + 0.06 \times 0.01 \times 0.99 = 0.000594 \approx p^2 + \varrho p \approx \varrho p, \tag{10.5}$$
$$p_{A|B} = 0.01 + 0.06 \times 0.99 = 0.0694 \approx \varrho. \tag{10.6}$$

We see that the joint default probability and the conditional default probability in equations (10.5) and (10.6) are dominated by the correlation coefficient ϱ.

10.1.5   Price bounds for FtD swaps

Some of the modelling problems that we will have to face can already be highlighted in the following simple example. We want to derive price bounds for a first-to-default swap on three reference credits A, B, C:

- Reference credits A, B, C.
- Default probabilities $p_A \leq p_B \leq p_C$, equal recovery rates.
- CDS rates $\bar{s}_A \leq \bar{s}_B \leq \bar{s}_C$.

---

[1] The fitted values then yield a default probability of 1.31% and an asset value correlation of 11.21%, which translates into a default correlation of approximately 6%.

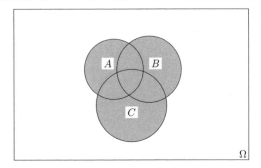

Figure 10.2 Possible default events for three obligors. Normal case

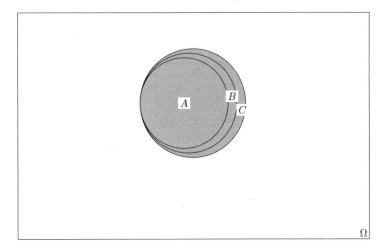

Figure 10.3 Possible default events for three obligors. Highest possible dependence

The possible default events are shown in Figure 10.2 The circles with labels A, B and C denote the states of nature in which the respective obligors default, the size of the circles indicates the probability with which these respective defaults occur. The random draw of the state of nature now corresponds to nature choosing a point in the rectangle, think of blindfolded Fortuna throwing a dart on the page. An obligor defaults if his circle is hit by the dart. Of course we can have joint defaults when the intersection of two or three circles is hit. The shaded area in the picture is the area in which the first-to-default swap has a payment to the protection buyer, it is the area that is covered by the circles.

The *worst case* for the protection buyer is the case when we have maximum correlation between defaults, as shown in Figure 10.3. (Because the default probabilities are not equal, the linear correlation coefficient will be $\neq 1$.) Given the ordering of the riskiness of the three obligors, this means:

- When A defaults, B and C default, too.
- When B defaults, C defaults, too.
- No matter which firms default first, C is always among them.

Thus, the price of the first-to-default swap must equal the price of the default swap on C:

$$\bar{s}^{\text{FtD}} = \bar{s}_C.$$

If we have *independence* between the three default events, we can easily derive the probability of no default: $(1 - p_A)(1 - p_B)(1 - p_C)$. Then, the probability of at least one default is:

$$p := 1 - (1 - p_A)(1 - p_B)(1 - p_C).$$

If joint default probabilities are low, we can approximate this to

$$p = p_A + p_B + p_C - (p_A p_B + p_A p_C + p_B p_C) + p_A p_B p_C,$$
$$p \lessapprox p_A + p_B + p_C \quad \text{for small } p_A, p_B, p_C.$$

Thus, the price of the first-to-default swap equals the price of a default swap on an asset with default probability p. In this case, the price of the FtD is approximately $\bar{s}_A + \bar{s}_B + \bar{s}_C$, but a bit smaller, because the true FtD probability is a bit less than the sum of the individual default probabilities (and because the protection buyer would refuse to transact at that price and buy the individual CDS instead). Furthermore, we abstract from the effects that are introduced by the cancellation of the fee streams (see the discussion below on the price for the case of disjoint default events):

$$\bar{s}^{\text{FtD}} \lessapprox \bar{s}_A + \bar{s}_B + \bar{s}_C.$$

In Figure 10.2, independence between the defaults of A and B means that the fraction of circle A that is overlapped by circle B is equal to the fraction of the whole rectangle Ω that is covered by B. If default probabilities are small in absolute value, the overlaps will be an order of magnitude smaller.

The following case is the *best case* for the protection buyer (Figure 10.4):

- No two firms ever default together.
- Default correlation $= -1$: if one defaults, the others must survive.
- Probability of one default $= p_A + p_B + p_C$.
- The protection of the FtD is as good as a complete portfolio of default swaps on A, B and C.

Thus, the price of the FtD swap is in this case

$$\bar{s}^{\text{FtD}} = \bar{s}_A + \bar{s}_B + \bar{s}_C.$$

In fact, $\bar{s}^{\text{FtD}}$ should even be a bit larger, because otherwise one could sell the three CDSs at $\bar{s}_A + \bar{s}_B + \bar{s}_C$ and buy the FtD at $\bar{s}^{\text{FtD}}$. If no default occurs, this position generates no profit and no loss. But if one default (A, say) happens after some time, the FtD and the CDS on A are knocked out and their default payments cancel, but we keep earning the CDS fees on B and C until the end of the term of these CDSs, although (by assumption) they cannot default any more if A has already defaulted. Of course this arbitrage is only a theoretical possibility under the assumption of mutually exclusive defaults. In reality the upper bound on an FtD swap will

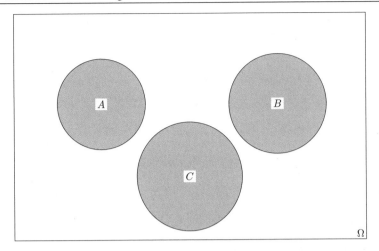

Figure 10.4 Possible default events for three obligors. Smallest possible correlation

always be the sum of the individual CDS rates. It would be extremely hard to convince an FtD protection buyer to pay a higher fee for the protection on the *first* default alone if he can buy individual protection on the whole portfolio for less than the fee of the FtD.

Summing up, we reach the following bounds on the price of a first-to-default swap:

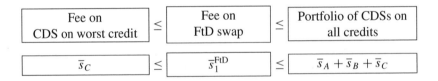

With low default probabilities and low default correlation the value of an FtD is usually closer to the upper bound than to the lower bound:

$$\overline{s}^{FtD} \approx \overline{s}_A + \overline{s}_B + \overline{s}_C,$$

but this bound is very coarse. These are the price bounds that we can infer without taking recourse to a theoretical model.

To derive these price bounds we had to consider the relative probabilities of eight events: the defaults of exactly $\{\emptyset, A, B, C, AB, AC, BC, ABC\}$, while we were only given three restrictions on the joint default probabilities: p_A for $A \cup AB \cup AC \cup ABC$, p_B and p_C similarly. Already in the three-obligor case, the determination of the upper and lower price bounds is not trivial. If we had 100 obligors, it would be impossible to keep track of all joint events without a formal model.

Thus, the fundamental problem when modelling joint defaults of a number of obligors is: Given implied default probabilities for the individual obligors A, B and C, which part of these probabilities refers to individual defaults, and which to joint defaults? Geometrically speaking we must model by how much the three circles in Figure 10.2 overlap.

10.1.6 The need for theoretical models of default correlations

Some structure in a theoretical model is indispensable for the successful assessment of the risk of default correlation. Models for default correlation must be able to explain and predict default correlations from fewer and more fundamental variables than a simple full description of the joint default distribution.

The first of these reasons lies in the data upon which the assessment of default correlation is based. There are several possible data sources, none of which is perfect.

- Historically observed joint rating and default events: The obvious source of information on default correlation is the historical incidence of joint defaults of similar firms in a similar time frame. We used such data in Section 10.1.1 when we analysed the evidence for default dependency in aggregated historical US default rate data. Such data is objective and directly addresses the modelling problem. Unfortunately, because joint defaults are rare events, historical data on joint defaults is very sparse. To gain a statistically useful number of observations, long time ranges (several decades) have to be considered and the data must be aggregated across industries and countries. In the majority of cases direct data will therefore not be available.
- Credit spreads: Credit spreads contain much information about the default risk of traded bonds, and changes in credit spreads reflect changes in the markets' assessment of the riskiness of these investments. If the credit spreads of two obligors are strongly correlated it is likely that the defaults of these obligors are also correlated. Credit spreads have the further advantage that they reflect market information (therefore they already contain risk premia) and that they can be observed far more frequently than defaults. Disadvantages are problems with data availability, data quality (liquidity), and the fact that there is no theoretical justification for the size and strength of the link between credit spread correlation and default correlation.[2]
- Equity correlations: Equity price data is much more readily available and typically of better quality than credit spread data. Unfortunately, the connection between equity prices and credit risk is not obvious. This link can only be established by using a theoretical model, and we saw that these models have difficulties in explaining the credit spreads observed in the market. Consequently, a lot of pre-processing of the data is necessary until a statement about default correlations can be made.

Thus, we do not have direct data on default dependencies, and the data sources that are available require a theoretical model which somehow gives the link between the data and the default behaviour of the obligors.

The second, and most important reason for the usage of default models is the fact that the specification of *full* joint default probabilities is simply too complex. While there are only four joint default events for two obligors (none defaults, A defaults, B defaults and both default), there are 2^N joint default events for N obligors. For a realistic number of obligors it is impossible to enumerate these probabilities, let alone specify a model which prescribes all these values explicitly.

These problems highlight the fact that we are faced with a different situation from the modelling problems in continuous random variables, e.g. share prices, FX returns, etc. If the

---

[2] Theoretically, two obligors could exhibit independent credit spread dynamics up to default of one of them, but still have very high default correlation. This point will be explained in detail later on.

processes are continuous, we can assume that they are jointly normally (or jointly lognormally) distributed.[3] Then, the $N(N-1)/2$ elements of the correlation matrix are sufficient to describe the dependency structure.

10.2 INDEPENDENT DEFAULTS

Assume the following (very simplified) situation.

Assumption 10.1 (homogeneous portfolio, independent defaults)

(i) *We consider default and survival of a portfolio until a fixed time horizon of T. Interest rates are set to zero.[4]*
(ii) *We have a portfolio of N exposures to N different obligors.*
(iii) *The exposures are of identical size L, and have identical recovery rates of π.*
(iv) *The defaults of the obligors happen independently of each other. Each obligor defaults with a probability of p before the time horizon T.*

Assumption 10.1 will be relaxed in coming sections.

We call X the number of defaults that actually occurred until time T. The loss in default is then

$$X(1-\pi)L, \tag{10.7}$$

the number of defaults multiplied by the exposure size and one minus the recovery rate. Therefore, to assess the distribution of the default losses it is sufficient to know the distribution of the number X of defaults.

10.2.1 The binomial distribution function

If defaults are independent and happen with probability p over the time horizon T, then the loss distribution of a portfolio of N loans is described by the binomial distribution function.

Definition 10.1 (binomial distribution) *Consider a random experiment with success probability p which is repeated N times and let X be the number of successes observed. All repetitions are independent from each other. The binomial frequency function $b(n; N, p)$ gives the probability of observing $n \le N$ successes. The binomial distribution function $B(n; N, p)$ gives the probability of observing less than or equal to n successes:*

$$b(n; N, p) := \mathbf{P}[X = n] = \binom{N}{n} p^n (1-p)^{N-n} = \frac{N!}{n!(N-n)!} p^n (1-p)^{N-n}, \tag{10.8}$$

$$B(n; N, p) := \mathbf{P}[X \le n] = \sum_{m=0}^{n} \binom{N}{m} p^m (1-p)^{N-m}. \tag{10.9}$$

---

[3] Joint normality or joint lognormality are strong assumptions and important risks may be overlooked in this specification (see Embrechts *et al.*, 2002). But they can serve at least as a first approximation to the true dependency structure.
[4] This assumption is not critical, we could also just consider the forward values of the exposures until T.

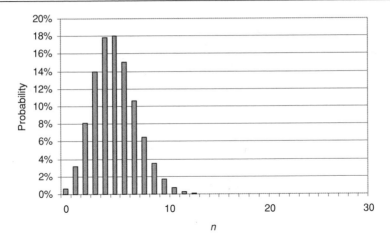

Figure 10.5 Distribution of default losses under independence. Parameters: number of obligors $N = 100$, individual default probability $p = 5\%$

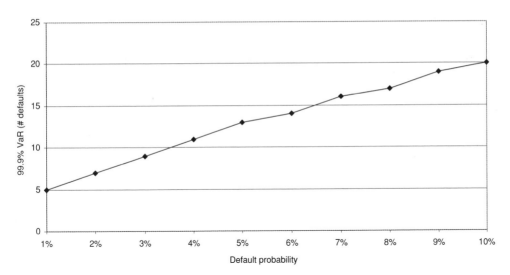

Figure 10.6 99.9% VaR levels of a portfolio of 100 independent obligors for different individual default probabilities

In our credit setting, the probability of exactly $X = n$ (with $n \leq N$) defaults until time T is $b(n; N, p)$ and the probability of up to n defaults is $B(n; N, p)$.

10.2.2 Properties of the binomial distribution function

An example of a typical loss distribution in the binomial case is given in Figure 10.5 for a benchmark portfolio with 100 obligors and independent default probability of 5%. The loss distribution has an extremely thin tail, the 99% VaR lies at 11 defaults, the 99.9% VaR at 13 and the 99.99% VaR at 15 defaults. As Figure 10.6 shows, these VaR numbers are not

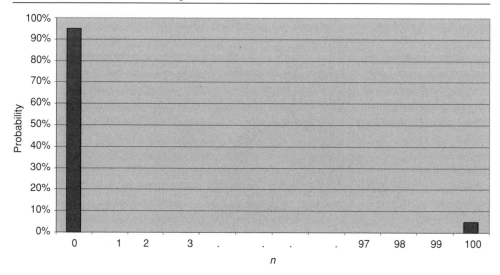

Figure 10.7   Default losses when defaults are perfectly dependent

significantly changed when different individual default probabilities are used. The bell-shaped form of the default loss distribution in Figure 10.5 is caused by the effects of the central limit theorem which ensures that the (suitably scaled) distribution function converges to a normal distribution function.

10.2.3   The other extreme: perfectly dependent defaults

The extreme case of default correlation is given when the defaults are perfectly dependent. In the situation of Assumption 10.1 this means that:

- *Either all* obligors default (with 5% probability),
- *Or none* of the obligors defaults (with 95% probability).

Figure 10.7 shows the distribution of the default events when defaults are perfectly dependent. Note that this situation is still compatible with the previously made assumption that each obligor defaults with a probability of 5%. VaR is not a meaningful statistic of the risk of the portfolio in this situation, as it takes the value 100 at all levels above 95%.

As both independence and perfect dependence are compatible with an individual default probability of 5%, these examples show that it is impossible to recover much meaningful information about the likelihood of joint defaults from the individual default probabilities.

When the individual default probabilities are not identical across the obligors it is possible to extract some information about the likelihood of joint defaults from the individual default probabilities, but not much. For example, the joint default probability of a certain set of obligors must be less than or equal to the smallest individual default probability of these obligors.

10.3   THE BINOMIAL EXPANSION METHOD

The binomial expansion technique (BET) is a method used by the ratings agency Moody's to assess the default risk in bond and loan portfolios. It was one of the first attempts to quantify the risk of a portfolio of defaultable bonds. The method is not based upon a formal portfolio default risk model, it can be inaccurate and it is generally unsuitable for pricing, yet it has become something of a market standard in risk assessment and portfolio credit risk concentration terminology.[5]

The BET is based upon the following observation. Assume we analyse a loan portfolio of $N = 100$ loans of the same size, with the same loss L in default and the same default probability $p = 5\%$. If the defaults of these obligors are independent, we know from the previous section that the loss distribution function is given by the binomial distribution function. The probability of a loss of exactly $X = nL$ (with $n \leq N$) until time T is (10.8):

$$\mathbf{P}[X = nL] = \binom{N}{n} p^n (1 - p)^{N-n} = \frac{N!}{n!(N-n)!} p^n (1 - p)^{N-n} =: b(n; N, p).$$

Let us now consider the other extreme. If all defaults are perfectly dependent (i.e. either *all* or *none* of the obligors default), we have:

$$\mathbf{P}[X > 0] = p = 5\% = \mathbf{P}[X = NL],$$
$$\mathbf{P}[X = 0] = 1 - p = 95\% = \mathbf{P}[X = 0].$$

The key point to note here is that this can also be represented as a binomial distribution function with probability $p = 5\%$, but this time only *one* binomial draw is taken and the stakes are much higher: a loss of NL if the 5% event occurs.

Thus we have the following results.

- Perfect independence is $N = 100$ obligors with loss L and loss probability $p = 5\%$ each. The probability of a loss X of less than x is

$$\mathbf{P}[X \leq x] = B(n; N, p),$$

where the parameters are:
- $N = 100$;
- $n = \lfloor x/L \rfloor$ ("rounding down", the largest integer less than or equal to x/L);
- $p = 5\%$.

---

[5] This section is based upon the description in Cifuentes *et al.* (1996), Cifuentes and O'Connor (1996) and Cifuentes and Wilcox (1998)

- Perfect dependence is equivalent to $N' = 1$ obligors with loss $L' = NL$ and loss probability $p = 5\%$. The probability of a loss X of less than x is

$$\mathbf{P}[X \le x] = B(n'; N', p),$$

where:
- $N' = 1$, an adjusted number of obligors;
- $n' = \lfloor x/L' \rfloor$ ($n' = 0$ here);
- $p = 5\%$.

Thus, if independence corresponds to $N' = N$ obligors with loss amount $L' = L$, and perfect dependence to $N' = 1$ obligors with loss amount $L' = NL$, it is convenient to approximate intermediate degrees of dependence as if we had $N' = D < N$ independent obligors with losses of $L' = LN/D$ each.

Definition 10.2   *Consider a portfolio of N obligors with a total notional amount (total potential losses at default) of K and average individual default probability p. The* BET *loss distribution with diversity score D is*

$$P^{BET}(x; N, K, D) := B(\lfloor x/L' \rfloor; D, p), \tag{10.10}$$

where $L' = K/D$. The parameter D is called the diversity score *of the portfolio.*

A diversity score of $D = 50$ in the previous example ($N = 100$) would mean that instead of considering 100 independent obligors with potential losses of L each, we now only consider 50 independent obligors with potential losses of $2L$ each. Equivalently, we could group the original N obligors in D groups and assume that all obligors of one group default at the same time (perfect dependence within the group), while we have perfect independence across groups.

Figure 10.8 shows the effect of a diversity score assumption on the loss distribution of the portfolio. The effect of the diversity score on the tail of the loss distribution is particularly

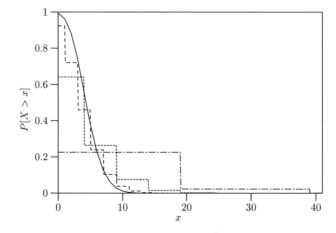

Figure 10.8 Loss exceedance probabilities for different diversity scores. Parameters: $N = 100$, $p = 5\%$, $D = 100, 50, 20, 5$ (solid, dashed, short dashed, dot dashed)

pronounced: the lower the diversity score, the more probability mass is allocated to the high-loss events. This effect is intended, portfolios with lower diversity scores are deemed to be riskier than portfolios with higher diversity scores. Not intended and quite unrealistic is the step-function shape of the probabilities. The lower the diversity score, the coarser the resolution of the loss distribution, the loss distribution can only be specified in multiples of K/D.

The crucial parameter driving the BET loss distribution is the diversity score. All information on default dependencies and risk concentration in the portfolio must be concentrated in this parameter. Moody's have developed a set of rules for the calculation of the diversity score for a given portfolio. Consider the following portfolio:

- N obligors, $K = \sum_{n=1}^{N} K_n$ total par value.
- p_n, K_n, I_n: obligor n's probability of default, par value and industry group.

First, a *weighted average default probability p* (or a weighted average rating WAR) is determined, to be able to treat all obligors as having identical default probabilities. How this is done will be described later.

The determination of the diversity score starts with an initial diversity score of $D = N$ (representing perfect diversification). This diversity score is adjusted downwards according to the following criteria.

- Exposure sizes: If the portfolio only contains exposures with identical notional amounts, the diversity score is not adjusted. In all other cases, large exposures represent concentration and carry a diversity score penalty.
  - Calculate the average par value K/N.
  - The adjusted relative contribution of the nth obligor is $\min\{K_n/(K/N),\ 1\}$.
  - The new diversity score is

$$D = \sum_{n=1}^{N} \min\{K_n/(K/N),\ 1\}.$$

- Industry group diversification: If several of the obligors belong to the same industry group (according to Moody's definition of industry groups), the diversity score is adjusted downwards as follows:
  - Allocate the bonds to their respective industry groups.
  - The "industry total" of companies within each industry group is the sum of the relative contributions of all companies in that industry group (exposure-weighted).
  - The diversity score is the sum of the industry group diversity scores according to Table 10.1. (The underlying assumption behind this table is that defaults on bonds within one industry group have a correlation of approximately 30%.)
- Regional diversification: For emerging market CDOs this takes the place of industry group diversification. Each region is treated as an "industry".

Table 10.1 Diversity score adjustments for industry groups. The industry total is the sum of the adjusted relative contributions of all obligors of this industry group

Industry total	1	1.5	2	2.5	3	3.5	4	4.5	5	5.5	6
Diversity score	1.0	1.2	1.5	1.8	2.0	2.2	2.3	2.5	2.7	2.8	3

Table 10.2   Weights for the calculation of the weighted average rating in the binomial expansion technique

Aaa	1	Baa1	260	B1	2 220
Aa1	10	Baa2	360	B2	2 720
Aa2	20	Baa3	610	B3	3 490
Aa3	40	Ba1	940	Caa	6 500
A1	70	Ba2	1 350	Ca and lower	10 000
A2	120	Ba3	1 780		
A3	180				

A portfolio consisting of N bonds all having the same par value, the same rating but each belonging to a different industry would have a perfect diversity score of $D = N$.

The second important parameter is the weighted average probability of default p. It is calculated as the "stressed" default probability of bonds with the same rating as the weighted average rating of the portfolio. "Stressing" usually means that the default probabilities are increased by two standard deviations of the average historical default probabilities.

The weighted average rating class of the portfolio is calculated as follows. Sum up the rating weights of Table 10.2, weighted by the exposure of the portfolio in this rating class. This number is divided by the total exposure of the portfolio to yield the WAR number. Then, again by looking up in Table 10.2, the weighted average rating is determined.

The rating weights in Table 10.2 increase exponentially as the credit quality deteriorates. There is a strong penalty on the inclusion of lower rated firms in the portfolio. For example, consider we had a portfolio of 100 obligors with WAR number 610 (all Baa3). If we add one Ba2-rated obligor, the WAR would rise to 617, and to regain a WAR of 610 we must add another two Baa1-rated obligors.

The third parameter is the expected loss in default. Again, this number is implied from historical experience and stressed.

Using these parameters, the loss distribution of the portfolio is specified as a binomial distribution as in Definition 10.2. If the portfolio is tranched into a CDO, the expected loss numbers can be calculated for each tranche of the portfolio using the probabilities of equation (10.10). Comparing these expected loss numbers to a table of historical expected losses per rating category yields the rating of the tranche in question.

When the expected loss is calculated, the timing of the cash flows can become important. Moody's assumes "front-loaded" defaults, i.e. that 50% of the defaults of the scenario occur in the first year, and the rest equally distributed over the life of the CDO. There are also additional minimum equity levels, e.g. in emerging market CBOs, a 20% minimum equity (subordinated) piece is required if the senior piece is to be rated A or higher. Furthermore, the results of the analysis are stressed against different recovery rate levels, default probabilities, timing of defaults, collateral coupons, etc.

While the BET is used to gain an approximative idea of the likely rating class, the actual rating assignment by Moody's is not an automatic process based upon the methodology outlined above. The portfolio and the payoff structure are still analysed individually for every rating assignment, and other qualitative features (like documentation, legal risk, etc.) are also taken into account. Thus, the procedure outlined in this section should not be taken as a recipe which gives you a guarantee to reach a particular rating by Moody's, it is just an explanation of how the author understood Moody's descriptions of their procedures.

Despite being a rough method and lacking theoretical justification for the many "adjustments" made to the model parameters, the BET does have its merits. The concept of the diversity score places restrictions and discipline on the pools that are issued. Typically, pools with homogeneous ratings and broad diversification over industry classes achieve the best ratings. Despite its shortcomings, the diversity score has become a market standard for communicating the degree of diversification of a portfolio.

The BET should not be used for pricing because that is not what it was developed for. The BET was designed to provide a conservative risk assessment. It contains assumptions that are inaccurate (but hopefully the many safety margins compensate for that), it is based upon historical experience and not on market data (which is good for risk assessment but not for pricing), and the resolution of the loss distribution is often not accurate enough. Finally, a time dimension is missing from the setup. In the following we will present better and more accurate methods to price CDO tranches.

10.4 FACTOR MODELS

10.4.1 One-factor dependence of defaults

In the previous section we considered a portfolio of 100 obligors who default independently from each other. Under independence, 99.9% of all loss events had less than 13 defaults, i.e. less than 13% of the portfolio. If the number of obligors is increased further, the diversification effect becomes even stronger, and the loss rate of the portfolio will be concentrated around the individual default probability of the obligors, which is 5%. In the limit we know that exactly 5% of the obligors in the portfolio will default, if they default independently from each other.

As we are considering a *static* model, we can reduce the data that we analysed in Section 10.1.1 to the histogram shown in Figure 10.9. Figure 10.9 shows the frequencies with which the given 12-month default rates for Moody's rated US corporate bonds were observed over the 30 years from 1970 to 2000. Clearly, this distribution does not resemble a concentrated distribution around a common average default rate (as predicted by independence), even though the number of obligors considered is very large. Again, this can only be caused by default correlation.

We will use a theoretical model in the following sections to derive a distribution of default rates which more closely resembles the empirical observations. We use a very simplified form of the so-called firm's value models due to Vasicek (1987). This approach is also used in Finger (1999) and Belkin *et al.* (1998), and extended in Lucas *et al.* (2001).

10.4.2 A simplified firm's value model

Assumption 10.2 (simplified firm's value model) *The default of each obligor is triggered by the change in value of the assets of its firm. The value of the assets of the nth obligor at time t is denoted by $V_n(t)$. We assume that $V_n(T)$ is normally distributed. Without loss of generality we set the initial asset values to zero $V_n(0) = 0$ and standardise their development*

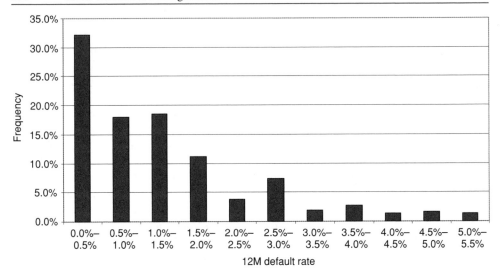

Figure 10.9   12-Month default rates of US corporate bonds 1970–2000

such that $V_n(T) \sim \Phi(0, 1)$. Obligor n defaults if its firm's value falls below a prespecified barrier $V_n(T) \leq K_n$. The asset values of different obligors are correlated with each other. The variance–covariance matrix[6] of the $V_1, \ldots, V_N$ is denoted by Σ.

This model is very similar in nature to the JPMorgan CreditMetrics model (see Gupton *et al.*, 1997), the only difference so far is that CreditMetrics incorporates rating transitions, while we only consider default and survival here. The qualitative conclusions that we will draw from the analysis of this model equally apply to CreditMetrics (with the appropriate adjustments). Linking this model to the firm's value approach it is a multivariate version of the Merton (1974) approach, where defaults only occur if the firm's value is below a barrier at the time horizon T. If the firm's value process is below the barrier at $t < T$ but recovers until T, the firm survives in this setup while it would have defaulted in the barrier setup of Black and Cox (1976).[7]

Note that in this setup we can still calibrate the model to reflect different individual default probabilities p_n over the time horizon by setting the barrier level to that level which replicates the given individual default probability. This level is

$$K_n = \Phi^{-1}(p_n). \tag{10.11}$$

The other calibration parameters are the $\frac{1}{2}N(N-1)$ elements of the covariance matrix Σ. These elements do not affect the individual default probabilities but only the joint default behaviour of the portfolio.

If $N = 100$, specifying an $N \times N$ correlation matrix is still a daunting task. A common trick to reduce the high dimensionality of the modelling problem is to introduce a small number

---

[6] The variance–covariance matrix coincides here with the correlation matrix.

[7] Of course a multidimensional version of the Black and Cox (1976) model is also possible, yet it should be noted that it will yield a different dependency structure from the one implied by fixed-time-horizon models.

of *factors* through which the dependency between the firm's values is driven. If there are M factors, the number of parameters left to specify becomes just $M \times N$ (which should be much less than $N(N-1)/2$ if $M \ll N$). These parameters are also known as *factor weights*. Here we take the simplest case and choose *one* factor (reducing the number of coefficients to N) and further assume *equal factor weights* across obligors, effectively reducing the dependency in the model to just one parameter.

Assumption 10.3 (one-factor model)   *The values of the assets of the obligors are driven by a common, standard normally distributed factor Y component and an idiosyncratic standard normal noise component ϵ_n:*

$$V_n(T) = \sqrt{\varrho}\, Y + \sqrt{1-\varrho}\, \epsilon_n \quad \forall\, n \le N, \tag{10.12}$$

where Y and ϵ_n, $n \le N$ are independent normally distributed random variables with mean 0 and variance 1 and $\varrho \in [0, 1]$.

Using this approach the values of the assets of two obligors n and $m \ne n$ are correlated with linear correlation coefficient ϱ. The important point is that *conditional on the realisation of the systematic factor Y, the firm's values and the defaults are **independent**.*

10.4.3   The distribution of the defaults

The systematic risk factor Y can be viewed as an indicator of the state of the business cycle, and the idiosyncratic factor ϵ_n as a firm-specific effects factor such as the quality of the management or the innovations of the firm. The default threshold K of the firm is mainly determined by the firm's reserves and balance-sheet structure. The relative sizes of the idiosyncratic and systematic components are controlled by the correlation coefficient ϱ. If $\varrho = 0$, then the business cycle has no influence on the fates of the firms, if $\varrho = 1$, then it is the only driver of defaults, and the individual firm has no control whatsoever. Empirically calibrated values of ϱ are around 10%.

In a boom we have fewer defaults than in a recession, but conditional on the state of the business cycle (i.e. once we know whether we are in a boom or a recession), the defaults and fates of the firms are independent from each other. The only effect of Y is to move the value processes V_n of all firms closer (or further away) from the respective default thresholds K.

In the following we assume that all obligors have the same default barrier $K_n = K$ and the same exposure $L_n = 1$. Following the intuition above, the distribution of defaults in the portfolio can be derived. First, the business cycle variable Y materialises, and conditional on the general state of the economy, the individual defaults occur independently from each other, but with a default probability $p(y)$ which depends on the state of the economy. This default probability is

$$p(y) = \Phi\left(\frac{K - \sqrt{\varrho}\, y}{\sqrt{1-\varrho}}\right), \tag{10.13}$$

where $\Phi(\cdot)$ is the cumulative normal distribution function. This can be seen as follows. The individual conditional default probability $p(y)$ is the probability that the firm's value $V_n(T)$ is below the barrier K, given that the systematic factor Y takes the value y:

$$
\begin{aligned}
p(y) &= \mathbf{P}[V_n(T) < K \mid Y = y] \\
&= \mathbf{P}\left[\sqrt{\varrho}\, Y + \sqrt{1 - \varrho}\, \epsilon_n < K \mid Y = y\right] \\
&= \mathbf{P}\left[\epsilon_n < \frac{K - \sqrt{\varrho}\, Y}{\sqrt{1 - \varrho}} \;\middle|\; Y = y\right] \\
&= \Phi\left(\frac{K - \sqrt{\varrho}\, y}{\sqrt{1 - \varrho}}\right).
\end{aligned}
\tag{10.14}
$$

The probability of having exactly n defaults is the average of the conditional probabilities of n defaults, averaged over the possible realisations of Y and weighted with the probability density function $\phi(y)$:

$$
\mathbf{P}[X = n] = \int_{-\infty}^{\infty} \mathbf{P}[X = n \mid Y = y]\,\phi(y)dy.
\tag{10.15}
$$

Conditional on the realisation $Y = y$ of the systematic factor, the probability of having n defaults is given by the binomial distribution

$$
\mathbf{P}[X = n \mid Y = y] = \binom{N}{n}(p(y))^n\,(1 - p(y))^{N-n},
\tag{10.16}
$$

where we used the conditional independence of the defaults in the portfolio. Substituting this and (10.14) into equation (10.15) yields:

$$
\mathbf{P}[X = n] = \int_{-\infty}^{\infty} \binom{N}{n}\left(\Phi\left(\frac{K - \sqrt{\varrho}\, y}{\sqrt{1 - \varrho}}\right)\right)^n \left(1 - \Phi\left(\frac{K - \sqrt{\varrho}\, y}{\sqrt{1 - \varrho}}\right)\right)^{N-n} \phi(y)dy.
\tag{10.17}
$$

Thus, the resulting distribution function of the defaults is:

$$
\mathbf{P}[X \le m] = \sum_{n=0}^{m} \binom{N}{n} \int_{-\infty}^{\infty} \left(\Phi\left(\frac{K - \sqrt{\varrho}\, y}{\sqrt{1 - \varrho}}\right)\right)^n \left(1 - \Phi\left(\frac{K - \sqrt{\varrho}\, y}{\sqrt{1 - \varrho}}\right)\right)^{N-n} \phi(y)dy.
\tag{10.18}
$$

Figure 10.10 shows the distribution of the default losses for our benchmark portfolio (100 obligors, 5% individual default probability) under different asset correlations. Increasing asset correlation (and thus default correlation) leads to a shift of the probability weight to the left ("good" events) and to the tail on the right. Very good events (no or very few defaults) become equally more likely as very bad events (many defaults). It should be noted that the deviation of the loss distribution function from the distribution under independence (i.e. zero correlation $\varrho = 0$) is already significant for low values for the asset correlation (e.g. 10%).

The most significant effect for risk management is the increased mass of the loss distribution in its tails. Figure 10.11 uses a logarithmic scale for the probabilities to show this effect more clearly. While the probabilities decrease very quickly for independence and very low

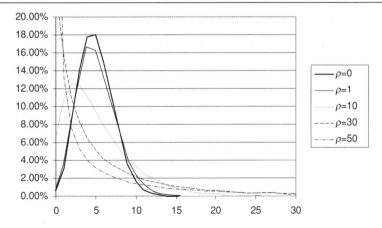

Figure 10.10 Default losses under correlation (one-factor model). Parameters: number of obligors $N = 100$, individual default probability $p = 5\%$, asset correlation ρ in percentage points: 0, 1, 10, 30, 50

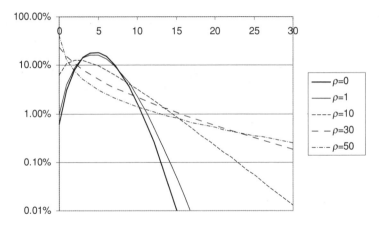

Figure 10.11 Default losses under correlation (one-factor model). Logarithmic scale. Parameters: number of obligors $N = 100$, individual default probability $p = 5\%$, asset correlation ρ in percentage points: 0, 1, 10, 30, 50

correlations, the probability of a joint default of 30 obligors is still above 10 bp for asset correlations of 30% or 50%.

The 99.9% and 99% VaR levels shown in Table 10.3 show the dramatically increased tail probabilities when correlation in the asset values is taken into account. The 99.9% VaR at a moderate asset correlation of 10% and an individual default probability of 5% is 27, which is worse than the 99.9% VaR of a portfolio of independent credits with a much higher individual default probability of 10% (the VaR is 20 in the latter case).

10.4.4 The large portfolio approximation

Even more tractability than in equation (10.18) can be reached if the number of obligors N tends to infinity.

Table 10.3   99.9% and 99% VaR levels as a function of
the asset correlation in the one-factor model. Parameters:
100 obligors, 5% individual default probability

Asset correlation (%)	99.9% VaR level	99% VaR level
0	13	11
1	14	12
10	27	19
20	41	27
30	55	35
40	68	44
50	80	53

Assumption 10.4 (large uniform portfolio)   *The portfolio consists of a very large $N \to \infty$ number of credits of uniform size. Let X now denote the* fraction *of the defaulted securities in the portfolio.*

Individual defaults are still triggered by the simple firm's value model, and conditional on the realisation of the business cycle variable Y individual defaults happen independently from each other. On average, in a large portfolio, we will therefore experience defaults on a fraction $p(y)$ of the obligors, where $p(y)$ is the individual default probability conditional on the realisation $Y = y$ of the business cycle variable. From this we can derive the distribution function of the loss fraction X. The individual default probability (conditional on the realisation y of the systematic factor Y) is given by equation (10.14):

$$p(y) = \Phi \left(\frac{K - \sqrt{\varrho}\, y}{\sqrt{1 - \varrho}} \right).$$

The large portfolio approximation justifies that conditional on $Y = y$ the loss X in the portfolio is given by $p(y)$ because:

$$\mathbf{P}[|X - p(y)| > \varepsilon \mid Y = y] \to 0 \qquad \forall \varepsilon > 0 \quad \text{as } N \to \infty. \tag{10.19}$$

If we know Y, then we can predict the fraction of credits that will default with certainty. Now we do not know the realisation of Y yet, but we can invoke iterated expectations to reach

$$\mathbf{P}[X \leq x] = \mathbf{E}[\mathbf{P}[X \leq x \mid Y]] \tag{10.20}$$

$$= \int_{-\infty}^{\infty} \mathbf{P}[X \leq x \mid Y = y]\, \phi(y)dy. \tag{10.21}$$

Using equation (10.19):

$$= \int_{-\infty}^{\infty} \mathbf{P}[X = p(y) \leq x \mid Y = y]\, \phi(y)dy \tag{10.22}$$

$$= \int_{-\infty}^{\infty} \mathbf{1}_{\{p(y) \leq x\}} \phi(y)dy = \int_{-y^*}^{\infty} \phi(y)dy = \Phi(y^*). \tag{10.23}$$

Here y^* is chosen such that $p(-y^*) = x$, and $p(y) \le x$ for $y > -y^*$. (Remember that the individual default probability $p(y)$ *decreases* in y.) Thus y^* is

$$y^* = \frac{1}{\sqrt{\varrho}}\left(\sqrt{1-\varrho}\ \Phi^{-1}(x) - K\right). \tag{10.24}$$

Combining the results yields the distribution function of the loss fraction X:

$$F(x) := \mathbf{P}[X \le x] = \Phi\left(\frac{1}{\sqrt{\varrho}}\left(\sqrt{1-\varrho}\ \Phi^{-1}(x) - \Phi^{-1}(p)\right)\right). \tag{10.25}$$

Taking the derivative of the distribution function with respect to x yields the corresponding probability density function $f(x)$:

$$f(x) = \sqrt{\frac{1-\varrho}{\varrho}}\ \exp\left\{\frac{1}{2}(\Phi^{-1}(x))^2 - \frac{1}{2\varrho}\left(\Phi^{-1}(p) - \sqrt{1-\varrho}\ \Phi^{-1}(x)\right)^2\right\}. \tag{10.26}$$

Obviously, infinitely large portfolios do not occur in practice, but the quality of the approximation is remarkable. In the present example (100 obligors, 5% individual default probability, 30% asset value correlation) the relative error in the tail of the distribution is around 0.1–0.2, i.e. the large portfolio value of the default distribution deviates by a factor of up to ±0.2 from the exact value. Given the uncertainty about the correct input for the asset correlation, this error is negligible in many cases.

Figure 10.12 shows the limit distribution of the default losses in the large portfolio context. For very low numbers of defaulted obligors (one or zero defaults) the approximation is incorrect

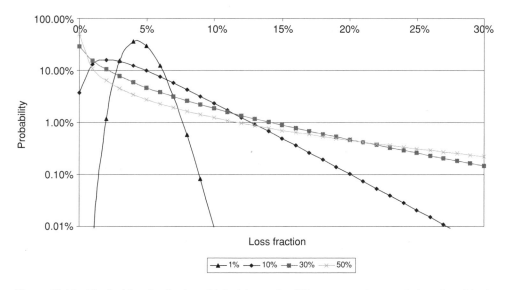

Figure 10.12   The limiting distribution of default losses for different asset value correlations, logarithmic scale

because these events are discrete in reality, but must be represented as continuous events in the infinitely large portfolio. The approximation also has problems with very low (less than 1%) asset correlation coefficients, again here the discreteness of the real world becomes noticeable. As the asset correlation coefficient tends to zero, the discrete distribution tends towards a binomial $b(n; N, p)$ distribution, while the distribution of the infinitely large portfolio tends to a default fraction of exactly p. Apart from this, the quality of the approximation is remarkable.

10.4.5   Generalisations

The results of Section 10.4.1 can be generalised to show the influence of some, seemingly innocent assumptions about the nature of the default process. More details can be found in Schönbucher (2000b).

The careful reader will have observed that in the derivation of the results for the loss distributions in Section 10.4.1 we never explicitly used the functional form of the normal distribution. We can therefore replace the normal distributions in Assumption 10.3 with other distribution functions and study the effects on the resulting loss distribution.

For example, we can replace the multivariate normal distribution of the firms' values V_n in equation (10.12) with a multivariate t-distribution. The t-distribution arises whenever the variance of a normally distributed random variable must be estimated; it can be considered to represent stochastic volatility in the firms' values. This will lead to "fat tails" in the firm's value distribution, and thus to a significantly increased level of joint default risk.

Alternatively, we can change the distribution functions of the systematic factor and the noise term. This will *not* affect the linear correlation between the values V_n and V_m of two firms (provided the second moments exist), but it may have a large impact on the default risk of a portfolio of obligors.

10.4.5.1   Multifactor dependence of defaults

The results of the previous section can also be extended to include more than one driving systematic factor for the development of the obligors' asset values. The model presented here is similar to that of Lucas *et al.* (2001).

Assumption 10.5 (multifactor firm's value model)   *The asset values of the firms are driven by J driving factors Y_j, $j \leq J$. Each factor j influences the value of the nth firm's assets with a weight of β_{nj}. Thus*

$$V_n = \sum_{j=1}^{J} \beta_{nj} Y_j + \epsilon_n,$$ (10.27)

where ϵ_n is the idiosyncratic noise of firm n.

Firm n defaults if its firm's value is below the barrier for this firm: $V_n \leq K_n$. The factors and errors are normally distributed with possibly positive correlations:

- $Y \sim \Phi(0, \Omega_Y)$: *the driving factors in firm's values,*
- $\epsilon_n \sim N(0, \omega_n^2)$: *idiosyncratic errors,*

and $(Y, \epsilon_1, \ldots, \epsilon_N)$ are independent.

Note that the assumption of uniform default probability across the portfolio has been given up.

The distribution function of the default losses can be written in closed form (see Schönbucher, 2000b), but its numerical implementation is often impossible because of the large number of summation elements in the formula.[8] Fortunately, in many practically relevant cases the number of summands can be reduced significantly.

10.4.6 Portfolios of two asset classes

As a simple example we consider the case where the portfolio of obligors can be decomposed into two classes of homogeneous obligor types.

Assumption 10.6 (homogeneous classes)   *Assume that the portfolio consists of two classes of obligors: C_1 and C_2. There are N_1 obligors of class C_1 and N_2 obligors of class C_2. Obligors of the same class have the same default barriers K_1 (or K_2) and factor loadings:*

$$V_{n_1} = \frac{1}{\sqrt{\beta_{11}^2 + \beta_{12}^2 + 1}} \left(Y_1 \beta_{11} + Y_2 \beta_{12} + \epsilon_{n_1} \right) \quad \text{for } n_1 \text{ in } C_1, \quad (10.28)$$

$$V_{n_2} = \frac{1}{\sqrt{\beta_{11}^2 + \beta_{12}^2 + 1}} \left(Y_1 \beta_{21} + Y_2 \beta_{22} + \epsilon_{n_2} \right) \quad \text{for } n_2 \text{ in } C_2. \quad (10.29)$$

The two factors Y_1 and Y_2 and the noises ϵ_{n_1} and ϵ_{n_2} are independently standard normal $\Phi(0, 1)$ distributed.

Note that we normalised the firms' values directly to an individual standard normal distribution. In many practical credit risk modelling problems the information about the obligors is given in this form. The obligors are classified into different risk classes by criteria like industry, country, rating, but within the individual risk class no distinction is made between the obligors. Similar classifications are also made by the well-known CreditMetrics (Gupton *et al.*, 1997) and Credit Risk+ (Credit Suisse First Boston, 1997) models.

The obligors' assets *within* one class are correlated with a correlation coefficient of ϱ_1 and ϱ_2 respectively, where

$$\varrho_1 = \frac{\beta_{11}^2 + \beta_{12}^2}{\beta_{11}^2 + \beta_{12}^2 + 1},$$

$$\varrho_2 = \frac{\beta_{21}^2 + \beta_{22}^2}{\beta_{21}^2 + \beta_{22}^2 + 1},$$

and the correlation of two obligors of different classes is

$$\varrho = \frac{\beta_{11}\beta_{21} + \beta_{12}\beta_{22}}{\sqrt{\beta_{11}^2 + \beta_{12}^2 + 1}\sqrt{\beta_{21}^2 + \beta_{22}^2 + 1}}.$$

---

[8] For 10 defaults out of 100 obligors there are $\binom{100}{10}$ summation elements, this is a number with 19 digits.

The calculation of the distribution function of the number of defaults in this portfolio now involves a two-dimensional integration over the possible values of the two factors Y_1 and Y_2. It is straightforward to generalise this approach to more than two classes of obligors.

Another generalisation of the model is the introduction of rating classes, which enables us to model changes in the market values of the assets in the portfolio before a default occurs. This approach is very close in spirit to CreditMetrics (Gupton *et al.*, 1997), and in the context of a large portfolio approximation was developed by Lucas *et al.* (2001). Closed-form solutions for the distribution of portfolio returns are not numerically feasible any more, but Lucas *et al.* (2001) provide an approximation.

10.4.7   Some remarks on implementation

It is not a coincidence that the setup of the model in equation (10.27) looks very much like a linear regression model. The only difference from classical linear regression is the fact that the firm's value V_n cannot be observed, but only the default/survival event. This situation is known as a *hidden variables regression problem* in the econometric literature, and the best-known methods for problems of this kind are *logit and probit regression*. In the case of normally distributed residuals ϵ_n we are dealing with a probit regression model. There is already a large literature on these models which can be directly used here, an introduction can be found in good textbooks like Greene (2000) (chapter 19), and the surveys of Amemiya (1984) and McFadden (1984).

As an alternative to the probit estimation of the fundamental asset value processes, one can calibrate the large portfolio distribution function (10.25) directly. Besides the average default rate p there is only one unknown parameter ϱ in equation (10.25). Given a historically observed distribution of default rates for a given industry/country/rating class one can imply these two parameters by fitting the distribution (10.25) to the historical observations. These parameters can then be used as asset value correlations and default probabilities in the models with fewer obligors.

This approach has the advantage of ensuring a realistic, historically confirmed shape for the distribution of default rates. Even if this approach is not taken, it should be used as a benchmark to check the results of the probit regression.

To illustrate this approach, we take the data on default rates of US corporate bonds from Figure 10.9, and fit the large portfolio distribution function (10.25) to these observations. To avoid overlapping time intervals we used only 31 observations of aggregate one-year default rates of US corporate bonds over the years 1970–2000. The log-likelihood function is easily derived from the density in (10.26), and maximisation with respect to the two parameters ϱ and p yields the estimated parameter values

$$\widehat{\varrho} = 11.21\%, \qquad \widehat{p} = 1.31\%. \tag{10.30}$$

The maximised log-likelihood function had the value -20.29. Figure 10.13 shows the fitted distribution function together with the data.

Figure 10.13 shows that even the very simplified one-factor large portfolio model generates an acceptable fit to the historically observed distribution of default rates. Using this model, the distribution can now be extrapolated into areas where no observations are available. Adding further explanatory variables (e.g. GDP growth) will also yield better estimates, as well as repeating the analysis with subsets of the observations, e.g. firms of the same rating class or industry.

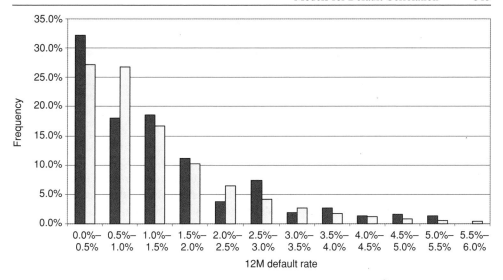

Figure 10.13 Maximum likelihood fit of the large portfolio model to Moody's one-year default rates. Left columns: historical frequencies. Right columns: fitted values

10.5   CORRELATED DEFAULTS IN INTENSITY MODELS

We used intensity-based models with great success in the pricing of single-name default risk: the intensity-based setup is particularly well suited to model rare events. Therefore it seems natural to try and extend the intensity setup to multiple obligors.

In this section we present three models that have been proposed to achieve this integration of default dependency and intensity-based individual defaults. The first approach is the most natural approach of correlating intensities, and the other two are attempts to improve upon this approach. None of the approaches is quite satisfactory. The first (correlated default intensities) cannot reproduce realistic levels of dependence, the second (joint default events) has an unrealistic distribution of defaults over time and is very difficult to implement and calibrate, and the third (infectious defaults) has a good intuition but again it is difficult to calibrate and lacks tractability.

There is a fourth intensity-based model (copula-dependent defaults) which is proposed in Section 10.8 because it requires some additional background on dependency modelling. In the author's opinion, this model dominates the other approaches, both in terms of realism and in terms of ease of implementation and calibration.

10.5.1   The intensity of the default counting process

Assume we are given a set of I individual obligors. For each $i \leq I$, the default of the ith obligor is triggered by the first jump of a point process $N_i(t)$ with intensity $\lambda_i(t)$.

To derive the distribution of the time of the *first* default of any of these I obligors, we make use of the fact that the time of the first default is the time of the first jump of

$$N(t) := \sum_{i=1}^{I} N_i(t). \tag{10.31}$$

At *each* default in the portfolio, N jumps upwards by the number of obligors who defaulted, usually *but not always* one. If there are no simultaneous defaults, $N(t)$ is again a point process. Regardless of the number of simultaneous defaults, the predictable compensator of $N(t)$ is

$$\int_0^t \lambda(s)ds = \sum_{i=1}^I \int_0^t \lambda_i(s)ds. \qquad (10.32)$$

We have $\mathbf{E}[N(t) - \int_0^t \lambda(s)ds] = 0$ for all t, and the integral of the intensity $\lambda(t)$ is a predictable process, so $\int_0^t \lambda(s)ds$ is indeed the predictable compensator of $N(t)$.

It should be noted that we did *not* need to assume that defaults occur independently or that the processes are Cox processes, or that only one obligor can default at the same time: (10.32) holds in general. Equation (10.32) also yields the intensity of N (if there are no joint defaults). This is our first result for this section:

If there are no joint defaults at the same time, the intensity of the default counting process of a portfolio of obligors is the sum of the individual default intensity processes.

It seems that there is not much more to be said about the joint defaults modelling in intensity models, after all everything reduces very conveniently to another point process with intensity. Unfortunately, there are some subtle points that destroy this bubble and force us to get knee-deep into the modelling problems. Here they are:

- The counting process N can increase by more than one at once, i.e. several obligors could default at the same time. Assume 10 obligors default jointly and have $\lambda_i = 1\% = const.$ Then $\lambda = 10\%$, but the probability of no jump of N until T is *not* $e^{-\lambda T}$, it is $e^{-\lambda_i T}$.
- Even if the N_i are all individually Cox processes, N does not have to be a Cox process.
- Even if the N_i are all individually Poisson processes, N does not have to be a Poisson process.

For these reasons, we now have to consider several modelling alternatives that have been proposed for the modelling of joint default events in intensity-based models.

10.5.2 Correlated intensities

The first possibility to incorporate dependency between two Cox processes is to introduce a correlation between the respective intensity processes, but to leave the processes independent otherwise.

Assumption 10.7

(i) The defaults of the obligors $i = 1, \ldots, I$ are triggered by the first jumps of Cox processes $N_i(t)$ with correlated intensities $\lambda_i(t)$.

(ii) Conditional on the realisations of the intensity processes $(\lambda_1(t), \ldots, \lambda_I(t))_{t \in \mathbb{R}_+}$, the processes $N_i(t)$ are independent *inhomogeneous Poisson processes with intensity* $\lambda_i(t)$ for all $i \leq I$.

Then we have for the joint default probability p_{AB} until T of two obligors A and B:

$$
\begin{aligned}
p_{AB} &= \mathbf{E}\left[\mathbf{1}_{\{A\}}\mathbf{1}_{\{B\}}\right] \\
&= \mathbf{E}\left[\mathbf{E}\left[\mathbf{1}_{\{A\}}\mathbf{1}_{\{B\}} \mid \lambda_A, \lambda_B\right]\right] \\
&= \mathbf{E}\left[\left(1 - e^{-\int_0^T \lambda_A(s)ds}\right)\left(1 - e^{-\int_0^T \lambda_B(s)ds}\right)\right] \\
&= 1 - (1 - p_A) - (1 - p_B) + \mathbf{E}\left[e^{-\int_0^T (\lambda_A(s)+\lambda_B(s))ds}\right] \\
&= p_A + p_B + \mathbf{E}\left[e^{-\int_0^T (\lambda_A(s)+\lambda_B(s))ds}\right] - 1,
\end{aligned}
$$

where p_A and p_B denote the individual default probabilities of A and B. We reach the strongest possible correlation in this setup if both intensities are perfectly correlated: $\lambda_A(s) = \lambda_B(s) = \lambda(s)$. Then:

$$
p_{AB} = 2p + \mathbf{E}\left[e^{-2\int_0^T \lambda ds}\right] - 1,
$$

where $p = p_A$. The linear correlation between the two default events is

$$
\begin{aligned}
\varrho &= \frac{2p + \mathbf{E}\left[e^{-2\int_0^T \lambda ds}\right] - 1 - p^2}{p(1-p)} \\
&= \frac{\mathbf{E}\left[e^{-2\int_0^T \lambda ds}\right] - (1-p)^2}{p(1-p)} \\
&= \frac{\mathrm{Var}\left(e^{-\int_0^T \lambda ds}\right)}{p(1-p)} \approx O(p)
\end{aligned}
$$

if we assume that the variance of the survival probability $\mathrm{Var}\left(\exp\{-\int_0^T \lambda ds\}\right)$ is of order p^2 at most. This is the case for most diffusion-based specifications of the intensity dynamics. For example, if we assume that the integral in the exponent is normally distributed (i.e. $\int_0^T \lambda(s)ds \sim \Phi(\mu, \sigma^2)$), then

$$
\begin{aligned}
\mathbf{E}\left[e^{-\int_0^T \lambda ds}\right] &= 1 - p = e^{-\mu+\frac{1}{2}\sigma^2}, \\
\mathbf{E}\left[e^{-2\int_0^T \lambda ds}\right] &= e^{-2\mu+2\sigma^2},
\end{aligned}
$$

and we reach

$$
\begin{aligned}
\varrho &= \frac{1}{e^{-\mu+\frac{1}{2}\sigma^2}\left(1 - e^{-\mu+\frac{1}{2}\sigma^2}\right)}\left(e^{-2\mu+2\sigma^2} - e^{-2\mu+\sigma^2}\right) \\
&= \frac{p}{1-p}\left(e^{\sigma^2} - 1\right).
\end{aligned}
$$

The default correlation that can be reached with correlated credit spreads in a diffusion setup is of the same order of magnitude as the default probabilities. In some applications this may be sufficient, but in many others it will be far too low, in particular if we consider that we had to assume the strongest possible correlation between the default intensities just in order to reach this small default correlation. This problem is worst for low default probabilities, low volatilities and correlations of intensities, short time to maturity, high credit quality and small numbers of credits.

The reason for the low levels of correlation is that the connection between two defaults is very indirect. Given issuer A defaults:

- λ_A was probably high.
- λ_B is probably high, too (caused by the correlation between λ_A and λ_B).
- Issuer B is more likely to default, too.

The only possibility of reaching significant levels of default correlation is the introduction of *joint jumps* in the default intensities.

If we allow for more complicated dynamics in the intensity processes, in particular joint jumps of the intensities, then the full spectrum of correlations can be reached. To see this, assume that λ_A and λ_B can jump to infinity with some probability p. Then, as soon as this jump is triggered, both A and B will default together, and we have a default correlation of 1.

10.5.3   Stress events in intensity models

The inability to achieve significant default correlations in intensity-based models with the "obvious" setup of Assumption 10.7 has sparked researchers to look for other ways of introducing stronger default dependency. Duffie and Singleton (1998) proposed the following approach.

Instead of correlating default intensities λ_A, λ_B introduce *joint default events*:

- N'_A with λ'_A – firm A defaults *alone*.
- N'_B with λ'_B – firm B defaults *alone*.
- N'_{AB} with λ'_{AB} – firms A *and* B default *together*.

In this setup, a default of each subportfolio is directly triggered by a jump process of its own. If we wanted perfect default dependence, we just have to set $\lambda'_A = 0 = \lambda'_B$ and $\lambda'_{AB} > 0$. Then, only joint defaults of the two obligors are possible.

We need to ensure that the specification of joint and individual default trigger processes is consistent with individual market-implied default intensities. For two obligors this means

$$\lambda_A = \lambda'_A + \lambda'_{AB},$$
$$\lambda_B = \lambda'_B + \lambda'_{AB}.$$

This approach can be represented more elegantly with a *marked Cox process*.

Define the *default event counting process* N', λ' with intensity

$$\lambda' := \lambda'_{A \setminus B} + \lambda'_{B \setminus A} + \lambda'_{AB}.$$

At each jump of N', we draw a *marker* X that defines the type of default event:

$$X = \begin{cases} A \setminus B & \text{with probability} & \dfrac{\lambda_{A \setminus B}}{\lambda}, \\[2mm] B \setminus A & \text{with probability} & \dfrac{\lambda_{B \setminus A}}{\lambda}, \\[2mm] AB & \text{with probability} & \dfrac{\lambda_{AB}}{\lambda}. \end{cases}$$

Formally, the original setup can be described as follows.

Assumption 10.8

(i) *There are J credit-relevant events. Event j is triggered by the first jump of a Cox process $N'_j(t)$ with intensity $\lambda'_j(t)$. The processes $N'_j(t)$ are independent from each other.*

(ii) *At each event $j \leq J$, a subset $A_j \subset \{1, \ldots, I\}$ of obligors defaults.*[9]

Under Assumption 10.8, the default intensity of obligor i is:

$$\lambda_i(t) = \sum_{j \,|\, i \in A_j} \lambda'_j(t). \tag{10.33}$$

Thus, to calibrate this model to a set of individual term structures of default risk, we must be able to evaluate expectations of the form

$$\mathbf{E}\left[e^{-\int_0^T \lambda_i(t)dt} \right] = \mathbf{E}\left[e^{-\int_0^T \sum_{j \,|\, i \in A_j} \lambda'_j(t)dt} \right]. \tag{10.34}$$

We encountered such expressions in the chapter on intensity-based models. If closed-form solutions exist, the evaluation of (10.33) should be possible. In particular specifications (for example in the framework of affine intensity-based models), closed-form solutions to (10.34) may be available even if the intensities $\lambda'_j(t)$ are correlated themselves.

With the approach of Assumption 10.8 we can reach arbitrary levels of default dependence, up to and including perfect dependence (if there is only one event which kills all obligors). This is a major improvement over the setup of Assumption 10.7, where the range of possible default dependencies was much more limited.

Yet, some problems remain also with the approach of Assumption 10.8. First, the specification of the intensities for the credit-relevant events is far from trivial. If a complete specification is desired, we will have to prescribe an intensity for every subset of the obligors, i.e. for every subset of $\{1, \ldots, I\}$. The number of subsets grows exponentially, it is

$$|\mathcal{P}(\{1, \ldots, I\})| = 2^I.$$

The average basket of an FtD swap contains 6 to 12 obligors, and this would mean specifying between $2^6 = 32$ and $2^{12} = 4096$ joint intensities. Obviously, these numbers are far too large, so we must find a way in which this number can be made manageable. If one is not willing

---

[9] Duffie and Singleton also allow for credit-relevant events that only cause jumps in the spreads of a subset of obligors but no defaults.

to make any simplifying assumptions on how the joint default intensities are specified in the model, the specification problem will become very difficult in particular if an additional calibration to individual term structures of default intensities is to be performed.

First, one can concentrate only on the *number* of joint defaults, e.g. there is one event that triggers k defaults, but *which* k obligors default is chosen at random at the time of default. Then only I events must be specified. This approach makes the number of events manageable but it represents a strong restriction on the dependency structure of the defaults in the model. Furthermore, we will run into a problem which is described in more detail below. The intensity of a k-defaults event cannot be determined from the probability of exactly k defaults alone: it will also interact with the intensities and probabilities of events with a smaller number of defaults.

Unfortunately it does not seem to be possible to delegate the allocation of intensities to one of the portfolio default risk models of the previous sections. Ideally, one would first run a factor model to reach the probabilities of the given number of joint defaults over a given time horizon, and then use these outputs in the intensity model to specify the intensity of the corresponding joint default events. This will *not* reproduce the distribution of the factor model because multiple individual default events can produce one joint default event.

For example, if the factor model gives the default probabilities $p_A = 5\%$, $p_B = 5\%$, $p_{AB} = 1\%$ over $T = 1$ a one-year time horizon, then it is tempting but wrong to specify

$$\lambda'_A = -\ln 0.95, \qquad \lambda'_B = -\ln 0.95, \qquad \lambda'_{AB} = -\ln 0.99.$$

Now the joint default probability is

$$p'_{AB} = (1 - e^{-\lambda'_{AB}}) + (1 - e^{-\lambda'_A})(1 - e^{-\lambda'_B}) = 1.25\% \neq 1\%.$$

The event of a joint default of A and B until T can also occur if the individual default events of A and B happen separately from each other, i.e. if both N'_A and N'_B jump over $[0, T]$. Thus, the probability p_{AB} of a joint default of A and B over $[0, T]$ is not $1 - e^{-\lambda_{AB}T}$. In higher dimensions this problem becomes even more complicated as many more different ways to the same default event must be considered.

It is possible to correct for this effect in the specification of the intensities, essentially we must reduce λ'_{AB} to account for the possibility that other default events can make up the joint default event AB. In principle a calibration to a fixed time horizon portfolio model is still possible, but very complicated. The intensities must be specified iteratively, starting from single-obligor intensities and increasing the size of the sets and taking into account the intensities of all subsets that were already specified. In practice such a procedure will be infeasible because the number of operations will grow exponentially.

The fact that we need to take recourse to another model for the actual *specification* of the joint default intensities shows that Assumption 10.8 is a modelling *framework* rather than a full model.

Another, more fundamental problem of this approach lies in the *time resolution* of defaults in this model. Here, joint defaults will most probably happen *at the same time*. Clustering of default times can certainly be an important risk in the model, but simultaneity of defaults seems a bit extreme, in particular if large numbers of obligors are involved. This problem could be avoided if joint default events only affected small numbers of obligors, but then this would largely eliminate the tail risk (the risk of a large number of obligors defaulting).

Furthermore, as everything happens almost instantaneously, we cannot have "crises" in this model. There may be a major joint default event that triggers the defaults of a large number of obligors, yet the default intensities of the other obligors will remain unchanged by this event. The event is over, they have not been hit, life goes on as before. This is obviously not what we observe in reality. Large defaults cause spreads (and therefore implied intensities) to increase across the board, and there is a period of crisis during which all obligors are at a higher risk.

10.5.4   Default contagion/infectious defaults

A model with a more realistic time resolution of defaults than the approach of Assumption 10.8 is the following idea by Davis and Lo (1999, 2001), and also Jarrow and Yu (2001), which tries to capture the effect of an increase in risk for other obligors that is caused by a large default.

Assumption 10.9 (infectious defaults)

- *Initially, the obligors have default intensities $\lambda_i(0) = \lambda$.*
- *At each default of one of the obligors, the default intensities of the other obligors are increased by a factor $a \geq 1$ to $a\lambda$; a is called the "risk enhancement factor".*
- *After an exponentially distributed time (with parameter μ), the default intensities return to λ.*

The fundamental idea is to let defaults occur in *bursts*, i.e. many of the defaults will occur in the period with high intensity $a\lambda$, while none of them will occur at exactly the same time. The model can then realistically reproduce clustering of defaults in time: credit crises and "recessions" are possible in this model.

Unfortunately, while the mechanism of the model is very simple to understand, the joint distribution of defaults that is implied by this model at a given time horizon T is hard to reach. But this distribution is necessary in order to understand the default behaviour implied by the model.

The Jarrow and Yu (2000) model is set up slightly differently. Here, there are two classes of obligors: large, key obligors and small, dependent obligors. If a key obligor defaults, this increases the default intensities of the dependent obligors, but not the converse. If a dependent obligor defaults, it has no effect on the default intensities of the other obligors. The authors said that they wanted to include symmetric dependency, but that the problem was too difficult. The default intensity of A depends on the defaults of B which in turn depend on the default intensity of B, which is a function of the defaults of A. This apparent circularity leads to a system of equations which must be solved simultaneously for all default intensities together.

It should be noted that the resulting joint process of the default indicators $(N_1(t), \ldots, N_I(t))$ is not a Cox process any more, because from the joint intensities we can draw conclusions about the default times. This causes many problems in the analysis of such models.

10.6   CORRELATED DEFAULTS IN FIRM'S VALUE MODELS

In the previous section we saw that intensity-based models encounter unexpected difficulties when trying to incorporate default dependence into these models. We do not expect such problems with firm's value models as we have already seen a very useful, working-fixed time-horizon version of the firm's value models in the form of the *factor models* presented in Section 10.4. Thus, there are two main tasks left to achieve: *calibration* to individual term structures of survival probabilities, and implementation of a realistic *time structure* of the defaults.

The firm's value approach does not exhibit the surprising difficulties we encountered in the intensity-based approach. We only encounter difficulties that were to be expected, mainly numerical complexity and the predictability of the default times.

For instance, the following, intuitive setup is indeed able to produce a complete range of default correlations. Consider the following simplest example, a variant of the Merton (1974) model with two obligors.

- Firm A: logarithmic value of assets V_A.
- Firm B: logarithmic value of assets V_B.
- Defaults only at T if $V_A < K_A$ or $V_B < K_B$.
- V_A and V_B follow Brownian motions:

$$dV_A = \mu_A dt + \sigma_A dW_A, \qquad dV_B = \mu_B dt + \sigma_B dW_B.$$

We now model the correlation directly as a correlation between the Brownian motions driving the firm's value processes:

$$dW_A dW_B = \varrho dt.$$

This can be rewritten as: $dV_A = \sigma_A dW_1$ and

$$dV_B = \sigma_B \left(\varrho dW_1 + \sqrt{1 - \varrho^2} \, dW_2 \right),$$

where W_1 and W_2 are independent Brownian motions. (Note the similarity with the firm's value model used in the factor models of Section 10.4.)

Without loss of generality we modelled the logarithm of the asset value process. Furthermore we can set $K_A < 0$, $K_B < 0$, $V_A(0) = V_B(0) = 0$ and $\sigma_A = \sigma_B = 1$. All these transformations only change the time and space scales. We also set $T = 1$ for the final time and neglect the drift terms (they can be absorbed into the default barriers). Then the final values are standard normally distributed:

$$V_A(T) \sim \Phi(0, 1), \qquad V_B(T) \sim \Phi(0, 1).$$

The individual default probabilities are

$$p_A = \Phi(K_A), \qquad p_B = \Phi(K_B),$$

where $\Phi(\cdot)$ is the standard normal distribution function. The joint default probability is

$$p_{AB} = \Phi_\varrho(K_A, K_B),$$

where $\Phi_\varrho(a, b)$ is the bivariate standard normal distribution function with correlation ϱ.

Now *all* default correlations are possible:

- $\varrho = 1 \rightarrow$ defaults perfectly correlated,
- $\varrho = -1 \rightarrow$ defaults mutually exclusive,
- $\varrho = 0 \rightarrow$ defaults independent,
- $\varrho > 0 \rightarrow$ defaults positively correlated.

This simple example can be extended to include more obligors by adding more correlated Brownian motions. As no intermediate defaults are permitted in the setup, this model can be considered as equivalent to the factor models that were explained previously.

Within the theoretical framework of the diffusion-based firm's value models, the local correlation between the firm's value processes must be identical to the local correlation of the firm's share prices. This can be seen as follows.

In all firm's value models, the share price is a function

$$E(V, t, K)$$

of the firm's value V, time t and some other parameters which are constant, here summarised in K. Let us assume that we have two firms A and B with lognormal, correlated firm's value processes V_A and V_B. Then the dynamics of the share prices are given by Itô's lemma:

$$dE_A = (\ldots)dt + \delta_A dV_A,$$
$$dE_B = (\ldots)dt + \delta_B dV_B,$$

where $\delta_A = \partial f(V_A, t, K_A)/\partial V_A$ and $\delta_B = \partial f(V_B, t, K_B)/\partial V_B$. We are interested in the local correlation coefficient so we can ignore the drift term. The local equity correlation is the number ρ_E which makes

$$dE_A dE_B = \sigma_{E_A}\sigma_{E_B}^T \rho_E dt.$$

The components of this expression are:

$$\sigma_{E_A} = \delta_A\sigma_{V_A} = \delta_A\sigma_A(1, \ 0),$$
$$\sigma_{E_B} = \delta_B\sigma_{V_B} = \delta_B\sigma_B\left(\rho, \ \sqrt{1 - \rho^2}\right),$$
$$dE_A dE_B = \delta_A dV_A\delta_B dV_B = \delta_A\delta_B\sigma_A\sigma_B\rho dt.$$

Substituting in the equation yields

$$\rho_E = \rho.$$

The local correlation between share prices should be equal to the local correlation between the underlying firm's value processes. Locally, we can consider a share of firm A as a portfolio of δ_A units of the firm's value of firm A. But (locally) constant factors like δ_A do not affect the correlation coefficient, so firm's value correlation should be equal to share price correlation.

Unfortunately, this theoretical result does not correspond to reality. In the calibration of the one-factor firm's value model in Section 10.4 we found in equation (10.30) that a firm's value correlation of $\varrho = 11.21\%$ yields a loss distribution which is roughly consistent with historical experience. Share price correlations on the other hand are significantly higher, values like 30% would be typical and even values of up to 60% are quite common in some sectors. There is no real resolution to this contradiction, it is an indication that the firm's value model may not fit reality as well as would be desirable. Possible explanations are that short-term share movements are mainly driven by liquidity, thus creating correlation in short-term time series which in reality is not there, or that there are different correlations whether we consider large, fundamental moves in the fate of the firms or small, daily movements of the share prices. Whatever explanation one prefers, the fact remains that the firm's value model does not seem to capture these features.

In order to achieve a time resolution of defaults and joint default events, Zhou (2001) extended this setup to include barrier defaults analogous to the Black and Cox (1976) model in the case of two obligors. Thus, firm A now defaults if its value falls below $C_A(t) = e^{\gamma_A t} K_A$, and the barrier for firm B is $C_B(t) = e^{\gamma_B t} K_B$.

If the default barriers grow exponentially at the rates of the drift terms, Zhou (2001) gives the following result.

Proposition 10.1   *Assume the firm's value processes follow lognormal Brownian motions*

$$d \ln V_{A;B} = \mu_{A;B} dt + \sigma_{A;B} dW_{A;B}$$

and let the default times be given as the first hitting times of the barriers $C_{A;B}(t)$ given above. Set

$$Z_{A;B} := \frac{\ln(V_{A;B}/K_{A;B})}{\sigma_{A;B}}.$$

Let $\gamma_A = \mu_A$ and $\gamma_B = \mu_B$. Then the probability of a default of either A or B until t is

$$p_{A \vee B} = 1 - \frac{2r_0}{\sqrt{2\pi t}} e^{-\frac{r_0^2}{4t}}$$

$$\times \sum_{n=1,3,\dots} \frac{1}{n} \sin\left(\frac{n\pi\theta_0}{\alpha}\right) \left[I_{\frac{1}{2}(\frac{n\pi}{\alpha}+1)}\left(\frac{r_0^2}{4t}\right) + I_{\frac{1}{2}(\frac{n\pi}{\alpha}-1)}\left(\frac{r_0^2}{4t}\right) \right],$$

where $I_\nu(\cdot)$ is the modified Bessel function of order ν and

$$\alpha = \begin{cases} \tan^{-1}\left(-\frac{\sqrt{1-\varrho^2}}{\varrho}\right) & \text{if } \varrho < 0, \\ \pi + \tan^{-1}\left(-\frac{\sqrt{1-\varrho^2}}{\varrho}\right) & \text{otherwise,} \end{cases}$$

$$\theta_0 = \begin{cases} \tan^{-1}\left(\frac{Z_2\sqrt{1-\varrho^2}}{Z_1 - \varrho Z_2}\right) & \text{if } (\cdot) > 0, \\ \pi + \tan^{-1}\left(\frac{Z_2\sqrt{1-\varrho^2}}{Z_1 - \varrho Z_2}\right) & \text{otherwise,} \end{cases}$$

$$r_0 = Z_2/\sin(\theta_0).$$

Proof.   For a proof see Zhou (2001).   □

Whether or not one would consider this result as a closed-form formula, in any case the implementation of this formula is far from trivial. We need modified Bessel functions of fractional (non-integer) orders, and must compute a series of these. Zhou (2001) also gives an even more complicated formula for the case of $\gamma_{A;B} \neq \mu_{A;B}$, this formula now involves an infinite sum over indefinite integrals of modified Bessel functions.

This is the limit of what can be reached in the search for closed-form solutions. For example, if the number of obligors is increased by just one, all these solutions break down. Furthermore, even the Merton (1974) setup with $n > 5$ obligors would require the evaluation of an n-dimensional cumulative normal distribution function for which no algorithms exist except brute-force numerical integration.[10]

The model of Zhou (2001) is *not* calibrated to any term structure of individual survival probabilities, and by choosing K and γ, one can only fit two parameters of the curve. On the other hand, the interpretation of the dependency between the defaults of the two firms is very nice, the number of parameters is just right (pairwise correlations), and there may be other sources for the parameter values (the same as in the factor models).

Hull and White (2001) introduced a method to calibrate time-dependent default barriers $C_i(t)$ to a given term structure of default *hazard rates*

$$h_i(0, t),$$

while retaining the fundamental model setup of Zhou (2001). The idea is that by choosing the values for the time-dependent default barrier, one can adjust the model in such a way that it reproduces the initial term structure of hazard rates while retaining the attractive correlation structure of the firm's value approach.

Hull and White (2001) proceed as follows.

1. Choose a time step Δt. Set $t_0 = 0$. Define
   - q_{ij}: the risk-neutral default probability of company j at time $t_i = i\Delta t$,
   - K_{ij}: the value of the barrier of firm j at time t_i,
   - $f_{ij}(x)\Delta x$: the probability that $V_j(t_i)$ is in $[x, x + \Delta x]$ *and* there has been no default by company j before t_i.
2. Initialisation:
   - Calculate $f_{1j}(x)$: It is just the risk-neutral transition probability of the value process of firm j over Δt.
   - Choose K_{1j} such that $h_j(0, t_1)$ is fitted.
   - q_{1j} follows from K_{1j}.
3. Iteration: At each t_i
   - Calculate $f_{ij}(x)$: this is an updating problem given $f_{i-1,j}(x)$. We must evolve these values forward according to

$$f_{ij}(x) = \int_{K_{i-1,j}}^{\infty} f_{i-1,j}(u) \frac{1}{\sqrt{2\pi}\sigma_i} \exp\left\{ -\frac{(x-u)^2}{2\sigma_i^2} \right\} du.$$

This equation gives the conditional density of $V_j(t_i)$, conditional on no default until t_{i-1} up to a constant factor.

---

[10] And even if an n-variate cumulative normal distribution function could be evaluated, there would be 2^N different events to evaluate – far too many for large n.

• The default probability over the next time step is

$$q_{ij} = \int_{K_{i-1,j}}^{\infty} f_{i-1,j}(u) \frac{1}{\sqrt{2\pi}\sigma_i} \exp\left\{-\frac{(K_{ij}-u)^2}{2\sigma_i}\right\} du.$$

Choose K_{ij} such that $h_j(0, t_i)$ and q_{ij} are fitted.

This procedure will ensure that *initially*, all term structures are fitted. It is numerically feasible because the fit can be done firm-by-firm, iteratively over all j. Nevertheless, there are other problems with this approach.

• The fitted barriers have an unrealistic shape. As seen in Chapter 9, diffusion-based firm's value models have predictable default times which cause the short-term credit spreads to converge to zero. This is forced by the fact that a diffusion process will only travel a small distance over a small time step almost certainly.

 Mathematically, this property has been well analysed. For Brownian motion it can be proven[11] that over a short time interval $[0, h]$, the Brownian motion will remain in a flat parabola of the shape of the square-root function $\pm\sqrt{h} \ln\ln h$. In fact, with probability 1 it will hit the parabola but not exceed it. For the calibration of a term structure of hazard rates with a positive short-term credit spread, this means that *the calibrated barrier level must also follow a square-root shape as $t \to 0$*. Furthermore, the calibration will be unstable, because the barrier level is either hit with certainty, or not hit with certainty. The fact that Hull and White (2001) use a discrete time step dampens most of these effects, but the fundamental problem remains.

• The fit will be wrong almost immediately after $t = 0$. We saw that the short-term credit spreads could only be fitted if the barrier approaches the current value of the firm's value like a square-root function from below. After one time step Δt, the firm will have moved away from the barrier (or it will have defaulted), thus causing the short-term credit spreads to drop to zero immediately. The short-term credit spreads are extremely *unstable* in this setup.

These problems do not arise because the model is multivariate, they would also occur if the same procedure was tried for a one-obligor firm's value model. There are better ways to incorporate a firm's value-based default dependency structure into an intensity-based setup, the copula approach.

10.7 COPULA FUNCTIONS AND DEPENDENCY CONCEPTS

In the previous sections we have seen a number of models which – some better, some worse – capture salient features of default dependency. Yet all these models have their problems. Some models (e.g. the factor models and Merton-type firm's value-based models with correlated asset values) are able to capture default dependency in a very intuitive way, but cannot resolve the *timing* of the default times in the portfolio. Others are indeed able to capture default timing,

---

[11] This result is known as the *law of the iterated logarithm*, see Karatzas and Shreve (1991).

but are extremely difficult to calibrate and implement (e.g. barrier-based firm's value models) or have a very large number of parameters (intensity-based approaches).

In this section we describe how one can combine a general default dependency framework with a calibration to a given set of individual term structures of credit spreads. This is achieved by separating the individual term structure of default risk from the default dependency model using *copula functions*. After an overview of copula functions in general, we first analyse the copula approach in a static setup. This will already give a lot of insight into the influence of the dependency structure on the distribution of a portfolio's losses. The real power of the copula method appears when this approach is extended into continuous time, using the copula transformation to generate dependent default times. This is analysed in the following section. Finally, we give an outlook over the effects of the different possible specifications of the dependency structure on the portfolio's risk and return profile.

In the following, vectors are denoted in **boldface x**, as are vector-valued functions **f(x)**. For functions that use vectors $\mathbf{x} = (x_1, \ldots, x_I)$ as arguments we use the following notation if we replace the ith component of $\mathbf{x}$ with y:

$$f(\mathbf{x}_{-i}, y) := f(x_1, \ldots, x_{i-1}, y, x_{i+1}, \ldots, x_I). \tag{10.35}$$

1 is the vector $(1, \ldots, 1)$ and $\mathbf{0} = (0, \ldots, 0)$. Comparisons between vectors are meant component-wise. Vectors of functions $F_i : \mathbb{R} \to \mathbb{R}$ are written as

$$\mathbf{F}(\mathbf{x}) := (F_1(x_1), F_2(x_2), \ldots, F_I(x_I)). \tag{10.36}$$

10.7.1 Copula functions

We want to model the default times of several obligors. There are two aspects to this. On the one hand we have to model the default dynamics of a single obligor and on the other hand we have to model the dependence structure of the defaults *between* the obligors. In this section we present some basic tools for the dependency modelling side of the problem and introduce the fundamental concept of a *copula function*. Further details on dependency modelling and copula functions and the proofs of the propositions in this subsection can be found in the excellent book by Joe (1997), and mostly also in the book by Nelsen (1999).

Definition 10.3 (copula)   *A function $C : [0, 1]^I \to [0, 1]$ is a copula if:*

(a) *There are random variables $U_1, \ldots, U_I$ taking values in $[0, 1]$ such that C is their distribution function;*
(b) *C has uniform marginal distributions, i.e. for all $i \leq I$, $u_i \in [0, 1]$*

$$C(1, \ldots, 1, u_i, 1, \ldots, 1) = u_i.$$

Copulas concentrate on the dependency, so the marginal distributions are irrelevant. They are set to uniform distributions because this makes the later incorporation of other marginal distributions straightforward, and we recover the benchmark case of the uniform distribution on $[0, 1]$ if we ignore the other $I - 1$ random variables. The reason why we can concentrate on the copula alone is given in Sklar's theorem. The starting point for understanding this theorem is the following elementary fact for continuous distribution functions F.

Proposition 10.2 *Let X denote a random variable with continuous distribution function F, then $Z = F(X)$ has a uniform distribution on $[0, 1]$. If U is a random variable with uniform distribution on $[0, 1]$, then $Y = F^{[-1]}(U)$ has the distribution function $F(\cdot)$.*

We have already made use of the second statement when we simulated normally distributed random variates in Excel. Excel only provides uniformly distributed random variates (in the function RAND($\cdot$)), but if we combine this function with the inverse of the standard normal distribution function NORMSINV(RAND($\cdot$)), we reach a standard normal random variate.

If we consider a whole set of I real-valued random variables, all information that we might possibly want is completely described by the joint distribution function of these random variables. The joint distribution F of the random variables $X_1, X_2, \ldots, X_I$ is:

$$F(\mathbf{x}) = \mathbf{P}[X_1 \le x_1, X_2 \le x_2, \ldots, X_I \le x_I].$$

Besides the joint distribution function, the (marginal) distribution functions $F_i(\cdot)$ of the X_i for $i \le I$ are also of interest:

$$F_i(x) := \mathbf{P}[X_i \le x].$$

The basic idea of the analysis of dependency with copula functions is that the joint distribution function F can be separated into two parts. The first part is represented by the marginal distribution functions of the random variables (the marginals) and the other part is the dependence structure between the random variables which is described by the copula function. Sklar's theorem below shows how this decomposition can be achieved for any set of random variables.

Theorem 10.3 (Sklar) *Let $X_1, \ldots, X_I$ be random variables with marginal distribution functions $F_1, F_2, \ldots, F_I$ and joint distribution function F. Then there exists an I-dimensional copula C such that for all $\mathbf{x} \in \mathbb{R}^I$:*

$$F(\mathbf{x}) = C(F_1(x_1), F_2(x_2), \ldots, F_I(x_I)) = C(\mathbf{F}(\mathbf{x})),$$

i.e. C is the distribution function of $(F_1(x_1), F_2(x_2), \ldots, F_I(x_I))$. If $F_1, F_2, \ldots, F_I$ are continuous, then C is unique. Otherwise C is uniquely determined on $Ran F_1 \times \cdots \times Ran F_I$, where $Ran F_i$ denotes the range of F_i for $i = 1, \ldots, I$.

Sklar's theorem states that for any multivariate distribution, the univariate margins and the dependence structure can be separated. The dependence structure is completely characterised by the copula C. We say that $X_1, X_2, \ldots, X_I$ have a copula C, where C is given by Theorem 10.3.

This separation also tells us that we can borrow the dependency structure (i.e. the copula function) of one set of dependent random variables, and exchange the marginal distribution functions for an entirely different set of marginal distributions. This is precisely what we are planning to do in the following sections.

By Theorem 10.3 the copula of $\mathbf{X}$ is the distribution function[12] of $\mathbf{F}(\mathbf{X})$, this is the multivariate analogy to Proposition 10.2. Furthermore, we are free to transform the X_i. This will not

---

[12] Watch the notation: $F(\mathbf{x})$ is the joint distribution function at $\mathbf{x} = (x_1, \ldots, x_I)$ whereas $\mathbf{F}(\mathbf{x})$ is the vector of marginal probabilities $(F_1(x_1), \ldots, F_I(x_I))$. As $\mathbf{F}(\mathbf{x})$ is vector-valued, the difference will also be clear from the context.

change the copula as long as all transformations are monotonously increasing. A monotonously increasing transformation of one component of the random vector will change its marginal distribution function, but this change in the distribution function will be reversed once it is operated upon by the new distribution function.

The following formal definition of a copula function is also frequently used, it looks a bit different and loses the direct link to the joint distribution of a set of random variables.

Definition 10.4   *A copula is any function $C : [0, 1]^I \to [0, 1]$ which has the following properties:*

1. $C(\mathbf{1}_{-i}, v_i) = v_i$ for all $i = 1, \ldots, I$, $v_i \in [0, 1]$ and for every $\mathbf{v} \in [0, 1]^I$, $C(\mathbf{v}) = 0$ if at least one coordinate of the vector $\mathbf{v}$ is 0.
2. For all $\mathbf{a}, \mathbf{b} \in [0, 1]^I$ with $\mathbf{a} \le \mathbf{b}$ the volume of the hypercube with corners $\mathbf{a}$ and $\mathbf{b}$ is non-negative, i.e. we have

$$\sum_{i_1=1}^{2} \sum_{i_2=1}^{2} \cdots \sum_{i_I=1}^{2} (-1)^{i_1+i_2+\cdots+i_I} C(v_{i_1}, v_{i_2}, \ldots, v_{i_I}) \ge 0$$

where $v_{j_1} = a_j$ and $v_{j_2} = b_j$ for all $j = 1, \ldots, I$.

At first it is not at all clear from Definition 10.4 that a copula function has any connection at all to the joint distribution of random variables. Looking more closely, the summation in this definition ensures that the copula can be used as a distribution function on $[0, 1]^I$ because it assigns non-negative weight to all rectangular subsets of $[0, 1]^I$.

Here are some more properties of copula functions.

Proposition 10.4

(i) *(Invariance to increasing transformations.) Let $\mathbf{X} = (X_1, \ldots, X_I)$ be a vector of random variables with copula $C(\mathbf{u})$. Let $f_i : \mathbb{R} \to \mathbb{R}$ be a family of I strictly increasing functions. Then $C(\cdot)$ is again the copula of $\mathbf{X}' = (f_1(X_1), \ldots, f(X_I))$.*

(ii) *Let C be an I-dimensional copula. The copula C is non-decreasing in each argument, i.e. if $\mathbf{v} \in [0, 1]^I$ then*

$$C(\mathbf{v}) \le C(\mathbf{v}_{-j}, v'_j) \quad \forall\, 1 \ge v'_j > v_j,\ \forall\, j \le I.$$

(iii) *(Fréchet–Hoeffding bounds.) Let C be an I-dimensional copula. Then for every $\mathbf{v} \in [0, 1]^I$:*

$$W^I(\mathbf{v}) \le C(\mathbf{v}) \le M^I(\mathbf{v}),$$

with

$$W^I(\mathbf{v}) = \max(v_1 + v_2 + \cdots + v_I - I + 1, 0),$$
$$M^I(\mathbf{v}) = \min(v_1, v_2, \ldots, v_I).$$

The Fréchet bounds are the copula functions for the largest possible positive and negative dependence. The functions M^I are copulas for all $I \geq 2$, they are the distribution function of $(U_1, \ldots, U_I)$ if all components are equal to one uniform [0, 1]-distributed random variable U, i.e. $U_i = U$. The functions W^I on the other hand are never copulas for $I > 2$. W^2 is a copula, it is the copula of $(U, 1 - U)$, where $U \sim [0, 1]$.

10.7.2 Examples of copulae

Copula functions are the most general way to view dependence of random variables, in many ways one might as well directly speak of "distribution functions". So this concept is much more general than linear correlation which often fails to capture important risks.[13] For mathematical analysis in full generality and to set up a modelling *framework* this is very convenient, but to build, parametrise and implement a model for a real-world phenomenon this generality allows far too much freedom. There are as many different copula functions as there are random variates on $[0, 1]^I$, an infinite plethora. Given the scarcity of data on default correlation, we must restrict ourselves to some convenient low-parametric families of copula functions. It is one of the great advantages of modelling dependency in a copula framework that it now becomes clear which restrictions we make when we choose, say, a Gaussian (or any other) copula. In this subsection we present some families of copula functions. In the end we will use the Gaussian and the t-copulae, but we could have chosen any other copula function, too.

The simplest example of a copula is the product copula which corresponds to the uniform distribution on $[0, 1]^I$. This copula is the *product (or independence) copula*, it is the copula that is common to all vectors of I *independent* random variables.

Definition 10.5 (product copula)   *The I-dimensional product (or independence) copula Π^I is given by:*

$$\Pi^I(\mathbf{v}) = v_1 \cdot v_2 \cdot \cdots \cdot v_I.$$

It is the copula of independent random variables.

Because the copula completely specifies the dependency structure of a set of random variables, independence of continuous random variables can be characterised by the copula. The random variables $X_1, X_2, \ldots, X_I$ are independent if and only if the I-dimensional copula C of $X_1, X_2, \ldots, X_I$ is:

$$C(\mathbf{F}(\mathbf{x})) = \Pi^I(\mathbf{F}(\mathbf{x})).$$

Like the Fréchet–Hoeffding bounds, the independence copula is an important benchmark case. In many applications, the normal or Gaussian copula plays an important role.

Definition 10.6 (Gaussian copula)   *Let $X_1, \ldots, X_I$ be normally distributed random variables with means $\mu_1, \ldots, \mu_I$, standard deviations $\sigma_1, \ldots, \sigma_I$ and correlation matrix R. Then*

---

[13] See Embrechts *et al.* (2002) for more details.

the distribution function $C_R(u_1, \ldots, u_I)$ of the random variables

$$U_i := \Phi\left(\frac{X_i - \mu_i}{\sigma_i}\right), \quad i \leq I \tag{10.37}$$

is a copula and it is called the Gaussian copula to the correlation matrix R *(where $\Phi(\cdot)$ denotes the cumulative univariate standard normal distribution function).*

The Gaussian copula is popular for several reasons. It is very easy to draw random samples from it, correlated Gaussian random variables are well known and their dependency structure is well understood, it has just about the "right" number of free parameters, and it is to some degree analytically tractable.

The following algorithm generates random samples from the Gaussian copula with correlation matrix R:

1. Generate $X_1, \ldots, X_I$ which are jointly $\Phi_{0,R}(\cdot)$ normal distributed with mean zero, standard deviation one and correlation matrix R.
2. Let

$$U_i := \Phi(X_i), \quad \forall\, i \leq I \tag{10.38}$$

where $\Phi(\cdot)$ is the univariate cumulative normal distribution function. Then $U_1, \ldots, U_I$ are C_R-distributed.

The flexibility of copula functions allows us to equip random variables with a Gaussian copula that are not normally distributed in their marginal distribution. For example, we could generate random variables that are exponentially distributed in the margin, but have a Gaussian copula function by generating the U_i as above and setting

$$Y_i := -\ln U_i.$$

Then $\mathbf{P}[Y_i \leq y] = 1 - e^{-y}$: the Y_i have an exponential distribution, but a Gaussian dependence structure.

There are $\frac{1}{2}(I-1)(I-2)$ free parameters in a Gaussian copula: the pairwise correlations of the X_i. This allows us to specify the dependence structure by specifying *pairwise* dependence between the different obligors. If the number of obligors is large (e.g. $I = 100$), this may still be too much freedom. In this case, a factor structure can be imposed (see e.g. Section 10.4) to reduce the number of unknowns. On the other hand, it is not possible to specify *additional* dependencies beyond the $\frac{1}{2}(I-1)(I-2)$ pairwise correlations.

Figure 10.14 shows the density of a Gaussian copula function where the original random variates had a correlation coefficient of $\rho = 50\%$. A particular feature of the Gaussian copula are the singularities at $(0,0)$ and $(1,1)$ which imply that the type of dependency changes between the corners and in the middle of the copula.

A variant of the Gaussian copula is the t-copula.

Definition 10.7 (t-copula) *Let $X_1, \ldots, X_I$ be normally distributed random variables with mean zero, standard deviation one[14] and correlation matrix R. Let Y be a χ^2-distributed*

---

[14] Mean and standard deviation are not relevant for the copula function.

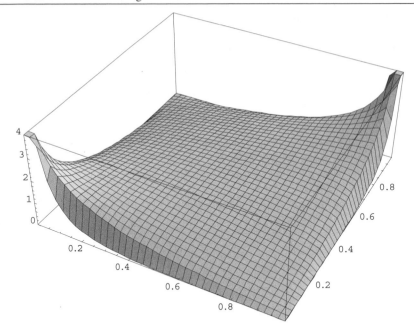

Figure 10.14 The density of a two-dimensional Gaussian copula where the original random variates had correlation $\rho = 50\%$

random variable with v degrees of freedom which is independent of $(X_1, \ldots, X_I)$. Then the distribution function $C_{v,R}(u_1, \ldots, u_I)$ of the random variables

$$U_i := t_v \left(\frac{\sqrt{v}}{\sqrt{Y}} X_i \right), \quad i \le I \tag{10.39}$$

is a copula and it is called the t-copula with v degrees of freedom and the correlation matrix R. Here t_v is the univariate Student t-distribution function with v degrees of freedom.

In the construction of the t-copula we used the fact that X_i/Y is t_v-distributed. The t-copula inherits almost all properties of the Gaussian copula, with the exception of *tail dependence*.

The formal definition of tail dependence is as follows.

Definition 10.8 (tail dependence) *If a bivariate copula $C(u, v)$ is such that*

$$\lim_{u \to 1} \frac{1 + C(u, u) - 2u}{1 - u} = \lambda_U > 0 \tag{10.40}$$

then C has upper tail dependence *with parameter λ_U. If*

$$\lim_{u \to 0} \frac{C(u, u)}{u} = \lambda_L > 0 \tag{10.41}$$

then C has lower tail dependence *with parameter λ_L.*

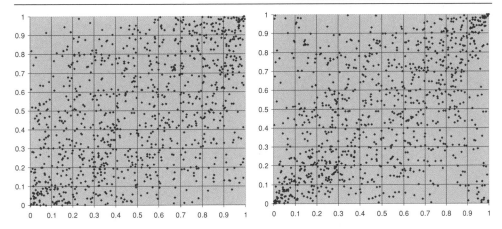

Figure 10.15   1000 samples from a Gaussian (left) and a t-copula (right): $\rho = 50\%$, $v = 2$

Essentially, lower tail dependence means that as $u \to 0$ the probability mass that is in the lower square $[0, u] \times [0, u]$ tends to zero like $\lambda_L u$, and not like u^2, the area of the square. This means that there must be a rather strong singularity of the copula's density in the lower left corner $(0, 0)$. Upper tail dependence means the same for a small square in the upper right corner $(1, 1)$. In a credit setup, we will be able to give another interpretation for upper tail dependence. The upper tail dependence parameter will be connected to the intensity of joint default events at $t = 0$.

Gaussian copulas are *tail independent*, i.e. the dependence modelled by the Gaussian copula disappears for joint extreme events (all U_i close to 0 or close to 1). Although it has the singularities at $(0, 0)$ and $(1, 1)$, these singularities are not strong enough to cause tail dependence. Extreme events occur almost independently from each other in a Gaussian copula setup. The t-copula on the other hand does exhibit positive *tail dependence*, here extreme events are dependent. The tail dependency parameters of the t_v-copula are

$$\lambda_U = 2 - 2t_{v+1}\left(\frac{\sqrt{v+1}\sqrt{1-\rho}}{\sqrt{1+\rho}}\right),$$

where ρ is the linear correlation between the two considered random variables. Figure 10.15 shows 1000 samples from a Gaussian copula and from a t-copula. For both graphs, the same bivariate normally distributed random variables were used, but for the t-copula these were mixed in addition with a χ^2-distributed random variable with two degrees of freedom. It can be seen very nicely that the samples from the t-copula cluster much more in the upper right and lower left corner than the samples from the Gaussian copula.

10.7.3 Archimedean copulae

Archimedean copulas have a very high degree of analytical tractability but the number of free parameters is very low, usually only one or two parameters can be adjusted. This is not sufficient if the dependency structure is to be modelled in more detail. Nevertheless, they can be very useful as test cases and there are generalisations of the Archimedean copula which allow for more freedom in the specification of the dependencies.

Definition 10.9 (Archimedean copula)

(i) *An* Archimedean copula *function $C : [0, 1]^I \rightarrow [0, 1]$ is a copula function which can be represented in the following form:*

$$C(\mathbf{x}) = \phi^{[-1]}\left(\sum_{i=1}^{I} \phi(x_i)\right), \tag{10.42}$$

with a suitable function $\phi : [0, 1] \rightarrow \mathbb{R}_+$ with $\phi(1) = 0$, $\phi(0) = \infty$.
(ii) *The function $\phi : [0, 1] \rightarrow \mathbb{R}_+$ is called the* generator *of the copula.*

Not every function ϕ is a suitable generator for a copula function, there are restrictions on the signs of the derivatives of ϕ which become more stringent with increasing dimension I. But in the following case the existence of the copula can be ensured.

If $F(x)$ is a distribution function of a positive random variable with $F(x = 0) = 0$ and $\hat{F}(y)$ is its Laplace transform, then $\phi(t) := \hat{F}^{[-1]}(t)$ is the generator of an Archimedean copula of dimension I for every $I > 0$. In fact, $\phi^{[-1]}(\cdot)$ must be a Laplace transform if it is to be an admissible generator for *any* dimension $I > 0$.

Definition 10.10 (Laplace transform) *Let Y be a non-negative random variable with distribution function $G(y)$ and density function $g(y)$ (if a density exists). Then:*

(i) *The Laplace transform of Y is defined as*

$$\mathcal{L}_Y(t) := \mathbf{E}[e^{-tY}] = \int_0^\infty e^{-ty} dG(y) = \int_0^\infty e^{-ty} g(y) dy =: \mathcal{L}_g(t), \quad \forall t \geq 0. \tag{10.43}$$

(ii) *Let $\psi : \mathbb{R}_+ \rightarrow [0, 1]$. If a solution exists, the inverse Laplace transform $\mathcal{L}_\psi^{[-1]}$ of ψ is defined as the function $\chi : \mathbb{R}_+ \rightarrow [0, 1]$ which solves*

$$\mathcal{L}_\chi(t) = \int_0^\infty e^{-ty} \chi(y) dy = \psi(t), \quad \forall t \geq 0.$$

(iii) *The distribution of Y is uniquely characterised by its Laplace transform.*

From equation (10.42) we can see that Archimedean copula models are *exchangeable*, i.e. the dependency between any two (or more) different variables X_i, X_j does not depend on the question *which* pair was chosen. For assessing portfolio credit risk in large, homogeneous portfolios this does not pose a major restriction, in fact it is a desirable property. For other, more realistic applications this may be too restrictive and the class of copulae must be extended.

Figure 10.16 shows 1000 samples from the Clayton and the Gumbel copulae, respectively. Both copulae are remarkable because they exhibit an asymmetric dependency structure: the Clayton copula exhibits lower tail dependency but no upper tail dependency, while the Gumbel copula has upper tail dependency but no lower tail dependency.

In Table 10.4 we give some popular specifications of the generator functions ϕ and their inverses $\phi^{[-1]}$, together with the inverse Laplace transform of the inverse generator, i.e. the density of the random variable Y.

Table 10.4   Some generators for Archimedean copulas, their
inverses and Laplace transforms

1.   Name: Clayton
$$\phi(t) = (t^{-\theta} - 1)$$
$$\phi^{[-1]}(s) = (1 + s)^{-1/\theta}$$
Parameter: $\theta \geq 0$
Y-distribution: Gamma $(1/\theta)$
Density of Y: $\dfrac{1}{\Gamma(1/\theta)} e^{-y} y^{(1-\theta)/\theta}$

2.   Name: Gumbel
$$\phi(t) = (-\ln t)^{\theta}$$
$$\phi^{[-1]}(t) = e^{(-s^{1/\theta})}$$
Parameter: $\theta \geq 1$
Y-distribution: α-stable, $\alpha = 1/\theta$
Density of Y: (no closed form is known)

3.   Name: Frank
$$\phi(t) = -\ln \frac{e^{-\theta t} - 1}{e^{-\theta} - 1}$$
$$\phi^{[-1]}(t) = -\frac{1}{\theta} \ln[1 - e^{-s}(1 - e^{-\theta})]$$
Parameter: $\theta \in \mathbb{R}\backslash\{0\}$
Y-distribution: logarithmic series on $\mathbb{N}_+$ with $\alpha = (1 - e^{-\theta})$
Distribution of Y: $\mathbf{P}[Y = k] = \dfrac{-1}{\ln(1 - \alpha)} \dfrac{\alpha^k}{k}$

Source: Marshall and Olkin (1988).

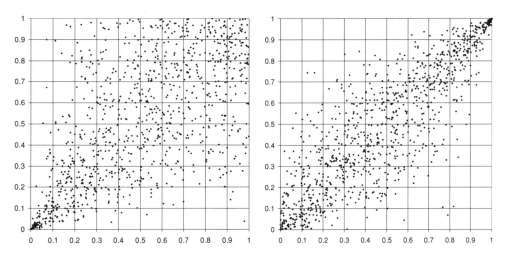

Figure 10.16   1000 samples from a Clayton copula (left, parameter $\theta = 2$) and a Gumbel copula (right,
parameter $\theta = 3$)

A highly efficient strategy for the sampling of a random vector X which has a given Archimedean copula as distribution function is the following algorithm by Marshall and Olkin (1988).

Theorem 10.5 (Marshall and Olkin, 1988) *Let $\phi : [0, 1] \to \mathbb{R}_+$ and its inverse $\phi^{[-1]}$: $\mathbb{R}_+ \to [0, 1]$ be continuous, strictly decreasing functions, where $\phi^{[-1]}$ is a Laplace transform for a strictly positive random variable Y. Follow the following algorithm:*

(a) Draw $X_1, \ldots, X_I$ i.i.d. uniformly distributed on $[0, 1]$.
(b) Draw the mixing variable Y with the following properties:
  * *Y is independent of $X_1, \ldots, X_I$;*
  * *Y's Laplace transform is $\phi^{[-1]}(\cdot)$.*
(c) Define

$$U_i := \phi^{[-1]} \left(-\frac{1}{Y} \ln X_i \right), \quad 1 \le i \le I.$$ (10.44)

Then the joint distribution function of the U_i, $1 \le i \le I$ is

$$\mathbf{P}[\mathbf{U} \le \mathbf{u}] = \phi^{[-1]} \left(\sum_{i=1}^{I} \phi(u_i) \right),$$

and the U_i have the Archimedean copula function with generator $\phi(\cdot)$ as distribution function.

Proof.   First note that for all $i \le I$

$$\mathbf{P}[U_i \le u_i \mid Y] = \exp\{-\phi(u_i)Y\}$$

and that the U_i are independent, conditional on Y. The claim of the proposition follows by using iterated expectations:

$$\mathbf{P}[\mathbf{U} \le \mathbf{u}] = \mathbf{E}\left[\prod_{i=1}^{I} \mathbf{P}[U_i \le u_i \mid Y] \right] = \mathbf{E}\left[\prod_{i=1}^{I} \exp\{-\phi(u_i)Y\} \right]$$

$$= \mathbf{E}\left[\exp\left\{ -Y \sum_{i=1}^{I} \phi(u_i) \right\} \right] = \mathcal{L}_Y\left(\sum_{i=1}^{I} \phi(u_i) \right)$$

$$= \phi^{[-1]}\left(\sum_{i=1}^{I} \phi(u_i) \right).$$ (10.45)

$\square$

The key point about the algorithm shown above is that *conditional on the realisation of Y, the random variables U_i are independent*. This conditional independence property was exploited in the proof of the algorithm, and it will also drive the results in the credit risk model. It has a similar function to the conditional independence which allowed us to derive the large portfolio loss distribution in the one-factor Vasicek model. In the context of the modelling of survival times, the mixing variable is also known as a *frailty* parameter, and models involving such parameters are known as *frailty models*. See e.g. Clayton (1978), Frees and Valdez (1998).

In all practical cases, the generator function ϕ is very easy to invert. If in addition the inverse Laplace transform of ϕ^{-1} is easy to calculate and to invert, all random variables in questions can be generated directly from a set of $I + 1$ independent unit random variables that are directly available on any computer system.

Frequently one encounters in the literature the suggestion to generate samples from copula functions using the *conditional distribution technique*. Intuitively speaking, this algorithm is as follows.

Draw a $[0, 1]$ random variable U_1. This is the realisation of the first component of the random vector. Next, derive analytically or numerically the conditional distribution of U_2 (the second component), conditional on the realisation of U_1. Draw U_2 from that distribution. Derive the conditional distribution of U_3, conditional on U_1 and U_2, and so on.

This algorithm fails very quickly if the number of dimensions becomes just moderately large (e.g. 10), because either the analytical expressions become impossible to handle, or because of numerical elimination.[15] We strongly advise the usage of the other sampling algorithms given above.

10.8   DEFAULT MODELLING WITH COPULA FUNCTIONS

10.8.1   Static copula models for default correlation

Because a copula contains all information on the dependency of the random variables concerned, this also applies to the 0–1 variables of default and survival of the obligors in a static portfolio credit risk model. Thus, copula functions provide the most general framework for static models of portfolio default risk.

A static model is based upon the following input data.

- T: A fixed time horizon. The model is a model of default and survival over $[0, T]$.
- $\{1, \dots, I\}$: The set of obligors.
- p_i for $i \leq I$: The individual (marginal) survival probabilities of the obligors.
- $C(u_1, \dots, u_I)$: The copula which describes the dependency of the defaults.

Given this input data, a scenario for the portfolio credit risk model can be generated as follows:

- Draw $U_1, \dots, U_I$ distributed with $C(\cdot)$ as distribution function. These variables control default and survival of the obligors as follows.
- Obligor $i \leq I$ is deemed to survive until T if and only if

$$U_i \leq p_i.$$

---

[15] Deriving the conditional distribution on the kth level involves taking k cross-derivatives of the distribution function. Each numerical evaluation of a derivative of a function involves the subtraction of two numbers very close to each other, and scaling up the difference. At each of these subtractions several significant digits in accuracy are lost. (For example, if we subtract the following numbers given with eight-digit accuracy, $0.12345678 - 0.12345677 = 0.00000001$, the result will only have one significant digit of accuracy.)

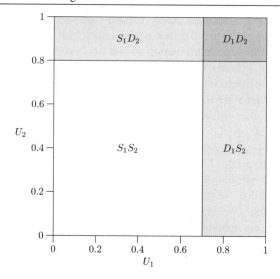

Figure 10.17   The static copula default model. In the white area both obligors survive, in the light grey areas one obligor defaults, and in the dark grey area both obligors default

The uniform marginal distributions of the copula ensure that the individual survival probability of obligor i is indeed p_i:

$$\mathbf{P}[U_i \leq p_i] = p_i.$$

Thus, the model is consistent with the given input data. Furthermore, C is the copula of the survival indicator functions.

Figure 10.17 shows the model setup for two obligors. The draw from the copula will be a pair of random numbers which can be viewed as the coordinates of a point in the unit square. If the draw falls into the white area (S_1, S_2) both obligors survive, if it falls in the light grey areas one obligor defaults: obligor 1 defaults in (D_1, S_2) and obligor 2 defaults in (S_1, D_2), and in the dark grey area (D_1, D_2) both obligors default.

It is now easy to give some interesting quantities in closed form:

- The *probability of no default* is

$$\mathbf{P}[U_i \leq p_i, \quad \forall i \leq I] = C(p_1, \dots, p_I).$$

- The probability of *survival of the first k obligors* is

$$\mathbf{P}[U_i \leq p_i, \quad \forall i \leq k] = C(p_1, \dots, p_k, 1, \dots, 1).$$

- The probability of survival of a given subset of obligors $I_S \subset \{1, \dots, I\}$ is

$$C(u_1, \dots, u_I) \quad \text{where} \quad u_i = \begin{cases} p_i & \text{if} \quad i \in I_S, \\ 1 & \text{otherwise.} \end{cases} \tag{10.46}$$

Thus, survival probabilities can be given directly. A given combination of survivals and defaults is more complicated to evaluate, and here we must iteratively build up the set of defaulted obligors. Let us call $I_S \subset \{1, \ldots, I\}$ the set of "survivors", and $I_D \subset \{1, \ldots, I\}$ the subset of "defaulted" obligors. Then we call

$$P(I_S, I_D) := \mathbf{P}[\{U_i \leq p_i, \quad \forall i \in I_S\} \text{ and } \{U_i > p_i, \quad \forall i \in I_D\}]$$

the probability that all obligors in I_S survive, and all obligors in I_D default. We require that $I_S \cap I_D = \emptyset$ but not that $I_S \cup I_D = \{1, \ldots, I\}$. We do not make a statement about obligors neither in I_S nor in I_D, they may default or survive. Then we can give a recursive recipe to calculate $P(I_S, I_D)$ for any given (disjoint) sets I_S and I_D.

Proposition 10.6 (recursive calculation of probabilities) *For any $j \notin (I_S \cup I_D)$ we have*

$$P(I_S, (I_D \cup \{j\})) = P(I_S, I_D) - P((I_S \cup \{j\}), I_D). \tag{10.47}$$

Thus, calculation of the probability of $P(I_S, I_D)$ requires knowledge of two probabilities $P(I_S, I'_D)$ and $P(I'_S, I'_D)$, where I'_D has one element less than I_D. As $P(I'_S, \emptyset)$ with empty default set is known from (10.46) for every survivor set $I'_S \subset \{1, \ldots, I\}$, $P(I_S, I_D)$ can be calculated recursively in $|I_D|$ steps.

As an example, consider the static one-factor firm's value model presented in Section 10.4. According to Assumption 10.2, a default of an obligor $i \leq I$ occurs if

$$V_i \leq K_i, \tag{10.48}$$

where the V_i are normally distributed with mean zero, standard deviation one and correlation matrix Σ. We can transform (10.48) to

$$\Phi(V_i) \leq \Phi(K_i) \quad \Leftrightarrow \quad U_i := 1 - \Phi(V_i) = \Phi(-V_i) \geq 1 - \Phi(K_i) =: p_i, \tag{10.49}$$

where $\Phi(\cdot)$ is the cumulative standard normal distribution function which also happens to be the marginal distribution function of V_i and (by symmetry) also of $-V_i$. Thus, $\Phi(V_i)$ has a uniform marginal distribution and the joint distribution of $\mathbf{U}$ is the Gaussian copula with correlation matrix Σ.

The multivariate firm's value model of Section 10.4 (which is essentially equivalent to the CreditMetrics model) can therefore be transformed into a copula model with a Gaussian copula function. We have thus found a common framework to compare different static default risk models against each other.

Nevertheless, the recursion formula is not always practical. If we tried to implement the recursion from Proposition 10.6 for this example using a Gaussian copula, we would encounter the practical difficulties that lie hidden in Proposition 10.6:

- It must be possible to efficiently evaluate the copula function with high accuracy.
- There must not be significant numerical elimination in the subtractions in equation (10.47). Thus, the portfolio should be small.

- The number of operations to calculate the probability of an event with n defaults is 2^n. Thus, the event concerned should not involve too many defaults.
- To calculate other probabilities (e.g. the probability of losing more than a given amount L), a large (potentially inefficiently large) set of possible default events must be evaluated.

For example, the first point is already a problem in the case of a Gaussian copula of dimension larger than 2. There are no efficient algorithms to evaluate a high-dimensional cumulative normal distribution function, but this is necessary to give the value of the Gaussian copula at a given point. It is possible to keep the problem under control in the one-factor setup with just one correlating factor, but even there a two-dimensional cumulative normal distribution function must be evaluated, which usually involves a numerical integration and which is not always accurate enough. And accuracy is necessary to control the numerical elimination when two almost equal numbers are subtracted from each other, as in (10.47).

Fortunately, there are other copula functions which do not have these problems. For example, the Archimedean copulae can be evaluated in closed form in any number of dimensions (provided the generator function and its inverse can be given in closed form, too). Therefore, for these copulae and moderately sized portfolios, Proposition 10.6 provides a viable recipe to infer relevant quantities about the distribution of the portfolio's losses, e.g. the probability of having *no* loss in the portfolio – an important quantity in the pricing of first-to-default baskets.

10.8.2   Large portfolio loss distributions for Archimedean copulae

Using the static setup, we can do even more than just calculate the probabilities of some events. The representation of Proposition 10.5 shows that the random variables of an Archimedean copula exhibit a factor structure which allows the derivation of a large portfolio loss distribution similar to the one derived by Vasicek (1987). We start with the following setup.

Assumption 10.10 (Archimedean copula finite portfolio)

- *All obligors have the same exposure size and the same loss in default. Thus, the number D of defaults is sufficient to determine the loss of the portfolio.*
- *Obligor i has the survival probability p_i until T.*
- *Obligor i defaults if and only if $U_i \geq p_i$, where U_i is generated by the algorithm of Proposition 10.5. We call the distribution function of Y $G(\cdot)$ and the density $g(\cdot)$ and assume that the density exists.*

In this setup, the loan loss distribution can easily be derived by conditioning on the mixing variable Y. *Conditional* on $Y = y$, the survival probability of an obligor i is:

$$
p_i(y) := \mathbf{P}[U_i \leq p_i \,|\, Y = y] = \mathbf{P}\left[\phi^{[-1]}\left(-\frac{1}{y}\ln X_i\right) \leq p_i\right]
$$

$$
= \mathbf{P}\left[-\frac{1}{y}\ln X_i \geq \phi(p_i)\right] = \mathbf{P}[\ln X_i \leq -y\phi(p_i)]
$$

$$
= \mathbf{P}[X_i \leq \exp\{-y\phi(p_i)\}] = \exp\{-y\phi(p_i)\}.
$$

If all obligors have the same unconditional survival probability $p = p_i$, $\forall i \leq I$ then the survival probability conditional on $Y = y$ is $p(y) = \exp\{-y\phi(p)\}$. The probability of k defaults and $I - k$ survivals in the portfolio is:

$$\mathbf{P}[D = I - k] = \int_0^\infty \binom{I}{k} p^k(y)(1 - p(y))^{I-k} G(dy). \tag{10.50}$$

Now, in order to reach the closed-form solution for the credit losses of a large portfolio, we make the following assumption.

Assumption 10.11 (large portfolio) *In addition to Assumption 10.10 we assume:*

- *All obligors have the same unconditional default probability p.*
- *The number of obligors I is very large ($I \to \infty$), the relevant quantity for the portfolio risk is the* fraction L *of defaulted obligors* in the portfolio.

By the law of large numbers, the fraction L of defaults will almost surely be $1 - p(y)$ in the limit of the very large portfolio, whenever the mixing variable Y has taken the value of y. Thus, the probability of having more than a fraction q of defaults in the portfolio is:

$$\mathbf{P}[L \geq q] = \mathbf{P}[p(Y) \leq 1 - q] = \mathbf{P}[\exp\{-Y\phi(p)\} \leq 1 - q] = \mathbf{P}[-Y\phi(p) \leq \ln(1 - q)]$$

$$= \mathbf{P}\left[-Y \leq \frac{\ln(1 - q)}{\phi(p)}\right] = \mathbf{P}\left[Y \geq -\frac{\ln(1 - q)}{\phi(p)}\right] = 1 - G\left(-\frac{\ln(1 - q)}{\phi(p)}\right).$$

This yields the following proposition.

Proposition 10.7 (large portfolio loss distributions) *The distribution F and the density f of the limiting loss distribution are:*

$$F(q) = \mathbf{P}[L \leq q] = G\left(-\frac{\ln(1 - q)}{\phi(p)}\right), \tag{10.51}$$

$$f(q) = \frac{1}{(1 - q)\phi(p)} g\left(-\frac{\ln(1 - q)}{\phi(p)}\right), \tag{10.52}$$

where G and g are the distribution and density function of the mixing variable Y.

In order to reach the large portfolio loss distribution for a specific choice of copula function all we need to do now is to substitute the distribution (or density) function of Y into (10.51) or (10.52). For the Clayton copula, for example, this would be the distribution function and the density of a gamma-distributed random variable.

Figure 10.18 shows the large portfolio loss distribution of the Clayton copula and contrasts it to the Gaussian copula. The individual default probability of the obligors is 5% in all cases, the parameter of the Clayton copula is 0.64 and 2.22, and the asset correlation in the Gaussian copula is 12% and 30.05%, respectively. These values were chosen so that on a *bivariate* level the two copulae give identical joint default probabilities. That is, the joint default probability of *two* obligors in the static copula model with a Clayton copula with parameter $\theta = 0.64$ is

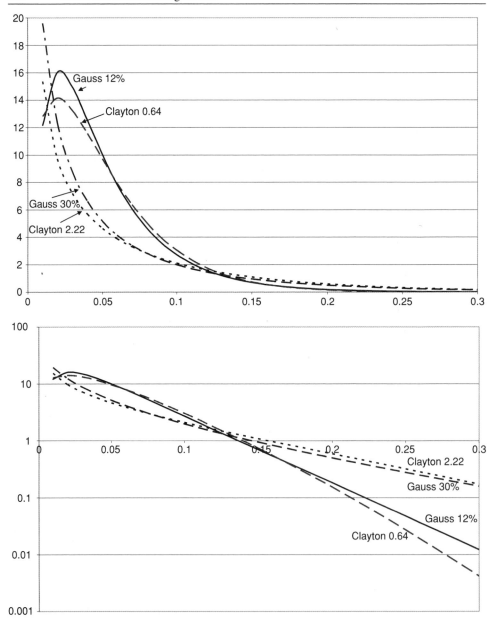

Figure 10.18 Large portfolio loss distributions for Gaussian and Clayton copula models in linear scale and log-scale. Individual default probabilities are 5%

0.3993%, and this is also the joint default probability of two obligors in a static copula model with a *Gaussian* copula with correlation $\rho = 12\%$. The same applies to the pair $\theta = 2.22$ and $\rho = 30\%$.

Of course, the joint default of only two obligors does not necessarily tell us anything about the likelihood of *large* losses which involve many more than two obligors. One example of this is given below, but it can already be seen in the diagram. The loss distribution of the Clayton copula is not exactly equal to the loss distribution of the corresponding Gaussian copula. Nevertheless, the agreement is surprisingly good, and there was no reason *a priori* to expect the two loss curves to be close to each other. If, for example, we had used the Gumbel copula instead of the Clayton copula, the picture might have been very much different. The Gumbel copula has upper tail dependence so we can expect many more joint defaults of *many* obligors in the Gumbel model. Having a large portfolio approximation ready therefore allows us to assess very conveniently whether the implications of a given copula on a portfolio's credit losses do indeed seem reasonable.

The log-scale diagram between the Gauss 12% and the Clayton 0.64 curves is a good example of the ways in which the implications of the two copulae may differ. While the *far* tail of the Clayton copula (i.e. for losses larger than 18% of the portfolio) is *lower* than the corresponding section of the tail of the Gaussian copula, the *medium range* of losses between 5% and 17% of the portfolio is actually *more* likely. It also has less mass at the average 5% loss, but more mass at the very good end of very low losses. The Clayton copula seems to put more weight on the very bad events, but less weight on the catastrophic events.

There are only very few points that any portfolio model must satisfy. First, the mean of all loss distributions must be at a common level (here 5%). Second, for independence we must have a concentration around the mean, and finally, as we move towards perfect dependence we must approach a distribution which has 95% mass at a default rate of zero, and 5% mass at a default rate of 100%. But the form in which the transition is made between these two extreme cases is entirely driven by the copula. In the case of the Gaussian and Clayton copulae, this transition has a roughly plausible shape but there are examples where this is not the case. The Fréchet class of copulae is constructed as a weighted average of the independence copula Π and the perfect dependence copula M^I. If the weight of the independence copula is $1 - \alpha$, then this copula implies that with probability $1 - \alpha$ we have perfectly independent defaults, and with probability α we have perfectly dependent defaults. In particular, with probability $5\% \times \alpha$ all obligors default and with $95\% \times \alpha$ none defaults. This is clearly a highly unrealistic choice of scenarios, nevertheless, we can choose α in such a way that – if we only consider default and survival of two obligors – we achieve a perfect fit to a given bivariate joint default probability.

10.8.3   A semi-dynamic copula model

In the static models of the previous subsection the copula approach may seem a bit contrived. The same models could have been set up without using copula functions as a framework, maybe even with a more convincing story to back it up. This changes now when we start moving into *dynamic* models of portfolio default risk. Here, the copula transformation becomes an extremely useful tool to connect the *times* of the defaults. I call the approach presented in this section only *semi*-dynamic because we first focus only on the generation of scenarios of joint default times, without considering the corresponding price dynamics of default hazard rates or defaultable bonds. Only if there is also a consistent specification of price dynamics will we call the model *fully dynamic*.

The basic idea how the static copula approach can be made dynamic is shown in Figure 10.19. Over a time horizon of T_1, we have a static copula default model which is characterised by the copula function and the survival probabilities $P_1(T_1)$ and $P_2(T_1)$ of both obligors. $P_1(\cdot)$ and $P_2(\cdot)$ are the survival probability functions of the two obligors which we assume to be

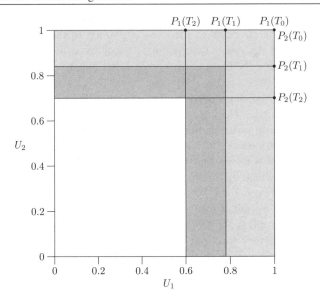

Figure 10.19   The static copula default model over two time horizons T_1 and T_2

continuous. Obligor 1 defaults before T_1 if $U_1 \geq P_1(T_1)$, and obligor 2 is defaulted at T_1 if $U_2 \geq P_2(T_1)$. In the figure the areas where these default events can occur is shaded light grey.

If we now change the time horizon to a later time $T_2 > T_1$, we must also change the survival probabilities of the two obligors to the survival probabilities until T_2, i.e. the survival probabilities are now $P_1(T_2)$ and $P_2(T_2)$. Obviously $P_1(T_1) > P_1(T_2)$ and $P_2(T_1) > P_2(T_2)$ must hold, i.e. we *decrease* the default thresholds. Thus we now have a copula default model with two lower default thresholds. The area in the figure where the sample (U_1, U_2) must fall in order to cause at least one default is now not only the light grey area, but the union of the light grey area and the deep grey area.

Now, the final step is to realise that there is no need to consider the static copula default model for $[T_0, T_1]$ and the static copula default model for $[T_0, T_2]$ as two completely separate models. They can be combined and we only need to draw one set of samples (U_1, U_2) from the copula. If (U_1, U_2) falls into the light grey area, we consider the default event to have occurred in $[T_0, T_1]$, and if it falls into the light grey *or* the dark grey area, the default was in $[T_0, T_2]$. More formally, let us denote by τ_1 and τ_2 the default times of obligors 1 and 2:

$$\tau_1 \in [T_0, T_1] \quad \Leftrightarrow \quad U_1 \in [P_1(T_0), P_1(T_1)],$$
$$\tau_1 \in [T_0, T_2] \quad \Leftrightarrow \quad U_1 \in [P_1(T_0), P_1(T_2)].$$

From these we can conclude that

$$\tau_1 \in [T_1, T_2] \quad \Leftrightarrow \quad U_1 \in [P_1(T_1), P_1(T_2)].$$

Analogous rules hold for obligor 2. If we now set $T_2 = T_1 + \Delta t$ and let the second time converge to the first time $T_2 \to T_1$, we reach:

$$\tau_1 \in [T_1, T_1 + \Delta t] \quad \Leftrightarrow \quad U_1 \in [P(T_1), P(T_1 + \Delta t)],$$
$$\tau_1 = T_1 \quad \Leftrightarrow \quad U_1 = P(T_1),$$
$$\tau_1 = P^{[-1]}(U_1). \tag{10.53}$$

Equation (10.53) tells us how we can determine the *exact* time of default of obligor 1 from a given value for U_1 and a given survival probability function $P_1(T)$.

We now have all the necessary building blocks in place to build a semi-dynamic model with general default dependency and given marginal (i.e. individual) term structures of survival probabilities.

Proposition 10.8 (semi-dynamic model) *Assume we are given:*

- *A term structure of survival probabilities $P_i(0, T)$ for each obligor $i \leq I$.*
- *A copula function $C : [0, 1]^I \to [0, 1]$.*
- *An algorithm to sample random vectors $U_1, \ldots, U_I$ with the copula C as joint distribution function.*

Then the simulation algorithm for the joint default events proceeds as follows:

1. Draw $U_1, \ldots, U_I$ from the copula C.
2. Obtain the default times $\tau_1, \ldots, \tau_I$ from

$$P_i^{[-1]}(U_i) = \tau_i. \tag{10.54}$$

3. Given this scenario of default times, simulate recoveries to each default, evaluate payoffs of the securities to price, etc.

Then the survival probability distribution function of each obligor $i \leq I$ is $P_i(T)$, and for each fixed-time horizon T the model is a static copula default risk model with copula $C(\cdot)$ and survival probabilities $P_i(T)$.

This algorithm was first proposed by Li (2000) for the special case of a Gaussian copula in the CreditMetrics framework. Essentially, we take the marginal, one-dimensional distributions of the default times (given by the survival probabilities) and link them with the copula $C(\cdot)$ to reach a joint, I-dimensional distribution of the default times.

A particularly convenient property of this algorithm is that we can identify the copula with the copula that we used for a static, fixed-time-horizon copula model. Thus, we can transfer the knowledge and calibration procedures that we know from the static setup and directly use that copula for the dynamic model.

For example, portfolio default risk models like CreditMetrics have a Gaussian copula structure if they are based upon the Merton (1974) firm's value model. These models are usually calibrated to the historical default experience of a country or industry group over a given (e.g.

one-year) time horizon. It may be argued that a copula of default events over a one-year horizon would look different from a copula of default times as it is used in this model. This is not the case because copula functions are invariant under monotonic increasing transformations of the marginals (see e.g. Li, 2000 or Joe, 1997). (If the transformation is monotonically decreasing, the copula of the transformed variables is equal to the *survival copula* of the original variables.) For many important cases (e.g. Gaussian copula, t-copula), the survival copula is identical to the original copula.

We now show that we can indeed directly derive the copula $C(\cdot)$ that we use in the model from historically observed default frequencies.

The indicator function of survival beyond the time horizon T can be approximated arbitrarily well by monotonous, continuously differentiable functions, for example cumulative normal distribution functions:

$$\mathbf{1}_{\{\tau_i > T_i\}} = \lim_{n \to \infty} g_{n,T_i}(\tau_i) =: \lim_{n \to \infty} \Phi\left(\frac{\tau_i - T_i}{n}\right).$$

For all n, $g_{n,T_i}(\cdot)$ is a strictly monotonically increasing function. Call $C_{g,n,\mathbf{T}}(\cdot)$ the copula function of the random variables $Y_{i,n} := g_{n,T_i}(\tau_i)$. By the invariance of copulae under strictly monotonous transformations, $C_{g,n,\mathbf{T}}(\cdot)$ will be equal to the copula of the default times $C_{\tau}(\cdot)$ for all n and for all choices of transformation function g and time horizons T_i.

Analogously, if instead of *survival indicators* we construct *default indicators*, we reach the *survival copula* of the default times. Again this result will hold independently of n or the approximation functions g or time horizons T_i. Thus, the copula will remain valid even if the limit is taken as $n \to \infty$.

In the limit as $n \to \infty$, the approximated default indicator functions will approach the default indicator functions themselves. We can therefore use a fixed-horizon default copula function in our model, for example the Gaussian default copula function of the CreditMetrics model.

10.8.3.1   Incorporating intensity models

A popular specification of the semi-dynamic copula model uses marginal survival probabilities that come from an intensity-based model.

- The marginal survival functions are given by a specification of a term structure of default intensities which is calibrated to market data as described in Chapter 3, or which is specified according to historical default hazard rates. Thus:

$$P_i(T) = \exp\left\{-\int_0^T \lambda_i(s)ds\right\}. \tag{10.55}$$

If default intensities are chosen to be constant, this reduces to

$$P_i(T) = \exp\{-T\lambda_i\}. \tag{10.56}$$

- A Gaussian copula is chosen for the default dependency, usually in the form of a factor model. Here there are several possible choices:

  (a) The simplest version is a one-factor model with constant weights of the form of Section 10.4. Although it is very simple, it often already gives quite realistic results.
  (b) If more realism is desired, an industry-class factor model can be chosen, where in addition to the one economy-wide factor of the one-factor model, additional factors are introduced: one for each industry group. This setup is usually sufficient for most applications, and is described in detail below. Because of its simple factor structure, it has the advantage of requiring only a small number of parameters and it is still possible to calibrate these models to historical default experiences as described in Section 10.4.
  (c) An alternative to the calibration to historical default experience is the specification of the correlation matrix based upon share price correlations between the obligors. This approach is taken in CreditMetrics "CDO manager" software for example. As we have seen before, share price correlations may be rather high when compared to historical default experience, so an adjustment of these correlations may be necessary.

- The default times are then given by finding the τ_i such that

$$\int_0^{\tau_i} \lambda_i(t)dt = -\ln U_i, \tag{10.57}$$

or in the constant intensity case simply

$$\tau_i = \frac{-\ln U_i}{\lambda_i}. \tag{10.58}$$

The industry-class factor model is set up as follows:

- We number the industry classes of the obligors from 1 to C and call $c(i)$ the industry class to which obligor i belongs.
- Next, introduce factors to describe the dependency. Y_0 is an overall dependency factor, while Y_c are the industry factors for $c = 1, \ldots, C$; ϵ_i are idiosyncratic noise terms. All these random variables are independent, standard normally distributed.
- Next, we set

$$V_i := a_0 Y_0 + a_{c(i)} Y_{c(i)} + a_i' \epsilon_i, \tag{10.59}$$

where the factor weights a_0, a_c and the noise weight a_i' are chosen in order to reach a realistic large portfolio default behaviour both within each industry class as well as within the whole economy.

- Finally, the copula transformation yields

$$U_i := \Phi \left(\frac{V_i}{\sqrt{a_0^2 + a_{c(i)}^2 + a_i'^2}} \right). \tag{10.60}$$

The Gaussian copula is by far the most common choice in practice, but other copulae could be used instead of the Gaussian equally well. The Gaussian copula has some attractive properties, in particular generating random samples from a Gaussian copula is straightforward and the number of parameters can be handled quite flexibly. Finally, two further helping factors are the nice "story" that can be told about the asset value correlations between the firms in the portfolio (although we have learned that this should be taken with a large dose of salt) and the dominance of the CreditMetrics framework which also uses a Gaussian copula.

This algorithm describes the mechanism with which *scenarios* can be generated for a Monte Carlo valuation of portfolio credit derivatives. An important (and complex) second step is the implementation of the payoffs that the instrument in question may have. If the instrument is a CDO with a complicated payoff distribution structure, this can easily be the numerically (implementation-wise) most complicated part of the algorithm.

We can now give another characterisation of *upper tail dependence*. Assume that we are given a two-dimensional copula $C(\cdot)$ with upper tail dependence parameter $\lambda_U > 0$ and two survival probability functions with the same intensity $P_1(t) := e^{-\lambda t}$ and $P_2(t) := e^{-\lambda t}$. Then the probability of a *joint* default of these two obligors until t is:

$$p_{12}(t) = 1 + C(e^{-\lambda t}, e^{-\lambda t}) - e^{-\lambda t} - e^{-\lambda t}.$$

We are interested in the intensity of a joint default of both obligors, i.e. the limit $\lim_{t \to 0} p_{12}(t)/t$. To calculate this, we first approximate $e^{-\lambda t} \approx 1 - \lambda t$:

$$\frac{1}{t} p_{12}(t) \approx \frac{1}{t} (2\lambda t + C(1 - \lambda t, 1 - \lambda t) - 1)$$

$$= \lambda \frac{1}{1 - u} (1 - 2u + C(u, u)),$$

where $u = 1 - \lambda t$. The limit of the right-hand side as $t \to 0$ (or $u \to 1$) is the parameter of upper tail dependence λ_U. Thus we have reached:

The intensity of a joint default of both obligors at $t = 0$ is the product of the upper tail dependence parameter and the individual default intensity:

$$\lambda_{12}(0) = \lambda \cdot \lambda_u. \tag{10.61}$$

This result only gives the intensity of a joint default of two obligors at $t = 0$. At later times, we must move to conditional distributions which is the topic of the next section.

Nevertheless, we can already give conditions for the *absence* of upper tail dependence. If the copula that is used in the model has a density which is bounded everywhere (in particular at the upper right corner $(1, 1)$), then upper and lower tail dependence must be zero, and consequently also the intensities of joint defaults; joint defaults at exactly the same time will have zero probability. If the only singularity of the density of the copula is at the corner $(1, 1)$, then we can only have a positive joint default intensity at $t = 0$ and the joint default intensity will be zero afterwards. Thus, joint defaults will again have zero probability.

In particular, with probability 1 the copula model with the Gaussian copula will not generate defaults at exactly the same time, nor will any copula model with an Archimedean copula which is generated by a Laplace transform or a t-copula.

There are of course copulae that do generate joint defaults, a trivial example is the copula of the default times in the "stress events" model of Section 10.5. Copulae that arise from models of this type are known as *Marshall–Olkin* copulae. For our application of modelling default dependency we do not really want to have joint defaults at exactly the same time; having clusters of close, but not identical, default times is much more realistic.

A copula model with positive dependency between the obligors will be able to generate clusters of defaults because the copula (and therefore the dependency) of the default times is the survival copula of the copula that was used in the model. If this copula has positive dependence, so will the default times, and they will tend to be more closely clustered than default times of independent obligors. But to fully analyse these properties of the copula models we need to move on to an analysis of the *dynamics* that are implied by the copula approach.

10.8.4 Dynamic copula-dependent defaults

The semi-dynamic copula default models already fulfil many needs for the pricing and analysis of portfolio credit derivatives. As scenario generator in a Monte Carlo simulation these models will yield prices that are consistent with the initial inputs, in particular the (individual) initial term structures of default intensities. But in order to fully understand all implications of a particular specification of a copula, we need to go one step further and analyse the consequences that the choice of copula has on the dynamics of the survival probabilities in the model. This was first done in Schönbucher and Schubert (2001), for more details and proofs the reader is referred to this paper.

Example 10.1 (a truly great trading strategy)   *A credit derivatives trader proposes the following strategy:*

Sell protection (CDS) on 10 names	$+10 \times 170\,bp = +1700\,bp$
Buy protection as one FtD swap on this basket	$-1500\,bp$
Net carry	$+200\,bp$

- *If a default should occur, one of the CDS and the FtD will be triggered.*
- *The default payment of the CDS is covered with the payoff of the FtD. We are ± 0 and we unwind the other CDS, so there will be no other losses.*

How do you react? Has this trader found a money machine? Or might there be something wrong?

Warning: This is not a recommended trading strategy!

Consider the trading strategy proposed in Example 10.1. The trading strategy sounds convincing at first, it has zero initial investment and seems to generate only positive or zero payoffs. But there must be an error – otherwise this would be an arbitrage opportunity (and I would never publish this strategy in a book!). So where is the problem with the strategy, where does it have a negative payoff?

The problem cannot lie in a scenario without any defaults. Here the strategy always makes money. So the problem must occur in a scenario with a default:

- The default payments of the defaulted CDS and the default payment on the FtD do indeed match. No problem here.
- The problem arises *when we try to unwind the **other** CDS*.

There is no guarantee that we can unwind the other CDS at the same price as we entered them, in particular if we have *default contagion* of the following form.

Definition 10.11 (default contagion)   *There is default contagion between obligors **A** and **B** if at a default of **A** the risk of default of **B** will jump upwards, and at a default of **B** the risk of default of **A** will jump upwards.*

If we have default contagion there is no way to make easy money using the strategy in the example, because we will lose our previous gains (and some more) once we try to unwind our position.

Let us now analyse the same example in the framework of a semi-dynamic copula model with *constant* and equal initial individual default intensities λ. That is, we set the initial survival probabilities to $P_i(t) := e^{-\lambda t}$. If we also set recoveries to zero, then the individual CDSs will initially yield a continuous fee of λ. On the other hand, the FtD will cost less than the sum of the CDS fees. The CDS fees seem to be constant (at least λ is), so it seems there was an arbitrage opportunity in the semi-static model. The resolution to this puzzle is that the default hazard rates (and thus the CDS fees) will in fact *not* be constant, although this cannot be seen directly in the semi-static model.

There is a set of "true" or "underlying" hazard rates h_i which are uniquely determined by the copula function and the "initial" intensities λ_i. These hazard rates reflect the progressive increase in information over time. While λ_i *was* the hazard rate of defaults of obligor i as seem from $t = 0$, it will *not* be the hazard rate later on if we take into account that we (and the market) learn new information as time proceeds. This new information is the information about default and survival of all other obligors in the model.

The result is a fully dynamic intensity-based model for the intensities h_i which is able to capture not only *default* and *survival* of the obligors in the portfolio but also:

- changes in the *risk of default*,
- changes in the *value or price* of the corresponding claim,
- the impact of the *timing* of defaults,

and which is equivalent to the semi-dynamic copula default model at $t = 0$.

Furthermore, as the "real" hazard rates h_i are uniquely determined by the copula and the initial λ_i this analysis opens another avenue towards the large, unsolved problem: "Which copula to choose?". We can now compare different copulae with respect to the dynamics they imply for the hazard rates h_i and (a) rule out those copulae whose dynamics are clearly unrealistic, (b) calibrate our copula to the dynamics of the h_i observed in the market.

10.8.4.1   Model setup

We use the following setup.

Assumption 10.12 (setup)   *There are I obligors. For each obligor $i \le I$ we define*

1. *The* (pseudo) default intensity $\lambda_i(t)$: *a non-negative stochastic process.*
2. *The* default countdown process $\gamma_i(t)$:

$$\gamma_i(t) := \exp\left(-\int_0^t \lambda_i(u)\,du\right).$$

3. *The* default trigger variables U_i: *random variables on* $[0, 1]$.
4. *The* time of default τ_i *of obligor* $i = 1, \ldots, I$:

$$\tau_i := \inf\{t : \gamma_i(t) \le U_i\}$$

and default indicator processes $N_i(t) := \mathbf{1}_{\{\tau \le t\}}$.

As seen from $t = 0$, the I-dimensional vector $\mathbf{U} = (U_1, \ldots, U_I)$ is distributed according to the I-dimensional copula

$$C(\mathbf{u}).$$

$\mathbf{U}$ *is independent of all other modelling variables, in particular it is independent of the λ_i.*

The reader should note how closely this setup resembles the "direct default time simulation" approach described in the chapter on Monte Carlo methods. This is not a coincidence, in fact it shows that the model can be implemented very efficiently, in particular if a Monte Carlo routine for a single-name intensity model is already in place.

So far this is the usual semi-dynamic copula modelling setup with the additional twist that the default intensities λ_i can be stochastic themselves. But as they are independent from U, this does not really change much.

10.8.4.2   Dynamics

Dynamics in the model arise from the way information is revealed. We consider two important cases:

- $(\mathcal{H}_t^i)_{t \in [0, \overline{T}]}$ –This filtration describes the information up to time t, *if we only observe default/survival of one obligor i alone.*
- $(\mathcal{H}_t)_{t \in [0, \overline{T}]}$ –Information up to time t, *if we observe default/survival of **all** obligors.*

Both information sets coincide initially at $t = 0$, but they are critically different later on. Figure 10.20 shows this effect: both observers learn that the default point is not in the shaded area. But while the left observer (who only has access to $\mathcal{H}_t^i$) can only learn from the survival and default of obligor $i = 1$, the other observer (with access to $\mathcal{H}_t$) also learns about the survival and default of all other obligors. This means that both observers will update their information differently.

The fact that both information sets coincide at $t = 0$ is extremely good news for the calibration procedure which takes place at $t = 0$. Although we are going to use the full information set $\mathcal{H}_t$ later on, at $t = 0$ we can calibrate the model as if we were going to use $\mathcal{H}_t^i$. But under $\mathcal{H}_t^i$, in Proposition 10.9 we just have I independent single-obligor models, where the default intensity is λ_i, and we can calibrate the dynamics of $\lambda_i(t)$ exactly as we learned to do it in the first chapters of this book.

Assuming positive dependence between the two obligors, the updating of the right observer will proceed as follows.

- t_0: Initially, there is no particular information.
- $t_0 \to t_1$: Obligor 1 has not defaulted, but obligor 2 also has not defaulted. Because obligor 2 is correlated with obligor 1 this is good news, so U_2 was not extremely high, either. This makes it more likely that (U_1, U_2) is somewhere further down. The distribution of (U_1, U_2) is the conditional distribution, conditional on $U_1 \le \gamma_1(t_1)$ and $U_2 \le \gamma_2(t_1)$.
- $t_1 \to t_2$: Obligor 1 has not defaulted (good), but obligor 2 has defaulted. This is very bad news. We now know U_2 with certainty (it is $U_2 = \gamma_2(t_2)$), and that is a high value.[16] The distribution of U_1, is now the conditional distribution of U_1, conditional on $U_2 = \gamma_2(t_2)$. Under this conditional distribution U_1 is much more likely to be high than under the conditional distribution just before default (i.e. conditioning only on $U_2 \le \gamma_2(t_2)$ and $U_1 \le \gamma_1(t_2)$).

If this updating is followed through rigorously, we reach the following results.

Proposition 10.9 (conditional survival probabilities)

(i) *Under $(\mathcal{H}_t^i)_{t\in[0,\overline{T}]}$ (i.e. if only obligor i is observed) and $\tau_i > t$, the survival probabilities are:*

$$P_i'(t, T) = \mathbf{E}\left[\frac{\gamma_i(T)}{\gamma_i(t)} \,\middle|\, \mathcal{H}_t^i \right] = \mathbf{E}\left[e^{-\int_t^T \lambda_i(s)ds} \,\middle|\, \mathcal{H}_t^i \right].$$

The intensity of $N_i(t)$ under $(\mathcal{H}_t^i)_{t\in[0,\overline{T}]}$ is:

$$h_i'(t) = -\frac{\partial}{\partial T} P_i'(t, T)\Big|_{T=t} = \mathbf{1}_{\{\tau^i > t\}}\lambda_i(t).$$

(ii) *Under $(\mathcal{H}_t)_{t\in[0,\overline{T}]}$ (i.e. if we can observe all obligors) and if no defaults have occurred so far, the joint distribution of the times $\tau = (\tau_1, \ldots, \tau_I)$ of default at time*

---

[16] Given the information one instance before, this is actually the highest possible value consistent with that information.

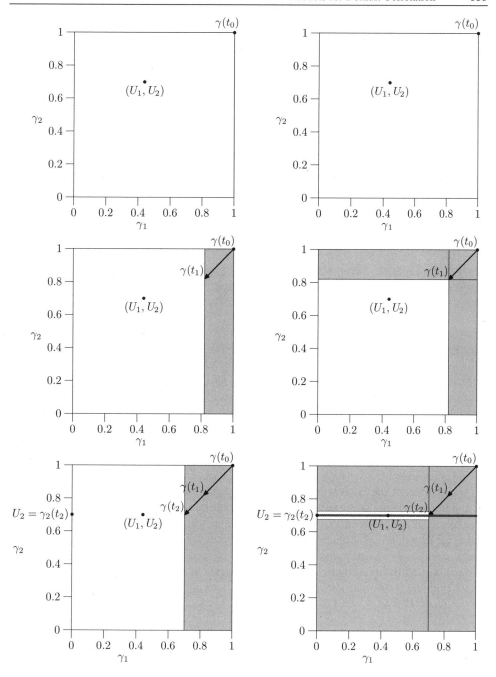

Figure 10.20   Progressive revelation of information to an observer only observing obligor 1 (left) and to an observer observing *both* obligors (right)

t is given by

$$\mathbf{P}[\tau \geq \mathbf{T} \mid \mathcal{H}_t] = \overline{F}(t, \mathbf{T}) = \frac{\mathbf{E}[C(\gamma_1(T_1), \ldots, \gamma_I(T_I)) \mid \mathcal{H}_t]}{C(\gamma_1(t), \ldots, \gamma_I(t))},$$

where $\overline{F}$ is the survival function of the default times.

(iii) The default intensity of obligor i is in this case $h_i(t)$, and not $\lambda_i(t)$:

$$h_i(t) = \lambda_i(t) \gamma_i(t) \frac{\partial}{\partial x_i} \ln C(\gamma(t)).$$

(iv) If the first k default times are known, the conditional distribution function of τ is (assuming sufficient regularity)

$$\mathbf{P}[\tau \geq \mathbf{T} \mid \mathcal{H}_t \wedge \{\tau_i = t_i \text{ for } 1 \leq i \leq k\} \wedge \{\tau_j > t \text{ for } k < j \leq I\}]$$

$$= \frac{\mathbf{E}\left[\dfrac{\partial^k}{\partial x_1 \cdots \partial x_k} C(\gamma_1(t_1), \ldots, \gamma_k(t_k), \gamma_{k+1}(T_{k+1}), \ldots, \gamma_I(T_I)) \,\middle|\, \mathcal{H}_t\right]}{\dfrac{\partial^k}{\partial x_1 \cdots \partial x_k} C(\gamma_1(t_1), \ldots, \gamma_k(t_k), \gamma_{k+1}(t), \ldots, \gamma_I(t))},$$

where $\tau_i > T_i$ for $i \leq k$.

For a proof see Schönbucher and Schubert (2001). This proposition shows how the conditional default probabilities change when the set of observed obligors changes. Default intensities are local default probabilities. As probabilities change if better information is available, so do default intensities.

We also see that the initially used default intensities $\lambda_i(t)$ only remain the default intensities if we restrict ourselves to the one-obligor case. Because $\lambda_i(t) = \mathbf{E}^P[h_i(t) \mid (\mathcal{H}_t^i)_{t \in [0, \overline{T}]}]$, the model is consistent.

At every default, the value of one U_i is revealed with certainty. The distribution function must be conditioned on this information, and this conditioning is done by taking a partial derivative. This allows us to find the change in default intensity h_i that is caused by this conditioning, and this is the essential step in the description of the dynamics of the default intensities.

Proposition 10.10 (dynamics of default intensities)   *If no default has happened until time t, and if λ_i has continuous dynamics, the default intensity h_i satisfies the following s.d.e. for any obligor $i \leq I$:*

$$\frac{dh_i}{h_i} = \frac{d\lambda_i}{\lambda_i} + \left(h_i\left(1 - \frac{C_{x_i x_i} C}{C_{x_i}^2}\right) - \lambda_i\right) dt - dN_i$$

$$+ \sum_{j=1, \, j \neq i}^{I} \left(\frac{C_{x_i x_j} C}{C_{x_i} C_{x_j}} - 1\right)(dN_j - h_j dt). \tag{10.62}$$

Here C_{x_i} denotes the partial derivative of C with respect to the ith argument, and $C_{x_i x_j}$ the second-order partial derivative with respect to i and j.

Similar dynamics can be written down for the dynamics of the hazard rate after some defaults have already occurred. Several observations can be made from equation (10.62).

First, the volatility of h_i equals the volatility of λ_i. This is an important fact also for the estimation of the semi-dynamic copula models with stochastic intensities because it gives the justification for estimating the volatility of λ_i from market data, although we can only observe h_i in the market. If we calibrate the drift of λ_i to fit a given initial term structure of defaultable bond prices, we have thus fully specified λ_i.

Second, Proposition 10.10 gives us a consistent description of the default intensities corresponding to the semi-dynamic copula model with copula C and hazard rates λ_i that we set out to find. We now have two alternative specifications of the same model:

(a) Use Assumption 10.12 to simulate default times.
(b) Use Proposition 10.10 to specify the dynamics of each obligor's default intensity. Simulate his defaults using this intensity process (e.g. using the Monte Carlo methods described earlier).

Both approaches will give us the same joint distribution of default times but only Proposition 10.10 will give us the correct dynamics of the default hazard rates under $(\mathcal{H}_t)_{t \in [0, \overline{T}]}$, i.e. full observation of all obligors' default and survival behaviour. Proposition 10.10 and the model setup in Assumption 10.12 are the two sides of the copula default risk modelling coin. As soon as we choose a copula and dynamics for λ_i, we have already fixed the "true" hazard-rate dynamics in equation (10.62). And if we just used the hazard-rate dynamics of equation (10.62), we would generate default times that have the same distribution as the ones generated directly from the copula.

The influence of the defaults of other obligors is contained in the summation term in the second line of (10.62). The size of the mutual influence between obligor i and obligor j is given by

$$\Delta_{ij} := \frac{C_{x_i x_j} C}{C_{x_i} C_{x_j}} - 1, \tag{10.63}$$

which mainly depends on the copula. The survival probabilities λ_i only have an influence insofar as they determine at which point the copula is evaluated. It can be shown that this expression is related to a dependency measure called *Kendall's tau*, and that it is positive if and only if there is locally positive dependence between the two default times.

Now, if obligor j does not default at t, then $dN_j = 0$ and we only have a drift influence of $-\Delta_{ij} h_j dt$ which is small but points in the right direction. No default of j and positive dependence between i and j leads to a *decrease* in i's default intensity.

If on the other hand obligor j should default at time t, then $dN_j = 1$ and there will be a relative jump in h_i by Δ_{ij} upward (given positive dependence). This effect is exactly the *default contagion* effect that was described earlier and which Davis and Lo (1999, 2001) and Jarrow and Yu (2001) also tried to model. While Davis and Lo and Jarrow and Yu directly tried to model default contagion, it now flows naturally out of the copula setup.

Finally, summing up the default intensities of equation (10.62) yields the intensity of the *first default* of the obligors:

$$h_{FtD}(t) = \sum_{i=1}^{I} h_i(t).$$

It is easily seen that $\int_0^t h_{FtD}(s)ds$ is the predictable compensator of the cumulative sum of all defaults $\sum_{i=1}^{I} N(t)$, so h_{FtD} is actually the cumulative default intensity of the portfolio.

We can now show how different copula specifications can be compared with respect to the dynamics they imply for the default hazard rates.

Example 10.2 (Archimedean copula) *Recall that an Archimedean copula function with generator function ϕ has the following representation:*

$$C(\mathbf{x}) = \phi^{[-1]}\left(\sum_{i=1}^{I} \phi(x_i)\right),$$

where $\phi : [0, 1] \to \mathbb{R}^+ \cup \{+\infty\}$, ϕ is invertible.

(i) The default intensity before any defaults is:

$$h_i(t) = \frac{\phi'(\gamma_i)}{C(\gamma)\phi'(C(\gamma))}\gamma_i\lambda_i.$$

(ii) At default $t = \tau_j$ of obligor $j \neq i$ the default intensity changes by a factor

$$h_i^{-j}(t) = \left(-\frac{C(\gamma)\phi''(C(\gamma))}{\phi'(C(\gamma))}\right)h_i(t).$$

(iii) The dynamics of h_i are:

$$\frac{dh_i}{h_i} = \frac{d\lambda_i}{\lambda_i} - \lambda_i dt - \left(-\frac{C\phi''(C)}{\phi'(C)}\right)dN_i$$
$$+ \sum_{j=1}^{I}\left(\left(-\frac{C\phi''(C)}{\phi'(C)}\right) - 1\right)(dN_j - h_j dt).$$

At default of an obligor j, the default intensities of all other obligors change by the same factor. The individual default risk is contained in $\phi'(\gamma_i)$, the default dependency $C(\gamma)$.

Example 10.3 (Gumbel copula) $\phi(x) = (-\ln(x))^\theta$ *for $\theta \in [1, \infty)$ yields the **Gumbel** copula:*

$$C(\mathbf{x}) = \exp\left\{-\left[\sum_{i=1}^{I}(-\ln x_i)^\theta\right]^{\frac{1}{\theta}}\right\}.$$

The default intensities for the Gumbel copula are:

$$h_i(t) = \left(\frac{\Lambda_i}{\|\mathbf{\Lambda}\|_\theta}\right)^{\theta-1} \lambda_i, \qquad h_i^{-j}(t) = \left(1 + \frac{(\theta-1)}{\|\mathbf{\Lambda}\|_\theta}\right) h_i,$$

where $\|\mathbf{x}\|_\theta := (\sum_{i=1}^I |x_i|^\theta)^{\frac{1}{\theta}}$ *stands for the* θ*-norm in* $\mathbb{R}^I$ *and* $\Lambda_i(t) := \int_0^t \lambda_i(s)ds$*. For constant* $\lambda_i(t) = \lambda = const.$ *we reach the following default intensities and jump sizes:*

$$h_i(t) = I^{-\frac{\theta-1}{\theta}} \lambda, \qquad h_i^{-j}(t) - h_i(t) = \frac{\theta-1}{I} \cdot \frac{1}{t},$$

$$h_{FtD} = I^{1/\theta} \lambda.$$

The Gumbel default intensity depends on the direction components of the intensity vector, normalised to 1 in $\|\cdot\|_\theta$. The first-to-default intensity has an interesting form: for constant λ_i it is time-independent itself, and the parameter θ controls whether it is closer to λ or to $I\lambda$. These results also carry through to the case with different (but constant) $\lambda_i \neq \lambda_j$, here we reach

$$h_{FtD} = \|\lambda\|_\theta = \left(\sum_{i=1}^I \lambda_i^\theta\right)^{\frac{1}{\theta}}$$

and $h_{FtD} \to \max\{\lambda_i, i \leq I\}$ as $\theta \to \infty$ (the case of perfect dependence), $h_{FtD} \to \sum \lambda_i$ as $\theta \to 0$. Thus, if a first-to-default rate was observed in the market, we could easily calibrate the Gumbel copula model to it by adjusting θ such that the observed market price is reached.

Unfortunately, the dynamics of the individual default hazard rates h_i do not share the nice properties of the first-to-default hazard rate h_{FtD} in the Gumbel model. If we regard the jump sizes as a function of time, we can see that the jump sizes tend to infinity as $1/t$ for early jumps (i.e. t small). Such a singularity at $t = 0$ is hard to justify, $t = 0$ is not a particularly risky time, it is simply the time at which we started to model. It is not surprising, though, because we already know that the Gumbel copula exhibits upper tail dependence.

Example 10.4 (Clayton copula) *The generator of the **Clayton copula** is* $\phi(x) = (x^{-\alpha} - 1)/\alpha$ *for* $\alpha > 0$*. Then*

$$C(\mathbf{x}) = \left(1 - I + \sum_{i=1}^I x_i^{-\alpha}\right)^{-\frac{1}{\alpha}}.$$

The hazard rates and their jumps are given by:

$$h_i(t) = \left(\frac{C(\gamma)}{\gamma_i}\right)^\alpha \lambda_i, \qquad h_i^{-j}(t) = (1+\alpha)h_i.$$

For constant $\lambda_i(t) = \lambda = const.$ *we reach:*

$$h_i(t) = \lambda \frac{1}{I - (I-1)e^{-\alpha\lambda t}}, \qquad h_{FtD}(t) = I\lambda \frac{1}{I - (I-1)e^{-\alpha\lambda t}}.$$

Irrespective of current time and default intensities, the Clayton copula model always exhibits *constant proportional* jumps in the default intensity of all other obligors if one obligor should default. This is a very intuitive and natural specification of the dynamics of the hazard rates and it also yields a new way to imply this parameter. If we believe that the credit spreads of firm X would jump by 60% if firm Y defaults, then we can model the default correlation between the two firms with a Clayton copula with parameter 0.6. We can now directly imply the parameters of something like a *market implied copula* from the *price dynamics* Δh_i of the default intensities.

Like the default hazard rate h_i, the first-to-default intensity in the Clayton model is not constant any more, but its development is well-behaved. It starts at $t = 0$ at $h_i(0) = \lambda_i(0)$ and remains bounded: for constant and equal λ_i it converges to λ/I, for constant but different λ_i all but the hazard rate with the maximal λ_i converge to zero, and the h_i of the maximal λ_i converges to λ_i.

Example 10.5 (Gaussian copula)   *In general and high dimensions it is not possible to give the parameters of the implied dynamics of the Gaussian copula, because there is no way to efficiently evaluate high-dimensional cumulative normal distribution functions. We therefore only treat the case of the bivariate Gaussian copula with correlation ρ.*

We call $x := \Phi^{[-1]}(u)$ and $y := \Phi^{[-1]}(v)$. Then

$$\frac{\partial}{\partial u} C(u, v) = \Phi\left(\frac{y - \rho x}{\sqrt{1 - \rho^2}}\right),$$

$$\frac{\partial}{\partial v} C(u, v) = \Phi\left(\frac{x - \rho y}{\sqrt{1 - \rho^2}}\right),$$

$$\frac{\partial^2}{\partial u \partial v} C(u, v) = \frac{1}{\sqrt{1 - \rho^2}} \exp\left\{-\frac{1}{2(1 - \rho^2)}(x^2 - 2\rho xy + y^2) + \frac{1}{2}(x^2 + y^2)\right\}.$$

From this and the bivariate cumulative normal distribution function the relative jump sizes can be calculated.

Figure 10.21 shows the size of the relative jumps in the intensity of obligor 1 in a Gaussian copula model, if the other obligor 2 defaults, as a function of the time of default of the other obligor. The parameters were $\lambda = 5\%$ and $\rho = 30\%$. Here we see a similar shape as for the Gumbel copula: again there is a singularity at $t = 0$ which decays as time proceeds. This singularity is caused by the singularity in the density of the Gaussian copula at $(1, 1)$, i.e. $(\gamma_1(0), \gamma_2(0))$. This singularity was not strong enough to cause upper tail dependence but is strong enough to imply highly unrealistic dynamics for the default intensities of the obligors. The same arguments apply here that already applied to the Gumbel copula. While some minor variations in the dynamics of the default intensities over time are probably unavoidable, there is no reason why there should be a singularity at $t = 0$. It seems that the Gaussian copula does not really fit the intensity-based marginals used in this model.

The t_v-copula will also exhibit similar jump sizes as the Gaussian and Gumbel models. In fact, as the t_v-copula has positive upper tail dependence the implied jumps in default intensities should be even stronger than for the Gauss copula.

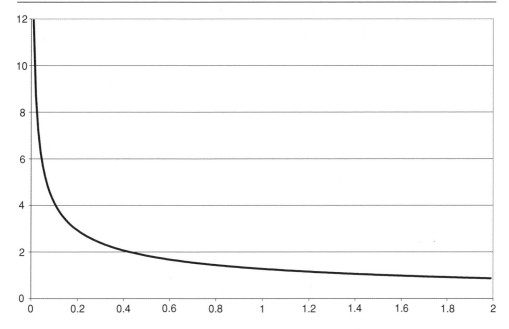

Figure 10.21 Relative jump sizes for a bivariate Gaussian copula with $\rho = 30\%$ and $\lambda = 5\%$ as a function of the time of the other obligor's default

10.8.4.3 Pricing of first-to-default swaps

Finally, we would like to demonstrate how a first-to-default swap can be priced numerically in the dynamic copula model. The copula approach is often a very flexible and convenient approach to price basket credit derivatives. For example, given the FtD intensities derived above for the Clayton and Gumbel copulae, an FtD swap can be priced exactly like a CDS, only we are now using the FtD intensity as default intensity process. Yet frequently, a numerical evaluation has its advantages.

The direct approach would be to simply simulate the default times of all obligors and then to determine the default time and identity of the first defaulted obligor:

1. Draw $U_1, \ldots, U_I$;
2. Simulate $\gamma_1, \ldots, \gamma_I$ and determine first default.

But if the copula $C(\cdot)$ is given in closed form and can be evaluated easily, there is also the *accelerated simulation approach:*

1. Draw only one $U^* \sim U(0, 1)$;
2. Simulate γ^* using the *intensity of the first default*;
3. Given γ^* directly evaluate the probability of first default.

Given individual survival probability processes

$$\gamma_1(t), \ldots, \gamma_I(t)$$

the *FtD survival probability process* $\gamma^*(t)$ is given by:

$$\gamma^*(t) = C(\gamma_1(t), \ldots, \gamma_I(t)).$$

The first default happens as soon as $\gamma^*(t) \leq U^*$. We can therefore simply define the *FtD hazard rate*:

$$h_{FtD}(t) = -\frac{d}{dt} \ln \gamma^*(t) = \sum_{i=1}^{I} -\frac{\gamma_i(t)\frac{\partial}{\partial x_i}C}{C}\lambda_i(t) = \sum_{i=1}^{I} h_i(t). \qquad (10.64)$$

This allows us to determine the distribution of the *time* of the first default. If we are also interested in the *identity* of the first default, we can use the following facts. Given that the first default has happened in $[T_k, T_{k+1}]$ with probability

$$\mathbf{P}[n \mid \text{1st default}] = \frac{C(\gamma^{-j}(T_k), \gamma_j(T_{k-1})) - \gamma^*(T_k)}{\gamma^*(T_{k+1}) - \gamma^*(T_k)},$$

the culprit was obligor j. In the limit as the time step sizes converge to zero we reach the following. If first default was at time t, the probability that the defaulted obligor was n is:

$$\mathbf{P}[n \mid \text{1st default}] = \frac{h_n(t)}{\sum_{i \neq n} h_i(t)}.$$

In fact, the problem is now reduced to the modelling of a single-name CDS with an (admittedly complicated) intensity process $h_{FtD}(t)$. If the copula allows sufficient tractability to derive a closed-form solution for the FtD intensity, we can give a closed-form pricing formula for the FtD in analogy to equations (3.26), (3.27) and (3.28). The reader is invited to substitute the example FtD intensities that were given in Examples 10.3 and 10.4 for the Gumbel and Clayton copulae into (3.28) and experiment with the inputs like λ, number of obligors I and dependency parameter.

Bibliography

Adams, K.J. and van Deventer, D.R. (1994) Fitting yield curves and forward rate curves with maximum smoothness. *Journal of Fixed Income*, 52–62.

Aguais, S., Rosen, D. and Smithson, C. (eds) (2001) *Enterprise Credit Risk*. Algorithmics Publications, www.algorithmics.com.

Altman, E.I. (1993) Defaulted bonds: demand, supply and performance, 1987–1992. *Financial Analysts Journal*, May/June: 55–60.

Altman, E.I. and Eberhart, A.C. (1994) Do seniority provisions protect bondholders' investments? *Journal of Portfolio Management*, Summer: 67–75.

Altman, E.I. and Kao, D.L. (1992) Rating drift of high yield bonds. *Journal of Fixed Income*, March.

Altman, E.I. and Kishore, V.M. (1996) Almost everything you wanted to know about recoveries on defaulted bonds. *Financial Analysts Journal*, Nov/Dec: 57–64.

Altman, E.I., Resti, A. and Sirone, A. (2001) Analyzing and explaining default recovery rates. Report submitted to the ISDA, Stern School of Business, New York University, December.

Amemiya, T. (1984) Tobit models: a survey. *Journal of Econometrics*, 24: 3–63.

Andersen, P.K., Borgan, Ø. and Gill, R.D. (1992) *Statistical Models Based on Counting Processes*. Springer Series in Statistics, Springer, Berlin.

Anderson, N., Breedon, F., Deacon, M., Derry, A. and Murphy, G. (1996) *Estimating and Interpreting the Yield Curve*. John Wiley & Sons, Chichester.

Artzner, P. and Delbaen, F. (1992) Credit risk and prepayment option. *Astin Bulletin*, 22: 81–96.

Artzner, P. and Delbaen, F. (1995) Default risk insurance and incomplete markets. *Mathematical Finance*, 5: 187–195.

Arvanitis, A., Gregory, J. and Laurent, J.-P. (1999) Building models for credit spreads. *Journal of Derivatives*, 6(3): 27–43.

Asarnow, E. and Edwards, D. (1995) Measuring loss on defaulted bank loans: a 24-year study. *Journal of Commercial Lending*, March.

Asquith, P., Gertner, R. and Scharfstein, D. (1994) Anatomy of financial distress: an examination of junk-bond issuers. *Quarterly Journal of Economics*, August: 625–657.

Aven, T. (1985) A theorem for determining the compensator of a counting process. *Scandinavian Journal of Statistics*, 12(1): 69–72.

Bakshi, G., Madan, D. and Zhang, F. (2001) Understanding the role of recovery in default risk models: empirical comparisons and implied recovery rates. Working paper, University of Maryland, November.

Belkin, B., Suchover, S. and Forest, L. (1998) A one-parameter representation of credit risk and transition matrices. *Credit Metrics Monitor*, 1(3): 46–56.

Bensoussan, A., Crouhy, M. and Galai, D. (1995) Stochastic equity volatility and the capital structure of the firm. In: S.D. Howison, F.P. Kelly and P. Wilmott (eds), *Mathematical Models in Finance*. The Royal Society/Chapman and Hall, pp. 81–92.

Bielecki, T.R. and Rutkowski, M. (2000) Multiple ratings model of defaultable term structure. *Mathematical Finance*, 10(2): 125–139.

Bierman, H. and Haas, J.E. (1975) An analytical model of bond risk yield differentials. *Journal of Financial and Quantitative Analysis*, 10: 757–773.

Björk, T. (1998) *Arbitrage Theory in Continuous Time*. Oxford University Press, Oxford.

Björk, T., Di Masi, G., Kabanov, Y. and Runggaldier, W. (1997) Towards a general theory of bond markets. *Finance and Stochastics*, 1(2): 141–174.

Black, F. and Cox, J. (1976) Valuing corporate securities: some effects of bond indenture provisions. *Journal of Finance*, 351–367.

Black, F. and Scholes, M. (1973) The pricing of options and corporate liabilities. *Journal of Political Economy*, 81: 637–654.

Black, F., Derman, E. and Toy, W. (1990) A one factor model of interest rates and its application to treasury bond options. *Financial Analysts Journal*, 33–39.

Bowler, T. and Tierney, J.F. (1999) Credit derivatives and structured credit: a survey of products, applications and market issues. Research report, Deutsche Bank Global Markets Research, Fixed Income Research, October.

Brace, A., Gatarek, D. and Musiela, M. (1997) The market model of interest rate dynamics. *Mathematical Finance*, 7(2): 127–155.

Brémaud, P. (1981) *Point Processes and Queues*. Springer, Berlin.

Brys, E. and de Varenne, F. (1997) Valuing risky fixed rate debt: an extension. *Journal of Financial and Quantitative Analysis*, 32(2): 239–248.

Burghof, H.-P., Henke, S., Rudolph, B., Schönbucher, P. and Sommer, D. (eds) (2000) *Kreditderivate – Handbuch für die Bank- und Anlagepraxis*. Schäffer-Poeschel Verlag, Stuttgart.

Carette, P. (1995) Characterizations of embeddable 3×3 stochastic matrices with a negative eigenvalue. *New York Journal of Mathematics*, 1: 120–129.

Chen, R.-R. and Scott, L. (1995) Interest rate options in multifactor Cox–Ingersoll–Ross models of the term structure. *Journal of Derivatives*, 3(2): 52–72.

Cifuentes, A. and O'Connor, G. (1996) The binomial expansion method applied to CBO/CLO analysis. Special report, Moody's Investor Service, December.

Cifuentes, A. and Wilcox, C. (1998) The double binomial method and its application to a special case of CBO structures. Special report, Moody's Investor Service, March.

Cifuentes, A., Murphy, E. and O'Connor, G. (1996) Emerging market collateralized bond obligations: an overview. Special report, Moody's Investor Service, October.

Clayton, D.G. (1978) A model for association in bivariate life tables and its application in epidemiological studies of familial tendency in chronic disease incidence. *Biometrica*, 65: 141–151.

Cossin, D. and Hricko, T. (2001) Exploring the determinants of credit risk in credit default swap transactions data. Working paper, University of Lausanne, May.

Cox, J., Ross, S. and Rubinstein, M. (1979) Option pricing: a simplified approach. *Journal of Financial Economics*, 7: 229–263.

Cox, J., Ingersoll, J.E. and Ross, S.A. (1985a) An intertemporal general equilibrium model of asset prices. *Econometrica*, 53: 363–384.

Cox, J., Ingersoll, J.E. and Ross, S.A. (1985b) A theory of the term structure of interest rates. *Econometrica*, 53: 385–407.

Credit Suisse First Boston (1997) Credit Risk+. Technical document, Credit Suisse First Boston. www.csfb.com/creditrisk.

Cumby, R. and Pastinte, T. (2001) Emerging market debt: measuring credit quality and examining relative pricing. Discussion paper 2866, CEPR, London, June.

Das, S.R. (1995) Credit risk derivatives. *Journal of Derivatives*, 2: 7–23.

Das, S. (ed.) (1998) *Credit Derivatives: Trading and Management of Credit and Default Risk*. Wiley Frontiers in Finance, John Wiley & Sons, New York.

Das, S.R. and Tufano, P. (1996) Pricing credit-sensitive debt when interest rates, credit ratings and credit spreads are stochastic. *Journal of Financial Engineering*, 5(2): 161–198.

Davis, M. and Lo, V. (1999) Modelling default correlation in bond portfolios. In: C. Alexander (ed.), *ICBI Report on Credit Risk*.

Davis, M. and Lo, V. (2001) Infectious defaults. *Quantitative Finance*, 1: 382–387.

Devroye, L. (1986) *Non-uniform Random Variate Generation*. Springer, Berlin.

Duffee, G.R. (1998) The relation between treasury yields and corporate bond yield spreads. *Journal of Finance*, 53(6): 2225–2242.

Duffee, G.R. (1999) Estimating the price of default risk. *The Review of Financial Studies*, 12: 197–226.

Duffie, D. (1988) *Security Markets: Stochastic Models*. Academic Press, San Diego.

Duffie, D. (1994) Forward rate curves with default risk. Working paper, Graduate School of Business, Stanford University, December.

Duffie, D. (1996) *Dynamic Asset Pricing Theory*. Princeton University Press, Princeton, NJ.

Duffie, D. (1998) Defaultable term structure models with fractional recovery of par. Working paper, Graduate School of Business, Stanford University.

Duffie, D. (1999) Credit swap valuation. *Financial Analysts Journal*, Jan/Feb: 73–87.

Duffie, D. and Huang, M. (1996) Swap rates and credit quality. *Journal of Finance*, 51: 921–949.

Duffie, D. and Kan, R. (1996) A yield-factor model of interest rates. *Mathematical Finance*, 6: 379–406.

Duffie, D. and Lando, D. (2001) Term structures of credit spreads with incomplete accounting information. *Econometrica*, 69: 633–664.

Duffie, D. and Singleton, K. (1997) An econometric model of the term structure of interest rate swap yields. *Journal of Finance*, 52(4): 1287–1321.

Duffie, D. and Singleton, K. (1998) Simulating correlated defaults. Working paper, Graduate School of Business, Stanford University, September.

Duffie, D., Schroder, M. and Skiadas, C. (1996) Recursive valuation of defaultable securities and the timing of resolution of uncertainty. *Annals of Applied Probability*, 6: 1075–1090.

Duffie, D., Pan, J. and Singleton, K. (2000) Transform analysis and asset pricing for affine jump diffusions. *Econometrica*, 68(6): 1343–1376.

Duffie, D., Pedersen, L. and Singleton, K. (2003) Modeling sovereign yield spreads: a case study of Russian debt. *Journal of Finance*, 58: 119–159.

Düllmann, K., Uhrig-Homburg, M. and Windfuhr, M. (2000) Risk structure of interest rates: an empirical analysis for Deutschemark-denominated bonds. *European Financial Management*, 6(3).

Eberhart, A.C. and Sweeney, R.J. (1992) Does the bond market predict bankruptcy settlements? *Journal of Finance*, XLVII(3): 943–980.

Eberhart, A.C., Moore, W.T. and Roenfeldt, R.L. (1990) Security pricing and deviations from the absolute priority rule in bankruptcy proceedings. *Journal of Finance*, XLV(5): 1457–1469.

El Karoui, N. and Lacoste, V. (1992) Multifactor models of the term structure of interest rates. Working paper, University of Paris VI, July.

Embrechts, P., McNeal, A. and Straumann, D. (2002) Correlation and dependence in risk management: properties and pitfalls. In: M. Demster and H.K. Moffatt (eds), *Risk Management: Value at Risk and Beyond*. Cambridge University Press, Cambridge, pp. 176–223.

Eom, Y.H., Helwege, J. and Huang, J.Z. (2000) Structural models of corporate bond pricing: an empirical analysis. Working paper, Finance Department, Ohio State University, Columbus, OH, October.

Finger, C.C. (1999) Conditional approaches for credit metrics portfolio distributions. *Credit Metrics Monitor*, 2(1): 14–33.

Finger, C.C., Finkelstein, V., Pan, G., Lardy, J.-P., Ta, T. and Tierney, J. (2002) CreditGrades. Technical document, Risk Metrics Group, Finance Department, Ohio State University, Columbus, OH, May.

Flesaker, B., Houghston, L., Schreiber, L. and Sprung, L. (1994) Taking all the credit. *Risk*, 7: 105–108.

Fooladi, I., Roberts, G. and Skinner, F.S. (1997) Duration for bonds with default risk. *Journal of Banking and Finance*, 21: 1–16.

Franks, J.R. and Torous, W.N. (1994) A comparison of financial recontracting in distressed exchanges and Chapter 11 reorganizations. *Journal of Financial Economics*, 35: 349–370.

Frees, E.W. and Valdez, E.A. (1998) Understanding relationships using copulas. *North American Actuarial Journal*, 2(1): 1–25.

Frye, J. (2000a) Collateral damage. *Risk*, Apr: 91–94.

Frye, J. (2000b) Collateral damage detected. Working paper, emerging issues series, Federal Reserve Bank of Chicago, October.

Frye, J. (2000c) Depressing recoveries. *Risk*, November.

Geske, R. (1977) The valuation of corporate liabilities as compound options. *Journal of Financial and Quantitative Analysis*, 12: 541–552.

Giesecke, K. (2001) Correlated default with incomplete information. Working paper, Humboldt Universität Berlin, October.

Greene, W.H. (2000) *Econometric Analysis*. Prentice Hall, New York, 4th edition.

Gupton, G., Finger, C. and Bhatia, M. (1997) CreditMetrics. Technical document, JPMorgan, April. www.creditmetrics.com.

Gupton, G.M., Gates, D. and Carty, L.V. (2000) Bank loan loss given default. Special report, Moody's Investor Service.

Hamilton, D.T., Gupton, G. and Berthault, A. (2001) Default and recovery rates of corporate bond issuers: 2000. Special comment, Moody's Investor Service, Global Credit Research, February.

Hamilton, D.T., Cantor, R. and Ou, S. (2002) Default and recovery rates of corporate bond issuers. Special comment, Moody's Investor Service, Global Credit Research, February.

Harrison, J.M. and Pliska, S.R. (1981) Martingales and stochastic integrals in the theory of continuous trading. *Stochastic Processes and their Applications*, 11: 215–260.

Heath, D., Jarrow, R. and Morton, A. (1992) Bond pricing and the term structure of interest rates: a new methodology for contingent claims valuation. *Econometrica*, 60: 77–105.

Helwege, J. and Turner, C.M. (1999) The slope of the credit yield curve for speculative grade issuers. *Journal of Finance*, 54: 1869–1885.

Ho, T.S.Y. and Lee, S.-B. (1986) Term structure movements and pricing interest rate contingent claims. *Journal of Finance*, 41: 1011–1029.

Houweling, P. and Vorst, T. (2001) An empirical comparison of default swap pricing models. Working paper, Erasmus University, Rotterdam, December.

Houweling, P., Hoeck, J. and Kleibergen, F. (2001) The joint estimation of term structures and credit spreads. *Journal of Empirical Finance*, 8: 297–323.

Hradsky, G.T. and Long, R.D. (1989) High-yield default losses and the return performance of bankrupt debt. *Financial Analysts Journal*, 38: 38–49.

Hull, J. (1989) *Options, Futures and Other Derivative Securities*. Prentice Hall, New York.

Hull, J. and White, A. (1993) One factor interest rate models and the valuation of interest rate derivative securities. *Journal of Financial and Quantitative Analysis*, 28: 235–254.

Hull, J. and White, A. (1994a) Numerical procedures for implementing term structure models I: single-factor models. *Journal of Derivatives*, 2(1): 7–16.

Hull, J. and White, A. (1994b) Numerical procedures for implementing term structure models II: two-factor models. *Journal of Derivatives*, 2(2): 37–48.

Hull, J. and White, A. (1995) The impact of default risk on the prices of options and other derivative securities. *Journal of Banking and Finance*, 19(2): 299–322.

Hull, J. and White, A. (1996) Using Hull–White interest rate trees. *Journal of Derivatives*, 4(1): 26–36.

Hull, J. and White, A. (2001) Valuing credit default swaps II: modeling default correlations. *Journal of Derivatives*, 8(3): 12–22.

Israel, R., Rosenthal, J. and Wei, J. (2001) Finding generators for Markov chains via empirical transition matrices, with applications to credit ratings. *Mathematical Finance*, 11(2): 245–265.

Jacod, J. and Shiryaev, A.N. (1988) *Limit Theorems for Stochastic Processes*. Springer, Berlin.

Jaeckel, P. (2002) *Monte Carlo Methods in Finance*. John Wiley & Sons, Chichester.

James, C. (1991) The losses realized in bank failures. *Journal of Finance*, XLVI(4): 1223–1242.

Jamshidian, F. (1995) A simple class of square-root interest-rate models. *Applied Mathematical Finance*, 2: 61–72.

Jamshidian, F. (1996) Bond futures and option evaluation in the quadratic interest rate model. *Applied Mathematical Finance*, 3: 93–115.

Jamshidian, F. (1997a) LIBOR and swap market models and measures. *Finance and Stochastics*, 1(4): 293–330.

Jamshidian, F. (1997b) Pricing of contingent claims in the one-factor term structure model. In: L. Hughston (ed.), *Vasicek and Beyond: Approaches to Building and Applying Interest Rate Models*. Risk Books.

Jarrow, R.A. and Turnbull, S.M. (1995) Pricing derivatives on financial securities subject to credit risk. *Journal of Finance*, 50: 53–85.

Jarrow, R.A. and Yu, F. (2001) Counterparty risk and the pricing of defaultable securities. *Journal of Finance*, 56(Oct).

Jarrow, R.A., Lando, D. and Turnbull, S.M. (1997) A Markov model for the term structure of credit risk spreads. *The Review of Financial Studies*, 10(2): 481–523.

Joe, H. (1997) *Multivariate Models and Dependence Concepts*. Monographs on Statistics and Applied Probability, Vol. 37, Chapman and Hall, London.

Johnson, N.L. and Kotz, S. (1969) *Discrete Distributions.* Distributions in Statistics, John Wiley & Sons, New York.

Johnson, N.L. and Kotz, S. (1970) *Continuous Univariate Distributions*, Vol. 2. Houghton Mifflin Co., New York.

Jones, E.P., Mason, S.P. and Rosenfeld, E. (1984) Contingent claims analysis of corporate capital structure: an empirical investigation. *Journal of Finance*, 39: 611–626.

Jonkhart, M. (1979) On the term structure of interest rates and the risk of default. *Journal of Banking and Finance*, 3(3): 253–262.

Karatzas, I. and Shreve, S.E. (1991) *Brownian Motion and Stochastic Calculus.* Springer, Berlin.

Karlin, S. and Taylor, H.M. (1981a) *A First Course in Stochastic Processes.* Academic Press, New York.

Karlin, S. and Taylor, H.M. (1981b) *A Second Course in Stochastic Processes.* Academic Press, New York.

Kijima, M. (1998) Monotonicities in a Markov chain model for valuing corporate bonds subject to credit risk. *Mathematical Finance*, 8: 229–247.

Kijima, M. and Komoribayashi, K. (1998) A Markov chain model for valuing credit risk derivatives. *Journal of Derivatives*, 6(1): 97–108.

Kloeden, P.E. and Platen, E. (1992) *Numerical Solution of Stochastic Differential Equations.* Applications of Mathematics, Vol. 23, Springer, Berlin.

Kreinin, A. and Sidelnikova, M. (2001) Regularization algorithms for transition matrices. In: S. Aguais, D. Rosen and C. Smithson (eds), *Enterprise Credit Risk.* Algorithmics Publications, pp. 43–60.

Kwan, S.H. (1996) Firm-specific information and the correlation between individual stocks and bonds. *Journal of Financial Economics*, 40: 63–80.

Lamberton, D. and Lapeyre, B. (1996) *Introduction to Stochastic Calculus Applied to Finance.* Chapman and Hall, London.

Lando, D. (1994) Three essays on contingent claims pricing. PhD thesis, Graduate School of Management, Cornell University.

Lando, D. (1998) On Cox processes and credit risky bonds. *Review of Derivatives Research*, 2(2/3): 99–120.

Lando, D. (2000) Some elements of rating-based credit risk modeling. In: N. Jegadeesh and B. Tuckman (eds), *Advanced Fixed-Income Valuation Tools.* John Wiley & Sons, New York, pp. 193–215.

Lando, D. and Skodeberg, T. (2002) Analyzing rating transitions and rating drift with continuous observations. *Journal of Banking and Finance*, 26: 423–444.

Lardic, S. and Rouzeau, E. (1999) Implementing Merton's model on the French corporate bond market. Presentation, AFFI Conference.

Last, G. and Brandt, A. (1995) *Marked Point Processes on the Real Line.* Probability and its Applications, Springer, Berlin.

Lehrbass, F. (1999) A simple approach to country risk. Working paper, West LB, May.

Leland, H.E. (1994) Risky debt, bond covenants and optimal capital structure. *Journal of Finance*, 49: 1213–1252.

Leland, H.E. and Toft, K.B. (1996) Optimal capital structure, endogenous bankruptcy and the term structure of credit spreads. *Journal of Finance*, 50: 789–819.

Li, D.X. (2000) On default correlation: a copula function approach. Working paper 99-07, Risk Metrics Group, April.

Linton, O., Mammen, E., Nielsen, J.P. and Tanggaard, C. (2001) Yield curve estimation by kernel smoothing methods. *Journal of Econometrics*, 105(1): 185–223.

Liptser, R.Sh. and Shiryaev, A.N. (1998) Elements of the general theory of stochastic processes. In: Yu.V. Prokhorod and A.N. Shiryaev (eds), *Probability Theory III.* Springer Encyclopedia of Mathematical Sciences, Vol. 45, Springer, Berlin, pp. 111–157.

Litterman, R. and Iben, T. (1991) Corporate bond valuation and the term structure of credit spreads. *Journal of Portfolio Management*, 52–64.

Liu, J., Longstaff, F.A. and Mandell, R.E. (2000) The market price of credit risk: an empirical investigation of interest-rate swap spreads. Working paper, Anderson School at UCLA, October.

Longstaff, F.A. (2000) The term structure of very short-term rates: new evidence for the expectations hypothesis. *Journal of Financial Economics*, 58: 397–415.

Longstaff, F. and Schwartz, E. (1992) Interest rate volatility and the term structure: a two factor general equilibrium model. *Journal of Finance*, 47: 1259–1282.

Longstaff, F.A. and Schwartz, E.S. (1994) A simple approach to valuing risky fixed and floating rate debt. Working paper 22–93, Anderson Graduate School of Management, University of California, Los Angeles, October (revised November).

Longstaff, F.A. and Schwartz, E.S. (1995) A simple approach to valuing risky fixed and floating rate debt. *Journal of Finance*, 50(3): 789–819.

Lucas, A., Klaassen, P., Spreij, P. and Staetmans, S. (2001) An analytic approach to credit risk of large corporate bond and loan portfolios. *Journal of Banking and Finance*, 25(9): 1635–1664.

Madan, D.B. and Unal, H. (1998) Pricing the risks of default. *Review of Derivatives Research*, 2(2/3): 121–160.

Marshall, A.W. and Olkin, I. (1988) Families of multivariate distributions. *Journal of the American Statistical Association*, 83: 834–841.

Mathieu, P. and d'Herouville, P. (1998) *Les Dérivés de Crédit*. Politique générale, Finance et Marketing. Economica, Paris, collection gestion edition.

McCulloch, J.H. (1971) Measuring the term structure of interest rates. *Journal of Business*, 44: 19–31.

McCulloch, J.H. (1975) The tax-adjusted yield curve. *Journal of Finance*, 30: 811–830.

McFadden, D. (1984) Econometric analysis of qualitative response models. In: Z. Grilliches and M. Intriligator (eds), *Handbook of Econometrics*, Vol. 2. North Holland, Amsterdam.

Mella-Barral, P. and Perraudin, W.R.M. (1997) Strategic debt service. *Journal of Finance*, 51.

Merrick, J.J. (2001) Crisis dynamics of implied default recovery ratios: evidence from Russia and Argentina. *Journal of Banking and Finance*, 25(10): 1921–1939.

Merton, R.C. (1974) On the pricing of corporate debt: the risk structure of interest rates. *Journal of Finance*, 29: 449–470.

Merton, R.C. (1977) On the pricing of contingent claims and the Modigliani–Miller theorem. *Journal of Financial Economics*, 5: 241–249.

Merton, R.C. (1992) *Continuous Time Finance*. Blackwell, Oxford.

Miltersen, K.R., Sandmann, K. and Sondermann, D. (1997) Closed form solutions for term structure derivatives with log-normal interest rates. *Journal of Finance*, 52(1): 409–430.

Morton, K.W. and Mayers, D. (1993) Numerical solution of partial differential equations. Oxford University Computing Laboratory, mimeo.

Musiela, M. and Rutkowski, M. (1997) *Martingale Methods in Financial Modelling*. Applications of Mathematics, Vol. 36, Springer, Berlin.

Neftci, S.N. (1996) *An Introduction to the Mathematics of Financial Derivatives*. Academic Press, New York.

Nelken, I. (1999) *Implementing Credit Derivatives*. Irwin Library of Investment and Finance, McGraw-Hill, New York.

Nelsen, R.B. (1999) *An Introduction to Copulas*. Lecture Notes in Statistics, Vol. 139, Springer, Berlin.

Nelson, C.R. and Siegel, A.F. (1987) Parsimonious modelling of yield curves. *Journal of Business*, 60: 473.

Nickell, P., Perraudin, W. and Varotto, S. (1998) Ratings versus equity-based credit risk models: an empirical analysis. Working paper, Bank of England.

Nielsen, L.T. (1999) *Pricing and Hedging of Derivative Securities*. Oxford University Press, Oxford.

Nielsen, L.T., Saá-Requejo, J. and Santa-Clara, P. (1993) Default risk and interest rate risk: the term structure of default spreads. Working paper, INSEAD.

Patel, N. (2002) The vanilla explosion. *Risk*, 2(Feb).

Pierides, Y.A. (1997) The pricing of credit risk derivatives. *Journal of Economic Dynamics and Control*, 21: 1579–1611.

Pimbley, J. (2000) The misuse of risk-neutrality in credit derivatives pricing. Conference proceedings, Risk 2000, Europe.

Protter, P. (1990) *Stochastic Integration and Differential Equations*. Springer, Berlin.

Rebonato, R. (1998) *Interest-Rate Option Models*. Wiley Series in Financial Engineering, John Wiley & Sons, Chichester, 2nd edition.

Rogers, L.C.G. and Williams, D. (1994) *Diffusions, Markov Processes, and Martingales*. Wiley Series in Probability and Mathematical Statistics, Vol. 1, John Wiley & Sons, Chichester, 2nd edition.

Sandmann, K. and Sondermann, D. (1995) A term structure model and the pricing of interest rate derivatives. *Review of Futures Markets*, 12: 391–423.

Sandmann, K. and Sondermann, D. (1997) A note on the stability of lognormal interest rate models and the pricing of Eurodollar futures. *Mathematical Finance*, 119–125.

Sarig, O. and Warga, A. (1989) Some empirical estimates of the risk structure of interest rates. *Journal of Finance*, 44: 1351–1360.

Schlögl, E. (1997) Interest rate factor models: term structure dynamics and derivatives pricing. PhD thesis, University of Bonn, Faculty of Economics.

Schmidt, W. (2001) Analyse und bewertung von credit default swaps. Working paper, Deutsche Bank, Global Markets, Research and Analytics, Frankfurt, March.

Schönbucher, P.J. (1993) Option pricing and hedging in finitely liquid markets. Master's thesis, University of Oxford, Mathematical Institute, September.

Schönbucher, P.J. (1996) Valuation of securities subject to credit risk. Working paper, University of Bonn, Department of Statistics, February.

Schönbucher, P.J. (1997) Pricing credit risk derivatives. Working paper wp-10, London School of Economics, Financial Markets Group, July.

Schönbucher, P.J. (1998) The term structure of defaultable bond prices. Discussion paper B-384, University of Bonn, SFB 303, August.

Schönbucher, P.J. (2000a) Credit risk modelling and credit derivatives. PhD thesis, Faculty of Economics, Bonn University, January.

Schönbucher, P.J. (2000b) Factor models for portfolio credit risk. Working paper, Department of Statistics, Bonn University.

Schönbucher, P.J. (2000c) A Libor market model with default risk. Working paper, University of Bonn, Department of Statistics.

Schönbucher, P.J. (2001) Factor models: portfolio credit risk when defaults are correlated. *Journal of Risk Finance*, 3(1).

Schönbucher, P.J. (2002) A tree implementation of a credit spread model for credit derivatives. *Journal of Computational Finance*, in press.

Schönbucher, P.J. and Schubert, D. (2001) Copula-dependent default risk in intensity models. Working paper, Department of Statistics, Bonn University.

Schönbucher, P. and Sommer, D. (2000) Analyse und modellierung von credit spreads. In: H.-P. Burghof, S. Henke, B. Rudolph, P. Schönbucher and D. Sommer (eds), *Kreditderivate – Handbuch für die Bank- und Anlagepraxis*. Schäffer-Poeschel Verlag, Stuttgart.

Schönbucher, P.J. and Wilmott, P. (1996) Hedging in illiquid markets: nonlinear effects. In: O. Mahrenholtz, K. Marti and R. Mennicken (eds), *ICIAM/GAMM 95: Proceedings of the Third International Congress on Industrial and Applied Mathematics, Hamburg, 3–7 July 1995, Issue 3, Applied Stochastics and Optimization*. Special Issue, Zeitschrift für Angewandte Mathematik und Mechanik (ZAMM), pp. 81–84.

Schönbucher, P.J., Epstein, D. and Haber, R. (1997) Pricing Parisian options. *ECMI Newsletter*, 22: 22–24.

Schwartz, T. (1998) Estimating the term structures of corporate debt. *Review of Derivatives Research*, 2(2/3): 193–230.

Scott, L. (1998) A note on the pricing of default swaps. Working paper 7, Morgan Stanley Dean Witter, Fixed Income Research, October.

Skinner, F.S. (1998) Hedging bonds subject to credit risk. *Journal of Banking and Finance*, 22: 321–345.

Svensson, L. (1994) Estimating and interpreting forward interest rates: Sweden 1992–94. Working paper 114, IMF.

Svensson, L. (1995) Estimating forward interest rates with the extended Nelson and Siegel method. *Sveriges Riksbank Quarterly Review*, 3: 13.

Tauren, M. (1999) A comparison of bond pricing models in the pricing of credit risk. Working paper, Indiana University, Bloomington, IN, March.

Tavakoli, J.M. (1998) *Credit Derivatives: A Guide to Instruments and Applications*. Wiley Series in Financial Engineering, John Wiley & Sons, New York.

Unal, H., Madan, D. and Guntay, L. (2001) A simple approach to estimate recovery rates with APR violation from debt spreads. Working paper, University of Maryland, February.

van De Castle, K. and Keisman, D. (1999) Recovering your money: insights into losses from defaults. *Standard and Poor's Credit Week*, June 16, pp. 29–34.

Vasicek, O. (1977) An equilibrium characterisation of the term structure. *Journal of Financial Economics*, 5: 177–188.

Vasicek, O. (1987) Probability of loss on loan portfolio. Working paper, KMV Corporation.

Vasicek, O. and Fong, H.G. (1982) Term structure modelling using exponential splines. *Journal of Finance*, 37(2): 339–348.

Waggoner, D. (1997) Spline methods for extracting interest rate curves from coupon bond prices. Working paper 97-10, Federal Reserve Bank of Atlanta.

Wilmott, P. (1998) *Derivatives: The Theory and Practice of Financial Engineering*. John Wiley & Sons, Chichester.

Wilmott, P., Howison, S. and Dewynne, J. (1993) *Option Pricing: Mathematical Models and Computation*. Oxford Financial Press, Oxford.

Yawitz, J.B. (1977) An analytical model of interest rate differentials and different default recoveries. *Journal of Financial and Quantitative Analysis*, 12: 481–490.

Yawitz, J.B. and Maloney, K.J. (1985) Taxes, default risk, and yield spreads. *Journal of Finance*, 40: 1127–1140.

Zhou, C. (1997) A jump-diffusion approach to modeling credit risk and valuing defaultable securities. Finance and Economics Discussion Paper Series 1997/15, Board of Governors of the Federal Reserve System, March.

Zhou, C. (2001) An analysis of default correlations and multiple defaults. *Review of Financial Studies*, 14(2): 555–576.

Index

DATE DUE

SEP 05 2006			
FEB 15 2008			
DEC 03 2007			
FEB 15 2008			
JAN 05 2009			
FEB 16 2009			
MAY 30 2009			
JUN 02 2010			
SEP 30 2009			